day	Money paid &c.	L.	S.	D.
	Lent Mess.ʳˢ Milon			
	and Florence, two			
	French Merchants			
	of Martinique, who			
	had been with a Cargo			
	of Arms & Ammunition			
	in Virginia, & had been			
	taken in coming from			
	thence, in July 1777. &			
	kept Prisoners eversince			
	just escaped from England,			
	and wanting wherewith			
	to help them down to Nantes,			
	Ten Guineas ————	240	.	—
	Recieved of M.ʳ Brown			
	Brought over 10	17	8.	0
	Paid Hatter for self & }	66	.	
	Servants			
	For W. T. Franklin —	24	—	
	& To Taylor for D.º — 2	52		
27	Paid Mad.ᵉ Brillon }	88	.	
	for Stockings for }			
	W. T. Franklin			
28	Advanced to W. T. F. }	96	.	
	to buy things for me }			
29	Lent le Baron de			
	Keltzendorff on his Note	100		
	he being in Distress, &			
	having as he says great			

day	Money...			
	Brought over 310 18			
26	Rec.ᵈ of W. T. Franklin			
	the Ballance of the Mo-	187.	1.	0
	ney furnish.ᵈ by M.ʳˢ			
	Adams for the Expense			
	of his Journey to Dieppe			
	for which I am D.ʳ to			
	Congress			

A Great Improvisation

On l'a vu désarmer les Tirans et les Dieux.

He has disarmed the tyrants and the heavens.

A Great

IMPROVISATION

FRANKLIN, FRANCE, AND THE
BIRTH OF AMERICA

STACY SCHIFF

HENRY HOLT AND COMPANY
NEW YORK

Henry Holt and Company, LLC
Publishers since 1866
115 West 18th Street
New York, New York 10011

Henry Holt® is a registered trademark of Henry Holt and Company, LLC.

Library of Congress Cataloging-in-Publication Data

Schiff, Stacy.
  A great improvisation : Franklin, France, and the birth of America / Stacy Schiff.—1st ed.
    p. cm.
  Includes bibliographical references (p.   ) and index.
  ISBN-13: 978-0-8050-6633-3
  ISBN-10: 0-8050-6633-0
  1. United States— Foreign relations—France. 2. France—Foregin relations—United States.
3. United States—Foreign relations—1775–1783. 4. Franklin, Benjamin, 1706–1790. I. Title.
  E183.8.F8S35 2005
  327.73044'09'033—dc22
                                       2004060615

Henry Holt books are available for special promotions and premiums.
For details contact: Director, Special Markets.

First Edition 2005

Endpapers: Two pages from Franklin's 1779 private cashbook, which include disbursements for the bath, the post, the hatter, the flower girl, and the servants at Versailles. The entries point up Franklin's light touch when it came to charitable giving, as well as his relaxed grasp of accounting.

Designed by Fritz Metsch

Printed in the United States of America

1 3 5 7 9 10 8 6 4 2

For Elinor Lipman

Contents

Contents

Cast of Characters

ADAMS, JOHN (1735–1826) Brilliant Massachusetts writer, orator, lawyer, statesman; austere, thin-skinned, fretful. Named to replace Deane as American commissioner to France, 1777. Recalled, 1779; returned to France months later. Assigned to secure a loan from the Netherlands, 1780; with Jay and Franklin, negotiated peace of 1783. Trailed through Paris a reputation for vanity and gracelessness.

ARANDA, PEDRO PABLO ABARCA DE BOLEA, CONDE DE (1718–1783) Spanish ambassador to France, out of favor with his own court. Set the gold standard for opulent living among the diplomatic corps.

BACHE, BENJAMIN FRANKLIN (1769–1798) Known as Benny. Eldest child of Franklin's daughter, Sally Bache, and her husband, Richard. Accompanied Franklin to France. To Geneva for school, 1779. Apprentice printer in Paris, 1784–1785.

BACHE, SALLY FRANKLIN (1743–1808) Franklin's only daughter. Every bit the unflappable "excellent female patriot" that one French officer applauded; collected funds and sewed shirts for American troops. Benevolent, capable, and dutiful in the extreme. Married Richard Bache, 1767. Mother of eight.

BANCROFT, EDWARD (1745–1821) Unofficial secretary to Franklin and the commission, 1776–1783. Native of Westfield, Massachusetts; physician, scientist, novelist, inventor. Highly congenial and gregarious, more so with a bottle of Burgundy. An impressive gourmand.

BEAUMARCHAIS, PIERRE-AUGUSTIN CARON DE (1732–1799) Incandescent, irrepressible secret agent, journalist, playwright, arms contractor. Initial conduit of military supplies from French government. Proclaimed himself the "agent, apostle, and martyr" of the American cause; acted all three parts to perfection. Intimate of Maurepas.

BRILLON DE JOUY, ANNE-LOUISE BOIVIN D'HARDANCOURT (1744–1824) Franklin's fluttery, porcelain-skinned neighbor, pianist, and composer. Wife of Jacques Brillon, mother of Cunégonde and Aldegonde.

CABANIS, PIERRE-JEAN-GEORGES (1757–1808) Medical student and poet, houseguest of and secretary to Madame Helvétius.

CARMICHAEL, WILLIAM (d. 1795) Widowed and wealthy Maryland native, self-appointed secretary to American commission. Member of Continental Congress, 1778–1779; accompanied Jay to Spain in 1780 as secretary. Swaggering and conniving; trusted least by those who knew him best. Even Mrs. Jay marveled over the "cloven foot."

CHAUMONT, JACQUES-DONATIEN LE RAY DE (1725–1803) Splendidly successful entrepreneur, Franklin's landlord and closest advisor. Principal private supplier of American aid. Advanced funds for d'Estaing's 1778 campaign; secured ships for Jones's 1779 expedition. Closely tied to Vergennes and Sartine.

CRÖY, ANNE-EMMANUEL-FERDINAND-FRANÇOIS, DUC DE (1718–1784) Decorated general and fortifications expert; named marshal of France in 1783. Dabbled in natural history, exploration, astronomy. Public-spirited and pious; confidant of Maurepas.

DEANE, SILAS (1737–1789) Son of a Connecticut blacksmith, Yale class of 1758. Dispatched by Congress to enlist French aid, 1776. Appointed with Franklin and Lee as American commissioner to negotiate a treaty, September 1776; recalled 1778. Returned to Europe in a private capacity, 1780. Combative, opportunistic lawyer, self-righteous and self-dramatizing. Childhood tutor to Bancroft.

DUBOURG, JACQUES BARBEU- (1709–1779) Kindhearted and excitable physician and writer, translator and publisher of Franklin's works in 1773. First contact for American emissaries in 1776. So vocal an America advocate that the abbé Morellet finally inquired what colony precisely Dubourg hailed from.

EDWARDS, EDWARD (1745–1821) Ingenious British spy, responsible on Tuesday evenings for secreting dispatches out of Franklin's house and to the Tuileries, to be sunk into the ground. Unconditionally trusted by the Americans; less trusted by his British employers, known to intercept his personal correspondence.

ESTAING, CHARLES-HENRI, COMTE D' (1729–1794) Franklin's across-the-lane neighbor and prominent admiral, commander of French squadron sent to America in 1778. Unpopular for having abandoned siege at Newport, 1778. Captured St. Vincent and Grenada; wounded at Savannah, 1779. Returned to Passy on crutches, December 1779.

FRANKLIN, WILLIAM (c. 1730–1813) Son of Franklin and an unknown mother, raised by Franklin's wife, Deborah. After 1763, royal governor of New Jersey. Arrested and imprisoned, 1776; exchanged 1778. Loyalist leader in London.

FRANKLIN, WILLIAM TEMPLE (1760–1823) Known as Temple, son of William Franklin and an unknown mother. Private secretary to Franklin during the French mission; returned to America in 1785. A poised, long-lashed, French-speaking version of his grandfather, who loved him "better than anything in the world."

GÉRARD, CONRAD-ALEXANDRE (1729–1790) Bilingual lawyer and diplomat, trusted undersecretary to Vergennes. Assisted in negotiations for and signed the French-American Treaty of Alliance, 1778. First foreign minister to the United States, 1778–1779. Brother of Joseph-Mathias Gérard de Rayneval, also a Vergennes aide.

GRAND, RODOLPHE-FERDINAND (1726–1794) In conjunction with his Amsterdam-based brother, Georges, America's banker and financial agent. Longtime collaborator of Vergennes. Franklin's next-door neighbor.

HELVÉTIUS, ANNE-CATHERINE DE LIGNIVILLE D'AUTRICOURT (1719–1800) Connoisseur of the arts, patron of the sciences, center of Franklin's social life in Passy. Blowsy, still-beautiful widow of Claude-Adrien Helvétius, Farmer General and philosopher. Franklin's most intimate link to the original Enlightenment cast, Diderot, d'Alembert, Condorcet, Turgot.

HEWSON, MARY STEVENSON (1734–1795) Known as Polly. Daughter of Franklin's London admirer and landlady, Margaret Stevenson. Walked down the aisle by Franklin in 1770; mother of three children; widowed in 1774. Angular-faced, well-read, unaffected.

IZARD, RALPH (1742–1804) Born Charleston, South Carolina, to a wealthy family of rice planters. Appointed American commissioner to Tuscany, 1777; never left Paris. Recalled 1779; served in Congress, 1782–1783. Athletic, smart, aristocratic, father of fourteen.

JAY, JOHN (1745–1829) Straight-spined New York lawyer. President of Continental Congress, 1778–1779; minister plenipotentiary to Spain, 1779–1782, though never received there; peace commissioner with Adams and Franklin, 1782–1783. Secretary for foreign affairs, 1784–1790.

JEFFERSON, THOMAS (1743–1826) Virginia statesman, author of Declaration of Independence. Appointed envoy to France, September 1776 (but declined), appointed peace commissioner to France, August 1781 (but declined), appointed peace commissioner November 1782 (accepted, but turned back as peace was already concluded). Arrived in France in 1785, to succeed Franklin as minister plenipotentiary.

JONES, JOHN PAUL (1747–1792) American naval captain. Given command of the *Bonhomme Richard* in 1779; defeated the British at Flamborough Head. Returned to America on the *Alliance*, 1781.

LAFAYETTE, MARIE-JOSEPH-PAUL-YVES-ROCHE-GILBERT DU MOTIER, MARQUIS DE (1757–1834) Against Louis XVI's orders, sailed to America as a French captain, 1777; returned 1778, as an American major general. Urged an invasion of Britain; lobbied for funds at Versailles; encouraged Rochambeau's dispatch; adopted Washington as his father. Led a New England battalion at Yorktown, 1781. Promoted to marshal, 1782.

LA LUZERNE, ANNE-CÉSAR, CHEVALIER DE (1741–1784) Gérard's replacement, popular and adroit French minister to the United States, 1779–1784.

LANDAIS, PIERRE (1731–1820) French seaman, commissioned captain in Continental navy, 1777. Given command of the Massachusetts-made *Alliance* in 1778. In that frigate joined squadron of John Paul Jones, 1779. Relieved of his command by Franklin, returned to it by Arthur Lee, 1780. Unbalanced if not insane. Court-martialed on return to America.

LA ROCHE, MARTIN LEFEBVRE, ABBÉ DE (b. 1738) Benedictine monk, librarian, and permanent houseguest of Madame Helvétius.

LAURAGUAIS, LOUIS-LÉON-FÉLICITÉ DE BRANCAS, COMTE DE (1733–1824) Professional eccentric and meddler, brigadier general, chemist, pamphleteer, Anglophile, aesthete. Friend of Arthur Lee.

LAURENS, HENRY (1724–1792) Leading Charleston merchant, president of Congress, 1777–1778. Resigned at outset of Deane scandal. Captured by British, 1780; appointed peace commissioner, 1781. Arrived in Paris November 1782, one day before negotiations concluded.

LAURENS, JOHN (1754–1782) Dashing son of Henry Laurens of South Carolina; aide to Washington. Special envoy to France, March 1781.

LAVOISIER, ANTOINE-LAURENT (1743–1794) A founder of modern chemistry, discoverer of oxygen. Gave six hours of his day to science while serving as a Farmer General; oversaw gunpowder monopoly. With his ebullient, English-speaking wife, frequently hosted Franklin at his table and in his laboratory.

LEE, ARTHUR (1740–1792) Virginia-born, Eton- and University of Edinburgh–educated doctor and lawyer. Appointed with Franklin and Deane as commissioner to negotiate a treaty and solicit French aid. Recalled in 1779; returned to America, 1780; served in the Continental Congress until 1784. Brother of Richard Henry, Francis Lightfoot, and William Lee. Like Franklin, a youngest son of a vast family. Unlike Franklin, a man of bilious temperament. Never married, as no woman could be found who met his standards.

LEE, WILLIAM (1739–1795) London alderman, 1775–1777. Appointed American commercial agent at Nantes, 1777; commissioner to courts of Berlin and Vienna, 1777. Received at neither; recalled, 1779. Older brother of Arthur Lee. Supercilious and strident.

LENOIR, JEAN-CHARLES-PIERRE (1732–1807) Omniscient chief of police and de facto mayor of Paris. Responsible for justice, order, and intelligence gathering, as well as cleaning the city streets, running its lotteries, stocking its bakeries, resuscitating its drowned, debunking its ghost stories. Closely allied at Versailles with his predecessor, Sartine.

LE ROY, JEAN-BAPTISTE (1720–1800) Director of royal laboratory in Passy; in contact with Franklin regarding his electrical studies as early as 1753. Studied ventilation and hygiene of prisons and hospitals. Among Franklin's most trusted friends.

LE VEILLARD, LOUIS-GUILLAUME (1733–1794) Witty, especially devoted friend and neighbor. Proprietor of fashionable mineral springs in Passy, under royal patronage.

LOUIS XVI (1754–1793) King of France. Succeeded to throne at twenty, on the death of his grandfather Louis XV. Married Marie Antoinette 1770; childless until 1778.

MAUREPAS, JEAN FRÉDÉRIC PHÉLYPEAUX DE PONTCHARTRAIN, COMTE DE (1701–1781) Eldest of Louis XVI's advisors and de facto minister of state. Nimble-tongued and flamboyant; his conversation very nearly a national treasure. A lukewarm proponent of Vergennes's American policy.

MORELLET, ABBÉ ANDRÉ (1727–1819) High-spirited political economist, writer, wit. First acquainted with Franklin in 1772, in England. Collaborated with Diderot and d'Alembert on the *Encyclopédie*. Elected
member of the Académie Française, 1785.

SARTINE, ANTOINE-RAYMOND-GUALBERT-GILBERT DE (1729–1801)
Brilliant minister of the navy, 1774–1780. Removed from his post in 1780,
having overspent on the French fleet and the American war. Particular
friend of Chaumont.

STORMONT, VISCOUNT, DAVID MURRAY, EARL OF MANSFIELD
(1727–1796). British ambassador to Versailles. Imposing, tenacious, and
immensely knowledgeable Scottish aristocrat.

VERGENNES, CHARLES GRAVIER, COMTE DE (1717–1787) Prodigiously
hardworking, influential French minister of foreign affairs, patron of
Beaumarchais. Famed for his ability to turn black to white overnight.
Concluded the French-American Treaty of Alliance, 1778. Known at Versailles for qualities that did not endear him there: thrift, industry, prudence, gravity.

WENTWORTH, PAUL (d. 1793) Audacious, artful master spy. With twenty
aliases, assorted disguises, and a host of invisible inks, eluded even the
peerless Paris police. Highly cultivated; in Beaumarchais's nervous opinion, "one of the cleverest men in England."

WILLIAMS, JONATHAN, JR. (1750–1815) Franklin's grandnephew and
former financial clerk, in London. Appointed commercial agent in Nantes
by Franklin and Deane, investigated at the Lees' request, 1777. Remained
in post unofficially, procuring American supplies and ships.

A Great Improvisation

Introduction

What then is an American, this new man?
—Crèvecoeur

In December 1776, a small boat delivered an old man to France. Typically after an ocean crossing his eyes brimmed with tears at the sight of land; he had just withstood the most brutal voyage of his life. For thirty days he had pitched about violently on the wintry Atlantic, in a cramped cabin and under unremittingly dark skies. He had barely the strength to stand, but was to cause a sensation. Even his enemies conceded that he touched down in France like a meteor. Among American arrivals, only Charles Lindbergh could be said to have met with equal rapture, the difference being that Lindbergh was not a celebrity until he landed in Paris. At the time he set foot on French soil Benjamin Franklin was among the most famous men in the world. It was his country that was the great unknown.

America was six months old, Franklin seventy years her senior. And the fate of that infant republic was, to a significant extent, in his hands. He sailed to France not for self-emancipation, as Americans have since, but for that of his country. Congress had declared independence without any viable means of achieving it; the American colonies were without munitions, money, credit, common cause. In the spring of 1776, foreign assistance had been debated as hotly as was independence. The two discussions were inextricably bound; to many the former qualified as the more palatable proposition. The best orator in Congress argued persuasively that a declaration of independence was a necessary step for securing European aid. In that light the document's name constituted a misnomer. It was drafted as an SOS.

"If I call Europe, what number do I call?" Henry Kissinger asked in the 1970s. In the 1770s the answer was obvious. Especially if you had a grievance with Britain, you called Versailles. How you did so was equally obvious, or would become so once others had fumbled along the way. You summoned the one man in the colonies possessed of that brand of sleek charlatanism known as social grace, the only one of the Founding Fathers familiar with Europe. Few Americans could have risen to Paris's diplomatic or conversational agenda, and even fewer could have done so with the requisite wit, in a language that approximated French. Whether Franklin could succeed in his mission was another question. In the annals of diplomacy his was an original one: Franklin was charged with appealing to a monarchy for assistance in establishing a republic.

In many ways he was splendidly suited to what would prove the greatest gamble of his life. He was very nearly too worldly for America; there were those in Philadelphia who found him suspect, as a century later Boston would find Edith Wharton fast. He happened to do a fine imitation of a French courtier. He knew better than to confuse straightforwardness with candor; he was honest, but not too honest, which qualifies in France as a failure of imagination. He left at home certain qualities on which America prides herself: piety, earnestness, efficiency. He was every bit as much the innocent abroad as Mark Twain, who covered his eyes at the Folies Bergère but who peeked. A master of the oblique approach, a dabbler in shades of gray, Franklin was a natural diplomat, genial and ruthless. He was enough accustomed to the foibles of man that he found no culture entirely foreign. He was possessed of a remarkably logical mind; the French would marvel over his ability to reduce any problem to its simplest terms. (The same gift allowed him to indulge in the ingenious and wholly specious argument, a staple of French conversation.) Above all he took with him to the Old World something for which the Old World had an insatiable appetite: personal prestige. He was the world-renowned tamer of lightning, the man who had disarmed the heavens, who had vanquished superstition with reason. Into Enlightenment Paris he rode on his own coattails. He was America's first international celebrity.

Unlike the other Founding Fathers, Franklin had no great taste for political debate. He was not a particularly adept politician; he left no political testament. (When his devoted younger sister requested copies of his essays on current events, he demurred. As they had served their purpose he had not kept them: "I could as easily make a collection for you of all the past parings of my nails.") It was on the power of personality that he traded. And he left in Paris a greater and more accurate imprint than he did in America, where the audience was more parochial and less discerning; the French mission stands not only as his greatest service to his country but the most revealing of the man. Franklin was at the height of his power, out of context, isolated, under surveillance, at odds with his colleagues. Hobbled by a foreign language, he was less subtle than was his habit. Those years belong literally to the Paper Age; there are two and a half times as many documents for Franklin's French sojourn as for the rest of the life combined. (And that is without factoring in intelligence reports, or ambassadorial dispatches.) The Parisian posting did not bring out the best in any of the American envoys, and Franklin was no exception: as much as does his charisma, his ingenuity, his silkiness, the flaws stand out in high relief. He could be negligent, manipulative, inconsistent, unmethodical, uncommunicative, vindictive, breathtakingly imprecise. Renowned for his overarching curiosity, he sought refuge in professions of ignorance. He set his colleagues' teeth on edge, none more so than John Adams's. Franklin's greatest enemies in France were his compatriots.

All births are messy, but America's was a particularly untidy and improvisational affair. Even among its most eminent minds, there were diverging objectives where foreign affairs were concerned. Washington's was to win the war without French troops. Adams's was to win the war without a political attachment to France. Franklin's was to win the war. He was nowhere more dogged, or more stubbornly idealistic. As has been said of him, "politically he was an American before it was really possible to be one." Misunderstood in European minds, America was barely united in its own. But America was an entity that Franklin saw very clearly, often to the point of delusion, and one in which he professed unwavering faith. "The greatest revolution the world ever saw is likely to be effected in a few years," he concluded when he had least reason to, following a humiliating, early encounter with the French foreign minister. When—seven years after she had declared it—America won her independence, Franklin wondered how it all could possibly have happened so quickly, and how he had been so lucky as to witness that miracle.

These were years in which the rules were different, when thirteen was a lucky number. Plenty of Frenchmen would have had trouble locating Britain's prize possessions on a map. Many believed that mythical arcadia either bordered Turkey or was part of India. The New World feared France's imperial designs rather than the other way around; it would be two centuries before the American refrigerator would be indicted as a threat to French domestic life. It was Franklin's job to fit a face to a nation that had none. And it was to be on the arm of a man Paris lauded as a frontier philosopher—a man who had never lived anywhere but in a city, who knew nothing of farming, and was as familiar with rural life as that other natural man, Montaigne, who claimed he could barely distinguish a cabbage from a lettuce—that America made her début on the world stage.

Always a generous soul, Franklin left his best years to his biographers. The outline for his unfinished *Autobiography* ends: "To France. Treaty, etc." This is the story of those four words, with emphasis on the last. Although its subject shied from doing so, Franklin's revolutionary odyssey has been examined before. In the simplified version, his is a kind of messianic entry into Paris that will precipitate a violent exit, thirteen years later, stage left, with noble French heads on pikes. In John Adams's worst nightmare, the story of the American Revolution assumed a different formulation: "The essence of the whole will be *that Dr. Franklin's electrical rod smote the earth and out sprung General Washington. That Franklin electrified him with his rod—and thence forward these two conducted all the policy, negotiation, legislatures, and war.*" In the romantic version, the French mission is reduced to a tale of baroque international melodrama, boasting a cast of aristocratic lovelies who transform Franklin into a debauched European. From there it is a short distance to the hostile misconceptions, in which Franklin is "the first to lay his head in the lap of French harlotry."

Certainly Franklin's French adventure taxes the more familiar version of the Revolution. It is not a pretty part of the seminal story; it is very near an insult to American ingenuity. At first blush the waltz with decadent Europe seems profoundly discordant. What could be more un-

American than the tale of an old man who went east? But American independence fell out of a conflict that was neither as neat nor as commonsensical nor as American-centric as one might like to believe. The majority of the guns fired on the British at Saratoga were French. Four years later, when the British set down their muskets at Yorktown, they surrendered to forces that were nearly equal parts French and American, all of them fed and clothed and paid by France, and protected by de Grasse's fleet. Without French funds the Revolution would have collapsed; by a conservative estimate, America's independence cost France more than 1.3 billion livres, the equivalent of $13 billion today. France was crucial to American independence, and Franklin was crucial to France. As it happens, his mission also conforms to the most genuine of American dramas, involving as it does three familiar elements: a borrowed identity, a getaway, and a swindle. At its center stands something equally homespun: a self-made, street-smart, civic-minded individual, who—roused by ideals crackling in the distance—harnesses those forces and wrestles them to the ground for closer examination, with his bare hands. To an eighteenth-century European mind, that was as wholly improbable as a republic that might endure.

I

The First Mistake in Public Business Is the Going into It

1776

If something foreign arrives at Paris, they either think they invented it,
or that it has always been there.
—*Horace Walpole*

Silas Deane was stranded in Paris, sick with anxiety, and nearly out of invisible ink. A spy trailed him mercilessly; the walls of every Left Bank café demonstrated an uncanny knack for recording—and rebroadcasting—his conversations. His frantic letters home met with stubborn silence. By his calculation, he was a month from bankruptcy. Having arrived in Paris on July 7, 1776, he had heard neither of self-evident truths, nor of unalienable rights, nor of the consent of the governed until October, and then only as the stuff of rumor. That solemn Declaration appealed to divine providence for support, but should providence prove less than forthcoming Deane was charged with a backup plan. "We look only to heaven and France for succour," a determined member of the American Congress announced that fall.

Deane, who would never confuse the two addresses, was in Paris on a discreet shopping expedition. His list was a short one. The eminently presentable Connecticut businessman was to procure clothing and munitions for an army of 25,000 men. While he was at it, a ship of war would come in handy, as would a sense of where officially neutral France unofficially stood on the issue of American independence. In exchange Deane had to offer only a young country's gratitude. He enjoyed no official title, no political powers, nor even the blessing of the Continental Congress. That assembly knew nothing of his assignment, which was at once public and private. The five-man Committee of Secret Correspondence, a forerunner of the State Department, had quietly dispatched Deane to test the political waters. A separate subcommittee empowered him to collect a percentage on the goods he acquired. To accomplish his clandestine errand, the thirty-eight-year-old Deane was advised to pass himself off as an Indian trader. No one, his instructions reminded him, had ever been challenged to justify a trip to Paris.

A lawyer and a two-time congressional delegate, Silas Deane was a contentious man, with a proclivity toward the shade in his business dealings. If anything those traits recommended him for a mission for which he was not otherwise remotely qualified. In his own analysis he found himself "so incapable of acting a tame, equivocal part, that I do not always act even a cautious one." Such was the envoy who presented himself at the notoriously difficult Parisian customs gates. Asked if he had anything to declare (the traditional answer was "See for yourself"), Deane confessed to precisely half of the four dozen bottles of claret in his carriage. His behavior was always patriotic even when it was not unimpeachably correct. His may have been an act of bravery, he reasoned, "but you know, Americans will smuggle."

Deane wrote his greatest burden down to his colleagues' incommunicativeness. "For heaven's sake," he that fall rebuked the silent, secret committee that had left him tilting single-handedly at windmills, "if you mean to have any connection with this kingdom be more assiduous in getting your letters here." He spent his time unspinning lies of every kind without knowing whether truth was even on his side. If nothing else it was common civility for the colonies to announce their independence to France. Congress's silence was all the more inexplicable in that that vital document had been drawn up with France prominently in mind. Without clothing, arms, ammunition, and money, the colonies were in no danger of waging a serious military campaign. Britain's historic rival had long appeared the likeliest candidate to assist in their struggle; sedition in America played as music to French ears. Where, then, asked Deane, were his instructions to approach Versailles with the news which had set all of

Europe chattering? If it preferred for another emissary to do so, the Committee of Secret Correspondence had only to say as much. He would be happy to step aside.

While it was next to impossible to transact business under these conditions—in addition to all else, France had just given birth to the word *bureaucracy*—a few trifles might help. It was one thing for all of Europe to have read of the Declaration of Independence two months before he did; the perils of the mail service were not unknown to Deane. But when such a document was, at long last, transmitted to Versailles in his care, surely it behooved Congress to do so with a little flourish. He was all for simple, republican manners, but these were the old kingdoms of Europe with whom his countrymen were dealing. Could there please be a little more pomp? The hunger for things American was moreover insatiable. Repeatedly Deane begged for a fine pair of Narragansett horses, an investment that should pay for itself with Marie Antoinette, a queen fond of parade. The request for other curiosities—"here where everything American is gazed at and where the American contest engrosses the attention of all ages, ranks, and sexes"—led to a congressional brainstorming session on moose, rattlesnakes, cranberries, woodchucks, and flying squirrels. "Is not this a pretty employment for great statesmen as we think ourselves to be?" sighed one member of that august body.

Words failed to convey his anxiety, sighed an addled Deane, who made no mention of the fact that in addition to being cold-shouldered and outmaneuvered, he was at a serious linguistic disadvantage. In his own estimation he could read and understand French moderately well but could write it not at all. If so he was a faster-thinking man than history has allowed; Parisians were famed for their ability to discourse on seventeen unrelated subjects before the Anglo-Saxon visitor could slip in a word edgewise. Deane left little record of his conversations, perhaps with good reason. When a critical nugget of information escaped, he protested that he could not have been the responsible party. As a rule, he was careful never to open his mouth before an Englishman. In a friend's estimation, that made Deane "the most silent man in all of France, as I defy him to utter six consecutive words of French."

That analysis was from one of the well-wishers, a man who spoke no English, who would argue that whole conversations could be sustained in that language with the use of a single word (*Goddamn*), but through

9

whom French sentences, paragraphs, voluminous memoranda coursed in streams, rapids, and cataracts; who devoted more lines to the American cause in 1776 than anyone else; and who would not only compensate for Deane's silence but had accomplished much of his mission before his arrival. Deane had not been in Paris two weeks when the French Foreign Ministry introduced him to Pierre-Augustin Caron de Beaumarchais, the flamboyant, scene-stealing playwright. Scene stealing was precisely what a government obliged to act furtively had in mind. Beaumarchais combined in one fair and lanky body the cunning of a Scarlet Pimpernel, the zeal of d'Artagnan, and the rectitude of the great gentleman burglar Arsène Lupin, the sprightly master of disguise. To Versailles he had already proved his mettle as a secret agent; Beaumarchais was the first person you called when you had a blackmailer on the doorstep. For a foreigner untutored in European affairs, who described himself as "moneyless, without credit, without friends," the incandescent Beaumarchais was a godsend. For a government eager to act without being said to do so—"one can connive at certain things but one cannot authorize them," went the Foreign Ministry's confidential self analysis—he was the ideal front man, as capable as he was expendable. And for the forty-four-year-old Beaumarchais, a consummate schemer—to whom the American cause beckoned both as a romance and as a business, and who, coincidentally, hoped to reingratiate himself with the ruling powers—it was a divine arrangement.

With a playwright's grasp of economics, Beaumarchais had already argued that a million livres advanced the fledgling country today would be alchemically transformed into eight million tomorrow, that every million Louis XVI invested in America would cost Britain 100 million. He also took it upon himself to expand the American army, assuring Versailles that George Washington commanded nearly 80,000 men. Irrepressible by nature, Beaumarchais was as fulsome in his I-can-get-it-for-you-wholesale overtures to Congress—whom he invited to look upon him as "one of the most zealous partisans of your cause, the soul of your success"—as he was swashbuckling in his assault on the French ministry. "Powder, guns," he pleaded with the powerful foreign minister at Versailles, who had covertly set him up in the procurement business. "My Lord, I have never wanted anything so much in my life." He was a very passionate man.

Concisely Beaumarchais articulated the prevailing ethos. "For the enemies of our enemies are more than half our friends," he reminded Deane's Stateside colleagues, with whom he carried on his own correspondence, of a very different tenor from the American envoy's. Under a false name, Beaumarchais gallantly assured the American Congress that—as if with a wave of his magic wand—he would "remove from the politics of Europe all obstacles that may oppose your wishes." And indeed it was through his unceasing maneuvers that cannonball, muskets, tents, and cannon began quietly to float, under cover of darkness, downriver from Abbeville, Strasbourg, and Metz, to the harbors of France. It was Beaumarchais who protested that Deane could not send artillery without qualified officers, which he could procure as well. You Americans have never made war before, he pointed out, and artillery was its most sophisticated science.

As Beaumarchais raced about frantically in his self-appointed role as fairy godmother, Deane relaxed somewhat into the comforts of Parisian life. He secured an additional million livres in explosives and uniforms from a dynamic, English-speaking businessman, willing to supply what the French government did not have on hand, and to do so on credit; Deane marveled at Beaumarchais's efficacity. The American's gratitude was boundless. The reprieve proved short-lived. As the year wound down, Deane discovered that a friendly official might just as well recommend overpriced saltpeter and second-rate munitions, that plenty of the "muskets for exportation" floating around France were as lethal to the man with his finger on the trigger as to the man at the end of the barrel. Given contracts as large as those he was signing, there was, he suddenly understood, ample potential for abuse. Nor were his concerns limited to the quality of the supplies, which Beaumarchais did not allow him to examine. In reminding Deane's employers that he was "better able than you to unfold the secret springs which give motion to states in this part of the world," the playwright went on to recommend that the colonists declare war on Portugal, a British ally. That would gratify Spain, who would rush to America's assistance. And while Beaumarchais's promise to remove any obstacle in Europe that might stand in the way of the American cause is such a resounding piece of velvet salesmanship it could be set to music, it ends on something of a discordant note. Have you realized, Beaumarchais inquired, that every word uttered in Congress is repeated verbatim in London? He was not the first to note that the Continental Congress consisted of too many members to keep a secret. Experience had already proved as much, which was why that assembly knew nothing of Silas Deane's errand. In despair one member asked if it might not make as much sense to fling open the Pennsylvania State House doors and hold their debates in public. John Jay would offer the best analysis later, to George Washington: "There is as much intrigue in this state house as in the Vatican, but as little secrecy as in a boarding school." Beaumarchais was however the only well-wisher who proposed the new republic address the problem by appointing a dictator.

To Deane's torments was added a steady stream of European officers bent on fighting in America. And although they longed to enlist, they did not care to serve as enlisted men. The French nobility included a fair number of eight-year-old majors and fourteen-year-old colonels, every one of them burning to be nineteen-year-old generals. By definition a French officer in 1776 was titled, and almost as much by definition Deane, a New England blacksmith's son, was flustered by the pageant of sonorous names. Soon enough he could describe his glittering mornings of dukes and generals and marquises and counts only as his *levées*. And soon enough it appeared from the American side as if Deane could not muster the courage to turn away any man whose name was preceded by *comte* or *chevalier*. While he had no authority to grant those applicants commissions, he did not desist from doing so. Aspirants of all rank imposed for his address on Jean-Charles Lenoir, the Paris chief of police, who routinely professed ignorance of the visitor's mission or whereabouts, while he knew perfectly well not only that the American had taken rooms at the Hôtel Grand Villars on the rue Saint-Guillaume, but what he had had for dinner and whom he had entertained before and after and when his letters had gone out by which conveyances and at what hour he had blown out his candle for the evening. The surveillance would have bothered any man and it unnerved Deane, with whose self-righteous streak a great number of businessmen had already collided, in Connecticut courtrooms.

As December neared the wet Parisian air grew chilly, and still Deane had had only two letters since the summer. He was as good as abandoned, expected to supply an army utterly lacking in clothing, arms, ammunition, or cannon, without a shilling to his name. Thomas Morris, the American commercial agent on whom he had been instructed to rely, proved useless, for the simple reason that, as Deane had it, he was prone to "paroxysms of intemperance and debauchery," there being but "very short intervals between the termination of one paroxysm and the commencement of another." (Deane could have elaborated further on the subject of young Morris, the half brother of the president of Congress. As a less chary soul noted: "He is drunk at least 22 hours of every 24 and never without one or two whores in company.") Everyone seemed to have better information than Deane, and it was universally bleak. He was not only low on the solution of tannic acid that made his words vanish from the page but frustrated by the effort those chemical washes required. His dispatches grew sloppy. It was next to impossible to make his voice heard over that of the popular and polished British ambassador, who weekly poisoned the waters at Versailles by hinting at a reconciliation between the mother country and her colonies, and who played up every American defeat in the finest drawing rooms of Paris. At some point on Tuesday, December 3, 1776, in over his head and sinking rapidly, Deane poured out his heart to John Jay, in Philadelphia. He was in an untenable situation, "without intelligence, without orders, and without remittances, yet boldly plunging into contracts, engagements, and negotiations, hourly hoping that something will arrive from America." Unbeknownst to him something had arrived, that very morning.

❦

Franklin's arrival could hardly have created a greater sensation. The welcome left something to be desired. That evening, under a wet mist, the half-demolished Philadelphian hobbled ashore in what he would remember as a wretched corner of Brittany, a lifeless hamlet of 2,500 people. He was seventy-five miles from the flourishing city of Nantes, where he had hoped to land. The stone and slate village was unimpressive but made for a happy sight; Franklin had spent four frustrating days bobbing about off the coast of France, admiring the rocky Breton coast from a distance, while the winds remained stubbornly against him. For a hefty sum a local fisherman agreed to row him to shore, with his two grandsons. In the dark the three made their way up the steep embankment to Auray's waterside inn. By nature Franklin was not inclined to dwell on the discomforts of life, but that December's distress would burn bright in his memory. The cold had been penetrating. The fowl on board having proved too tough for his teeth, he had subsisted primarily on salt beef; he blamed his diet for the boils that had erupted over every inch of his upper torso, including his scalp. He was dotted with scabs. For the first hours on land the soil of France spun underfoot.

There was no one on hand to greet him, for the simple reason that no one in France knew he was coming. The letters heralding his arrival lay at the bottom of the Atlantic. With difficulty the next day he located a post chaise in a neighboring town. The conveyance compared poorly with the carriages of England and its three horses were far from fresh, but the transaction was an amicable one. Years earlier Franklin had noted that French drivers were as mercenary as their English counterparts but that theirs was a more polite brand of thievery. Since the post was to depart that evening he spent his morning with pen in hand. "You will be surprised to receive a letter from me dated in France, when neither of us had been expecting such a thing," he wrote his closest Parisian friend, the learned physician Jacques Barbeu Dubourg, in a lovely piece of under statement. To Dubourg he entrusted as well the note that released Silas Deane from his misery. He sent word separately to Thomas Morris, the Nantes agent whose drunken antics so perturbed Deane and who happened to be in London on a spree. Franklin was heading discreetly and indirectly to Paris, he warned Deane who—like Dubourg—received his mail only after the post office had read and copied it. In that art too the French were superior to the British. It was universally agreed that no one sealed and resealed an envelope as adroitly as a Frenchman. "I propose to retain my incognito," Franklin assured Deane, saddling his beleaguered colleague with another impossible task. Repeatedly and nervously, Deane assured the influential and artful French foreign minister, Charles Gravier, comte de Vergennes, that it was not his fault if every man with a correspondent in Paris had something to say on the subject of Benjamin Franklin.

It is doubtful that Congress knew whom they were sending to France; Franklin alone had some sense of who he was in that country. In America he was a printer, a publisher, a civic force, a businessman, a colonial agent. The Franklin known to the French, the Franklin who had briefly visited Paris in 1767 and 1769 was—in Voltaire's description—the discoverer of electricity, a man of genius, a first name in science, a successor to Newton and Galileo. Franklin had made his first French friends through those pursuits. Dubourg, who raced to Deane's door with the Auray envelope in hand and who counted as one of America's earliest proponents, had long before published some of Franklin's experiments. (No less ingenious than his American correspondent, the pale-complexioned, open-faced Dr. Dubourg was the designer of a lighting rod umbrella, for the protection of wary pedestrians.) Long before Franklin's arrival, the highly literate physician had begun to kindle interest in an American revolution. In 1775 he declared himself the Don Quixote of the American cause. That Beaumarchais had demoted him to Sancho Panza did not dull his ardor; Dubourg was that rare thing, an entirely affable zealot. He was also garrulous and fast-talking and excitable, and on learning the astonishing news of his friend's arrival he sent word all over Paris. The tamer of the lightning bolt was on French soil. It may have been unclear where exactly America was, but the scientific community had been utterly transfixed by the foreigner's account of having killed a turkey on the far bank of Philadelphia's Schuylkill River with electricity.* That he might now be attempting a similar experiment across a wider body of water did not immediately present itself as the reason for the great man's arrival.

In a conveyance only slightly less cramped than the cabin in which he had sailed, Franklin made his way east that afternoon. He was accompanied by his son's son, sixteen-year-old William Temple Franklin, known as Temple, and by his daughter's seven-year-old, another Benjamin, known to his Philadelphia household as Benny. The woods of Brittany were dark, and neither grandson would have been much charmed by the driver's succulent account of the gangs of murderers who infested them, a danger magnified either in translation or in pursuit of a healthy tip; the French countryside was in truth admirably well patrolled. From the road Franklin imposed on Deane to arrange for Parisian lodgings, preferably in his own hotel. The two boys would need their own room but could share a bed.

Meanwhile Franklin detoured to Nantes, where he was to collect his luggage, and where he had arranged a line of credit. He had some business

---

*Dubourg had elicited that account, with a very different question: Could Franklin devise a method for tenderizing meat with electricity? Franklin thought it possible but had not investigated. Instead he offered detailed instructions for electrocuting a turkey, an art unfamiliar to most statesmen. Fowl so slaughtered were, Franklin noted, uncommonly tender.

to transact too in that bustling city. The able captain who had delivered him to France had been instructed that his first priorities were the comfort and safety of his distinguished passenger. In the event that Captain Lambert Wickes and his sixteen-gun sloop of war were to find themselves in a position to capture a British ship, Wickes was to solicit Franklin's advice. Anyone who knew Franklin knew where he stood on that matter; he saw a great advantage in some well-choreographed buccaneering. By his instructions he was as well to be complicit in it. Upon delivering his passenger, Wickes was to capture any vessels he could off the coast of England. Franklin was to see to it that the ports of France were open to him on his return. "Let Old England see how they like to have an active enemy at their own door; they have sent fire and sword to ours," read Wickes's heated mandate.

A first opportunity had presented itself as Wickes's sloop neared the coast of France. Attack amounted virtually to a linguistic necessity: Wickes's brigantine was the *Reprisal*, and before her sailed the *George*. Hours later an Irish brigantine crossed the *Reprisal*'s path. By the time Wickes arrived in Auray he had in his possession valuable stores of flaxseed and brandy, lumber and tar. In Franklin's mind danced visions of 4,000 pounds sterling of munitions, but the exchange would involve some finesse; as he well knew, such sales violated the law. Long-standing treaties prohibited France from so much as harboring vessels belligerent to England in her ports. At the same time, Franklin was under instructions to test the limits of French hospitality. And so in the prosperous, teeming port of Nantes, where he was feted and doted upon by a host of starry-eyed merchants, all of them offering crash courses on the politics and policies of France, he did his best, in the name of patriotic corner cutting, to arrange his sales.

❧

In the face of a major decision Franklin advocated an exercise he termed "moral algebra." Make a list of pros and cons and allow it to marinate for a few days. Gradually jettison the entries that equal each other—canceling out multiple arguments that amount to a single one in weight—and endorse the column in which a balance remains. In his view changes of heart resulted from the failure to assemble all arguments at once; it was natural to favor the most recent set of reasons at the expense of the best. The exercise was perhaps a necessary invention for a man able to debate either side of an issue with equal conviction, a quality known in some circles as open-mindedness. When it came to the decision to send Franklin—portly, balding, and seventy—to France in the role of seductive ingénue, the congressional balance sheet would have been almost absurdly asymmetrical. Having retired from the printing business twenty-eight years earlier, Franklin had dedicated himself to civic, scientific, and political pursuits. A one-man booster club, he had been instrumental in paving and lighting Philadelphia's streets, founding her hospital, establishing her library, police force, fire brigade, sanitation department, militia. No one in the colonies could rival his administrative experience. As crucially, he was a genius at fund-raising. His winning technique appealed to equal parts envy, guilt, and shame, all in the name of the higher good. He could make a sale and leave the purchaser without a trace of buyer's regret. Two years of formal schooling stood behind those accomplishments; algebra was not something Franklin had ever encountered in a classroom, where he had failed arithmetic, twice. He never went to college, a wrong he has been said to have redressed by founding one.

The least provincial of Americans, he was also among the best traveled. Appropriately it was Franklin who had seen to it that maps of the world hung in the Pennsylvania Assembly. He was the sole American with any substantial experience of foreign affairs, having served for fifteen of the previous twenty years as a colonial agent in London. Returning to Philadelphia only in May 1775, he had been halfway across the Atlantic—the address corresponded to his state of mind—when the first shots were fired at Concord and Lexington. Ten months later he made a punishing trip to Quebec to persuade the Canadians to join America as a fourteenth colony, a visit that left him with an enduring set of designs on that northern neighbor. On the London return he had sworn never again to cross the ocean; the Canadian excursion had left him more dead than alive; he had already vowed many times to retire from public service. On the other hand—and there is no question in which column this would have figured on Franklin's personal ledger—both missions had proved dismal failures. All his good work in London to preserve what he liked to think of as "that fine and noble China vase, the British empire" had not only proved vain but ended in indelible public humiliation. He had stood stone still while excoriated, before a jeering audience, by the solicitor general of England. The Canadian mission had proved futile from the outset.

Probably Franklin realized that what passed in England for "conceit, wrong-headedness, obstinacy, and passion" could go a long way in France. Certainly he was very aware of France waiting ardently in the wings, where she had been brooding since 1763. From the French and Indian War France had emerged in debt and shorn of virtually all her American territories. Worst of all, she felt publicly and indecently disgraced, displaced as the preeminent European power, despite a population three times as great as England's. Having signed that peace, Vergennes's predecessor, the duc de Choiseul, sat back to plot his revenge. The American colonies seemed a likely instrument; over the decade prior to 1776, France studied an American insurrection more scientifically than did the colonies themselves. While there was no love lost between the two foreign ministers, Vergennes too saw 1763 as a mere pause in hostilities. He spoke of that treaty only with a shudder. In 1775 he had dispatched a representative to Philadelphia to investigate whether America might be inclined to engage in that time-honored French sport: baiting the British. Franklin had been one of the five men present at the secret, late-night assignations with that emissary, outside the city. None of those overtures made Franklin an advocate of an alliance. Long after he had mastered the art of Parisian tipping, acquired a maître d'hôtel, and invested in French linens, he remained firmly convinced that it was beneath America's chaste dignity to run about "suitoring for alliances."

Why did he go? He was at all times eminently pragmatic; Franklin had after all founded both Philadelphia's first fire brigade and Philadelphia's first fire insurance company. And as far as an alliance went, he was plainly in the minority. John Adams, the forty-year-old Massachusetts congressman who understood European politics as well as anyone in America, was among the first to argue that the colonies must apply to a European power for war supplies, an idea that "was too much for the nerves of Congress," in which assembly "the grimaces, the convulsions were very great." Initially Franklin joined in those grimaces. Over the next year most members of Congress came around, to find themselves more united behind the idea of foreign aid than behind a declaration of independence.*

Few outside of Congress knew how desperate the military situation actually was in 1776. The 78,000 men whose courage Beaumarchais exalted—his math tutor deserves a statue in America—were in fact closer to a bedraggled pack of 30,000. It was said that they might soon enough scare the British away by their very nakedness. And that wretched band was not only barefoot and hungry but without munitions. Nine months into the war the country was nearly destitute of gunpowder, to the despair of General Washington. When he had finally found his way to a Parisian desk, Franklin explained that the American army had not five rounds of powder to a man. "This was kept secret even from our people," he confessed. "The world wondered that we so seldom fired a cannon. We could not afford it." England had done her best to suppress manufacturing in the colonies, prohibited from trading with other powers while under British rule. Not a single man in North America could boast of any engineering expertise. Franklin was as appalled by this state of affairs as anyone, but envisioned an alternative solution. What had happened, he wondered early in 1776, to the underrated bow and arrow? Muskets were unreliable at three hundred yards. No smoke occluded an archer's vision; a flight of arrows made for a terrifying sight.

Meanwhile the man who until eighteen months earlier had committed himself to preserving that noble China vase resorted to more traditional diplomatic means. Having seen Deane dispatched to France, he had accompanied John Adams and South Carolina's Edward Rutledge to Staten Island to discuss a peace with Admiral Richard Howe, a meeting at which Adams observed all the Franklinian qualities that would make his colleague the ideal envoy to a monarchy. The Philadelphian summoned pitch-perfect ripostes "with an easy air and a collected countenance, a bow, a smile, and all that naivité which sometimes appeared in his conversation and is often observed in his writings." It was Adams as well who—in explaining Franklin's Canadian departure—best articulated his suitability to the French mission. Franklin had to his

---

*The order of priorities was clear to many in Europe. One savvy German diplomat went so far as to suggest that Congress had been led into the Declaration by dreams of powerful French and Spanish aid.

credit a "masterly acquaintance with the French language, his extensive correspondence in France, his great experience in life, his wisdom, prudence, caution; his engaging address; united to his unshaken firmness in the present American system of politics and war." This was not the same Franklin whom Adams would rejoin in Europe. From the New Englander's point of view, Franklin suffered the fate of all provincial ingénues who debark in Paris. He was everywhere applauded, Adams could not refrain from clucking later, like an opera girl.

Which was very little how Franklin saw himself. By the fall of 1776, when it had become apparent that someone would need to represent America in France, to discuss an alliance, to bolster Deane's efforts, and to add import to the delegation, Franklin readily packed his papers, laid in provisions and bedding for the trip. He made it sound as if he had nothing to lose, whereas he had as well something to gain. Twenty years earlier he had expressed his conviction that life, like a play, should finish with a rousing last act. And so engaging in his best imitation of the modest everyman that he was not, on either count, he agreed to undertake the mission with a great sigh of insouciance. "I am old and good for nothing; but, as the storekeepers say of their remnants of cloth, 'I am but a fag end, and you may have me for what you please,' " he shrugged, when complimented on the honor. The tone is familiar; it is the same note of faux diffidence Franklin sounds in his *Autobiography*, when the eminent statesman begs to be forgiven the invertebrate digressions that are to follow.

That he should have been sent to France made perfect sense. That the French should have received him as they did made perfect sense as well. The reasons were different, however. A citizen of the world and a statesman at home, Franklin was piquantly American, a scientist and philosopher abroad. The obvious man for the job on one side of the ocean, he was the ideal man on the other. Louis XV had been among the first to congratulate him on his electrical discoveries, well known throughout Europe, where he had been received with kudos. And if science was in Paris the fashion of the day, there was no greater laboratory than North America. So too were dreams of the innocent and primitive New World. It could be said that the French were in love with the concept of America and a man named Franklin before either of them materialized. They made certain that, at least in the latter case, the reality conformed to the idea.

Moreover the metropolis Franklin entered at the end of 1776 was not yet home to any American community. He was France's first real rebel, different from Silas Deane not only because Franklin trailed behind him an illustrious past but because he lacked Deane's establishment airs and Yale degrees. To European eyes, Deane was as much an Englishman as an American. Franklin was the genuine article. Conveniently, he looked the part. Even among his compatriots he conformed to the image of the venerable philosopher. The wide, heavy-lidded, hazel eyes, the vast dome of a forehead, seemed to radiate wisdom and virtue. A solidly built, jowly, bull-necked man—he dubbed himself "Dr. Fatsides"—Franklin liked to think he projected an air of placid contentment, and indeed it seemed that serenity and goodwill had etched themselves across his plush, pleasant face. "Persuasion and goodness sat on his lips, and the benignity of the whole was remarkable," noted one admirer, speaking for countless others, of a man who was by no means conventionally handsome. France loves ingénues, and France loves underdogs, and there is no better kind of ingénue underdog than a seventy-year-old winner.

Franklin knew that his name had been a passport in France for years. As early as 1769 friends reported that they were welcomed everywhere with open arms on his account; Deane discovered that that distinction was the best recommendation a man could claim in Paris. It introduced where titles failed. If Franklin knew he was vilified in London as the insidious "chief of the rebels" he would have known too the effect of that epitaph on his stock in France. Nowhere was his compound status as emblem, as thinker, as chief rebel on better display than in a letter penned from one Enlightenment bookend to another, just as its subject lent his life savings to Congress and bid his Philadelphia goodbyes. "You know that Dr. Franklin's troops have been defeated by those of the King of England. Alas! Philosophers are beaten everywhere. Reason and liberty are poorly received in this world," wrote Voltaire to d'Alembert. And Franklin's symbolic power only increased as he crossed the ocean. Unwittingly, Congress sent France a sort of walking statue of liberty.

⁓⧉⁓

As a general rule, news about Franklin traveled infinitely more quickly than did the seventy-year-old emissary. And word of his improbable appearance spread with lightning velocity. Before Deane had so much as expressed his relief and delight on the occasion, the French government was frantically putting out fires. Vergennes, the all-seeing foreign minister, could barely conceal his discomfort. Franklin's arrival, in a vessel belonging to a nation at war with Britain, which had taken prizes, when Beaumarchais had munitions piled high in three ports, threatened to reveal the embarrassing double game at Versailles. Meanwhile French officers bragged loudly in cafés and theaters of having secured their government's blessing to serve in North America. Quickly Vergennes commanded the Paris chief of police to extinguish all talk of public solidarity for the rebels. Lenoir was to see to it that any Frenchman who declared as much be arrested, as conspicuously as possible. Forty-eight hours later Lenoir reassured the foreign minister that every proprietor of a café or gaming club had been or would be notified, but made clear too what he was up against. "Dr. Franklin's landing in Nantes has created an extraordinary sensation," he observed dryly.

Few were as flummoxed as Silas Deane, who had been angling in vain for an appointment with Vergennes and who found himself as discomfited by the surge of enthusiasm as he had been disabled by its absence. It was true that Dr. Franklin was in Nantes, he wrote the minister, but he himself had as yet no clue to his compatriot's mission. Nor had Franklin offered any elucidation. Surely Deane could not be held accountable for any indiscretions. He protested that he had been prudent in the extreme while others—the finger pointed meaningfully at Dubourg—had not been. The temperature of the reception was not lost on Franklin, who enjoyed in Nantes only a glimmer of what was to follow, but who reported— modestly to Congress, with an audible purr of gratification to his sister— on the civilities with which he had been met, the impressive visits he had received. No flying squirrel or woodchuck could have caused such a commotion.

Deane was alone in professing ignorance as to why the "chief of the rebels" had washed up unexpectedly on French soil. Everyone else in Europe was an authority. The newspapers assigned Franklin the age he doubtless felt after the debilitating journey: Europe marveled that the eighty-four-year-old, as distinguished for his scientific achievements as for his dedication to his cause, had braved the crossing. Soon enough he was reported to be seventy-four, although he remained "an old man who will brave any danger to serve his country." The nature of those services occasioned much dispute. Franklin had come for his health, the climate of France being gentler than that of America. He had come to supply his grandsons with a European education. He had come to see his works published. Much depended on where the papers were printed, and by whom. It was equally asserted that Franklin had sailed as a fugitive, having quarreled with Congress, to protest his countrymen's decision to reconcile with England, to discuss a commercial treaty with France, to nurse a private grievance, to sue for peace with the British, to secure his bank account, to ensure that future American generations were "Frenchified." Silas Deane had not exaggerated when he claimed that all eyes were on America, and they turned now to Franklin. The diplomatic corps drilled Vergennes for an explanation in vain, although their ignorance did not curtail their speculations. The Portuguese ambassador reported on Franklin's plans to retire to a Swiss château with his fortune of 800,000 livres. As no one could be so foolhardy as to capture a British ship, the Saxon ambassador doubted Franklin could conceivably even be in France at all. According to the Sardinian envoy, Franklin had fled America with his family, having deluded his countrymen with talk of a foreign mission. All waited breathlessly for Franklin to divulge his plans. When interrogated, he was reserved. He had come to finish his days in France. It had not yet been established that this was what good Americans did, but the answer was an irreproachable one.

While he remained unforthcoming—if he set pen to paper again in Nantes after his first full day there, no record remains of his having done so—he noted with satisfaction that the prevailing opinion appeared to be that he had come to negotiate with the French and that that idea gave his hosts much pleasure. Judging the temperature to be warm, he added a little kindling of his own. While he was opaque as to his own motives, he was wildly expansive on the subject of his country's resolve. Washington's sustained retreat was of little consequence. Their compatriots were wholly uncompromised and universally determined to persevere. Long Island—where Washington had suffered a late August thrashing at the hands of General William Howe—afforded the British no strategic advantage. They would need an army of 200,000 men to subjugate a people so stubbornly attached to their freedom. Short of that the war would stretch on for a decade. The American army was in fine shape and lacked for nothing. It was repositioning itself and would fight on indefinitely; by spring it would number 80,000 expertly trained men. The farther the British troops penetrated the continent, the more resistance they would encounter. "I have helped them here to recover their spirits a little," Franklin assured Congress the morning after—unknown to anyone in Europe—Washington, reeling from an unbroken string of defeats, scrambled to the Pennsylvania side of the Delaware River, and days after Congress had fled, bag and baggage, to muddy Baltimore, to hold sessions in a deserted tavern.

Above all a man of the press, Franklin appreciated the value of misinformation. And he had demonstrated an early gift for creative dissembling. At the age of seventeen he had staged a dress rehearsal for the slipping of oppressive familial chains. Having determined to escape Boston to make his way in the world, he had hatched a surefire—if entirely fictitious—alibi. He advanced the rumor that he had got a girl pregnant and was pressured to marry her. In 1776 that was one of the few explanations not trotted out to explain why he had risked a perilous trip across an ocean "porcupined" with enemy cruisers, at the least propitious time of year, when the English would have taken every delight in hanging him.

No one tracked Franklin's progress over the 230 well-maintained miles that separate Nantes from Paris as assiduously as did Lord Stormont, the charismatic, beautifully mannered British ambassador in Paris. From his splendid baroque town house on the Right Bank Stormont reported breathlessly on the swirl of rumor, which he leavened with his own sound opinion. It was indeed likely that Franklin traveled as a secret agent, and on a crucial mission. Nor did Stormont underestimate him: "As he is a subtle, artful man, and void of all truth, he will in that cause use every means to deceive, will avail himself of the general ignorance of the French to paint the situation of the rebels in the falsest colours, and hold out every lure to the ministers to draw them into an open support of that cause. He has the advantage of several intimate connections here"— Stormont knew precisely who they were, having arranged for all of their mail to be intercepted—"and stands high in the general opinion." In short the man was dangerous. Stormont genuinely regretted that some English frigate had not met and dispensed with Franklin on the high seas.

That bitterness seeped out in the course of a long and tempestuous discussion at Versailles, the seat of the French government, to which Stormont dashed in protest. Vergennes did little to oblige him, shrugging off the clandestine aid to which every diplomat in Paris was privy. Stormont was willing to play the dupe for only so long; ultimately he eased the minister into a corner. As the French police were so vigilant about the corruption of their subjects, how was it that they were permitting rebel emissaries to engage French officers? And how did Vergennes account for his absurd café-and-gaming-club edict, which had only generated more publicity for the Americans? The Frenchman swore that the police chief had mistaken his intentions. Stormont blustered on, to be interrupted by Vergennes, who seemed suddenly to have located his excuse. He could post notices in all the cafés of France but he could not single-handedly regulate the "wild, roving disposition" of his countrymen. It was that same appetite for adventure that had historically carried them to all the corners of the globe. A handsome and imposing man, with a lofty manner, Stormont emerged from the interview visibly shaken. The next morning Vergennes wrote to London, to request that his ambassador tend to a little damage control. According to the *London Chronicle*, the Americans had obtained permission to arm privateers in French ports. Could his envoy publish an anonymous article protesting that falsehood? Vergennes would prefer that the English entertain no such suspicions at such a time.

Meanwhile Stormont worked himself into a froth. As he feared, reports surfaced that the insidious Franklin had turned up in Versailles, where he painted a delightfully rosy picture of the rebels' affairs. Stormont could perfectly envision the traitor waltzing through Vergennes's courtyard offices, spinning his web of lies. Within days the ambassador announced that the deed was done. He had it on good authority that Franklin had effectively turned Vergennes's head by offering up Britain's greatest treasure: the exclusive trade of North America. That alarm echoed in London, where stocks fell on the news of Franklin's surprise appearance. The sole defect in Stormont's flurry of fevered dispatches was that Franklin was still in Nantes. He had been in Versailles only once in his life, in 1767. Awed by its magnificence, he had also revealed himself to be every inch an American. The plumbing, he had noted, was in an abject state of disrepair.

⁓⁂⁓

Only on Sunday, December 15, did Franklin begin to clatter his way east, at a leisurely pace, across smooth roads and through impeccably cultivated fields, along the luscious banks of the Loire, to Paris. He found the drive enchanting. Stormont was far from alone in having conveyed him prematurely to the capital; especially in a country that was still without daily newspapers, hearsay had a long and distinguished history. Many men—Vergennes and police chief Lenoir foremost among them—felt they could shape it, but only one volunteered to position himself squarely in its path. Naturally that was the same versatile dramatist who two months earlier had reminded the French foreign minister that he held the destiny of the world in his hands.* Should Vergennes fail to take advantage of this historic opportunity, his ministry would be immortalized as a laughingstock in their children's history books. A comparable opportunity to crush England was not likely to present itself for another thousand years.

Beaumarchais had heard the sensational news in Le Havre, where he was devoting ten hellish days to loading American supplies, under more than the usual duress. His relationship with Franklin was to begin under an unlucky star. Given the tumult occasioned by the American's appearance, Vergennes thought it wise to prohibit the departure of Beaumarchais's ships. Beaumarchais had other ideas; between the time that hints of that embargo arrived and the actual edict did, he put more than one hundred men to work through two sleepless nights. Chaos ensued. What was intended for one vessel was loaded in another; the inventories bore no relation to the invoices. But by December 14, three-quarters of the supplies were loaded and safe in the *Amphitrite*. The other two boats would be unloaded publicly, reloaded when the clamor had subsided. "I am about to begin by changing the names of the ships, and the rest will be done silently and under cover of darkness," Beaumarchais calmly assured Deane, while preparing a tantrum for Versailles. How was it that one office could tacitly clear the decks for his enterprise while another publicly rescinded his permission to sail? As he did so the *Amphitrite* slipped out to a spurious destination. Beaumarchais made every effort to see to it that no one aboard ship had in his possession a single incriminating scrap of paper, for which he scoured the port as well. He followed the boat for some distance along the coast, to remind its captain again of the premium on secrecy. Those efforts he vaunted without mentioning the play rehearsals

---

*Or as Beaumarchais put it later, "God is a Bourbon."

he directed that week, which rendered all precautions futile. No one in Le Havre happened to subscribe to the conviction that a certain Monsieur Durant was the author of *The Barber of Seville*. Ultimately Stormont would thank Vergennes for having entrusted his affairs of state to Beaumarchais, who made Stormont's job so easy. The remark elicited only a twisted smile.

Having set out from Le Havre in the north at the same time as Franklin from the west, Beaumarchais hurtled to Paris in a nonstop, bone-rattling forty hours. The 120-mile sprint nearly incapacitated him, but—buckling over with fatigue, one foot out of the carriage—he fired off a missive to Vergennes on December 16, before turning in for the evening. The commotion caused by Franklin's arrival was extraordinary. And he knew of only one man who could tame the frenzy. Already Beaumarchais had advised Deane "to go and meet his friend, to lock him up until my return, and not to let him speak nor give letters to anyone until I had the honor of forewarning you, *Monsieur le comte*, and of taking your orders regarding the matter." He had traveled day and night expressly "so as not to keep Monsieur Franklin locked up too long." His efforts had paid off; Franklin was expected only the following day. Rest easy, Beaumarchais assured Vergennes, who rarely rested and was less often at his ease: "I have everything under control, with the exception of the idle Parisian gossip that neither you, nor I, nor the King, nor the heavens, can keep from circulating."

On waking, Beaumarchais reminded Deane to sing the praises of his covert operation to the new arrival. Franklin's appearance threw more than a few wrenches in the works, and the apprehensions showed. Would Beaumarchais need to renegotiate everything with the new envoy? Would Deane's contracts be invalidated? Of course if Franklin was the man Beaumarchais supposed him to be, he would rely on the playwright for his first and best advice as to his political conduct. This was another of Beaumarchais's leave-it-to-me letters: "No one knows better than I the perilous ground on which we tread, you and I." The perilous terrain was only too familiar to Deane, who suffered as well from afflictions he did not think his French associate could cure. Deane had heard that one of the outbound vessels was an inferior ship, that her captain was unfamiliar with the American coast and generally too inebriated to transact business. Surely Beaumarchais did not mean to destroy the faith between the two countries by taking advantage of him?

And so it was with Stormont remonstrating, Deane fretting, Beaumarchais hyperventilating, the *Amphitrite*, unbeknownst to all, contemplating an about-face on the high seas, Captain Wickes and the *Reprisal* paralyzed as the Loire froze around them in Nantes, and all of Paris speculating, that Franklin forged his way calmly across the plains of western France, to Paris. He made it as far as Versailles on Friday afternoon, December 20, where, exhausted, he settled in for the night. From the Auberge de la Belle Image he dispatched a courier to ask what Parisian arrangements Deane had made. That was the very question that preoccupied the city; every morning Franklin was said to have arrived, and every evening to be expected. Lenoir could have answered the query in detail: Deane had booked a second apartment at the Hôtel d'Entragues on the rue de l'Université, where Deane now occupied an extensive suite on the first floor. Rarely was anything so absurd that Lenoir desisted from reporting it to Vergennes, but with this frenzy he drew the line. He was not alone. Within weeks Franklin would observe that he had read seven paragraphs about himself in the papers, of which six were lies. Not that he had any intention of correcting them.

On receipt of Franklin's note Deane hurried to Versailles to fetch his colleague. The two were little acquainted but the embrace could only have been a warm one. Franklin had been the author of Deane's original instructions, and was one of the few to know of the supplies Deane had obtained. Already with Franklin's arrival, Deane felt like a new man; he had as well summoned Arthur Lee, the third American commissioner, to Paris. The envoys' instructions were simple and, from Vergennes's perspective, unsurprising. Without having met, the fifty-six-year-old French minister and Franklin had seen eye to eye for some time, resorting to the same incendiary metaphors. From the start Vergennes had been a less reluctant player. The Franklin who in 1767 had sidled past the Swiss Guards of Versailles, brilliantly attired six-footers with plumed hats and red pantaloons, was a Franklin profoundly devoted to King George III. Not only was he a proponent of empire, but he believed his own king to be far superior to that of France. To that conviction he held firm until the eleventh hour, disapproving of France's eagerness to undermine relations between Britain and her colonies. A decade later he was happy to exploit that enthusiasm, of which no one was so early a champion as Beaumarchais. It was to him that America owed her first grant of foreign aid, or so Vergennes made it appear. Beaumarchais had single-handedly lobbied for and obtained the first assistance a month before Deane set foot in France. That was an unsolicited million livres, sent to America by the king of France via the playwright, on May 2, 1776. A month later that million was matched by the king of Spain, who was perfectly clear about his motives. The funds, the French ministry noted, were granted "to the end of reciprocally weakening both the English and the colonies, so as to destroy the one and to hold the other in check." For discretion's sake, Vergennes saw to it that the actual proclamation was transcribed neither in his hand nor in that of his secretary but by his fifteen-year-old son. Already the French government was hiding behind pubescents and playwrights.*

The trip from Versailles was a quick one; Deane showed the newcomers around their rooms at the Hôtel d'Entragues early on the afternoon of December 22. As he did so the carriages lined up at the door, discharging callers of every station. Few actually managed to secure interviews, but all were assiduously catalogued by Lenoir's agents, who recognized among them prominent sons of some of the oldest families in France. The next morning brought with it the clamor of the street and the clang of bells, and, from London, the blue-eyed, sandy-haired Arthur Lee. Thomas Jefferson had been elected to serve with Franklin and Deane; he who claimed he would go to hell for his country declined to go to Paris, however. He had a pregnant wife in fragile health. Arthur Lee, a thirty-five-year-old Virginian based in London, was named in his stead. Lee was a patriot of the first rank, already serving as a confidential correspondent to Congress. A well-educated lawyer and doctor, he was ideally suited for the mission in every way save for his personality, which was rancid.

The three men were equally ranked but Franklin loomed largest, by three decades the elder statesman and by virtue of his popularity the figurehead. In the eyes of Stormont, who until now had had to contend with only one rebel on his turf—"a warm, wrong-headed man" whom he did not believe capable of making any serious inroads at Versailles—Franklin's stature was the most dangerous weapon in the American arsenal. Already his magic was in evidence. Such fervor did Franklin's cause excite that a young rake was said to have managed a difficult seduction in the last days of 1776 by dressing as a Quaker and announcing himself, to

---

*The disguise was a transparent one. The hand of Constantin de Vergennes is slightly larger than that of his father, from which it is otherwise indistinguishable.

a woman who read and dreamed only of America, as an apostle of liberty. His humiliated victim was advised to retreat to a convent and to steer clear of newly arrived Philadelphians.

Toward noon on the twenty-third, Franklin and Deane rode out to Passy, a leafy village west of Paris, to dine with Jacques-Donatien Le Ray de Chaumont, who would become America's unofficial contractor general. A tiny, curly-haired man with an immense fortune, Chaumont enjoyed all the court connections that the well-intentioned Dubourg did not. Even better, the inveterate speculator harbored a vicious hatred of the British. Already Chaumont enjoyed a close working relationship with Deane, whom he had supplied with cloth and saltpeter, the active ingredient in gunpowder; already the British spies—remarking on the "extravagant zeal" with which the fifty-one-year-old threw himself into the American cause—had assigned him a code number. He made himself endlessly available over the next hectic weeks, supplementing the crash course in French politics that Franklin had begun in Nantes. One of Chaumont's first acts of kindness was to weigh in on a personal matter. What to do with Benny? His grandfather's vague plans amounted to seeing that the seven-year-old acquire a taste of French manners, after which he might be shipped off to friends in England. Benny was entrusted for several days to Chaumont, who introduced him to a local boarding school, in which Benny enrolled. Temple Franklin headed out to Versailles in Chaumont's carriage the following afternoon.

The three commissioners notified Vergennes of their appointment to negotiate a treaty of amity and commerce—her love and her money being the two greatest enticements a young republic could offer—and requested a meeting in a letter carried by Temple on Christmas Eve. Slipping the note into his pocket, Vergennes asked the young man to call for his answer the next morning. By messenger, Temple requested his grandfather's permission to spend the night in Versailles; simultaneously, Vergennes applied for the king's permission to meet with the Americans. That left the three commissioners to celebrate the holiday—and Deane's thirty-ninth birthday—on the rue de l'Université. It could not have been a quiet affair, Franklin having been overwhelmed by visitors from the minute he alighted in Paris. Nor was there much cause for celebration; Franklin arrived in Paris to hear of the defeat at White Plains. Few in London would have leapt to take up General John Burgoyne on the bet he offered that week from his comfortable club. He wagered he would be home from America, victorious, by Christmas Day 1777.

That evening Vergennes—by all accounts happiest when celebrating with his files, at his massive rosewood desk—sat down again to write his London ambassador. He was to concede only that Franklin was in France, instructed Vergennes, whom Stormont had already observed to be a master of the language of the philandering spouse: "He avoids direct falsehood, but does not avoid evasion." Otherwise the trusted comte de Noailles, the French ambassador, was to cloak himself in ignorance. If pressed further about the American's status, Noailles should reply—"as if in jest," Vergennes specified—that that would depend entirely on the British. Having closed that door, Vergennes proceeded to open the service staircase. Louis XVI granted him permission to receive Franklin, with the proviso that the foreign minister do so with the greatest of caution. Accordingly Vergennes impressed the need for perfect secrecy on the Americans. Franklin must be understood to be in France purely for family reasons. Were he to visit Versailles he must conceal his identity, a rather tall order. So long as Franklin respected those conditions, the French minister would be happy to meet and talk with him.

Vergennes opened the Saturday meeting in the south wing of Versailles with the formulaic diplomatic welcome. To each of the emissaries he extended a compliment: most lavishly on Franklin, for his celebrity, his achievements, and on the honor of receiving him on such a vital mission; on Deane for his prudence; and on Arthur Lee—whose name Vergennes had forgotten by the next morning, but who was charmed by the reception—for the zeal he had exerted from his London base. The French minister made clear the need for the Americans to lie low, to avoid giving umbrage to England. Simultaneously he assured his visitors that France's ports would be open to them. While it was common knowledge that thirty thousand fusils and two hundred fieldpieces were at that moment making their way directly from the king's arsenals to America, Vergennes affected utter ignorance of the matter, from which the envoys took their cue. Franklin reported on American affairs; offered to set his request for a commercial alliance to paper; and correctly asked if it would not be proper to extend his overtures to the ambassador of Spain, as the French and Spanish—ruled by Bourbon kings—were bound by family compact. Vergennes readily agreed. He was well aware of Franklin's reputation for duplicity, trumpeted loudly about Paris by the indefatigable Stormont. He was also much taken by the American, whom he found a cool-headed man of tact and intelligence. He was highly congenial, his conversation honest and unassuming. The straightforwardness was especially striking. Vergennes was particularly relieved that his caller already understood that he could not sell Wickes's prizes in France, which Franklin assured him he would not dream of doing.

Vergennes emerged from that conversation bewildered by the modesty of the Americans' demands, however. The deputies requested no privileges that they did not already enjoy. If they had done so in the name of decorum, theirs was a highly laudatory approach. But was it not equally possible, reasoned the statesman who had made it his business to peel words from their meaning for nearly four decades, that the Americans were attempting to manipulate Britain through the good graces of France? Their agenda remained to be seen. "In any event," concluded the man in whose casino there had of course been no gambling, "we have our principles here." He did some intriguing of his own that December morning, warning the Americans off both Dubourg and Beaumarchais, to whom delicate matters were not to be trusted. How imprudent, he frowned, for the playwright to have meddled in the Americans' affairs! As expected, Beaumarchais's variegated past served its purpose. The repudiation of the formerly penniless playwright, trading under a fictitious name with fictitiously named ships dispatched to fictitious ports, was all too easy. When senior members of the diplomatic corps clucked about Beaumarchais—they complained even to Marie Antoinette—Vergennes insisted he had neither any dealings with the playwright nor any interest in acquiring any. The official line when Lord Stormont next called to remonstrate about the irregular shipments of arms and clothing was simple: agitated English hand wringing was met with expert French hand washing. What was the government meant to do? France was full of adventurers. Merchants sold their goods to whomever they chose. But that matériel may end up in North America, insisted the British ambassador, hotly. "Wait now, they're not there yet," came the soothing reply. Stormont met only with nonchalance at Versailles. So someone had trusted some money to Beaumarchais. What could be expected of people like that?

On December 29, Franklin requested a meeting with the conde de Aranda, Spain's ambassador to France. He suggested that Franklin call after dark that evening. Aranda entertained the Americans in his private study, the opulence of which would have dazzled even after Versailles; few in Paris lived more extravagantly than the ambassador, who took pains to conceal both from his colossal staff and his family the delicate conversation. It was tough going. "Franklin speaks very little French, Deane less, and Lee none," went the Spaniard's appraisal, although with some twisting of tongues the four more or less managed to communicate. Franklin reported on his visit to Versailles, assured Aranda that he indeed had the full powers of Congress, and made a stirring case for America's resolve. He also attempted to maneuver his way around time-honored treaties. Could Spain extend safe harbor to American vessels and permit them to sell captured cargos in her ports? Aranda reminded his visitor of what Franklin well knew—both were impossible—and attempted some reconnaissance of his own. He had had little luck wrangling information out of Vergennes. Was the overnight in Versailles a coincidence? Had Franklin had any prior communications with the French court? Under interrogation Franklin proved deft. "Either because of the language barrier or because of some reserve on his part, I got nowhere," Aranda conceded. He emerged as puzzled as Vergennes. Everyone knew the Americans to be in dire straits. Why, then, did they not beg for aid and protection?

They did so promptly enough. Franklin, Deane, and Lee wasted little time before submitting a second list of considerations, "much more specific although less enticing," noted Vergennes, and hardly the last he expected to hear on the subject. The way things were going he would not be surprised if Franklin had come to inveigle France into war. For every moral and practical reason he found that proposition uninteresting in the extreme, a distaste he conveyed to Madrid. Neither kingdom had any reason to play mercenary. Nor was it in either of their interests to provoke the British, less so for the sake of an unproved country. It was established fact that republics were self-serving, less likely to honor their engagements than were monarchies. All might end with the Americans accepting a separate peace, leaving France vulnerable to her ancient rival. The colonies demonstrated little cohesion, and Congress no particular authority; Vergennes would never be convinced of that body's capacity to rule or govern.

(His confidence would not have been enhanced had he known that Congress that week requested a copy of Franklin's instructions, misplaced at their end.) As for the American people, they had no friendly feeling toward the French, whom they had fought only thirteen years earlier, and who counted among the more foreign of foreigners.

Vergennes's authority flowed directly from the king, and it was twenty-two-year-old Louis XVI who enjoined his foreign minister to reply to the Americans in a way that did not entirely extinguish their hopes. The time was simply not ripe for open intervention. A secret two million livres would soften that blow, agreed Vergennes, who simultaneously made a contorted case that it would be contrary to the dignity of a great power to resort to back channels. Beaumarchais very keenly felt the approach of that cold front, although his attention was riveted by the disaster in Le Havre, to which the *Amphitrite* unexpectedly returned on January 3. The recriminations flew fast and furious, and in every direction. The vessel had been judged less than seaworthy, and too small for its crew. Its inadequate provisions had spoiled. Not a man aboard knew the coast of North America. While the December cry from America was that independence hung by France alone—"Our fate is in your hands," went the plaintive refrain, to the Paris commissioners—the much-needed muskets and cannon and powder and tents and uniforms sat sullenly and flagrantly in a French port. The best that could be said of the business was that it was "originally well-imagined, but execrably executed."

A first crop of robust antipathies took root immediately. From an American point of view, the fault was already that of flirtatious France, an ambivalent suitor who had done too little too conspicuously, alarming England while ruining America's chances of making a match elsewhere. Deane—felled after Christmas and well into the New Year by a spectacular fever, which left Franklin handicapped in his dealings—could only groan anew that his disappointments would fill volumes as, ultimately, they would. The *Amphitrite*'s return occasioned a second embargo; there was a limit to how many times Beaumarchais could rechristen the same ship. A friendly Marylander whom Deane enlisted to review the catastrophe in Le Havre ranted against the playwriting purchasing agent: "God preserve us from trusting our money to such beings!" As for the inventive Dr. Dubourg, the Marylander's verdict was simple: "I heartily wish that we might get rid of him."

On that count Beaumarchais agreed wholeheartedly, scrambling toward center stage, and lashing out at both his perceived competitors. If Dubourg was a bumbling gossip, the energetic Chaumont was greed personified. Between the excitable doctor and the rich entrepreneur there was no affection either. Franklin left the tangled matter of personnel to Deane, a snub Beaumarchais felt keenly. No one could imagine his torment, the jilted savior wailed to Deane on a day he might have been celebrating; his ex-mistress, still living under his roof, had given birth to a healthy baby girl. "My dear Sir," Beaumarchais sighed, consumed by his own labors, "politics only rewards success. Best efforts earn only a bitter smile." It was a quite brilliant summation, and more of a prophecy than either Franklin or Vergennes could have imagined.

II
Half the Truth Is Often a Great Lie
1776–1777

It's easy. Pretend to know what you don't, and pretend not to know when you do. Hear what you don't understand and don't hear what you do. Promise what you cannot deliver, what you have no intention of delivering. Make a great secret of hiding what isn't there. Plead you're busy as you spend your time sharpening pencils. Speak profoundly to cover up your emptiness, encourage spies, reward traitors, tamper with seals, intercept letters, hide the ineptitude of your goals by speaking of them glowingly—that's all there is to politics, I swear.
—Beaumarchais, The Marriage of Figaro

Franklin would swear that an American "set down in the tourbillion of such a great city as Paris must necessarily be for some days half out of his senses." He knew of what he spoke; his first priorities were four good engineers and a host of munitions, but the French capital had ideas of its own. Immediately the city closed in on him. The envelopes had piled up in advance of his arrival; there was every reason why the former post-master general should have cursed the efficiency of the Paris mails. They arrived nine times daily. The stream of visitors was unrelenting. Almost indecently early on the first morning, the comte de Broglie, one of the great schemers of France, sent up his card. Broglie had made his name in the Seven Years' War, and headed up Louis XV's secret diplomatic service. More recently he had convinced Deane that he should assume command of the American army, which he proposed to do gratis. Broglie was so given to backroom manipulations that some in Paris credited him with having single-handedly instigated the American Revolution. Franklin granted him an interview.

Secrets did not keep in the rented rooms of Paris, and either out of a dim hope of privacy or (as the informers preferred to see it) out of discomfort, Franklin began to cast about for more suitable accommodations after two nights in Saint-Germain. Much of Christmas Day was devoted to exploring other neighborhoods in quest of a private apartment. The search continued into the New Year; on January 2, the American contingent moved down the street to the Hôtel d'Hambourg—"the English tongue is spoke," trumpeted the ads—on the fashionable rue Jacob. The move gave Lenoir his own cause to celebrate. The chief of police rarely wanted for a source in a city in which his payroll included doctors and clergymen and scullery maids—among his reports came weekly catalogues of the city's sexual escapades—but the Hambourg's maître d'hôtel was particularly devoted to him. The caliber of the callers remained impressive, but it was Lenoir's impression that the plague of visitors abated somewhat at the new address.

From Franklin's point of view it seemed that every merchant in France had a proposal too delicate to be trusted to paper but which America could not refuse. His hotel doubled as a mail drop for unsolicited advice and fervently solicited favors. One kind soul cautioned him against signing any document not drafted in English. Another charted the leaks in Beaumarchais's operation and how information wound its way to the British ambassador. A third offered an enlightened analysis of affairs as they stood. In the future Franklin would be well advised to trust in the professionals alone; Beaumarchais's recklessness had been costly. Nor was Vergennes likely to welcome any proposal to menace England. On that count Franklin was urged to be relentless. His anonymous correspondent emphasized a cardinal rule of the Old World: If in America the interest of the majority prevailed, in Europe the interests of the majority yielded to that of the few. The French people loved liberty like no other people on earth. But the general will of the populace was worthless; the government would determine its own course of action. Franklin recognized that counsel as sound. He endorsed the missive, "good advice."

His anonymous advisor's last paragraph must have had a special resonance to the man who dined out nearly every day during his first Parisian weeks. If Franklin chose to disguise the true object of his mission by accepting the flood of invitations that came his way he would eat well but not secure a cent for Congress. He would be wise to remain on guard "against the hollow puffery of the mighty, the scientists, and the women, each of whom will have some protégé to recommend." The counsel was good but not expansive enough. Franklin's reputation was immense; his protection slim; the hotel porter either eminently impressionable or bribable. It was to be a solid month of slate-gray mornings and fleeting, raw afternoons before the chaos began to subside and Franklin could think of tending to his correspondence. He was far from defenseless however, and as must anyone who expects to accomplish anything in that voluptuous city, he settled on a few ways to resist Paris's charms.

"The first thing to be done in Paris is always to send for a tailor, peruke maker, and shoemaker, for this nation has established such a domination over the fashion that neither clothes, wigs, nor shoes made in any other place will do in Paris," observed John Adams, who found himself trapped at home on one occasion when his barber was unavailable. No French porter or washerwoman or scullery maid deigned set out in the morning with unpowdered hair. Jefferson was to complain that he would prefer to cut off his locks than to surrender what would doubtless amount to a year of his life to hairdressing. And the dictatorship was absolute. The Parisian metamorphosis extended to buckles (delicate, preferably jeweled) and ruffles (obligatory lace, even if filthy and tattered), and stockings (white silk). Inevitably the new arrival in the French capital was greeted by an obsequious crew of tailors and hairdressers and language tutors and dance masters. In the event that he failed to summon them himself, his servant did for him.

The Franklin of 1767 had embraced his instant transformation, taking delight in the dapper figure he cut in his light French wig. He teased that he felt so much the Frenchman that he was tempted to pursue fashion to its Gallic end: he contemplated seducing his neighbor's wife. The Franklin of 1776 took equal delight in resisting the tyranny of fashion, largely for practical reasons. About certain things he was fastidious; he had long preferred to shave himself rather than submit to the "dull razors and the dirty fingers or bad breath of a slovenly barber." His head was covered with an unsightly scruff, better concealed by a plush fur cap, which Franklin pulled down low, to his eyebrows. As he wore the hat indoors, he may have meant for it to deflect his own scratching hands. And it was cold in Paris, not that any self-respecting Frenchman deigned to cover his hair.* The effect of his sartorial heresy was by no means lost on Franklin, more radical in his dress than in his demeanor. He relished the effect his marten fur worked among the powdered heads of Paris. His hosts were more eloquent yet on the subject. The uncoiffed head put them in the mind of Plato or Cato. It did not hurt that the fur hat bore some resemblance to that of Rousseau. And the French could not help themselves; this was a century that wrote its history in its hairstyles. The plumed headdresses that were the order of the day in December inevitably yielded to the *coiffure à la Franklin*, in which every effort was made to sculpt hair into the shape of a backwoods hat.† As much as the marten fur connoted a happy primitivism, in published reports it was soon enough upgraded to sable. In London the Tory press took the imagery in the opposite direction, describing Franklin's Parisian attire as a "Canada fur-cap" and "bear skin pelisse."

The cap was very much in evidence as he made his first important social outing. A foreigner's French fortunes depended on the initial drawing room he entered; under the wing of the eminent scientist Jean-Baptiste Le Roy, Franklin launched his conquest of Paris from a vast yellow and red silk salon that qualified as Europe's preeminent newsroom. If good taste has an epicenter, its Parisian address in 1776 was the Saint-Germain apartment in which the blind, eighty-year-old marquise du Deffand held court twice weekly. Her information was generally better even than Lenoir's. In other respects the rue Saint-Dominique was an unusual choice of drawing room. On her deathbed four years later, Madame du Deffand would beg forgiveness for having disobeyed all ten commandments and having indulged in the seven mortal sins—she had been one of the most illustrious libertines of her day—but having embraced the American cause did not figure among her transgressions. A committed Anglophile, she favored

---

*Soon enough word went around that Franklin had attempted to acquire a wig like everyone else, but that his American head had stubbornly defied French dimensions. "Sir, it's not my fault. Never has there been a head as large as yours," protested his defeated barber, in a tale Franklin trotted out to illuminate the absurdity of fitting head to wig instead of the reverse, to his mind a lovely kernel of procrustean logic. The papers extracted a different moral. "It is to be sure a large head," they conceded. "But it is also a great head."

†The tribute was not as high-minded as it might seem. After the king's zebra arrived, head-to-toe stripes were the rage, too. A generation later the first giraffe came to town, immortalized in the 1827 *"coiffure à la girafe."*

Stormont over the rest of the diplomatic corps. Nor had she any interest in or understanding of politics. For all the splendor and wit of her salon she was unable to make it past the first pages of Gibbon, who bored her to tears.

The still-beautiful hostess knew a newsworthy caller when she received one, however, and when a snowy Monday brought Franklin to her doorstep she was all attention. In his fur cap and his equally remarkable spectacles—only in 1830 would a French sovereign sink to such unstylish depths, too late for Louis XVI, who stumbled myopically through his reign—Franklin was seated at Madame du Deffand's side, before the fire. The tiny empress of opinion occupied her celebrated high-backed armchair. On Franklin's other side sat Madame de Luxembourg, who had also emerged from a scandalous past to dominate society. Most of the rest of the company consisted of a glittering array of aristocratic liberals. It was a curious gathering, enough so that friends wondered if perhaps some kind of complot was being hatched before Madame du Deffand's unseeing eyes. Among her guests was the former French foreign minister Choiseul. His presence in the same room as the incendiary American did not seem entirely coincidental. Stormont played up the encounter at Versailles, fully aware that Choiseul's name was as toxic in Vergennes's office as was Franklin's in his. Surely, asserted the British ambassador, Vergennes's enemies were leading Franklin into some sinister plot.

Franklin emerged from the visit with flying colors. His composure was exemplary, his silence amidst the chattering beau monde so novel as to be intimidating. Here was a city that had the corner on volubility and fashion and a visitor who resisted her on both counts. Doing so required no contortions on Franklin's part; words came always more easily to him on the page than in person. Even after years in Paris his deliberate responses could be preceded by eight- to ten-minute pauses. To a lesser man that would have spelled a social death, but from the start Franklin broke the rules and France returned the favor. In the theaters, the drama took place in the audience as much as on the stage; the Parisian curtain went down again, and the overture was replayed, if the king of Sweden happened to take his seat late. Franklin quickly caught on to the fact that performances were punctuated by outbursts of applause, in which he joined; only later did he learn that he had lustily applauded himself. His behavior may not have spoken well for his modesty but nor did it earn him the censure heaped upon the Moroccan ambassador for having yawned his way through a performance. In a society of elaborate, unbending rules there must have been an unnerving round of faux pas. Only a few have survived, and those courtesy of a Tory sympathizer; Franklin may have had the temerity to tackle asparagus with his fingers, and to cut with his knife instead of his spoon. The evidence points generally to his having embraced France with an ease and calm that only raised his stock. There are no strains of mortification or self-pity in his account of having called on the prince de Masserano and having been ushered in instead to see the princess, still in bed.

Insofar as he picked up the pieces from Silas Deane, Franklin did so discriminately. Beaumarchais was an immediate casualty. Dubourg had nothing good to say of him; Vergennes had made clear his disapproval. From all fronts came accounts of the playwright's imprudence. Deane observed that Franklin left the covert shipping operation entirely to him; Beaumarchais felt only the insult of the powerfully turned back. Wildly he begged for an explanation of the mystery behind Franklin's "bizarre and dishonest conduct." He was left to make scenes with Deane and Lee about defective cannon, about American ingratitude, about the meddling of philosophers in foreign affairs—all while he continued to coax boats out of French harbors, through a web of lies, and toward America. His neglect also left Franklin's hands clean, which meant it was easier for him to play his assigned role. On the evening of January 4, 1777, Franklin met again with the Spanish ambassador to Versailles. To the conde de Aranda's question—has France provided you with any help?—Franklin replied with perfect innocence. A private company had supplied arms, ammunition, and officers. France's assistance was limited to noninterference, a statement Aranda knew to be as adept as it was false. Franklin was equally disingenuous on another front. Aranda had heard that the Americans were interested in a treaty. How could they offer one up, when they were not yet independent? Was aid not their more immediate need? Franklin replied that a treaty would allow the colonies to identify their true friends. He was not soliciting aid. Doing so was inappropriate and, as yet, entirely unnecessary.

He battled the aspiring officers, the merchants, and the advice givers less ably; Franklin was a congenial man without any great gift for solitude. When the duc de Cröy, a noted naturalist and much-decorated military hero, called in mid-January, Franklin received him warmly, even before he understood that Cröy roamed freely among the ministerial offices at Versailles. Impressed with his vigor, the duc found Franklin "a large and immensely attractive man." The fur hat and the spectacles worked their usual magic. Cröy breathed not a word about the insurgents or affairs of the day, limiting the discussion to electricity and, finally, the weather. Was it true, asked the distinguished general, that Philadelphia was colder than Paris, despite their relative latitudes? It was both hotter and colder, replied Franklin, explaining: "Our Delaware River, more than twice the size of yours, freezes in the winter, in one night." (It would be nearly three months before he would have any inkling of the use General Washington had made of that ice floe on Christmas evening, when he led two thousand men in darkness, through sleet and snow and roaring winds, to the first victory of the war.) Soon enough Franklin's reserve— what had passed in America for his "perpetual taciturnity"—became in French "his sublime reticence." In prattling Paris it was noted that Franklin did something extraordinary. He listened. And any word that did escape his lips sped instantly around the kingdom. Hence his theory that God had visited the scourge of war upon America to chastise her for her devastating beauty made the tour of France and—via the ambassadorial corps—all of Europe. So did Franklin's disappointments. It was a terrible thing, quite unfair indeed, he grumbled loudly, regularly, and falsely, that he had not been accorded an interview with a single French minister.

Stormont argued that Franklin's language had already sunk him; nothing but duplicitous statements issued from the arch-rebel's mouth. The excitable British ambassador fell prey to a syndrome to which Franklin was immune: Stormont was expert at hearing what he wanted to hear. When word reached him that the French minister of the navy had referred to Franklin as "a first-rate scoundrel," Stormont instantly rushed off a confidential dispatch to London. Regularly he disseminated reports that Franklin was in Europe as a fugitive. On Wednesday, January 15, Stormont reiterated his news of the previous week, which he had forced on the rest of the diplomatic corps. No fashion in Paris survived the French attention span. Franklin's hour had passed. Already, trumpeted Stormont, he was eclipsed by an Italian composer. The ambassador should perhaps have been more catholic in his dinner invitations. That week the papers reported that the gift of the season was a Franklin portrait for the mantel, where he functioned as a sort of household god. Soon enough it was difficult to find a French coachman or chambermaid unfamiliar with the arch-rebel's image, "and who did not consider him as a friend to humankind."

Also that Monday the king granted the American commissioners their 2 million livres, without interest, payable when "the United States are settled in peace and prosperity," a gift so secret that the envoys vaguely credited it to unnamed private hands when exuberantly notifying Congress. (The king's largesse would never be committed to paper on either side. Nor would Conrad-Alexandre Gérard, the young, bilingual undersecretary who delivered the happy news, sign his notes to the commissioners. Nor would any document connecting the French court to the rebels ever be entrusted to American hands.) While Stormont reported on Franklin's discussions with the French tobacco monopoly—which he was pleased to see went nowhere—no word of that official transaction ever crept into his voluminous correspondence. Instead he railed about French interference in the American tobacco trade, which he held to be nearly as seductive as Dr. Franklin himself.

The French made no mystery of their interest in Stormont; in a city in which police surveillance was universal, no one was more closely trailed than the British ambassador. Very little eluded Lenoir's agents, part gumshoes, part gossips, who knew when His Excellency took his fencing lesson, his Italian lesson, his dinner; when he was in a good mood, when he went out to ride, when his teenage wife was pregnant; what was in his mailbag. Even Stormont's informers were informed upon. French police intelligence was legendary, as was the average Parisian's interest in the affairs of his neighbors. If that was not actually an indigenous French trait, Lenoir did all he could to cultivate it. The adage went that when two Parisians talked a third inevitably listened. (Precisely nine days elapsed between Franklin's assuring Aranda that the colonies were in no immediate need of assistance, and the arrival of a very different report. Someone in Franklin's confidence assured the Spanish ambassador that "Congress did not want to come humbly begging or manifest extreme need, as they feared incurring onerous obligations.") Franklin knew well there was a price to be paid for appearing on every mantel in France. When asked later to meet a dubious emissary in central Paris he was very clear about the burden of his celebrity. He could not put in an appearance at Notre-Dame without any conceivable business there.

In both his terseness and his aversion to intrigue he was well suited to his mission. At the same time he was alarmingly casual about security. Mid-January found William Carmichael, the dashing young Marylander who was to attach himself to the mission as Deane's secretary, in Le Havre, sorting out the *Amphitrite* fiasco. "If you ever expect secrecy from a Frenchman, woman, or child, you merit being abused," he sputtered. "The secrets of the women are sometimes indeed worth having, but as from them you run the risk of infection, so from the close whisper of the men you are suffocated with garlic." In less offensive terms Franklin was repeatedly warned that he was surrounded, that his papers lay about his rooms too openly, that his every move was monitored. Given the Parisian ability to spin a tale out of whole cloth, suggested one friend, did it not behoove his grandson to spend a half hour every day filing papers so as to shield them from prying eyes? That helpful soul was himself a British spy.

To his counsel Franklin replied with a logic all his own. He made no experiments with invisible ink. He who had taught himself languages as a youth, who amused himself with mathematical puzzles during tedious meetings, proved useless with cipher, which he found more trouble than it was worth. (He had a point. Most of the various ciphers used by the Americans seemed to frustrate only their intended recipients.) Franklin barely participated in the masquerade which would transform Beaumarchais into Roderigue Hortalez and Arthur Lee into Mary Johnston and John Adams into Ferdinando Ramón San. When pressured to adopt a cryptonym early in 1777, the man who would write as Alice Addertongue and Sidi Mehemt Ibrahim chose to wrap himself in the plain brown cloak of Monsieur François. As for the swarm of spies, Franklin was grateful for and in no way surprised by the information. But as it was impossible both to prevent that surveillance and to determine exactly who one's false friends were, he intended to live by a rule that he had long observed. "It is simply this," he shrugged, "to be concerned in no affairs that I should blush to have made public; and to do nothing but what spies may see and welcome. When a man's actions are just and honorable, the more they are known, the more his reputation is increased and established. If I was sure therefore that my *valet de place* was a spy, as probably he is, I think I should not discharge him for that, if in other respects I liked him." He had, he insisted, nothing to conceal. Already his method had produced results; he had thrown Stormont off the trail. Franklin also seriously underestimated the perfidy of those around him. As a result, some of his best friends were spies.

⤙⋇⤚

The Paris into which Franklin rode in 1776 was at once the most opulent city in the world and the Calcutta of its day. A decade earlier Franklin had himself marveled at the city's "prodigious mixture of magnificence and negligence." His was a more indulgent analysis than that of Voltaire, who reduced the European capital to "an appalling luxury and a hideous misery." Approached from the tree-lined Versailles road, as Franklin entered it, Paris was almost blinding in its pearly splendor, a twinkling constellation of steeples bathed in hazy light. After submitting to the customhouse interrogation, the visitor continued down the sloping, elm-lined Champs-Elysées, through a field dotted with pavilions, cafés, and flower beds.* A collection of handsome town houses and manicured gardens gradually materialized to the south, while to the north windmills spun over the green hill of Montmartre. The effect was of a majestic family of eagles taking flight. At the foot of the Champs-Elysées stood the largest public square in existence, the newly created heart of Paris, presided over by an immense equestrian statue of Louis XV. Beyond his balustrade a bridge led to the immaculately groomed paths of the Tuileries, which gave on to the palace of the Louvre. The view was a wonder, a thrilling triumph of design. To Philadelphian eyes it would have been particularly imposing. French visitors to America noted that the only building of any distinction in that provincial city was the prison.

If Franklin found the vista a reward for the monthlong trip across a cold sea he left no record. Nor did the man who was so much to thank for the clean, cobbled, and well-lighted streets of redbrick Philadelphia

---

*It is unlikely that Franklin attempted any of Deane's misdemeanors at the barriers of Paris; this was the man who forever linked death with taxes, and that when addressing a Frenchman. Moreover, his American accent had disarmed those green-coated inspectors before.

leave any lasting impression of what followed. The visitor who ventured on into the heart of Paris—confined in the 1770s to an area a third its size today—discovered a very different city, a dim, bustling, steaming, fetid, brimming, deafening madness. Eighteenth-century Paris generally registered with the visitor as an assault on the senses; entire terraces of the Tuileries, lengths of the quais, public stairways repelled visitors with their odor. From the tangle of dark, congested streets rose a stench that crawled up the visitor's nostrils and took noxious hold. Rain produced only a sulfurous steam. "All the splendors vanish before you," noted a keen observer, "yielding to the impression that the sewers of every city on earth meet in Paris, to spew forth their most vile refuse." The streets amounted to pungent rivers of filth, their mud so acidic that it rotted through a dress or a stocking in the course of an evening. It gave rise to a herd of young men who threw themselves on the spattered pedestrian with their brushes, a breed so agile they doubled as theatrical stunt men.

The slippery stew which was a Paris thoroughfare accounted for the city's most singular danger. No man who had the means walked through the filth of the streets, and no man who had the means hired a driver with any respect for the individual who did. A stroll through Paris was an exercise in skulking in doorways and leaping into shops and running for one's life so as to avoid the fate of the thousands sacrificed each year to carriage wheels. Every day brought accounts of children crushed by coaches; so common were the collisions that the fines for legs, thighs, arms had been codified. How actually to navigate the Parisian filth on foot was a secret known only to natives. One of the finer amusements of the city was the sight of a Parisian "vaulting across a river of blood with his three-tiered wig, his white stockings, and his brilliantly decorated suit, navigating the filth on tiptoe, and fending off the assault from the drain pipes with his taffeta parasol." Stiletto heels were a clever solution, but red stilettos made for the most sensible choice. The blood from the butcher's shop discolored anything in its wake. The average Parisian, it was noted as early as the 1770s, preferred his dog to a clean stairwell.

If nighttime Philadelphia was thought the quietest city on earth, daytime Paris could stake claim to the noisiest. The rush of carriages and the bark of their escorts made for a vigorous percussion section; the melody was carried by the city's ambulatory bazaar. The piercing cries of the hat seller and the fishmonger and the water carrier and the umbrella boys and the chimney sweep and the coffee ladies—two sous a cup, from the urns strapped to their backs—produced an extraordinary wall of sound, a perpetual clamor. Half unintelligible to the educated Parisian, the idiom of the streets was unfathomable to the foreigner. The visitor who was not flattened by the sound of the city was soon enough worn through by its vivacity. It was commonly accepted that Paris goodbyes were interminable, compliments fulsome, the smallest transaction cause for eternal discussion. And the French language was happy to accommodate the chronically voluble Parisian, who even in the native opinion "generally speaks at great length without saying anything, or rather, in saying nothing." As the straight-shooting Arthur Lee had it, the French tended "to talk much, do little, and protract everything."

How that would have sounded to the Boston native who had begun his journalistic career as Silence Dogood can easily be imagined. Franklin so much deplored the habit of "saying little in much" that he would propose a law against padding books. Encounters of old men and old worlds are not notoriously successful; in the initial embrace Franklin was equitable, however. In the first place, caught as he was in the social whirl of the first months, his luggage still somewhere between Le Havre and Paris, his time cannibalized by strangers, the mood at Versailles difficult to gauge, he committed little of personal substance to paper. The transcription of documents for Aranda and Vergennes consumed his first weeks, as Deane was out of commission, and Franklin unwilling to delegate the task. There were to be none of the Paris "is the very dirtiest place I ever saw" expostulations of Abigail Adams, none of Jefferson's "I find the general fate of humanity here most deplorable." If Paris existed only in the writing of Benjamin Franklin, all of eighteenth-century painting and sculpture, architecture and theater would be lost, just as the arts would wither were Poor Richard taken at his plodding, prosaic word; Franklin was alarmingly blind to the aesthetic, at least in its inanimate form.

He knew already the extravagances of London, to which he had not been immune; years before he became an arch-rebel, he had designed a coat of arms for his carriage. Those luxuries were unknown to John Adams, who had never before been abroad when he arrived in Paris and began to rant over its alabaster and mirrored impurities. Franklin had seen it all before. It may have mattered less to him because he had; it may have mattered less because he had no eye for it in the first place. It cannot have been invisible to a man who spent his early childhood in a two-room clapboard house and who, for all his crest designing, never forgot as much. It was perhaps on that count that Paris and Franklin would prove best suited to each other. They were composed of equal parts gravitas and raffishness. Mostly though the earthy Franklin took to Paris—a city that before him Rousseau, Smollett, and Walpole could not leave quickly enough—because he needed to. At the time of his arrival he loved his country and hated England, probably with equal passion. What he felt about France could wait until later, and did.

What did he know about France, America's traditional enemy? He may have provided many Frenchmen with their first taste of America, but Franklin had himself so long profited from Gallic collaborations that his arrival could nearly be termed a homecoming. He claimed to have learned about dealing with his fellow men from the immensely popular *Port-Royal Logic*; two decades before Descartes, Antoine Arnauld had argued that "common sense is not really so common." A powerful and avid swimmer, Franklin had mastered all the strokes in Thévenot's illustrated *The Art of Swimming*, one of the first texts on the subject. The mathematical puzzles with which he had conjured as a Pennsylvania Assembly clerk too were French, from a seventeenth-century text. Franklin set out to improve on the numeric columns that added up to identical sums in every direction, producing what he rather gloriously described as "the most magically magical of any magical square ever made by any magician."* In his Pennsylvania stove experiments, he had followed the lead of a Frenchman. The Academy of Bordeaux in 1749 had formulated the compelling question that had ultimately made Franklin's name: Was there any link between electricity and thunder? From his late twenties Franklin had read French; to Philadelphia's first subscription library he donated a volume of Montaigne. He knew Voltaire's pages on religious tolerance. Early on a pattern had established itself: The ideas came from France and the execution from America, as Franklin the faux Quaker—in his sense and sensibility, a joint production of Voltaire and Rousseau—now proved. There

---

*It fell to a Frenchman to catch the errors in Franklin's magical masterpiece. That man was the invincible Dubourg.

was every reason why the apothegms of Poor Richard were nearly as familiar to the French as to the Americans. Franklin had been lifting liberally from La Rochefoucauld and Rabelais for years.

It is doubtful that Franklin knew how to lift a French glass (with thumb and two fingers only) or how properly to enter a salon (with bows all around, the caller took the seat to his hostess's right, to make sparkling conversation until vacating his perch to the newcomer). But what he possessed in spades, and what was prominently on display, was a majestic suppleness, always a rare quality, the more so in a man of his age. He was equally comfortable with a lack of clarity. Public opinion might well be divided over whether he was in Paris to underwrite or undermine a revolution, but that was of no concern to Franklin. The conjectures "amuse those that make them, and some of those that hear them; they do me no harm, and therefore it is not necessary that I should take the least pains to rectify them." He was held in high esteem by the Catholics, by the Church of England, by every religious denomination, each of whom happily claimed him as one of their own; a monochromatic blur amid the brilliant plumage of Paris, he was so commonly taken for a Quaker that even Dubourg labored for some time under that impression. (He did not like his friend any the less when disabused of it.) A satiric paper ultimately concluded that Franklin owed much of this mileage to the fact that he had no religion at all, which in a churchgoing sense was exact. (He had lasted five Sundays as a Presbyterian.) That may have made it easier for him to swallow what was for may of his countrymen the bitter pill of cozying up to a Catholic country. Some members of Congress still shuddered at the prospect of doing business with "Papists," even if the Roman Catholic in question happened to be an artillery expert. Worshipped throughout Paris as someone he decidedly was not, the new envoy comported himself as Benjamin Franklin. He liked himself too much to pose as anyone else. His religion while in France was America, and he adapted his rituals to suit the Parisian faithful.

He was quick to decode the language of the day, which was persiflage. What passed for good manners in France amounted in the Anglo-Saxon view to fawning. It took Franklin little time to grasp that "You must come to dinner" meant "I hope never to see you again," that one was "prodigiously obsessed" with a subject in which one was at best mildly interested. No minor transaction could take place without recourse to the words "conscience," "honor," and "faith," words that rarely went to market in America. Lush bouquets of compliments bloomed spontaneously, distributed themselves widely, and signified nothing. That Franklin well knew; he could be held responsible for a riotous explosion of bad poetry. So much was overstatement the order of the day that Franklin would tease that the French tongue was in danger of wearing itself out. It was noted that the French tended to treat their affairs of state like bagatelles, their bagatelles like affairs of state. Franklin adapted easily, no great stretch for the man who had been a seventeen-year-old satirist.

In parsing the customs of the country he relied heavily on the tiny, pock-faced Chaumont, whose interests were as diverse as his energy was boundless. Few branches of business failed to engage the high-powered Frenchman. He had established a tannery, a glassworks, a flour mill, a saltpeter manufacture, a limestone quarry, and a textile mill, and held interests in coal-mining and grain-importing enterprises. Over the first weeks, Franklin saw Chaumont more regularly than any other of his new acquaintances. Clearly he felt as comfortable entrusting America's needs as Benny's schooling to the lively entrepreneur, who was busily procuring thousands of barrels of saltpeter for the American cause. Chaumont had every reason to be sympathetic to his friend's housing woes; he saw firsthand that Franklin was subject to perpetual interruption and close surveillance. The envoys had been instructed to establish a residence in the French capital that was consistent with their dignity as public representatives but it was to be years before anyone in Philadelphia understood what that meant; congressional delegates did not count among the readers of the popular 1777 novel *The English Fortnight in Paris, or The Art of Bankrupting Oneself in No Time*. Franklin's hotel bill would have accounted for half his salary. A coach and horses could easily subsume the other half. As the proprietor of one of the two most spectacular estates in Passy, Chaumont was in a position to offer an alternative to ruinous hotel life. By the end of January he had convinced Franklin to move to apartments in an outlying villa on the grounds of the Hôtel de Valentinois, as his guest.

The arrangement suited everyone, perhaps Vergennes—who helped to orchestrate it—most of all. His was the no-fingerprints school of diplomacy, and discreet communication with the American was next to impossible when Franklin sat in plain view of every spy in Paris. Vergennes much preferred him hidden away behind linden and lime trees, with a difficult-to-find back door, through which emissaries could slip discreetly. Two miles west of the center of Paris, the village of Passy, today part of the sixteenth arrondissement, was that much closer to Versailles; Chaumont's hospitality allowed Franklin to move at once nearer to the maze of European policy and farther from that of the fetid city streets. The benefits to his host were equally great. Franklin's proximity guaranteed Chaumont privileged status among those jockeying to supply the needy Americans; quite literally it put his market in his backyard. By default he became the primary go-between with Versailles. And as he did everything he did with conviction, that meant he was not above listening at Franklin's door when he felt it necessary. "Doors and walls are fool's paper," Franklin had observed, in the guise of his almanach-writing alter ego, Poor Richard. They were especially so in Passy, where the landlord had his own substantial stake in the American contest.

Having been awarded a series of lucrative sinecures over the years, Chaumont had bought the furnished Valentinois property for a princely sum, from the duc de Choiseul's younger brother. In the clear light of revisionism, he claimed to have done so expressly to lodge the American commissioners, but as he made the purchase in August of 1776—when Franklin had not yet been appointed, and Deane was comfortably ensconced in Saint-Germain—his memory may have failed him. His ingenuity did not. Chaumont had long been interested in ceramics, and established a workshop at his Loire château for the talented, pint-sized Italian sculptor Giovanni-Battista Nini. Early in 1777 Nini began to turn out terra-cotta medallions of Chaumont's celebrated guest, which traveled throughout Europe. Chaumont claimed half the net profits of the medallions; Nini soon discovered that he could not keep up with demand. It was less than Chaumont deserved for having so adroitly served the American cause. He removed Franklin from circulation, while keeping him always in the public eye.

For Franklin, juggling foreign policy with family concerns, the Valentinois solved a multitude of problems. Chaumont's hospitality came rent-free. With the good faith of a good businessman, he promised he would sacrifice himself no longer when America could afford to pay. It was agreed between the two men that Franklin would reimburse his host for all meals he and his guests took with Chaumont's family; the lodger assumed the costs of entertaining at his villa. Had there been a Mrs. Franklin at his side the arrangement would have been unnecessary, but Deborah Franklin had died two years earlier, when her husband's London existence had been in the hands of his capable and adoring London landlady. That winter he felt his wife's loss acutely, which may say all that need be said about Franklin's marriage. The relationship was one very much founded on practicality.* Fortunately Chaumont had a witty wife and four lovely daughters, of whom the eldest was happy to release Franklin from the quotidian details, looking after the horses and supplying clean linens, stocking up on firewood and tracking down the occasional piano, assistance that was particularly welcome as there were no set prices in France. Franklin had as well his grandsons' interests to consider. Seventeen-year-old Temple would be living with Franklin, who for all his offhandedness was well aware of what Jefferson would observe: "While learning the language in France a young man's morals, health and fortune are more irresistibly endangered than in any country of the universe." This was after all a city with over fourteen thousand registered prostitutes, an army larger than was, at times, General Washington's.† Benny's boarding school was in Passy, which meant the seven-year-old would be able to join his grandfather on weekends. Deane and Lee were invited to settle at the Valentinois as well but for their own reasons kept their distance, or at least their partial distance. Lee remained his own man, initially installing himself in a rue de Richelieu hotel. By April Deane had joined Franklin in Passy, while signing a one-year lease on a luxurious second apartment in Paris, overlooking the place Louis XV.

Chaumont's estate was a sumptuous home in a sumptuous location, a half hour's ride from central Paris. Accessible by carriage or ferry, Passy consisted of four royal châteaux, a collection of handsome estates, a parish church, a settlement of a few hundred inhabitants, and three paved

---

*When the two joined households in 1730, Deborah Read was in fact Franklin's ex-fiancée. He returned to her—after a failed marriage suit elsewhere—with respect, out of a sense of duty, and with an illegitimate son, whom the able-bodied Deborah raised.

†Borrowing a page from Beaumarchais, Abigail Adams would inflate that number to 52,000. And John Adams would outdo Jefferson. The delights of Paris aside, "there is everything here too which can seduce, betray, deceive, corrupt and debauch."

streets. It was home as well to several renowned mineral springs, on the terraced grounds of the spirited and jovial Louis-Guillaume Le Veillard, soon to be a Franklin intimate. A short walk from the Valentinois stood the royal scientific laboratory, stocked with an array of microscopes and telescopes and under the direction of Le Roy, who shared Franklin's encyclopedic interests. At its western edge the town bordered a royal forest, today the Bois de Boulogne. Perched atop a hill, since considerably leveled, Chaumont's property stood a few hundred yards above the Seine. Franklin's address would have been the rue Basse.*

On Chaumont's eighteen acres stood a vast country estate and several outlying buildings, among them a two-story, neoclassical garden pavilion, a five-minute walk from the main house. In that structure Chaumont installed the Americans. A more salubrious accommodation would have been difficult to imagine. Franklin strolled down a gallery of paintings and sculpture to his apartments. A half-hidden pathway connected his back door to the quiet village; the pavilion gave on to a formal, terraced garden of chestnut and linden and acacia trees. Beyond Chaumont's belvedere lay commanding views of Paris, of the Champ de Mars and the Invalides, of the towers of Notre-Dame, of the hills of Saint-Cloud and Meudon, and of the tip of the Ile de Cygne. All was subdued, airy, and scenic. Immediately Passy began to function as a mail drop for "M. François," although it would be a month before Franklin managed to extricate himself from Paris and transfer his effects to the Valentinois. From its roof a lightning rod soon sprouted, in 1777 the closest thing to an American flag. The motto over Chaumont's door read, "*Se sta bene non se muove*," which a later American tenant translated, overly literally, as "If you stand well, stand still." There Franklin remained, in as close to a rustic retreat as this frontier philosopher ever managed.

~※~

Franklin was clear about his expectations for Passy. He hoped "there to find a little leisure, free from the perpetual interruption I suffer here by the

---

*Doubtless it would have amused the man who could debate either side of an issue that the street had recently borne another name. Around 1770, when the landowner at the top of Passy's main thoroughfare hoped to make a point, the rue Haute was turned on its head to become the rue Basse. It is today the rue Raynouard.

crowds continually coming in, some offering goods, others solliciting for offices in our army, etc. etc." In that desire he was disappointed. He had been in Passy only forty-eight hours when he agreed to meet, late on a Sunday afternoon, with a distinguished historian, poet, and diplomat. What he did not know was that he owed the urbane chevalier de Rulhière's call to his campaign on behalf of a Polish friend, whom Rulhière believed to be an invaluable asset to the American cause. The visitor was irritated to find Franklin as unforthcoming as he was uninformed. He did not know who the vaunted Kazimierz Pulaski was; he did not have the funds to settle Pulaski's debts and send him to America; he was most unhelpful. Pointedly Franklin explained that he had "refused so many people of every nationality who have come to offer themselves to him that he was unwilling to give an example the least effect of which would expose him to renewed importunities." He knew that while the colonies needed every manner of matériel, from flints and musketballs to buttons and rope, the one thing they did not want was men. In this case Vergennes weighed in. Pulaski sailed early in the summer.

What began as a trickle of applications swelled to a spring torrent. To a large extent Franklin had himself to blame, his presence having fanned excitement for the American cause to a fever pitch. Republican ideals figured nowhere in the picture; any grasp of the word *liberty* was purely phonetic. Military distinction was the currency of the realm, and since 1763—France having been achingly, stubbornly at peace—her noble sons had been without any means to enrich themselves. Franklin bore the brunt of the pent-up frustration. It was unrelenting and original and often comic, at least to someone who did not have the most illustrious names of France beating down his front door. America beckoned as well as the perfect place to warehouse the unregenerate sons of respectable families until they grew into a little sense, a strategy to which Franklin was not blind: "Frequently if a man has no useful talents, is good for nothing, and burdensome to his relations, or is indiscreet, profligate and extravagant, they are glad to get rid of him by sending him to the other end of the world." At times he must have felt as if he were running an exclusive reform school.* One aspirant's

---

*Franklin was particularly charmed by the young courtier sent his way with an appeal from his mother: "Sir, if you in America have the secret of reforming detestable individuals who are the torment of their families, I beg you to send the bearer of this letter there." According to Franklin, the little-loved son fought for and died in America.

qualifications were these: He was "well-born, tall, agile, and handsome." Another burned only to fight the English once again before he died. A third admitted he was no genius and had never borne arms, but had ambition in spades. Some appeared on the edge of hysteria. A Lille aspirant happy to serve with pen or sword proposed his services as a musician, an accountant, or a bad poet. On one application Franklin scrawled "mad," on a second "wild." The correspondents were by no means universally French. They were Walloons and Russians and Poles. Three Peruvians offered up their services. They wrote in every language of Europe and often in ingenious hybrids thereof. Each and every one was unflinchingly brave and irreparably moral and deeply ambitious, but could not be expected to make war at his own expense.

Nor did Franklin's friends show him much mercy. Even Dubourg tested his limits. When he exceeded them, Franklin—more of a scorekeeper than he let on—reminded the good doctor that he was harassed without reprieve, from morning to night: "The noise of every coach now that enters my court terrifies me. I am afraid to accept an invitation to dine abroad, being almost sure of meeting with some officer or officer's friend, who, as soon as I am put in good humor by a glass or two of champagne, begins his attack on me. Luckily I do not often in my sleep dream of these vexatious situations, or I should be afraid of what are now my only hours of comfort. If, therefore, you have the least remaining kindness for me, if you would not help to drive me out of France, for God's sake, my dear friend, let this your twenty-third application be your last."

Generally he managed to remain silent, or coolly noncommittal. As the weeks wore on the tenacity proved even more than an equable man could bear, however. To a Franconian aspirant who took it upon himself to upbraid the dignitary for his silence, Franklin extended a memorable lesson in etiquette, doubtless intended for the previous two hundred intruders as well: "Whoever writes to a stranger should observe three points; 1. That what he proposes be practicable. 2. His propositions should be made in explicit terms, so as to be easily understood. 3. What he desires should be in itself reasonable. Hereby he will give a favorable impression of his understanding, and create a desire of further acquaintance. Now it happened that you were negligent in *all* these points." Ultimately he would avail himself of a sort of non-reference letter, but he would never entirely adjust to the patronage system of Europe, even when he had begun to exploit it himself.

Had Franklin known that Deane's more liberal dispatching of officers would result in one of the greatest public relations disasters of his Parisian stay, he would doubtless have exploded sooner. As late as April 1777, Franklin queried Congress as to whether he should encourage applicants. He had not yet heard the collective groan going up in America against the French arrivals. On the day that he blasted the young Franconian, Congress pointedly requested its Paris commissioners to discourage any foreigner in search of military employment. The difficulties extended beyond the language barrier; just because Congress did not want the officers who could not speak English did not mean it wanted the ones who could. By August Washington was pleading with Franklin to spare him future mortification. There was no money to pay the hordes who descended on America, their pretentions rarely borne out by their experience. They quarreled endlessly about rank; they compromised morale. The commander in chief well understood that he was putting Franklin in "a delicate and perplexing" position. He also begged him not to so much as offer up a line of recommendation. In Passy the barrage continued.

To those wishing to serve were joined applications from every friend of liberty, commerce, or both, in every corner of Europe. A dazzling array of benevolent souls could supply top-quality blankets, shoes, beer, folding tables, healing powders, at enticing prices. And then there were the inventors. It seemed that even Dr. Franklin had his limits when it came to ingenuity. "The number of wild schemes proposed to me is so great, and they have heretofore taken so much of my time, that I begin to reject all, though possibly *some* of them may be worth notice," he concluded, on a day when he entertained, in succession, the creator of a miraculous, self-propelled tobacco-cutting machine; the genius behind a plan to land six hundred men in the British Isles, to burn and ransom towns; and the inventor of a sort of Trojan horse contraption, in which a cavalryman could conceal his arms.* The same afternoon brought an essay on the properties of fire, written in English "with a little tincture of

---

*The assault was not entirely unfamiliar. "I don't know what it is about our home," Franklin quoted his wife as having complained years earlier, in Philadelphia, "but not one madman sets foot on the American continent without proceeding directly to our front door."

French idiom." The author, whose name rang no bells with Franklin or with anyone in France, where he was to play a role in a different revolution, was Jean-Paul Marat. Some of those visions were no more far-fetched than the ones hatched by the American commissioners themselves. Early in the year a great deal of attention went to a scheme to occupy a Mediterranean island, for use as an American naval base. Deane recruited a deranged pyromaniac to burn an English shipyard. He contemplated inciting an Irish rebellion. As if not to be outdone, Arthur Lee—whose imagination was undeniably more fertile than either of his colleagues'—proposed they send an emissary to the emperor of China.* The idea of the youngest republic appealing to the oldest despot made some kind of romantic sense to him. He was gratified that Franklin did not reject the idea out of hand.

What did stick in Franklin's craw was the posture of supplicant. The father of self-reliance was an unhappy beggar, one especially wary of taxing Vergennes's patience. He was never to waver in his conviction that asking for help was the worst way of obtaining it. From the start he held that America's best interest lay in allowing France to act in what she considered to be her own best interest. He felt he could afford to be patient; he was certain France would never abide the colonies' return to British dominion. From Vergennes's office through January and February came only the scrape of artful foot-dragging. As much as France yearned to wreak revenge on England, neither her finances nor her navy were in a state that would allow her to do so. Franklin's reaction was to take some obvious steps forward—in the absence of any word from Congress, the commissioners determined to have six ships built, to send Arthur Lee to try his luck at the court of Madrid, to purchase additional, secondhand munitions from the arsenals of France—and to desist from all solicitations. He entrusted matters of matériel entirely to Deane. So long as the French government continued to turn a blind eye, commercial affairs could remain in the hands of various private individuals, Chaumont foremost among them. In the weeks before and immediately after the move to Passy, Franklin continued in his social

---

*For his part Beaumarchais championed some prearranged piracy. In his caper, two American corsairs would sail for San Domingo, where they would "capture" the cannon and artillery intended for them. Afterward they would be loudly disavowed by Congress.

rounds, made his first visit to the prestigious Académie des Sciences, and toured the king's libraries. Several foreign diplomats called on him, ostensibly to discuss scientific matters. But he assumed a low profile politically.

In that strategic withdrawal everyone read what he wanted. Beaumarchais—still waiting for a dinner invitation from the discourteous envoy, alternately moping and raging against ingratitude, inaction, ineptitude—questioned Franklin's resolve. If he could sow doubts about Franklin's constancy he could pave the way for his new and improved Franco-American financial scheme. And so it suited him to insinuate that Franklin entertained British offers of reconciliation. (Beaumarchais also provided what appeared a perfectly valid excuse for his sour humor: "No one but me does anything around here for the good of America.") Stormont cheerfully noted that Franklin seemed lost; he passed on word that the American had been rebuffed by Versailles. Members of the ambassadorial corps breathed a collective sigh of relief. If France could resist Franklin's advances, peace would prevail. War with England was not in anyone's best interests; the rest of Europe was happy to believe Franklin shut up in his Passy sanctuary.

But it was Vergennes, who presumably advised Franklin on the tactical shift, who wrung the most mileage from it. Just before the move to Passy the French minister shared his supposed mystification over the emissary's behavior with his ambassador in London: "I still don't know what Dr. Franklin has come to accomplish among us. When he first arrived it seemed possible that he had an important mission. Suddenly he has closeted himself with the philosophers. If he contemplates some political objective, it is not with the King's ministers but rather with those who are opposed to them. Evidently, opposition is his natural element." Vergennes could easily understand how much Franklin's presence in France rankled in London; the glimpse of American stocking was provocative indeed. But before casting any stones the British should be reminded of the hero's welcome they had extended to the Corsican rebel Pasquale Paoli. Weakening a power by assisting her defiant colonies was an established European practice, and in 1768 England had been only too happy to supply the Corsicans in their Paoli-led battle against the French. (Versailles had threatened to retaliate by inciting rebellion in New York and Boston.) In any family there is an old misdemeanor that can be trotted out when useful. This would be Vergennes's.*

In London the comte de Noailles took his superior's words at face value. Franklin should hardly be devoting himself to philosophical pursuits at such a time. His efforts on his country's behalf were decidedly lackluster. At the risk of appearing the American's apologist, Noailles thought he could shed some light on his lack of ambition, however: "Franklin's customary strategy when landing on unfamiliar ground is to display for a short while the greatest inactivity. He speaks little and when he does, addresses only general subjects, or those relating to literature and science, in which he is exceedingly well-versed. Accordingly, long after his return to America many suspected him of having succumbed to the proposals of the British ministry, although he had never engaged in any kind of deceit or double-dealing. His extreme reserve alone encouraged those predisposed to do so to entertain suspicions. Finally he broke his silence, since which time American independence has had no more forceful advocate." That was indeed the manner in which Franklin had conducted himself in 1775, when there had been much whispering about his allegiances. Of course, conceded Noailles, the situation was different this time. If the doctor was following along a path other than the one Vergennes had indicated for him he was seriously deluded.

Vergennes's censure would have rung true were it not for the fact that the papers of Europe reported that Franklin had withdrawn to his Passy redoubt and was consorting with all the wrong people, at his country's expense. The foreign minister was among the most influential men in Europe and among the handful of those in France whose mail was secure; he had near-total control over the French press. Had he not intended for the story of Franklin's retreat to circulate it would not have. And it is notable that

---

*The parallel had not been lost on Franklin. In 1769 he weighed in eloquently on the Corsican situation, in the guise of a Frenchman writing to London: "You English consider us French as enemies to liberty: You reproach us for endeavoring to reduce Corsica to our obedience. . . . The Corsicans are not so remote from us as the Americans are from you; they never enriched us by their labor and their commerce; they never engaged in our wars, and fought as brothers, side by side with us, and for us, bleeding in the same cause; they never loved and honored us; they are not *our* children. . . . Yet at this very moment, while you are abusing us for attempting to reduce the Corsicans, you yourselves are about to make slaves of a much greater number of those British Americans." Not coincidentally, Paoli, Pennsylvania, is five miles west of Philadelphia.

in the course of the same week he treated Stormont to an unsolicited confession. "I will deal confidentially with you, I never conceal what I do," ventured Vergennes, before revealing, two months after the fact, that he had indeed met with Franklin. He had done so only a single time, however; in his position it was incumbent on him to receive everyone at least once.* He had read Franklin the riot act—otherwise known as the Treaty of Utrecht, which prohibited France and England from sheltering ships belligerent to the other power in her ports, or permitting them to sell prizes—and assured the American of the king's determination to observe that 1713 treaty to the letter. Vergennes did a fine imitation of the reformed philanderer, but the rules of the game remained unchanged. He continued to assure the British ambassador of France's honorable intentions while Stormont—who had a perfectly good ear—heard only massive duplicity. From every quarter he amassed incriminating reports of America-bound munitions. And he was hardly oblivious to the activities of Captain Wickes and the *Reprisal*, who in their intrepid privateering had occasioned Vergennes's sudden and irregular fit of honesty.

With the Americans Vergennes persisted in handing down Stormont-appeasing edicts and then watching with almost perverse pleasure as the rebels maneuvered their way around them. Franklin was happy to engage in that divertissement; on February 24 the commissioners reassured Vergennes that they had ordered no American prizes into French ports and were engaged in no sales—if Captain Wickes had proceeded differently he had done so without their knowledge or orders, and would be reprimanded—when the opposite was true. In early March they were sternly reminded of the Utrecht terms, after which they celebrated Wickes's five successful winter cruises. Naturally, they wrote Congress, Wickes's brazen privateering—it was essentially licensed robbery—had caused "some trouble and uneasiness to the court, and must not be too frequently practised." In the next sentence, Wickes has been ordered out again, with an armed consort. Had Vergennes hewed to the laws of neutrality, he would no more have allowed Wickes into a French port than

---

*Earlier Vergennes had warned Stormont that he would not be able to refuse a meeting with Franklin: "A minister's residence is like a church. Anyone can enter, although there is no guarantee he will be absolved."

monies out of the French treasury. As Franklin well appreciated, *charade* is a word of French origin.

***

Stormont, Vergennes, and Franklin were involved in the same business: the parsing of each other's inflections, late-night callers, and mailbags for the slightest glimmer of partisanship. Franklin had on his side nerves of steel and the patience of an old man. This was a slow-moving game, with plenty of bluffing; he was a slow-moving man, and naturally poker-faced. He was also seriously handicapped. He was feeling his way in a baroque world, in which he did not entirely comprehend what was said. He was under constant surveillance, at the mercy of every kind of intriguer. Among them figured even Silas Deane's landlady, related by marriage to the French minister of state, the shrewd and regal comte de Maurepas, not as much a friend to America, or Franklin, as Deane's landlady might have liked. She managed to prevail upon the elderly Maurepas to make a risky trip to Passy. All was set for a visit via the back door. At the last minute the plan was discovered and aborted, leaving Maurepas feeling betrayed by all. He would never afterward summon a shred of confidence in the Americans.

Repeatedly the commissioners came up against the same problem they had in Congress, save that in a city of thousands of paid informers the problem manifested itself differently. As they began to navigate the seas of conflicting advice and interests and to circumnavigate the loudly conflicting egos, the Americans were left largely to fend for themselves, with the assistance of one very capable secretary. Over the summer Deane had summoned from London a well-traveled, thirty-three-year-old Massachusetts native whom he had tutored as a boy. A physician by training and a novelist and inventor by vocation, the portly, idiosyncratic Edward Bancroft spoke excellent French and was as gregarious as he was well informed. He was delighted to assist Franklin—the two hailed from similar backgrounds and had been friendly in London—as unofficial aide. Generally Bancroft wore a displeasing frown, which a good bottle of wine, or a sufficiently sardonic remark, could transform into a luminous smile. All agreed that he had "a clear head and a good pen"; the most agreeable of companions, he was eloquent in the extreme.

Of the three commissioners Franklin had the greatest experience setting words to paper, but that craft was nothing compared to the art of a master diplomat. Vergennes was famous—if not particularly beloved—for his ability to stall any decision. He remained on high alert with the Americans, whom he trusted to convert anything they could into a rumor of war. With as much at stake, Stormont was privy to the best information but did not count on the intelligence of the cunning American, whom he was quick to write off, along with his colleagues, as a band of thieves and muggers. He drove himself wild attempting to decode Franklin's signals, reporting on his incendiary language, his conciliatory language, either of which qualified equally well as "the lie of the day." He felt, and sounded, as if he were chasing his tail. He was entirely abashed when a piece of paper turned up cataloguing French assistance to the rebels. It concluded, "This is what is happening, while the comte de Maurepas hypnotizes the British ambassador with entrancing speeches." Humiliated, Stormont conceded that his dispatches fell under two heads: "The title of the first might be 'this is what I'm told,' the title of the second, 'this is what is happening.' I am heartily sorry that the articles of the second column agree so ill with those of the first."

Franklin had no intention of entertaining any kind of conciliatory language, as he had made clear to a February caller intent on soliciting as much. Sir Philip Gibbes, a West Indian planter, appealed in Passy both to his honor and to his emotions. In Franklin's mind things had already gone too far for any kind of rapprochement; he regretted that Britain seemed intent on the destruction of the Americans. It was true, he admitted, that together the two countries constituted a formidable whole. There was however a crucial distinction between the two nations, argued the man who had projected decades earlier that America's population would double every generation.* (This was the same news Choiseul's spies had sent back from the colonies in the 1760s. Those American children swarmed like ants.) In the darkest hours Franklin banked on the numbers game. As 150,000 new Americans were born every year, he wagered that his country could outgrow all the mischief that Great Britain could inflict on her. With

---

*His prediction held true until 1890. And Franklin's 1751 prediction that the American population would equal that of Britain in a century was exactly on target, although not for the reasons he had envisioned.

asperity Franklin informed his caller that the colonies understood precisely what they were doing, "for we know that separated both countries must become weak; *but there is this difference, Great Britain will always remain weak; America after a time, will grow strong.*" The question of independence was nonnegotiable.

He had a priceless asset in his popularity. His powers in no way abated with the retreat to Passy, at least not so long as there was anyone with an imagination still around. Soon enough rumors circulated that "Dr. Franklin had invented a machine the size of a toothpick case, and materials that would reduce [the cathedral of] St. Paul's to a handful of ashes." That mechanism would be followed by his mythical battery of deflecting mirrors, to be installed at Calais. With them Franklin was to burn the British navy to a crisp. He was said to have concocted a chemical brew that would "smooth the waves of the sea in one part of the globe, and raise tempests and whirlwinds in another," a statement that was not altogether inaccurate. Nor was it exclusively on those apocalyptic powers— the gifts of Newton, Prometheus, and Galileo rolled into one—that Franklin traded in his most momentous role. As a publisher, he knew that in a country with a daily newspaper news happens daily. And so he indulged in a tradition to which William Randolph Hearst would be indebted: Europe supplied the papers—in a happy coincidence, the first Parisian daily was born in January—and Franklin supplied an American war, which as far as he knew was a fiction. Early in February, with the news of defeats at Forts Washington and Lee, Stormont marched around Paris crowing that the Americans were beaten, destroyed, annihilated. The evidence was indeed entirely on his side: as far as Europe was aware, Washington had not won a battle since America had declared her independence. Two-thirds of Britain's army and half her navy were in the colonies. Franklin dismissed any setbacks as temporary glitches. "All the better, the English will be trapped in the end!" became his regular refrain.

Nor did he confine his propaganda to foreign ears. From the start he was sanguine on the subject of French goodwill while sparing the Committee of Secret Correspondence from such annoyances as double-dealing French officers or Versailles fence sitting or Beaumarchais's laments. He wrung hope from Vergennes's driest pronouncements. To the chicken-and-egg riddle of American independence and French aid he offered his own pragmatic solution: He misrepresented each side to the other. As he did so his voice occasionally rose from the page like a clarion call, as it did from a detailed March dispatch on horse saddles and interest payments: "All Europe is for us," announced Franklin, taking another kind of liberty, in addressing the Committee of Secret Correspondence. "Tyranny is so generally established in the rest of the world that the prospect of an asylum in America for those who love liberty gives general joy, and our case is esteemed the cause of all mankind. Slaves naturally become base as well as wretched. We are fighting for the dignity and happiness of human nature. Glorious it is for the Americans to be called by providence to this post of honor." Lest his anthem miscarry, Franklin replayed the same stirring notes later. America had before her a glorious task. Already she was the country God loves best. Franklin may well have been crowned the modern Pythagoras, Prometheus, Cicero, Socrates by the French. But—never a man to let a metaphor or parable slip by—on the only other occasion on which he adopted a pseudonym in France, he reached further back in time. He signed himself "Mr. Moses."

III

Three Can Keep a Secret,
If Two of Them Are Dead

1777

What is optimism? Alas, it is the mania for pretending that all is right,
when in fact everything is wrong.
—*Voltaire*, Candide

The news from America was very bad. Mercifully, little of it reached Franklin. His rhapsodic dispatch of March 12, 1777, began with a familiar enough plaint: more than four months had elapsed since he had sailed to France, during which time not a line had arrived from Philadelphia. Two days later the first dispatches arrived, with new instructions. Urged to pursue the French court more aggressively, the commissioners were authorized to offer up territorial inducements in exchange for military assistance. Immediately Deane requested an audience at Versailles. He heard nothing for days, and eventually found that the lure of half of Newfoundland and of American aid in conquering the British West Indies were insufficient to turn Vergennes's head. The minister confined himself to apprising the insurgents—the exonym was easier on monarchical ears than *rebels*—that the king did not share their impatience. Vergennes was too much the diplomat to reveal the full catalogue behind France's reluctance to rise to the bait. Tempting though the British islands might be, France was not in an acquisitive mood. France and Spain had already

agreed that were hostilities to erupt, they had no intention of being perceived as the aggressors; the rest of Europe watched closely. And Vergennes could not shake his doubts about an unproved, irresolute, and
fractious new people. It seemed unlikely that a barely credible government could resist the disparate enthusiasms of its people.

Franklin was not unaware of the last of those concerns, to which he
spoke as eloquently as he could. To lend a legitimacy to the new republic
and to blunt British propaganda, he saw to it that an early draft of the Articles of Confederation was translated and published in Europe. That
publication returned to his doorstep the duc de Cröy, a particular intimate
of France's brilliant naval minister. On examining that document, Cröy
was as troubled as Vergennes. How could an unwieldy expanse of seven
hundred leagues of coastline manage to cohere? His doubts extended further still. Where Vergennes would remain pessimistic about any serious
future for America, Cröy fretted that the Declaration of Independence
transformed a commercial outpost into a military state, one that might
soon enough menace all of Europe. On February 17 he took his questions
to Franklin, whom he found alone and writing, and eminently hospitable.
As a pretext for his call Cröy proposed that the two observe the electrical
experiments being performed in Paris. Newly recovered from a painful
episode of gout, Franklin accepted for a time when the weather might
prove milder. He took the opportunity to advertise not his own scientific
accomplishments but what they said about America. To think that in less
than a century his country had distinguished itself in the sciences and its
commerce. How little time was necessary to the formation of a great empire, marveled the man who had read his own way through the book-
shelves of Boston, when an educated people stood at its foundation!

Struck anew by the clarity with which the appealing patriot expressed
himself, Cröy dove right in. Might he offer a word on affairs of the day,
which, out of discretion, he had not previously allowed himself? Franklin
urged him on. To Cröy's contention that America's bid for freedom
would ruin her, Franklin countered that English commerce had hardly
constituted a blessing. It had been so heavily restricted as to have been
onerous; it had cost America more than it had brought her. Cröy confessed that he had studied the war carefully from every military
standpoint—over the previous decades he had commanded troops along
nearly every coast of France—and concluded that all depended on the

colonies' ability to stand together. He had already foreseen that Washington was fighting a war of attrition, in which tenacity mattered more than victory. Now he predicted that the American general would lose both Philadelphia and Boston in the coming campaign. Franklin labored to convince him otherwise: "We were poorly armed. We will be better off this summer, in a state to resist more capably, and I believe that our determination will not be lacking." Cröy was dubious, especially given what he termed American languor. Since Franklin's departure three colonies had fallen into British hands. It was ludicrous to think that the greatest army in the world could be outmaneuvered by "the division of the young New Hampshire attorney, the battalion of the Rhode Island blacksmith, or the guns directed by the bookseller of Boston." Meanwhile, noted Cröy, the French ministry affected not to know Franklin. So long as there remained a question as to the colonies' resolve, Europe would have nothing to do with him. "Everyone will aid you secretly, but no one openly!" he averred. Crossing his arms, Franklin rose vigorously to the challenge. "Europe will do as you say and we'll see what happens," he replied. "It's up to us to make the effort." His language was altogether different from that of his countrymen, panting nervously after a French alliance.

He was not privy to the full extent of Vergennes's concerns, nor did he appear to apprehend the rather unassailable logic of Vergennes's Spanish counterpart, who argued that France and Spain would be best served by sitting out the war entirely. The British and the Americans were best left to destroy each other. Yet more trenchant was the argument that the French should *join* the British against America, dividing the spoils. Franklin did however recognize that no begging or blandishment would induce Versailles to engage in the contest as it stood. France waited in part for an American victory on which to bank, while Washington banked on French aid with which he might deliver a victory. To that stalemate Franklin brought two great talents: an ability to temporize, and an ability to extemporize. He continued his campaign undaunted, and all over town. The rebels were well provided for. The casualties at Forts Lee and Washington were not what the British claimed, for the simple reason that the Americans had not had as many men defending those strongholds. British atrocities only further embittered his countrymen, assuring a longer and bloodier war. At the end of May Franklin assured the Committee of Secret Correspondence that while nothing had been signed at

Versailles, there was little cause for alarm: "Feeling ourselves assisted in other respects cordially and essentially, we are the more readily induced to let them take their own time, and to avoid making ourselves troublesome by an unseasonable importunity." This was the wisdom of the independent-minded man who had never legally wed his wife of forty-four years. He had no objection to accommodating himself to a common-law marriage now.

In part Franklin's was a master strategist's bow to human psychology. Rebuffed, he played hard to get. In part the calm reflected his ambivalence about foreign aid. He grasped instinctively that the very presence of the man the London press anointed "the old veteran in mischief" a comfortable drive from Versailles was, in the short term, poison enough for the British to swallow. He was not wrong. Stormont threw regular tantrums, insisting that Franklin be expelled without delay. Vergennes dreaded the outbursts even while he entirely enjoyed the ambassador's discomfort; from the start Vergennes was convinced that the only danger greater than not helping the Americans at all was not helping them enough. By spring he was soliciting Spanish suggestions for means by which the two countries might actively intervene in the American crisis without violating treaties or precipitating a war. He was baffled, but hoped that his Spanish counterpart might prove more imaginative. All the will in the world was there. Of those deliberations neither the Americans nor the inflamed French public had any hint. To them Versailles presented an obdurate front.

On the American side the distress was palpable, the humor dark. "You being at so great a distance may probably think we ought to have destroyed Mr. Howe's army by this time, and we undoubtedly should had we an army to do it," the financier Robert Morris wrote the commissioners, at the end of March. In the estimation of its commanding officer, that army was wasting away. Given the lack of munitions, the desertions, the discontent, and the disease, it barely constituted an army at all. As the year dragged on, wise and benevolent France emerged in America as specious, unreliable, and slow-moving France. Even as Morris sat down to commit his despair to paper relief was in sight, however: The first of Beaumarchais's provisions were unloaded the following morning on a New Hampshire pier. Against all odds and despite every variety of headache, a fresh batch of deceptions, and a set of frayed nerves, Beaumarchais had ten boats headed to America by the end of the month, a Herculean feat that would raise his stock at neither end. Still he flapped about in a tireless attempt to curry favor. On a good day he needled Vergennes. On a darker one he buried him under an assault of agitated, unsigned briefs, on the lost opportunities, on the pittance the American effort would actually require, on the odious parsimony of France, on the grief that was consuming him.* Was it not time they stopped vacillating between a timorous "It's too soon" and a defeatist "It's too late"?

Nor did he confine his assaults to Vergennes. Beaumarchais was something of a pet of Madame de Maurepas and of her husband, the natty, seventy-six-year-old minister of state. It is doubtful that anyone else in France would have had the audacity to instruct a minister to press the American case on a twenty-two-year-old king, "whose heart is formed, but whose politics are still in the cradle"; Beaumarchais was speaking, after all, of an absolute monarch. Then again it is doubtful that such a glorious cross-fertilization of dramaturgy and foreign policy could have taken root in any other than Beaumarchais's overheated mind. In that March communication he articulated his own three goals for France, among them the "abasement of the English in the union of France and America." There he cribbed from his own work. Beaumarchais had already created a frothy comedy featuring a pompous old guardian. That hapless gull intends to marry his beautiful young ward for her fortune but finds his scheme upset by the cleverest character on stage, the servant Figaro, a silver-tongued figure of perpetual motion. That Beaumarchais should have been rehearsing *The Barber of Seville* in Le Havre while shipping off the tools that might permit England's young ward to slip her uncomfortable chains was almost too delicious. Given the obstacles thrown in his path, the ingratitude that greeted his quick-witted capers, there was every reason why he should send the nimble Figaro back to wreak his revenge in a virtuoso encore.

As Beaumarchais pressed Maurepas to talk some sense into the French monarch, Deane assumed a different tack. Barring a fresh infusion of funds, he insisted, the colonies would surely settle with Great Britain. On that fear he and Arthur Lee played heavy-handedly, sounding a different

---

*Beaumarchais signed his name only when he feared that distress, or fatigue, had disfigured his handwriting. It never did. And his inimitable style was signature enough.

note from Franklin's stately calm. They let it be known at Versailles that a British emissary had pressed them hard for reconciliation. Did the Americans really mean to make themselves the pawns of Bourbon political ambitions? The price of a peace was simple; the colonists had only to commit to wage war against those powers. Vergennes was unconvinced by the reports; it hardly made sense that England would confide her secrets to enemy hands. Still, it was dangerous to ignore any proposition that included a joint Anglo-American assault on Bourbon interests, especially when the British were expanding their fleet, the most powerful in Europe. He admitted to being "in a state of some perplexity over the intentions of the British government, which seems at once bent on war and peace." Across the Channel the British viewed their implacable foe with the same mystification. The French appeared not to know their own minds.*

William Carmichael, the voluble, restive secretary, adapted least well to the impasse in Paris. He was one of the Americans abroad who regularly overreached his commission, or more precisely his lack thereof: Finding himself in Europe in 1776, the independently wealthy Marylander had volunteered his services. Of Franklin's colleagues he was the first to convert frustration at French inertia to anti-French pronouncements. Carmichael went nightly to the opera, the theater, the masked balls, but found there was little to do with his days but pine for his London girlfriend, whom he had not seen for months and to whom he was achingly faithful. (Or was until June, when he at least confined his exploits to "ladies of the first quality.") Publicly and privately he began to seethe, and to offer up tirades against the French. He was judged ripe for the plucking by British intelligence, who understood that he was both familiar with all the secrets at Passy and unable to handle his champagne, "which sets him chatting like a madman and completely off his guard."

The overtures were made under cover of darkness at the place

---

*Later Vergennes offered a masterful explanation for his policied nonpolicy: "Only small minds formulate plans and act according to a methodical routine." Had Louis XVI acted consistently, the British would have more easily sabotaged him. There was little truth to the British temptation to declare war on France. There was more truth to the French posture, for which a name would be coined only many years later, when Prime Minister Léon Blum adopted a policy of "elastic nonintervention" toward the Spanish Civil War.

Vendôme, by the most gifted of British spies. He offered Carmichael a handsome bribe were he to succeed in effecting a reconciliation between England and the colonies. Carmichael stood his ground, less on account of his integrity than his pride; he preferred to double-cross and back-stab without inducement. And his loyalty by no means tempered his impatience. It began to corrode his respect for Franklin, whose best lines Carmichael merrily appropriated even while he bemoaned his lassitude. Soon enough he was asserting that neither Deane nor Franklin was capable of performing the job with which he had been entrusted. (The criticism did not prevent him from being unfailingly deferential to Franklin in person.) Carmichael could not bring himself entirely to dismiss Franklin's opinions, although he knew them to be out of keeping with those of his constituents. "He thinks we shall derive resources from our distress, like the earth-born giant Antaeus, who derived new strength from his falls. I think he trembles for fear his propositions should be accepted. He wishes no European connection," wrote the disgruntled secretary, yet to learn that diplomacy was less colorful than soldiering. At the end of a sultry spring his blood boiled over. "I had rather be sent home to fight manfully, or to make peace politically, than to be in this miserable shilly-shally way here," he erupted. In his disgust he put money on the British troops taking Philadelphia. He would have only three months to wait before collecting on his wager, by which time Franklin had far greater problems on his hands than a frisky, insinuating secretary.

~ン~

In mid-March 1777, Franklin received the happy news of Washington's December successes at Trenton and Princeton, modest victories, but the first hints that the British might not be invincible. They represented as well a small tribute to French aid; Washington's men had been partially equipped by Beaumarchais. At about the same time Congress learned of the safe arrival of its illustrious envoy. That constituted a miraculously efficient exchange of information. More often Franklin worked amid the tides of conflicting information that had driven Deane to the brink; even the omniscient Madame du Deffand threw up her hands in despair. All the American reports contradicted themselves. Safe conveyances were few and far between. Unsafe conveyances defeated the purpose. "When you hear not so often as you wish, remember, our silence means our safety," the Committee of Secret Correspondence—now doing business as the

Committee for Foreign Affairs, although Franklin, who had never mastered the original name, was not to know for months—soothed the envoys, whom they understood to be starved for news.

To remedy the situation the commissioners proposed a regular packet service, an idea championed by the indomitable Chaumont, one of the leading shipowners in France. He would supply the boat and the insurance and assume all risk, in exchange for the right to ship goods to America in the same vessel. A contract was signed on April 1; two months later, the *Mère Bobie* set sail with a first set of dispatches. She made an eventless westbound crossing, to fall prey to an English frigate on her return. Per his orders, the captain threw his dispatches overboard. And so the off-kilter duet began anew. Having not heard from its Paris delegates since the spring, the Committee for Foreign Affairs wondered after their silence, in December 1777. What had happened to the plan for the monthly packet? Essentially it ended with the *Mère Bobie*, which was to say for the duration of the war. It was not unusual for Franklin to go six months without news from America. For the year that followed not a single one of his missives reached Congress.

As the man who had streamlined postal service over the loose-limbed expanse that so troubled the duc de Cröy, Franklin would have marveled—had he known of it—over the speed with which news hurtled from his own desk to that of George III. Hobbled by the lack of communication between Philadelphia and Paris, American efforts were further crippled by the unimpeded flow of information from Paris to London. The *Mère Bobie* was a case in point. The British knew of the packet service days after it was arranged. In the extracting of information no cost was spared, no channel unexplored, no underworld character neglected. As the commissioners prepared sensitive documents for America, Edward Bancroft, the Massachusetts-born secretary who was as familiar with the inner workings at Passy as anyone, traveled to England, where he was arrested. Franklin and Deane knew he would be interrogated mercilessly. The only consolations were that Bancroft had beautifully covered his trail and was a champion tale spinner. At the end of May Franklin was crestfallen to learn that the Nantes banker who oversaw America-bound stores had turned over his most recent dispatches from the colonies to the enemy. His replacement upheld the tradition, making a regular habit of removing all American correspondence from the post and delivering it to Stormont.

The two most spectacular heists of the summer took place not in Paris but in Berlin and Le Havre. Having made a futile trip to Spain, Arthur Lee set out at the end of May to approach Prussia about a commercial treaty. In Berlin his diary was filched from his room and raced to the British embassy, where dinner guests exchanged knives and forks for quills and paper and set to copying. Days later an unabridged narrative of Franklin's four months in Paris appeared in London. Lee had been the victim of the simplest of crimes; the burglar had climbed in through his hotel window. He was mortified. His mood failed to improve on the return to Passy, where he discovered that Deane had installed himself in the Valentinois rooms on which Lee had earlier set his sights. Establishing himself a few miles away at Chaillot, he set to grousing about security at Passy. "We have no time or place appropriate to our consultation, but that servants, strangers and everyone was at liberty to enter and did constantly enter the room while we were talking about public business and that the papers relating to it lay open in rooms of common and continual resort," Lee protested.

Nor did he feel that his fellow commissioners exhausted themselves conveying his mail to him, as he explained to Joseph Hynson, an American sea captain who complained equally of Deane's and Franklin's neglect. The two seemed disinclined to grant Hynson any substantial errand. Lee assured the downtrodden captain that he could not account for his colleagues' distrust, although soon all three commissioners would be called upon to account for their confidence. Lee's note of solidarity was the last of eight months of confidential correspondence to be bundled up and sent in Hynson's care to the coast, from which it would sail to America. Hynson delivered the pouch to Le Havre but its contents to Great Britain. In its stead a stack of clean white paper sailed in a waterproof wrapper to Congress, where the substitution went undetected until January. In London the head of the British intelligence service, Undersecretary of State William Eden, sat down on October 20 to a feast of dispatches.*

For that lapse Franklin was rebuked by Congress; the captain on

---

*Hynson's astonishing coup brought him a rich reward but little admiration from his superiors. "He was an honest rascal, and no fool, though apparently stupid," went the British assessment. Congress was left to wonder whether it had been duped by the French or the British; it was clear to all that the crime was too sophisticated to have been the work of one of their countrymen. No American, went the congressional reasoning, would have thought to send a decoy bundle.

whom Hynson had preyed was a simple man, by no means equal to the trust placed in him. He also happened to be a distant cousin of Franklin's. As fine a nepotist as the eighteenth century produced, Franklin had for years stocked the colonial postal service with his relations. When Jonathan Williams, a twenty-seven-year-old grandnephew working in the London sugar business, paid a visit, Deane prevailed upon him to travel to Nantes to survey the outbound stores. Soon enough Williams was installed in that port as commercial agent, in Thomas Morris's soggy stead. An accountant by training, Williams was hardworking and well intentioned, if entirely naive. At the same time, Franklin had his limits when it came to familial bonds. Over the summer of 1777, his own son, the former Loyalist governor of New Jersey, languished in a Connecticut prison.* A year after America had declared her independence, William Franklin applied for parole so as to visit his ailing wife. Washington denied the request. At no time did Franklin—who could very well have written Washington—urge clemency. Rather he burned with rage at what struck him not only as a misguided stance but as an insulting one. It was to that anger that Temple owed his trip to France, so intent was his grandfather on removing the sixteen-year-old from his father's influence. With equal vigor Franklin washed his hands of the innocent captain who had been Hynson's dupe. Were he a traitor he should be hanged, family or not.

He applied none of that vigor to security at the Valentinois, where it seemed that anything could penetrate the garden pavilion but the news, and where Franklin affected a blithe invincibility. Repeatedly that spring he dined unwittingly with Eden's right-hand man. In early July an odd, repulsive-looking caller talked his way past Franklin's porter and into the Valentinois apartments. Someone in the house met the ill-dressed character on the stairs and—alarmed by his demeanor—accompanied him to the second floor. Introduced to Franklin, he insisted on being left alone; the suspicious friend half retreated. The visitor muttered a few incomprehen-

---

*As had his father, William ran away from home at an early age. The difference was that in William's case, Franklin fetched him back. The independent streak persisted however; cautious and conciliatory by nature, William failed to develop a taste for his father's radical politics. He was unconvinced that a revolution was either viable or desirable, at which point his father turned his back on him. Some months later the order went out for William's arrest. He landed in prison on July 4, 1776.

sible remarks, finally inquiring, awkwardly, if the envoy had any diamonds of which he might like to divest himself. Only then was he seized
by the shoulders and bodily ejected from the house. Once the incident had
been reconstructed there was general agreement that the intruder had
been a hired assassin. He was almost certainly an emissary of Stormont,
who over the previous weeks had met privately with a burly, ill-dressed
individual of the same description, lodged at a dubious address. Franklin
was rattled by the encounter, which put at least a temporary damper on his
nonchalance. At his request Lenoir stepped up police surveillance at
Passy.

The single item that seemed to elude Lenoir's agents was the leak
through which bundles of paper escaped the Valentinois weekly. Every
Tuesday afternoon exhaustive reports of what had transpired in
Franklin's house seeped into Paris. On the south side of the Tuileries they
were stuffed into a bottle and lowered by twine into the hollow at the foot
of a tree. The other end of the twine was knotted to a peg at the tree's
root. After dark Stormont's secretary drove to the garden, where he
fished up the dispatches, depositing Stormont's side of the correspondence in a bottle under a neighboring boxwood. At the British embassy
the Passy documents were moistened with a dark chemical solution, revealing their contents in red. So it was that Chaumont's packet service
had been compromised from the start; that the quiet assurance Vergennes
extended to the Americans was loudly broadcast to London; that the
British knew every time Vergennes warned Franklin that there was a mole
in his household. Generally he went by the name Edward Edwards. He by
no means exaggerated when he confessed later to having kept the English
informed of "every transaction of the American commissioners; of every
step and vessel taken to supply the revolted colonies with artillery, arms,
etc.; of every part of their intercourse with the French." That catalogue
conforms perfectly to his instructions, although Edwards could have
boasted as well of having smuggled a fair number of original documents
out of Franklin's office. With reason the Valentinois has been called a
branch of British intelligence. Between the visitors and the staff, information coursed through the stately house as if through a sieve.

Nor was Franklin alone in his obliviousness. Shortly after the move to
Passy, two British spies managed to position themselves near him, but as
neither was told of the other's identity they informed equally well on each

other. So it was that on April 6 the British Secret Service's efforts to recruit Hynson were carried back to the Secret Service by another agent. He wrote in haste, as he was decamping with Deane for the rue Royale apartment, and no bag was yet packed. "There is one Hynson here, a simple fellow who was followed by Colonel Smith and Vardill and was offered great rewards if he would mediate a pacification between Great Britain and America *and give information of the secrets of the latter*," he reported, unnecessarily, as Smith and Vardill were also on Eden's payroll. (The latter distinguished himself as the only minister among Eden's operatives. For his faithful treachery he would be awarded a Chair of Divinity.) Probably of greater value was the agent's disclosure that the French police alerted the Americans to each of Hynson's interviews with Lord Stormont, further proof of French disingenuousness. Why the commissioners trusted Hynson at all under the circumstances remains a mystery.

William Eden's Secret Service was notoriously sophisticated, and the Paris informers strikingly motivated. In an age when the thinnest of lines separated diplomacy from intrigue, when the interception, copying, and resealing of letters qualified as standard operating procedure, Eden's agents went the extra mile, recklessly diving into closets, emptying locked drawers, filching seals and calling cards. In one case an agent purloined Franklin's mail while it was in transit with a fellow agent's wife. At the head of his network Eden installed an impeccably educated, hugely resourceful American named Paul Wentworth, the highest-handed of the lowlifes. It was he who had arranged the secret meetings with Carmichael at the place Vendôme; it was he who recruited Edward Edwards. The charismatic Wentworth traveled around Paris with his own personal cipher and recipes for a host of invisible inks. He alone could elude Lenoir's surveillance. He had no fewer than twenty aliases and nearly as many addresses, but doubtless his most effective weapon was one on which that most articulate of Parisians commented. "He speaks French as well as you," Beaumarchais warned Vergennes, "and better than I." Nor was Wentworth sent to Paris with the limited resources of Franklin, Lee, and Deane. His base was a London mansion, where he had years earlier counted Franklin among his guests. Eden urged him to live comfortably in Paris, to seduce his sources, and to take a mistress, which Wentworth did, although he appeared wholly indifferent to the mistress. His greatest love was rather for his own respectability. While he energetically speculated on the London stock market, he could not abide being called a spy. He was indignant to find himself hounded by Lenoir's agents, like a common informer.

Regularly Wentworth crossed and recrossed the Channel, bearing intelligence of every kind, most of it alarmingly accurate, and all of it months before any such reports washed up in America, if ever they did. With Lee's papers the British had a clear view back to Vergennes's first meeting with the Americans. Hynson's heist brought them fully up-to-date. If anything, Eden was handicapped by the profusion of intelligence that came his way. Sometimes it seemed that his deceivers were paid by the word; a dispatch might begin, "Nothing to communicate," and yet run on for four pages. And sometimes too the operative detail slipped through the most closely woven net. In March came the report that someone "of the first birth and fortune, not high in the army, who though he has never spoken to Deane or Franklin, but with Carmichael only, is upon the eve of his departure" to fight in America. He had requested a command but no pay. Only one pertinent detail baffled. The informer could not unravel his name. King George, who pored assiduously over the Paris reports, caviled that the spy's narrative was foggy at best, and that "writing is not his forte."

⚜

Lafayette sailed for America on April 20, in a medium-size ship for which he had paid, and with an entourage of twelve officers. Through Deane, he had entered the American service as a major general. The British would continue to stumble with his name; meanwhile the nineteen-year-old marquis adopted a perfectly revealing alias. Gilbert du Motier de Lafayette chose to disguise himself as Gilbert du Moutier Natif de Chavaniaque. Even for the sake of a republic he was not yet able to leave his *particule* at home; for a surname he borrowed that of the family château. His given name posed no trouble to a Frenchman of 1776. The teenage orphan stood in possession of one of the country's great fortunes. He stood too as the logical culmination of dynastic principles. He was the nephew of the French ambassador to Great Britain, the comte de Noailles. The governor of Martinique was Lafayette's relation, as was the governor of Bordeaux, as was Marie Antoinette's first lady-in-waiting, as was the comte de Ségur, as was the French ambassador to Spain, as was, more distantly, the comte d'Estaing. Indeed, Lafayette was bound to so much of France he may have felt it obligatory to bolt.* He was a perfect emblem of his generation on two additional counts. His family history amounted to a neat recapitulation of the century's. His young father had been killed by a British artilleryman serving under a general who—two decades later—was to die in his bed in Virginia, when a French cannonball sailed through his window. And Lafayette had been a colonel since childhood, without seeing active service. "To injure England is to serve my country," went this aristocrat's noble battle cry; liberty, fraternity, and equality were nowhere in view, and when they materialized would only trip him up. His flight from France perfectly illuminated the ministry's position. Alarmed by his plans, Lafayette's family prevailed upon the king to forbid all French officers from serving in the colonies. Those who had departed were instructed to return posthaste. The order went to Minister of State Maurepas and naval minister Gabriel de Sartine to be duplicated. Somehow it went missing on Sartine's desk.

The April departure was not particularly romantic. Lafayette was violently seasick and desperately homesick; he left a high-profile dynasty to conjure with the fact that they were now related to a fugitive when for years they had thought they were related merely to a dullard. From London Noailles wrote to ask Vergennes if his nephew's rash departure compromised his position. He felt particularly exposed, as he had two days earlier dispatched a closely reasoned, confidential memo to Vergennes in which he enumerated his reasons why France should dismember England. Vergennes had strong feelings about honor as about filial loyalty—he was a coldly exacting father—but could not have been more graceful in his reply. He thanked Noailles for his communication while resisting his logic. He was disinclined to take a more active role in the American contest for the present. As for Noailles's impulsive nephew, he expressed only compassion. He also went out on what was even for supple Vergennes a dangerous limb. He thought it perhaps best if he not mention that departure to the king. Already the foreign minister had his hands full with Lafayette's flight. "Lord Stormont appears to be in a very bad temper about it," he

---

*He could have been said to have taken French leave, save that a Frenchman who makes an unceremonious departure does no such thing. He is said to *filer à l'anglaise*.

observed, venturing as close as he ever did to drollness. "He has a talent for giving much importance to very small matters."

A gawky and indolent-seeming major general, Lafayette took with him not a word of English and left behind a pregnant wife. But his departure caused a sensation second only to the December arrival; he left Franklin to bask in a burst of refracted enthusiasm. While the government position was that Lafayette had committed a first-rate idiocy, unofficially even the authorities admired his derring-do. From London his indulgent uncle soon chuckled, "Luckily his age can excuse great follies," surely not the position he adopted on his official rounds. Madame du Deffand was of the same school: "Of course it's madness, but it does him no dishonor. On the contrary, it bespeaks courage and a thirst for glory." While his family wrung their hands, the rest of society—faced with the need to decide if a man who abandons a beautiful wife and a life of luxury for the sake of adventure was a knight-errant or a madman—came down squarely in the first camp. A sulky Stormont ascribed much of the frenzy to feminine weakness, as indeed it was; the women of Paris were gaga over Lafayette's feat.* And the women of Paris constituted a dominant force. They kept the salons, which was the equivalent of running the newspapers.

Franklin's spirits could only have been buoyed by the pro-American sentiment that bubbled noisily in Lafayette's wake. To many that caprice carried more weight than did all the accumulated aid; Lafayette's was a very imposing name indeed. And it helped considerably that Franklin's hands were clean. Lafayette had had no direct contact with him, having plotted instead with Carmichael, in a series of long carriage rides. Vergennes had to work far harder than Franklin to distance himself from Lafayette's folly. The people of France had already succumbed to what the British papers termed the "American malady," which they had contracted in part from Franklin. Word that Congress had ordered a lead statue of George III to be melted down for musket balls was received ecstatically in Paris. On a day when Franklin rode to Versailles on undisclosed business and Lafayette retched as the waves rolled by, abbé André

---

*One Lafayette family member went so far as to admonish the adventurer's father-in-law. Were he to lift a finger to undermine his son-in-law he could surrender all hope of marrying off his remaining daughters.

Morellet, the effervescent polemicist and intellectual gadfly, warned a British minister of the French obsession with American affairs. "There is more support for American independence in Paris than in the entire province of New York," he asserted. Already a game of one-upmanship began to color Franco-American affairs. By 1780 a French volunteer would swear that there was greater commitment to the American cause in the cafés of Paris than in all of Washington's army.

The right arm of an autocrat, Vergennes had no obligation to heed public opinion, which it was rather his responsibility to control. He was however well attuned to it, and made it his business to remain so. Officially he acknowledged pro-American sentiment only when shrugging off the rumors Stormont deposited on his doorstep. On May 13 the British ambassador called on him at home, to confront Vergennes with a faultless set of details of ships fitting out for America. The Frenchman was shocked, shocked. He would make all the proper inquiries. Clearly the king's ministers were the only ones in France to be uninformed of what was happening in their ports, chided Stormont, who, more gently, expressed his hope that France was not preparing for war. Squirming, Vergennes went the disingenuous route, reminding Stormont "that there is an unaccountable enthusiasm in favor of the Americans, and you know how the public rails at us for not falling in with *that* frenzy." To his assertion Stormont made no reply. He did not feel it incumbent on him to offer Vergennes "compliments at the expense of truth."

It was Stormont's task to embarrass the French with evidence of their specious neutrality while convincing them that the British were triumphing in America. On both counts in 1777 the truth was entirely on his side. Vergennes's evasions were one kind of torture. That Paris should prove so receptive to Franklin's propaganda was another. The day after Stormont's conversation with Vergennes the Americans were heard boasting that Versailles would go to any lengths and run any dangers rather than see the colonies reduced to their former dependence. Stormont burned with rage. Since March, fumed the ambassador, Franklin had "industriously propagated the wildest and most extravagant accounts of the flourishing state of the rebels and the defeat and distress of our army. These accounts are greedily received by those who wish them true. It does not require a man of Franklin's art and duplicity to impose upon those who love so much to be deceived." Stormont was very much of the mind that—barring an accident—the rebels would surrender before the French could make up their minds about whether to intervene in the contest. Franklin was of the mind that—barring an accident—his country would win the war on their own before the French could make up their minds.

⁓⅏⁓

Paris was however by no means as fertile as he might have liked. As a newspaperman—and as a man who had every interest in pleasing the court—he was hemmed in by the government stranglehold of the French press. Every aspect of the business in which Franklin got his start and made his name was regulated by the state. The number of printers in France was tightly controlled; in 1777 Louis XVI prohibited printshop workers from assembling, from pooling their funds for any common cause, or from establishing professional associations. Funeral and wedding announcements alone were printed without government permission; a team of 160 discerning readers spent their Tuesdays and Fridays vetting every manuscript and foreign volume headed toward publication. Before the censors came a handbook for governesses, a volume comparing the relative merits of French and German mineral waters, a treatise on Turkish literature, a text on Mexican cures for venereal disease, and the prophetically titled *The Discovery of America: For and Against*. Piles of books were routinely confiscated; it was common for one newspaper to report that another's publication had been temporarily suspended, having offended someone or other at Versailles.

Nearly every writer with whom Franklin associated during his Parisian stay had seen the inside of the Bastille at least once. An *embastillement* could be worth the discomfort; generally the prisoner emerged to admiring applause and vigorous sales. Voltaire had served his first prison stint in 1717, when eleven-year-old Franklin, his formal schooling behind him, watched his older brother set up the press to which Franklin would be apprenticed the following year. He spent many hours in France with the ebullient abbé Morellet, a small man with a concave face, less original than Franklin but of similar spirit. Had the friendship not been cemented in England in 1772, it surely would have been by the abbé's description of his Bastille holiday, one he nearly solicited. In the course of his two-month incarceration Morellet read eighty novels from the prison library, all of Hume and Tacitus, and translated a Latin chemistry text. "Except at mealtimes," he remembered, "I read or wrote, with no other distractions than that resulting from my urge to sing and dance by myself, to which I succumbed several times daily." He admitted to having been sustained by the fame that waited on the other side of the prison walls. Persecuted, he would be famous. The volumes of the great Claude-Adrien Helvétius, whose widow was to become a Franklin intimate in 1778, had been burned publicly. There was some irony in the fact that the single most confiscated book of the age was the abbé Raynal's *Histoire des deux Indes*, a volume that did more to propagate misconceptions about North America than any other of the eighteenth century. With Rousseau and Helvétius, Raynal made up the triumvirate of most frequently seized samizdat.

It was a system that cried out for abuse, and in that it was not disappointed. If the canny Bostonian or Philadelphian was both publisher and postmaster, the canny Parisian was both bookseller and police agent. The influential publisher of the abbé Raynal waged an all-out public relations assault on Versailles before issuing an expanded edition of his irksome title in 1780, after which Vergennes and Maurepas arranged for the police to ignore its sale in central Paris. Beaumarchais had to lubricate the system every time he hoped to open a play. (To Lenoir's mind, the playwright set the censor-defying gold standard.) For the most part it made sense to sidestep rather than to violate the industry's constraints. The best French papers were published in—or were said to be published in—Leyden or Utrecht or London. These were the papers in which one might read of Lafayette's departure, which would have been news to the officially sanctioned *Journal de Paris*.* A virulent campaign had been necessary to get the city's first daily paper off the ground in January 1777; to stay off the ground that morning paper, read both by the king and by Franklin, confined itself to freak accidents and medical miracles and eclipses and recipes for rat poison and competitions for plans to keep the streets of Paris clean.

The attempt to stanch the flow of news created a deluge of illicit papers and scandal sheets and satires, the kind of thing that Vergennes might summon from London in the eighteenth-century equivalent of a brown paper bag, and that, for all its scurrilousness, Louis XVI heartily enjoyed

---

*In the official press Lafayette and his cohorts went unnamed, or were said to have succumbed to a sudden and violent desire to master the art of navigation.

as well. These were the curiously well informed publications that were not above weaving actual accounts of Franklin's progress at Versailles with imaginary dialogues, in which Franklin was asked to explain, for example, what an austere and principled republic was doing with a scamp like Beaumarchais. ("Deane is managing him carefully," came the quasi-fictional response, with a loud sigh.) To that stranglehold came a man who could not afford to offend; whose career had been jump-started when his older brother's publications had landed him in a filthy jail cell; who had left straitlaced Boston because he had made himself a little "obnoxious" to the authorities. In his new circumstances Franklin evinced enormous restraint. For all his claims about "all Europe being for us" he understood that advertising rebellion in an absolute monarchy is a sticky business. Fortunately he had in his court something more valuable than his own pen. Well before Franklin's arrival, Vergennes had launched a publication to counteract English propaganda. The Tory press in London was as rabid as it was prolific, and at greater liberty to infect French minds on the subject of America. Over the next years it would report in convincing detail on the surrenders of the American army, the captures of Washington, the recurrent deaths of Dr. Franklin.

Congress implored its envoys to stanch "the tide of folly and falsehood" emanating from London, but did not for a minute believe the French court fell for such nonsense. They themselves were above such invented tales. Vergennes was not. And while he had no interest in educating the people, he had plenty of interest in neutralizing the British roorbacks. As he arranged for the first American funds in 1776, he gave his blessing to a new periodical, the *Affaires de l'Angleterre et de l'Amérique*. It was as rich in fiction as the British press, but its fictions were of the pro-American variety. Along with a commentary penned by a Dutch banker in London—who was in fact a French statesman in Versailles—the "Antwerp" paper delivered a running account of Great Britain's quarrels with her colonies. The 1776 draft of the Articles of Confederation that Franklin swore elicited such admiration appeared in the *Affaires*, as did the constitution of the state of Pennsylvania, as did, over the course of 1777, five additional state constitutions as well. Franklin's original compositions were limited to several minor pieces. More often and more effectively, he simply funneled information to sympathetic sources. In any event there was no outpouring of prose from

America's foremost newspaperman in that delicate first year, when Vergennes choked on any text that might explicate the principles of the American Revolution by way of "an indecent and absurd" swipe against monarchy. He suppressed even a quatrain Dubourg composed to accompany a Franklin portrait.* A dedication to a scholarly text met with the same fate.

Franklin was to learn that—in a city in which the most reliable newsmonger was the barber—he could make his literary mark in oblique ways. On Tuesday, June 17, he opened his copy of the *Courrier de l'Europe*—the London-based paper circulated in France courtesy of Beaumarchais, who had lobbied hard for its distribution—to read a contribution from the venerable abbé Raynal. Raynal provided a meticulous account of Mary Baker's trial in a Connecticut courtroom, for having produced a gaggle of illegitimate offspring. So eloquently did the hapless defendant argue her case that one of her judges rose to the rescue and married her. The story had appeared earlier in Diderot as well, but its inclusion in Raynal's text clinched its validity. Evidently Silas Deane questioned Mary's own legitimacy at dinner one day with the abbé, who briskly defended himself. Deane was mistaken. The story was authentic, protested the gravel-voiced sage. He had documentary evidence. Franklin listened to the debate for some time, silently shaking with laughter, before setting Raynal straight. He had invented Mary himself as filler for his paper in 1746. She was then Polly Baker. At last the ex-Jesuit relented, conceding that he preferred Dr. Franklin's mistruths to anyone else's truths, a statement that fairly summed up Paris's attitude toward the muted propagandist in 1777. From Polly's triumphant European tour Franklin elicited his own moral. What a slippery thing was history! Thirty years had suffered to transform fiction into fact.[†]

⤜✖⤛

On April 24 *The Way to Wealth* came before the censors. Already Franklin's compilation of proverbs had bowed to local mores. In its Pari-

---

*"The pride and pedestal of the new hemisphere / Waves of the ocean all obey his whim; / He quells or directs as he pleases the thunder / He who disarms the gods can he fear Kings?"

[†]Given the botch that was made of current affairs, Franklin was left to deduce that ancient history too must be riddled with errors.

sian edition the compendium of Poor Richard's wisdoms became *The Science of Good Richard, or The Easy Way to Pay Taxes*. (It could be argued that had the colonies known a painless way of paying taxes they might not now be at war with the mother country. And, for that matter, that the British might not have levied those taxes in the first place were it not for the expenses Britain had incurred battling the French in America, a war she believed she had waged to protect her colonies from French designs.) In many editions the volume included a transcript of Franklin's 1766 interrogation by the British Parliament as well as the Pennsylvania state constitution, a document that would be credited solely to him. Attaching those treatises to Poor Richard's earthy wisdoms was an interesting way of slipping them into the drinking water, akin to Franklin's plan for seeding appeals to the better sense of the Hessian mercenaries in America with tufts of tobacco. In any event the censor did not balk, at least over the political pages. "This short volume could be in better taste, but its message is sound, and I see no risk in its publication," he ruled. Sold in the streets for four sous—two cups of street-corner coffee, or slightly more than a loaf of bread—the volume proved a bestseller. By the end of 1777 the clear-eyed wisdoms of Poor Richard rained down from French pulpits, a twist even Polly Baker would have enjoyed.

It was not only his title that made Poor Richard—and by extension Franklin—an honorary Frenchman. He may well have devoted a great amount of ink to virtue and order, but he checked those concepts at the door of the beau monde; he made it clear that he was not too good for that world, an interesting assignment for a candlemaker's son set down amidst an enameled aristocracy. There was nothing of the "dry, moral, utilitarian little democrat" about Franklin in Paris. America's first humorist, he had long before observed that Robin Hood's songs outsold David's psalms. This was a society in which even impertinence was admissible so long as it was clever, and Franklin was happy to comply. He had his salty streak; he was generally flirtatious. There was something touching in the patrician duc de Cröy marveling over the colonist's wisdoms, just as there must have been some delight for Franklin in finding that two of America's most dedicated supporters were the duc de la Rochefoucauld, the affable, English-speaking great-great-grandson of the aphorist, and his mother, the redoubtable duchesse d'Enville, by general consensus the smartest woman in France. It was the unassuming thirty-four-year-old la Rochefoucauld who both undertook the translations of the American constitutions and introduced Franklin to Anne-Robert Turgot, among the original laissez-faire economists and a family intimate. The sober Turgot came to appreciate what la Rochefoucauld identified as one of the greatest weapons in Franklin's arsenal at a time when the immediate front was one of propaganda, and the master propagandist's style cramped: "The pleasure of his company," recalled the young duc, "defied description." In a country that preferred comedy to tragedy, that gaiety served Franklin inordinately well. So familiar did it make him that he was claimed by the Franquelin family of Picardy. It was inconceivable that anyone possessed of Franklin's joie de vivre was not blessed with French ancestors. The sprightliness of mind, the merriment, the embrace of fancy were not Anglo-Saxon qualities.*

His high spirits saved Franklin throughout 1777, a year that began with confusion and uncertainty and dissolved into a string of very real disasters. Franklin's habit had been to set a day aside for his correspondence, a routine that did not adapt well to Passy, given the intrusions. All the same—occupied with every variety of opaque and unraveling scheme, in Paris at least several times a week—he felt he had never worked so hard in his life. He routinely put in twelve-hour days, which had not been his habit even when he was younger and intent on advising Americans how to succeed in business by really trying. It was all a great improvisation: He was inventing American foreign policy out of whole cloth, teaching himself diplomacy on the job, while serving as his country's unofficial banker. He directed American naval affairs, such as they were. In the spring he launched a campaign about which he felt passionately and would pursue vigorously, although it did not figure in his official instructions: He appealed to Stormont for an exchange of prisoners. After a February overture had met with silence, Carmichael carried a second request to the Hôtel de Deux-Ponts at the beginning of April. Stormont was not an insensitive man—devastated by the death of his first wife, he had traveled across Europe with her heart in his luggage—but he returned the envelope unopened. On it he scrawled: "The King's ambassador receives

---

*For the same reason the Tory press discounted his mission. "Dr. Franklin is a man of austere manners, little suited to the pliability of courts, or the genius of the French nation," predicted one political broadsheet. The argument was valid, but the paper had the wrong American.

no applications from rebels unless they come to implore his Majesty's mercy." Franklin resubmitted the envelope, for what he suggested might be a more mature response. He found the reports of London's abominable prison conditions infuriating. Few projects would mean as much to him over the next years, and few would so defy his best efforts. The exchange fell victim to bad faith, as well as to Franklin's inability to hold in French ports any sizable number of British prisoners whom he might barter for his countrymen. The humanitarian concern partly accounted for his continued enthusiasm for privateering.

In only one other realm was he so consistently defeated in France, although for that one he bore sole responsibility: The Passy accounts were a quagmire. Four years before the Paris departure Franklin had confessed to a growing distaste for such matters and a related tendency to neglect them, both of which were on open display in Passy, where they increased in proportion to the disorder. Louis XVI's contributions to the American colonies passed through the hands of Ferdinand Grand, a meticulous and powerful banker whose estate conveniently abutted the rear gardens of the Valentinois. (As convenient, Grand happened to be an intimate of Vergennes, and a close friend of Chaumont.) Franklin left the large calculations to Grand and the family expenses to Temple, while making no attempt to improve on Deane's bookkeeping. A calculation of prisoners to be exchanged might well figure on the back of a shopping list. In mid-May Jonathan Williams, newly installed in Nantes, traveled to Passy to settle accounts with his granduncle. He stayed two weeks, during which a great number of matters were discussed but the bookkeeping was not. It began muddily, and ended chaotically. Franklin knew as much but resisted all of Arthur Lee's attempts to review their finances, until finally Lee threw up his hands in frustration.

If in the Philadelphia of his youth Franklin had recognized the value of seeming to work hard, he quickly mastered the essential French art of accomplishing much while appearing to accomplish little. Industry and efficiency were still foreign concepts in a world calibrated in glory and style; Maurepas did not mean to flatter his colleague when he labeled the decidedly unjovial Vergennes a machine. (Vergennes's reputation as a drone so irritated him that when one of his aides calculated that he put in eleven-hour days, Vergennes insisted he scale back the figure.) Few were aware of the actual drudgery Franklin faced daily, and to which he often devoted several hours in the middle of the night. The paperwork alone was appalling. The barrel-chested envoy never appeared to bend under his burden, just as he never offended his hosts by arriving punctually, as did his countrymen; he had removed to a world in which tardiness practically constituted an art form. His Passy friends admired his most French of abilities: "At whatever moment you called," remembered a young neighbor who did so regularly, "he always made himself available." Dr. Franklin, the eminent scientist, who would spend much of the year apologizing for the dilatoriness of his correspondence, always had an hour for you. In particular he would drop everything for a game of chess. He was a ruthless opponent. He was also one who played to his public. During one match against an ancient duchess he made a rather unorthodox capture. "We do not take kings so," his high-born companion corrected him. "We do in America," replied Franklin.*

The exception to the open-door policy was the portraitists, who quickly found their way to Passy and just as quickly wore Franklin out. He well understood, and was not displeased to acknowledge, that his very person qualified as propaganda. While Lee debated a trip to Florence or Berlin so "that I might not be idle," while Carmichael chomped at the bit, while Beaumarchais and Deane scurried about designing uniforms for men who were of stouter proportions than those of France,† Franklin submitted to a number of sessions with Jean-Jacques Caffieri, whose terracotta bust would be universally admired by the throngs at the Salon that fall. Among likenesses Caffieri's ranks with the best; his is a resolute, sharp-eyed Franklin, a realistic figure who might well move chess pieces around the board while his opponent was out of the room, as did its model. By June an idealized portrait by Jean-Baptiste Greuze was on view as well. The renowned Greuze was thought to have outdone himself. The Duplessis portrait displayed at the Salon that year would meet with the

---

*The witticism flew around the kingdom, as did the version in which Franklin, lost in thought, quietly placed his king in his coat pocket. To his opponent's stupefaction he replied that he would now prove that the party without a king would win the game. Of course either move might qualify as a highly competitive player's graceful way of evading defeat.

†The commissioners' directives for the hundreds of thousands of uniforms were clear. Their quality was to be consistent with that of the French army, but the greater part of them were to be "of the largest sizes, and made to button as far as the waistband and not sloped away so as to be incapable of covering the belly in cold or rainy weather, let the fashion of Europe be what it may."

same ecstasies; this was art criticism as elegy. Pierre-Samuel Du Pont de Nemours, the liberal economist whose ideas on population and on taxation dovetailed neatly with Franklin's and who would eventually emigrate to America, found in the visage of this seventy-one-year-old Hercules both a firmness of character and an inalterable serenity. His gloss on Franklin's wrinkles was telling. They denoted gaiety, tenderness, and pride, but none betrayed a hard life. "It would appear that his labors have never taxed his nerves," Du Pont marveled, redefining sangfroid. The artists did; ultimately the force of Franklin's popularity would imprint his likeness on matchboxes and teacups and candy dishes and fabric and walking sticks. Franklin was soon stiff from posing; he directed those requesting a sitting to copy their predecessors, preferably Duplessis. He acknowledged the French mania with more gratitude than weariness, however. "This popularity has occasioned so many paintings, busts, medals and prints to be made of me, and distributed throughout the kingdom, that my face is now almost as well known as that of the moon," he informed his sister.

Given the attention it could be onerous to venture out. As one diplomat noted, Franklin had no place to hide. His January visit to the Académie des Sciences caused a sensation; the lecture may or may not have been audible amid the uproar. Franklin was escorted to the assembly's second-floor meeting rooms at the Louvre by his next-door neighbor Le Veillard, who had earned a medical degree so as to promote the curative powers of his Passy springs. The witty Le Veillard served as both companion and bodyguard, necessary even among a distinguished gathering of educated men. The contributor to a New Jersey paper offered a slightly inflated account of the difficulty with which Franklin moved about Paris: "The curiosity of the people to see him is so great that he may be said to be followed by a genteel mob. A friend of mine paid something for a place at a two-pair-of-stairs window to see him pass by in his coach, but the crowd was so great that he could but barely say he saw him."

The darling of Paris curtailed his public appearances accordingly, with one exception. He made regular late-afternoon visits to a white, canvas-covered barge that floated on the Seine opposite the Tuileries. For a nominal sum, visitors could immerse themselves there in a tub of heated mineral water. Pot-de-Vin's bathhouse was not Paris's most luxurious establishment, and Franklin was surely unaware that it was the city's premier gay bathhouse. He relaxed in its spotless rooms for two-hour stretches not only because water had long been his natural element, or because the prolonged soaks brought relief to his skin condition; he luxuriated especially in what he perceived to be his naked anonymity. It was his impression that he was known at Pot-de-Vin's simply as "an Englishman with grey hair," which was not how anyone else would have described the man whose reputation was said to rival that of Newton or Voltaire. When an English peace emissary requested a meeting in the fall, Franklin directed him to the one spot in Paris he felt inconspicuous: the steam at Pot-de-Vin's.

～✤～

The psoriasis was as tenacious as it was troublesome. Boils covered every part of his body and left his linens spotted with blood. Franklin experimented with pills until his gums began to weaken; after three teeth fell out he discontinued the medication altogether. (He had been ingesting mercury.) Otherwise, save for a ten-day assault of gout, an inflammatory form of arthritis, he found himself in robust health in his country retreat. "The air of Passy and the warm bath three times a week," Temple observed of his grandfather, "have made quite a young man out of him. His pleasing gaiety makes everybody in love with him, especially the ladies, who permit him always to kiss them." On every level the Chaumonts tended to Franklin's comfort. Twenty-three-year-old Marie-Françoise saw to it that the garden pavilion was staffed and supplied; the maître d'hôtel arranged for regular deliveries of provisions. Vast quantities of strawberries and cream, healthy shipments of Roquefort and Parmesan and leeks, rabbit and wild duck, made their way to the Valentinois door. In his first weeks Franklin discovered an apple pie of which he was inordinately fond, innocent still of any symbolism. His appreciation of French fare appears to have been as healthy as his knowledge of its preparation was scant. He ate with gusto—his kitchen turned out chicken with eggs and pancakes and plum pudding and turkey with oyster dressing—but was surprised to discover that he never suffered from heartburn. That he attributed to the fact that there was no butter in French sauces.

While Mademoiselle Chaumont saw to his creature comforts, her father—who regularly entertained a table of twelve or fifteen—introduced him to the neighbors, to become the mainstays of Franklin's social life. Le Veillard brought with him the stunning Madame Brillon, from down the street; the versatile Le Roy handed him on to the scientific community. Always a man who delighted in gathering family, natural or synthetic, around him, Franklin took great comfort in the presence of his grandsons. Benny was released from school on Sundays, on which afternoon Franklin, flanked by the two young men, entertained at home. The eldest child of Sally Franklin Bache, Benny was a handsome, black-eyed eight-year-old, who viewed his grandfather with undiluted awe. He weathered the dislocations of the first months admirably, making rapid strides in French. There was nothing particularly unusual about an American undertaking the European trip with a child in tow; a French education was considered far superior to anything available in the colonies, as Silas Deane's son and Arthur Lee's nephew were among the first to discover. More unorthodox was the fact that Franklin abandoned his plan to enroll Temple in a foreign university and took it upon himself to recruit his elder grandson as his personal secretary.

Nor did it help that illegitimate children seemed to run in the family.* Around the time of Franklin's marriage, William was born to another woman, whom Franklin never identified, and who was probably a household servant. (The peccadillo does not figure among Franklin's errata in his *Autobiography*, a volume ostensibly addressed to the result of that slip.) The extent to which Franklin took William's betrayal to heart could be measured by the tears he shed in the Bois de Boulogne one day over his second son, whom he had lost decades earlier, at the age of four, to smallpox. He attributed his emotion to a simple conviction. "I still imagine that this son would have been the best of my children," he explained, not a statement likely to cross the lips of a gratified parent. The defection of the elder son was all the more painful in that the two men had been best friends. And William had continued the family tradition, siring Temple while in England, a secret kept from the family

---

*In the spring Jonathan Williams, Franklin's grandnephew in Nantes, blurted out what he had long wanted but been too embarrassed to: He had fathered a son in England. He pleaded guilty to stupidity but not malevolence. The child, for whom Franklin cared at one juncture in Passy, was referred to within the family as Williams's nephew.

for years. Temple discovered he was a Franklin only at fifteen, when, in a sort of fairy-tale encounter, the grandfather who had materialized in London uprooted him to Philadelphia. That was evidently to be his fate, as he was wrenched again from his home, against his wishes, by the newly appointed Paris commissioner. And so off to France sailed Temple, a pawn in the game of a father and son who had been off speaking terms for the better part of a year. Of all the odd filial dramas played out over a very patriarchical contest, that of the three Franklin generations may have been the most quietly devastating. It was all the more poignant for Franklin's unwillingness to engage with it. He could not tolerate family disputes.

Temple's service solved two of Franklin's most pressing problems. There was at least one member of the Passy household on whose loyalty he could unequivocally rely. And the apprenticeship allowed Franklin to streamline his operation. In that respect he was a rock-ribbed American: It was his belief that government should be economical and efficient, which ran counter to the custom of the country. "I'm not surprised," he confided in a friend, "that the French Ministers have so much trouble concluding even the most insignificant matters, given the colossal size of their staffs. They only complicate things to the point of making them interminable." He had no patience either for the strangling brand of paperwork that could be relied upon to prolong business, a weight Temple assumed. Whether the eighteen-year-old would have been a candidate for the secretarial post was not even an issue. A slimmer, sleeker version of his grandfather, Temple had had no opportunity to distinguish himself for his originality. Nor had he yet—in his one year of collegiate life— evinced either ambition or discipline. If Franklin thought he might cure those habits with an introduction to the foreign service, he did so only incidentally. In the immediate he needed a secretary.

Temple's devotion freed his grandfather as well to focus on the dinner table diplomacy at which he displayed such virtuosity. There Franklin showcased his talent for *l'art de vivre*, the greatest of French disciplines, one still unknown in puritan America, where it too nearly resembled enjoying oneself. The dulcet home life in Passy would prove his salvation during a war of nerves. It also opened him to a torrent of abuse. He demonstrated more patience than was seemly in a revolutionary; he lived rent-free in a spectacular estate; he refused to play the cipher-and-pseudonym game; he staffed his disorderly mission with family; he was worshipped by foreigners to an indecent degree; he was too tolerant, too charming by half. It was through Temple that he would be made to pay for those sins.

IV

The Cat in Gloves Catches No Mice
1777–1778

*I've always found the secrets of government to be easier to penetrate than
those of individuals.*
—Beaumarchais to Vergennes, July 14, 1775

July 4, 1777, brought with it no cause for celebration. That Friday Stormont
was instructed to deliver an ultimatum to Versailles. Franklin and his colleagues brazenly continued to encourage cruises against the British, from
French ports. It was less a lucrative business than an effective one. The raids
impressed the rest of Europe and sowed terror among the British. Franklin
made no effort to disguise his pleasure that the proud ruler of the seas could
be insulted on her own coasts; he had moreover every reason to flaunt French
complicity. The cruises continued despite a rebuke in May, and after the fear-
less Irish-born Gustavus Conyngham was imprisoned in June, for having
captured an English mail packet. Meanwhile Captain Wickes and his cohorts
sailed around Ireland, raided or destroyed seventeen vessels, drove up insurance rates, and generally left British shipping in a shambles—all despite the
treaty that the French "pretend to hold sacred," as Deane had it.

Franklin was by no means solely responsible for the irregularities; in
French hands the Treaty of Utrecht was an eminently malleable thing.
Naval minister Sartine advised the captain of a Maryland privateer to

anchor just beyond the port of Cherbourg, where he might auction his prizes outside French territory. Tipping the collective hat, a French admiral in Brest improvidently returned the salute of a rebel ship. Rather too loudly it was arranged through Sartine that any American privateer requesting entrance to a French port should smash the water casks aboard ship so as to feign a leaky vessel. "Scarcely more could be done if there was an avowed alliance betwixt France and them, and that we were in a state of war with that kingdom," went the July explosion in London. That news would have startled the commissioners, who only dimly sensed France's favor, and had all but abandoned hope of an alliance. They had, however, precipitated a major diplomatic crisis.

On July 8 Stormont headed to Versailles, to make clear to Vergennes that peace would not survive such subterfuges. The meeting was a tempestuous one. Stormont remonstrated hotly, and at length. Vergennes was chilly and curt. Discussions over the previous weeks had been only slightly more cordial. Vergennes had been provoked into an unguarded admission that one of his representatives met regularly with Franklin; Stormont had offered a rattled tribute to Franklin's manipulative genius. Whatever the American was, "he is anything but a fool," sputtered the ambassador. He was outraged to have learned, just before the July showdown, of the arrival of Beaumarchais's supplies in New Hampshire. To Stormont's mind 30,000 guns, 400 tons of gunpowder, 5,000 tents, and 60 pieces of field artillery surely represented the greatest succors ever afforded by a nation pretending to be at peace.

Vergennes lost little time reprimanding the Americans for behavior that flew so egregiously in the face of their December promises. "You are too well-informed, Gentlemen, and too discerning, to be unaware of how deeply this behavior undermines the King's dignity, and offends the neutrality he claims to profess," he chided, making very clear his expectation that the Americans would both apologize and desist from embarrassing themselves in the future. His letter was a model of diplomatic restraint, with which he was pleased. He felt he had resisted all temptation to condescend. At the same time he burned with very honest rage, and let it be known that he had no desire to see the commissioners again. His indulgence had been sorely tried already. He had only just begun to bail out Beaumarchais, who had spent the funds with which he had been provided for America many times over, on credit. By the end of the summer Vergennes's bill came to a million livres.

His disfavor was keenly felt in Passy, where Franklin drafted an abject apology. Matters got worse before they got better, however, and that before the commissioners had any inkling of the reception their enthusiastic exports were receiving in America. After an eight-week trip, Lafayette had arrived in Philadelphia to a glacial July welcome on the State House steps. The knight-errant was essentially told to go home. He owed that American politesse largely to the behavior of the French recruits who had preceded him, a tetchy, rank-obsessed band of adventurers who strained every congressional nerve. Deane's year of good intentions and rank ineptitude threatened to catch up with him, but the poorly choreographed double game the American commissioners played with the privateers did first. The restless Conyngham sailed from Dunkirk in a new and larger vessel on July 16, and—baldly disobeying his very precise orders—made several quick captures. As the majority of his crew was French, Sartine's collusion was immediately suspected. The infraction sent Stormont barreling back to Versailles, threatening war were the Americans not instantly ejected from French ports. Vergennes obliged him with a search warrant for William Hodge, who had outfitted Conyngham's cutter. Hodge was hunted down and trundled off to the Bastille, the first American to enjoy that privilege. Franklin pleaded for his release in every office—Hodge was the finest of Americans, a devoted partisan of a worthy cause—but he did so in vain. Vergennes categorically refused even to receive Franklin. A sop to Stormont, Hodge remained in the Bastille for six weeks.

Vergennes was sorry to have been so severe, but he had already been more patient with the troublesome Americans than they had any right to expect. If they asked nicely, he would of course explain his position. But he could not much help their predicament. They knew very well why Hodge sat in the Bastille. Franklin and his colleagues had failed to grasp a fundamental tenet: One did not lie to the king of France. In his second rebuke the foreign minister felt no need to desist from highhandedness. And he enhanced his slap, adding to it the accusation of ingratitude, high on his list of reasons to distrust republics. "I think our sentiments of friendship have not made a deep impression on them," he concluded of the insurgents. The American commissioners would have agreed, but for different reasons. Neither Anglo-Saxon constituency was happy, and for once King George could be said to have spoken for Franklin. The day after Vergennes's outburst, the British sovereign observed, "It is very irksome to find the conduct of the French so very changeable; whether from duplicity or timidity, it is equally distressing." That official double-jointedness was on public display in the August Salon, to which Franklin paid a morning visit with Madame Brillon. His own bust featured prominently in the dazzling Louvre exhibition space, as did a piece he had commissioned for Congress, a marble monument to a young American general slain by the British at the 1775 siege on Quebec. Discerning Parisians were quick to note that the bust bore no caption, a craven tribute to British sensibilities.

In truth Vergennes felt anything but spineless that week. As the American commissioners nursed their wounds and braced for peace, the French foreign minister—unbeknownst to them, and despite the reprimands—prepared for war. Already he had briefed Louis XVI on the dangers of assisting the colonies insufficiently and on the advantages of more aggressive support, especially at a time when the French fleet was returning from its cod fishing and the Spanish fleet from Mexico. The colonies could never be perfectly tranquil; the British presence in Canada would keep them always in check. He anticipated a rupture with Britain with a barely disguised relish, one shelved whenever Stormont came to call. France had begun outfitting eight new warships; to the British ambassador's mind, that rearmament, various hints in the press, and the privateering firestorm pointed in a single direction, a concern he shared with Vergennes on August 19. In a silken bit of salesmanship—this was Vergennes in his element—the smiling French minister reminded his caller of a few laws of the eighteenth-century universe. The French court did not divulge its plans in advance to the newspapers. Stormont should bear in mind that the age of miracles was past; French troops could not walk upon water, either to rescue North America or to invade Britain's islands. For that a navy was required. And as everyone knew, that of the king of France happened to be off fishing. As for the French infatuation with the rebels, Stormont should rest assured that it derived neither from love of America nor from enmity toward England. The root was far deeper, hinted Vergennes, without bothering to explain. To the temperate English mind the allusion could be to only one thing. If there was one commodity as objectionable as Gallic duplicity, it was Gallic hotheadedness, defined by Stormont as "that licentious spirit that prevails in this country, and that no doubt is one of the principal causes of the enthusiastic madness in favor of the American cause, which every man you meet with has espoused, though he is free to own that he does not understand, and has not so much as attempted to understand, the question."

Days later the news of the British capture of Ticonderoga arrived, although it was not that defeat that came between Vergennes and the war for which he agitated. The unlikely angel of peace was a profligate Irish stock speculator informally attached to Stormont's embassy. The strapping Nathanial Forth had a passion for back staircases, the more disreputable the better; even the slippery Carmichael thought him a "low-lifed criminal." The British Foreign Office imposed Forth on Stormont as a favor to Maurepas, who did not find his weekly sparring matches with the starchy British ambassador as invigorating as did Vergennes. As much at home in the beau monde as the demimonde, Forth was an inspired choice for the assignment. As Vergennes noted, the notorious libertine was an emissary who could be put forward equably so as to be equably disavowed, a practice with which he had some familiarity.

It was Forth who made a secret August trip to Versailles to clear up the privateering mess with Maurepas, and it was Forth who—pressing for a speedy French answer—returned to London early in September with comforting news. Maurepas, he claimed, acceded to his every demand. The French pledged to abandon the Americans; peace was guaranteed. That news did more to demolish the hopes of the envoys than had the loss of Ticonderoga. The London stock market rallied; a new serenity reigned in the street. In that serenity Vergennes glimpsed Britain's clever new strategy; England would lead the Americans to despair by forcing France to be brutal with them. He felt himself to be in a new and ticklish bind. Were Versailles to throw over the Americans, France would not only facilitate a reconciliation but—for the first time he betrayed a hint of confidence in the future of the colonies—would surely "instill in the American heart a hatred and vengeance of which we would not be long in feeling the unhappy effects."

The privateering crisis had been averted, but to Vergennes's mind a greater one now loomed. He thought it imperative that France secure the confidence of the insurgents. And that he no longer felt could be done with the gentlemen at Passy, whom he had come to find pigheaded in the extreme, blindsided by their ideals, resistant to discussions of anything other than their glorious independence. Not only were they unreasonable, they were suspicious and indiscreet. Their art consisted equally of interesting France in their contest and of compromising her with England. "Everyone does what he has to do," Vergennes conceded, but if the Americans' duty was to "embrace anything that might benefit their cause, ours is not to allow ourselves to be carried further than it is in our interest to go." He resolved to persuade the Passy delegation to sign treaties of amity and commerce with France and Spain *after* they had won their independence, at which point the Bourbon powers would stand as guarantors of their sovereignty.

In the meantime, he sounded out the Spanish. As no rupture with England could take place before the return of the Bourbon fleets, there was ample time to make an end run around Franklin. Why not send a secret emissary to America? The man for the job was someone intelligent, adroit, and distinctly unflamboyant, who could divine the insurgents' true sentiments on French and Spanish support, an opinion which Vergennes did not feel came to him unembellished from Passy. As important, that agent would be able to answer the questions that so bedeviled the French ministers, and on which Franklin had not sufficiently satisfied them. Was this country for real? Did it have either consistency or resolve? Vergennes had no expectation of a reasonable discussion at Passy, where there was much discontent with French pandering to England. Reports had it that there was some dissent among the American ranks. And the mood was evidently grim at the Valentinois, which the nuance-friendly Vergennes—a man who saw strategies in wallpaper patterns, especially when they covered Anglo-Saxon walls—suspected might well be a ruse as well.

⁓

Disaffection was indeed the operative emotion at Passy, where the stalled state of American affairs in Europe had begun to take its toll. Franklin barely needed to say a word; both the French and the English spies noted a change in his disposition. In his years of huckstering and cajoling and lobbying and wheedling he had known impasses before, but never when so much was at stake; this dithering season of half-promises and quarter-efforts constituted a torture. Insofar as was possible, he attempted to work within the confines prescribed, and to bow to local mores. He ordered the privateers back to North America until tempers cooled. When his grand-nephew met with obstacles in the purchase of a frigate for supplies, Franklin commiserated: "It is vexing for men of spirit and honor accustomed to a different mode of conducting business to be trifled with, and as I may say, to be jockied by such a *finesse*. But we must for this time submit." He also advised Williams to surrender the vessel; increasingly the mood was one of resignation. Weekly came reports that Franklin's spirits were low; that he was uncommonly silent; that when he did speak, he spoke of France with diminishing fondness. The police agent stationed outside the Valentinois noted that the finest carriages in France continued to roll up to the door, that Franklin met regularly with arms and uniforms manufacturers, prominent scientists, and provincial officials. At the same time it did not escape the agent's attention that as September passed, "Mr. Franklin seems to have lost a great deal of his exuberance, and appears much preoccupied."

On the afternoon of September 7, Franklin received a visit from the comte de Lauraguais, a French officer and one of the more convincing eccentrics in Europe. Lauraguais had on his side fluent English; he was also possessed of a spirited, independent mind and an ungovernable tongue, both of which had made him an intimate of prisons all over France. Too restless for the military, the forty-four-year-old aesthete dabbled in science, in literature, in politics, in agricultural studies. His application of the sciences indicates why he was no natural for court life. To the sober Académie des Sciences Lauraguais would report on an experiment he performed in his Normandy fishpond. He beheaded six ducks, then replaced them in water, where they continued to swim happily. "This struck me as all the more interesting," concluded Lauraguais before an assembly accustomed to drier discourses, "as it might begin to explain the workings of an infinite number of things in France."*

---

*The loss of his mistress to a tedious prince led to an equally inspired bit of logic. Heartbroken, Lauraguais queried four doctors as to whether one could die of boredom. Several attested to the fact that one could. Lauraguais then consulted a number of prominent lawyers. If someone caused you nearly to die of boredom, did you have a legal right to banish that person from your home? Two attorneys conceded that would be just. Lauraguais submitted these reports to the prince, who naturally challenged his rival to a duel, which, alas, did nothing to displace him in the affections of their mutual mistress.

It was this colorful character who sailed into Franklin's rooms in early September to dine with the demoralized commissioners. As on most matters, Lauraguais's view of the American context was unconventional. He trusted the insurgents as little as he did their mother country, an opinion he presumably kept to himself. He was less discreet with Franklin's side of the conversation, every syllable of which he shared with Vergennes. Franklin may have surmised as much; while his colleagues were more critical, he spoke devotedly of Vergennes and Maurepas. After several glasses of wine Franklin also unburdened himself with much emotion. "There is nothing better to do here than drink," he lamented. "How can we fool ourselves that France might understand America better than Britain? How can we fool ourselves that a monarchy will help republicans, revolted against their monarch? How can your ministers believe what they cannot understand?" He was heartsick. He sorely regretted having failed to interest Versailles in a commercial alliance, which would have been so much for the good of both countries. And while he understood that the French court feared for her colonies if America succeeded too well, he believed France could delay but by no means prevent that success. He sounded neither the serene, unflappable Franklin of legend nor the man who trembled lest his proposals of a foreign alliance be accepted.

As authentic as it may have been, his bad mood made for good strategy. It could be dilated upon, or dismissed, at will. That was the kind of posturing in which Franklin actively engaged; it had nothing to do with his accidental apotheosis as the reborn Newton, or the original Quaker. His bout of despair would ease through the loan the Americans formally requested at the end of September, a request over which Franklin labored for weeks. His application was laced with a perfectly legitimate sense of defeat. Never had the French court seemed so ill disposed toward America. Deane had practically to force himself on Vergennes. On both the military and the financial fronts the situation was dire. The commissioners had no money. All Paris knew that General Burgoyne was marching toward Albany and General Howe toward Philadelphia, from which two-thirds of that city had fled in terror. Washington's men were in retreat. The American cause appeared futile.

At the same time Vergennes did not believe he could afford to alienate a people who felt already sacrificed and abandoned. Their frustration with Versailles only strengthened the British hand. France must compensate for her severity with secret funds. He argued that she restrict the sale of American prizes, keep their ships out of her ports, and, simultaneously, tether the colonies to France through her generosity. A loan was not a viable option, as the insurgents had nothing with which to secure it. Was it not more in keeping with the dignity of a great power to make an outright gift? Vergennes too was playing a game. He ran his thoughts past his Spanish counterpart, only to reveal—days later—that the Americans had submitted precisely such a request, one he knew well was forthcoming. It seemed that America would not be compromised by her too honest and trusting nature when she had friends around like the comte de Vergennes.

Instead America was compromised by her own representatives. When he could be found, Thomas Morris, whose binges had so driven Deane to despair, remained America's official agent in Nantes. The local merchants were only too happy to ply him with liquor and assist with his accounts. Every visitor to that city passed on news of his misdeeds, along with their astonishment that the commissioners should entrust their affairs to a drunkard. The astonishment was all the greater as it was common knowledge that Robert Morris had removed his own business from his brother's unsteady hands; the financier's vote of nonconfidence made the commissioners appear particularly inept. Deane and Franklin had made known their displeasure, only to earn a reprimand from Morris, humiliated before Congress. Morris felt moreover that Franklin was to have kept an eye on the half brother whom he looked upon as a son.

Franklin tended to avoid any affair that combined the personal with the unruly, but could not escape on the late September Saturday when a disheveled Thomas Morris turned up on the doorstep. His brother had shared with him the commissioners' censure and his outrage at it, which Morris publicized in Nantes. He then headed to Passy to excoriate Franklin. At the Valentinois he offered up his brother's tattered envelope, stained and soiled. As soon as Franklin had read the document through he opened fire. Franklin had overstepped his bounds in denouncing him to Congress. Thomas Morris despised him, and would henceforth treat him only with contempt. To the storm of abuse Franklin replied coolly. He was delighted to be respected by men who were themselves respectable, but remained utterly "indifferent to the sentiments of those who are of a contrary character." Morris proceeded to waltz around Paris maligning his colleagues. He by no means overestimated his powers. Pointing up the divisions among the Americans undermined their legitimacy at a time when they were struggling desperately to prove it. After the one-two punch of Ticonderoga and the Morris imbroglio, went the British reasoning, the court of France would surely have had its fill of amateurish Americans.

Franklin handled the mess as he handled most such debacles. He observed only that Congress might support the credit of the foreign envoys as those envoys supported the credit of Congress. While Morris continued to disgrace them, Franklin refused to say more, a true measure of his fury, which could most often be read in his silence. He was unwilling to submit to an additional "rap over the knuckles."* Unfortunately the Morris skirmish was part of a larger conflict, with which Franklin had no choice but to grapple. Months earlier a congressional committee had appointed Arthur Lee's elder brother as commercial agent. That left William Lee, Jonathan Williams, and Thomas Morris, their authority deriving from different sources, to tend to the same business in Nantes, at a time when the disposing of prizes was already a contentious issue. Not having received official word of Lee's appointment, Franklin—who appears to have made himself unavailable to the bushy-browed William Lee for as long as possible—insisted that the new agent remain in Paris until the notification arrived. For his part, Lee showed no particular impatience to settle in Nantes. The situation ultimately resolved itself at the end of the year, when Congress dispatched Lee to try his hand at soliciting support in eastern Europe; when Thomas Morris drank himself to death; and when Williams resigned his position, with, apart from those of the deceased, hard feelings all around.

The pileup in Nantes had its parallel in Passy, where Lenoir's agents noted that the American ranks swelled. Rooms were prepared (although ultimately not occupied) for William Lee in August, for Silas Deane's

---

*Surely Congress had simply neglected the matter, argued a colleague, who read no reproof into their silence on the Morris matter. Franklin demurred. Badly stung by Robert Morris's reprimand, he refused to meddle further. Knocking on closed doors was one thing, hurling himself against brick walls another.

brother in September. August also brought Ralph Izard, the tall, fine-looking scion of a prominent South Carolina family, dispatched to represent his country in Tuscany. By the end of September Franklin was presiding over a table that, supplemented by family members, numbered at least fifteen. It was an unharmonious group. Lee had fallen out with the blustery Carmichael when the Marylander declined his invitation to serve as secretary in Berlin, from which Lee returned convinced that Deane had been slandering him. Having advanced the mission funds out of his own pocket, Carmichael did not see why he had not been reimbursed, or why he should continue to be saddled with business but no commission. The bulk of the secretarial work fell to the indefatigable Bancroft. Eloquently conversant in many of the same fields that so absorbed Franklin—Bancroft's obsessions ranged from poisons and inks to electric eels—he diligently acquitted himself of his responsibilities but threatened to leave, having neither been paid for weeks nor granted an official title. Jacobus van Zandt, an English spy masquerading as an American businessman, angled for the job. Probably the least gifted of Eden's agents, van Zandt ate regularly, as George Lupton, at Franklin's table. Carmichael's refusal to join Lee introduced a rogue commissioner into the picture; Lee had traveled to Berlin with forty-year-old, Princeton-educated Stephen Sayre, with whom he fell out, and who remained in Berlin. Sayre spent the next years passing himself off as an official American envoy from one end of Europe to the other. Even Vergennes, whom Franklin begged to intervene, refused to assist on that count. (Although Franklin could not have found it so, Sayre's excuse was charming: "I must look on myself as a modern Don Quixote, going about to protect and relieve the virtuous in distress.") And each of these colleagues—Sayre included—wondered after his salary, when the mission was strapped financially.

On September 14, Franklin waged a serious but losing battle with the naval ministry. He emerged convinced—or convincing those whom he knew to be listening most attentively—that French promises were illusory. He hinted that he was soon to leave, as the climate might no longer be safe for him. Not only for public consumption, Deane acknowledged that the mission was "greatly embarrassed" and "well-nigh discouraged," which did nothing to improve internal relations. Beaumarchais took a drubbing from Franklin and Deane, who blamed him for Hodge's incarceration. Secrecy continued to defy the Americans at every step. Original papers from Deane's Paris apartment made their way to Versailles at a most delicate juncture; Vergennes was deliberating a grant of aid, contingent on absolute secrecy. With the approach of fall the envoys found themselves desperately overdrawn. Franklin recommended they cancel their contracts and sell off the supplies waiting to be shipped to America. Louis XVI graciously bought the immense frigate they had ordered to be built in Amsterdam but could not afford to complete. On October 1 Beaumarchais paid a visit to the Valentinois and found it a gloomy place indeed. If he did not know as much already, he would have learned that morning of the death of Deane's young wife, news Deane had been left to pluck from the newspapers. Beaumarchais found Franklin reeling from the word that an American privateer had been captured and its captain killed. What afflicted him more greatly yet was the irresolution at Versailles, about which Franklin quizzed the visitor closely. Beaumarchais played the eternal optimist. It was, he reminded Vergennes afterward, all a sort of confidence game. He upheld his end of the chain, which ran directly from Franklin to Congress to the American people.

Well aware of the responsibility of keeping that chain bright, Franklin made no public concession to despair. It was as essential that he appear buoyant in Paris as that he convince Vergennes that the Americans were perilously close to sinking. Through September and October the papers reported him to be in good spirits; especially with the news that General Howe had occupied Philadelphia, it was imperative that he remain so. Around town he was as wildly applauded as ever; there was no intermission in the odes, the encomia, the ovations. Publicly Franklin conceded that America no longer counted on any rupture in her favor but remained undeterred. The colonies had only their union and their resolve, but those weapons, he insisted, were infallible. His countrymen could hold out for thirty years. He was colorful in his pronouncements. Philadelphia would prove a grave for the British troops. That city was of no strategic importance. Washington would blockade the roads; the Delaware would freeze; the British army would be cut off from its own ships. He argued—in a line for which Jefferson would get the dubious credit, speaking of a different revolution—that "civil wars in the political systems, like bleeding to the human body, or thunderstorms in due season, are salutary." In the sole surviving letter to his family that miserable fall he focused on his good health, the comfort he took in his grandchildren, his agreeable friends and lodgings in Passy. He knew what documentary evidence of Dr. Franklin's sagging spirits was worth on the open market.

※

Two convictions sustained him through that bleak season, in which the weather remained complicit; November disappeared under a murk of fog. While Deane concluded that the ineptitude of Congress and the deceit of France were greater evils than anything Britain might have to offer and began to lean toward reconciliation, Franklin held fast to the belief that America should win her independence on her own. He confessed to having dreaded the idea of France espousing the American cause too warmly, which would sap her of her vitality and ingenuity at the start. Arthur Lee had heard Franklin expound on that theme often enough, but even he must have been taken aback by Franklin's rhapsody of October 25, 1777. In his rooms that day Franklin argued that the manner in which the entire American Revolution had thus far proceeded represented "such a miracle in human affairs that if he had not been in the midst of it, and seen all the movements, he could not have comprehended how it was effected." Everything about it defied logic—and everything about it gave cause for concern—and yet he remained adamant that "the greatest revolution the world ever saw" would likely soon be complete. To his conviction in American self-reliance Franklin joined a fierce belief in the value of perseverance. As a teenager he had observed that success bred presumption and that presumption bred inattention. On the other hand misfortune fostered care and vigilance, by which losses might be reversed. He codified those rules at the chessboard, to his mind a metaphor of life and, especially, of war.

To Franklin's rules he might have added that a man reveals a great deal of himself on that checkered square. Already his single-mindedness had earned him the wrath of his neighbor, the captious and outspoken Madame Le Roy. Detaining her scientist husband at a game, Franklin had thoughtlessly sent Madame Le Roy home alone, after eleven at night, in the rain, with his umbrella. He got his umbrella back, with a fierce reproach. Nor did Franklin religiously observe his own rules. Although he would write that it was rude to exhibit one's impatience at the chessboard, he was an unreconstructed drummer of fingers on tables. Chaumont called this to his attention. Did his friend realize that he himself had a very bad habit? What was it, asked Franklin? Chaumont demonstrated the annoying piano playing, only to hear a dismissive: "Oh that! My dear, it's trivial, and not worth mentioning." As in most things in Passy, he was indulged. Madame Brillon cosseted him as much as anyone, and it was to her that Franklin dedicated his essay on chess, a tribute to her civilized approach to the game. That quality was particularly in evidence on November 29, when Franklin and Le Veillard began a ferocious match in her bathroom, while she soaked in a covered tub. (Presumably the fire burned brightest there, or Madame Brillon craved the company.) It was an entirely waterlogged hostess who emerged hours later. Franklin was shocked to discover after his short walk home that he had kept her nearly to eleven; he had lost all track of time. "Never again will I consent to a match in your bathroom," he swore, in an apology irresistible as much for its text as for its type. He wrote his neighbor in a flawless imitation of her own penmanship.

While Franklin focused on the chessboard, Arthur Lee directed his single-minded attention to the defects of the Passy mission. He wrote to Congress of the problems of combining political and commercial agents in the same men. He was not the first to warn—as he did the day of Madame Brillon's bath—that if some changes were not made, American affairs in Paris "must end in total confusion and disgrace." Repeatedly he had endeavored to establish responsible accounting and regular business hours at the Valentinois, in vain. Only recently Franklin had again set a date for which he failed to appear. Lee was deeply suspicious of Jonathan Williams, who had been established practically overnight in Nantes while Lee was in Berlin, when neither Franklin nor Deane was authorized to make that appointment. (Lee was right.) The three commissioners diverged as well in their opinions of France. When they conferred at the end of November, Deane insisted it was time to issue an ultimatum. Either they were to count on the immediate support of the Bourbon powers or they would reconcile. Franklin took a more temperate stand. Such a threat might well lead France to abandon the American cause in anger. Lee feared that such a declaration would scare away the monies already granted.

That disunion was the least of Franklin's problems. For weeks the commissioners labored over an abject and very necessary apology to the Spanish court for their privateering excesses. It sat on Vergennes's desk for final approval when word came that an American ship had captured an English one in French waters. Versailles was now as offended as Madrid. On November 23, tails between their legs, the Americans promised truly, meekly, to behave. They suggested to Congress that America simply forgo all future privateering. They were earning a reputation as pirates. As they drafted that dispatch, they received the horrifying news that Captain Wickes and his crew had perished at sea, off Newfoundland. There was no movement on the prisoner relief front, a subject that infuriated Franklin more than any other. Bravely he continued in his public stance, by which all disasters were setbacks and all defeats skirmishes, but on that front too he waged a losing battle. "The Americans are doomed," announced a sympathetic paper, predicting that even Franklin's eloquence could no longer salvage Washington's reputation. "The Americans' friends here, already a little bored by their so-called caution, will now disdain them as fervently as once they admired them." For the first time Franklin was in the same boat as Beaumarchais, who squawked that he was as good as battling the English, the Americans, the French, and the Atlantic Ocean, all at once.

～✦～

It took a very great deal to upstage Franklin but—especially at a time when the American contest began to devolve from impossible dream to lost cause; the eighteenth-century Anglo-Saxon visitor to Paris seized always on the Gallic preference for burlesque—a brawny, cross-dressing dragoon officer with an alluring pout did the trick. The chevalier d'Eon was not the only transvestite in the newspapers, but he was the only one who had distinguished himself with a sword and as secretary to the French embassy in London before disclosing his little secret.* A long negotiation preceded her return to France, to which Vergennes testily agreed on the condition that the chevalier dress as was proper for her sex. That fall the chevalier returned to the family château and to the mother he

---

*It was on d'Eon's account that Beaumarchais was in London in 1775, where Arthur Lee would infect him with his American passion. Beaumarchais's secret mission was to relieve d'Eon of some incriminating papers, during which exchange he claimed to fall victim to another passion: that of d'Eon for him. Even the nimble Beaumarchais had difficulty resisting the advances of that demented woman, who "drank and smoked and swore like a German trooper."

had not seen in decades, a woman who for forty-nine years had labored under the illusion that she had given birth to a son. There was some tussle about wardrobe—Could d'Eon alternate between wardrobes? (No.) Could she wear her military decorations on her dress? (In the provinces, only.)—and much tussle with it. "I'm doing my best to walk in pointed toes and high heels, but have nearly broken my neck more than once," the chevalier griped to Vergennes, who devoted nearly as much time to d'Eon as to American affairs, and who scoffed that the former bored him to tears.

In that he was alone. All the eyes of France turned in the chevalier's direction on Sunday, November 23, when she was presented at court, in her new guise. It was almost inevitable that Mademoiselle la chevalière d'Eon, in white gloves, diamond necklace and earrings, would, as jaws dropped all around, herself fumble with her wig. She spent Mass madly readjusting her coiffure. Versailles was captivated as this flat-chested, muscle-bound individual continued to leap manfully from her carriage unassisted by any equerry, as she ascended stairs four at a time, all in the work of France's premier dressmaker. Even Voltaire fell victim to d'Eon's "amphibian" appeal, pleading for details. Not only to justify their attention to the sideshow, the ambassadorial corps observed that d'Eon was spending an inordinate amount of time in Vergennes's office.

Paris was thus transfixed when Beaumarchais rode out to Passy on Thursday morning, December 4, 1778. As Temple remembered it, the playwright had come to share his woes. He swore that he was the next to be sacrificed on the altar of Stormont's protests, when his only crime was to have followed Vergennes's orders. As Beaumarchais remembered it, he called at Passy having heard that an American messenger was en route from Nantes. In any event, Chaumont, Beaumarchais, and the commissioners were assembled—and Beaumarchais was or was not anticipating his imminent slaughter—when thirty-year-old Jonathan Loring Austin rode into the Valentinois courtyard at eleven-thirty. He had left America but four weeks earlier. He had not alighted from his horse when Franklin cried out, "Sir, *is* Philadelphia taken?" "Yes, sir," replied the rider. Franklin turned in defeat, his hands clasped behind his back. "But, sir, I have greater news than that," Austin called to the retreating figure. "General Burgoyne *and his whole army are prisoners of war!*"

At no point in his life could Franklin have wished more for a rack of printer's type. All hands set to copying the joyous report of the Battle of Saratoga, which Franklin carefully plumped up for French consumption. To Burgoyne's stunning defeat he added the imminent ruin of General Howe, encircled by Washington's men in Philadelphia. Within hours Temple carried word to the Brillon household, where the entire family leapt to embrace him. In their jubilation the Brillons begged to congratulate Franklin in person, but Temple discouraged them. His grandfather had his hands full. (The musical Madame Brillon settled for composing a triumphal march, "to cheer up General Burgoyne and his men, as they head off to captivity.") Events moved speedily at Versailles, where Vergennes's undersecretary, Conrad-Alexandre Gérard, was dispatched to pay a midnight call of congratulations at the Valentinois. As usual no one moved with the celerity of Beaumarchais, who raced back to Paris with the banker Ferdinand Grand to share the news. So relentlessly did he urge on his driver that the carriage caught on a stone and overturned in the street. Out flew Beaumarchais, in a shower of glass, on the rue des Petits-Champs. He was cut all over his face and body; a shard of window lodged in his right arm. He had nearly broken his neck. (Grand suffered a dislocated shoulder and a fractured collarbone, for which Beaumarchais apologized profusely.) Even as he spit blood the playwright continued to wail about his cursed affairs. In the end it would not be his postilion who killed him, he swore, but the America-doubting Maurepas.

As Beaumarchais nursed his wounds, Franklin reveled in the extraordinary and touching accounts of Burgoyne, impeccable in full dress and gold epaulettes, surrendering to Major General Horatio Gates, in a plain dark coat, his officers in fantastical uniforms of their own invention. In Passy Franklin took to clapping his hands together and exclaiming, "Oh! Mr. Austin, you have brought us glorious news!" The manner in which that news was reported—in cafés as well as the corridors of power it took precedence over all other, and introduced talk of war with Britain—spoke to its import. Paris's daily paper reported on Beaumarchais's accident but not on Saratoga. The premier gossip sheet did the same (adding only that, typically, Beaumarchais had exaggerated his mishap for dramatic effect). The news of Saratoga fell to the foreign press, although not all of it emanated from foreign sources. From the couch on which he recovered in central Paris, Beaumarchais submitted to Vergennes his account, for the London-based *Courrier de l'Europe*.

By December 6 Vergennes had already written several times to the court of Madrid, with whom any French action would have to be coordinated. Here was precisely the situation he had hoped to avoid; he was unsure whether he should mourn or rejoice. He needed to collect his thoughts—something to which Vergennes rarely confessed on paper— but within twenty-four hours of Austin's arrival had resolved that one way or another, there was not a moment to lose. He and Maurepas were agreed that it was imperative that France solidify her relationship "with a friend who could be useful if bound to us, dangerous if neglected." The next day Undersecretary Gérard was back on the Valentinois doorstep. Would the Americans care to renew the overtures they had made to France a year earlier? Franklin set to work, dusting off the treaties with which he had sailed.

Temple found that the news of Burgoyne's defeat "was received in France with as great demonstrations of joy as if it had been a victory gained by their own arms." To a great extent it was. Insofar as the men to whom Burgoyne surrendered were clothed and armed by France, Saratoga represented a triumph for Chaumont and Beaumarchais and those merchants whose clandestine aid Vergennes had underwritten. Jubilant though the atmosphere at Passy was—and the congratulations poured in from all over; these were times when a portrait of George Washington was worth more than a shipment of truffles—it is doubtful that anyone savored the news as much as Vergennes. The victory was as much his as anyone else's. With it his double game edged closer to a self-serving triple game; even while he kept Saratoga out of the newspapers, he had lent the fledgling nation a viability that made America an attractive partner at Versailles. Only the extended family resisted the grooming. To Madrid, Saratoga was meaningless. The conde de Floridablanca, Vergennes's Spanish counterpart, remained firm in his conviction that the wisest course of action was to continue to fund the insurgents covertly, so as to allow the British and Americans to demolish each other. To his mind there was no greater urgency to the American situation than there had been four months earlier. Vergennes owed his position to a reputation for slavish, unimaginative conservatism, which he maintained in all realms save one: his tiny, irritating grudge against the British Empire. Still, he was circumspect. Stormont would not catch him glorying in England's embarrassment. With delight Vergennes pictured the blush that would cross Stormont's face for having a short time earlier mocked the cowardly Americans. The gloating minister then caught himself: "But we must not be petty."

Pettiness was not in Franklin's repertoire. If indeed Austin's news made him weep with joy, as one report had it, he handled the American victory as coolly as he had handled the defeats. His grace was of the utilitarian variety: He made one of his first acts the propagation of the courageous exploits of the French officers in America. (Among those who had distinguished themselves were the unwanted Lafayette and the unknown Pulaski, who had ridden straight up to the enemy with a pistol.) That made for a nice counterpoint to the manner in which the British press reported on the Ticonderoga debacle, from which, those papers claimed, "the French officers had fled, if it was possible, even faster than the Americans." Franklin was entirely in his element, which is to say he picked up his pen; per Gérard's request, the application to the French court fell to him. He did not work with the intensity Lee would have liked, devoting two days to what his impatient colleague noted was a rather short document. By it hung a young country's fate, and to it Franklin applied a year's worth of frustrations; in his brief application he reminded the court that given the secrecy in which French aid had been cloaked, America had as yet no inkling of the king's generosity. By contrast she was soon to hear plenty on the severity with which the king treated her privateers. Essentially he restated America's 1776 application for a treaty of amity and commerce, but Lee was correct on one count: To Vergennes's mind, the actual text of Franklin's application mattered little.

Already there was a palpable change of temperature at Versailles, as Temple discovered when he delivered his grandfather's appeal on the evening of December 8. Vergennes received him personally, with uncommon warmth. He promised an answer in forty-eight hours. The same day at dinner Ferdinand Grand observed that Vergennes had for the first time referred to the Americans as "our friends" rather than "your friends." A seismic shift was read into that amended pronoun. In his glory Franklin attended the Académie des Sciences lectures that week, a program that included everything from a study of longitude to a discourse on sulfur formations. He was much fussed over afterward, when two women detached themselves from the crowd and begged to congratulate him on the news. Franklin accepted their good wishes with open arms but then spotted another woman who appeared unmoved by his presence. Was she really going to withhold her favors, he challenged? She allowed herself to be embraced as well, another victory, reported the *Courrier de l'Europe*, for the Americans.

The welcome was nearly as effusive at Versailles, to which the deputies were summoned on December 12. Once they had assembled, Gérard's servant conveyed them to Vergennes's country home, outside town, where the foreign minister and his aide awaited. Vergennes applauded their triumph and spent some time discussing the two armies, after which he appealed to Franklin for his predictions. Franklin assured him that the British would tire of their effort and that America would emerge victorious. Vergennes read through their proposed terms of the alliance, in which he was pleased to see that no new demands had been inserted. He explained why France and Spain had been unable to welcome earlier overtures; not being themselves sure of the consistency of Congress, the commissioners could not be surprised by the failure of other powers to take their side openly. While he assured his callers that the king would be happy to entertain their proposals, he labored to disabuse them of their naiveté. For France to enter into a commercial treaty was no innocent act. It was tantamount to a declaration of war against England, something Vergennes begged the envoys to acknowledge plainly. Were they to negotiate, it was imperative they begin in good faith. France, he promised, would take no advantage of their situation. She would attempt nothing that was not in the new nation's best interest. While on the subject, he thought he might point out that the Americans were fooling themselves if they felt they could ever preserve peace in North America so long as the British retained a foothold there. They would sow dissension in their ranks, and destroy their country.* As instructed, Vergennes ended the conference with the request that the envoys do nothing to hasten the premature birth of their independence. It would be three weeks before he had an answer from Madrid.

The conde de Aranda, as fond of an American war as he was out of favor with his own court, was waiting for Vergennes when the deputies emerged. Having counseled prudence and patience, Vergennes broke into

---

*That was the converse of the argument Vergennes used with Spain, whom he hastened to assure that Canada would remain always a check on America.

a sweat of urgency. (He was preaching to the converted. A dyed-in-the-wool Anglophobe, Aranda had been ready to wage war a year earlier.) If Vergennes had hesitated on Austin's arrival, he had in the course of the week made up his mind. France and Spain could ally themselves with America or abandon her entirely, but one way or another, he convinced himself, they would be embroiled in a war with England. (The British did not share that conviction, and would drag their feet on the subject as long as they could.) Certainly events gnawed at him: Vergennes had just learned that Parliament was to discuss peace proposals when it reconvened after the holidays, on January 20, 1778. Accurately or not, a German paper had Franklin crowing that the opposition speeches in London comforted him more even than would a vast French fleet. The Americans made perfectly clear that they preferred a French to a British relationship; all the same, were France not soon to offer support, they hinted they might well find themselves seeking solace elsewhere. Before any British delegate had made contact with Franklin, Vergennes had compressed his thinking into a neat formula. The first to recognize American independence would be the first to garner the fruits of the conflict.

As it happened, the line was Beaumarchais's, and not one of recent vintage. While America's premier munitions supplier sulked in the background—was he who had done more than anyone for America ever to see a penny in return?—his voice on the foreign policy page grew louder and clearer. Three days after his accident he was finally up and about. He delighted in the American victory, the effect of which was staggering—the English in Paris dared not show their faces—but was none too happy with his insurgents. Having delivered supplies that helped to make Saratoga possible, the *Amphitrite* had returned with her first cargo. It was claimed by Franklin. There was no question that those goods belonged to Beaumarchais, who shared his outrage with Versailles. Beaumarchais made clear that he had long distinguished among the honest Deane, the insidious Lee, and—it was the most cutting insult in his vocabulary—the taciturn Dr. Franklin. He could not so much as prevail upon Franklin for an appointment, much less elicit a reply to a letter.

Vergennes spent as much time managing the thin-skinned playwright as he did foreign policy that week. His patience held out for five days. On

December 16 he sent Gérard to assure the Americans that a treaty would indeed be made. France waited only for Spain. For his own benefit and for Madrid's, Vergennes spent the next weeks harping on the twin threats: He cared to be neither the victim of Britain nor the laughingstock of Europe. Both were ideas that had originated as much with Beaumarchais as with the British Parliament. And in their light everything appeared quite differently. To buttress his arguments, Vergennes enlisted an unusual ally; suddenly he was the servant of public opinion. The French people were all for a treaty with the Americans. They called loudly for one. To the Spanish court he sang as well the praises of the bold American privateers who had caused him—and continued to cause him—such headaches. With what spirit they had harassed English shipping! Imagine what they could do with the French and Spanish fleets behind them! As Vergennes labored to impress this inverted logic on Madrid, Paris began to fill with peace emissaries. The race was on.

⁓🙟⁓

No sooner had the news of Saratoga reached London than volunteers began lining up to sound out Franklin on peace terms. There was much discussion as to who the proper emissary might be. Sir William Pulteney, a hugely wealthy and distinguished Whig, felt strongly that only an aboveboard negotiation could succeed. He did not believe that Franklin would incline to France over England but knew him also to be much exasperated; a trusted friend would be the most effective envoy. Undersecretary of State Eden was of a different mind, concerned that any official proposal would be used for leverage at Versailles. Accordingly the first to the doorstep was not to be someone aboveboard at all but Paul Wentworth, in Beaumarchais's alarmist opinion "one of the cleverest men in England." To the master spy Eden conceded that the war was going poorly, but on it would go. Britain intended to continue until her resources gave out. On the other hand, this might well be the moment to end a taxing contest. "We have often been asked here, 'Do you mean anything short of unconditional submission?' I wish to answer that question by putting another to those who are in the confidence of the colonies. 'Do you mean anything short of unqualified independence?'" If the answer was no, the colonies could look forward to a decade of unsuccessful war. Equipped with a fair supply of white ink, Wentworth checked into his rue de Richelieu hotel on December 12, which put him in Paris before the Americans had yet visited Vergennes's country home.

That day Wentworth engaged in a little negotiation of his own. By anonymous note he requested a clandestine interview with Deane, known to be the most conciliatory of the Americans. Wentworth waited in his coach at the gates of Passy for his answer; Deane could not be lured into a secret meeting, but offered to receive his correspondent the next morning, at his rue Royale apartment. There the two began an eleven-hour conversation, one they continued in a neighborhood café the following day. To some extent Wentworth had chosen his delegate well. He and Deane were fellow Freemasons, and the British envoy appealed to shared ideals, in which Deane delighted. He made no secret of his disgust for France. Personally he would prefer a farm in America to a French dukedom. As for Dr. Franklin, he too felt most closely bound to Britain and the British, "and frequently tread over the ground of his enjoyments there, with tears of regret for the separation." At the same time the colonists were so intent on independence that the North would surely fight on even were the South to capitulate. Deane fended off Wentworth's advances with an effusion of self-righteousness. He reveled in America's future and her courage, inviting Wentworth to admire the pluck of an ill-dressed militia who, mounted two to a horse, sustained by only the barest of provisions, had faced cannon with bayonets. That rosy portrait of "republican pride" irked Wentworth less than did a new habit of Deane's. "He had collected historical maxims in a diary, from which he is always quoting," snorted the spy.

Agreeing finally to confine future discussions purely to treaty terms, the two made a date to talk a few days hence. Wentworth's presence in Paris was more eloquent even than his winning command of language, however; while Franklin declined Wentworth's invitation to meet, he shared his note with Vergennes. Two days elapsed between the arrival of that document in Versailles and Gérard's December 16 visit to Passy, to assure the deputies that France would enter into a treaty. Simultaneously Vergennes set out to ascertain the true nature of Wentworth's errand. Beaumarchais was already on the trail; it was a measure of the foreign minister's concern that he judged that surveillance insufficient. He assigned another agent to the case, a dissolute pamphleteer whose gambling debts Vergennes had settled. Jean-Louis Favier was familiar to Wentworth, who quickly unburdened himself. It was demeaning to be taken for a common spy. Friends disavowed him; he was badgered even at the opera. Especially after Deane missed their next interview, Wentworth complained that the Americans were to blame for the cloud of suspicions that had settled upon him. Favier reminded his old friend that it had been hazardous to make contact with Deane in the first place. In turn Wentworth sheepishly confided that he hoped to keep his meetings secret only from the British. He sent money to his family in America through the Passy agents, on whom he relied for market tips. He was most displeased that Deane declined to join him in a new stock scheme, from which the envoy refrained not on account of any scruples, but because he already had his hands full speculating with a number of other people, including Chaumont, Beaumarchais, and Grand. Favier emerged from Wentworth's fabulous oration with his head splitting, feeling, for good reason, "like a blind man at a fair."

Vergennes did as well, and to observe the shape-shifting Wentworth at closer range—he assumed that the speculating was a pretext for a negotiation—invited the agent to dinner. Favier reminded Wentworth of that honor when next Wentworth complained of the indignity of being taken for a spy. Clearly he was in favor. He had nothing to fear. The comte de Vergennes had indeed been polite, agreed Wentworth, admitting that "his dinner was sumptuous, his wines exquisite and served with profusion, but that he could not drink them with a good heart while thinking whom he had been taken for." Presumably to restore his pride—it was an odd day when the spies complained of being shadowed, and officials turned down stock schemes because they were already overcommitted—Stormont arranged for Wentworth to be presented at court. He was much pleased by the ambassador's attention but questioned his tactics. The high-strung Stormont should learn to contain himself. It would be wiser to ease off a little, so as to catch the French napping.

Wentworth was equally censorious of the Americans, having divined that they had presented a proposal to Versailles, currently making its way to Madrid. They had proved themselves "unfaithful in friendship or politic, and devoid of that heroic pride that scorns to take advantage of a foe." Franklin was left to defend himself from allegations of bad faith not with the upright Wentworth, whom he shrewdly refused to see, but with the hysterical Beaumarchais, who arrived with the same charge on the morning of December 24. Tears in his wide hazel eyes, Beaumarchais heaped his fury over the *Amphitrite* stores on Franklin and Lee. By all rights that cargo was his. He waved his agreement of 1776 at Franklin, who countered that Deane had had no commission at the time he had entered into it. Insisting they were in total darkness on the matter, the envoys called in Lauraguais, the great aesthete. For his own reasons Lauraguais gamefully attested that Beaumarchais's munitions had been intended as a gift. Beaumarchais was left to pour out his outrage to the Committee for Foreign Affairs, in America. He would not mention Dr. Franklin's unconscionably discourteous behavior were it not now to extend to his appropriating the *Amphitrite* cargo: "Would you believe, Gentlemen, that this deputy, a man of the greatest merit, genial with everyone in this country, and endlessly dining out among individuals entirely indifferent to your republic, would you believe, I ask, that this deputy has not had, in the year he has been in France, the decency to set foot a single time in my home?" He pressed his point by signing his letter "Secretary to the King," a title that sounded all the more impressive to an assembly unaware that some nine hundred Frenchmen affixed it to their name. At the same time Beaumarchais vowed not to confuse Franklin with his country, probably the only man in France to desist from doing so. For his part Franklin relinquished the cargo, a symbolic gesture, as by Beaumarchais's calculation America owed him millions. The *Amphitrite*'s indigo and rice represented a meager 150,000 livres. Beaumarchais could only quote Voltaire—"Injustice in the end produces independence"—but might more aptly have reversed the terms.

Meanwhile Franklin was "all life and full of spirits." He flew exuberantly from one end of Paris to the other, leaving Wentworth to choke on his "parading and gasconading." To friends Franklin sent a holiday gift in the form of the newly printed *Bonhomme Richard*, his advance man. His language was bold. England was like an eagle, he maintained, whose wings cast shadows over America and India. "We have severed one," he asserted, "and it is now up to France to sever the other." Mockingly he compared Britain's propositions with those tendered by an officer about to slaughter a man, in the heat of a battle. On his knees, his victim begs for mercy. Replies the officer: "Ask for whatever you wish. I will grant you anything, except your life." A regular procession of emissaries trooped to Passy to sound him out; an attempt was made even to suborn Chaumont, who had been listening at keyholes anyway. (He reported the offer to Vergennes—who obsessively monitored every English footstep—and went back to listening at keyholes.) Christmas Day found Franklin at the beautiful home of his neighbor, the charming, forty-six-year-old Admiral d'Estaing. D'Estaing's hatred of England bordered on mania; already he had formulated a French campaign in the event of war. In his company Franklin proposed the toast of which he was to become master. All over Paris that week he lifted his glass to offer, with a flourish, "And if you please, we'll add a perpetual and everlasting understanding between the house of Bourbon and the American Congress."

At his Christmas table d'Estaing introduced Franklin to the Portuguese ambassador to France, Vicente de Sousa Coutinho. Five days later the two men met at the Valentinois, in the company of a translator. Out of deference to their English allies, the Portuguese had closed their harbors to American ships. Franklin made an impassioned case for humanitarian principles—surely the Portuguese did not mean to cause shipwrecks—and for a pacific future for the two nations. To some extent he was cleaning up after his messy colleagues. American privateers had taken a Portuguese ship, and Deane had spoken with much hostility of that kingdom. Hinting broadly at a Franco-American alliance, Franklin reminded Coutinho that were Portugal to remain unaccommodating, she would have an additional enemy in her future. The conversation was revealing of Franklin the negotiator: He did his best to propose a face-saving way for Portugal simultaneously to accommodate new and old friends. Despite his assurances, Coutinho remained skeptical that the Americans would continue to fight. He was taken entirely with Franklin and with his lyrical riff on the principles to which the young republic was committed, however. Given "his urbanity and the sweetness of the expressions he used," Coutinho wondered if Dr. Franklin might not have a point. It appeared to the ambassador that it would take very little to make the Americans happy.

In his euphoria Franklin got a little carried away, suggesting at a party he threw on January 5 that he contribute the week's consecrated bread to the neighborhood parish. Why not offer up thirteen brioches, the first loaf decorated with the word *liberty* rather than the traditional figure of the king? The two churchmen at the table shuddered at the thought. Franklin was reined in on the occasion by the chevalière d'Eon, who spent the week commuting between Passy and Versailles, and had come to dinner with her plan for an invasion of the British Isles. An expert on boundaries, she reminded her host that it was hardly wise to brandish a word, barely ten miles from Versailles, which "the court neither loved nor wished to be acquainted with."

Franklin relinquished that project but otherwise made himself entirely available, indecently so in some opinions. While Wentworth paced in the wings, the New Year began with a barrage of peace feelers from England. "There were 13 carriages at Franklin's door when I waited upon him, the owners of which were making proposals of every kind," noted one envoy. A vast array of sample merchandise crowded his front hall. "I know the door is still open for reconciliation," insisted yet another, who met with Franklin during the first week of January, and who emerged from his discussion to warn against all procrastination. Franklin made child's play of everyone's fears; the diplomatic corps could report on nothing but British anxiety that the French were negotiating with the insurgents and on French anxiety that the British were doing the same. "Mr. Franklin plays his game," warned the Swedish ambassador, who like all of France's friends on the Continent saw no reason whatever for her to rush into an American engagement. It would handsomely benefit the insurgents, but represent "a grievous catastrophe for France." For Vergennes the New Year began on an especially harrowing note. With alarm, Grand, Chaumont, and Beaumarchais each warned of the arrival of a formidable envoy. James Hutton, a roundly admired, sixty-one-year-old religious leader, an intimate of King George and an old friend of Franklin's, was in Passy, a houseguest of Grand. Hutton was empowered to grant the Americans anything they asked, short of independence. Already he and Franklin had had a two-hour conversation that was observed to be as affectionate as it was animated.

Hutton and Franklin spent all of January 3 together, in the course of which Franklin evidently informed his old friend, "You have only left us the option of perishing by you or with you: we have chosen the latter alternative." (If he did so he did so at blaring volume. A blessing to anyone at the keyhole, Hutton was deaf even with his ear trumpet.) The two made so little headway that Hutton was searching still for an opening as he said his goodbyes. Stepping into his carriage in the Passy courtyard he inquired one final time if there was not some shred of hope for a reconciliation. Franklin regretted that there was not. America had been a tender and loving daughter, but having been mistreated at home, she was now to be married. On that note Hutton rode off, dissolved in tears. He suspected that Vergennes had already maneuvered the Americans into a treaty. Chaumont suffered from the opposite anxiety and needled Vergennes. British negotiations were brisk; he prayed they could trust in Franklin's good faith; the Valentinois swarmed with emissaries. "I observe much eagerness to entertain proposals," trembled Chaumont, "and I am afraid." His disquiet rang all the more loudly in Versailles given a small omission on Franklin's part. He had neglected to mention Hutton's visit to Vergennes. Vergennes played that news for all it was worth. Word flew to Spain that while France patiently awaited her answer, Franklin busily negotiated in Passy with "a man of genius." To which Vergennes added the kicker. He did not have that information from the American.

While Franklin was playing the belle of the ball he consented finally on January 6 to an interview with Wentworth. It was very nearly a humanitarian gesture. Paralyzed by events, chilled to the bone by hours of surveillance in a hackney coach, Wentworth was reduced to playing the French lottery. Edward Edwards, his best source at the Valentinois, had been away; Vergennes dealt exclusively with Deane or Franklin, which left Wentworth out in a more penetrating cold. To avoid the prying eyes both of his servants and of the French police, he had taken to collecting his mail and composing his dispatches between midnight and three in the morning. He was tripping over Forth and another secret agent, who had very nearly blown his cover. And was it not time for a raise for this miserable assignment? As for the frank conversation on which Eden banked in London, there was little hope. By code name Wentworth surveyed the options: "72 [Franklin] is taciturn, deliberate, and cautious; 51 [Deane] vain, desultory, and subtle; 116 [Lee] suspicious and insolent; 117 [William Lee] peevish and ignorant; 111 [Izard] costive and dogmatical; all of them insidious, and Edwards vibrating between hope and fear, interest and attachment." All the same he headed out to Passy for what was billed as a discussion among private friends. Franklin had stipulated that Wentworth was to make no offers of bribes. Nor was he himself to be expected to make any proposals, although he would discuss any that Wentworth cared to make. The visit was stage-managed in advance as well; at Wentworth's request, Deane was to enter the room as if by accident once the interview was well under way.

Franklin received Wentworth warmly that January Tuesday. He had barely cleared his way through his visitor's hail of compliments, however, when he set to bemoaning the time lost to insulting propositions and half-hearted negotiations. He worked himself into a froth on the subject. Wentworth begged him to separate private from public grievances. Franklin denied that personal considerations had any bearing on his distemper, talking a blue streak about England's barbarous behavior, her treatment of American prisoners, her burning of American towns. Nothing his visitor said put an end to his desultory tirade, the conclusion of which was that any number of European powers were wiser and more candid than England. The savages of North America were more civilized. At last Wentworth calmed Franklin enough to exact a promise that he listen to a confidential proposal, at which juncture he read Eden's plan for qualified independence. Franklin remarked on the document's good sense and asked after its author, which information Wentworth refused to divulge. Franklin then strayed off on a tangent about Hutton. Again Wentworth restrained him, reading the terms aloud a second time. Would Franklin be willing to negotiate in London if passports could be arranged? He would. Two hours having elapsed, Deane entered on cue and Chaumont hosted a lovely dinner, at which there was much banter about America's brilliant future. No detail or nuance of the visit was lost on the keen Wentworth, who may or may not have noticed in the thick of it that he had gleaned absolutely nothing of Franklin's thinking. What he did notice was Franklin's behavior: "I never knew him so eccentric; nobody says less generally and keeps a point more closely in view. But he was diffuse and unmethodical today." This was the same Franklin who the previous day had headed off another British envoy with a demure "We are new at treaty. Advantage may be taken of our incapacity."

It was a stunning performance, strictly speaking also an unnecessary one. Before twenty-four hours were out Vergennes and Stormont had arrived at opposite conclusions. At ten the next morning the panicked British ambassador swore that a Franco-American treaty was en route to

Congress. Hours later, in a meeting of the King's Council held in Maurepas's bedroom, where the minister of state was laid up with gout, Vergennes convinced Louis XVI that there had better be such a treaty. He did not care to let an 800-mile trip to Madrid deprive him of a once-in-a-lifetime opportunity. At his eldest minister's bedside, Louis XVI agreed to pursue a military and a commercial alliance with the Americans without waiting for Spain. Much though he may have overdramatized Chaumont's reports, Vergennes's distress was authentic. He was convinced that war with England was imminent were France to ally herself with the Americans or not, a conviction Franklin routinely buttressed. Already English insolence had reached unacceptable heights; Britain had begun to seize French boats, on the pretext that they carried American cargo.

That assertion was true but flimsy compared with another statement Vergennes made on January 8: "I don't know that I could survive the humiliation of signing the passports these deputies would request of me to travel to London." More than anywhere else his foreign policy was encapsulated in that uncharacteristically emotional line. Even if it were accurate that the colonies and mother country were within a hairbreadth of reconciling, there was no particular reason for the French to ally themselves with the Americans. Nor was there ever valid reason to suppose that the Americans and the British would together fall on France. The Anglo-American threat to the French West Indies was very much the MacGuffin of the tale. The stale idea had been kicking about since the 1760s, reheated by Arthur Lee and appealingly garnished by Beaumarchais, a slab of specious reasoning that kept the plot in motion. French trade was the cloak of respectability in which was wrapped raw prejudice. "In what better policy can one engage than in that our enemy fears the most!" Vergennes bellowed on January 8, having trotted out every argument in the book except the one closest to the heart of the matter: France suffered from an incapacitating case of wounded pride. Fundamentally America would owe her independence to a French tradition of grandeur, to her sense that she stood at the center of world politics, and to the kick in the teeth England had dealt that heady concept in 1763.

As intent as was Vergennes on an American alliance in 1778, he would engage later in some subtle buck-passing. In all accounts of foreign affairs that issued from his offices afterward, the Americans approached the

French in December 1777, when in truth Vergennes had come calling on Franklin. In those pages Vergennes respectfully reminded the king that, at their decisive conference, His Majesty had called upon the bedridden Maurepas for his opinion. Maurepas excused himself. The matter had been discussed to death. It was time for his sovereign to issue an order. And, too, Vergennes would argue disingenuously that their American overture had been an act of perfect moderation. Nothing about it implied war—precisely the opposite assurance Gérard pressed upon Franklin, Deane, and Lee when he met them on the rue Royale that Thursday. Retrospectively, Vergennes inserted as well a cry in England for an American peace and a French war. (The buck-passing would continue all the way to the top. Years later, Louis XVI—twenty-three years old at the time Vergennes clinched his deal—was heard to argue that his ministers had taken advantage of his youth.*) Maurepas alone failed to wash his hands of responsibility, although he had less opportunity to; he would be dead in several years' time. And until the last he equivocated. Four days before the bedroom conference he met with Forth, who submitted an extraordinary proposal. The special envoy could promise peace with England if Maurepas would expel Franklin and Deane from France. Already a dangerous arms race was on; an agreement was in both countries' best interests. "And what will you give us?" asked Maurepas. "What will you have?" countered Forth, whom Maurepas left with the impression that France might still throw over the Americans in exchange for a juicy part of Canada. For his part, Maurepas promised to speak to the king.

If ever he did so the conversation came to naught. Nor did Forth leave France without further assisting Vergennes in his campaign. The Englishman returned to London shortly thereafter, Vergennes reported, "but had the indiscretion, in the course of an orgy preceding his departure—where as was his admirable custom, he got drunk—to share with one of his fellow debauchees two letters from Lord North." Those documents, Vergennes assured Madrid, indicated that England was set on a French war. The carousing was perfectly probable—Forth left France

---

*In the short term he justified himself eloquently to his uncle, the king of Spain. It was a war he undertook not for the sake of conquest or glory but, Louis XVI assured Charles II in 1780, "to restore the honor of my oft-insulted banner, and to assist an oppressed people who have come and thrown themselves in my arms."

as well with nine hundred bottles of champagne—but the documents could only have been figments of Vergennes's imagination. In the end he would be reduced to courting Spain as assiduously as Franklin had courted France. If the Americans could continue to be strung along with vague promises, Vergennes assured Madrid, he would do so. But, the foreign minister was sorry to say, those days were over. With or without the Spanish navy, it indeed appeared—as Franklin assured one of the envoys for whom he performed his damsel-in-distress act—"that the dependency of the colonies was gone forever, like the clouds of last year."

V

There Is No Such Thing as a Little Enemy

1778

There are people whose defects become them,
and others who are ill served by their good qualities.
—*La Rochefoucauld*

Briefed in advance by Deane, Gérard rode to the rue Royale on the evening of January 8, to meet with the American commissioners. There was one subject on which Deane had been unable to enlighten the undersecretary, however; Franklin had had the wisdom not to share the details of his Hutton discussion. Gérard opened the meeting by cross-examining Franklin, to no avail. Finally he changed tack. He was eager to resume negotiations but needed first to exact a promise of absolute secrecy. The Americans must vow not to shop around any piece of the proposal he had come to impart. All three fell silent until Franklin weighed in. Sourly he observed that the regularity with which secrets were divulged in France was indeed extraordinary, but that he and his colleagues were blameless. A polite arm-wrestle ensued, after which Franklin consented to Gérard's terms, with a plain "I promise." Gérard had come with two questions: What would France need to do to prevent the deputies from succumbing to "the bait of a false peace and a mutilated or precarious independence"? What would work the same effect on the American people? From his long-winded oration Franklin inferred that Louis XVI was poised to declare war, a decision he applauded. Gérard stopped him cold, insisting that while the king would not refuse to wage war on America's behalf, Franklin was putting the cart before the horse. He pressed hard on the point, as Franklin ably pressed back. Gérard's were thorny questions. They would require some deliberation.

Ultimately it was agreed that the deputies would confer privately. Gérard excused himself for an hour; in his absence Deane and Lee set to sniping about details while Franklin set to writing, interrupting his colleagues to read his draft. Gérard returned to Franklin's discourse on the manifold difficulties the Americans had met with in France and the futility of their best efforts, a speech that ended with the assurance that an immediate conclusion of a treaty of amity and commerce "would close their ears to any proposal which should not have as its basis entire liberty and independence, both political and commercial." Franklin was utterly taken aback when Gérard revealed that the king would be pleased to enter into such a treaty immediately. His Majesty embraced the opportunity to offer both worlds an example of his disinterestedness. Even in that glorious and affecting moment Gérard could not resist adding that the court hoped all the same that America "would not inherit the pretensions and the greedy and bold character of their mother country, which had made itself detested."

Vergennes's deputy promised documents within a matter of days. The agreement would bind the two countries in perpetuity and might well spell war; in that event, France would not lay down arms until Britain was expelled from North America. The deputies heard out the remainder of his terms with rapture, Franklin extolling their wisdom and justice. Gérard was not surprised; Deane had tipped him off in advance to Franklin's enduring interest in Canada, on which the Frenchman meaningfully dwelt. Gérard was himself pleased, on leaving, to obtain a draft of the document Franklin had read to him. His fear of dealing with an elusive man was much in evidence: "I was very glad to have this additional sort of engagement to bind the Doctor as much as possible." Only at the threshold did Gérard note that Franklin had alluded to treaties with France and Spain. Was that, he asked, at the end of a grueling five hours, an essential condition?

Franklin was dumbfounded. Recovering himself, he admitted with some emotion that he had always understood France and Spain to be acting together. It was now Gérard's turn to be elusive. He sugar-coated the alarming news that France was negotiating alone, at least for the present. The answer, as Gérard well knew, effectively sidestepped the question, and allowed everyone to say his goodnights on the warmest of terms shortly before midnight. In Versailles Vergennes was less than entirely pleased by his secretary's account of the evening. "These people show themselves infinitely more troublesome and more sullen than we could have believed," he caviled. He was accustomed to more bowing and scraping, astounded that Franklin could have had the gall to militate for a French declaration of war. He hoped the Americans might prove more tractable in the future.

It was Franklin who had waited thirteen months for France to make an honest woman of America but Vergennes in the end who could not hurry the marriage along quickly enough. He had no need of a frantic letter from Beaumarchais, but that was what landed on his desk hours after Gérard's debriefing. Beaumarchais was sleepless on the insurgents' account. What on earth was Vergennes waiting for? Did he not know that Burgoyne's officers had shed tears of relief at the considerate treatment they had received at American hands? If Vergennes could make his proposal to Congress first, any English overture would sound like jealousy. Should a particularly difficult American be impeding Vergennes's negotiation—if that envoy intended to leak information, so as to precipitate a reconciliation with England—the insomniacal Beaumarchais would be only too happy to spirit him away. (Lee had no such intentions.) And while Vergennes paced nervously, Wentworth stood by open-mouthed at the speed with which events proceeded. He had it on good authority that a French treaty was to be signed before Parliament reconvened. Doubtless that was Vergennes's goal, although he would be foiled by Franklin.

Negotiations began in earnest only on January 18, when Gérard submitted draft treaties to the Americans. They spent the next days reviewing them, at a pace that made Vergennes quiver. Given the simplicity of the documents and the insurgents' need for a powerful ally, could they not move with a little more celerity? Stormont certainly did, making a news-gathering dash around Paris while the Americans deliberated. On the afternoon of January 22 he materialized in Vergennes's office, having heard that the French and Spanish were coordinating a surprise attack on British-held Gibraltar. Vergennes claimed utter ignorance of any such assault.* The ambassador hazarded a more delicate question. Departing from diplomatic idiom, he asked outright if the French and Americans had entered into an alliance. Vergennes confined himself to a few remarks on the fecundity of the public imagination. Stormont balked. Where were the vigorous denials he knew so well? Playing nervously with his fingers, Vergennes replied that he hewed to only one inviolable law in his office, which was never to offer a ministerial response without prior orders of the king. He had no great hopes of having deluded Stormont, who indeed left Versailles perfectly convinced of what the Frenchman had half attempted to hide from him. Stormont had never seen him so flustered.

Stormont derived no greater satisfaction from Maurepas, who held off his visitor with the banter on which he had staked his reputation. What was the source of the ambassador's panic? Stormont pronounced himself unable to discount what was being discussed in the king's carriages. "But do you know what is being said in the queen's carriages?" parried Maurepas. He sent Stormont off with a few words of advice: "Remember that in politics those who know the most say the least; fools alone talk and believe." (Stormont would have been wise to consider the source. The French minister was one of the century's preeminent conversationalists.) He did not share with Stormont the apprehensions he had catalogued for the king. Maurepas remained unconvinced that Franklin and his colleagues acted with any solid authority; that they would, in their divisions, desist from using French offers to their own ends; that Congress, in which the British freely meddled, would ratify such a treaty; that even if that body was to do so, the nation at large would honor a pact with a country which did not share her language, her religion, her mores.

Beaumarchais attempted to allay each of those concerns in a document over which he labored all week. His finances were in a precarious state and he was dying of heartbreak, but before he expired he intended to elucidate

---

*Versailles was a large palace, but Vergennes made it seem a boundless one. Whenever Stormont inquired about what was happening down the hall, in the offices of the naval or war ministers, Vergennes pleaded ignorance. He did the same with Stormont's treaty imputations, begging for elucidation: " 'You,' explained Vergennes, 'live in the world. I lead the life of a hermit, and scarce ever stir out of my closet.' " Whatever could Stormont be alluding to?

France's options for Vergennes. He advocated recognizing American independence but bypassing the delegation in Passy. A masterful secret agent should be dispatched promptly to America. That much seemed a fair if self-serving suggestion, but Beaumarchais continued on in his ambitious staging of foreign policy as *opéra bouffe*. With the Passy delegation insulated from all British advances, French troops should be massed along the coasts of France, and the navy deployed. Portugal was to be detached from England and incorporated into the Bourbon pact; the Turks were to be incited to declare war with Russia, so as to force the Russians to redeploy their armies from the north to the south. As Russia's ally, England would be forced to send troops to defend the north, to hold Austria at bay.*

Meanwhile the Americans grappled with the treaties and with each other. Lee made the astute point that France guaranteed American independence only on condition of waging war. Did that not constitute an invitation for the English to focus on the destruction of America, while granting idle France the favor of her commerce? Franklin countered with the proposal that France subsidize the colonies at a rate of a million pounds sterling a year so long as the war continued against them alone; Lee pointed out that their doing so could not prevent the utter devastation of America. And so it went, in a marathon of discussion and translation and copying of which Arthur Lee—the only lawyer among the three— confined himself primarily to the first, while Franklin translated and Temple produced the drafts. Lee bogged down particularly in the treaty articles concerning molasses, on which issue he clashed with Deane. By their instructions, the commissioners were to arrange for duty-free molasses from the French West Indies. When Gérard asked what concession America might make in return, Franklin—generally allergic to tariffs—

---

*Beaumarchais was very much playing to his audience. If Maurepas stumbled over American consistency, Vergennes wrestled as carefully with the situation in eastern Europe. He had his eye always on the Russians, his rivals in Polish affairs; his three undersecretaries, Gérard included, were Poland experts; he himself had served for years in Constantinople. So much more preoccupied was Vergennes with Poland and expansionist, British-allied Russia that it has even been suggested that American independence arrived as a sort of by-product of eastern European politics. Certainly the ambassadorial corps at Versailles speculated with as much concern about the existence of a Franco-Prussian treaty as to what those emissaries viewed as Franklin's shameless attempts to lure France into American affairs.

suggested that both countries agree to forgo export duties of any kind. Lee violently objected. To his mind that exacted more of America than of France. To break the deadlock Franklin suggested that Izard and William Lee, Congress's appointees to Tuscany and Prussia, be consulted. As both men were southerners, their opinions would be particularly valuable. The idea offended Deane, who did not see why additional parties should be left to adjudicate a matter that had been entrusted to the three commissioners.

All the odium that was to color Franklin and Lee's future relations could be seen in the scrimmage that followed. Franklin deferred to Lee's position, eager neither to delay the treaty nor to reveal any dissension in the ranks. Lee squirmed at the concession, which he saw as an artful means of throwing the consequences of the wording on his head. His senior colleague subsequently assumed a different tack: "Dr. F[ranklin] then, in a certain soft, smooth accommodating manner, which he can assume at pleasure, said, 'Well, suppose we just propose it, and then say that we are very willing to give up both the articles.' " Doubtless this was the same tone the Portuguese ambassador had heard as "sweetness." It was the very fluidity that, coupled with his natural reserve, served Franklin in place of any formal diplomatic training. To Lee—who felt himself manipulated into a corner, and whose taste ran to the bitter—it was as suspect as it was sickening.

Most galling to Lee was the desultory fashion in which Franklin worked. Repeatedly Lee called at Passy to find his colleague out or gliding past him, on his way out. It never occurred to him that Franklin might be avoiding him, or that he might be in no particular hurry to finalize a French treaty. Certainly Franklin made what appears to be considerable effort to avoid discussing politics with Lee, at one juncture steering him away from a discussion of the Saint Lawrence fisheries with a discourse on the effect of sunlight on vegetables. On Friday, January 23, Lee arrived at the Valentinois in tandem with a young Frenchman. Franklin ushered the visitor into the small room in which Temple was copying out the treaties. Lee surveyed the room afterward, to discover "the treaty upon the table, and the young Frenchman close to it." Secrecy was impossible under such circumstances. He was only further mortified to find Franklin away again the following evening, when Temple greeted him. The seventeen-year-old allowed that his grandfather's dining out every day seriously slowed the course of business, and that he was to be out again next morning. "A very unpromising state of things," added Lee, lips audibly pursed, "when boys made such observations on the conduct of their grandfathers."

Franklin had little incentive to hurry. No sooner had Hutton returned to London than he brokenheartedly begged his American friend for some hint, some proposal, any proposal that might reconcile the two countries. Hutton would do his best. Here too Franklin dragged his feet. Vergennes recognized his genius, as, grudgingly, did Stormont. "They play us off against one another," Stormont warned, adding, "Franklin's natural subtlety gives him a great advantage in such a game. It is easy to see that in such a situation peace between England and the House of Bourbon hangs by the slightest of all threads."

By the end of January the commissioners had at last ironed out terms with Gérard. Six million livres were granted on the twenty-eighth, occasioning much joy in Passy. Vergennes had less reason to celebrate; on February 4 he learned that Spain declined to be party to a Franco-American alliance. The refusal failed to dampen his ardor; documents were signed on Friday evening, February 6, in ministry offices on the quai des Théatins, across the Seine from the Louvre. When Franklin rode back to Passy late that evening he did so with two signed treaties in his carriage. The first, of amity and commerce, was the most-favored-nation agreement that the colonies had long sought. The second established the military alliance on which Vergennes insisted, to be triggered in the event of a French war with England. That treaty guaranteed that neither signatory would consider a peace until American independence was established. At the same time France renounced any claim on Canada, and the Americans guaranteed French possessions in the West Indies. Two years earlier, when the colonies had been primping for this very moment, flirting with a declaration of independence and assessing their chances with foreign powers, John Adams had asked: "Are we to be beholden to France for our liberties?" That question resolved, his colleagues began to grapple with something more troubling. Could it be morally right to transmute French affection into a European war? wondered Robert Morris. Six months later, Franklin held the answer to both queries in his hands. It was the greatest triumph of his career.

It was Vergennes's intention to keep the treaties entirely under wraps until they were ratified in America, which put the European unveiling on the calendar for the end of April or the beginning of May. The French minister belonged to that breed of men who pride themselves on their sense of humor although unable to tell a joke; deep in his very undramatic body he appears to have had as well a taste for the theatrical flourish. Had war not already broken out by May, he imagined brandishing his startling commercial treaty, to Europe's astonishment. He much relished the idea of exiling Stormont, so much a nuisance to him. The British ambassador had no need again to hound Vergennes to report, on the evening it was concluded, that an American treaty had been signed. (Unbeknownst to him, Edward Edwards claimed to have had a copy of the commercial treaty in London forty-two hours after its seals were set to paper, a feat that would have made him the envy of every French aristocrat who sent his laundry across the Channel. Under the best of circumstances, that was a five-day trip.) Rumors of a treaty surfaced regularly throughout February, only to be snuffed out, by rational men, as so many false alarms. France had no conceivable reason to offend Britain. If all else failed, the skeptical Maurepas would surely blunt Franklin's incessant petitions. Nothing could induce France to enter openly into the American contest, the Venetian ambassador assured his court as, from London, Noailles warned Vergennes that he understood a treaty to have been signed on February 8.

Franklin was exultant. His dispatches could have been dictated by Vergennes; they were without exception odes to French benevolence. On no count had Louis XVI attempted to take advantage of a young country in distress, with whom he had negotiated as if she were a mature and prosperous power. It was to be hoped that Congress would approve and ratify the documents without delay. At the same time, Franklin could not help but rattle the hinges a little. On February 12 he finally mailed off a letter he had composed ten days earlier, in response to Hutton's frantic appeals. Surely his advice was academic, but given Hutton's persistence here it was. Only with a change in attitude could Britain hope to recover America's affection. That change could clearly be signaled by throwing into the bargain Canada, Nova Scotia, and the Floridas. While he was at it, Franklin sent a copy of that letter to his old friend David Hartley, a left-leaning member of Parliament who had come to the relief of American prisoners in London. Hartley had expressed his fervent hope that "nothing ever persuade America to throw themselves into the arms of France." Franklin obliged Hartley in his language: "America has been *forced* and *driven* into the arms of France." Into that metaphor he loaded a subtle announcement. America would make a dutiful and honorable wife. He had no doubt "that her husband will love and honor her, and that the family from which she was so wickedly expelled will long regret the loss of her."

Of all the European powers, only the Spaniards knew the truth of what had transpired on the quai des Théatins and remained clear-eyed as to the transaction. To their minds, Franklin had led Vergennes down the primrose path. Anything Spain did openly to assist the colonies would furnish Britain a pretext to pounce on its possessions, which Madrid had no fleet at hand to protect. And for that predicament the Spaniards had their ally to thank! The deluded French minister had backed them into a corner. He had been not only foolhardy but clumsy; in gratifying France's *amour-propre*, he had injured that of Spain. Left to feel that Vergennes had treated his country like a shabby province of France, Spain's foreign minister was apoplectic. In his pique he enunciated a truth no one else dared utter. By entering into the American contest, France was acting like Don Quixote.

~☆~

The trials of the next weeks were to be Vergennes's. Days after the treaties had sailed to America, Stormont casually revealed to him that conciliatory bills were to be submitted to Congress, by a commission headed by the Earl of Carlisle. Those bills offered the colonies the equivalent of home rule within the British Empire. The move provoked disbelief all around. To a sympathetic London observer, the idea that the British might, on bended knee, acknowledge wrongs done to their rebellious colonies was without parallel in any history, ancient, modern, or fairy.* Vergennes heard Stormont out less with surprise than alarm, noting with relief that the proposal stopped short of granting American independence. He had already endured one set of palpitations that week, when Franklin worked overtime to stamp out rumors that the colonists had rec-

---

*Franklin had an additional reason to view Parliament's February 17 about-face with astonishment. Always attuned to anniversaries, he had, on February 17, 1775, personally offered to reimburse the cost of the tea dumped into Boston Harbor, on the condition that England grant precisely what she now proposed.

onciled with England. The British, Vergennes should understand, were toying with them.

British duplicity worried Vergennes less than did her command of the seas. While the ocean was wide open for their rivals, it was studded with obstacles for the French. The man before whom 1763 burned brightly at all times claimed that he preferred not to dwell on the past, but he kicked himself all the same that he had already lost a month. He should have had a treaty in America already; it would be too cruel for the Americans to escape him now. He was busy torturing himself with that anxiety when Deane rushed to see him late on the evening of February 26. The ship that had been dispatched to America with news of a pending alliance had been forced back to France after six weeks at sea.* Hastily Vergennes arranged for another vessel, but his discomfort was palpable. It announced itself in a philosophical note. "We most often understand the value of time only when we are in a position of having to regret its loss," he sighed.

At Passy the return of the *Belle Poule*—slated to play a more significant role soon enough—provoked a different, pettier sense of anxieties. Arthur Lee upbraided Deane and Franklin for not having informed him immediately of the ship's return. Franklin explained that their colleague had hurried to Versailles minutes after the news reached Passy that evening. In any event there had been neither time nor reason to consult in such an obvious crisis. "We think Mr. Deane deserves your thanks, and that neither of us deserve your censure," Franklin replied evenly. Lee next raised a larger concern. Given the disastrous delay, was it not imperative that the French court publicly acknowledge the commissioners, and with them American independence? Nothing else would so powerfully frustrate British overtures. A public acknowledgment would reach America by a thousand channels, while their private dispatches might never arrive. Accounts of French severity with American privateers would meanwhile wash up quickly enough. Lee's was a valid point, and he enlisted the colorful Lauraguais to lobby on its behalf, the two having more or less squared off against Beaumarchais and Deane. Lauraguais pursued the matter at Versailles. Given Lee's admirable zeal, surely Vergennes

---

*So intent was Versailles on secrecy that it had led the *Belle Poule*'s captain to believe he was sailing from Bordeaux to Brest. He learned his true destination only on the high seas. Insufficient provisions, coupled with violent winds, sent him back to shore.

could understand how bored he was, isolated in his country home, "and seeing no one but M. Gérard and the occasional girl."

It was precisely that admirable zeal that Vergennes had come to distrust. While the papers filled with talk of war, the last thing for which the foreign minister had patience was a choosy beggar, especially one he suspected of indiscretion. News traveled with its usual efficiency around France, as was particularly clear that March; in a sight that ranked alongside Britain's astonishing about-face, eighty-four-year-old Voltaire returned to Paris in a blaze of glory after decades of exile, a nearly posthumous apparition of the most famous Frenchman in the world. Delegations flocked daily to his Saint-Germain doorstep. Every cup of bouillon, every scrambled egg, every spoonful of bean purée that passed Voltaire's shriveled lips qualified as national news. To Vergennes's burdens was added the difficulty of keeping an explosive treaty under wraps when all of Paris freely discussed the queen's menstruation, the king's erections, and Voltaire's urination.

Buoyed by a diplomatic success that had been not only sweeter for its deferment but all the more beneficial as well—even Vergennes admitted that the Americans had obtained better terms for their delay—Franklin was a man about town like never before. He who would write that there would never be a good war or a bad peace was now daily awaiting the former (which he well understood had its basis in the latter, the craw-sticking one of 1763). It could not happen soon enough for his taste. He was all grace and charm when with some embarrassment the duc de la Rochefoucauld disinvited him from a concert to be held at his mother's. The duchesse d'Enville had remembered that Lord Stormont and his young wife were to be in attendance. Perhaps this was not the most opportune moment for a meeting? Franklin good-naturedly bowed out; his calendar was in any event full, rather impracticably so.

On March 16, after a testy meeting with Lee, Franklin paid a call of which he could not have overestimated the symbolic value. Temple in tow, he made a second pilgrimage to the quai des Théatins. Past the entryway griffins and into the pale stone courtyard of Number 27 he rode, as would everyone of note in Paris that month, to pay homage to the man who had done so much to establish the legend of the good Quaker—and with him Benjamin Franklin—in France. Confined by a fever to his bed,

Voltaire greeted his guest in bathrobe and nightcap. The contrast between his gaunt and hollowed frame and the corpulent, ruddy American was extreme. Franklin had admired Voltaire's sparkling prose as early as 1764; Voltaire had followed Franklin's work nearly as long. The two men who had risen by their wits on different continents worshipped at the same altars, at those of common sense, liberty, and tolerance. Satirists and critical thinkers both, they read neither earthquakes nor lightning bolts as divine commentary. To Voltaire's mind the illustrious caller was "the worthiest man in America, and perhaps in Europe." He did his best to dust off his English for the occasion, only to be bullied back into French by the twenty people who crowded his bedroom. They hung on his every word. Voltaire hesitated not a second when Franklin, who knew already how much he had sanctified his cause, asked Voltaire to bless Temple. The anticlerical rationalist preaching to the confirmed agnostic, it made for a curious gesture; evidently the coreligionists could not help themselves. Voltaire offered up three words, "God and Liberty," a benediction that reduced the assembled crowd to tears.* In a thousand permutations, the encounter found its way into every paper in Europe, which carried no report of Voltaire's next caller. He was for once blessedly slow-moving. An hour after Franklin had excused himself from Voltaire's side, Stormont arrived to pay his respects.

Franklin and Voltaire would find themselves in a room together again at the end of April, at the Académie des Sciences. The presence of the two numinous icons was not enough for the assembly, which clamored for them to embrace. The philosophers suffered a few moments' awkwardness, until it became clear that they were at their public's mercy. Only after they had planted kisses on each other's cheeks did the tumult subside. By general assent this was nothing short of the embrace of Sophocles and Solon, with Franklin in the role of the Athenian statesman. Again the two were a study in contrasts. Franklin appeared in a drab yellow suit and with a white hat so incompatible with Paris fashion it could only have been imported from Philadelphia. The impish Voltaire amounted to a desiccated pile of bones. It was not a shining hour for the authors of the

---

*Years later, Temple would use that phrase on the seal with which he closed his envelopes.

day's presentations; as assemblies were limited to two hours, the scientific discourses were cut short. Nor was the triumph of reason entirely secure. In one newspaper, the account of that Enlightenment apotheosis preceded the story of the cat who had installed herself on a bird's nest. Her brood emerged as half cats, half chicks.

Through the next weeks the two elderly men divided between them the acclaim of Paris. "The moment they appear in a theater, or on the street, or at any of the academies, a great ovation follows. Princes come and go, unnoticed, but when Voltaire sneezes, and Franklin rejoins 'God bless you,' it begins all over again," scoffed one onlooker. At a mid-March concert the applause for Franklin was deafening. When he joined a prominent lawyer and his family for a sensational courtroom trial, the Parliament erupted with cheers at his arrival and departure. The tribute continued as an ecstatic crowd carried Franklin through the rooms of the law courts, down the staircase, into the courtyard, along the street, and to his carriage. The reception was the same everywhere. It confirmed the impression, well before any revelations had been made, that he was on comfortable terms with the French government.

There were plenty of delights in French society for Franklin—at a lavish ball, reported one paper, "There were many young and beautiful women, and each of them in turn paid him homage, kissing him, despite the glasses glued to his nose"—but he wrung the most mileage in England. He had long been an entity Parliament preferred to wish away, as that body made abundantly clear in dispatching peace commissioners to America. Franklin was firm on that point to the ever-hopeful Hartley. If the English were sincere in their professions of peace, why did they overlook the three men sitting in Paris? His answer could easily be found in that week's iconoclastic, London-based *Annales Politiques*. The House of Commons had addressed the very issue. British humiliation at prostrating themselves before the rebels was great enough.* Assuming that posture on French soil was unthinkable. What would Europe think? Europe would not fail to notice England's toadying were it to happen several universes away, was the editor's reply. Much of the Continent already

---

*Already the British papers had carried the mortifying news that Hutton had thrown himself at Franklin's feet, sobbing, to beg for peace.

assumed that England would recall her troops from America, to fall full force on France.

If the Atlantic looked comfortably broad from the British Isles, it appeared impossibly so from France. The momentous dispatches of December 18 sailed again early in March. With them Franklin sent a jocular personal letter to a friend in Boston. Deane had recently expressed his hope never to see the inside of another court; Franklin alluded more subtly to the deficiencies of his Parisian existence: "I live here in great respect, and dine every day with great folks; but I still long for home and for repose." It was a cold spring; he thought longingly of old friends, and of a good Indian pudding. His was a rare hint of regret—he had been violently and explicitly homesick during the London years—but the wistfulness paled in comparison to the commissioners' greater disquiet. Given the *Belle Poule* fiasco, it was now very likely that the British articles of reconciliation would arrive in America before the French treaties. Surely there must be a way to persuade Vergennes to make an immediate announcement, so as to head off the Carlisle commission's chance of success? The benefits of keeping the treaty secret were entirely England's, Lee astutely noted, the benefits of making it public entirely France's. On the evening of March 5 the three pursued the case with Gérard, who admitted that the French court hesitated only for fear that Congress might repudiate the alliance after it had been announced. Doing so "would subject France to infinite disgrace, and probably occasion a mortal enmity between the two people." The Americans assured him that there was no reason to believe that Congress would reject the treaty.

The next day Vergennes tentatively floated the idea past his Spanish ambassador but knew already he could not wait for Madrid any more than he could a ratified treaty. He was buckling under the strain. His appetite had evaporated; his nerves were shot. On March 10 the treaty of alliance alone went to Noailles in London, who was instructed to submit it, without commentary, to Lord Weymouth, the British secretary of state for foreign affairs. Noailles did so on the thirteenth. The effect exceeded Vergennes's wildest dreams. Tears of anger glistened in Weymouth's eyes. King George denounced the pact as a formal act of aggression, and recalled his ambassador. French troops headed to Cherbourg, despite the fact that Louis XVI trusted that George III would find in the treaty only proof of his "constant and sincere commitment to peace."

Stormont packed up the Hôtel de Deux-Ponts in haste. His departure was delayed by a feud with his landlady, who objected to his slipping out of his lease and threatened to foreclose on his carriage; both sides summoned their lawyers. (In a generous light the tussle could be construed as an act of republican solidarity. Stormont had leased the magnificent town house from the widowed duchesse de Forbach, a great admirer of Franklin. Whatever her motives, the duchesse must have brilliantly entertained her American friend with the details of the contretemps.) Stormont took no leave at Versailles, but on the eve of his departure stopped in to say goodbye to Madame du Deffand, who found him devastated. She worried he would be blamed in London for not having prevented the course of events. He had been all-seeing, also outmaneuvered. Noailles followed the same protocol in London, but not without one jarring encounter. "Is it possible," King George asked the French ambassador, the resentment thick in the air, "that the King, your Lord, has signed this treaty?" Noailles assured him he had. "Surely he understands the consequences?" asked the British sovereign. "Yes, Sire," replied Noailles, "the King is prepared for any eventuality." At which King George turned his back on the ambassador.

The first gust of ill wind blew into Versailles in the athletic form of Nathanial Forth, come to remind the French ministers that one does not double-cross a double-crosser. In Maurepas's office he hurled the traditional diplomatic parting gift—a fine portrait of Louis XVI surrounded by diamonds—to the floor. How could Maurepas have deceived him? And how could Maurepas have dishonored France "by signing a treaty with rebels and pirates"? Lamely Maurepas protested that his hand had been forced but that all would be well in the end. Off marched the strapping Forth to Vergennes, who pretended at first not to know him. Forth lost no time in accusing the foreign minister of having entered into an American alliance for the sake of his own stock manipulations. Vergennes reminded the spy where he stood and to whom he addressed himself. "I have entered the cabinet of a lackey, and I am speaking to a stockjobber," spat Forth, who did not hesitate to torch an already burned bridge. Vergennes threatened the Englishman with arrest, to which Forth shot back that he had copies of the minister's accounts in his pocket. Alarmed, Ver-

The port of Auray, which provided Franklin his first glimpse of France in 1776. Evidently the town appeared less idyllic in the dead of winter and in the dark; Franklin would remember it as a wretched corner of Brittany.

The comte de Vergennes (bottom left), the architect of American independence and among the most powerful—and best informed—statesmen in Europe. The foreign minister inevitably knew who in Paris was short on funds and had sent his domestic to pawn what, who suffered indigestion from having overindulged in *dindon aux truffes*, whose mistress had thrown her diamonds from the window.

Caron de Beaumarchais (bottom right), dramatist, secret agent, arms runner. The colonies had no more vocal advocate at Versailles, including, in Beaumarchais's opinion, their own representatives. "No one but me does anything around here for the good of America," he sulked in 1777.

ABOVE LEFT: Le Ray de Chaumont, Franklin's landlord and America's unofficial contractor general, "greed personified" in Beaumarchais's book, a "grasping man" in John Paul Jones's. To Franklin he was simply America's first and best friend.

ABOVE MIDDLE: America's first envoy to France. Along with uniforms, matériel, and munitions, Silas Deane supplied America with the first party scandal in her history.

ABOVE RIGHT: Franklin's sensible and learned unofficial secretary, Edward Bancroft. "His first appearance is not agreeable," allowed Abigail Adams, "but he has a smile which is of vast advantage to his features, enlightening them and dispelling the scowl which appears upon his brow."

The decorous British ambassador to Paris, whose manners deserted him only when it came to Franklin. Lord Stormont could not warn often enough that the American was a dangerous and dangerously seductive man, who "can assume any shape," and to whom nothing came more naturally than "artifice and fraud."

Three views of the Hôtel de Valentinois: at top, the garden façade of the main house; middle, a garden vista; bottom, the façade giving on to the Seine. Early in 1777 Franklin occupied a pavilion at the far end of the garden. Two years later Chaumont moved him to the right wing of the main house, more opulent rooms, with sweeping views of Paris.

"Perhaps no stranger in France has had the good fortune to be so universally popular," Franklin noted, and the paraphernalia bore him out. The ivory box, top right, joins his image to that of Voltaire, the only man who could be said to rival his popularity, and who here adopts his headgear, which both men inherited from Rousseau. The snuffbox, bottom left, derives from the Duplessis image to which Franklin directed the portraitists. Set in gold, on tortoise shell, it was a gift to Georgiana Shipley, who teased that she could even discern a hint of a smile in the image. In the toile de Jouy fabric, bottom right, Franklin carries a banner that reads: "Where liberty dwells there is my country."

Madame and Monsieur Brillon as they appeared in 1763, the year of their marriage, which Franklin did his best to undermine. By 1781 he was reminding Madame Brillon that he had called on her at least twice a week, every week, for four long years, "a constancy that would seem to entitle me to favors I have never managed to obtain. But one cannot help but act madly when one loves madly."

Madame Helvétius, whom the widowed American would have liked to have made the second Madame Franklin.

The three greatest banes of Franklin's French existence, his colleagues and countrymen Arthur Lee, Ralph Izard (bottom right), and William Lee (bottom left).

ABOVE LEFT: The only extant image of Benny Bache, who at seven sailed from Philadelphia with his grandfather. Franklin returned him to his parents eight years later, at which juncture Benny—apologizing for his tentative English—billed himself as an "Anglo-Français."

ABOVE RIGHT: William Temple Franklin, Franklin's beloved grandson and his underpaid secretary during the French years. A very able assistant, in John Adams's assessment, if one also—as John Jay noted—with a pronounced fondness for "dress and diversions."

William Franklin, Temple's father, and until 1776 royal governor of New Jersey. Well before Franklin sailed for France the two men were off speaking terms. Loyalist William went his own way coolly, remarking that if his rebellious father was determined to set the colonies on fire, William trusted that "he would take care to run away by the light of it." Franklin would disinherit him, twice.

ABOVE LEFT: Vergennes's trusted aide, Conrad-Alexandre Gérard. Having negotiated the treaty of alliance, Gérard lobbied hard to become the first French envoy to the United States; were anyone else named he threatened to resign. He got his way.

ABOVE RIGHT: One rendering, in porcelain, of Louis XVI proferring America her independence. Franklin would not have quibbled with the iconography. To Adams's dismay, his colleague consistently referred to the French monarch as America's father.

The place Louis XV, the newly created, octagonal heart of Paris. Deane lodged at the corner of the rue Royale, just north of the statue of Louis XV. In the eighteenth century as today, the foot of the Champs-Elysées was on the left and the Tuileries on the right. This engraver reverses them.

gennes backed down. Forth left him with a threat: "If you ever dare to arrest me, I will see that you yourself are arrested."*

Franklin would have known nothing of Forth's tantrum, or of the state of Vergennes's nerves. He had reason for flutters of his own that Thursday, having been notified by Gérard that he would be presented at Versailles the following morning. Franklin held up well in the public eye, but this was the kind of appearance that could cause a poised and independent-minded beauty a month of agony. If the magnificence of Versailles did not affect Franklin the import of the occasion certainly would have: His introduction to Louis XVI was America's introduction to the world stage. And the audience for her feat that chilly morning was immense. Not until President Woodrow Wilson's drive down the Champs-Elysées would an American political figure attract so wide-eyed a French following, the difference being that the cheers that greeted Wilson in 1918 were cheers for peace. In terms of world affairs there was no question what Franklin represented, although there was a great deal of question about whom he represented. His recognition at Versailles stood so far outside the diplomatic norms as to throw the ambassadorial corps into a tailspin; Europe's emissaries were left to scramble with the riddle of how to receive or not receive a nonaccredited ambassador whose very existence was an offense to Britain. The cringing Swedish ambassador planned to fall in behind Spain. The conde de Aranda—pouting over orders that prohibited him from so much as speaking to an American—promised that no matter when Franklin called, Aranda would be out. The Russian envoy made equally clear he would not receive Franklin. No one took the opposite stand.

A cut-rate ceremony was consequently designed at Versailles, which was not so brilliant that day as legend has it. Nor was Franklin so drab. He ordered an expensive new suit for the occasion, although he was not the last American to discover that his best sartorial efforts came to naught in France. The court chamberlain evidently hesitated before admitting the swordless caller in the plain brown velvet suit, a white hat under his arm,

---

*Forth alleged that Vergennes speculated with Grand, who would have been the likely candidate. And if Vergennes was speculating, he did so in the company of nearly every American in Paris except Arthur Lee and Franklin. If indeed he played the market, Vergennes did so with less vigor or talent than he brought to diplomacy. He left a modest estate.

glasses perched on his nose, a scattering of hairs gracing his head. It was a singular, and sensational, getup for Versailles. "I should have taken him for a big farmer, so great was his contrast with the other diplomats, who were all powdered in full dress, and splashed all over with gold and ribbons," confessed one onlooker. Up the stairs of the palace and down the gleaming parquet of the Hall of Mirrors Vergennes led the delegation of twenty, a body that comprised all the Americans in Paris, including the ubiquitous Edward Edwards and several naval officers. They appeared to be falling in behind their patriarch. The duc de Cröy had no difficulty locating Franklin amid the throngs awaiting the king's *levée*; the American stood beneath the Veroneses in the king's antechamber, surrounded by admiring courtiers. Cröy cleared his way to his friend with an epigram: "Only the man who discovered electricity can electrify both halves of the world!," a comment that would quickly be mangled, so that the distinguished French general would have to remind everyone that he had said "electrify," not "inflame," the world. Either way he knew well that France was playing with matches.

At noon the massive gold and white doors to the king's room opened, and Vergennes ushered the deputies past the Swiss Guards and halberds at the door. As Louis XVI rose from his prie-dieu, Franklin found himself looking into the mild blue eyes of the only other consistently underdressed man in France. The young king's hair hung loose to his shoulders; his attire was both perfectly undistinguished and in a state of disarray. In Lee's view there was a distinct lack of forethought to the reception; he was correct in that a fully accredited minister would not have been presented to the king at the door of his cabinet, without the diplomatic corps on hand. To Franklin the words with which he had entered Louis XVI's chambers on March 20, 1778, may have eclipsed all else. For the first time he heard himself announced as a deputy of the United Provinces of North America, rather than of the thirteen colonies. And the French monarch addressed Franklin with more care and grace than he was known to possess. "Please assure Congress of my friendship. I hope this will be for the good of the two countries," offered Louis XVI, in a high nasal tone. With dignity Franklin thanked the French sovereign, replying: "Your Majesty can count on the gratitude of Congress, and on her commitment to the engagements into which she enters." To which, tears glinting in his eyes, he added a flourish: "If all monarchies were governed by the principles which are in your heart, Sire, republics would never be formed." Louis XVI was not a monarch who generally had a great deal to say to the foreign envoys; at Vergennes's prompting he did, however, offer up a compliment on the Americans' comportment in a precarious situation, after which the delegates were led away, to call on the king's ministers. That afternoon Vergennes threw a sumptuous dinner for the Americans. In distinction to his king, he did so with the ostentation he would have accorded a full ambassador. There was at once a great friendliness and an uncomfortable artificiality to the banquet. It was carefully seated, with Franklin at Vergennes's side, in Stormont's customary place.

Everything about the day was irregular, as Franklin was well aware. The British ambassador had not yet removed himself from Paris, which he had been expected to leave much earlier but where he had been detained by his landlady.* And yet, as the duc de Cröy noted, already Versailles had replaced him with a rebel chief who hailed from a nation that did not yet exist. To Cröy's mind the presentation had its troubling side. France had recognized the emissary of a country with whom she had no ratified treaty, in defiance of a power with whom she was not at war, for the sake of creating a republic that might very well one day devour Europe. She could well be creating a monster. The duc shared his anxieties with Maurepas, who offered up a rather stark explanation. No one wanted another war; the decision had been an arduous one. "But Franklin having skillfully convinced us that America was going to reconcile with England, and that we would be cut off from the tobacco trade, may have led us by the nose," concluded the still-reluctant minister, adding, "And strangely enough, on that may turn the fate of America." There had been no master plan. Without Franklin's maneuvers, conceded Maurepas, there would have been no treaty.

The festivities continued with a dinner for fifty at Chaumont's; the next morning Franklin was back at Versailles, where he braved a fawning, murmuring, jostling crowd to gaze upon Marie Antoinette and the rest of the royal family. That afternoon Gérard hosted the twenty-six-man American delegation. Arthur and William Lee threw a celebratory dinner

---

*Lady Stormont begged to head off the following evening but her husband was firm in his conviction that it would be undignified to do so under cover of darkness. The couple finally departed on March 22.

in Chaillot. It was probably during that week that Franklin made a graceful, futile, attempt to diffuse the spotlight. An enormous cake celebrating the Americans' triumph arrived at the Valentinois, bearing the legend *le digne Franklin*. Surely the inscription, explained the senior envoy, amounted to an awkward misspelling of the three commissioners' names. There was plenty to celebrate, as the drama at Versailles had, in the words of the versatile Edward Edwards, "united all parties, and now we see unanimity and vigor." The spy nearly suffocated on the goodwill.

Franklin was ebullient, although he left no more record of his high spirits than he did of the Veroneses or the matchless beauty of Versailles. "Never have I seen a man as happy, as jubilant as was M. Franklin, the day that Lord Stormont, the English ambassador, left Paris on the occasion of our rupture with his court," remembered the scientist Le Roy. "We dined together, and he who was usually so calm, very serene, seemed to me that day another man altogether, transformed by the joy he radiated." It fell to a later innocent abroad to offer up a window on his elation. There were innumerable canvases at Versailles, of which most were battle scenes. And in only one solitary frame, noted Mark Twain, a century later, was anything pictured but a great French victory.* Plenty in Europe were happy to bet on that record, sanitized though it was. "Never has England been in so perilous a position," warned one ambassador, predicting that if France made no mistakes, England was lost. Franklin left no record either of the semantic divide he crossed on March 20. As of the next day, no one spoke of the "thirteen states," but of the "United Provinces." America was a republic rather than a rebellion.

~~✺~~

No sooner had the Americans prevailed at Versailles than the mission began to disband. In truth it had already imploded. Is it true that one of us has been recalled? Lee had inquired of Franklin early on the morning of March 13. From the other side of town Vergennes heard that day from a

---

*Irwin Shaw would identify a variation on that theme: "Many of the streets of Paris are labeled for battlefields on which Frenchmen have conquered, and you wonder what it must do to the spirit of a city to have the sound of triumph on their lips every time they give an address to a taxi driver, and whether they would be different today if, along with the avenue Wagram and the avenue de Friedland, there were a boulevard Sedan, a rue Waterloo, and a place of the Surrender."

different source why it was imperative he acknowledge the American treaty at once. For him Beaumarchais decoded the tangled state of affairs within the American mission. Lee's jealousy had mutated into a sulfurous hatred of Deane, an obstacle to Lee's ambitions. In libertine dinners—Beaumarchais knew well how the turn of phrase would irritate Vergennes, who had a horror of prurient details creeping into his ambassadors' dispatches—Lee freely expounded on his equal distrust of France and England. He was as happy to exploit one power as the other. And he missed no opportunity to blacken Deane's reputation in America, by way of straightforward jeremiads and backhanded insinuations. With two older brothers in Congress, Lee enjoyed ample means with which to do so.

His fortunes allied with Deane, Beaumarchais had every reason for defending him. Meanwhile Lee and Lauraguais argued vociferously that the matériel Beaumarchais had shipped had been sent to America compliments of the king. The two did so effectively; within a matter of weeks the most theatrical speaker in Congress—he happened to be Richard Henry Lee—would throw up his hands in bewilderment over Beaumarchais's bill. Congress understood those munitions to be the gift of France. Why, then, was a private individual dunning America? On that scabrous issue the personal animosities spilled open. At least I don't sashay around Paris with the king's orders looped around my neck in a gold locket, fumed Lauraguais, mocking Beaumarchais. At least I don't see to it that my name is trumpeted in every café in Paris, fumed Lee, mocking Deane. It might all sound trifling, warned Beaumarchais, but the personal vendetta was heavy with political repercussions. He and Deane were known to be most closely attached to the French alliance. Lee—Beaumarchais too was anything but a fool—had close connections in England. Unable to offer up a scenario without casting and stage-managing it as well, Beaumarchais forged on in his analysis for Versailles. To sacrifice Deane to his personal enemies was to sacrifice the French alliance to America's. Were Deane heading back, it was essential that he do so with every honor France could bestow. As usual, there was not a moment to lose. Coincidentally or not, that was the day Vergennes chose to drop the bombshell that was the news of the alliance in Noailles's lap, for English consumption. It is very likely that Deane's recall—for which Congress provided not a syllable of explanation—had accelerated the happy announcement.

The commissioners had hinted at their incompatibility as early as March 1777, in a line that may have slipped past Congress. By December they begged to be relieved of each other. The pre-Christmas festivities evidently brought with them some kind of collision, as Deane and Franklin separately mentioned their distress. Franklin lay the blame for the kinks in the operation at Lee's feet, allowing that some members of the commission were by nature captious and choleric. They were now five in Paris, well-meaning men all, "but our tempers do not suit, and we are got into disputes and contentions that are not to our credit, and which I have sometimes feared would go to extremes." He alluded to slanders that would make their way to America but that he trusted Congress would read in context. He also made himself clear: "I wish most sincerely that we were separated." Deane simply exploded. He could no longer live with or do business with the Lees, nor did he know a man who could. He had had enough of his fellow commissioner's pugnacity, his suspicions, the "rude and disgusting manner in which he constantly spoke of the French nation." Lee ridiculed and cursed the French daily before his servants, every one of whom happened to be a spy and a gifted reporter. Early in December Deane had attempted in vain to clear the air with his colleague; after the holidays he gave vent to a year's worth of grievances. He and Lee had clashed over every decision before them. They came to blows even over the lapels and number of buttons on an American army uniform. As for the blue and brown fabrics Deane ordered for Washington's men, Lee insisted that they must be red, as "no troops ever fought so well in any other color." The issues were occasionally more lofty, and more knotty. Paranoid by nature, Lee seized early on to the flow of information, which he believed detoured around him. He had a point. As early as September 1777, Franklin shared little with anyone other than Deane. The two took to meeting Gérard at midnight, so as to elude their colleague.

Izard and William Lee leveled the same charge against their uncommunicative colleague, although their situation was complicated by the fact that they were not officially members of the Paris mission. (It was additionally complicated by the fact that they had been sent to Tuscany and Vienna but that Congress, in an oversight, had made no provision for their salaries. This left them dependent on Franklin, who had no authority, and less inclination, to apply meager American funds to commissioners with substantial personal fortunes, neither of whom was serving at the court to which he was assigned.) And while it was true that Franklin had no obligation to confer with colleagues whose commissions were elsewhere, it was equally true that he preferred not to do business with men who disagreed with him, disagreeably. William Lee railed that he knew nothing of American affairs until that news had been in half the papers of Europe. (He was reduced to applying for news to George Lupton, a British spy.) He may have imagined that there were dispatches to be shared but was not wrong about the lack of communication. He also recommended that Congress try to persuade Portugal to open her ports to American vessels, a request to which Franklin had already seen, without having breathed a word to his colleague.

One person Franklin had neglected when the glorious Saratoga news arrived on December 4 was Ralph Izard, sick in bed in Paris. Izard stepped avidly into the role of malevolent godmother, attaching that oversight to his own litany of grievances. He bounded to Franklin's door to discuss his misdeeds. Those the thirty-five-year-old South Carolinian dissected with all the moderation of which he was capable. Franklin acknowledged each of his colleague's points, apologized for all of them, and promised to modify his conduct accordingly—after which Izard found his behavior to be yet more egregious than before. He sputtered that Franklin and Deane were intoxicated by power. Removed as he was from his constituents, Franklin showed no signs of being "guided by principles of virtue and honor." France, Izard charged, had utterly skewed the great man's moral compass.

The control of information created as much enmity as did its brisk flow. "How does it happen that what passes at Versailles is always so accurately known in London?" Beaumarchais asked, pointing directly at Arthur Lee. Lee's suspicions fell on Bancroft, who—the hardest-working member of the mission, and as a trusted housemate of Franklin's, one privy to better information than Lee—was incensed by the attack on his integrity. Vergennes warned repeatedly of a traitor at the Valentinois, fingering Lee's young secretary. The secretary was indeed a double agent, but Lee insisted on his innocence. Instead Lee wrote by every mail of Franklin's carelessness, his indolence, his wickedness, his arrogance. By spring, frustration blistered into revulsion, negligence into criminality. Why should Franklin hesitate to support the commissioners for Tuscany and Vienna when he was only too happy to disburse funds "plenteously and without account to dependents, favorites, relations, and for private purposes?" William Lee inquired of his brother, Richard Henry. Arthur Lee went so far as to insinuate that Deane and Carmichael had together arranged for the Hynson heist, with Franklin's collusion.* Izard blamed Franklin for the naval infractions; he had nearly had the Americans expelled from France. If one issue was loaded, the next was booby-trapped. And so tempers flared over the disposal of Thomas Morris's effects; over the discussions of Jonathan Williams's fate, from which Franklin abstained (How can you abstain out of delicacy when you "have put near a million of public funds in his hands?" screeched William Lee, who made a perfectly valid point); over the invective churned out by the Loyalist press, behind which the Lees saw the only man they personally knew to be so adept with the English language. If any single charge could be discerned in the general mudslinging it was speculating, or stockjobbing, of which nearly everyone involved in the American cause stood accused by someone. Yet again the former postmaster general suffered for the mail. His colleagues wrote often from outside France. Their vitriol got through. Franklin's letters—which were unconscionably rare, although that was one flaw on which the Lees never settled—did not.

As much as the commissioners stood united in their patriotism they were divided in their notions of a future United States of America. And over those premonitory fissures geography loomed most largely. Arthur Lee shared Franklin's belief that Canada was critical to America's fortunes, but for different reasons. To his mind Canada represented a check upon the overly aggressive New England states, which "might otherwise combine in time to subjugate the rest of America." When he thought of his country he thought of Virginia. He could not get past the idea that two of the three commissioners behind the alliance hailed from New England, a region with little to export and with a commensurate interest in duty-free molasses, a treaty term that continued to rankle. (At his insistence, it was finally omitted.) Alone among the Americans in Paris, Franklin entertained the truly radical notion that he was fighting not for a colony but

---

*Elsewhere Lee admitted that Congress had been fortunate not to have heard from its commissioners; the interceptions had spared that assembly a thousand disappointments. Deane went further still. He suspected that his countrymen might not have continued the war had they known of the stonewalling at Versailles.

for a confederation of colonies, and a set of ideals. He also had less use for kings than any other American abroad.

Lee grappled too with an uglier issue. He had been affronted to return from Berlin to find Deane installed in his stead in Passy. The insult was all the greater when the usurper happened to be the son of a Connecticut blacksmith. "The sending persons over here who were neither bred nor born gentlemen in such respectable characters was either a great folly or a great contempt of those to whom they were sent," he snapped, eager to protect Versailles from the unwashed masses, and failing to recognize that in the eyes of the court, the Americans were all of them hopeless provincials. Equally stifling to William Lee was the idea that the Passy parvenus were reaping fortunes from the war. Meanwhile representatives who hailed from America's landed gentry received barely enough to live on. He could not bear the fact that Franklin's grandnephew, "from being a clerk in a sugar bake-house in London, is become a capital merchant here." His brother sniffed that penniless Bancroft, also a former clerk, now kept a house, a mistress, and a carriage. (The mistress happened to be Mrs. Bancroft.) Deane was "a dirty Scotch peddlar." It was to be hoped that in future Congress would send representatives who were gentlemen, fit to move in proper circles. While deploring Franklin's and Deane's "ample appointments," the Lees and Izard made a specialty of proposing a more sensible deployment of commissioners. Surely Dr. Franklin was better suited to the less taxing court of Vienna. As the French court was the "great wheel that moves them all," Arthur Lee preferred to take charge of it himself. In their reassignments the three sounded like nothing so much as pedigree-obsessed members of the European nobility.

While Vergennes never complained about those humble origins, he did complain of Lee. He wished "to be done with this deputy, who is prickly, and an Englishman to his very fingertips." The Americans' banker, Ferdinand Grand, shared his aversion. Was it not possible at least to spirit Lee off to the Spanish border? The two appealed to Aranda, who was less than helpful. They could not send Lee away just because he was impossible. Moreover, he had influential relatives. Vergennes settled for requesting that Franklin spare him from his colleague. The detour was not without analogy among diplomatic professionals; Maurepas's allergy to Stormont had brought the hard-drinking Forth to Paris. And Aranda was so much at odds with his court that Madrid routinely asked Vergennes to withhold information from its own ambassador. The divisions at the American mission were more critical, however. Those five men were the representative of a nation laboring to impress its consistency upon the world. It was highly detrimental to their interests that they offered instead a public spectacle, familiar to every café-goer in Paris. Well before Congress heard the first blows, the British relished their ringside seats. As early as September 1777, Wentworth predicted of the Valentinois: "They will soon have a civil war among themselves."

Chaumont wrote the dysfunction down to British mischief-makers, although even he had to admit that the Americans had offered plenty of help. Deane credited Carmichael. The ingratiating Marylander had indeed played all sides, worming his way into the confidence of each of the commissioners by denouncing him, in turn, to his colleagues. In the end only Izard had a good word to say about him. William Lee refused to be alone in a room with Carmichael; he so distrusted Carmichael that he made it a point never to supply him with any scrap of his handwriting. Carmichael was lucky however; William Lee hesitated to condemn anyone who could be counted on to testify against Deane in Congress. All the same Lee viewed Carmichael's February departure with relief. He predicted that the uneasiness and bickering would subside now that the fomenter made his way to America. In that he was deluding himself. A week later, his own brother unleashed another broadside. Dupes of Beaumarchais, his colleagues appropriated funds, intercepted mail, and delayed America-bound munitions for the sake of their private ventures.

Three weeks later Arthur Lee posed his question about Deane's recall. Franklin's response was telling. Deane would indeed be heading back to America, although that news was not yet official. Franklin may have been attempting to deflect a query that Lee lobbed his way all the same. If Deane had had news of his recall on March 4, why had he been presented to court as an American commissioner sixteen days later? The exchange set the tone of the next weeks, when Franklin—who guessed that Deane owed his recall to the insinuations of his enemies—refused to gratify those men. Even Stormont knew already that Deane was to return to America, to be replaced by one "George" Adams. Deane was reluctant to make the trip, not overly tempted to run the gauntlet with one enemy on the high seas only to confront another in Congress; Franklin counseled him to head off posthaste so as to clear his name. Neither man yet had an inkling that Deane owed his recall primarily to his having inflicted on America a plague of officers as expensive as they were unwelcome.

On March 31 Deane slipped quietly out of Paris under an assumed name. And he indeed headed off well armed. With him went a gold snuffbox from Louis XVI, an endorsement from Franklin, and a testimonial from Bancroft. In Bancroft's opinion the recall was infinitely regrettable; Congress did nothing for its reputation abroad by censuring a diligent man. Bancroft had seen every letter to and from Deane since his arrival as well as every related scrap of paper, had been constantly in his company, privy to every piece of business. He could affirm that Deane had "labored indefatigably and incessantly in the public service, and for the public good, and that he has suffered more toil, perplexity, and embarrassment than you can possibly imagine or I explain by letter." The greatest testimony to Deane's effectiveness was however the fleet that came with him for America's deliverance, of which no American apart from Franklin had the slightest hint. And Vergennes made a very public show of the court's favor. He saw to it that Deane sailed home in the flagship of Admiral d'Estaing's seventeen-ship squadron.

As the alliance would need to be protected from Tory tampering on the American side as well, Vergennes resolved to appoint a French envoy to Philadelphia. His right-hand man, the bilingual Conrad-Alexandre Gérard, begged for the assignment. Separately he made his way to Toulon, to join d'Estaing. That information Franklin also withheld from Lee. He had every reason for secrecy; Vergennes had requested as much, and it was essential that Franklin prove America's commitment to the alliance. He had occasion to do so again at the end of March. Two days before d'Estaing sailed, Franklin met a new British emissary in his Saint-Germain hotel. William Pulteney, the Scottish member of Parliament, finally got his turn; he was in Paris to discuss an eighteen-point peace proposal, which he presented on the condition that his terms never be divulged should they prove insufficient. They were the most liberal yet; Franklin wasted no time in rejecting them. He also made two revealing offers. Arthur Lee should be consulted, as he might well entertain a different opinion. And Franklin felt under an obligation to consult the French ministry, with whom any peace would need to be coordinated. Pulteney's response was an unequivocal no on both counts. Franklin saw to it that the propositions went to Vergennes all the same, adding that the terms would "probably have been accepted, if they had been made two years ago." He had by no means forgotten that Lee was in Paris. Nor did he hesitate to break his word for the sake of French relations. Whether he would sacrifice those relations to an irritable colleague was a different matter.

The explosion in Chaillot was immediate. Lee was left to learn of Deane's departure and of Gérard's appointment from the Frenchman. How was it possible that Franklin had kept this news from him?, Lee erupted on April 2. He reminded Franklin that they lived fewer than ten minutes apart, not something Franklin often had the luxury of forgetting. Lee had been at Passy as recently as the eve of Deane's departure, when he had inquired directly about communication with America. His colleague had been both silent and deceptive. For that Lee eviscerated him: "Is this the example you in your superior wisdom think proper to set of order, decorum, confidence, and justice?" He could not more effectively have misled a public enemy. It was entirely true that he had been silent, Franklin promptly confessed: "I do not like to answer angry letters. I hate disputes. I am old, cannot have long to live, have much to do and no time for altercation." He went on to warn Lee of the dangers of his corrosive mind, "which is forever tormenting itself, with its jealousies, suspicions and fancies that others mean you ill, wrong you, or fail in respect to you. If you do not cure yourself of this temper it will end in insanity."

The next day brought a diatribe from Izard, the first in a lacerating series. Izard demanded in writing Franklin's reasons for having concealed the treaties from him. Franklin put him off until the following week, sitting down again to address Lee. Lee's charges were serious ones. Franklin had served many publics, all of them faithfully. He had kept Deane's trip secret because he had been requested to. The papers were at Passy not for any sinister reason, as his colleague charged, but because Deane and Franklin lived together and transacted most of the business. He was perfectly willing to account to Congress "for this my terrible offense of being silent to you." Not only had he ignored Lee's letters, he had burned them. (That was untrue.) He had no need of being lectured as if he were one of the servants.

To the departing Deane he described his torture at the hands of a colleague he had already privately portrayed as deranged. "His disorder seems to increase," Franklin noted, "for he raves not only against you and me, but seems to resent the court's sending a minister to Congress without advising with him. I bear all his rebukes with patience, for the good of the service. But it goes a little hard with me." Chaumont testified as well to Franklin's suffering at the Virginian's hand, adding that Congress would be better served without a deputy in Paris at all than by an arrogant madman like Arthur Lee. He was right to distinguish between the two Americans. Equally vituperative though it was on both sides, there was a crucial difference in the exchange. Franklin never sent his angry letters.

On April 26 Izard dispatched his secretary to Passy, with another riot act. Franklin barely glanced at it before asking after the allegations. The secretary obliged. Franklin calmly explained that Izard would have his letter but that business came first. He also informed Izard's secretary that his employer's complaints were so legion he would soon need a volume to respond to them all. He volunteered some advice: People who write angry letters should hold on to them until they had reflected sufficiently on the contents. Izard appreciated that counsel as much as he had an earlier piece of Franklinian wisdom: It was, he volunteered, wise "always to *suppose* one's friends *may be right*, till one *finds* them wrong, rather than to *suppose them wrong* till one *finds* them right." That maxim Izard threw back in his face, accusing Franklin of having himself violated it.

Izard never got the satisfaction of a letter nor Lee the sparring partner for which he hungered, which only confirmed Franklin in his reputation of artful wickedness. "His tricks," Izard would alert Congress, "are in general carried on with so much cunning that it is extremely difficult to fix them on him," a line that qualifies as the most admiring Izard ever devoted to Franklin. Izard was persuaded that the French would long before have entered into an American alliance had the colonies only sent fitter representatives. To the contaminated mind of Arthur Lee, Franklin was so shrewd about avoiding decisions, so generally dilatory, so prone to idleness, that he would have postponed the American Revolution if he could have. He ranked Franklin "the most corrupt of all corrupt men." From William Lee's correspondence it is difficult to tell if America's greater enemy was "the old mule" which was Great Britain or "the old fox" which was Ben Franklin. Franklin had no doubt that Lee was lunatic, an opinion seconded by Chaumont and Grand, but which diagnosis Jonathan Williams thought overly charitable. Deane took to writing off the Lee brothers as one sect; to them Franklin and Deane constituted another. Even the servants took to quarreling.

It was by those hostilities that Franklin was consumed as the treaty of alliance sailed to America, and as the rest of Paris speculated about a different set, on which subject everyone was an oracle but no one knew a thing. It had generally been assumed that the Franco-American alliance would spark an open confrontation. Weeks later, as tempers flared in Passy, France and England glowered uneasily at each other across the Channel. With Europe's attention fixed upon them, neither power was particularly inclined to make the first move. In Paris the joke went that the minister of the navy wanted a land war, the minister of the army a naval war, and Maurepas no war at all. For her part England seemed to be doing her dignified best to turn her back on any open confrontation. As early as the day of his court presentation, Franklin predicted that the two powers would come to blows only on American soil.

In the midst of that gathering storm forty-two-year-old John Adams arrived in Bordeaux. After six torturous weeks at sea he was to make two unwelcome discoveries. He had not yet disembarked when he learned that the treaty he had been sent to negotiate had been concluded before he had sailed. And he was on land for only a matter of days when he heard that all was not well among his countrymen; there was evidently a "dryness" among the Paris commissioners. Franklin had a different word for it. As soon as he and Adams were alone together in Passy he dilated on the "coolness" that prevailed between him and Lee, with whom it was impossible to do business. Franklin's relationship with Adams had been very much the opposite; the two had worked easily together since 1775. They had lived in close company while serving in Congress; on their 1776 trip to Staten Island they had shared a bed. They had been part of the five-man team that produced the Declaration of Independence. Adams had been among the first to advocate a French alliance; the treaty now wending its way to America was based on his handiwork. The plump, pale-complexioned Adams offered another solace as well, in the form of a commodity rare in Paris. "The Boston manner, turn of phrase, and even the tone of voice and accent in all please, and seem to refresh and revive me," Franklin would acknowledge later. With what could only have been delight he welcomed his brilliant and determined colleague, and his Yankee cadences, to the Valentinois, where he made Deane's former rooms available to Adams and to ten-year-old John Quincy Adams.

Days after the new commissioner was installed Izard too poured out his heart to him. Adams knew the South Carolinian to be proud and irritable but was all the same taken aback by the outburst. With recourse to the words "pillage" and "fraud," Izard denounced Franklin, Deane, and every man, French or American, with whom they had associated. He swore "that Dr. Franklin was one of the most unprincipled men upon earth: that he was a man of no veracity, no honor, no integrity, as great a villain as ever breathed." He described for Adams the balancing act that had confounded him on his arrival the previous summer, one Adams did not yet realize he was to inherit. "I wished to be on the side of Franklin and Deane," explained Izard, "but the former was too wise to be my dupe, and treated me with reserve; the latter too haughty to be guided by me, and treated me with contempt." He had been left with no choice but to ally himself with Lee.

Lee alone was quiet, at the instruction of his older brother. From Vienna William Lee advised they not hurry Adams into taking their side. They were wiser to lead him gently, as he "has too high a sense of himself" to appreciate being driven by others. This was the man who complained incessantly of Franklin's schemes. Carmichael and Deane, that "nest of wretches," might well be gone, "but still the oldest is left, who can breed mischief enough for twenty worlds," William Lee warned Congress at the end of May. There was "rather more of animosity among the Americans here than I remember to have seen anywhere else," Adams would conclude by summer's end.

~✼~

Silas Deane's run of poor luck continued. Since his wife's death, he had hoped to arrange for their only child to join him in Passy. Thirteen-year-old Jesse Deane drove into Passy with John Adams; he missed the father from whom he had been separated for years by a matter of days. Franklin assumed responsibility for him, seeing to it that Jesse was enrolled in school with Benny and John Quincy Adams.* As quickly

---

*"Children," Franklin held in France, "are to be treated like people who arrive from foreign countries, who must be gently instructed in the customs of ours."

Franklin folded the owlish John Adams into his debilitating rounds, sweeping him off to meet the la Rochefoucauld family in their baronial home. He did so before Adams yet felt appropriately outfitted for any kind of Parisian outing. That anxiety would underline the difference between the two envoys, one of them self-conscious about his attire, the other confident that fashion would follow him, both of whom were right. Franklin also sent Vergennes word of his new colleague, bearing with him the news that Congress was warmly disposed toward ratification of their treaty. Adams's arrival was in that respect a blessing additionally to the French minister, wrangling with Spain. He knew well the question on which Madrid stumbled: Would the Americans be either so stupid or so clever as to betray a nation that rose to their aid? At Versailles Franklin did his best to bolster Vergennes's confidence, billing the congressional resolutions that traveled with Adams as irrefutable proof that "America had not been acting a double part, which some of our enemies have most maliciously accused us of." (Presumably Vergennes was less pleased by some embroidering that Franklin affixed to his North American report. Franklin assured others at Versailles that week that the Canadians would not be long in joining the thirteen colonies. "We've kept a spot for them," he maintained.)

Vergennes welcomed Deane's replacement to Versailles twice during his first week in Paris, the second time for a Monday *levée* of naval minister Sartine. After the ceremony a rehabilitated Maurepas joined the Americans in Sartine's office, where he asked if Adams spoke French. Franklin answered for him: "A little, and if one speaks slowly and clearly." It was a generous appraisal of a man who in his diary admitted that conversations were impenetrable to him. The question came up again a month later, at Adams's presentation to Louis XVI. Having tended to his wardrobe, Adams entered the king's gilded bedroom in the obligatory wig and dress sword; nonetheless he came at Versailles to understand what it felt like to be an Indian chief on display. He was powerless before Louis XVI's verbal torrent. Nor was he put at ease by the king's sole query in his regard. Did he speak French? inquired the sovereign of the exotic specimen. "Not a word," went the answer, at which Louis XVI breezed past Adams and into the next room, confirming the verdict to be tantamount to one of savagery. It was no wonder that the new envoy devoted every spare minute to his French, which he studied like a schoolboy.

Franklin did little to promote those studies. Adams's social calendar began with a festive and extravagant dinner at the Brillons, in the course of which he admired the sweet charms of Madame Brillon, the thirty-three-year-old beauty to whom Franklin found himself increasingly attracted. The children's plain-faced governess joined the family as well. Adams was shocked later to learn that this graceless individual was Monsieur Brillon's lover. He heard as well that Madame Brillon consoled herself with Franklin's friend Le Veillard, which was almost certainly less true. How this was arranged without any slitting of throats was beyond his comprehension. "But I did not know the world," sighed Adams. While he was no expert on French mores he knew his American etiquette; he saw that Franklin had needlessly offended some of his compatriots in Paris by failing to return their calls. He was even less punctilious about his accounts, which—if ever they existed in any formal incarnation—had either been lost or lay in confused heaps in his rooms.

To that anarchy Adams applied himself, requisitioning a set of ledger books. At the same time he attempted to unravel the tangle of personalities. Hourly he received reports on the animosities that divided his compatriots. He felt that Deane had perhaps attended to his own business as much as America's. He had lived too extravagantly (his expenses were about 50 percent greater than Franklin's), "but he was active, diligent, subtle, and successful, having accomplished the great purpose of his mission to advantage." Deane had won the confidence of the court where Lee made a career of damning the French publicly. While Franklin was more temperate in his language, Adams surmised that he felt no less bitterness toward his colleagues than they toward him. He had heard aspersions cast on Franklin's character before but had always known him to have acted honorably. It was all "a rope of sand" on which Adams could get little grip. He was without any books, documents, letters that might guide him. He felt himself a double stranger: to the country, language, and manners of the French, and to those of the Americans in Paris.

While Adams grappled with the ledgers, Franklin fielded another peace emissary, in the form of the tireless David Hartley. Their late April conversations were not ones to which Adams was privy, with good reason; the new Paris commissioner took an instant dislike to the member of Parliament, whom he took for a spy, and a vain one at that. Evidently he did little to hide his aversion; while Adams felt he comported himself civilly, Hartley found him "the most ungracious man I ever saw." With every argument he could muster, Hartley implored Franklin to renounce the ill-advised alliance. The Americans could expect nothing but bad faith from the French. Hartley did so not only with Franklin but separately with Lee; the difference between a diplomat and a politician can be read in their responses. To Vergennes Franklin reported that he had politely fended off Britain's offer: "And that if she made war against France on our account, a peace with us at the same time was impossible; for that having met with a friendship from that generous nation when we were cruelly oppressed by England, we were under ties stronger than treaties could form to make common cause, which we should certainly do, to the utmost of our power." Lee cited Hartley's claim that France had never done anything for America and could not be trusted, preferring to convey to Vergennes Britain's spite rather than America's goodwill. Vergennes heartily applauded Franklin's stance, convinced that the envoy could not have conducted himself with "more nobility, more candor, or more firmness." In his book the compliments came no higher. He promised to report back on his own meeting with Hartley, who he suspected would attempt a double game, as indeed Hartley did. Noble, candid, and firm, Vergennes offered up his regrets. France was no more disposed to renounce America than was America to renounce France.

The next week an eccentric peace offer landed on the floor of Franklin's rooms, lobbed through a window grate. Its author proposed an American government of two hundred peers, to be appointed by the king. Yet again Franklin was reminded that he had nothing to gain from consorting with a people whose laws, government, and religion differed so radically from America's, and "who heartily despise you already." He replied with a lengthy manifesto, vetted by an admiring Adams, and intended more for Vergennes's eyes than anyone else's. Franklin could not be duped into believing France capable of bad faith. He had no reason to think she despised America, even less to believe that she would cheat a young country. He was indignant at the author's intimation of a bribe. The man whose French friends were universally titled jeered that he had no use for peerages, "a sort of tar-and-feather honor, a mixture of foulness and folly." Franklin's mysterious correspondent requested a midday meeting at Notre-Dame, near the statue of Saint Christopher, where Franklin would recognize him by the rose in his hat. As Franklin refused to be lured along such "crooked dark paths," Lenoir and three special agents explored them in his stead. The emissary turned out to be a British army captain whose mission came to naught, save for having allowed Franklin to prove to Vergennes yet again how eloquently and how honorably he held to their as-yet-unratified alliance.

Vergennes did his part as well for the fledgling relationship, lifting a floodgate or two. At the end of April he authorized a print featuring Franklin in his role as America's liberator, a print prohibited only six months earlier. The torrents of enthusiasm were now permitted to flow freely, along carefully defined channels. In a city that speculated daily about the whereabouts of d'Estaing—his operation was nicknamed "the campaign of destiny"—Franklin's stock had never been so high.* He found it more difficult yet to shrink from the spotlight, its intensity sanctioned by Vergennes. Franklin was not adverse to flattery, but made very clear how he felt that attention should be directed. When Antoine Borel submitted to him the allegorical composition in which Franklin played the central role, he reminded the artist that he could by no means approve such a thing. Congress deserved top billing. In that discussion Franklin may best have put his finger on an issue that would color the Parisian years. He well understood that in France it would be considered an approbation, but "in my own country it would hurt my character and usefulness if I were to give the least countenance to such a pretention."

"I have long been accustomed to receive more blame, as well as more praise, than I have deserved," Franklin had observed, without noting that there was, in that equation, some cause and effect. Adams observed both as he conjured with the disorder at Passy. Probably for the best he had not been on hand when Franklin—recently inducted into the most eminent of the Masonic lodges—had escorted the fragile Voltaire into the ceremony on his arm. (On that occasion Voltaire inherited the apron of the lodge's founder, Helvétius, an apron that Franklin would inherit later.) Despite

---

*It brought to the doorstep a new rush of would-be emigrants, who had in common their inability to take no for an answer. One young architect dreamed of building in America. If there was no stone he would work in brick. If there was no brick he would work in wood. The manufacturers of playing cards and the expert wine growers and the writers of constitutions and the invisible-ink makers who yearned to be Franklin's countrymen were one thing, but he must have found it painful to discourage the enterprising printer who found himself stymied in France. All six of the licensed printers in his region had children who were slated to take their places.

his attempt to curtail all outings for the sake of the American accounts, Adams was very much on hand for a Passy dinner that concluded with a piece of theater. The cast consisted of the envoys' hostess in the role of the muse of history, and two guests, cast as North America and the genius of liberty. The presentation opened with North America reading *The Way to Wealth*, and ended, by way of a eulogy of that volume's author, with the curtains parting to reveal his distinguished portrait. Of the playlet Adams left no account in his diary, a book he was already attempting to keep in French. And which he soon abandoned, judging there to be too many spies in the house, his own servants first among them.

He was quick to grasp that European women were a different breed—exquisitely groomed, outspoken, well educated, brilliantly accomplished—and that they flocked irresistibly to his co-commissioner, who flirted outrageously with the greatest beauties of France. He warned Franklin that he intended to convey as much to America, and did: "My venerable colleague enjoys a privilege here that is much to be envied. Being 70 years of age, the ladies not only allow him to embrace them as often as he pleases, but they are perpetually embracing him." Adams was not the first to report on these tributes, one honor which Abigail Adams hoped would elude her husband. A visitor who accompanied Franklin for a walk in the Bois de Boulogne noted that he did so with an entourage, "and all the ladies both old and young were ready to eat him up." (Franklin only shrugged on the subject. Someone had let out that he liked the ladies, and the French were the most obliging people in the world.) Adams by no means begrudged his colleague his appeal, rather making light of French-women's "unaccountable passion for old age." His greater quibble against Franklin was that he always had the carriage, which meant that Adams could get to the theater less often than he liked.

Generally Adams reserved his misgivings for the French; from the start he was on the alert for European designs on America. He was down-right pained by a comment Vergennes made one afternoon, as he escorted Lee and Adams from his offices to those of the minister of the army. In the bustling courtyard of the château of Versailles, amid a sea of sedan chairs, the three exchanged bows with a decorated French marshal. "That is a great general, Sir!" exclaimed Lee. "Ah," rejoined Vergennes, "I wish he was in command of your army." Alarm bells went off in Adams's head. Silently he vowed to sacrifice his life before he "voluntarily put on the chains of France when I am struggling to throw off those of Great Britain." He had already begun to shudder at the thousands of abbés who had attached themselves to the French aristocracy, off whom they lived in a conversation-bolstering, court-jestering, patina-providing brand of parasitism; he was shocked to discover that *Jesuit* was not, in Europe, a dirty word. It was his conviction that a country's moral temperature was most accurately read in the deportment of its women. And this was a man who in his first Passy weeks dined with a prominent couple and a bishop, the latter of whom was the wife's lover. For that privilege money changed hands. Adams watched the trio like a hawk throughout the meal. He skidded up against a divide that Franklin had identified linguistically the previous year, when collaborating with la Rochefoucauld on the translation of the state constitutions. There was no word for *industry* in eighteenth-century France. (*Assiduité* was the closest equivalent Franklin could locate, after a bout of head-scratching.) Business in Paris, observed Adams, consisted primarily of ceremony and pleasure.

Seven weeks into his stay the frustration began to show. "Our affairs in this kingdom I find in a state of confusion and darkness that surprises me. Prodigious sums of money have been expended and large sums are yet due," he conceded. Lee articulated the same sentiment differently. All was "disorder and dissipation," and he could be held accountable for none of it. Adams was happy to embrace the responsibility but less eager to be sucked into the vortex of ill will generated by his colleagues. Surely one commissioner would be more effective than three. As Franklin had the confidence of the French court and of his own people, it was incumbent on his colleagues to respect him. Nothing could be clearer to Adams, who soon discovered that the enmity was not so reasonably tamed. Any agreement was impossible. Franklin refused to so much as have Izard in his home.

~·~

On June 17 a different kind of squall erupted. The French and British fired at each other when the *Belle Poule* met a British frigate in the English Channel; a second engagement followed days later. It was a murky beginning—there was no formal declaration of hostilities, and never would be—but the two countries were at last at war. Up went the hair of Paris, three masts and all, into a *coiffure à la Belle Poule*, when but six months earlier the *coiffure à l'insurgent* had been prohibited. The youth of

France was put out of its misery, although the chevalière d'Eon was not: "I was perfectly happy to remain in a skirt in peacetime, but now that we are at war this is untenable," the erstwhile dragoon officer groaned. The announcement would bring to Franklin's doorstep a different parade. Now that a zealous Frenchman could serve with his own army, Franklin appeared as a recruiting officer for the rest of Europe.

The news brought as well a ten-page screed from Izard. Franklin had no right to have agreed to French demands for secrecy, he foamed; he had done nothing about the "scandalous abuses" at Nantes; he had entrusted America's business to Temple, the son of a Loyalist, and to Bancroft, a speculator. Quoting scripture and verse, citing the Greeks, invoking Kubla Khan, Izard pronounced Franklin a tyrant. "An ear poisoned with flattery listens with reluctance to the voice of truth," hissed Izard, to the man who—in a Paris delirious with war fever—could barely make it from the door of the Opéra to his carriage without seeking refuge from the bombardments of applause that followed him. While Izard lobbed his grenades, Franklin focused instead on Versailles, to which he was summoned. Spain offered to mediate between France and England, a proposal that several French ministers welcomed. Expertly Franklin played his role, saucily reminding the Spanish envoy that the king of England might prove less reasonable than the king of France. In any event France would do nothing without the United States, nor the United States without France.

Spain would fail where John Adams was to succeed with a more difficult mediation. Adams defused tensions at Passy enough to clear the way for a spirited July 4 celebration. His intention was to invite all the Americans in and around Paris as well as the new nation's best friends; Franklin drew the line at Izard, however. To the South Carolinian and the other members of the community whom Franklin petulantly omitted from his guest list, Adams extended an invitation in his name only. The day passed happily, with an elaborate feast, fetching floral arrangements, a gaggle of American children, and without incident of any kind. Only afterward was the company critiqued, on two counts. Izard complained that the Americans had been slumming; no princes or dukes or cardinals had graced their assembly. (For that Adams was unapologetic. American finances hardly allowed them to entertain on such a level; they would have appeared ridiculous.) At the same time Adams conceded that Franklin consorted with a brand of people of whom many in the kingdom disapproved. By definition the liberal aristocracy and the intelligentsia, they included their share of rabble-rousers. That was unfortunate. It was also the work of Vergennes and Sartine, who had led Franklin directly into that company, the one most intent in 1778 on the American experiment.

On July 6 Franklin shared with Vergennes the triumphant news that France's treaties had been greeted with universal joy by Congress, who had turned England's conciliatory bills away with equal indignation. Initially Congress had been puzzled by Britain's haste to submit its conciliatory bills; the French treaties—which arrived eight days later, unheralded and unexpected, after nearly a year of silence—resolved the mystery. "France by her open candor has *won* us more powerfully than any reserved treaties could possibly *bind* us," wrote Richard Henry Lee and James Lovell, the two delegates who had heard the most elaborate accounts of Franklin's misdeeds. They were signing the documents now and could discuss the details later. On July 17 ratified treaties were exchanged in Versailles. Days later Franklin wrote Congress at length, on a number of matters. He sang Deane's praises. Insofar as the disputed molasses articles were concerned, he believed the language inconsequential. To strike it was by contrast to send up a red flag; it was a signal that America intended to engage in trade wars. He offered his own compelling case against tariffs: "To lay duties on a commodity exported which our friends want is a knavish attempt to get something for nothing. The statesman who first invented it had the genius of a pickpocket." The nations that practiced that art invariably suffered; Franklin cited among his examples a certain ill-advised tax on tea. Moreover, America produced no commodity not manufactured elsewhere. Under the circumstances, leveling any kind of export duty amounted to folly: "It is a meanness with which I would not dirty the conscience or character of my country."

Quite naturally his explanation led him to another kind of meanness. Could Congress really intend to keep three representatives at Versailles? In truth they were four, as the Tuscan ambassador lived in Paris. And they were about to be five, as William Lee was headed back from the court of Vienna, which refused to receive him.* The envoys undermined both

---

*For political reasons, both the courts of Vienna and Berlin had refused to receive Lee. The Grand Duke of Tuscany followed the court of Vienna's lead. Izard was invited to reside in Florence as a private individual but chose not to, for reasons of his own. He never left Paris.

each other and their country's credibility. Business took three times as long as it should; correspondence languished; opportunities were lost. They were costing Congress a fortune, while gratifying the spies of Paris. Those were the practical considerations. About the personal ones Franklin was forthright, and composed. Evidently it was an impossibility to find three men so even-tempered that they might live together without quarreling. Would Congress please separate them?

Having for so long looked to France for an alliance, the colonies received in its wake a second, less welcome Passy import. On June 8, 1778, Henry Laurens, the president of Congress, read with horror the Lees' charges against Silas Deane. "I know all the gentlemen yonder, some of them very intimately, know their tempers and habits and I think I can mark out causes, but I can only deplore their impolitic and I was going to say schoolboy jarrings," he warned General Washington, who had himself only just heard of those far-off battles. Already Laurens braced himself for the brawl that was to spill out of the Valentinois and across the ocean, into Congress. Franklin's mission was to produce the vital alliance on which American independence rested, its magnitude best articulated that summer by Adams: "The longer I live in Europe, and the more I consider our affairs, the more important our alliance with France appears to me. It is a rock upon which we may safely build." The mission also produced the first party scandal in American history.

VI

Admiration Is the Daughter of Ignorance
1778

In Paris they just simply opened their eyes and stared when we spoke to them in French! We never did succeed in making those idiots understand their own language.
—*Mark Twain*, The Innocents Abroad

Word of the alliance on which America's independence would be founded—her bedrock, her polestar, her salvation—arrived in Philadelphia without a moment to spare. It was very nearly too late. One friend tactfully confided that it was a relief to hear Franklin was all the rage in Paris. Popularity was said to count for everything in that city; it was hoped to be "a good prognostic of your political success. To tell you the truth, we begin to be a little out of humor at the delay of the Bourbon princes." In fact colonial impatience with France had reached a breaking point. As the president of Congress saw it, America's "artful specious half-friends" had done nothing but manipulate the Passy commissioners like puppets on a string. From Valley Forge George Washington fulminated against the indecision at Versailles. He was primed for drastic measures. Was it not time, he contended on April 21, 1778, either to dispatch new commissioners or to issue an ultimatum? He had greater reason to remonstrate than anyone, having withstood a miserable winter with a smallpox-infested, half-naked army, famished and on the verge of disbanding. A week after his outburst

Gérard sailed into Philadelphia, to an extraordinary welcome. "You have come to our rescue," came the cries from the banks of the Delaware, before the Frenchman had yet disembarked. "When you need us, we'll come to yours."* Swiftly and unanimously Congress ratified the treaties at a special Saturday meeting on May 4. Washington set that Monday apart as a day of celebration, ordering up fireworks and parades, thirteen-cannon salutes and gills of rum. The 11,800 men who joined him in the cheer "Long live the king of France!" were half of them still without shirts, but both army and commander looked livelier than they had since the outset of the war. "The favorable issue of our negotiation with France is matter for heartfelt joy, big with important events, and it must, I should think, chalk out a plain and easy road to independence," Washington exulted.

In that the circumspect commander in chief rather overstated the case. Word of a Franco-American treaty indeed caused a sensation—as far away as Saint Petersburg it was the talk of the town—but even those who had the most to gain from it swallowed misgivings. A fervent patriot of French Huguenot descent topped that list. Days before the treaty reached Congress, John Jay felt he would still prefer a connection with Britain to one with any other power on earth. Old England had after all sheltered his ancestors from religious persecution—by Catholic France. In 1778 it was not necessary to be a Huguenot to subscribe to anti-French prejudice; such was the enduring suspicion of France that when Silas Deane proposed a professorship in French to his alma mater in 1778, the Yale authorities found themselves dubious about (and in one case violently opposed to) the idea. Even when America's linguistic isolationism gradually gave way—Harvard taught French after 1787, and Yale recognized it officially in 1825—there were those who reflexively felt it should be kept from the ladies. Where the French language went, depravity, frivolity, and indolence were sure to follow.

Franklin was fully aware of the potency of that ingrained prejudice. Along with the treaties for Congress went a letter to his old friend the Reverend Samuel Cooper, the silver-tongued pastor of Boston's Brattle Square Church. Franklin sang the praises of Louis XVI and urged

---

*It would be 139 years until Colonel Charles Stanton's "*Lafayette, nous voici!*" but already the promise was there. Stanton's July 4, 1917, tribute would be reprised in 1944, by American troops landing in France.

Cooper to do his utmost to eradicate all lingering bias in America. (He pressed the same point with Congress, but Cooper would be the more active party. He spent the next three years on Vergennes's payroll, propagating pro-French sentiment from his Boston pulpit.) With Vergennes's blessing, he also rushed word to the European papers that the French treaties met with an ecstatic reception in America. Congress offered up prayers for the king, queen, and royal family. As swiftly, they prohibited prayers for the king of England. Franklin knew well how to hold a grudge and delighted in the fact that—to the world's astonishment—America had landed not only a powerful patron, but the one guaranteed to cause the British the greatest discomfort. Even a sympathetic Whig felt that sting. To be ruined by France was more than even the most liberal of Franklin-admiring Englishmen could bear. To a Tory the charade in which America and France engaged played as something else. It was a fraud perpetrated by self-deluding peoples who actively despised each other, a "farce of union and friendship." With it the Loyalist press had a field day; decades of blind prejudice gave them plenty to work with. The misguided Americans had made a Faustian bargain. Theirs was a reckless act of miscegenation. It took no time at all to produce a Dr. Franklin who had converted to Catholicism and was delivering boatloads of priests to America daily.

Franklin fixed his attention not on the fictitious priests but on his friend d'Estaing, who had sailed from Toulon on April 13. Franklin had estimated that that squadron would reach America by June 22 at the latest, but d'Estaing anchored off the Delaware only on July 8. He missed striking a decisive blow at a British convoy by a matter of days. As Franklin spoon-fed news of America's jubilation in the alliance to the French press d'Estaing sailed north, where he prepared to face a smaller British fleet off Newport. A storm intervened, followed by a squabble over where the French admiral should refit. Against the advice of the American generals, d'Estaing retreated to Boston. He left in his wake something more resilient even than the glorious French fleet of which General Washington had so long dreamed: a bumper crop of resentment. What to make of a navy that fled at the first sign of danger? These new allies, fumed the Americans, were useless. The feelings were mutual. D'Estaing could not bring himself to look upon the Rhode Island militia as soldiers. (Lafayette assured him that they could be relied upon to distract and discomfit the enemy, while "the French did the fighting.") The alliance toward which Franklin, Deane, and Lee had worked for eighteen months yielded anti-French demonstrations and riots, and claimed as an early casualty a foreign lieutenant who attempted to break up a Franco-American scuffle. (He was buried quietly, after what may have been the first Catholic Mass to be said in Boston.) An officer serving with Lafayette described for his mother the prevailing colonial sentiment. The Continental Army burst with cabals and intrigues. The sniping against General Washington was relentless. It was all just like Versailles.

On no other count could White Plains be said to resemble the French court, and therein lay a great deal of the difficulty. The "honeymoon of national matrimony" was short-lived, and from its first embrace an awkward affair. On hearing of the treaties Lafayette threw his arms around Washington—a man no American dared slap on the back—and deliriously planted kisses on each of his cheeks. Held together by a shared and (on one side) short-lived antipathy toward Great Britain, the partnership was founded on various illusions about the past and a general misunderstanding of the future. Even Lafayette assumed that Washington would one day be appointed dictator. He noted that the two nations were off to a wobbly start. The ingratitude of the Americans was particularly deplorable. He pronounced himself incensed to "have personally been put in the position of hearing the name of France spoken without respect, and perhaps with disdain, by a herd of Yankees from New England."*

While it was universally agreed that the Americans were helpless without the French, there was no love lost between the officers of the two nations. One foreigner described Washington's troops as being "English as regards Frenchmen, but Americans toward the English." Another noted that officers of the two nations rarely fraternized, which was for the best: "Their character being so different from ours, we should inevitably have quarreled." Gérard discovered that Washington commanded an army half

---

*As usual, that officer made for a walking litmus test. To a French audience, Lafayette's exploits continued to be the stuff of romance. When Lord Carlisle scoffed that the colonists had allied themselves with "an enemy to all civil and religious liberty," Lafayette felt that his nation's honor had been impugned. He challenged the English peace commissioner to a duel. To French ears that rang out as his most glorious exploit yet. To both sets of Anglo-Saxon observers, the gesture was absurd.

the size of what that envoy had been led to believe. On contact the formidable American militiaman—in great part a Beaumarchais–Vergennes coproduction—melted into myth as well. A closer inspection revealed the American militia to be an unreliable body of indeterminate size, with a hideously unprofessional sense of discipline. That untrained body of slow-moving citizens, noted one foreign officer, "assemble only when the danger is imminent; and flee when it becomes great." By no stretch did the rebels represent the militarily invincible ally that Vergennes had promised. Instead the French officers stifled their laughter. Mounted on the scruffiest horses they had ever seen were the country's tailors and apothecaries, who resembled nothing so much as "a flock of ducks in cross-belts."

For the misunderstandings d'Estaing bore less blame than did Rousseau and the prolific abbé Raynal. The degree of misconception on both sides was staggering. The average Frenchman not only attached America to Turkey but marveled at the skin color of the natives and wondered what language they spoke. No one had done as much as Raynal to impress upon France an American continent peopled by degenerate, feebleminded iguana eaters. It was not unusual for a French volunteer to expect to be greeted on arrival in the New World by panthers. A rosy overlay of idealism attached itself to that dreary picture, hand-tinted by Rousseau. An Eden of spartan simplicity, America beckoned as a refuge from decadent, byzantine Europe. Count after marquis after duke would discover that it was easier to be besotted by republican sobriety from a Parisian drawing room. Few Frenchmen were able to survive a New England Sunday, to be spent in prayer; it brought to mind nothing so much as the Inquisition. One Frenchman was arrested for having dared to play the flute on the Sabbath. Nor did any of them recover easily from the sight of a judge or a doctor tending his own garden. Before the year was out Congress outlawed attendance at theatrical productions, which distracted from the war effort. Even Lafayette came close to defying the law.

The divide between the two worlds seemed unfordable. The women of America labored under the illusion that they were to be flirtatious until they landed a husband and paragons of virtue thereafter, when every self-respecting Frenchwoman subscribed to the opposite approach; what passed for gallantry in one country was commonly known as adultery in the other. (Lafayette's great friend the duc de Lauzun had the time of his life explaining to one colonial beauty that he was indeed married, but only a little bit so, hardly enough to bear mention.) The allegations were familiar: The American coffee was undrinkable, the food inedible, the people overly familiar and bizarrely peripatetic. The appetite of the American was matched only by his ignorance concerning the meal before him. He ate whenever he was so inclined. The questions were direct; the children spoiled; the women graceless and unshapely, if uncommonly clean. American women were aged by twenty and decrepit by thirty-five, whereas everyone knew a Frenchwoman was twenty-nine until she was sixty. It was difficult to distinguish the rich from the poor; and as for the very poor, there were none. How was the comte de Ségur to explain himself when he was asked by a Rhode Island villager what his father did for a living? Even a diplomatic Frenchman—grappling with the forces that had so shaped Benjamin Franklin—was left to long for a land where people thought about something other than utility. The mercantile spirit infected everything; the mania for commerce was inexplicable. America was a cultural wasteland, its people devoid of conversation.

The citizens of Boston labored very hard to be sociable. They turned out en masse to admire d'Estaing's fine fleet, his eleven ships of the line and his five frigates, as brilliant a sight as had graced Boston Harbor for some time. To their surprise those ships were manned by a strapping, ruddy-faced crew and a cadre of vigorous officers, hardly the pygmy barbers and dancing masters of legend. Still, an American knew what he did about Frenchmen, and when Cambridge's most successful businessman hosted a formal dinner for the foreigners he welcomed them with brimming tureens of their national dish. With his first spoonful, one of the guests fished up a full-grown, brilliantly green Massachusetts frog. "*Mon Dieu! Une grenouille!*" he exclaimed, holding up his catch and passing it, by a hind leg, to the gentleman at his side, who did the same, until the well-inspected creature reached d'Estaing. An examination of the bowls before them revealed that each officer had been similarly favored; the Frenchmen could not contain their mirth. "Why don't they eat them?" wondered their crestfallen host. He had dispatched emissaries to every swamp in Cambridge.

To innocent misunderstanding was added a reservoir of ill will, courtesy of Deane's early recruits, who by 1778 had sailed or were sailing home, bearing with them almost universal disaffection for France's new ally, which had afforded them little compensation or decoration. Congress reciprocated, one of its more eminent members roaring that he was tempted to drown Silas Deane for having sent over the French recruits. He preferred the most ignorant American officer. Incompatibility seemed a given. From Passy Franklin sent on to Versailles the best press he could from the late summer papers, along with his synopsis: "They contain particular accounts of the great harmony between count d'Estaing's fleet and the people of the country."

Even with ratified treaties in hand, Vergennes fretted that Congress would fail to honor its engagements. Both Adams and Franklin reassured him, but the foreign minister entreated Gérard to tend very carefully to France's new friend. Gérard could not have taken his instructions more literally. He set up shop sixty paces from the Pennsylvania State House, plainly visible from his front windows. And he filed exhaustive dispatches, at least 150 massive letters in sixteen months. As a consequence Vergennes knew far more of America's deliberations than did Franklin, and generally far earlier. From their end Franklin and Adams reminded Congress that while war had not officially been declared, it was considered to be under way; the French treaty was therefore in full force. In this the two commissioners rushed the season a little, a distortion clearly intended to hold Congress to its obligations in the face of a rumored defection. Even under Franklin's own roof ancient antipathy died hard. Sufficiently lubricated with his preferred Burgundies, Edward Bancroft, a virtuosic eater and drinker, went at his favorite whipping posts. Above all he excoriated the Bible and Christianity, but he reserved a special place in his diatribes for the royal family, the intrigues and idiocies of Marie Antoinette in particular. Ralph Izard too felt it his duty to expatiate on France's conduct, equivocal at best, more often offensive. Lee looked positively docile by comparison, although he strongly objected, on philosophical grounds, to demonstrations of gratitude toward America's benefactor. Anticipating the congressional request, Franklin and Adams applied to Vergennes for a portrait of Louis XVI. Given the magnitude of the alliance, "we conceive it would be highly pleasing to our constituents to have a portrait of His Majesty to be kept where Congress sits," they flattered Vergennes in November. Lee found the idea so distasteful he refused to sign the letter.

As with most marriages of convenience, there was something missing from this one. Few were able to effect Franklin's eminently limber aboutface. He who had in 1754 envisioned a confederation of American colonies to repel French attack threw himself wholeheartedly into an alliance of the opposite flavor. He then never looked back. When he stubbed his gouty toe against rock-solid prejudice he did not howl in pain but labored to chip away at, to ease around, the obdurate stuff. He had his work cut out for him. Even when he had ample opportunity to revise his opinion, the abbé Raynal, for instance, continued to insist on the inferiority of the North Americans, a stunted species hailing from a dark and degenerate country.* He expounded on the subject at dinner one day, in binational company at the Valentinois. Franklin prided himself on hewing to a cardinal rule of human relations—"Never contradict anybody"—but on this occasion indulged himself. He invited all at his table to rise, "to see on which side nature had degenerated." To a man, the five stunted specimens of the New World towered over the pillars of the Old, mere shrimps by comparison. ("In fact," elaborated the perennially diplomatic Carmichael, "there was not one American present who could not have tossed out of the windows any one or perhaps two of the rest of the company, if this effort depended merely on muscular force.") The abbé remained unconvinced by this meaningless display; it took more than one proof to demolish an age-old argument. "Great men," he assured the five-foot, ten-inch Franklin, "are everywhere the exception." Nor was the influential abbé of much help with the alliance. Esteemed by many as a political oracle, Raynal predicted that France would pollute America, to which she would impart a legacy of intrigue and dissipation. The kernel of the argument was perfectly sound; no one would subscribe to it more fervently than John Adams, who fretted daily over American susceptibility to the plague of Europe. It remained to be seen only which world would contaminate the other.

Vergennes resorted to his usual tactics to calm the waves stirred up by d'Estaing. The *Courrier de l'Europe* found itself banned as a punishment for printing that unhappy story. The foreign minister was less successful in staving off the news that roiled Paris. With France's entry into the war,

---

*Raynal followed in the tradition established by the great naturalist Georges Buffon, the first to espouse the view of an insalubrious, benighted New World. (He was also among the first to request that Franklin's work be translated into French.) According to Buffon, the most attractive men were those found between the fortieth and fiftieth degrees of latitude, a measure into which France fits snugly, as does America north of Philadelphia. By Buffon's logic, even a house pet transported from the Old to the New World would be smaller than its progenitors. It seems almost unnecessary to add that Buffon stood not quite five feet tall.

the Americans endured defeat after defeat. Far more than Franklin, Vergennes had staked his reputation on that partnership. He had already nearly destroyed his career with an earlier misalliance: While posted to Constantinople he had had the temerity to marry without having applied for the king's permission, permission he knew would not have been granted.* With this second unconventional match Vergennes opened himself to attack from his enemies at Versailles, who over the next years happily bludgeoned him with the senselessness of it. In 1778 he wrangled especially with the turmoil the American treaty had created in another alliance. The Spaniards howled on in indignation. What benefit could Vergennes possibly hope to extract from an American war? By every measure Spain preferred to mediate a peace between England and America than to fight a war against either power.

Even while Franklin met with the Madrid envoy charged with a mediation, he and Adams assured Congress that there was every likelihood that Spain would soon join France. Nothing could have been further from the truth. Spain continued to rant about French impetuosity as Vergennes continued to denounce Spanish irresolution. Over and over Vergennes reminded that court that she had nothing to fear from an independent neighbor on the far side of the ocean. There was no likelihood of American power or prosperity; it would be centuries before that republic assumed any place in world affairs. Even then its ascendancy was dubious; the north and south of the country were incompatible. "I vow to you that I have only the feeblest confidence in the energy of the United States," he assured his Madrid ambassador, a statement that may even have been true.† He certainly

---

*The future Madame de Vergennes and the mother of the comte's two sons was a widowed Franco-Greek commoner. The marriage left Vergennes isolated at court, where he was looked upon as a sort of exotic plant, a foreign minister who was himself rather foreign. He was all the more so for his unwavering devotion to his wife. There was some irony in the fact that the Frenchman most responsible for bringing America into existence was—by virtue of his work habits, his marital fidelity, his impatience for frivolity—himself a misfit at court. He preferred always his modest house in town to his fifty-eight rooms at the palace.

†Vergennes too came down on the side of Raynal. America was unlikely to develop any expansionist tendencies for years. And before that age came, "our vices will have been introduced among them by more intimate contact, to retard their growth and progress." Much later Prime Minister Clemenceau seized on that very pathology: "America is the only nation in history which has managed to pass directly from barbarism to degeneration without the customary interval of civilization."

subscribed to another he never shared with Franklin and Adams: It was essential that Canada remain always in English hands. Out of deference to Spain, Vergennes entertained that power's December proposal for a truce, an idea he discussed at length with Franklin. He chose not to include Lee and Deane in those negotiations, in the course of which he was able to extract a concession from the senior envoy: Franklin allowed that a truce would procure America the time to hone her constitution and perfect her government. The idea would be acceptable, so long as the Bourbon powers granted America their protection in the interim. In that discussion Vergennes was humoring France's ally. The futility of a truce was evident to him—and doubtless to Franklin, too—from the start. But there was no question that Spanish reluctance left France in a bind. Only together did the two powers outnumber the English on the high seas.

Vergennes felt his vulnerability all the more strongly as Gérard's reports from Philadelphia began to pile up in Versailles. The members of Congress, observed Gérard, owed their position to zeal rather than talent. There were more divisions among them than he could enumerate. "It pains me to have to report, Sire, that the birth of America is not attended by personal disinterestedness or financial propriety," sighed the Frenchman. Franklin heard similar reports in the fall from William Carmichael, who had been chosen to represent Maryland in Congress. The assembly was rent by dangerous divisions. It was inconceivable that so many talented men could accomplish so little. Carmichael submitted his verdict via Lafayette, whose Parisian return the Marylander advised Franklin to manage carefully. It was imperative he stress at Versailles how well loved was the major general in America. In a ceremonial bit of alliance bolstering, Franklin was authorized to commission a sword, to be presented to the marquis with America's gratitude. Carmichael made it clear that that order should be entrusted only to Lafayette's personal sword maker, whose address he enclosed.

Carmichael's instincts were sound. The ocean did as much for Lafayette's reputation as it did for Franklin's, absolving each man of the sins ascribed to him by his countrymen. The irony was that in their iconic exchange France should rally around Franklin, frontier philosopher and everyman, while the Americans should anoint as the face of republican liberty a man who—a simpleton at home—they took to be the consummate French aristocrat.

"There is certainly scarce any part of a man's life in which he appears more silly and ridiculous than when he makes his first onset in courtship," Franklin had remarked, as a precocious sixteen-year-old. With months of artless bluffing and calculated innocence, he had spared his country that embarrassment. He left no record of what he thought of late-life seductions, though he left ample evidence of their intensity; over the summer of 1777 he engaged in a little suitoring of his own. Ever practical, he ventured only a short distance down the rue Basse and into a household he knew to be rather misaligned. More quixotical, he fixed his sights on the rosy-cheeked, doe-eyed, infinitely accommodating Madame Brillon, at thirty-three the age of his daughter. Two decades earlier Anne-Louise Boivin d'Hardancourt had married the burly, white-haired Jacques Brillon de Jouy, a rough-edged country squire of her father's generation, more of a talker than a wit. For Franklin she elucidated the simple tribal laws behind that match. The fortune of the bride was deposited on one side of the scale, the fortune of the groom on the other. When the scale balanced, the parents shook hands. In such a way was a budding young girl joined to a partner who was already—Madame Brillon had trouble with the next few words—spoiled "by his debauchery."

Well before she acknowledged any marital mismatch, well before she discovered that her husband was amusing himself with the governess of their two teenage daughters, she inserted herself boldly into her new neighbor's path. Le Veillard introduced her early on to Franklin, but Madame Brillon's self-consciousness got the better of her; she remained hopelessly tongue-tied. She begged Le Veillard to help her to redeem herself, to which end she applied an acknowledged talent. A peerless harpsichordist, Madame Brillon composed chamber music and socialized with accomplished musicians. She owned one of the first pianos in Paris, sent to her by J. C. Bach. Could Le Veillard kindly obtain for her sheets of the music Dr. Franklin so enjoyed? Her rendition of a Scottish air—like her bold, Saratoga-inspired regimental march—may have charmed Franklin, but to his mind her personal graces eclipsed her talent. To John Adams she was simply "one of the most beautiful women in France." In life as in her orchestrations, she aimed for grace and simplicity, succeeding at least on the first count. She was an exemplary specimen of an exemplary breed, that perfectly calibrated confection of steel and silk which is a well-bred Frenchwoman.

Franklin succumbed immediately, first to the Brillon household, where he spent several hours every Wednesday and Saturday, soon enough to his golden-haired hostess herself. Of the intoxicating combination of three Brillon women and their keyboards, the tea, the chess, the sparkling conversation, he drank heartily; after a forty-nine-year marriage to the many-chinned and large-boned Debbie, nearly illiterate and entirely un-couth, the hours with Madame Brillon represented nothing less than a late-life conversion from beer to champagne. The fresh-faced Madame Brillon cited Molière, she lent Montaigne, she knew her Homer. Refine-ment was her basic instinct.

Franklin reveled in the twilight view from the Brillons' landscaped ter-race, which magnificently overhung the Seine; there was nothing more exquisite than the silvery light that hung there at the end of an afternoon. He designated that household his personal opera as he rarely attended the one in Paris. At that address he escaped to a sanctuary out of time; de-parting from habit, Franklin neglected to date his letters to Madame Bril-lon, an oversight he abhorred in others. And soon enough the original American self-corrector entrusted his friend with the task of reforming his soul, in the course of which he merrily ambushed her. There was one transgression for which he intended to atone not at all. "I mean the one that forbids us to covet our neighbor's wife. A commandment which (I confess) I have consistently violated (God forgive me) every time I have seen or thought of my kind confessor; and I fear that I shall never be ca-pable of repenting of this sin, should I even obtain full possession of my confessor's person," he explained, before coming to his senses: "But then, why should I be so scrupulous, when you have promised to absolve me even of future sins?" Would the most effective way to banish that tempta-tion not simply be to satisfy it? Madame Brillon held off the assault with a felicitous reference to Monsieur Brillon but found that her vanity got the better of her. Franklin's only real sin, his only unpardonable one, was to have shared his affections with the other Parisian ladies.

He offered no apologies, opting for a different tack. Their bond would be exclusive if Madame Brillon would be more obliging: "You renounce and exclude arbitrarily everything corporal from our amour, except such a merely civil embrace now and then as you would permit to a country cousin. What is there then remaining that I may not afford to others without a diminution of what belongs to you?" Over the next months he continued in his efforts to nudge, ease, reason, and wrestle the relationship to another plane. As devoted to Franklin as she was neurasthenic—a current of air could send her sailing over the edge and to her bed, where she spent long intervals—the tremulous Madame Brillon held her ground. Having concluded a treaty with her nation, Franklin suggested an accord with his neighbor. He might well have the weaker hand, but he was also the wiser party. And indeed his proposed articles were entirely self-serving, binding Franklin to love no woman other than Madame Brillon while stipulating that in her company he "shall do anything he pleases." He leaned heavily on that condition, as he did on his remaining loyal so long as Madame Brillon remained agreeable. At the same time he conceded that infidelity was unlikely, as "I despair of ever finding any other woman I could love with equal tenderness."

His exacting terms gave way to a little spat about who loved whom more. Already Franklin had adopted the regular refrain of "I love you furiously, indeed too much." He stood ready to grant her anything in the world. She continued to withhold favors. Every exchange returned to the same issue. At the end of one Wednesday afternoon Franklin took his leave at seven-thirty, a half hour earlier than was his custom, while Madame Brillon was showing some ladies around her gardens. They had bored her to tears, and she was as furious with them for having detained her as with her admirer for having escaped. He pleaded utter fatigue, having risen at four in the morning, made a sweltering midday trip into Paris, and attended to a full schedule of business. Having nodded off on one of her garden benches in mid-conversation, he felt it only decent to retire. He dragged himself home, to crawl into bed before eight. In formulating his apology he dwelled not on his engagements but on another excuse: "Half an hour spent with an old man who is not allowed to put it to its best use is a mighty small matter, and you should not get angry over small matters." He would attempt to overstay his welcome later in the week, when he would take as his cue to leave Madame Brillon's refusal of a kiss.

The siege continued through the summer of 1778, a scorcher that drained the rivers of France, withered the crops, and seared the livestock. Paris was three months without rain and miserable in the heat; the parched visitor to the city found himself enveloped in a cloud of dust.* Franklin escaped the sweltering city one August day with Madame Brillon for a visit to the Moulin-Joli, an enchanted island in the middle of the Seine. The property of a financier and amateur of the arts, Claude-Henri Watelet, the Moulin-Joli consisted of a brilliantly perfumed and tamed landscape, to which one crossed on a bridge of flowers. Franklin succumbed there to an uncharacteristic bout of melancholy; characteristically, he both set it to paper and harnessed it to a cause. The Watelets shared their luscious paradise with a breed of tiny mayflies known as ephemerae, fated to hatch, mature, mate, and die within a matter of hours. In the shade of a hot afternoon, the tinkle of French conversation in the distance, the seventy-two-year-old envoy settled down to observe the insects at closer range, and—well attuned to their evanescence—to eavesdrop on their conversation. He preserved his thoughts in a shimmering letter to Madame Brillon, polished over the following weeks, the first of the airy French riffs that were to be known as his bagatelles.

Into this one he threaded his frustrations and disillusionments. One elderly fly, Franklin professed, had separated himself from the company of his peers. Poignantly that venerable insect grappled with the good fortune that had granted him a remarkable 420 minutes of life. Generations had come and gone, but 7 or 8 minutes remained still to him. As he savored his last dewdrops he mused that all his political and philosophical struggles had been in vain. He could take pleasure neither in his modest accomplishments nor in the posthumous fame that friends assured him would one day be his. "To me, after all my eager pursuits, no solid pleasures now remain but the reflection of a long life spent in meaning well, the sensible conversation of a few good lady-ephemeres, and now and then a kind smile, and a tune from the ever-amiable *Brillante*," concludes Franklin's entomological alter ego, for whom even resignation doubles as seduction. In that valedictory spirit Franklin offered as well a new twist on an old theme. The allegory was a variation on one he had read fifty years earlier,

*For that turn of affairs Franklin was blamed, in an accusation that spoke to the very different powers with which he was credited by the two nations. As his colleagues submitted their regular indictments to Congress, the farmers of France damned Franklin for the catastrophic drought. Marie Antoinette was pregnant; in the popular imagination Franklin had "electrified the weather to accommodate the Queen, whom he promised no more storms until her delivery."

which endorsed virtue as the recipe for immortality. For virtue, Franklin now substituted pleasure.

Madame Brillon received his offering at her mother's country estate in western France, to which she coaxed Franklin early in September. Over two fall weekends the friends grappled toward a definition of their relationship, discussed at length on the accommodating meadows of Normandy. Madame Brillon's solution was simple. She had lost her father as a young girl. Franklin was abroad without his daughter. She proposed a mutual adoption, from which Franklin was to emerge as "Mon cher Papa."* Good-naturedly Franklin accepted the proposal, although not without conceding that he would need to modify his passions accordingly. Theirs was in any event to be an unorthodox father-daughter relationship. Madame Brillon's soul called out for Franklin. She loved him more with each passing day, more than anyone had or would love him. She preferred for him to read of her devotion in her eyes rather than in her letters. Franklin prided himself on the comb his daughter Sally had given him twenty years earlier; Madame Brillon begged him to accept her own, for the next twenty years. After his second visit she refrained from tidying his rooms, which bore his traces. In his absence the Normandy lawns faded, the streams flowed sluggishly. Each Wednesday and Saturday without him was a torment. Back in Passy, Franklin could not pass her empty house without regret. All was a wasteland without her. Nor did the new relationship spell an end to all indulgence. "Do you know, my dear Papa, that people have criticized my sweet habit of sitting on your lap, and your habit of soliciting from me what I always refuse?" she inquired. Franklin apologized for any trouble he had caused her, an apology she batted away. She had no misgivings. On the other hand, propriety could not be ignored. He was by no means to conclude that she loved him less if she sat on his knee less often.

Madame Brillon had no monopoly on the emission of conflicting signals. Even while Franklin pursued her, he made it clear that he was probably not much longer for the French world. Quietly—so quietly that his colleagues had no hint of it—he had requested new instructions of Congress. As the chestnuts ripened in Passy he began to anticipate a return. He played that eventuality for all it was worth. "As one day I will have to

---

*In her half-literate letters, Debbie Franklin had by contrast addressed her husband as "My dear child."

go back to America, without hope of seeing you ever again, I have occasionally thought that it would be wise to wean myself from you by degrees, to see you first once a week, then once every two, then once a month, etc., so as to diminish my immoderate desire to be in your enchanting company," Franklin wrote his French daughter. His trial run ended in defeat: "I find that absence, instead of diminishing, only augments this desire." There being no other remedy for his disease, he would be over that evening. At the same time he began to order type for the press he was setting up at the Valentinois, a sure sign that he was settling in.

~~~

For many months the commissioners had kept a close eye on the Netherlands; a republic with a Protestant population and a free press seemed a natural partner for a fledgling democracy. In the fall of 1778 the task of making a formal overture fell to Franklin. He found the prospect distasteful. Persistent though his campaign on the rue Basse might be, he recognized indecency when he saw it. "I think that a young state like a young virgin should modestly stay at home, and wait the application of suitors for an alliance with her; and not run about offering her amity to all the world, and hazarding their refusal," he explained. He resisted all pressure to submit that appeal, ostensibly as doing so before America had been formally recognized by the Netherlands amounted to an exercise in futility.* As his colleagues urged him to make the Holland trip he hit on a flawless strategy to subvert it. On October 20 he consulted Vergennes. Personally he believed such an expedition premature and unwise. But of course Vergennes knew best. "If you would be so good as to offer your advice, I will adapt my conduct accordingly," Franklin wrote disingenuously. He had his reprieve by return mail. Vergennes discouraged him from leaving, a pardon at his end as well; in Franklin's absence the foreign minister would be left to do business with his colleagues. For a second time Franklin deferred to French logic over American, a tactic guaranteed to inflame his critics.

---

*He had taken a very different tack earlier in the year, when it had seemed as if Deane might attempt the Amsterdam errand. At that time Franklin thought the ground ripe and the application foolproof.

And indeed as the heat abated, Izard revived his anti-Franklin campaign. He began as well to cast his poisonous net further. Was he the only one who noticed that France was being awfully stingy? For that too he faulted Franklin. In Izard's opinion, America's great and good ally would have been more generous "had things been properly conducted by those who ought to have thought less of themselves and more of the public." In his crusade Izard clashed even with Adams who—bent on keeping the peace—reminded him that he was, in Paris, trespassing on the commissions of others. The Tuscan envoy who was never to see Tuscany riled Vergennes too, applying to France to guarantee any loan Izard might procure in Italy. Vergennes rejected the application out of hand, which did not prevent Izard from resubmitting it, or Vergennes from rejecting it, again and again.

Some clue as to how Franklin weathered the attacks can be read in the correspondence with Madame Brillon, with whom he shared his tribulations, and who grappled with a diplomatic crisis of her own. In the spring she discovered her husband's infidelity; he was smitten with a girl whom Madame Brillon had taken in when the girl's parents had disowned her. In her moment of need Madame Brillon rushed a note to Franklin. Could he devote an hour to her behind closed doors? Indeed he could and did, twice that week, putting aside various pieces of business to consider the clutch of incriminating letters and to console his dear friend in her distress. (The distress was compounded by Chaumont's suggestion that the treacherous governess find employment with Franklin, to ease tensions in the Brillon household.) Gently Franklin reminded his fair neighbor that it is not in our power to reform the personalities of those around us. While it paid to be sensitive to one's own faults, it was fruitless to be afflicted by those of others. He devoted a great deal of effort to a follow-up letter, in which he reiterated Poor Richard's counsel of thirty years earlier: "Doing an injury puts you below your enemy; revenging one makes you but even with him; forgiving it sets you above him."* Madame Brillon tearily swore to do her best to follow Franklin's advice. She was without any

---

*It is notable that Franklin found Monsieur Brillon's crime to consist in having allowed himself to be led astray by "the lure of others." Brillon had a keen eye for the female form, in all its permutations.

confidence in her strength to adhere to it, however. She sank into a puddle of despair, in which she spent several months. She was strong only in Franklin's presence.

He was less easily daunted. "I think with you that there are many hardships in life. But it seems to me that there are many more pleasures," he reminded his friend, at a time when much conspired to undermine his equanimity. To his trials were added those created by the arrival in Paris of a man whom Lenoir's agents described admiringly as "an affluent pillar of the community, a vigorous, lively, and gallant man," but who was to cause Franklin a headache every time he set foot on land. John Paul Jones, the debonair, Scottish-born sea captain, turned up in Paris at the end of July, to spend the next weeks petitioning for a ship. He would assume command of anything that would sail. He found inactivity lethal; he had no desire to be "thought a knight of the windmill." The thirty-one-year-old was his own best advocate; Franklin succumbed quickly to what he could describe only as "the strange magnetism of his presence." Behind the scenes Franklin attempted to arrange a cruise with Sartine, but again found himself funneling American ardor into sclerotic veins. And as before his efforts were sabotaged by the zeal of his countrymen. Gustavus Conyngham precipitated another diplomatic crisis at the end of September, when he seized a Swedish ship loaded with Spanish cargo. Spain's indignation came to Franklin via Grand, to whom Franklin submitted his response. The banker both translated the apology and ladled into it a second helping of humility.

Early October found Franklin in a meditative mood, setting his hand to the commission's accounts as well as to an appraisal of his health. Madame Brillon and the steamy summer had proved tonics; his psoriasis had abated. He was nearly free of boils. He resolved to drink in moderation, a resolution to which he held whenever it was convenient to do so. It was no less on account of Adams that Franklin was left to feel as if he had "as much vigor and activity as can be expected at my age." Finally he had a colleague with whom he might discuss both the commission's business and its quotidian demands in a sane and orderly way; the Massachusetts lawyer was equally at ease in ancient history and modern bookkeeping. He was less comfortable at Passy. Franklin and Lee were indeed men of opposite temperaments—"The one may be too easy and good natured upon some occasions, the other too rigid and severe upon some occasions.

The one may perhaps overlook an instance of roguery, from inadvertence and too much confidence. The other may mistake an instance of integrity for its opposite"—but they were both of them honest patriots. Adams vowed to absorb the strains and to quarrel with no one. He could not help but stumble over the resulting inefficiency, however. It drove him to distraction. He found it difficult to get Franklin's attention, more difficult yet to extract a decision. Typically Franklin refused to sign a dispatch until Lee had signed it first. There was no central place for the commission's papers nor anyone to keep them in order, which meant that with each man pulling what he needed at any given time business was continually stalled. It also left Adams, to whose rooms the papers migrated, to assume the role of glorified clerk.

On October 10 Adams proposed that the three envoys move in together. Lee contended that the commission should properly establish itself in Paris, an idea Franklin rejected. Adams saw no need even to submit to his senior colleague Lee's subsequent proposal that a room and a regular meeting time be set at Lee's address, an effort Adams knew would be futile. He judged it senseless as well: "It can not be expected that two should go to one when it is as easy again for one to go to two; not to mention Dr. Franklin's age, his rank in the country, or his character in the world; nor that nine-tenths of the public letters are constantly brought to this house, and will ever be carried where Dr. Franklin is." The logical solution would be for Lee to move to the Valentinois, where Adams kindly offered up his rooms. He would decamp to the library and the adjoining chamber. Not only would the arrangement save America untold sums, provide a thousand opportunities for discussion, and greatly accelerate business, it would do wonders for their tarnished reputation. A room could be set aside for business, and regular hours set. Until Congress sent one, Temple could be promoted from Franklin's personal aide to commission secretary. The appointment would be provisional: "But in the meantime young Franklin writes very well, keeps papers in good order, and can be of more help than he currently is," submitted Adams, surely not unaware that the Lees and Izard already resented Temple for angling for the job. "I would so like to cultivate a harmony," declared the newest envoy, proposing a regular meeting at nine in the morning and anticipating by a matter of days Congress's injunction to its envoys to behave.

Lee resisted Adams on every count. In addition to all else, the Virginian who condemned Franklin's dilatoriness found it inconceivable that he might dress, breakfast, and attend to both his family and his correspondence by nine. "I find 11 o'clock the soonest I can engage for," Lee demurred. He pointed as well to the impropriety of lodging gratis under the roof of a private individual, especially one he suspected of meddling with his mail. Here diplomacy entirely failed Adams. He made more of an effort than Franklin, but despite his best efforts the miscommunications, misapprehensions, and misrepresentations piled up. In their requests for aid, at Versailles and elsewhere, the commissioners worked at cross-purposes. Arthur Lee attempted various end runs around Franklin. A scheduling change failed to reach Lee in time, which left him waiting for hours at Versailles on a day when his colleagues had postponed their appointment. The state of Virginia commissioned an independent representative to procure arms in France, entrusting him to the Lees. As the brothers were unavailable, Franklin stepped in, locating three willing merchants. All three offers evaporated once Lee assumed control of the transaction, leaving Franklin to apologize for the mess. Nor did Franklin and Adams act always in perfect concert. The two disagreed as to how to handle the returning David Hartley, the peace-promoting British member of Parliament. Adams felt his trip should have been forbidden; there had been enough of private individuals. Franklin reminded his colleague that it was not in their power to forbid anyone's trip to Paris. Might it not make more sense simply to decline any private conversations with Hartley?

Adams was undone by these tensions, over which he "sighed and mourned and wept," and which, with all the best intentions in the world, he could not defuse. Franklin soldiered on quietly. He made no further complaint to Congress. The first hint that relief was in sight came late in November, when rumors reached him that he had been named sole American commissioner. It would be some time before official word arrived, unleashing a new wave of acrimony. In the short term he dispatched a letter to Polly Hewson, the daughter of his beloved London landlady, with whom he longed for a reunion. It seemed he would be staying in France. Would she bring her mother to Passy, to run his house? "I should be happy in her and your company," he added, unnecessarily. He had spent some of the merriest years of his life in the Stevenson household, where he had written the closest predecessor to a bagatelle, in the form of a mock household gazette. That the Stevensons perfectly understood the demands of their eccentric lodger was clear from his next letter. Could Margaret Stevenson please send to Paris "the copper pot lined with silver to roast fowls in" that he had left in London? He would be grateful too for his fossilized mastodon teeth, which would stupefy some of his Parisian friends.*

As the French posting took on an air of permanence, Franklin tended as well to a piece of unfinished business at a different address. Madame Brillon had finally consented to become his wife—in paradise. Franklin gave a little thought to the arrangements. By his calculation, forty years would elapse before his friend joined him in the next world. He wanted her word of honor that she would neither forget him nor renew her vows with Monsieur Brillon in the meantime. An eternity of mere kisses and bi-weekly visits was unthinkable. Still under fire for her sweet habit of perching on his lap ("The tongues do wag in this rotten country," sighed Madame Brillon), she knew her man. She was his in paradise on one condition. He was not to spend the wait ogling the virgins. "I want a faithful husband when I take one for eternity," she warned, having already assured her fiancé that, at their future address, all music would consist of Scottish airs, all games would be chess, all Englishmen righteous, all menus composed of Franklin's favorite roast apples, and that everyone would speak the same language.

⤝⤞

It was on the shoals of language that another partnership began to founder. Born twelve miles from each other, hard-driving, book-loving, middle-class sons of Massachusetts, staunch patriots both, John Adams and Benjamin Franklin had recourse to two very different vocabularies in France. That idiomatic divide was on display at the Valentinois on December 4, when the commissioners met to discuss their next appeal to Vergennes. Without Versailles's help America could not meet the interest expense on her loans. Adams was eager to press for a more robust naval commitment, which Franklin was loath to do; he was all too well aware that the French navy had suffered its share of embarrassments, d'Estaing chief among them. Adams had no qualms about open French wounds. By

---

*Relocating to Paris struck the Stevenson women as an "airy scheme." Were there no other, the war presented obstacle enough.

the end of 1778 the British had mobilized their entire navy. Surely, he insisted, France could bear a reminder that it was in her best interest to support the United States? And surely Franklin did not intend to ask her to do so purely "as a *matter of mere grace?*" Adams was altogether unimpressed by America's ally, which "did not treat us with any confidence, nor give us any effectual assistance."

Franklin violently disagreed. He would entertain no such reproof. France had acted impeccably, opening her coffers and providing a fleet. That fleet, Adams countered, speaking equally for Lee, had been useless, the subsidies pitiful. If the French had meant for d'Estaing to be effective, they would not have wasted six weeks readying his ships in Toulon. A fleet from Brest, on France's west coast, could have reached America in that time.* Again Franklin objected. Toulon had been chosen expressly to conceal d'Estaing's destination. At any other port the British would have guessed his designs and intercepted him immediately. Lee protested that the British had not been fooled for a minute. It was time to remind Versailles that immediate aid to America was the sound basis of their foreign policy. Franklin flinched from his colleagues' highhandedness, insisting they postpone their decision until he could impress upon them the wisdom of a more graceful approach. He was adamant that they should ask a favor first. Ultimatums could wait until later. The delicacy was admirable, but his stubbornness also seriously delayed the application. Not until January did a letter finally go to Vergennes, so much worked over that it was not even dated. Adams prevailed; the document made a succinct case for a powerful fleet to be sent to America. Vergennes ignored it.

From that December 4 discussion Adams and Franklin went their separate ways, never again to converge. Two evenings earlier an immense aurora borealis had thrilled Paris. In a dazzling display, flashes of red and yellow had streaked across the sky, which for three hours exploded from every direction with vibrant color. Probably it was no accident that— days after having heard hints of his extended posting—Franklin seized the opportunity to attempt his first scientific treatise in French. Customar-

---

*John Paul Jones agreed. In his opinion, detaching the squadron from Toulon had cost France "an excellent chance to establish American independence and strike a blow that would have brought Great Britain to her knees."

ily the aurora borealis was thought to rise from the earth; Franklin sat down to make a rather fanciful case for its emanating from a buildup of electricity in polar regions.* He drafted his argument in English, which he rendered into very literal French. The abbé de la Roche, a learned ex-Benedictine, then corrected and refined the piece, after which Le Roy vetted the pages as well; this was rather like having both Strunk and White on the job. Franklin assigned his editors a substantial task; as Madame Brillon put it, "If your French is far from pure, at least it is very clear!" And crystal clear it was when Franklin dined at Vergennes's home that week, in the company of a celebrated Croatian mathematician and the Tuscan chargé d'affaires. Franklin made no attempt to buttonhole the French statesman in his lucid, impure tongue. Instead he held forth authoritatively on d'Estaing. Rumors that the French admiral was blockaded in Boston were unfounded. He was on the high sea, asserted Franklin, his speech a shining tribute to benevolent ignorance. (And one that happened accidentally to be accurate.)

While Franklin conjured with the idioms of science and diplomacy, Adams retreated to his rooms to articulate two frustrations that now collided, with a burst of frenzied energy. He had been of various minds about France since his arrival. Much as he marveled over the opulence and the pleasures of that kingdom, he did not think it seemly to succumb to them. Of the conviction that elegance and virtue are natural-born enemies, he discovered that he was by no means a natural-born Frenchman. He danced badly; he was incapable of flattering; he did not play games; he had eyes only for his wife. Even when Franklin was good enough to leave him the carriage, Adams found his trips to the opera less nourishing than he had hoped: "I always wish, in such an amusement, to learn something." The eye and the ear might well be indulged, but there was little in those productions that engaged the intellect. A month into his stay he found himself debilitated by the profusion of marble and silk and velvet and alabaster. France was too rich for his blood. Of a concert of religious music he concluded, "There was too much sound for me." It remained to be seen who was the authentic puritan: Franklin, who seemed never to

---

*Even for the time the argument was far-fetched. Franklin was unfazed, remarking of the piece: "If it should occasion further enquiry, and so produce a better hypothesis, it will not be wholly useless." Generally he had no particular investment in being right.

notice those splendors, or Adams, ur-wowser, who railed against them and who bragged—there is also a foppery of morals, warned Franklin—that no one could live as cheaply as he.

In France Adams came to play the Poor Richard of the pair. It was he who rose at five to tend to the relentless demands of the commission; he who wrestled with the paperwork; he who devoted every spare moment to his conquest of the French language.* Dining out six nights a week, Franklin rose at a more civilized hour and breakfasted at eight. After his four cups of light tea he was immediately overwhelmed by callers; he tackled business in fits and starts. Adams was the journeyman diplomat. In France that industry translated into neither applause nor results; this was a country in which a Bostonian's reputation was not enhanced by an overly great devotion to discipline. (Edith Wharton would discover as much a century later, when a visiting duchess sniffed, "It's too orderly at her house.") And Adams applied his prodigious energies as intensively to his own self-improvement as to the American mission. His pursuit of an education appears to have served as his conversational gambit in Paris, where he was, as ever, an omnivorous reader. Dining with Franklin one lovely afternoon at the spectacular country estate of a French minister, Adams inquired after the purest writers of French. He left with a list, thereby establishing another American tradition. The following day he quizzed a tablemate as to who was the best historian of France. He imposed next on the newly arrived Valentinois clerk for the authors of the best French prosody. From that well-spoken young man he extracted as well the titles of the best Italian and German dictionaries. None of this fantastic intelligence gathering boosted Adams's stock. If the Paris posting failed at times to bring out the best in Franklin, what it brought out in earnest Adams was a mile-wide streak of pedantry.

In no arena was the contrast between the two men on better view than in their approach to the French language. On that front Franklin was as realistic and as flexible as on any. He would acknowledge that a man plunging into a language not his own instantly sacrifices half his intelligence; where that left him in the land of badinage and rodomontade is

---

*Sent to represent America in Paris in 1788, Gouverneur Morris said it all when—in a different context—he noted that France was "oppressive to industry but favorable to genius."

only too easy to imagine. How good was his French? He read it perfectly and spoke it poorly. On his arrival he stumbled badly in conversation. At the same time he had no trouble making himself understood, save when he preferred not to be. His pronunciation left a great deal to be desired. Double-barreled French names always flew past him. A man of few words, he was further disabled by Parisian volubility. "If only you Frenchmen would only talk no more than four at a time, I might understand you, and would not leave an interesting party without knowing what you were talking about," he grumbled. He observed that the bifocals he invented in Passy improved not only his vision but his aural comprehension. On the page he veered from the clumsy to the chimerical. His was the brand of freestyle French permitted only to those of exceptional talent or beauty who, attempting to clamp their jaws around the French language, are understood—regardless of the results and by virtue of their very audible disregard for their inhibitions—to be acknowledging with every mutilated syllable the superiority of France.*

But Franklin was adverse neither to making mistakes nor to asking for help. "For 60 years now, masculine and feminine things—and I am not talking about modes and tenses—have been giving me a lot of trouble. I used to hope that at the age of 80 I would be free of all that. But here I am, four times 19, which is mighty close to 80, and those French feminines are still bothering me," he carped to Madame Brillon, an explanation worth a lifetime exemption from Gallic grammarians. He got only encouragement for his unorthodox diction. His neologizing, his awkwardness, insisted his friends, merely improved the language. He was equally deft in his vocabulary. And so he forged on; for the first time in his life, he went to the right schools. Grand and Chaumont routinely assisted with official communications. Within a relatively short period Franklin could rely on Temple to compose a near-perfect French letter. Much of the time a young French clerk was also at hand. Le Veillard

---

*The retrospective report card offered up by one tough twentieth-century grader is nothing to brag about. Franklin took home a hard-earned A− in oral comprehension, a B− in spoken French, and a downright F for his written skills. That failing grade came with the caveat that Franklin's error-riddled compositions were however utterly clear. In a nutshell, that was also why they were not French.

pitched in for formulaic niceties. At the end of December 1778, Madame Brillon returned to him a previous letter, to which she had taken a red pencil at his request. A willing pupil, Franklin marked it "Exercise in French No. 5 Letter to Mme. B. transcribed and corrected by her" and copied out a list of his most egregious mistakes. This was Franklinian efficiency: grammar lesson as billet-doux.

A garrulous man, a born orator, and a brilliant polemicist, John Adams came up against a brick wall known as the French language. Where Franklin sidled around that structure, defying genders (the creator of *Le Bonhomme Richard* was perfectly capable of prefacing the masculine *homme* with the feminine *bonne*), tripping over prepositions, merrily sending pronouns and antecedents their separate ways, ducking under the subjunctive, Adams hurled himself against it. He had already complained of the curse of the voluble. "They talk very loud, very fast, and all together," he had observed in 1774, of New Yorkers. And he had earlier confessed to being mortified by his own ineptitude in French: "I find I can neither express my own thoughts in it nor understand others." By 1776, when an alliance with France topped his list of American priorities, he had further cause to regret his deficiency. He begged Abigail to see to it that their children master the lingua franca of the civilized world. For all his inadequacy there was, however, no such thing as a speechless John Adams. The reticences of a Franklin or a Jefferson grated on his ear. So taken was he by oratorical flourishes that Adams found himself spellbound before the abbé Raynal, who struck him—even at a time when Adams could not quite tease a glimmer of meaning from a French conversation—as the most eloquent man in France. That was one word for it. More commonly, Raynal was considered an old windbag. His listeners had been known to fake objects falling from the ceiling so as to escape his bombast.

While talk was Adams's lifeblood, he attended a very different language school from Franklin's. Alone in his room he waged a methodical assault on French grammar, with the result that he had no one to talk to. (He admitted later that he had made an egregious mistake.) And while he devoted every available hour to his French lessons, his independent study bore slow fruit. It would be a year before he could converse with a shopkeeper, or uphold his end of a conversation with a very patient partner.* Having buried himself in Molière en route to France, Adams continued in his dedication to the written word. Franklin, the man of the press, devoted himself to the spoken word. Asked whether he thought a mistress or the theater the better school of language, Adams cast his vote for the latter.

The divide disguised a more essential truth. One man was trying very hard, while the other did not appear to be trying at all. Eight days after his arrival in Paris, Adams registered his disillusionment at the state of Franklin's French, which he had assumed was fluent.† He was startled to note that his colleague's grammar was inexact, even more surprised to hear Franklin confess, when queried, that he paid no attention to the stuff. That invited some sleuthing on Adams's part: "His pronunciation too, upon which the French gentlemen and ladies compliment him, and which he seems to think is pretty well, I am sure is very far from being exact." It is difficult to read in that line which was the greatest offense: Franklin's inadequacy; the high marks French society bestowed on this teacher's pet; or his seeming obliviousness to the preferential treatment. In settling the matter Adams could not always procure the satisfaction he came increasingly to crave. He was delighted to hear their landlord contradicted over a 1779 dinner table, when Chaumont asserted that Franklin spoke excellent French. He did nothing of the sort, protested a French diplomat. Days later that diplomat further endeared himself by elaborating: "You speak slowly and with difficulty, like a man who searches for his words; but you don't sin against pronunciation. You pronounce well. You do so far better than Mr. Franklin. He is painful to listen to." The triumph was short-lived. The envoy's straight-shooting secretary reminded Adams, as

---

*Adams gets full credit for the headlong assault on the French language. Another Founding Father cringed at the very idea of a Paris appearance, given his ignorance of the tongue: "Remember my good friend," he enjoined Lafayette, "that I am unacquainted with your language, that I am too far advanced in years to acquire a knowledge of it, and that to converse through the medium of an interpreter upon common occasions, especially with the *ladies*, must appear so extremely awkward, insipid, and uncouth, that I can scarce bear it in idea." That craven soul was George Washington, half Franklin's age when he begged off.

†The deficiencies served their purpose. "Women, especially, flocked to see him, to speak to him for hours on end, without realizing that he did not understand much of what they said, because of his scant knowledge of our language," laughed Le Roy.

Adams often needed to be reminded, of the uses of flattery. The secretary then leveled with the American. Both Adams and Franklin spoke French badly.

It was one thing for Adams to admit, as he did often over the first months, that the French language was unintelligible to him, another altogether to read in the papers that he had no French. He was mortified by the figure he cut, especially rankled by his portrait in a London paper: "They make fine work of me—fanatic, bigot, perfect cypher, not one word of the language, awkward figure, uncouth dress, no address, no character, cunning hardheaded attorney." He did not note that that derision issued from the Loyalist press, which was far more scathing when it came to Franklin. To Adams the most irritating charge was that he was "disgusted with the Parisians." Of all the accusations that one may have been closest to the truth, although "disgust" was less the word than "aggravated." France was not proving the vigorous, munificent ally on which he had counted. Over the fall he formulated a theory about that restraint: The Americans' intramural squabbles were to blame. The commissioners had not been assertive enough. Their timidity compounded French misgivings.

While at one end of the Valentinois Franklin labored to convert his thoughts into the language of the realm, at the other Adams inveighed against American complaisance toward her new ally. The frustration had been building; he had just permitted himself a tirade against the effects of fame. Was it possible to succeed in public life with any degree of modesty? Must a man have his statue and picture made, and encourage the mob to gape at him, in order to succeed?, he huffed, without naming names. He did not need to; Franklin's shadow was inescapable. Adams could not have picked up a newspaper that week without reading of his illustrious colleague, hailed as "the founder of the New World," at a highly dramatic, late-night Masonic tribute to Voltaire. Franklin turned up as well—along with police chief Lenoir and a host of academicians and ministers—for the much-publicized banquet of the pharmacologist Antoine Parmentier. Every course, from soup to dessert, was potato-based, the toasts made with a potato vodka. Franklin's role in the pantheon was reconfirmed in November by a masterful Fragonard allegory, in which he appeared as a Michelangelo-inflected Zeus. Chief of the gods, Franklin directs the punishment of tyranny and avarice from his celestial throne,

America seated at his feet, the genius of France sheltering him from above. While Adams well appreciated the European value of that popularity, by early December the inflated reputation began to gnaw at him. The dilatoriness, the complaisance, the dabbling in shades of gray took their toll. Adams was of the sorry school that expected meetings to yield decisions, decisions to yield actions, and actions to yield results. He had done his best to adapt to their mismatched pace; he had tread carefully among his colleagues. What evidently put him over the edge was the rumor that Franklin would be staying on in Paris. He concluded that that could only be to the detriment of their country.

On December 7 he unburdened himself, to his cousin Samuel Adams, the fiercest of New England patriots. John Adams was constitutionally unable to mince words; while his cousin was a political ally of the Lees, Adams would concede only that Arthur Lee was a man of integrity. It was also true that "he cannot easily at all times any more than your humble servant govern his temper, and he has some notions of elegance, rank and dignity that may be carried rather too far." Lee was, and had been, a difficult colleague. On the other hand Franklin had been accommodating to a fault. It would come as no surprise to Samuel Adams that Franklin "loves his ease, hates to offend, and seldom gives any opinion until obliged to do it." He was as determined a man as any, "yet it is his constant policy never to say yes or no decidedly but when he cannot avoid it." (Adams was unaware that he had not only delineated a silence-loving school of diplomacy but at the same time underlined Franklin's suitability for the French court. It was said of Vergennes that his only political principle was his resolution never to give a decisive answer.) Franklin was overrun by hordes of callers and a correspondence that flowed from every corner of the globe, little of which pertained to American business. Nor was that all: "There is another thing which I am obliged to mention. There are so many private families, ladies and gentlemen that he visits so often, and they are so fond of him that he cannot well avoid it, and so much intercourse with academicians, that all these things together keep his mind in such a constant state of dissipation, that if he is left alone here, the public business will suffer in a degree beyond description, provided our affairs are continued upon the present footing." Both America and France were likely to regret the reappointment of this indolent, acquiescent man. Adams's solution was simple. Were Franklin to be left alone in Paris, he should be provided with a secretary but relieved of all naval, mercantile, and fiscal responsibilities.

Nothing would have made his colleague happier. By default Franklin had become overseas secretary of the Treasury and chief purchasing agent. He so resisted naval affairs that he appears not to have realized for some time that they fell in his department. The continued snags with privateers and prizes exhausted him. No man would be comfortable with John Paul Jones breathing down his neck for weeks on end. The greater irony in Adams's outburst—aside from the fact that he continued to collaborate, live, and dine, on what appear to have been easy terms, with the man whose indolence, dissipation, and neglect he announced to America—was that in his denunciation he spared Silas Deane. The original commissioner might well have been ambitious and opportunistic, but as far as Adams could ascertain he had never acted improperly.

Adams knew nothing of the fact that there was equal discomfort in Vergennes's office over the American match. Beaumarchais continued to vent his spleen about the ungrateful Americans, with whom he refused to have any future dealings as long as his nemesis was in place, "the bilious Arthur Lee, with his yellow skin, green eyes, yellow teeth, and hair always in disorder." Chaumont too reminded Vergennes of his American woes. He had sheltered that country's ministers from the ambushes that awaited them in Paris. He had stopped at nothing in the name of their far-off crusade: "I fete everyone who is an American. I run continually after the ministers to inform them of what it is important they should know. I fend off all emissaries from the court of London. I have rejected all idea of doing business with Congress directly or indirectly, in order not to be taxed with having personal interests." His allegiance had yielded but one result: He was in financial straits. And Madrid showed no more inclination to succumb to an American passion than she had at the beginning of the year. Her stubbornness weighed increasingly on Vergennes, who found he could not even motivate his own privateers. Without the Spanish navy, they felt the sea was British. Spain's assistance was if anything more vital than it had been in March; Vergennes had banked on a quick and decisive victory, which d'Estaing had not delivered. The foreign minister was clear about his doubts; in mid-December he suppressed the production of a play called "La Fête Bostonienne," scheduled for 1779. He prohibited the performance on the grounds that the production treated too delicate a subject.*

Even Franklin sounded a rare note of disenchantment. A year had passed since the heady news of Saratoga, and America remained at England's mercy. Twelve months earlier he would have bet his entire fortune on there being not a single American city in British hands. He was alarmed to see how very wrong he was. Despite his country's hard-won acquisition of "a great faithful and beloved friend and ally," the British held New York, the Carolinas, and Georgia. Their fleet controlled the coast. The residents of the Valentinois were left alone with their disappointment at Christmas, when the temperature plummeted and a snowstorm ferocious even by Massachusetts standards blew in. The roads were impassable, the mails at a standstill. Adams felt he had been posted to Greenland. The howling winds were to be succeeded soon enough by a tempest from the west, one that would wrench the new republic apart. With recourse to nearly the same adjectives with which Adams denounced Franklin, George Washington condemned Congress. All was a quagmire of partisan strife. Surveying the wreckage of American affairs, the commander in chief of the Continental Army groaned: "Our affairs are in a more distressed, ruinous, and deplorable condition than they have been in since the commencement of the war." It was a far cry from the plain and easy road to independence down which he had thought his country headed six months earlier.

---

*His predicament found a literal expression early in December. At Louis XVI's command, the entire court was masked and costumed for a brilliant ball on twenty-four hours' notice, Sartine transformed into Neptune, Maurepas into Cupid. Vergennes, who found such frivolities nearly as distasteful as did Adams, obligingly sported a spinning globe on his head. And he downed his late-night hot chocolate while sandwiched between maps of England and America. He wore the American map in front.

VII

Success Has Ruined Many a Man

1779

Calumny, Sir. You don't realize its effectiveness. I've seen the best of men pretty near overwhelmed by it. Believe me there's no spiteful stupidity, no horror, no absurd story that one can't get the idle-minded folk of a great city to swallow if one goes the right way about it—and we have some experts here!
—*Beaumarchais*, The Barber of Seville

It was to be a curious axiom of the French years that the higher Franklin rose in the public pantheon, the lower he sank in the estimation of his colleagues. To what extent was he complicit in either? The mythmaking assumed a life of its own, which he did little to foster, and nearly as little to deter. The Fragonard etching issued from the same source as the prohibited "Fête Bostonienne," the full-throated surge of enthusiasm for France's new ally, whom she was to rescue from the clutches of insidious England. That ardor would put three enduring images of Franklin on display in the 1779 Salon, which he graced in an engraving, a terra-cotta bust by Jean-Antoine Houdon, and an oil by the leading court portraitist.

How much was Franklin to blame for the antagonisms at Passy? A January 1779 contretemps was revealing. On the first business day of the New Year, Ralph Izard applied to Franklin for his salary. The father of five and the husband of a very pregnant wife, his monies tied up in South Carolina, Izard found himself in a precarious spot. Franklin turned him down flat. Demands of every kind rained down on him, from interest on French loans to the furnishing and refitting of ships. The British had at long last agreed to a prisoner exchange program; Franklin hoped to direct monies to the relief of those men, half-starved and penniless. Less than a year earlier he had provided Izard with what he believed an extravagant sum for his Florence trip, a trip the Tuscan envoy had never made. Franklin saw no reason why Congress should support Izard's growing family. "You are a gentleman of fortune," he reminded the South Carolina rice planter, who was possessed of estates on both sides of the Atlantic and rarely omitted an opportunity to mention as much. Like the Lees, Izard hailed from one of the first families of the South; his income was far greater than Franklin's substantial one. "You did not come to France with any dependence on being maintained here with your family at the expense of the United States in the time of their distress and without rendering them the equivalent service they expected," Franklin chided. Under the circumstances he felt it made more sense for Izard to reimburse him.

Franklin attempted to impress his logic on Adams and Lee, in vain. They thought he was being unreasonable. Congress had been tardy in doing so, but had clearly instructed him to support "the commissioners at the other courts of Europe." To his side Franklin recruited a preposition. As William Lee was not *at* the court of Vienna nor Izard *at* the court of Tuscany, he had no obligations toward them. Izard took his case to Grand, the Americans' banker. How could he fulfill his responsibilities if he was compelled to leave Europe for financial reasons? He had been a model of frugality, having supported a family on a more modest sum than had ever sustained them abroad. Very civilly, Grand declined to help. Izard had no choice but to draw finally on a public banker, whose bill he presented for payment at the Valentinois. There he happened upon the three commissioners together. Out of deference he handed his draft to Franklin, who remained deaf to all entreaties. Over his objections, Lee and Adams accepted the bill.

Franklin sat down afterward to justify his conduct. He was enough concerned to draft two explanations but not enough so to send them; four months would elapse before he would address his colleagues' discontent. He had no intention of causing either Izard or William Lee any distress. Nor did he feel he had in any way violated his instructions, as those gentlemen charged. Had he erred, he submitted himself to Congress's censure. Izard was notably less confined in his indignation. He reported immediately on Franklin's "insolence, falsehood, and brutality." Surely

Congress would not "calmly suffer their authority to be insulted, their instructions evaded," by one contemptible and haughty individual? No honorable man could work with Franklin, sputtered Izard, yet unaware that he was sputtering to a man who—an ocean away—had already fallen victim to the squalls in Passy.

As often as not, Izard was blinded by the smoke of his overheated indignation. He was a difficult colleague. He was also right about a great number of things. Franklin *was* elusive and unforthcoming. He knew his Machiavelli well enough to have written a satire of it. Effortlessly congenial, he could also be callous, and cavalier. Of his humility he could say only that he was proud. He was observed to turn white with fury, although he billed himself as "cool and phlegmatic," which was telling too. By nature he was a critic and a satirist, tendencies toward which his father had thought him dangerously inclined. Even friends knew him to be factious. He was after all a man who owed his place in history to a series of collisions with authority: a brutal one with his brother, which took him to Philadelphia; that with a Philadelphia printer, which had helped him to make his fortune; America's with Britain, which guaranteed his legend.

He was offhanded to a fault in Paris, where the crush of business was overwhelming to a man half his age, and where his desk could function as a sandtrap. And as Izard discovered, Franklin could be highhanded. But he was not underhanded. Izard and Lee were wrong only in assigning Franklin malevolent ends; he was no more guilty of profiting at America's expense than he was of conspiring against his colleagues. At the same time he was sorely remiss in applying his diplomatic skills to the one front that called out so desperately for them. Later he conceded that much ill will could have been averted had he tossed a compliment or two in Izard's direction. He shunned confrontation as fervently as his colleagues embraced it. (The aversion went hand in hand with his altruism. It was his distaste for proprietary quarrels that dissuaded him from patenting his inventions.) Izard insisted that he wished to avoid disputes with Dr. Franklin, while assaulting him regularly. Franklin smoldered silently and shied from his rage, which was not helpful either.

The intelligent if querulous Izard touched too on an emotion that— once aroused—was powerful in Franklin. He was vengeful. Already he had vowed that if he was to found a religion it would include neither pardons nor repentance. He would go so far as to locate a loophole in the biblical injunction. "We are commanded to forgive our enemies," the eagle-eyed Franklin noted, "but we are nowhere commanded to forgive our friends." Were further reminder of the limits of his compassion necessary, both Franklin and Izard could read, as their January saga played itself out, of the exchange of an eminent prisoner. After two years of captivity, William Franklin, the former royal governor of New Jersey, was released from prison. Franklin expressed no sympathy for his forty-eight-year-old son who—in taking up arms against him—angered him more even than had Great Britain. Mutual friends would keep Temple apprised of his father's welfare, cautiously routing their letters around Franklin, who remained firm in his conviction that the filial bond trumped all others. He had no intention of forgiving a son who felt differently nor any interest in communicating with William, when later he reached London. The uncompromising stance was a fine quality in a revolutionary. It bore mixed results closer to home.

His prominence too rankled his colleagues, well aware that in his company they appeared as his assistants. Through February 1779 John Adams was of the mind that no one could focus Europe's attention as well as Franklin and that—disproportionate though it might be—his acclaim was both beneficial to America and entirely merited. Franklin's reputation was long and great. Adams's was still in its infancy. What irritated was less the monopoly of attention than the discrepancy between the man and the myth. The benevolent hoaxer with the twinkle in his eye and the gift for priceless repartee was less a fount of free-flowing republican ideals than a stubborn monument of volcanic anger. He ruled by fiat; the Enlightenment embodied was a bully at home. The distance from America only heightened tensions in Passy. As his dissenting colleagues saw it, there were no checks on Franklin's behavior. As Franklin saw it, he was operating in a vacuum, forced to make sweeping decisions in areas far outside his expertise, with no hope of guidance in Europe and little in America.

Relatedly or not, his psoriasis returned with the Izard flareup. Itchy eruptions spread outward from his back, to colonize new areas. And that was before he had heard that Deane had made himself the toast of London. On his return to America, Deane twice appeared before Congress, which treated him shabbily and evinced no interest in pursuing his deposition. In frustration Deane took his case to the American people. The

December 5, 1778, *Pennsylvania Gazette* carried his blistering attack on the Lee brothers. Deane charged that in Paris Arthur and William "gave universal disgust to the nation whose assistance we solicited"; he denounced even Richard Henry Lee, in Congress, with whom he credited that body's neglect of foreign affairs. Tucking self-pity and self-righteousness neatly aside, Deane thereby passed off personal vendetta as public service. He professed himself duty-bound to enlighten the American people. The Lee brothers, he implied, labored behind the scenes for a reconciliation with England, at France's expense.

Deane's inflammatory words fell on a volatile body already hot with regional frictions. (It was no accident that the French mission was composed in the first place of a southerner, a New Englander, and a Philadelphian.)* The radical faction of Richard Henry Lee and Samuel Adams—the first was Congress's most dazzling orator, the second its most accomplished arm-twister—had long harbored suspicions of France. Prior to Deane's outburst, those suspicions were confined to closed rooms and top desk drawers. With the *Gazette* publication they came tumbling out into the open; Deane initiated a full-scale war in the press, and a congressional feud that brought business to a standstill. This one offered something for everyone: misappropriated funds, foreign intrigue, money laundering, abuse of power, fraud, personal vendetta, profiteering, all of it spiced by ideology. It was easy for his opponents to argue that Deane had prospered at America's expense, as public and private business was already conflated to an extraordinary degree. Chaumont was no original in that respect, nor was he remotely as enterprising as Franklin's old friend (and Deane's business associate) Robert Morris, the Pennsylvania merchant prince who dominated every continental committee in charge of supplies.

Four days after Deane's publication, Henry Laurens resigned as president of Congress. He could not contain his disgust. John Jay was elected to replace him. In the ensuing fracas Thomas Paine rose to Arthur Lee's defense. As secretary to the Committee for Foreign Affairs, Paine was uniquely placed to do so; unfortunately, in defending Lee, he divulged a

---

*It may not have been accidental either that to the French mind, New England was the intolerant province where Quakers were persecuted; the South a shadowy realm where slavery was practiced; Philadelphia a utopia on earth.

host of classified information. Paine published the news that the French had provided American aid prior to the alliance. Perfectly true though it was, that revelation impugned the honor of the king of France. With it Gérard, the French envoy, stepped in, embroiling himself in a maelstrom to which he too would be sacrificed. (It did not help that he was often seen walking the Philadelphia streets with Deane.) On January 12, 1779, Congress passed a resolution censuring Paine and confirming that the king of France had contributed not a single button to the American cause prior to the alliance. Ultimately Gérard forced Paine's resignation.

Entirely lost in the din of accusations was Washington's report to the Board of War. He now had quantities of French fabric in hand to clothe much of the American army.* That was only the first of many ironies. Deane's recall owed nothing to his most serious missteps, to the impenetrable deal with Beaumarchais, to the mismanagement of funds, even to the profiteering of which Lee ranted on in Paris. So far as Congress was concerned, Deane had simply burdened his country with more majors, colonels, brigadiers, and major generals than they knew what to do with—an idea that had originated not with Deane but with Lee. And Deane would succeed in jeopardizing the very relationship he had suffered so miserably to cement. While he aimed at his former colleagues, it was primarily the Franco-American alliance that he imperiled.

On January 2 his jeremiad appeared in the British press, which thrilled to the sight of Congress imploding over factions devoted to their various European representatives. Franklin heard of the celebration from the London-based, Maryland-born shipping agent Thomas Digges. "What egregious fools must the Americans have been after suffering such hardships and severe struggles to thus divide among themselves," scoffed Digges, who could not help but thank Franklin. The London markets had risen on the news of the paroxysms in Congress; he was a far richer man thanks to his compatriots' folly. In Paris Lee and Adams braced for the fallout. Learning in February that Deane's philippic was scheduled for a forthcoming issue of the *Courrier de l'Europe*, the two lobbied Vergennes to prohibit its publication. Presumably because he did not think the French minister in need of his counsel, Franklin declined to join in their

---

*Beaumarchais's ships had provided cloth and supplies, primarily of Chaumont's manufacture, for thirty thousand men.

request. His reluctance convinced Lee that his colleague would stop at nothing to defame him.

To Adams's mind Deane had succeeded where the British had failed. "I confess it appeared to me like a dissolution of the constitution," he lamented of the publication. It seemed likely not only to thrust America into a civil war but to cost her the confidence of France; he did not see how her ally could ever trust America again. On the morning of February 8 he allowed himself a tantrum at the Valentinois, where he compared Deane to a wild boar, who "ought to be hunted down for the benefit of mankind." He got less satisfaction than he might have liked from Franklin, who refrained from judgment, or from levelheaded Grand, who preferred to dissect Lee's paranoia rather than Deane's grandiosity. In his distress Adams stumbled toward the obvious conclusion: "All the Parisian evils were American." Within a matter of days he convinced himself that his senior colleague bore some responsibility for Deane's atrocity. Franklin had been utterly deceived by the younger man, to whose vanities he was blind. Adams professed himself duty-bound to mention that shortsightedness to Vergennes and did so, submitting a long defense of Lee without alerting either of his colleagues. Tartly Vergennes suggested that the Americans settle their differences among themselves. In truth, the foreign minister parsed the infighting closely. Its implications for France were huge. Had Deane broken the revolutionary stride? The ex-commissioner's greatest critics were after all those men who stomped their feet loudly on the State House floorboards over the impropriety of a French alliance.

Adams submitted his heartfelt letter to Versailles by special messenger on Friday morning, February 12. Hours later, and in advance of Vergennes's flinty reply, he had his relief. At four that afternoon a Lafayette aide-de-camp arrived, bearing a set of congressional dispatches. Among them was confirmation of Franklin's appointment as sole plenipotentiary to the court of France, a rank equivalent to modern ambassador. Franklin headed out immediately to Versailles. Returned by the same dispatch to life as a private citizen, Adams communed with his diary. The appointment—which he had essentially recommended—came to him as a tonic. With one "masterly measure" Congress had at last done away with the crippling dissensions at Passy. Such was his initial reaction. Within the week he sounded a different note. Shunted aside, he was ready to fault

Franklin for more than his smoldering silence, his chaotic record keeping, his reluctance to tangle with the abysmally complex. He had been less than rigorous on any number of fronts. Most of all he had too much enjoyed his prominence. There was suddenly on Franklin's part "a monopoly of reputation here and an indecency in displaying it which did great injustice to the real merit of the others."

With the Lafayette-borne dispatches came as well the first explicit accounts of Lee and Izard's attempts to abuse Franklin in Congress. Franklin was cut to the quick to learn that his own state alone had voted against his new appointment. And the Lees had fixed on a most pernicious means of impugning his integrity. How could America trust its most delicate affairs to a representative who employed as his secretary the son of a Loyalist? Close on those dispatches came a diatribe from the long-silent Beaumarchais, who had been pursuing his case in Congress, with meager results. He had reached the end of his rope. Should the Americans persist in their shabby treatment he was ready to sue. Did Franklin really want a bailiff on the Valentinois doorstep? Nothing would make the British happier. Simultaneously William Lee added a new accusation. In naming Franklin sole commissioner, America had exchanged one tyrant for another. In lieu of King George his country placed itself at the mercy of King Ben. So it was that the twin evils against which Franklin battled in the French imagination—Fragonard had him prevailing over tyranny and avarice—were those with which his countrymen accused him of leaguing. The adulation from the French side only reinforced the argument.*

Meanwhile the discord among the commissioners and the divisions they cracked open in Congress were splashed over the European papers.

---

*Franklin's position was brilliantly illuminated by thirty-six-year-old Jean-Paul Marat, the ambitious, convention-defying doctor who assiduously courted him; Franklin's sanction was equivalent to Académie admission. Prevailing upon mutual friends, Marat managed finally in April 1779 to assemble several prominent scientists and the American minister plenipotentiary in his darkened laboratory near the Invalides. Through a microscope he trained a beam of light, surrounded by a cloud of oscillating shadows. (Marat claimed to have isolated "igneous fluid," an element of fire.) His conclusions were rather far-fetched, but his demonstration in many ways confirmed the obvious. Franklin leaned in that spring morning to expose his bald head to the beam of light. A wreath of undulating shadows danced around the familiar pate. "They looked like those flames which in painting symbolize genius," commented one academician. Given those effusions there was every reason why Adams should grumble that Franklin was universally thought to have effected the American Revolution with his electric wand.

As Adams sighed and wept and mourned over the Lee–Deane fallout, so did some of America's best French friends. To the reform-minded Turgot, the American Revolution appeared to be sputtering out, yet another false hope. His dear friend Franklin was laid up with gout, amusing himself with his writing. It was around this juncture that the new minister plenipotentiary channeled some of his rage into a satire, to remain secret for decades. On the page Franklin reduced Ralph Izard to the letter "Z," a "little, hissing, crooked, serpentine, venomous" entity, obsessed with his placement in the alphabet, which he considers consistent neither with his station nor with his ability. Intent on redress, "Z" petitions for nothing less than a wholesale reform of the alphabet. There was a name for this brand of infectious disease. "The Americans are already terribly European," sighed the worldly Turgot.

~☙~

Franklin was delighted with the new appointment, particularly pleased—again he was the bane of the overachiever's existence—to have obtained it effortlessly, and without "magnifying my own service or diminishing those of others." He took some immediate measures, engaging in a three-day letter-writing spree, consolidating the public papers, and amending the commission's forms to the first person singular. Over Lee's objections, he put Bancroft in charge of the prisoner exchange negotiation. He began a daily log of his correspondence, a prosaic exercise that lasted two weeks. He ordered up a magnificent vicuña suit, presumably for his presentation in his new capacity at Versailles. Vergennes expected that ceremony to take place immediately; confirming Franklin in his appointment would solder the alliance. Both men were to be disappointed. Franklin was stricken by a searing attack of gout on February 17 and—after a brief respite—laid up again for the first three weeks of March. He continued to entertain callers, or tried to; the pain was excruciating. He admitted that in the grip of the sickness he "could neither write nor think of anything." His frustration was great, eager as he was to make a fresh start. Wistfully he acknowledged the discrepancy between his new title and his curtailed abilities.

On March 1 he profited from his brief respite between attacks to make a trip to the baths. On his return he found the duc de Cröy waiting for him in his rooms. The general found Franklin feeble and much diminished, evidently also on the road to recovery. He was ravenous—with his visitor he polished off a few fat slices of cold meat, washed down with some good wine—while he had eaten next to nothing over the previous weeks. After the meal the two men decamped to Franklin's office, its walls plastered with maps, all of them familiar to Cröy, pleased to find himself at the center of American operations. Franklin took up the issue of recalcitrant Spain, who sat on the sidelines with her fifty-five ships of the line. She did not, he mused, offer a very promising advertisement for family compacts. Darkly he confirmed what his visitor already knew: America was broke. He could hardly bring himself to call more regularly for assistance at Versailles, where he was loath to make himself unwelcome. Cröy exhorted him to persist. "I will try to see M. de Maurepas," conceded Franklin, his right foot still pulsing, "but I dread his staircase!" Cröy was struck by this rather vivid embodiment of the crippled American cause, all the more so because he saw Franklin as the creator of that republic. The new minister plenipotentiary allowed himself as well a comment on the snarled relations at Passy. Franklin shrugged off the divisions that roiled the American community. "Petty disputes between particular persons about private interests, there are always in every country: But with regard to that great point of independence, there is no difference of sentiment in the Congress," went his party line.

A man who saw opportunity everywhere, Franklin persisted in viewing his malady as he did the slings and arrows of his colleagues: It qualified as a remedy rather than a disorder. As such he turned it entirely to his own ends. The diplomatic corps fretted anew at the American intrusion into the corridors of power; with Franklin's elevation to minister, he would make regular Tuesday pilgrimages to Versailles and formal calls on his fellow ambassadors. The courts of Europe had done their polite best to resist all shameless American schemes for recognition. Surely Franklin did not expect his visits to be returned? Having heard whispers of that disregard—to which rumor many attributed the delay in the presentation—Franklin settled on a simple solution. He resolved to disappoint his colleagues' project by visiting no one. Privately he deemed it preferable to be thought "rude or singular" than to be insulted. Publicly he held that he had no intention of bowing to anyone's discomfort but his own. The tenderness in his feet might keep him from Versailles. The qualms of Europe would not.

When introduced finally on March 23, the newly appointed minister plenipotentiary of the United Provinces of America therefore presented his credentials and executed his three bows before Louis XVI but refrained from making the customary calls. He thereby spared his colleagues from embarrassment and himself from disgrace; the gout stood as his defense. The day was full enough. Franklin paid homage to the royal family, and dined with Vergennes and Lafayette. He was pleased by the gracious reception, afterward utterly disabled for a week. Over the next months he did not miss a Tuesday. Nor did he refrain from making his presence felt. He expressed American gratitude to France at every opportunity, heralding the king's wisdom and magnanimity. He spoke glowingly of Washington's army, waxing eloquent about victories still unknown in Europe and, occasionally, in America. When British propagandists sowed apprehensions in the French government, as they did with savage regularity, Franklin strode in on tender feet to uproot them.

Days before the presentation at Versailles, Franklin received a congratulatory call from William Lee, newly returned from Germany and Holland. Lee hoped to prevail upon Vergennes for assistance in heading off a fresh infusion of German mercenaries, as well as in inducing other powers to recognize American independence. Franklin judged both applications futile. He was equally disinclined to help Lee in pursuing Virginia's separate request for arms. Observing that Franklin had refused to pay his recent bills, Lee wondered whether he might count on more generous support in the future. He had already let his secretary go. Franklin replied that he had no money. Finally Lee reminded America's representative that Congress had ordered them to get along, if for no other reason than to neutralize Deane's acidic publication. Evidently Franklin countered, "Congress should set us the example by their own conduct." Both sides clung to their (perfectly valid) opinions. Franklin had no interest in pursuing any competing demands at Versailles. He justified his severity in reminding himself that Lee had a private fortune and ample personal credit. Lee concluded that Franklin was intent on starving him out. He would resign if he could—Izard had already requested a recall—but refused to leave America's fate in the hands of what his family generally wrote down as "the corrupt hotbed of vice at Passy." He professed himself dutybound to thwart the pilfering and plundering and plotting in Passy.

Separately Arthur Lee dilated on Franklin's misdeeds. Nothing less than the salvation of America depended on his recall. If Congress truly meant to support additional ministers in Europe, it would need to supply funds through other channels. Franklin would always find a way to circumvent orders. Lee felt he could prove Franklin's depravity; he had attempted to suppress various papers, clear evidence of corruption. In applauding the British-born Paine and his attack on Deane, Izard lamented that America "should stand in need of protection from an adopted son against the assaults of so many of her own unnatural offspring," a sweeping condemnation of the carelessly conceived Franklin family. To be fair, the point was as germane to the Passy commission as were William Lee's and Ralph Izard's personal fortunes. If the class issue bubbled always close to the surface, it did so from both sides.

Confronted by Arthur Lee about the mission's papers at the end of March, Franklin lost his magisterial cool. He had no intention of withholding any documents from Lee. He was always meticulous with public papers. That may have constituted an exaggeration, but the accusation that Franklin was profiting from America's war effort was egregious (as was Lee's allegation that Jonathan Williams had diverted more than 100,000 livres of public monies to his own ends). Generally Franklin indulged his detractors with no such loss of control. He was above such pettiness. Or so he claimed; he knew well that his very imperturbability made for a gratifying revenge. "They quarrel *at* me rather than *with* me; for I will not quarrel with them. They write me long abusive letters which I never answer, but [I] treat the gentlemen with the same civility when we meet as if no such letters existed. This I think most prudent for a public character but I suspect myself of being a little malicious in it, for I imagine they are more vexed by such neglect than they would be by a tart reply." Convinced of his own blamelessness, he trusted in the wisdom of Congress. His faults he sloughed off on the French. He had done no harm, "but my too great reputation and the general goodwill this people have for me, the respect they show me and even the compliments they make me, all grieve those unhappy gentlemen; unhappy indeed in their tempers, and in the dark uncomfortable passions of jealousy, anger, suspicion, envy and malice." In that "state of damnation" he intended to leave them, having no inclination "to reverse my conduct for the alleviation of their torments."

At the same time he broke his own rule, denouncing at a distance. He assured the Committee for Foreign Affairs that he made it "a constant rule to answer no angry, affronting or abusive letter of which I have received many and long ones from Mr. Lee and Mr. Izard," a comment that constituted a rebuke in itself. And while he proposed to leave his associates "to hiss, bite, sting, and poison one another," he conceded that they had hit a nerve. He was startled by the assault on Temple, all the more so as he felt it to his credit that he had "rescued a valuable young man from the danger of being a Tory, and fixed him in honest republican Whig principles." The attempt to sever him from his grandson was as cruel as it was impracticable. Why would anyone "deprive an old man sent to serve his country in a foreign one of the comfort of a child?" Temple served impeccably. Franklin was convinced he would go on to be of great service to their country. In any event, faced with the choice, he would sooner part with the job than with the child. The attachment was all the fiercer for the loss behind it; Franklin received reports over the same weeks of William Franklin's involvement, from London, in a vicious Loyalist retaliation on New Jersey. "It is enough that I have lost my *son*, would they add my *grandson!*" cried the new American minister.

To his management of his colleagues there was a counterexample, and it came in the form of a fresh-complexioned, red-haired Frenchman not previously known for his social graces. As punishment for having left the country against the king's wishes, Lafayette spent the week of his return under house arrest. He was ordered to see only family, but as that constituted most of the court the sentence was meaningless. His penance consisted in having to sit still while he accepted congratulations from everyone of importance in France. He met Franklin for the first time late in February, at which juncture the two men began to discuss a variety of projects, all of them ill-fated. Presumably Lafayette stood behind the proposal Franklin submitted to Vergennes for a joint summer attack on Rhode Island, one that went notably wide of Franklin's instructions. He knew little of Washington's aversion to involving French troops in North America but well understood that he was charged with sending none; he never mentioned the imprudent request to Congress. What was obvious to him were the difficulties of a joint operation. Days after petitioning Vergennes, Franklin found himself in correspondence with Pierre Landais, the French captain who had, for symbolic reasons, been given charge of the Massachusetts-built *Alliance*. Landais had heard he was to return to America with a crew supplemented by his countrymen. He vetoed the idea. "Frenchmen and Americans being mixed together, not understanding one another, having different discipline, manner of living etc. can never act well in concert, but will always disagree," he demurred, an argument to which Franklin was sympathetic.*

While Lafayette attempted to loosen the purse strings at Versailles, he channeled his energies into a project that would preoccupy Franklin throughout 1779, in various configurations. The time seemed ripe for a raid on England. Her coasts were deliciously, defenselessly open. Four to five thousand men, Franklin calculated, could wreak some extensive damage there. It was very much a long shot, and one on which Franklin largely deferred to Lafayette. He delighted however in an observation he shared with his avid collaborator. In the history of warfare, impossible schemes often succeed for the very fact that "nobody expects them, and no precautions are taken to guard against them." Those same Herculean maneuvers reflected most gloriously on their commanders. This one was vexed twice over, warned Franklin: "For there is not only a junction of land and sea forces, but there is also a junction of Frenchmen and Americans, which increases the difficulty of maintaining a good understanding." Fortunately the bit-champing John Paul Jones was at hand. His petition for a ship had finally paid off; at Chaumont's intervention, he was given command of a decrepit fourteen-year-old merchant ship, armed and christened the *Bonhomme Richard*. Franklin briefed Jones on the pitfalls of that delicate, Lafayette-led maneuver: "There is honor enough," he promised, "to be got for both of you."

That joint venture too came to naught, but left an enduring legacy. Late in March Sartine joined the *Alliance* to Jones's squadron, a decision that—meant to accommodate one burning patriot—seriously inconvenienced another. John Adams waited impatiently in Nantes to sail home on the pristine *Alliance*, into which his baggage had been loaded. There was only

---

*The Rhode Island plan came to naught. Of a second Franklin–Lafayette coproduction nearly as little evidence remains. Together the two began to compile a list of British atrocities, to be illustrated and published in a bound volume, a chilling work of propaganda. The British had incited slaves to murder their masters and Indians to scalp frontiersmen; they had executed men who had surrendered; they had burned American cities. Unlike Franklin, Lafayette had actually witnessed many of those depredations. Nonetheless it was he who reminded Franklin that a little moderation might be in order. Lafayette despised the British as much as anyone, but even he had to concede that as a people they were no worse than the rest of humankind.

so much Cicero translating he could do with John Quincy; already he felt the sting of his superfluity. On April 28 he learned that his May departure was to be postponed, news that Franklin passed on with apologies but without elucidation. He attempted to soften the blow by hinting that it would be safer for Adams to return in a vessel that did not include a "mixed crew," and in which he would have the company of the new French ambassador. (Having compromised himself in the Deane affair, Gérard was coming home, to be replaced by Anne-César de la Luzerne.) Late in April Franklin promised that Luzerne—an even-tempered and politically astute colleague, and an ideal traveling companion—would turn up in a few days. The new envoy did so only on June 11.

Reports that Franklin's new appointment was a torture to Adams had been false in March but were only premature by April. In Nantes he felt himself to have been left kicking and sprawling in the mud; he took comfort in the news that Passy was out of favor, little frequented by his compatriots. He predicted that Franklin would not be up to his new assignment. And as the delay was never properly explained—Adams might have been mollified by word that the *Alliance* had been ordered to join the squadron Jones was assembling—he found himself susceptible to a bout of Lee-borne paranoia. He had, after all, been rather mysteriously transferred from a swift sailer (the *Alliance* was one of the best frigates around) to a slower, less well armed vessel. Clearly he was the dupe either of Jones's ambitions or of Franklin's misconduct.* "Does the old conjurer dread my voice in Congress?" Adams wondered. "He has some reason for he has often heard it there, a terror to evil-doers," continued America's ranking vigilante, deducing that Franklin had something to hide. Adams sailed from France finally on June 17, all the while huffing about his ex-colleague.

In the end the *Alliance* would cause Franklin nearly as many headaches as its namesake. In a different humor Adams might have alerted Franklin to the erratic behavior of the ship's captain, on whose pinched physiog-

---

*It seemed that few Americans could make of Paris a city of brotherly love. Adams said his goodbyes early in March, but not without developing an aversion to the soft-spoken, keen-eyed John Paul Jones, who talked as handsomely of America and her affairs as anyone in France. Jones's gold epaulettes were too much for Adams. (They were a French touch.) For his part, Jones would dub the sober, balding New Englander "Mr. Roundface."

nomy and paranoid ravings he had ample time to meditate. With his February arrival in France, Landais had saddled Franklin with a difficult conundrum; he had arrived from Boston with thirty-eight disaffected sailors. As the de facto judge of the admiralty, if one operating before American naval law was yet established, Franklin was left to decide what to do with a crew of mutinous seamen. A court-martial was out of the question, since it required more officers than were at hand; as Sartine made clear, the conspirators could not be tried in French courts. Again Franklin's conciliatory powers failed him. Chaumont was dispatched to Lorient, to discover that the *Alliance*'s officers were ready to devour their high-strung captain. He wished Franklin could put in an appearance; his "paternal benediction" was sorely needed. Chaumont was tempted to review his ancient history, to see if other great revolutionaries had quarreled so insistently among themselves when they had an enemy at hand. The American squabbles struck him as unrelenting indeed: "And in truth, from your country I have as yet seen no one but Your Excellency who is moderate and wise. As such, you have won our respect, and I think that without you we would not have so much loved the people of the New World." Lafayette was of a similar mind, although he applied for relief to a different address. So great was the bitterness between the American camps in Paris that he hesitated to visit either Lee or Franklin. "For God's sake," he pleaded with George Washington, "prevent their loudly disputing together. Nothing hurts so much the interests and reputation of America than to hear of their internecine quarrels."

~※~

As Adams vegetated in Nantes, Franklin emerged from the spring rains in an expansive mood. Chaumont's garden hung heavy with peas and cherries, delivered up by the basket to the Valentinois; from those lilac-scented grounds Franklin reached out with unusual warmth to old friends in America. The rays of the spring sun can very nearly be felt on his pages. A run of good health and good weather coincided finally with some good news: On June 21, Spain at last declared war on England. Her priorities were better left unexamined. The king of Spain determined to go to war, laughed the wags, not altogether inaccurately, because the British had mangled his attempts at mediation. He most distinctly did not go to war for the sake of America, to whose independence Madrid made no commitment. Instead Spain held France, by a secret convention signed in April 1779, to her own priorities: an invasion of England and the return of Gibraltar. It was to that rock that American independence, unbeknownst to Franklin, was now chained.

With much energy Franklin threw himself into plans for a sumptuous Independence Day celebration. He printed invitations on the press he had quietly been setting up at the Valentinois, in operation as of the late spring, distributing his envelopes far and wide. For a party that was equally to mark his formal introduction to the American community as its sole representative he invited even those who labored for his recall. Arthur Lee and Ralph Izard both attended the Independence Day gala, held on Monday, July 5. The celebration was the most elaborate of Franklin's Passy stay, probably of his life. His forty guests—the list included Sartine's and Vergennes's representatives, French officers from the American army, the marquise de Lafayette, Ferdinand Grand, close friends from Passy, and the prominent Americans in Paris—sat down to a table decorated with rented porcelain ornaments, flower vases, and silver platters. Franklin's kitchen turned out a profusion of meats and fowl, including two varieties of pigeon; lavish quantities of gooseberries and strawberries, figs and melons, and an impressive quantity of wine were consumed that day, amid dozens of flickering lanterns. Over the banquet table presided a full-length portrait of Washington, holding aloft the Declaration of Independence and the Franco-American treaties, while trampling underfoot Britain's conciliatory bills. (Lafayette had brought the painting with him from America.) Of the seven bilingual toasts, five went to France. Franklin commissioned a respected poet to compose a piece for the occasion; it was delivered by a choir, who extolled the courage of the allied forces. A band of musicians followed with military airs, after which Franklin treated his guests to a ball. They were sent home with party favors, including *La Science du Bonhomme Richard*.

The festivities confirmed Franklin both in his new appointment and in his role as capacious host. That was assumed to be a rare quality in a republican, as was one other. In Nantes Adams had bridled at a talent he thought less than flattering in a Philadelphian. "He has the most affectionate and insinuating way of charming the woman or the man that he fixes on," he noted of his former colleague. "It is the most silly and ridiculous way imaginable, in the sight of an American, but it succeeds, to admiration, fulsome and sickish as it is, in Europe." Yet again Adams articulated better than anyone else a cultural divide with which Franklin wrangled, publicly and personally. By the laws of one side, he was a man who could work eight days straight without any repose aside from a brief nap in his armchair. By the laws of the other, he was monumentally indolent, meticulous only about his social calendar. To one world America's minister plenipotentiary held court in royal splendor at the Valentinois; to the other his was a spartan existence. The duc de Cröy marveled over the frugality of his table, the modesty of his quarters, the paucity of his staff. The household help consisted of a maître d'hôtel and two manservants; Franklin borrowed Chaumont's carriage when in need. His kitchen worked no wonders; years into his stay his pantry was notably bare of most of the linens, china, and glassware considered essential to a well-set Parisian table. He could not have cost Congress less.*

Franklin ministered not only to two constituencies but to his own off-kilter standards as well. He expressed an easy admiration of the French, "a most amiable nation to live with," and a people without any vice aside from the occasional frivolity. Agreeable though they might be, the French were not the people to whom he cared to entrust the education of his ten-year-old grandson, however. Shortly after the new appointment, Franklin elected to separate Benny from his Passy friends. He claimed that Benny had got as much out of the local pension as he could, but had other concerns as well. The clergy ran the schools of France, in which boys said their prayers in Latin, made the sign of the cross, and confessed regularly. "As he is destined to live in a Protestant country, and a republic, I thought it best to finish his education where the proper principles prevail," explained the man who could find no fault with France, in regard to Benny.

---

*The truth of the matter is perhaps best left to a grateful and hungry ten-year-old American. On Sundays Franklin received his countrymen, a guest list that inevitably included a group of schoolboys. Having paid their respects to Dr. Franklin, they were left to romp in the immense gardens of the Valentinois until mealtime. They never missed a week. One son of Robert Morris found that Franklin could not have been more welcoming, or less affected. Although not in livery, the staff was dressed neatly and tastefully. Franklin's table, by contrast, was both excellent and luxurious. As the school fare was neither, remembered Thomas Morris, "we indemnified ourselves by pocketing, with the Doctor's approbation, from the dessert, after the guests had left the table, cakes, raisins, almonds, and dried preserved fruits to last us during the greater part of the week."

To his daughter Franklin broke the news that her son spoke a foreign tongue better than his own. After some deliberation Franklin enrolled Benny in a Geneva boarding school, to which he made the five-day voyage with a diplomat friend of his grandfather's. A regent of the Calvinist academy volunteered to supervise the boy's studies. Serious and placid, Benny went off happily, or so Franklin liked to believe. He promised all parties that he would visit Geneva in the spring.

At the same time Temple showed every sign of having inherited his grandfather's charm, in two languages. Already he was mastering French arts and breaking French hearts. His service irked many, although no one could say he was anything other than highly competent. He was as well enormously dedicated. He had seen to voluminous correspondences and every variety of errand, embarking without complaint on a last-minute, midwinter, 500-mile wild-goose chase to the coast of Normandy. (It was a quick trip, but not so hurried that he failed to manage a romance.) As the plans for the invasion of Britain evolved, so did the idea—cooked up by the two younger men—that Temple might make a very capable aide-de-camp to Lafayette. Franklin professed to miss Benny and knew he would be handicapped without Temple, but encouraged the project. The ministry of war granted Temple permission to don a French uniform; Lafayette promised Temple active duty, at his side. In early September the invasion was scuttled, on account of sick crews and unfavorable winds, leaving John Paul Jones to head out alone for a cruise with a small squadron in the refitted *Bonhomme Richard*. The man who sent Benny away to make him a good Presbyterian was clear about his disappointment. He thanked Lafayette—the major general was three years Temple's elder—for his willingness to mentor his grandson. The experience would have been incomparable. "I flattered myself too, that he might possibly catch from you some tincture of those engaging manners that make you so much the delight of all that know you," Franklin assured Lafayette.*

Franklin's colleagues were not alone in exposing decadence where there was none. An unfrivolous woman and a dutiful daughter, Sally

---

*Temple left no record of his disappointment over the aborted mission, of which his only souvenir was an epaulette design. Lafayette held up remarkably well given his vow that were France to invade England, and he not there with his countrymen, he would hang himself.

Franklin rarely asked anything of her father, but that spring applied to him for lace and feathers. She was to attend a ball at which General Washington would be present. Franklin berated her. Her request, he railed, "disgusted me as much as if you had put salt into my strawberries. The spinning, I see, is laid aside, and you are to be dressed for the ball!" If Sally wanted feathers they could be found in the tail of any American rooster. As for lace, were she to wear her cambric ruffles as long as did he, they would pass for lace soon enough. Doubtless Sally bore some of her father's pent-up frustration with French levity, as did his countrymen; having heard myriad (and inflated) reports of how mores had changed since the war began, he raged against the burgeoning American taste for superfluities. Sally's lashing was all the more severe as Franklin felt he had a reputation to uphold. Since he was forever preaching frugality, "I cannot in conscience or in decency encourage the contrary, by my example, in furnishing my children with foolish modes and luxuries."* He sent the practical items she requested but not the rest. It is notable that Sally's higher-standards letter is the same in which her father informs her that his likeness is all the fashion on snuffboxes. And it is notable too that the season of Franklin's opulent July 4 celebration was the same in which Congress deliberated the proper manner in which to commemorate the holiday. Was a day of fasting not more appropriate than one of fireworks?

The cultural divide promised to subsume some of Franklin's best efforts. By the end of the summer the gold sword he had commissioned for Lafayette was ready. Jacques Brillon and Temple journeyed together to present it to the American hero, preparing in Le Havre for the British invasion. Franklin made certain that an account of that instrument—magnificently wrought in gold, its scabbard engraved with scenes from Lafayette's glorious career—appeared in every European paper. Even while it taxed the congressional budget, the sword failed to impress. It could not hold its own against the baubles that Louis XVI routinely handed out.† Aware of a gulf that was to yawn more widely as 1779 drew

---

*With other people's children the tune was very different. "What do you want from Paris? Name it," he essentially commanded Georgiana Shipley, the twenty-four-year-old daughter of Jonathan Shipley, in England.

†The sword had cost 4,800 livres, or a tenth of the sum on which Izard had supported his family for fifteen months.

to a close, Franklin swatted away the derision. "It only proves," he rejoined, unflinching, indomitable as ever, "that everyone has his own way of seeing things."

~~~

"A benevolent man should allow for a few faults, to keep his friends happy," Franklin would observe. The second half of 1779 proved him a prince of bonhomie. At the end of July, Nicolas-Maurice Gellée, the well-mannered, nineteen-year-old clerk who had arrived with glowing references a year earlier, resigned his position. With his curt demission letter he returned the key to his rooms. Evidently Franklin harbored some doubts as to the young man's loyalties, doubts he never bothered to explain. He preferred instead a gentle (and disingenuous) letdown, professing that he did not have enough work for someone of Gellée's abilities. It was abundantly clear to the young secretary that the truth was quite different. He appears to have tangled himself up in his loyalties to Adams and Franklin, only the former of which survived his employment. And shortly after Gellée's stormy departure Franklin confirmed that there was every reason for secretarial help. "You have found out by this time that I am a very bad correspondent," he apologized to Lafayette, vigorously petitioning for American aid at Versailles. "As I grow old I perceive my aversion to writing increases, and is become almost insurmountable." Congress had already discerned as much. Over the summer it reprimanded Franklin for his silence. Doubtless he had already guessed what that reproach made painfully clear. The Deane debacle opened him to every manner of accusation.

Vergennes knew the extent of that damage—and the sordid details of the "spirit of assassinating innuendo" that prevailed in America—well before Franklin. In the wake of the Deane firebomb Congress appointed a committee to examine the nation's foreign affairs, universally agreed to be in a deplorable state. That committee recommended a discharge of all Paris personnel and a fresh start. Gérard was left to engage in some expert maneuvering. He made it his business to impress upon Congress how little Versailles was tempted to do business with Arthur Lee. The French court wanted reasonable men at the helm. Franklin came in for some very rough treatment, which Gérard viewed with some astonishment. "I fear that the ease with which he has allowed himself to become embroiled in various collegial disputes will lead Congress, despite itself, to sacrifice him to the opposition," he warned Vergennes.

Franklin had been officially presented at Versailles as American minister plenipotentiary on March 23. Hours later, the Committee for Foreign Affairs submitted to Congress its careful report on the "suspicions and animosities" that plagued the Paris mission. The charges against Franklin were straightforward. Lee maintained that he withheld information. He was responsible for disorder and dissipation in the public accounts; he was lining the pockets of Williams and Chaumont. (Chaumont had not only advanced funds for d'Estaing's campaign but partially outfitted Jones's squadron as well.) Izard held "that Mr. Franklin is not a proper person to be trusted with the management of the affairs of America, that he is haughty and self sufficient, and not guided by principles of virtue or honor." Indeed everyone had his own way of seeing things.

In a series of bitter and protracted discussions over the next weeks Congress debated Franklin's recall, dissecting his character in detail. (A curious number of those who inveighed against him had their own ambitions for careers abroad.) Gérard was dubious that he would survive the initial vote, and with reason; days later, several supporters claimed to have had second thoughts. They resolved to reopen the issue. "I must warn you," Gérard wrote Vergennes in mid-July, "that neither of the two parties has in Dr. Franklin the confidence that his intelligence and his integrity deserve. Factionalism rules, and he has distanced himself too much from any group to be entrusted with its interests." Franklin was severely battered in the debates, which raged on for months. He prevailed in the end less because of any real enthusiasm for his merits than because of a lesser-of-evils check on regional interests and rival ambitions. Ultimately Izard and William Lee were recalled, although neither man was required to return home. Franklin remained in place in Paris; Arthur Lee retained his appointment to Madrid; and Deane was allowed to return to Europe. The debates segued into a fall vote for a peace commissioner, a discussion for which Vergennes was responsible. He knew that Franklin's instructions did not include the power to negotiate a peace and—with mediation in the air—preferred they did, a consideration Gérard conveyed to Congress. The request backfired. The North supported Adams and the South threw itself behind John Jay, and, reported Gérard, "neither one nor the other mentioned Dr. Franklin."

Vergennes suffered especially for that abuse. So instrumental was Franklin to the alliance, so much had he become synonymous with it, that the preservation of his reputation was almost more crucial to the French minister than it was to America. Vergennes had long assumed that Spain's entrance into the war would cement the collaboration; in the end he was terrified that she might work the opposite effect. Madrid's motives for helping America were so inconsistent with France's, and so incompatible with America's, as to render France suspect. Perhaps the Bourbon powers indeed had designs on the unsteady new republic. It was to convince America of the king's good intentions that Vergennes pushed for a joint military operation; Lafayette had repeatedly to remind him that the Americans were by no means eager to welcome French troops on their shores. If the minister intended to send men he would need first to create the desire. Otherwise they would be met very coolly indeed. The major general warned of a hurdle greater even than the delicacy of such a maneuver: "I cannot deny that the Americans are somewhat difficult to handle, especially for a Frenchman." From Vergennes's point of view, the siege against Franklin came at a most inopportune time.

Everyone tried to capitalize on that stain, out of ambition if not animosity. In it Lafayette glimpsed a chance at a diplomatic career, attempting a mid-August detour around Franklin. As England daily feared an invasion, was a peace negotiation not in the offing? Lafayette knew that Franklin's instructions prohibited him from concluding any such treaty without submitting it to Congress. And Franklin's name was tainted in America. "If Mr. Franklin sends the treaty," Lafayette reminded Vergennes, "his enemies in Congress will attempt to belittle it and will defeat the treaty itself in order to harm a single person." On the other hand, should Franklin be left out of the loop, his supporters would suspect foul play. Only a man who enjoyed the confidence of all parties stood a chance of success. He was himself prepared to head off immediately, with no formal title, for as long as was necessary. America had done nothing but shower him with kindnesses. She had been far less generous with her own representative.

Franklin knew nothing of Lafayette's proposition, having been questioned by him only as to Britain's leanings toward peace. Of those he was not optimistic. As for his feelings about Congress, he neither succumbed to Vergennes's anxieties nor picked up the pace of his correspondence. He saw no particular reason to address himself to the depths of the Atlantic Ocean, he explained at a time when his employers wondered why they had not heard from him in seven months. He made no secret of the fact that he was under fire in his home country. His friends commiserated. The economist Turgot, himself an ex-minister, was of the opinion that "the Congress has used Franklin shamefully, and did not deserve him." If a British earl who set himself up in the espionage business can be believed, Franklin confessed himself equally dissatisfied with Congress and with Versailles. Neither irritation distracted him from the game at hand. He was too busy ratcheting up his hatred toward England. News of the British burning of defenseless Connecticut towns obliterated his last shreds of moderation.

He was protected as well by a calloused ego. "But one is not to expect being always in fashion," he remarked, as he had the first taste that— with the return of the dissatisfied French officers, the demise of American credit, and the Deane fallout—the cult of Franklin had begun to dim. The July 4 festivities ushered in a season of cynicism. There had always been skeptics at Versailles, where many viewed the American contest purely as an impediment to the Paris–London mail; 1779 gave them their platform. As admiring as the French had been of a people they barely knew, they were perfectly well acquainted with their own foibles. And the time had come to be embarrassed by the unseemly fawning. "Monsieur Franklin is pursued, followed, admired, adored everywhere he shows himself, with a mania, a fanaticism, which while flattering to him, reveals as well that the virtues and great qualities of our nation will always be counterbalanced by a frivolity, an inconsequence, and an enthusiasm too extreme to be sustained," clucked one paper, days before the July 4 gala and two weeks too late for the relief of John Adams, finally westbound on the *Sensible*, a frigate that could have been named for him.

Adams was not alone in caviling with his colleague's near-mythical status; the lightning directing could be as offensive as the thunder stealing. Franklin lent his name to an array of causes. Not all were as neutral as Parmentier's potato feast, or as civic-minded as the commission to protect Strasbourg's cathedral from lightning. Franklin discovered in 1779 that in his attempts to deflect the errant lightning bolt he was himself singed in the process. (The phenomenon would have been familiar. *Conductor* and

nonconductor were words of his coinage.) In no realm was that more pronounced than in his association with the Paris Freemasons. Franklin had
very effectively hustled his way into a Philadelphia lodge in 1731; not
having been welcomed, he slighted the Masons in the *Gazette*. He was
quickly enough initiated, after which the Masons received excellent press.
In Paris the reception was much the opposite. The most lettered of Paris
lodges, that of the Nine Sisters, welcomed Franklin with open arms; its
members were limited to distinguished artists or thinkers. He was a credit
to that solemn, semisecret institution, whose ideals were his own: A
brawny arm of the Enlightenment, the Masons committed themselves to
the equality of men, to the liberal exchange of ideas, to the useful, pure,
and moral life. By both inclination and calculation, Franklin had every
reason to join an anticlerical society that numbered among its members
many of America's most fervent French supporters. For the same reasons,
the lodge enjoyed an uneasy relationship with the government and a
patently hostile one with the church. Evicted from its headquarters and
nearly outlawed in 1779, the order recruited Franklin to a leadership position. He accepted on the condition that he be exempt from any ceremonial
functions; he was not even in attendance at the August fete to mark his appointment. The lodge that had nearly been forced out of existence was
granted a miraculous reprieve hours before his term began, however.

The potshots aimed in his direction for having busied himself with that
elite boys' club gave way to the kind of flak of which Franklin was himself the acknowledged master. Through 1779 he found himself the butt of
satirical pamphlets, publications remarkable as much for their mordant
wit as for the quality of their information. From the far side of the Channel came the much-savored, impossible-to-find, and consequently very
costly *Green Box of M. de Sartine*. Masquerading as a collection of documents the naval minister had mislaid at a tryst, the pamphlet ridiculed
both Franklin and America. Its author offers up the diatribe Franklin
would have been well entitled to deliver on his awkward court presentation. The pope dismisses him as a Quaker. The Spaniards are too enamored of South America to receive him. The Russians are slavishly bound
to England. He has been made to feel the laughingstock of Europe. Humiliated, he pours out his rage to Sartine: "In short, Sir, I am insulted in
all the languages of Europe. My religion is satirized in Italian. My politics
in Spanish and Dutch. I hear Washington ridiculed in Russian, and myself

in all the jargon of Germany. I cannot bear it. Make Europe civil to America, or I'll follow Silas Deane."

Franklin was not the only satirist to recruit an entomological narrator. Longer-lived than his mayfly, the self-educated hero of *The Story of a French Louse* is every bit as worldly. He has derived superior strength and vigor (and a mastery of the English language) from his sojourn on the chevalière d'Eon's uncommonly sweaty head. It is in the chevalière's labyrinthine coiffure that the louse travels to a Valentinois dinner. Toward the end of the meal he emerges to find himself face to face with His Excellency Dr. Franklin, a wart-covered, double-chinned grotesque, with bulbous nose and oversized spectacles. The gifted spy listens in as—thirteen toasts into the evening—the chevalière privately serenades Franklin. The American responds with a kiss and a request for an assignation. (The account squares perfectly with the "corrupt hotbed of vice at Passy" that the Lees decried.) Alas the enterprising louse has no opportunity to continue his surveillance, as a violent motion detaches him from d'Eon's spinning head and sends him sprawling in Franklin's garden. Ultimately he finds asylum with Beaumarchais, again to encounter Franklin, delivering an urgent appeal for enhanced French assistance, so as to drive the British once and for all from North America. The parasite proves himself marvelously well versed in Franklin's early years, especially as he had not yet had the pleasure of reading Franklin's *Autobiography*, only a portion of which had been drafted. On a number of prominent heads the louse continues in his rounds, ably reporting that Franklin is not only a lecher and a dupe of Beaumarchais, but a profiteer as well.

The Loyalist press in America could hardly improve upon that formula. In its pages Franklin, the consummate courtier, makes an easy peace with Europe. In its October 20, 1779, issue, the *New York Gazette* reported on Franklin's activities: "Since Dr. Franklin has ceded Canada and Florida to the French and Spaniards, it is to be hoped he will give New England to the Pretender, and make the pope archbishop of North America, that the whole continent in the end may go to the devil." ("Truth, candor, and decorum" was the paper's motto.) Increasingly the friendly fire was indistinguishable from those assaults. Both were happy to place Franklin between Prometheus and Prospero; there is always something immoral about tampering with the heavens. The charge of "charlatanism" trailed happily behind; it was a short step from magus to mountebank. Even in America, the acknowledged sorcerer's magic could be held against him in 1779. "Dr. Franklin's knowledge in electricity does not prove him to be acquainted with the politics of the courts of Europe, nor does his leading the lightning with a thread prove he has led us into any secrets of the British Court," carped one newspaper. Aboard the *Sensible* John Adams was delighted to hear it said that while Dr. Franklin had many educated French friends, had made an indelible impression on Paris, was charming, brilliant, and witty, and an accomplished man of letters, he was hardly a statesman. "He is," allowed Adams, "a great philosopher, but as a legislator of America he has done very little. It is universally believed in France, England, and all Europe, that his electric wand has accomplished all this revolution but nothing is more groundless."*

Adams provided no resistance when the conversation aboard the *Sensible* wound its way around to the fate of illegitimate children in America. In France, it was remarked, they were barred from the army and from government. Adams conceded that no such prohibitions existed in America but—he admitted to have urged the line of inquiry along—that such children "were always attended by a mark of disgrace." Aware that he may have overstepped his bounds, he justified his remark in his diary. He professed himself duty-bound to be frank about his colleague, however great his merits. And on his arrival in America he shed any second thoughts he might have entertained on that subject. He ranted freely. His picture of Franklin was perfectly consistent with the infidel philosopher pilloried in the Loyalist press, all the more dangerous for his talent, his urbanity, his ecumenicalism, his scientific prowess, an immoderate wizard gloating with ambition and orchestrating a revolution for his own ends. Having overpowered the heavens, he was poised to continue his heist on earth.

---

*In a more magnanimous mood, Adams expanded on the formula: "The history of our revolution," he lamented in 1790, "will be one continued lie from one end to the other. The essence of the whole will be *that Dr. Franklin's electrical rod smote the Earth and out sprung General Washington. That Franklin electrified him with his rod—and thence forward these two conducted all the policy, negotiation, legislatures, and war.*" To his list of offenders he would later add Jefferson, who "ran away with the stage effect, and all the glory of it." At all times on the alert for false idols, Adams worried as well that Washington was too much of a god in America. Having garnered fewer votes than Washington in 1789, Adams was also the man who felt that being voted runner-up (which in his day was vice president) to the most popular man in America constituted a "stain" on his honor.

In 1779 Franklin remained blessedly ignorant of Adams's cavils; it is doubtful that he felt more than a pleasurable sting from the satiric louse. America's falling stock alone preoccupied him. Neither d'Estaing nor Washington had provided a military victory around which to rally; a year of minimal results and of mixed feelings wound down to a perfect stalemate, and a bleak Morristown winter. The disappointment was palpable at both ends. Franklin had a public relations disaster on his hands with the returning French officers, who "endeavor to give an idea here that our nation does not love the French." He begged for capsule summaries of each man's career so that he might better deflect the criticisms. Meanwhile French interest in America's struggle had largely evaporated. It had always run parallel to a coursing Anglomania, which in 1779 surged ahead. Franklin was more likely to have been cut to the quick by the assertions of futility that crept into the Parisian discourse. Those were the assaults that took their toll, rather than the acerbic verse that beseeched Franklin to take good care of himself—while also making himself a little less ubiquitous. That author's request was only too easy to fill in the fall of 1779, when Franklin turned his attention to two labors that would occupy the better part of the next year.

~~~

From every direction came accounts of the deprivations of Washington's men, half of them naked, two-thirds of them starved. Franklin could not have been surprised then by the shopping list Congress submitted to him in the fall. The extent of the thirty-eight-page inventory was however staggering, however. Along with a frigate, a ship of the line, and 49,000 uniforms, the 1779 requisition included clarinets and trumpets, spoons and sheet music, paint and thimbles. It not only took Franklin's breath away but literally left him speechless: He was unable to translate some of the more technical items into French. Friends proved equally baffled. Franklin devised finally an intelligent solution, sending to London for samples of each item, to be either matched or copied. He had less success with Vergennes. Franklin applied to the minister with his inventory on September 18, begging for a speedy answer. A week later he hazarded a second plea. America's enemies profited handsomely from her dashed hopes; he was uncommonly anxious. Vergennes was sympathetic to the demand but floored all the same by the enormity of the request. It represented one-tenth of the French government's annual budget. He pursued Franklin's case with Spain—the most reliable road to peace lay in fortifying Washington's troops, rather than in attempting an invasion of the British Isles, Vergennes argued—but hurtled up against a familiar obstacle in Madrid. As ever, Spain preferred to assist America only insofar as she might reduce the colonies to a state of anarchy.

In the end Franklin managed to procure three million livres in aid, the bulk of which he determined to devote to cloth and uniforms. He entrusted the order to Jonathan Williams, as eager to please, and as much preyed upon by interfering colleagues, as ever. Was he to fill the order for blue uniforms turned up with white, as Congress requested, or with blue turned up with yellow, as Lafayette preferred? Congress ordered hats laced with white; Lafayette insisted on black. Franklin assured his grand-nephew that Congress had been very precise. He was to follow its orders. Williams hewed to the congressional directives on all but one count. That assembly had requested the uniforms to be sewn from preshrunk cloth. Given the weather in Brittany, if he were to soak the cloth it would never dry. Nervously, he promised to have the uniforms made with shrinkage in mind.

Days after Franklin submitted the colossal request to Vergennes, John Paul Jones and his four-ship squadron came across the Baltic fleet in the English Channel. A year earlier Jones had proposed an attack on that very convoy; by nightfall he was engaged in the grisly battle off Flamborough Head that would make his name. It was on September 23, from a cauldron of smoke and a sinking ship, that he was purported to say, as he surely did not: "I have not yet begun to fight." (By contrast, Franklin said nearly everything attributed to him, but borrowed much of it from others.) Jones fought a splendid battle from the blazing *Bonhomme Richard*, the deck slick with blood, cannon, muskets, and grenades exploding around him. Two hours into the engagement he assumed help to be on the way when the *Alliance*, Landais at the helm, detached itself from the darkness; Jones's astonishment was great when, shortly after nine at night, a series of broadsides ripped into the flames of the forecastle. "For God's sake! Wrong ship! Stop firing!" yelled his men, to no avail. The thirty-six-gun *Alliance* continued in her assault. Indeed in the course of the encounter the *Alliance* managed to blast the *Bonhomme Richard* not once but three times, killing several men before melting again into the mist, during the battle's climax. The *Bonhomme Richard* would not survive but Jones emerged from her wreck a hero; from Amsterdam, where he sought refuge, came reports of his instant celebrity. Ecstatically Franklin assured him that nothing but his "cool conduct and persevering bravery" was spoken of at Versailles. Landais, who had a very different account of the evening, emerged as a villain. "Either Captain Landais or myself is highly criminal and one or the other must be punished," an indignant Jones bellowed to Franklin, following the one thrilling American naval victory of the war. Already Jones had declined the Frenchman's invitation to duel.

Yet again the perversely named *Alliance* plunged Franklin into the kind of fracas he most abhorred. A livid Sartine ordered him to summon Landais for questioning, on charges of insubordination. Were it not for the Frenchman the *Bonhomme Richard* would not be sinking under the North Sea. In fits and starts, through November, Franklin led an inquiry into Landais's conduct, an opportunity he embraced halfheartedly, feeling himself both out of his depth and dangerously beyond his authority. It was notable that he exceeded his commission on other occasions—the request for a joint attack on Rhode Island was a case in point—but resisted doing so when those matters were unpalatable. Disciplining a French officer on French soil was highly impolitic. (The situation was all the more charged as the two ships had already once collided, on a June cruise, after which Landais had vowed to kill Jones. From the outset of their recent adventure, in which Landais joined only intermittently, he had ignored every one of Jones's signals.) Franklin showed no great incentive to get to the bottom of the matter, concerned mostly with heading off a duel, and a scandal. Landais challenged Jones's allegation that he had intentionally fired on the *Bonhomme Richard*, an argument to which Franklin, after a flurry of affidavits, succumbed. Ultimately he would suspend judgment in the matter, which not only occupied a great deal of his time but pointed up the need for someone in Paris qualified to serve as consul, which Congress had not provided.

As much as anything the *Bonhomme Richard* fiasco painfully drove home yet again the difficulty of coordinating a joint effort. Franklin thirsted for revenge on British soil, but—frustrated by the mortal enmity that separated Jones and Landais—could only conclude that there were "so many inconveniences in mixing the two nations together that I cannot encourage any farther proposal of the kind." Uncertainly he felt Congress out on the idea of dispatching a French regiment to America. (He also soft-pedaled his disappointment regarding Jones's cruise. Dramatic it had been, but disappointing, too; the richest British prizes had escaped during the battle.) Preferring endeavors that united men, he tended to a more manageable assignment, lobbying Sartine for the release of an American sea captain in French prison, dying for love of his French fiancée. The damsel in distress, as Franklin termed her, paid him a call; he could resist neither her pleas nor the couple's rapturous love letters. To Sartine he communicated his ardent desire that the obstacles to the union be removed, and "that there were a great many more matches made between the two nations, as I fancy they will agree better together in bed than they do in ships." On that count the American proved more of an idealist than his French counterpart, who took a cooler view of the proposed alliance. Sartine discovered that the groom had acted less than honorably with his intended—and evidently with a slew of other intendeds as well.*

A more sensitive man might have read something into the *Alliance* having sunk the *Bonhomme Richard*; from the point of view of nomenclature, the assault was painfully apt. A discomfort with French assistance, somehow embarrassing or tawdry, and with which Franklin was so intimately bound, began to haunt him. He was unfailingly courteous, begging funds in Versailles on the same March Thursday that, three thousand miles away, his compatriots sputtered rudely about a French alliance. His mincing metaphors were themselves out of sync with those of his colleagues. As a friend of the Adamses rumbled in November: "The way to insure the lasting regard of France is by showing independent virility instead of colonial effeminacy." It was a far cry from suitoring for alliances. The dashed hopes only fostered further dissent. The combined fleets of France and Spain were to have swallowed up England, Scotland, and Ireland. What had come to those exertions? As if in answer, d'Estaing limped back to Passy early in December, fresh from the New World, on

---

*Had Franklin checked his files he would have been further disabused of his romantic streak. The same lovestruck captain had petitioned him a year earlier. He had a wife and family in Nantucket.

crutches. He had failed at Newport in 1778 and again, at Savannah, in 1779. Franklin's friends joked that they hoped Versailles might in future provide America with addresses of some more gifted admirals.

On December 13 the affable, liberal-minded Dubourg died after a brief illness. The man who had introduced Franklin to France and been among the first to propose that Louis XVI appoint himself the noble defender of America, Dubourg had claimed to want only one thing before he died: a Franco-American alliance. That he got, for better or worse. His devotion to America also bankrupted him. He left no children, but had taken under his wing a nephew who was an aspiring doctor. Dubourg had withdrawn the teenage Jean L'Air de Lamotte from his medical studies so as to have a confidential secretary for his American affairs. The boy was now without funds or prospects, as a mutual friend reminded Franklin shortly after the December funeral. Could Congress either assume his medical school tuition or compensate him for his loyalty to the American cause?

Franklin spared the American government from that conundrum by taking on L'Air de Lamotte himself, installing him at the Valentinois. He doubtless inclined all the more toward generosity as he had now lived three years in expectation of the secretary Congress had promised but never delivered, leaving him to rely on Temple. An official appointment remained lost in a thicket of party politics; it seemed impossible to settle on a candidate acceptable to all factions. And when a compromise did emerge—as it did that fall in the form of Henry Laurens's son John, a Washington aide—the honor was shrugged off. Laurens warned his son the post was not one for "a man tender of his reputation." (John Laurens tried to atone for his decision by proposing Alexander Hamilton, who was no more able to muster the requisite seven votes than any other candidate.) Franklin would be the only American to be posted in Paris without clerks voted for and paid by Congress. The collaboration with L'Air de Lamotte was yet another that bore blighted results. The congenial secretary remained in Franklin's service for five and a half years, regularly mangling syntax and miscopying documents, with the purest of intentions.

Year's end brought with it word of several new arrivals, at least some of them welcome. At two in the morning on Christmas Eve Lafayette dashed off a note to Franklin from Saint-Germain. The American hero could not contain his excitement, of which he wanted Franklin to be the first to know; the marquise had given birth to a son, to be christened George Washington Lafayette.* Hours later Franklin heard that Congress had elected John Jay minister plenipotentiary to Spain. That was a Christmas present of a kind; Jay's appointment put Arthur Lee out of a job. Delighted though Franklin would have been by that prospect he by no means facilitated his colleague's departure. On the last day of 1779 he proved as obdurate as he had been with Izard in January, peremptorily refusing Lee's request for funds with which to settle his Parisian accounts.

From London came rumors of a third arrival. Word on the street had it that John Adams was headed back to France, with powers to negotiate a peace. Franklin dismissed the chatter out of hand, seeing in it only a ruse designed to provide a little holiday cheer for the London exchange. (It worked the desired effect.) And if America was in a mood for reconciliation he was decidedly not their man. "You began the war," he practically shouted across the Channel, "and it belongs to you to propose putting an end to it." Only once the rumors were confirmed did he change his tune. If Congress did not trust him with such a negotiation it was doubtless because that assembly knew his feelings about peace. He so abhorred war that he was likely to be lax in his terms. At the same time he added, unwilling to entertain any hints that France and Spain stood poised to take advantage of an enfeebled America, all parties should rest assured that he found the "destruction of our whole country, and the extirpation of our whole people, preferable to the infamy of abandoning our allies."

---

*The Lafayettes would christen their next child Virginia, moving Franklin—always a fan of fertility—to quip that the couple still had twelve colonies to go. All the same he counseled against saddling anyone with the names Massachusetts or Connecticut, perhaps tipping his hand a little. (The Lafayettes had no more children.) He was curiously silent about the name his daughter chose for the son she bore in 1779. Franklin's third Bache grandson was christened Louis, a name then unknown in America.

VIII

Everyone Has Wisdom Enough to Manage the Affairs of His Neighbors

1780

In Paris everything is very slow. Also, when dealing with the bureaucracy, the man you are talking to is never the man you have to see. The man you have to see has just gone off to Belgium, or is busy with his family, or has just discovered that he is a cuckold; he will be in next Tuesday at three o'clock, or sometimes in the course of the afternoon, or possibly to-morrow, or, possibly, in the next five minutes. But if he is coming in the next five minutes he will be far too busy to be able to see you today.
—James Baldwin

His seventy-fourth birthday brought Franklin around to the conviction that he would not live to see the end of the war. At the same time, undaunted, he hatched a plan. "Being arrived at 70 and considering that by traveling further in the same road I should probably be led to the grave, I stopped short, turned about and walked back again; which having done these four years, you may now call me 66," he informed a longtime friend, mightily pleased with his technique. He judged himself to be in the pink of health; he felt no less vital than he had a decade before. Doubtless it helped that he was fresh from a tutorial with Le Veillard's kittenish daughter, eager to instruct him in the ways of his adopted country. The teenage Geneviève Le Veillard had located certain deficiencies in Franklin's education: "Of course you know many important things. You have traveled, far and wide. You know men well. But you have never ventured into the head of a young French girl! Well, I shall tell you her secret," promised Geneviève. When she protested that she did not want to be kissed, she meant she did.

Toward the end of 1779 Chaumont moved Franklin from the garden pavilion to the right wing of the Valentinois proper, more luxurious rooms with a broad view over the Seine; Franklin's paneled, marble-floored quarters were linked to the Chaumonts' by a portrait gallery. It was, he admitted, "a lofty situation," and he very palpably longed for someone with whom to share it. While he hoped still to tempt Polly Hewson to make the Parisian trip, he simultaneously burrowed more deeply into French life. Again the signature suppleness was on brilliant display. For Madame Brillon he drafted, late in 1779, a whimsical piece called "The Whistle." He approved entirely of his friend's paradisiacal arrangements, but the truth remained that they had both of them some time still to live in this world. To do so happily Franklin cited a lesson he had mastered early on, as essential to a seven-year-old Bostonian as to a Parisian septuagenarian. In his youth he had dearly overpaid for a coveted whistle; his chagrin entirely outweighed the pleasure of the purchase. It was essential to keep one's priorities in check.

He followed that exercise with an all-out offensive, penned on or just after January 1, 1780. Already he had begun to divide his neighborly attentions between Madame Brillon in Passy and a very different address down the hill in Auteuil, to which he gravitated with increasing frequency. The philosopher Claude-Adrien Helvétius had left behind a stunning and vivacious sixty-year-old widow, as unfettered by nerves or convention as Madame Brillon was a prisoner of both. The blue-eyed, alabaster-skinned, Anne-Catherine de Ligniville d'Autricourt Helvétius was by no means a first-rate intellectual—her spelling was deemed on par with that of her cats; she tended to dive headlong into a conversation and thrash about with all her might—but had all the same inherited her husband's exalted circle of liberal-minded scientific, literary, and political celebrities. His Masonic lodge held its initial meetings in her living room; among her earliest admirers was the sober, awkward Turgot, who had proposed marriage both before and after Helvétius, and who remained an intimate. Franklin marveled at Madame Helvétius's popularity, which he attributed not to any intellectual prowess but to her unbounded charm. She was indeed an unpretentious delight, as unfussy and forgiving as Madame Brillon was oversensitive and prone to defeat. And she was a beauty. As one of her more elderly admirers put it upon meeting her in a state of relative undress: "Oh, to be 70 again!" Those qualities combined to make the twenty-minute walk to Auteuil an irresistible one, perhaps more irresistible even than the scatty Madame Helvétius intended. On one occasion Franklin and Temple took her up on a breakfast invitation that their hostess either forgot or assumed her neighbors would. They were left to fend for themselves, without staff or provisions. Inevitably the outcome was a bagatelle, Franklin's "Bilked for Breakfast."

Madame Helvétius was a woman for whom a country retreat and solitude were very different things; hers were three of the most populated acres of Auteuil. Even in an age when lapdogs were operagoers, when Frenchwomen shared their hot chocolate with pet monkeys, Madame Helvétius carried animal loving to an extreme. She began her day by distributing crumbs to the birds in the acacia outside her bedroom window; she doted on her chickens, her canaries, her dogs, chief among them Pompon. An armada of angoras presided over her immense blue-and-white second-floor salon, filled always with abundant bouquets and inundated with light. From September to June Madame Helvétius saw to it that the eighteen cats were regally attired in satin and fur-lined brocades, finery in which they roamed the household, magnificent trains rustling behind them. Their decorum vanished at mealtime, when partridge and chicken breasts arrived on white china, to be greeted by a storm of hissing and mewling. Madame Helvétius's claws came out too for the visitor who dared to occupy any of the angoras' favorite perches among her sea of stained sofas. Generally she could be found in her favorite velvet armchair, her curly hair in a state of perfect disorder, one of her overdressed animals on her underdressed lap.

In the pavilion at the edge of her lushly and haphazardly plotted garden she lodged a different collection. There she installed two great admirers, the blond, blue-eyed abbé de la Roche, a slow-moving classicist whose only other passion in life was old books, and the long-faced, high-minded Pierre Cabanis, a medical student and poet, something of an adopted son. (To Madame Helvétius's embrace of the animal kingdom there was one exception. She had no use for women, including her own daughters.) Along with the sharp-tongued abbé Morellet, who installed himself in the main house two to three nights a week, Cabanis and la Roche assisted Madame Helvétius in her social rounds. As such they became the instruments of Franklin's courtship of the Auteuil establishment, not one he felt compelled to conduct in private. It was to twenty-two-year-old Cabanis that Franklin transmitted an early message to their mutual friend: "If this lady is pleased to spend her days with Franklin, he would be just as pleased to spend his nights with her. And since he has already granted her so many of his days, of which he has so few remaining, she seems an ingrate for never having granted him a single one of her nights, which have been utterly wasted, having made no one happy except Pompon."

The consorts further animated an exuberant household. For one late 1779 evening, the teetotaling abbé Morellet coined a drinking song in Franklin's honor, assigning to his revolutionary fervor a cause that eluded even the most perverse critics at home. The intrepid American battled for that most elevated of human liberties: the right of the American people to drink French wines. As the "abbé Franklin," Franklin countered with an essay of his own. (In his high-spirited romp through the Bible he purported to prove the equation of *vino* with *veritas*. Only he would have titled the exercise "Sundry Moral and Philosophical Christian Reflections, sacred and profane, substances better mixed in France than in America.") Franklin remarked repeatedly on the affinity he felt for the late Helvétius, a disciple of Locke and a longtime correspondent of Voltaire. Like Franklin, Helvétius focused in his work on the civic spirit and on the pursuit of happiness, radical ideas for eighteenth-century Europe. And in the company of the philosopher's widow Franklin seemed eager to prove one of Helvétius's maxims: "It is worth being wise only so long as one can also be foolhardy." In Auteuil the abbé Morellet sang Franklin's favorite Scottish ballads, in French, while Franklin accompanied him on the glass harmonica, for a select few, once the footmen had been dismissed.

In the course of one such lighthearted evening Franklin suggested that he and Helvétius, two men who had so much in common, add Madame Helvétius to their mutual interests. The suit was emphatically rejected; Madame Helvétius protested that she had every intention of remaining faithful to her great husband's memory. "The Elysian Fields" was delivered to Auteuil the following morning. In that tale a distraught Franklin throws himself into bed upon the rejection. His dreams carry him to paradise, where he seeks out Helvétius. He grills the visitor on the war, on religion, on liberty, and on the French government, but at no juncture inquires after his widow. Franklin reveals that he has left her but an hour earlier. Does the philosopher not care for her news? Helvétius declines. He has found a new wife, not as beautiful, perhaps, but with as much spirit and good sense as his first, and infinitely devoted to him. She is at that moment off collecting the best nectar and ambrosia to be had, for his delectation. Franklin wastes no time in informing Helvétius that his widow is more faithful than he. She has had many suitors, each rejected out of hand. He himself loves her desperately. Helvétius commiserates with Franklin on his plight and offers up a solution—Franklin should enlist la Roche to argue against his cause, as Madame Helvétius has a marked tendency of doing the opposite of what the good abbé suggests—when the new Madame Helvétius returns from her ambrosia gathering. She is none other than Debbie Franklin, although this Mrs. Franklin has no time for her husband of forty-four years. Coolly she indicates that she has moved on. The moral is abundantly clear. "Let us avenge ourselves!" Franklin entreats his dear friend in Auteuil, not for the first time proposing a match based on spite.

How seriously he intended the proposal remains a matter of conjecture. He may have courted as ardently before, but never on paper; Madame Brillon and Madame Helvétius were his most literate conquests, and he rose splendidly to the occasion. There is no question of his affection for Madame Helvétius, the only woman he outpaced in correspondence. Made of sturdier stuff, that devotion would outlast even his fondness for Madame Brillon. At the same time Franklin was no stranger to the time-honored ploy of asking for something he deeply desired without any honest expectation of receiving it, a brand of courtship known to those with much to gain and little to lose, or the already married. And a suitor who thought his proposition in any danger of being accepted would have had some incentive to keep it private. Someone corrected the piece for Franklin, who polished it carefully. He was proud of it, enough so to have the composition published in April, when all Paris could enjoy his sprightly wit. That too was unusual behavior for a spurned suitor. For those reasons "The Elysian Fields" has been read as an exercise in style, or as proof that literature came first with Franklin. He may have been less embarrassed by the rejection than pleased by its implications. It was not every day that an American rebel could court a distant relative of Marie Antoinette.

All the same there seems little question that his remarks were intended earnestly. At no juncture did Franklin relent in his campaign. At the end of the year he was leveled by another attack of gout, which confined him to the Valentinois for nearly six weeks. With the onslaught came a familiar, crippling pain in his foot and leg, followed by an acute tenderness. Madame Helvétius arranged for his rooms to be cleaned; that they offended her relaxed sense of order spoke to their neglect. She was afterward thanked not by Franklin but by the Valentinois flies. In having ordered the cobwebs swept away, Madame Helvétius had banished the spiders who nested in Franklin's woodwork. She had restored the flies' happy existence. It would be idyllic with but one small adjustment: For their sake, could she and Dr. Franklin please join households?

Madame Helvétius held Franklin off with a weapon close at hand. She teased him about his profligacy. This was flirtation as sport; it was good for the circulation. Nor was she alone in goading Franklin. Her houseguests did too. Morellet badgered Franklin about an Auteuil seating arrangement. His friend considered himself an enlightened free trader. How then could he justify his monopolizing ways? Madame Brillon had more reason to begrudge Franklin his attraction to Auteuil than anyone; it was one thing for Franklin to grant her rival a Wednesday when he might have been with her, another thing altogether for him to make alternate plans for the afterlife. He had after all borrowed the idea of a paradisiacal encounter from her. (Madame Helvétius quipped that it was going to be one very crowded paradise.) It fell to the younger woman to upbraid Franklin for allowing his wisdom to "be perpetually broken against the rocks of femininity." And as she pointed out, he did not so much permit it to do so as enjoy for it to do so. While he was the first to confess to the "bad habit I have long had of doing everything that ladies desire me to do," Franklin impishly held his own. He offered up his Euclidian proof that the man who is constant to many women is in fact more constant than the man who is constant only to one.

As much as Madame Helvétius may have resisted Franklin's petitions there was no question of her devotion. For her American friend she broke one of her cardinal rules, venturing to Passy weekly for dinner, with her retinue, when otherwise she strayed little from her own grounds.* He broke his rules too, sitting for a portrait for Madame Helvétius when he had sworn never to do so again. He knew of nothing more tedious. If the

---

*It was one of many small tributes. From a coffee-drinking country Franklin elicited the ultimate compliment: On his account the women of France mastered the art of brewing tea.

marriage proposal fell on deaf ears, it was at the very least proof that Franklin had mastered something of the local idiom; "semi-serious declarations of love" have been called the small change of eighteenth-century conversation. He had made himself at home, more of a feat than it seemed.* The Franklin who had always been fastidious about personal hygiene yielded to a world in which the well-bred Parisienne thought nothing of spitting and hawking in the street, of swabbing her armpits before an audience.

John Adams counted Madame Helvétius and Madame Brillon chief among his colleague's distractions, from which "he came home at all hours from 9 to 12 o'clock at night." And Amazons and angels it very much was when the Old and New Worlds faced off in the forms of Madame Helvétius and Mrs. Adams. The American would set eyes upon a real Frenchwoman for the first time shortly after her 1784 arrival, when Madame Helvétius swept carelessly into the Valentinois, a blowsy blur in a black shawl and straw hat. She managed only to cry out: "*Ah! Mon Dieu! Where is Franklin? Why did you not tell me there were ladies here?*" before running from the living room, in what might equally well have been disappointment or fright. "When she returned, the Doctor entered at one door, she at the other, upon which she ran forward to him, caught him by the hand, '*Hélas* Franklin'; then gave him a double kiss one upon each cheek, and another upon his forehead," observed Mrs. Adams, whose eyes grew wider yet at the dinner table. The exotic specimen was placed between Franklin and Adams. "She carried on the chief of the conversation at dinner, frequently locking her hand into the doctor's and sometimes spreading her arms upon the backs of both the gentlemen's chairs, then throwing her arm carelessly upon the doctor's neck." She might well be the rich, respectable widow of a distinguished thinker, as Franklin assured her, but Mrs. Adams saw before her only repellent gauze rags and unkempt hair, a decaying monument to impropriety. The sole American to whom Madame Helvétius could be compared was a madwoman.

Matters did not improve after dinner, when Madame Helvétius settled

---

*The manners and mores of a Frenchwoman left many an American befuddled and discomfited; Jefferson may have said it all by falling in love with an Englishwoman while in Paris. He reduced the difference between the women of France and America to the contest between "Amazons and angels."

jauntily on a settee, exposing more than a little ankle. From her perch she covered Pompon with kisses. "She had a little lap dog who was next to the Doctor her favorite," observed Mrs. Adams, who nearly fainted dead away when Pompon left a puddle on Dr. Franklin's floor, which Madame Helvétius casually mopped up with her sleeve. The Massachusetts minister's daughter vowed to remain a shut-in were this indecency the norm.* Curiously enough her reaction had been anticipated years before, when a celebrated philosopher imagined what a sober, liberty-loving republican might make of Paris were he to be dropped down amidst the best company. "How would he be surprised at seeing every one there treat public affairs with indifference, and warmly employ themselves about nothing but the fashion, a novel, or a little dog," mused Helvétius, in 1758, well aware that his countrymen were in no danger of shedding their reputations as a "trifling, giddy-brained people."

Franklin came to a somewhat different conclusion. He made no secret of enjoying the company of the ladies, time permitting. He evinced no qualms about immorality; he is reputed to have been the first American to own a copy of Cleland's *Fanny Hill*. But utility remained his middle name. "The purest and most useful friend a man could possibly procure was a Frenchwoman of a certain age, who had no designs on his person. They are so ready to do you service, and from their knowledge of the world know well how to serve you wisely," he noted. It was a very different analysis from that offered up by the thirty-nine-year-old Franklin who—making a cynical case for taking an older woman to bed—had observed that all cats are gray in the dark.

On January 30, 1780, Franklin was joined at his Sunday dinner by a well-traveled New Yorker who had arrived in Paris the previous evening. Peter Allaire was a London-based merchant in his late thirties who had for some

---

*Abigail Adams measured the world by her husband's infallible barometer. "The manners of women are the surest criterion by which to determine whether a republican government is practicable in a nation or not. The Jews, the Greeks, the Romans, the Swiss, the Dutch, all lost their public spirit, their republican principles and habits, and their republican forms of government, when they lost the modesty and domestic virtues of their women," Adams concluded, after his years in France.

time plied a profitable trade in the most exotic locales. Since the war, he had confined himself to the flow of merchandise and intelligence between England and France. At various times he attempted to interest Franklin in his schemes, most recently in acquiring a fever-reducing chemical powder for the Continental Army; Allaire proposed to ship quantities of his miracle substance in bulk to Calais. Franklin resisted that offer, as he had Allaire's appeals to serve as an American agent in London—his dubious wares appeared superior to his information—but welcomed the New Yorker all the same to the Valentinois. To that address Allaire was trailed by a spy sent by Beaumarchais, who had it on good authority that the visitor's loyalties were suspect. Beaumarchais was all the more concerned on Monday, when the New Yorker paid him a call. Allaire claimed to be in Paris for business reasons, as well as to serve as secretary to John Jay, who he insisted was in town. (He was not.) In nearly the same breath, Allaire added that London believed the American cause to be lost. Beaumarchais was enough disturbed to turn over surveillance to the professionals. Meanwhile Allaire arranged to have an enticing package sent from his Saint-Germain hotel to Passy, bestowing on Franklin a copy of William Eden's *Letters to Carlisle*, an account of the failed American peace mission. Along with the volume he sent something equally guaranteed to please: a bottle of aged Madeira, a Franklin favorite.

The days that followed were hectic ones for Franklin, who saw to it that L'Air de Lamotte, the new clerk, was installed at Passy, and who braced himself for more company; as it turned out, John Adams was indeed expected. Adams rolled into Paris finally on February 9, having spent twice as long on a harrowing, overland trek from Spain as he had crossing the Atlantic in a leaky vessel.* He settled in the hotel in central Paris where he had first alighted in 1778. The next morning he paid a call at the Valentinois, but without revealing the purpose of his mission, about which Franklin did not inquire. If he thought the matter would come up when he escorted Adams to Versailles that week he was mistaken; Adams breathed not a syllable of his business to Vergennes, whom the Americans found cheerful and relaxed. Franklin trusted that a letter from Congress would elucidate matters soon enough. If he felt vulnerable he did not reveal as much.

---

*He had spent all of three months at home, in which time he drafted, nearly single-handedly, the Massachusetts state constitution.

He was by no means altogether complacent. He was terrified by the louche Allaire, who he suspected was in Paris to poison him. (The conditions were right. As has been noted, Madeira is flavorful enough to cloak an additive, and Allaire's fever powder contained a cousin of arsenic.) Evidently Franklin trusted in his own instincts and in Lenoir's talents—he had as well the versatile Bancroft at hand, an expert on poisons—as he made no immediate move to have Allaire apprehended. He was biding his time. On February 14 Temple presented him with Allaire's request for documents with which to leave Paris. Did Franklin care to grant them? "NO," Franklin replied emphatically. The next morning Allaire's hotel breakfast was interrupted by two of Lenoir's men. They spent several hours searching his rooms, after which they escorted the visitor to police headquarters. They found nothing incriminating, but Allaire's papers, it was explained at police headquarters, would need to be reviewed carefully. That would take time. Allaire was dismissed courteously, or so he believed, until he realized he was being courteously escorted to the Bastille. Atypically, he was incarcerated at the request of the prison chief, a Franklin friend.

Only after ten days of solitary confinement was Allaire led to an interrogation room, where prison officials and chemists awaited him. The bottle of Madeira was produced and uncorked. Allaire was offered a tumbler of the nutty liqueur. He swallowed it blithely, and had at the end of his inquisition enough self-possession to ask that his regards be conveyed to Messrs. Lenoir and Franklin. Less for that impudent remark than on suspicions that he was a British spy, he spent the next months in the Bastille, subjected to a second interrogation (held amid a collection of instruments of torture), and deprived of all contact with the outside world. He was released finally late in May and expelled from France, doubtless to Franklin's relief. His uncharacteristic panic aside, he had no need either of a new, murderous enemy or for an American to be locked up in the Bastille on espionage charges, an embarrassment to the cause.*

The image sullier would turn out not to be Allaire but Franklin's intermittent colleague, who felt neither need nor obligation to enlighten Franklin as to his mission. Even if he had some inkling of Adams's dis-

---

*Allaire was indeed on the British payroll, although it is by no means clear that he was an assassin.

tress over the 1779 departure, Franklin had no reason to believe Adams to be anything but a loyal and straight-shooting compatriot. As for Adams having maintained a separate address on his second visit, Franklin would have been hard pressed at the Valentinois to accommodate his colleague, who in 1780 traveled with an entourage of six. (In addition to his servants, Adams had with him two young sons and two secretaries.) All the same, lacking any assurances to the contrary, it would have been reasonable to assume that he was in Paris as a corrective to, if not as a replacement for, Franklin. That was the conclusion at which members of the diplomatic corps arrived quickly enough, having heard that there was dissatisfaction in America with "the dawdling manner, and some say the self-serving spirit, of Dr. Franklin."

Yet again Vergennes was better informed about American affairs than was that country's minister plenipotentiary at the court of Versailles. Vergennes had learned of Adams's arrival in Spain soon after he made landfall, although he was for some days uncertain as to whether the envoy was heading to Paris or to Madrid. He devoutly hoped it was not the latter; at a time when the war effort seemed stalled, the last thing he needed was for a hot-blooded patriot to discover that his country had in Spain an indifferent ally. He was relieved then when Adams turned up in Paris, less so when Adams ultimately revealed his mission. He was entrusted to negotiate both a peace and a commercial treaty with Great Britain. Vergennes had in part himself to blame; when he had requested an American peace commissioner, he had not for a minute dreamed he would end up with John Adams. And the timing was dismal. Adams was approximately two years too early, and devoid of all talent for waiting offstage for his cue. For his part, he was to regret having solicited advice at Versailles, where a flabbergasted Vergennes let him know that it was in neither ally's best interest to hint at a peace under the present circumstances. (In London, Adams's very presence in Europe was read as a surrender.) Nor was it wise for the new envoy to make any formal announcement of his second commission. To solicit a treaty of commerce at such a time was, warned Vergennes, to "busy oneself furnishing a house before the foundation is laid."

Adams was all the same gratified by the reception at Versailles when several days later Franklin took him to confer with Vergennes, Sartine, and Maurepas. "I never heard the French ministry so frank, explicit and decided, as each of these were, in the course of this conversation, in their declarations to pursue the war with vigor and afford effectual aid to the United States," a delighted Adams assured Congress. Clothing and arms for fifteen thousand men were being assembled; a fleet was to supplement those ships already in the West Indies. Moreover, Jay had safely arrived in Spain, where he was to negotiate a Spanish treaty. The *Alliance*, now under the command of John Paul Jones, was being readied to sail with American supplies.

It was by those arrangements that Franklin was consumed, rather than by the riddle of Adams's mission. As France prepared to send six thousand men to America under the legendary comte de Rochambeau, finances remained the major preoccupation in Passy. Jones lobbied hard to make various repairs to the *Alliance*, leaving Franklin to beg for mercy: "But let me repeat it, for God's sake be sparing, unless you mean to make me a bankrupt." (Jones complied, but not without a whimper. He would be frugal. He would convey Lee, Izard, and their families to America. He would deliver Franklin's uniforms. But he was in dire need of a new first lieutenant, his own being a drunkard.) Franklin fended off additional strains in the form of state representatives dispatched to Paris to solicit funds, requests that interfered with his own. He was strapped as it was. "But the number of agents from separate states running all over Europe and asking to borrow money has given such an idea of our distress and poverty as makes everybody afraid to trust us," he warned Congress, fully aware that his was an unpopular position.

Shorthanded and overwhelmed though he was, his spirits were good. On February 21 the French government settled on Lafayette to deliver the news of Rochambeau's expeditionary force to America; the first installment of a new loan came through; Franklin was pleased with the stores he had obtained. He and Adams enjoyed cordial relations. He did not begrudge Adams his discretion, nor did Adams badger him; he sounded no note of reproach against Franklin in his voluminous correspondence of those months, when, by his own count, Adams dispatched ninety-five letters to Congress, more, he could not help but note, than all of the European envoys combined since the Revolution began. (It helped that Adams had two well-educated secretaries and no immediate responsibilities.) "We live upon good terms with each other," Franklin allowed, "but he has never communicated anything of his business to me, and I have made no inquiries of him, nor have I any letter from Congress explaining it, so that I am in utter ignorance." In a forward-thinking mood he proposed a joint European tour to George Washington. "You would on this side [of] the sea enjoy the great reputation you have acquired, pure and free from those little shades that the jealousy and envy of a man's countrymen and contemporaries are ever endeavouring to cast over living merit," he wrote, continuing on to offer one of his most eloquent anthems to America's future. He was himself feeling liberated from those shades, two of whom were scheduled to depart shortly. He did not fool himself as to what those exports would mean for the alliance in America, however, and warned friends of the spirit of enmity in which Lee and Izard headed off: "Not being liked here themselves, they dislike the people. For the same reason indeed they ought to dislike all that know them." With neither man did he permit himself behavior of which he might be ashamed. Both came to the Valentinois to say their goodbyes. Franklin sent them off civilly, without letting on that he knew anything of their indictments. Nor did he choose to trust either with his dispatches.

~⚡~

Even rid, as he believed he was, of Izard and Lee, Franklin found himself refereeing contests among the staunchest of American patriots. Repeatedly Chaumont and Williams, rivals in supplying Congress, came to blows. At the end of March Chaumont discovered that Williams planned to ship trunks of gold, lace, and silk in the military convoy, of which every inch was already spoken for. He delivered a savage reprimand. Meanwhile Jones, scheduled to command the *Alliance*, separately questioned Chaumont's integrity. The entrepreneur was both wildly indiscreet and reluctant to disburse payments, claiming that the government was in arrears with him, as indeed it was. "And if the people remain much longer dissatisfied I tremble and *let him tremble too* for the consequence!" thundered Jones, prevailing on Franklin to run interference. (Franklin felt powerless to help. Chaumont was Sartine's man. And as long as France was paying the bills, France was entitled to call the shots.)

The situation was complicated by the fact that a portion of the American stores were meant to be sent with the French fleet preparing to sail under Rochambeau but arrived too late in Brest to be included in that May 2 departure. By which time Franklin had begun to bleat about the muddle:

He was at a great distance from the ports, knew not what to advise about the cloth or the small arms or the powder that refused to load itself into boats, "and yet everybody writes me for orders, or advice, or opinion, or approbation, which is like calling upon a blind man to judge of colors." He knew only that those things were all desperately needed in America. Increasingly he fell back on an excuse not often associated with Franklin: his ignorance. At the outset of the French and Indian War he had ingeniously provisioned General Braddock's army, but that was on a smaller scale and in a different language. By 1780 he could indulge only in a roundelay of buck-passing. The business of cargoes, the fitting out of ships, the purchasing of supplies, the payment of crews, the distribution of prize monies were all of them out of his sphere. He washed his hands of them.

With the supplies being loaded into the *Alliance* at Lorient was Arthur Lee, whom Jones was to convey to America. Also at hand was the ship's former captain, the erratic Pierre Landais, whom Franklin had not cashiered, preferring to leave his fate to an American court. "I find him so exceedingly captious and critical, and so apt to misconstrue as an intended injustice every expression in our language he does not immediately understand, that I am tired of writing anything for him or about him, and am determined to have nothing further to do with him," Franklin vowed on March 1. He could not have guessed that Landais was to occupy him night and day for the remainder of the spring. Also on March 1 Franklin asked that Jones return to the French captain the personal effects Landais had left on the *Alliance*. If Landais wished to sail to America to obtain a trial, he could find a place on any of the many boats heading out. Instead Landais lobbied to return on the *Alliance*. It was his rightful command, and the crew disliked Jones. Franklin was astonished: Those same officers had earlier mutinied against him, he reminded Landais. Franklin suspected that the Frenchman was harassing him so that he would refuse him, of which he would make a great deal in America. And as that appeared to be what the peevish captain so desired, he obliged. Landais could not have the *Alliance* back. Franklin would defend himself against any charges the captain cared to make against him at home. Landais could hardly reproach him the inquiry he had held over the *Bonhomme Richard* incident, as the Frenchman attempted. Franklin had kept his opinions entirely to himself, so as not to prejudice any future trial. (In fact he had done one better: He had actually defended Landais to all parties.) He would leave the assessment of Landais's military conduct to the professionals. If the captain truly wanted his personal opinion he was happy to offer it, however. Franklin thought him imprudent and litigious. Had he twenty ships of war at his disposition, he would, he assured Landais, entrust none of them to him.

Sounding embarrassed and beleaguered, Franklin labored to explain the delay in the *Alliance*'s departure to Congress. He could make no promises as to when she would sail. The same day the ship's officers reminded him that they had six weeks earlier applied to him for wages and prize money, as well as to be returned to America, where they longed to be. They still awaited word. Franklin replied that as he had no authority to rule on prizes he had simply sent the officers' wages. Already he was bending the regulations a little. As for their newfound loyalty to a captain against whom they had mutinied, he was stupefied. He had already placed another man in command. "Take in good part this friendly counsel of an old man, who is your friend. Go home peaceably with your ship. Do your duties faithfully and cheerfully. Behave respectfully to your commander, and I am persuaded he will do the same to you," advised Franklin, in this case not only colorblind but tone-deaf. His homily fell on the ears of a disappointed crew who were broke, hungry, and homesick, and without any affection for the hard-driving Jones. With the same mail went a note to Landais. Franklin was flabbergasted to find him still meddling with the *Alliance*. Landais refused receipt of the letter. Addressed as it was to the former commander of the *Alliance*, it was clearly not intended for him.

The next exchange sent Franklin scurrying to Versailles for help with what was becoming more a crisis than an embarrassment. He stood between two American-commissioned officers, of different nationalities and at daggers drawn, fighting for command of a ship called the *Alliance*.* And not only did Landais's officers reaffirm their solidarity for their original leader, but Franklin heard as well from the ship's crew. All 115 men requested that Landais be restored. Chaumont at his side, Franklin applied to Sartine for assistance. Two orders went out immediately. Landais

---

*Already Landais had taken to trailing Jones about town, sword in hand, intent on the duel to which he had challenged the American months earlier. "Shut the door," Jones cried to one visitor, having narrowly eluded Landais on the Lorient street. "I do not know how to fence and I do not want to be killed by that rascal."

was to be apprehended and imprisoned. And the French government undertook to facilitate Jones's departure in the *Alliance*, which Franklin enjoined him to effect immediately, in appropriately Jones-worthy rhetoric: "You have shown your abilities in fighting. You have now an opportunity of showing the other necessary part in the character of a great chief, your abilities in governing."

On June 12 Jones read his orders to the crew of the *Alliance*, who appeared satisfied. Several hours later he went ashore. In his absence Landais's men ejected Jones's officers from the ship and placed his crew in irons, in the hold. To fervent cheers Landais then boarded the *Alliance*, by what he claimed were orders of Congress. Behind his coup some were quick to spot "a certain industrious genius" who—in perfect opposition to Franklin's repeated orders—had advised Landais. There was only one man in Europe perverse enough to prefer that his country suffer a little longer than that Franklin claim any additional glory. While there was as yet no evidence at hand, it seemed safe to venture, as did one of Franklin's friends, that "Mr. Lee is at the bottom of this affair."

Jonathan Williams was of the same conviction, as he made abundantly clear to Lee's twenty-two-year-old nephew when he ran into him in the street days later. He hurled a loud insult in the younger man's direction. As Williams refused to apologize, there was only one means of recourse. Arthur Lee sent his seconds to challenge Williams to a duel, an invitation that was accepted with relish, though not one that was sanctioned by Passy. The two men faced off in Williams's rooms on June 20. Damaging though he had been to Franklin on every other count, Lee missed his shot at four yards; his bullet lodged in the wall. Williams—perhaps more sensitive to the spectacle of two Americans drawing on each other when they had enemies to battle elsewhere—fired out the window, and the matter was considered honorably settled in Brittany. At Passy it was anything but. Having again conferred with the experts at Versailles, Franklin ordered Landais to leave the *Alliance* immediately. The ship's officers were to report to Jones. He also ruled that Jones was under no obligation to transport Lee to America, should he feel the voyage might be in any way endangered by that passenger. He needed no convincing that Lee had crossed the line from malicious to criminal. Once again he offered up insanity as Lee's only excuse, predicting that "if some of the many enemies he provokes do not kill him sooner, he will die in a madhouse."

Jones chose not to confront Landais after the coup, but rather to journey to Paris for Franklin's orders. He was gone for a matter of days; on his return to his ship he met with a most extraordinary sight. Landais had moved the *Alliance* out of harbor. And Jones received impertinent letters not only from Landais but also from Lee, who argued that Franklin was exceeding his orders in commanding the Frenchman to relinquish command of his ship. As Jones saw it, Lee was angling for nothing less than a little Franco-American bloodshed. He offered Franklin a little advice of his own: "And as a friend who really loves you, I must tell you that I am persuaded your malicious rivals leveled the blow against you rather than me."

Per orders from Versailles, a boom was lowered across the harbor to prevent Landais's escape. The port citadel stood under orders to fire should the *Alliance* attempt to pass; Jones was supplied with a small flotilla of warships. Called upon to yield up the *Alliance*, Landais threatened: "If you come within reach of my cannons I will sink you!" Weighing gross insubordination against the ramifications of the French firing into an American ship, Jones relented. He saw to it that the flotilla turned back and that the boom was raised. Unhappy though he was with that turn of events, he explained that "my humanity would not suffer me to remain a silent witness of bloodshed between allied subjects of France and America." To do otherwise was to play into Lee's hands. In Passy Franklin appealed for advice to John Adams. In his opinion Lee was right, legally speaking. Franklin could not remove Landais from his command, as Congress had not granted the Navy Board itself that authority. Nor was there yet sufficient admiral law to adjudicate such a case in Europe. In the absence of either a code of law or a tribunal, Adams advised Franklin to submit the entire mess to Congress, as quickly as possible. Meanwhile Landais refused either to sail without his prize monies or to return the half-loaded *Alliance* to port. "Thus does this fool and madman sacrifice the dearest interests of our country, by following the pernicious councils of your late colleague," moaned Jonathan Williams, searching frantically for a replacement ship.

Landais's impudence left Franklin to conjure with the various schemes that Chaumont, Williams, Jones, and each of their associates proposed to convey the abandoned stores, schemes by which he was utterly bewildered. Again he protested that those arrangements lay utterly outside his domain and beyond his expertise. He was right on both counts, wrong not to have exerted more energy to unravel them; a younger man might have made the trip to Lorient. As much as Franklin yearned to free himself of maritime matters, their import was driven home to him on June 23, when he received the devastating news that Charleston had been taken. The work of a vast naval force, that defeat was the worst of the war; within months nearly all of South Carolina would be overrun by the British. At court and elsewhere Franklin held his head high, insisting that Charleston was another Philadelphia. The city would be difficult for the British to maintain. It was of no strategic advantage. In truth he was much concerned; with Charleston went five thousand American soldiers, four American ships, and three hundred pieces of artillery. Worse, the defeat seriously compromised American stock at Versailles, the more so as that news followed word that Congress had in March depreciated American currency from 40 to 1. In America a bushel of corn sold for a sum in the neighborhood of $150. In France any merchant who had in a substantial way assisted the American war effort was ruined.

While Franklin's self-control was such that he could make it through an entire dinner without reference to either calamity, the frustration manifested itself on the page. At Chaumont's intervention, Louis XVI provided a second ship for the additional Lorient stores. Franklin's landlord had seriously underestimated, however; the *Ariel* was too small for the goods at hand. There were no further options. Franklin instructed Williams to send what he could immediately, and without deluding himself as to any easy cooperation between Jones and Chaumont. That was impossible, as was any new squadron project, which he prohibited his nephew from so much as mentioning to him. "I have been too long in hot water plagued almost to death with the passions, vagaries, and ill humours and madnesses of other people. I must have a little repose," he exploded.

That was not to be, as the Landais saga continued. Stubbornly the captain held out for his monies, threatening Franklin that the blame for the *Alliance*'s unconscionable delay would fall squarely on his head. The former *Bonhomme Richard* crewmen begged for mercy; they were in irons, on half-rations, and did not care to sail home as prisoners. (And these, Jones pointed out, were the same men who had fought so bravely at his side at Flamborough Head.) Jones continued to claim as much of Franklin's attention as his delinquent rival, having been indiscreet enough to blame Landais's escape on the French. He grumbled that the Lorient officers had behaved "rather like women than men." Franklin firmly reproached him. Had Jones stayed aboard his ship he would not have lost the *Alliance* in the first place. He would be well advised not to blame his men: "Hereafter, if you should observe on occasion to give your officers and friends a little more praise than is their due, and confess more fault than you can justly be charged with, you will only become the sooner for it a great captain. Criticising and censuring almost everyone you have to do with will diminish friends, increase enemies, and thereby hurt your affairs."

Landais harangued Franklin for the last time on July 7, setting sail hours later. The departure brought with it little immediate relief, not only because of the six hundred tons of desperately needed merchandise he left behind. Franklin emerged from the crisis to find himself embrangled in another. While his attention had been diverted by the fiasco in Lorient, Adams had been busying himself with Vergennes in Versailles. Over the spring Adams had begun to fret not only that France pursued the American war halfheartedly but that her allies had no interest in seeing a powerful new nation rise in the west. In that clear-eyed assessment he included Vergennes, who he believed intended "to keep his hand under our chin to prevent us from drowning, but not to lift our heads out of water." From the start the air between the two men was thick with mutual suspicion: Vergennes was of the belief that he was dealing with a tactless, inflexible amateur who practiced slapshot diplomacy, while Adams was convinced that the sinuous, velvety Vergennes thought little of him or of America. Matters came to a head after a long June conversation about the currency devaluation. As Jones recoiled from an open confrontation in Lorient, Adams opened fire in Versailles. Vergennes let it be known that France categorically opposed such a measure unless America provided an exemption for French merchants. In response Adams buried Vergennes in an avalanche of papers, defending Congress's fiscal decisions, and offering various pointers on how France might conduct her war effort. Where, by the way, was the promised military support? Rochambeau and his army may well have been sent to Washington's assistance, but what was the French navy doing in the West Indies rather than in North American waters? The colonies would never prevail so long as Britain ruled the seas. Adams promised to avail himself of all future opportunities to enlighten Vergennes on foreign policy.

"It is hard that I who give others no trouble with my quarrels should be plagued with all the perversities of those who think fit to wrangle with one another," yelped Franklin, his hands full of the Landais mess, and shortly before he heard from a disgruntled Vergennes. On June 30 the French minister asked Franklin to alert Congress to its representative's activities. Franklin indulged in some immediate damage control. While he remained noncommittal on the issue of the currency devaluation—surely no French creditor should be made to suffer—he reassured Vergennes that Adams did not speak for America as a whole. His countrymen had only respect for and gratitude to France. It seems he did not press the case with Adams, who days later, in an interminable discourse, reminded Vergennes of the dangerous remnants of anti-French sentiment in America. Many of his compatriots would be only too happy to return to British dominion. Naturally a few men-of-war along the coast could obliterate that lingering prejudice once and for all. And too the ships would disprove the arguments that France did not mean to assist America in any substantive way. For the lack of coordination between the two envoys Franklin was as guilty as Adams, but it was the younger man who blundered on. Why exactly should he not enter into talks with the British? He made a passing nod to humility, asserting that he did not believe himself qualified to "give my poor opinion and advice to his Majesty's ministers," only to continue on to do precisely that. He corrected Vergennes's assertion that America had never solicited France's help. But of course we did, Adams reminded Vergennes, unable to abide the harmless illusions that make for happy marriages.

It was Adams who fired the salvos but Franklin who was left to grapple with the fallout. In light of the rout of Charleston, the devaluation, the fiasco at Lorient, there was a shrinking reserve of American goodwill at Versailles. Franklin himself was said to be in the king's disfavor. Vergennes had had more than his fill of Adams, as he let his relentless correspondent know, brutally terminating their relationship with what Adams would refer to later as a second flaming thunderbolt. At the end of July Vergennes observed that Franklin alone was an accredited minister to France. In future he would deal exclusively with him. There was nothing diplomatic about his message, which he thought he had already delivered, and brusquely did again: "The King has not stood in need of your promptings to tend to the interests of the United States." Adams had long had trouble parsing French compliments, but he understood that affront.

To Franklin went the bundle of Adams's collected writings. Vergennes now insisted Franklin notify Congress of his colleague's behavior. That assembly could determine if he was equal to his task.*

Again Franklin reassured Vergennes that it was unthinkable that either Congress or the American people shared his colleague's sentiments. He further separated himself from Adams, reminding Vergennes that his compatriot had early on resolved not to consult him in any of his writings, "a resolution that I believe he will keep, as he has never yet communicated to me more of his business in Europe than I have seen in the newspapers. I live upon terms of civility with him, not of intimacy." To the relief of all concerned, Adams was at the time of that statement en route to Holland (although addressing missives still to Vergennes on the day of his departure). He was off, he informed Franklin, to investigate "whether something might not be done to render us a little less dependent on France." It was a trip of which both Franklin and Vergennes disapproved, and one that should have driven home how much gratitude to France truly was in order. Adams would spend two years in Holland before he could boast of results.

As promised, Franklin alerted Congress to the offense his colleague had given. He made clear that he did so with reluctance and at Vergennes's request, but did not mince words. He had already stressed how inconvenient it was to have two ministers, affecting different voices, at one court. Adams's arrival had been premature. And with no business to occupy him, Franklin noted crisply, Adams "seems to have endeavored supplying what he may suppose my negotiations defective in." Louis XVI was a young king, bent on glory, and proud of his benevolence in delivering up an oppressed people. Surely America could allow him that pleasure. To do otherwise was not only improper and unbecoming but potentially disastrous. While Adams had been in America more recently than had he, Franklin did not feel he was misjudging their countrymen's sentiment, and stated his philosophy succinctly: "It is my intention while I

---

*The French minister had no illusions on that count: "As for myself, I anticipate that this plenipotentiary will only incite difficulties and vexations, because he has an inflexibility, a pedantry, an arrogance, and a conceit that renders him incapable of dealing with political subjects, and especially of handling them with the representatives of great powers, who assuredly will not yield either to the tone or to the logic of Mr. Adams."

stay here, to procure what advantages I can for our country, by endeavoring to please this court."

That statement stood too as an effective means of heading off the Lee and Izard attacks that he knew to be imminent. Hiding behind an allegiance to France was not necessarily a safe place to be, as Franklin himself acknowledged in writing of his insubordinate colleague: "He says the ideas of this court and those of the people in America are so totally different, as that it is impossible for any minister to please both." At the same time he had no choice but to deliver up to Congress a brief version of another tangled history. He hoped Landais and his mutinous crew would arrive safely, although they carried with them but a negligible fraction of the ten thousand uniforms, fifteen thousand guns, and two thousand barrels of powder he had assembled. Jones was headed out imminently with more. The greatest part would follow in a large vessel, Franklin promised, without any mention of dates.

Landais indeed made a rapid westbound crossing, with increasing signs of mental disequilibrium. On the high seas he and Lee quarreled over a prize portion of the turkey carved up at the officers' table, a dispute that led the *Alliance*'s ex-captain to swoop down upon the ex-commissioner, whom he threatened to kill with a carving knife, a scene that amply supported Franklin's assertion that both men were lunatics. (He deemed the American lunatic the more dangerous one.) By the time the *Alliance* reached Massachusetts Bay its men had again mutinied; their unbalanced captain had to be hauled bodily from the ship. Court-martialed in November, he was found guilty of having left France without Franklin's permission. With that imbroglio the Franklin–Lee feud reached its tentacles into the dimmest of corners. The charge was lessened as Landais was found to have done so on the advice of Lee, "a gentleman learned in the laws and high in office."*

---

*Otherwise Lee did his friend few favors. Landais was convicted on several counts, among them that of having transported personal items in a military vessel. Those goods belonged to Lee, who was never censured for having claimed precious cargo space aboard a military transport for his carriage and household effects, which crossed the ocean at government expense. Landais went on to serve briefly in the French navy, only to be stripped of his command, for insubordination.

"Try if you can beat this business into my head," Franklin challenged his grandnephew, as he grappled with the shambles of the shipping affair. He could not fathom what precisely Chaumont was doing at the heart of the operation. As matters stood, Williams drew for his funds on Chaumont, who in turn drew on Franklin. To Williams, Chaumont explained that as Franklin's political capacity was incompatible with any commercial transactions, he had stepped in to manage the latter. To Franklin, Chaumont explained that he had inserted himself into the operation as a financial guarantor. So shaky was American credit that no goods would be forthcoming otherwise. No mention was made of the fact that—in his role as conduit—Chaumont was in an ideal position to control the whole enterprise. More to the point, it was unclear precisely who had placed him there. A necessary fixture in 1776, he was a hindrance by 1780. While Franklin could not bring himself to distrust his warmhearted landlord, he knew him to be overly ambitious. His grandnephew should be careful, "for sometimes people drag down with them their best friends." As Chaumont's credit dissolved entirely, Franklin reverted again to nautical metaphors. Holding his landlord up as a cautionary tale, he warned Williams "never to go out of your depth in business, for the best swimmer may be seized with a cramp."

At all cost he determined not to wade into those murky waters. And, relatedly, over the second half of 1780 nothing so forcefully defied his best efforts as did the shipment of stores to America. Franklin tore his hair out with frustration. He regretted even having asked for the *Ariel*; he did not believe she would ever sail. He was flummoxed by the "mad management" of the entire matter. He could not often enough protest that he was ill suited for, unacquainted with, woefully ignorant of, unversed in mercantile matters, that he had no aptitude for accounts. On August 9 he assured Congress that John Paul Jones and the *Ariel* were to sail immediately, with 146 crates of arms and 400 barrels of powder. Another ship would follow with arms for 15,000 men and with 10,000 uniforms. That was one of Franklin's more optimistic assessments. It was also one to which he joined a fervent plea, begging Congress again for a consul to relieve him of maritime and commercial affairs. He did not stop to separate inability from unwillingness; he knew he was out of his element, which was enough for him.* "I, in all these mercantile matters, am like a man walking in the dark. I stumble often and frequently get my shins broke," he wailed. For having played only to his strengths—by nature Franklin was a streamliner and a simplifier, while everything about the procurement business was baroque and protracted—the price to be paid in America would be greater still. Vergennes thought Franklin unimpeachably honest, but loath to exercise the authority necessary to tame his unruly compatriots. Jones thought him too lenient, especially when it came to disciplining one refractory French naval officer. Adams found his touch so light as to be invisible.

If there was one American who might have sympathized with Franklin's Sisyphean labors it was the man who had known a similar set firsthand, four years earlier. Franklin replenished his liquor supplies in mid-August so as to welcome Silas Deane back to Paris, to which he returned as a private citizen. He was delighted by the August 20 reception, which went some way toward soothing his congressional wounds. Nothing so much drove home the disconnect between the two worlds; a pariah in America, Deane was warmly feted in Passy, where he reclaimed his old rooms in the garden pavilion. Never for a minute had Franklin doubted his probity; quietly he continued to defend him. For his part Deane found his former colleague in fine form. If anything, the doctor seemed to grow younger every day. On the subject of the American cause the ex-commissioner was not nearly so sanguine. Congress, he reported, was discredited in Europe, and individual Americans stigmatized. "It is almost as great a disgrace to be known to be an American as it was two years since an honor," he swore. The depreciation of Continental currency had done more harm than had the British army. French enthusiasm for the cause had vanished. Deane had an axe to grind, and away he energetically ground.

He took special pride in Adams's falling out with Vergennes, snorting that his successor had made himself as obnoxious at Versailles as had

---

*He often regaled French friends with his story of the tailor who winds up in Newgate, condemned to hang for having stolen a horse. In prison he meets a horse thief, who asks how he was apprehended. On hearing of the crime the thief exclaims: "But you're not a horse thief, then?" The new arrival concedes that he had simply availed himself of an opportunity. "Then what in God's name," scolds the professional, "possessed you to steal a horse?"

Arthur Lee. Nor was that all. Deane saw in Adams's behavior a plot to upend the French alliance and to reconcile with England. Why otherwise, in a moment of crisis, had Adams chosen "to boast and threaten where he ought to soothe and conciliate"? Grappling as he was with the shipping fiasco, Franklin made no attempt to distance himself from his ex-colleague's ravings. The two dined together regularly, which allowed Deane to broadcast Franklin's sentiments, amplified and slightly contorted. So Deane was able to assure the Madrid-based John Jay that in Franklin's opinion, Adams was "actually mad, and more so, though in a different way, than ever Lee was." The Americans made utter fools of themselves, sending separate states to trip over each other soliciting European funds, when the country as a whole had no credit. Deane was back in Passy for only a matter of weeks when he began to expatiate on another matter. With friends like France, America might need Britain after all. From there it was a short step to outright defeatism.

On that count Deane, Congress, and many at Versailles were in perfect accord. American affairs had never seemed so dismal. At Versailles it had escaped no one's notice that the French had now fought a series of perfectly futile campaigns. (Some wrote that down to the fact that every year France waged the campaign she should have waged the previous year.) The duc de Cröy believed it time to give up. Vergennes deplored American infighting; his allies' obsessions with their personal affairs seemed to take priority over their independence. Noting that Franklin himself seemed oddly silent—his energies were wholly directed to the logjam in Brittany—some predicted a September reconciliation between Britain and her colonies. Rubbing his eyes in disbelief, Deane blamed his countrymen. Congress pointed fingers elsewhere. Franklin's August 9 letter was one of precisely three that his employers would receive from him in 1780. In March he had promised only a partial fulfillment of Congress's shopping list; in May he reported on his troubles conveying the supplies; in August he further elaborated on those obstacles. Covertly, and with the British at his back, Beaumarchais had done far better.

The accusations against Franklin came at a time when he was moving heaven and earth to mediate between the feuding Chaumont and Jones; coaxing long-warehoused supplies to Lorient; and—with dread—pleading with Vergennes for a new loan. The *Ariel* sat still in harbor; if that ship had disappointed because it was too small, the Chaumont-acquired,

1,200-ton *Marquis de Lafayette* complicated affairs because it was colossal. It made no sense to send the vessel to America half empty, especially when there were caches of supplies languishing in French warehouses. Chief among those were 100 tons of American-owned saltpeter.* Unfortunately the saltpeter was in Saint-Malo, on the northern coast of Brittany, and the *Lafayette* was in Lorient, on the southern coast; the transport of the explosive was highly restricted by the state. Obtaining a permit was no easy feat; even in its infancy, bureaucracy had an iron grasp. Franklin overcame his dislike of asking favors, calling in a chit with his good friend Antoine-Laurent Lavoisier. Best remembered for his discovery of oxygen, the gentle, gray-eyed Lavoisier had worked early on in meteorology, with city lighting, on water supplies. He and his English-speaking wife regularly welcomed Franklin to their sunny laboratory near the Bastille, where young Madame Lavoisier painted Franklin's portrait. Conveniently, Lavoisier also happened to be one of the four men in France who controlled the country's gunpowder supply. (It was thanks to his pioneering experiments that France made the best and cheapest powder in the world.) Waiving a regulation or two was the least the public-spirited chemist could do to thank Franklin for having advised him on how to protect the French arsenals from lightning, on which project the two men had twice collaborated.

Both countries were running low on funds, as was any French merchant who held American debt. By October Chaumont was bankrupt. He pleaded his case not with Sartine but with his successor in the naval ministry, Sartine too having been sacrificed to an overextended budget. At the intersection of those teetering worlds stood Franklin, tin cup tremulously extended. The bills rained down on him from every direction. In addition to all else, Jay and Adams were relying on him for funds. (Jay was to spend thirty murderous months on the periphery of the Spanish court, where he was never received, without securing a penny of the five million dollars for which he was sent. The assignment was self-defeating from the start: On the one hand he was to solicit funds from Spain. On the other he was to assert America's right to the Mississippi, which right the Spaniards opposed.) Franklin was himself so close to ruin he could not sleep, "and

---

*By way of comparison, the colonies had in hand some 30 tons of gunpowder when they began the war.

so much indisposed by continual anxiety as to be rendered almost incapable of writing." He had warned against riding a free horse to death months earlier, but to no avail.

With a reluctance he described as "almost invincible," Franklin again prevailed upon Vergennes for funds. To his immense relief he met with a warm reception. He turned as well to a more original approach, drafting a proposal—it has been called a sort of primitive, reverse Marshall Plan—that would allow Congress to settle a portion of its debt by supplying French troops with provisions in America. America might be cash-poor, but her 1780 harvest was uncommonly bountiful. The king of France did not think it fair to accept such a barter. "You will not wonder at my loving this good prince," crowed Franklin, just back from Versailles, to John Jay. "He will win the hearts of all America." He emphatically believed it his nation's interest, and duty, to please, which conviction led him finally to tackle an onerous task. On October 8 he alerted Adams to the fallout—or at least some of the fallout—of his assault on Versailles, relegating that unsavory news to a last paragraph, and omitting to mention that he had alerted Congress. Delicately Franklin offered up a thought concerning Adams's letters: "If they were the effects merely of inadvertence, and you do not on reflection approve of them, perhaps you may think it proper to write something for effacing the impressions made by them." (The suggestion in no way appealed.) That same October day, from New Jersey, Washington replied to Franklin's invitation for a European tour. It was tempting, but by no means an immediate option. Domestic affairs were dire. America needed either an immediate infusion of French monies or peace. Lafayette was more graphic. "We are naked, shockingly naked, and worse off on that respect than we have ever been." Franklin could have no idea how appalling it all was. The war effort was closer to collapse than at any other time. They were without uniforms, money, gunpowder. Where *was* everything?

❧

The supplies that Washington and Lafayette had every reason to believe would turn up daily were still in France. Having made two false starts, Jones and the *Ariel* were again in Lorient; the *Lafayette* was not yet loaded. It was amply clear to Franklin that there was to be no relief in sight from his end for the American winter. He did not succumb to despair but did succumb, just after Jones's second return, to a disabling attack of gout. For the next three weeks he barely stirred from his bed, where he was much visited by Madame Helvétius's devoted houseguest, the poetry-writing Cabanis. The mild-mannered medical student in part explained how Franklin survived those wretched weeks. For him Franklin trotted out his earliest memories and pet theories, an oral preview of the *Autobiography*. He explained that he considered ill humor a vice. To prove his point he penned an essay, ably translated by his attentive visitor. In "The Deformed and Handsome Leg," Franklin noted that the world divided into two camps. To some, defects were always more pronounced than were beauties. Franklin advised steering clear of those discontents, "particularly when one finds oneself entangled in their quarrels." Typically, he believed a peevish disposition could be corrected. It amounted to nothing more than a bad habit.

He was proud of the piece, which he submitted to Madame Brillon. As ever she proved an inspiration, on the page if not in person. Throughout the fall she too was confined to bed, by nerves. The correspondence along the rue Basse flourished accordingly, with Monsieur Brillon as go-between. Franklin found the arrangement unsatisfactory; he wished he had wings to carry his friend off, or at least to peck at her window. He missed her dearly. From her sickbed Madame Brillon sent Franklin a fable, "The Sage and the Gout," a piece he much admired. Its hero eats lustily, exercises infrequently, and devotes an inordinate amount of time to chess and the ladies, for which the gout takes him to task. Franklin could hardly quibble with the assessment but could improve on it; chaste though it remained, the relationship proved as fertile as ever. At midnight on October 22 he picked up his pen to compose "The Dialogue Between the Gout and Mr. Franklin." He had a score of his own to settle with Madame Gout. Did she really need not only to torment him but to slander him as well? She made him appear a gourmand and a drunkard. Those indulgences, counters Franklin's quick-witted scourge, were perfectly acceptable in a man who exercised reasonably. Franklin did no such thing. A Valentinois morning consisted of a few sedentary hours given to books and worthless newspapers, followed by a hearty breakfast. Then Franklin would settle in at his desk, immobile until lunch. And what then of the Brillons' magnificent one hundred steps? Franklin had spent three hours at that household several times a week all summer, installing himself on the upper terrace, extolling the magnificent view, luxuriating in the glow of the setting sun, and calling for a teapot and a chessboard, without venturing from his seat until nine o'clock. He then only compounded his crimes by summoning his carriage, to convey him the five hundred yards home. The carriage would be better off burned, or lent to the poor.

Several weeks after its composition, the bagatelle went down the street to Madame Brillon, along with the three volumes of Montaigne Franklin had borrowed. He could not resist challenging his neighbor's essay on one point. Her Madame Gout reasoned poorly if she supposed that his time with the ladies contributed in any way to his malady. He could prove that the opposite was true: "When I was a young man, and benefited more from the favors of your sex than at present, I had no gout. Therefore, if the ladies of Passy had a little more of the Christian charity that I have so often and so futilely recommended to you, I would not have gout now." Delighted by his composition, Madame Brillon was appalled by his logic. He might just as well argue that there was a causal link between tossing himself out the window and not breaking his leg. She railed too against those who had retouched his French. It was better off without their fussy intrusions. Franklin begged to differ on both counts. How was he ever to learn to write her language properly if he did not submit to some lessons?

At the end of November he was finally up and about, walking feebly, assisted by a set of crutches. He emerged from his convalescence to find that the *Lafayette* had budged no more than had he. The military news was similarly bleak. His friend Horatio Gates had suffered a career-ending string of defeats. From London came the curious tale of Benedict Arnold. Just as Madame Brillon assured him that he spoke better than anyone else even in a language he knew only imperfectly, he found himself utterly unable to comprehend Chaumont's French. The entrepreneur concocted a financial scheme of stunning intricacy, of which no one could make head or tails, but which appeared a means to renege on his agreements. In frustration, Franklin requested a few explanations on paper. He heard the same day that Vergennes had procured for him an extra million livres, news that came as a relief but did nothing to move the supplies languishing in Brittany, which provoked further collisions between Williams and Chaumont. Chaumont insisted on submitting the dispute to a team of arbitrators, a proposal that Franklin approved. At the same time he made his priorities clear: "For God's sake, finish it somehow or other. The delays in sending the clothing have been an immense prejudice to our affairs in America. The army is naked." He had no idea that a new congressional order—and something of a reprimand—was en route to Paris.

The bungled affairs at Lorient exacted a toll on both home fronts. In Passy Franklin and his landlord took to passing each other in stony silence. Despite his conciliatory efforts, Franklin found Chaumont "cold and dry." And just as Franklin believed the matter resolved, Chaumont lobbied for a second panel of arbitrators. With a coldness and dryness of his own Franklin pointed out that the process could continue endlessly, until every merchant in France had been consulted. He reminded Chaumont that the tragic delays in shipments had hardly been of his making. He had more than the usual reason to be overly scrupulous: "You know that I have enemies, who have left here, and who are now in America, ready to denounce and demolish me if I give them the least occasion to do so." Chaumont displayed little mercy, taking his case to Versailles. There Vergennes chastised Franklin for having been inexact in his accounts. "Affairs among friends," the French minister counseled, were to be "transacted with rigor but amicably and with indulgent allowances."* Franklin promised to make every accommodation in his power, only to be assailed by Chaumont on the return home. He was close to frantic.

On December 18, twelve months after Vergennes had granted the funds with which to address America's most urgent needs, the *Ariel* sailed from Lorient. Franklin could only conclude that there had been some kind of jinx on the enterprise. To Lafayette he muttered vaguely that "a number of unforeseen and unaccountable accidents have delayed and prevented it from time to time." Most of the stores were now en route. The remainder was to follow shortly. He made no mention of the fact that the remainder amounted to a million livres in cargo, the largest single shipment. It was all of it too late for Washington, whose men were to shiver through the worst winter of the war without any help from France. And it

---

*He himself was paying heartily for his American enthusiasm that month. Having bailed out Beaumarchais, Vergennes was protecting Chaumont from bankruptcy proceedings. Within a matter of weeks he would arrange for the entrepreneur to be lodged at Versailles, to escape his creditors. Deane too was without funds. Amicably and indulgently, Vergennes asked Grand to supply him with 12,000 livres.

was too late as well for Franklin. On January 10, 1781, he learned that Congress was to vote for his recall.

As for the *Lafayette*, it loaded finally in February, at a very different pace from the brisk tempo Beaumarchais had adopted in 1776. The Lorient crew boarded the arms and ammunition, the clothing for nearly twenty thousand men, the ten thousand blankets, as if sleepwalking. Carrying the most expensive of Franklin's cargoes and the one that had cost him the greatest distress, the *Lafayette* set sail late in March. It was captured at sea. Six months later, Franklin's fifteen hundred bags of saltpeter were sold at auction, in London.

IX

The Sting of a Reproach Is the Truth of It
1780–1781

It is better to be humbled than ruined.
—Edward Gibbon

Franklin literally dragged himself around Versailles that Christmas season, chilled to the bone, half lame, wincing from the pain in his feet and knees. Like the rest of the diplomatic corps, he did so in flopped hat and long black coat, in mourning for the Austrian empress, Marie Antoinette's mother. He distributed his end-of-the-year tips—he received exemplary service at the palace, with good reason—but suffered miserably. He begged off of a December 26 dinner with Vergennes. He tried but failed to call on Maurepas, defeated by the climb to his second-floor office. January 9 found Franklin unable to attempt even an abbreviated version of his rounds. He simply stayed home. The following day he learned of the recall discussion. He had heard something of the batteries that had been opened against him in America from the ever-obliging Carmichael, now posted to Spain, as Jay's secretary. Franklin continued unperturbed. "If my enemies would have a little patience, they may soon see me removed without their giving themselves any trouble, as I am now 75," he cracked, a proposal that indicated how little he understood his enemies. They were not patient men. And by the end of 1780 they were rabid.

Infected by his brothers, Richard Henry Lee had for some time subscribed to the school that the political salvation of America depended on Franklin's recall. "How long, my dear friend," Lee inquired of Samuel Adams, "must the dignity, honor, and interest of these United States be sacrificed to the bad passions of that old man under the idea of his being a philosopher?" In addition to all else, Lee was incensed that Franklin had recruited Chaumont to assist with the Landais hearings. The owner of a French privateer had thereby sat in judgment of the captain of an American ship. Nothing could be more insulting to the dignity of a sovereign state. Surely the French must question the new nation's wisdom in allowing herself to be so miserably represented, thundered Lee, unaware that this was one of the few points on which the French did not question American sagacity. Lee was equally appalled to learn that his youngest brother had entrusted his return to a ship sailing under Franklin's authority. There was little of which he did not believe America's minister plenipotentiary capable.*

The coup de grâce fell to Arthur Lee. On December 7, 1780, he submitted to Congress a litany of Franklin's misdeeds, read in that assembly the following day. Franklin neglected his duties; he corresponded illegally with the British, through his son; he was guilty of fraud and embezzlement. It pained Lee to say as much, but there it was: "The truth is that Dr. Franklin is now advanced in years, more devoted to pleasure than would become a young man in his station, and neglectful of the public business." That business he sloughed off on Chaumont, Bancroft, and various others, "persons notoriously unfit for such trust." Already Congress had devoted an inordinate amount of time to sorting out Deane's charges of 1778, a scandal so embarrassing that every effort was made to destroy the records of those debates. Lee did his best to resurrect them.

Franklin indulged his enemies on two counts. The supplies Congress had requested in 1779 were nowhere in sight; he indeed appeared either inefficient or negligent. And while few believed all the allegations, Franklin's mystifying silence seemed to indicate that he was not overly involved in public affairs. There was some irony to Ben Franklin's committing

---

*It helped that Arthur Lee had hinted at (unfounded) attempts on Franklin's part to have him committed.

political suicide with his reluctance to set pen to paper: He owed his worldly success to his ability to compose a flawless sentence; he could not often enough stress the efficacity of the written word. Certainly he knew he was delinquent. With what sounds like admiration, he acknowledged that Adams was writing up a storm. Franklin was responsible for any number of odes to industry, also for some of the finest procrastinator's credos ever written; he always thought himself lazy, the more so as he aged. He could not have been unaware of the ramifications. His aversion to communicate was the despair of his friends and the delight of those who argued—Massachusetts and South Carolina led the charge—that any representative would be preferable to Franklin, who had "by his non-chalance and the influence that his surroundings have had on him, lost the cause of America in France."

Lee's assault forced the issue. Congress had resolved to appeal to France for a special cash loan of 25 million livres; quickly that assembly agreed to send a new envoy to obtain it. Again the honor fell to Washington's twenty-five-year-old aide John Laurens, who again would have preferred to decline it. A brilliant young lieutenant colonel much admired by all, Laurens had on his side impeccable credentials, including a grasp of French and a European education.* His father, the former president of Congress, was a flourishing South Carolina planter. The choice of the new envoy's title occasioned substantially more debate. Luzerne, the French representative, heard of the resolution after it had passed but before the position was filled; he managed to tone down the appointment without involving himself directly in the debate. He did so less out of loyalty to Franklin than out of loyalty to his king. In the back of his mind was the idea that if Louis XVI meant to deny Laurens's request, it would be easier to rebuff a lesser dignitary. From their side the Lees labored to restore the "pomp and glitter" of the appointment. Proposed initially as a special envoy, Laurens was upgraded to "minister in conjunction with our

---

*Like Franklin's son, John Laurens studied law at the Middle Temple in London. And like William Franklin, John Laurens got a girl pregnant while abroad. Laurens married the child's mother before leaving the country; William Franklin left both mother and child behind. He first expressed an interest in Temple around the time the boy was six, when Franklin was posted to London and Temple still five years away from knowing that he shared a family name with that eminent American. Did it make sense, wondered William, for his son to be brought back to America? Married but childless, he proposed to pass Temple off as a poor relation.

minister plenipotentiary at that court," the last nine words of which title the Lee faction managed to eliminate before Laurens sailed. Whatever the billing, it was clear to all that the appointment implied "a want of confidence in our minister's attention, abilities, or something else." Many feared it would wreak havoc. Surely an active, intelligent secretary—the kind of assistant with whom every lesser envoy in Europe had been supplied, and with whom even Laurens headed off—was a more effective solution.* Insofar as a moderate voice could be heard in the din, it was that of New York's Gouverneur Morris. "In a word," warned Morris, "we have sent a young beggar instead of the old one."

There was palpable concern over how Franklin would take the news. With Laurens Washington dispatched a make-nice letter, explaining that Congress felt it necessary to send someone with firsthand knowledge of the military scene to plead America's case. Franklin should rest assured that the aide was wholly disposed to avail himself of his advice, something that figured nowhere in Laurens's instructions. That letter constituted a masterpiece of restraint for a commander in chief whose army was on the brink of dissolution; on the same day that Franklin learned of the recall discussion, Washington acidly reminded a New York friend that mutiny was a rather natural consequence of asking an army to serve without pay, clothing, or provisions. The only man with intimate knowledge of both fronts laid on soothing hands as well. Lafayette explained to Franklin that his request for a secretary had been subsumed by party politics. Laurens was heading over as part of a compromise. Vocal enemies, the marquis reminded Franklin, were an inevitable feature of a popular government. He should not forget that he had innumerable admirers too. Wistfully Franklin replied that Lafayette was far luckier than he. The marquis had no enemies in either world.

Franklin's detractors were not all of them in America that winter. With Chaumont under ministry protection in Versailles, his creditors threatened to close in on the *Lafayette*. That left Franklin with few options. Against Chaumont's objections, he offered the lease of the ship to the French government. Vergennes was not immediately helpful. Relations with Chaumont continued frosty until the morning of January 25, when

---

*In April 1781 another abortive attempt was made to provide Franklin with help, after which the matter was never again broached.

the landlord appeared on Franklin's doorstep and cheerfully demanded breakfast; unexpectedly, monies had come through from America, although it would be some weeks still before that reprieve had any effect on the *Lafayette*. And through the rain of bills Franklin was much displeased to make out new American envoys, dispatched to Europe to solicit individual state loans. He made no new friends by reminding the Virginia representative that foreign affairs should be left entirely to Congress. Until the last minute he failed to inform that envoy that he would have no luck borrowing money in Genoa at a 3 percent interest rate; that republic had already refused twice as much. Why had he not said as much sooner? groaned the envoy, before whom Franklin shrugged. It had not occurred to him. He took the same unhelpful position with former congressman James Searle, dispatched by Pennsylvania with a mile-long shopping list. Searle was shocked to discover how low America's stock truly stood in France. There was barely a businessman willing to negotiate with him. A few dinners at the Valentinois convinced him that the blame lay under Franklin's roof. There the irreverent Bancroft gleefully insulted Lee, while Chaumont disserted wildly on Congress's defects.* As Franklin was unapologetic about his distaste for private state loans and as Chaumont and Bancroft appeared eager to discourage everyone's business but their own, it was clear to Searle that his mission was doomed. "Alas, sir, there are, I fear, Arnolds in France, natives of America," he concluded, in writing to Philadelphia.

On February 13 Franklin informed Searle that Laurens was en route to Paris. Searle was overjoyed. He had come to France as a Lee ally; nothing about Franklin's behavior had converted him. He made no mention of the tone in which Franklin delivered that news, which he could have read only as a very public, very humiliating blow. With it Franklin moved quickly, crafting a masterpiece of last-ditch, deathbed fund-raising. It was impossible to conceive of America's distress, he reminded Vergennes, citing Lafayette and Washington, and marshaling arguments on which four years of assistance had been based. To neglect America, he stated more baldly than he had since 1776, was to guarantee that England would

---

*Chaumont had good reason to do so. Already he had lost at least five America-bound vessels; the *Lafayette* alone cost him 500,000 livres. And by 1781 his bills to the new republic were worthless.

become the terror of Europe. Spain had disappointed all expectations; Congress was in danger of losing the confidence of the American people. Franklin permitted himself even a brief detour into melodrama. "I am grown old," he concluded. "I feel myself much enfeebled by my late long illness; and it is probable I shall not long have any more concern in these affairs."

He was fortunate in that the combined offenses of the Lees and the Adamses were every bit as effective as his own eloquence. Vergennes was as offended by the Laurens mission as was he. As much to spite Franklin's enemies as to gratify America, the French minister determined immediately to grant additional funds. He also directed Luzerne to sing Franklin's praises. It was purely out of esteem for and confidence in its minister plenipotentiary that Vergennes now resolved to help America out of her financial embarrassment. "Let them judge by my gesture, which is entirely personal, if the behavior of this minister has endangered the interests of his nation, and if anyone other than he could have obtained the same advantages," he blared.

That anyway was the version for congressional consumption. Privately Vergennes added a few lines that were as damning as all of Arthur Lee's wild imprecations combined. His esteem for Franklin aside, Vergennes continued, "I am nonetheless obliged to admit that his age and his love of tranquility leave him with an apathy incompatible with his responsibilities. With all the more regret I see that in crucial matters this minister is silent, whereas his service should require him to communicate his opinions to Congress." (In Franklin's place, Vergennes had been the author of incessant, thirty-page missives.) Why did Congress not simply provide its envoy with an intelligent, capable secretary? Could that post not be confided to Laurens? Vergennes could have been writing for the *Pennsylvania Gazette*, which saw the situation the same way. "If Dr. Franklin was really incapable of doing any part of our business at the court of France, he was unfit to be our minister, and he ought to have been recalled, and another person sent in his room," argued that paper. Assuming he was able, why was Congress adding a second man, at double the expense? Always the issue of how America looked in the eyes of the world weighed heavily. What must Europe think to see a twenty-five-year-old supersede a minister plenipotentiary! The French minister and the Pennsylvania paper differed in only one essential condition. If, against his wishes, Congress was determined to replace him, Vergennes implored Luzerne to see that Franklin was not succeeded by John Adams. The polished Luzerne, who had spent forty-seven days in close quarters with Adams on the Atlantic, took his point.

In Passy Franklin did what any self-respecting manager would do. He passed on the alert, chastising Williams for his inattention to the *Lafayette*. His grandnephew should remember that Franklin was under fire in America: "You should therefore double your diligence, and omit nothing in this affair that may give satisfaction to Congress." He reminded the admirer who buried him in the usual deluge of compliments that he was not singly responsible for eradicating North American tyranny. The Revolution was the work of a great number of brave and capable men. He was happy to claim but a small share, he demurred, just as Congress called in reinforcements. He pressured Vergennes for a decision. What could Congress expect from Versailles? He settled his private accounts; he put his house in order. And—having obtained from Vergennes both a new loan and the promise of an additional, outright gift of 6 million livres, the single greatest gift of the war—he submitted his resignation. Forty-eight hours later, John Laurens arrived in Paris.

~✳~

When precisely Franklin made his decision is unclear. He was too much the professional to have spoken of it beforehand to Vergennes, who did not share everything with Franklin either. Only at their March 10 meeting did the French minister reveal that the king was considering mediation offers from both the Russian and the Austrian courts, to which he wondered if Congress might be amenable. He omitted to mention that he too had drafted plans for a settlement in the event the spring campaign failed; a large fleet was to sail shortly with the comte de Grasse, after which France could afford no more American adventures. From the start Vergennes had banked on a speedy and decisive war. Around Versailles he was known to be at the end of his rope, fraught and exhausted on the American front.

Franklin presented his reasoning to Congress as perfectly straightforward, although it could not have been anything of the kind. It represented a departure from his first principles. He preferred to think of himself as someone who did not quit, as a man proudly "deficient in that Christian virtue of resignation." He had secured this new grant—bestowed by

Louis XVI as "a signal proof of his friendship," and despite France's own crushing expenses—against all odds. If he was feeling vindictive, he could derive some satisfaction from Vergennes's stipulation that the new monies bypass Congress. They were to be drawn on directly by Washington and spent by Franklin in France; there was no faith in any American board or committee. (He had balked at that condition, to be informed that it was Louis XVI's explicit order. Franklin could dispute the issue only to a point, he explained to Congress, "every donor having the right of qualifying his gift with such terms as he thinks proper.") He would submit a list of the most urgently needed supplies on Laurens's arrival. There was as yet no sign either of him or of the consul Congress had finally managed to send, who would be lost at sea, and replaced only at the end of 1781.

"I must now beg leave to say something relating to myself, a subject with which I have not often troubled the Congress," Franklin continued, on March 12. He was seventy-five years old and infirm, for which he blamed the business that chained him to his desk. In a bravura bit of thunder stealing—he as good as took the words from his enemies' mouths—he admitted to a "great diminution in my activity; a quality I think particularly necessary in your minister for this court. I am afraid therefore that your affairs may some time or other suffer by my deficiency. I find also that the business is too heavy for me and too confining." He could not adequately serve as consul, judge of the admiralty, merchant, banker, and minister. Even at that delicate juncture the humor was irrepressible. "I do not know that my mental faculties are impaired; perhaps I shall be the last to discover that," he offered. He had served the public in one way or another for fifty years; he hoped now only for repose. That he proposed to take in France. The last sea voyage had nearly killed him, and he had no great desire to wind up in an English prison. To his reminder of his half century of service he added a request. Temple had lost out on the legal education for which Franklin had (at least in retrospect) intended him. Franklin's task would have been impossible without his grandson, who was diligent, discerning, genteel, and perfectly bilingual, and who in four years had served quite an apprenticeship. Could Congress find a secretarial position for him at a European court, so as to groom one very capable American diplomat? In a single document Franklin therefore violated two of his steadfast rules, having vowed years earlier never to ask, refuse, or resign an office.

What kind of shape was he truly in? He mentioned the resignation solely to John Jay, in part because he trusted him, in part because he hoped that the New Yorker would succeed him. The Madrid-based Jay was unaware of how much Franklin's health might be compromised but was very clear on the subject of his colleague's intellectual capacity: He was both unerringly lucid and highly attentive. (Jay also shivered to think how America would appear in the eyes of the world if she alone failed to appreciate the magnitude of Franklin's achievements.) All the same, there was undeniably some fumbling at the Valentinois. Vergennes promised a loan of 4 million, which Franklin reported as 3 million. Not for the first time, there was some distress in the paperwork. Franklin was punctual for his March 10 meeting with Vergennes but by the next morning had unaccountably misplaced the notes with which the foreign minister had supplied him, for which he bashfully requested a replacement. (The original surfaced shortly after he had done so.) That week the *Lafayette* was at last ready to sail; Franklin did not realize that its captain awaited his orders, inadvertently delaying the ship's departure by several days.

For much of that distress Congress was as responsible as was Franklin. One secretary, or consul, could have obviated a thousand mishaps. And as Jay made even more clear than Franklin, it was next to impossible to direct America's affairs abroad in the absence of a foreign secretary, another appointment that stymied Congress. At the same time, Franklin had learned little from his experience with Lee and Izard. The relationship with Searle blistered into open warfare. Soon enough the zealous Pennsylvanian took to boycotting the Valentinois, strutting about Paris in a green uniform with enormous epaulettes, huffing about Franklin's obstructionist behavior. He insisted that French arms had done more harm to America than had foreign mercenaries. He met his toxic match in Silas Deane, a man obsessed. Daily Deane wrote one friend or another, promising not to touch on politics, only to find himself caught up in that current before he had composed a full page. In company he could speak of nothing else. To his mind America was already ruined. He despaired of Congress, France, Spain, and America, in no particular order. So much did the currency devaluation debase America that the country stood now "like a common prostitute among chaste and respectable matrons." Only by relinquishing independence could she redeem herself. He churned the entire history over so many times that finally he whipped up a conspiratorial version. The French had always intended to abandon America, hence the lack of a paper trail. And hence the desultory military effort. D'Estaing had been sent not to rescue America but to establish a foothold there. The very fact that the new monies were granted payable to Washington proved Deane's septic point. The French schemed to take the American general and his army into their pay, thereby making them subservient to Versailles. French malevolence aside, how could a cluster of jealous states work together in the first place without falling into anarchy or civil war? By March 1781 Deane sounded like nothing so much as Lord Stormont at his apoplectic, prealliance best.

What was this man doing in Franklin's household, privy to his negotiations, and—as Searle observed—raging at the dinner table against the false idol of independence? Franklin could be blinded by loyalty and softhearted to a fault; even as eyebrows lifted at the stream of literature that issued from his address, he continued to defend his heretical houseguest. As he would again learn while drafting his recall request, he was generally at the mercy of his trusting disposition. In England Thomas Digges, the Maryland expatriate to whom Franklin had directed monies for the relief of American prisoners, absconded with the funds. Franklin recoiled in pain. "If such a fellow is not damned, 'tis not worthwhile to keep a devil," he cried, having blindly trusted in a man with more than thirty aliases. And evidently there were villains everywhere. Simultaneously Temple discovered that he had been robbed, calling in the police to report that a trunk in which he kept a quantity of silver and rolls of Spanish coins had been pilfered. By removing the nails on the underside of the case, someone had relieved him of the currency, worth about 2,000 livres. Although depositions were taken and the trunk carefully inspected, the case went unsolved. Petty theft was a fact of Parisian life but the extent of it clearly eluded Franklin, who had about him the languor of the optimist. Testimony to his tolerance—or inattention—came from a curious source. "In certain matters," noted Silas Deane of his ultraindulgent host, "the Doctor is no more of a philosopher than the rest of the world."

Toward other laws of French life Franklin remained either willfully blind or prone to misreading. For years he had, in his convivial way, expressed his devotion to various friends by suggesting matches between their respective children or grandchildren. (Benny had been married off at the age of six to Polly Hewson's youngest daughter, age one, and thereafter referred to as Franklin's "granddaughter elect.")* He bound his retirement plan to Temple's future, which he decided, before or after plotting the geography of his own, lay in France. That idea he pursued with both of the Brillons in April. Was it not eminently sensible for twenty-one-year-old Temple to marry their elder daughter, sixteen-year-old Cunégonde? The youngsters were fond of each other. Cunégonde would make a wonderful wife, and the fresh-faced, long-lashed Temple was well on his way to becoming a distinguished gentleman. Franklin admitted to an ulterior motive. He hoped in such a way to reinforce the bonds of the familial friendship; the vote was for clan over coupledom. He broached the topic with Temple, a dutiful child who responded as such. His only objection was that he did not care to be separated by an ocean from his grandfather. Franklin assured him that were Temple to marry Cunégonde, he too would remain in France. Temple was delighted. He would be thrilled if his grandfather would arrange the marriage.

Franklin felt he thereby addressed one of Monsieur Brillon's two concerns about the match. The second was of religion. To that objection Franklin applied the creed he knew best: reason. Every faith, he held, had in common five principles. A God had created and governed the world; he was to be worshipped; the best way of serving God was to do good among men; the soul was immortal; in the future if not in the present, vice would be punished and virtue rewarded. Comparing sect and ritual to the wrapping of a standard French pastry—the pâtissier was just as likely to wrap his confection in red as in yellow paper, with a wool as with a flax string, none of which had any bearing on his goods— Franklin concluded that religious fundamentals were identical. The differences, he assured the Brillons, were but paper and string. Evidently Franklin had forgotten Madame Brillon's lesson about the marital scales; his argument betrayed a solid misapprehension of French life. And religion was by no means a simple matter of paper and string. In 1781 a Protestant had no legal rights in France. He was excluded from some of

---

*Having himself tried but failed to land a wealthy wife, Franklin was not above prospecting for chances for those he felt in need. In 1777 he had advised Jonathan Williams to cultivate a particularly successful French merchant, not only for business reasons, but on account of his daughters. Franklin fared less well with his own children, making very clear his disapproval of both Sally's and William's choices.

the least significant employments. He could not hope to so much as enter the Ecole Militaire.

Madame Brillon let Franklin down gingerly. Temple had everything to recommend him. He was much loved in her household. But he could not reasonably decide to settle in France when everything attached him elsewhere. The Brillons would need a son-in-law who could assume Monsieur Brillon's post; he must be familiar with French law and custom, and a Catholic. (They got one, eighteen months later. As it turned out, Brillon took a dislike to his new son-in-law, whom he dismissed as nouveau riche. The irony was not lost on Temple, left to suffer a rejection for a proposal that had not been his in the first place.) This Madame Brillon explained plainly but tactfully, assuring Franklin that the extent of their devotion could be read in the pains it cost them to refuse him. Congress would indulge in no such niceties when considering its application regarding Temple, which Franklin—had he reread his correspondence, or been less enamored of his grandson—might have seen would touch a nerve. On that continent the son of a Loyalist who had somehow acceded to a post that no one else wanted and Congress could not fill was—Abigail Adams did not share Madame Brillon's delicacy—"a mere white curd of asses' milk."*

Neither in eighteenth-century America nor in Europe was there any aversion to dynastic politics—it was Franklin's own effective influence peddling that had established his son as a royal governor—and yet in 1781 his timing was off. He lobbied tirelessly for Temple, courting everyone who he believed might have an influence on Congress, just as he was being denounced for pursuing a personal agenda at America's expense. Indeed Franklin broached the topic with John Laurens, no natural enemy to nepotism, shortly after his March 14 arrival. Laurens seems not to have mentioned the calumnies leveled against Temple on account of his grandfather; he spoke freely however of the stain Temple bore on account of his Loyalist father. Sympathetic to Franklin's ambitions, he suggested an effective means of clearing Temple of any prejudice. Why not send him to Congress, a body wholly unacquainted with him? That was a trip Temple

---

*Mrs. Adams rose to poetic heights when it came to the Franklins. Later in the year she wrote off the family as "wicked unprincipled debauched wretches, from the old deceiver down to the young cockatrice." (A cockatrice is a hybrid monster of legend, hatched by a serpent, from the egg of a cock.)

had long hoped to make. Paradoxically the Franklin-inspired devotion that would make the reputations of so many young Frenchmen—to have fought in America in the eighteenth century was to have fought in the Resistance in the twentieth—was to deprive one young man of his obvious future. And the devotion continued to cripple. Franklin thanked Laurens for the suggestion but did not feel he could spare Temple long enough for him to make the trip.

In his retirement plans Franklin made but one reference to Benny, a slightly guilty-sounding promise to "attend more nearly to his education." Presumably Benny would return to America with his grandfather, but he was otherwise a victim of a habit Madame Helvétius ably codified: Franklin tended to forget those not at hand. The correspondence with the eleven-year-old was spotty and formulaic, an ungratifying exchange of homages for homilies. The world divided into two camps, Franklin reminded Benny, in a do-you-want-to-be-a-garbageman-when-you-grow-up letter. The first had the luxury of education and took pains with it. The second either had no schooling or neglected it, and were as a consequence "poor, and dirty, and ragged and ignorant, and vicious, and live in miserable cabins or garrets, on coarse provisions." He exhorted the young Genevan to waste no opportunity to improve himself. And the letters were not only infrequent (if his grandfather was too busy, could Temple not write, pleaded Benny?) but generally free both of news of Benny's friends and of hints of a visit from his grandfather.

The results were predictable. Unmoored, Benny grew morose. He distinguished himself over his first eighteen months in Geneva neither for his academic prowess—a steady diet of Greek grammar did nothing for him—nor for his shining personality. Unsmiling and taciturn, he took poorly to criticism, applied himself haphazardly, and failed to ingratiate himself with his classmates. He found little delight even in a casual game of cards. Academically he was remarkable mostly for his indolence, to the extent that when he won a Latin prize he shrugged that he had done so by accident. Painfully shy, he made little social effort; he was delighted to be spared from a dance when a fire broke out at the house where it was being held. (He was equally delighted to be able to slip away without helping to extinguish the blaze.) Benny complained of too little spending money, not without reason. He had less than his classmates. While Franklin applied himself to Temple's future, a gulf widened with Benny. Soon enough he had forgotten his English, and Franklin—who resisted regular hints from Benny's parents that he might enjoy a trip to Geneva—had lost track of how old precisely the boy was.

Benny could only have felt further isolated in his first Swiss year as he promptly lost the amiable guardian to whom Franklin had entrusted him. And in a turn of events to which Franklin paid little attention, revolution broke out in Geneva in February 1781. It was a dress rehearsal for the French Revolution but an orderly affair; removed nightly to safety, Benny was spared most of the disturbances that paralyzed the city. (He did manage a glimpse of a firing squad, when a Piedmontese soldier was administered last rites and executed by his own comrades, for theft.) There was some irony in the fact that that fourteen-month-long insurrection was the only revolution Franklin's grandson was to witness. There was some too in Vergennes's having supplied troops to quash the Swiss insurgency even as he underwrote the American contest. Both were bids for more democratic representation. The nimble minister addressed them not in terms of their politics but "by reason of their attitudes toward France." Geneva too was uncomfortably close. America was worlds away. In any event the French public never heard of the former. Vergennes saw to it that it never made its way into the papers.

※

At Versailles Vergennes plied the new American envoy with questions as to the state of the colonies and their military potential. What, precisely, was the condition of the American army? John Laurens's answer was that it should have been 34,000 men strong but that General Washington had only 13,000 men in his command. All was in a state of suspension. Laurens pressed for ships rather than troops, passing on the message that Washington so clearly articulated: "It may be declared in a word that we are at the end of our tether, and that now or never our deliverance must come." Continental currency was virtually worthless, and the government without any remedy. The British may have poked fun at America for being kept by France, but she was not being kept in very high style.

Nothing about the next weeks would have made Franklin regret his decision to retire or to hesitate to support a colleague who might enable him to do so. Nearly every day for a month Laurens was at court, where he was as persistent as he was charming. In Vergennes's office there was some discussion of the American mission as a whole; the young South Carolinian assured Franklin that no other man could be more effective in Europe than he. All he needed was a fine secretary, to relieve him of the drudgery of the office. (It was rich advice from the man who had declined the appointment.) In turn Franklin assured his poised and indefatigable colleague that Congress could find no better set of hands. He wished Laurens could succeed him. (Laurens replied that he had no yearnings to be a diplomat. Moreover, he would not succeed Franklin unless Franklin would pass on both his mantle and his abilities.) Even if he had felt otherwise—and there is no indication that he did—Franklin had every reason to embrace this special envoy. Nothing but bad blood had flowed from the Paris mission; Laurens constituted a sort of walking reproach. And the two were in an awkward situation, the more so as Franklin had accomplished Laurens's object before his arrival. There were no further funds to be obtained, as Vergennes made clear.

As the impressive lieutenant colonel made clear on hearing as much, he was indeed not cut out for a diplomatic career. Displeased to learn that the French had no intention of offering additional aid, Laurens lost no time in making his irritation felt. Vergennes was willing to write brashness down to inexperience until the early May morning when—it was an unseasonably warm spring, and Laurens a particularly animated young man—the heat seemed to rush to his head. He traded appeals for threats; this was liberty on the barricades. Vergennes snapped. The young man might care to remember that he was no longer delivering orders in a military camp but addressing the minister of a monarch who was, if anything, well disposed to his cause. Laurens chafed at the implication that France was doing America favors, by one account reaching for his sword, which he threatened to brandish unless his demands were satisfied. Vergennes reminded him that his colleague had no quibbles with France, to which Laurens countered that he had been at the front lines. Dr. Franklin had not. He then swept off, threatening to address himself directly to the king, which in defiance of all protocol he did, pressing an envelope into Louis XVI's hand at the next *levée*. The approach was not ineffective. The following morning Laurens was summoned to discuss the assembly of supplies, which he managed brilliantly in the days that remained to him. He made a hasty departure, but returned to America with three cargoes of military provisions and a miraculous 2.5 million livres in silver, an impressive bounty for a mere ten weeks in Paris.

To Franklin, closer to the intricacies of the business, the mission wore a different complexion. He was left to do a great deal of feather unruffling at Versailles, where he was stunned to discover after Laurens's May departure that he had "given more offense than I could have imagined." Franklin made quick work of those embarrassments, which he did not mention to Congress. Yet again he was to be more effective at the French court than with his countrymen, however. The casks of silver with which Laurens sailed were those Franklin had obtained. And Laurens left him with a throbbing headache in the form of twenty-three-year-old Major William Jackson, Laurens's secretary, meant to purchase and ship the military stores. That business Jackson arranged from Amsterdam, with the assistance of a Rotterdam-born, South Carolinian commodore, Alexander Gillon. Jackson did so in a most spendthrift fashion, saddling Franklin with bills ten times greater than what he had authorized, at a time when he was in a financial crisis unlike any he had known. Already he had borrowed French funds months ahead of schedule, and still he could not cover Adams's and Jay's expenses. He was under the impression that Jackson was spending monies acquired in Holland; to his "monstrous surprise" Franklin discovered that Jackson was instead drawing on him. Consequently Franklin was left without funds to pay America's bills, due on July 10. To preclude that crisis he prohibited Jackson from shipping his gold and silver to America. It was a dire measure, but the credit of America stood to be demolished otherwise. Besides, Franklin had no faith in Gillon. A former associate of Izard, Gillon had assisted in the *Alliance* mutiny and was an acknowledged rabble-rouser. Were he to be entrusted with the shipment, Franklin suspected that the stores would see England before they saw America.

In attempting to avert that catastrophe Franklin was afforded a glimpse of how the Laurens mission would be viewed in America. Jackson threatened him with a scandal. And he implied that Laurens had secured the exceptional 6 million livres gift. That assertion he shared with Adams, in Amsterdam. From Adams's desk word went out immediately that Laurens had "done more for the United States in the short time of his being in Europe than all the rest of their diplomatic corps put together." The reproach was too much even for Franklin, who defied Jackson to set the record straight. The dispute produced another of his irate, unsent letters, penned on July 10, a day he had been dreading. Jackson might care to remember that Franklin had some experience with public affairs, which enabled him "to judge better than you can do, who are a novice in them." He was unwilling to take responsibility for the expenses the secretary was running up in Amsterdam. Nor was Jackson enhancing America's reputation by tossing about conjectures and suspicions in public. "Credit is a delicate, tender thing, capable of being blasted with a breath," Franklin reminded him. Normally he would not stoop to setting a record straight, but here it mattered: "Who obtained the grant is a matter of no importance, though the use I propose to make of it is of the greatest. But the fact is not as you state it. I obtained it before he [Laurens] came. And if he were here, I am sure I could convince him of the necessity of leaving it." Mounting a high horse, not one usually in his stable, Franklin derided Jackson's "superior airs." Had it not been for Franklin, Jackson would have had no business in Europe in the first place. Jackson came around soon enough; within a matter of months he was apologizing profusely. Franklin had been correct both in prohibiting the shipment and in mistrusting Gillon, who slipped out of Amsterdam without the two vessels of American supplies. Jackson managed his apology only after escaping the commodore's attempt to hold him prisoner.

In the end the young beggar made more of a hash of things than had the old beggar. And yet from a certain perspective Laurens's mission appeared a dazzling success; it was far preferable to believe in his manly saber rattling than in Franklin's alluring legerdemain. Not only was Franklin never thanked for having headed off the greater part of a disaster, but Congress entertained a motion that he be censured.* The debacle left a bitter taste in his mouth, confirming him in two opinions. It had for some time been unclear to him whether Adams was friend or foe; he made an attempt to flush out his allegiances early in the summer, but forced no declaration. He could have read something into Adams's brief July visit to Paris, during which Adams discussed mediation offers with

---

*Laurens was unanimously commended. Jackson became assistant secretary of war.

Vergennes but steered wide of his colleague. In that light the hair-trigger endorsement of Laurens was revealing. Certainly the blowup left Franklin to discourse anew on the thanklessness of public service. While he was delighted to hear in July that Congress had appointed his friend Robert Morris superintendent of finance, he could congratulate Morris only with some acid advice. "The public is often niggardly even of its thanks," he warned, "while you are sure of being censured by malevolent critics and bug writers, who will abuse you while you are serving them, and wound your character in nameless pamphlets, thereby resembling those little dirty stinking insects, that attack us only in the dark, disturb our repose, molesting and wounding us while our sweat and blood is contributing to their subsistence." Days after Jackson had offered his abject apologies, Franklin was meditating still on the pettiness of human nature. It was uncanny, but there were those who "cannot bear that another should distinguish himself even by greater usefulness." They would prefer to give credit to "a man that lived 3000 years ago, or at 3000 leagues distance, rather than to a neighbor or even a friend."

Of the happier side of the equation he had a fresh taste shortly after submitting his resignation. The comtesse d'Houdetot, a homely, sentimental version of Madame Helvétius and something of a monument herself, lured Franklin ten miles out of Paris for a fête champêtre in his honor. It was generally through its women that Franklin brushed up against the original cast of the Enlightenment, and Madame d'Houdetot was a case in point. Celebrated as the Sophie of Rousseau's *Confessions*, she was an intimate of Diderot, the abbé Galiani, and others, whom she coaxed to her magnificent estate that April afternoon. The largehearted, verse-spouting hostess helped Franklin from his carriage with hymns to liberty. Those paeans followed him as he made his way slowly through a garland-laden park, to an elaborate picnic. Between each of seven glasses of wine Madame d'Houdetot's friends recited couplets to their exalted guest, who—three thousand miles away—was being vilified by his countrymen. At the end of the afternoon Franklin planted on the Sannois estate a Virginia locust, a tree to which Jefferson would pay his respects several years later. A full orchestra accompanied Franklin back to his carriage, the illustrious company singing in chorus. It was an afternoon of which he left no account but did not need to; Madame d'Houdetot saw to it that the pastoral apotheosis appeared in all the papers.

That excursion may have been the most newsworthy but was not the only one he made that summer, when—in anticipation of his recall—Franklin liberated himself from his desk. He was both more mobile and more social than he had been in some time. He contemplated even a tour of Italy and Germany, in part to reward Temple for his faithful service. He allowed himself to rove a little in his mind, imagining the pleasures of various London reunions. As always he was overwhelmed by demands—why did everyone imagine he had "a mint of money" at his command?—but allowed himself finally the various diversions Arthur Lee had so long decried. His interests were as catholic as ever. While he could not devote to science the time he wished, he managed all the same to coauthor a report on lightning conductors, read at the Académie des Sciences. He indulged in a spirited discussion of Native American language and orthography, to which he added an aside on the history of the compass. With a Swiss mining engineer who spent a week at Passy he shared his new ideas for a stove and a lamp. (He proposed using atmospheric pressure to tamp down the smoke, something that plagued him for years at the Valentinois.) He meditated on hospital ventilation and on the persistence of infection in cadavers. The Passy press grew, augmented by a British-made copying machine, the invention of James Watt, and one by which Franklin was fascinated. (As the importation of all printing equipment was forbidden, the machine was smuggled into France as a "scientific apparatus.") He experimented with various papers and inks so as—the Revolution in a nutshell—not to be dependent on Watt's. And he shared his experiments in that realm with a French friend, who by the fall had improved on Franklin's technique. He found time even for the highly original Patience Wright, a London-based New Jersey native who had gained some renown as a molder of wax figures. The mile-a-minute talker made regular trips to Passy that summer. An imposing, angular woman with an athletic stride, flashing green eyes, and a fierce set of cheekbones, Mrs. Wright cut quite a figure in Paris, where she marched about regally and loquaciously, without a syllable of French. Having made Franklin's acquaintance years earlier in London, she had little trouble convincing him to allow her to coax his likeness from a blob of wax, warmed in her lap. A visiting American subsequently prevailed upon Franklin for an old suit, in which the effigy was dressed. It went on to make sensational appearances in armchairs all over France and England, clinching Franklin's reputation for self-composure.*

When the naturalist and historian the abbé Soulavie came to call, Franklin speculated on the physical upheavals of the earth's surface, venturing a parallel between the two realms. In the physical as in the political world, he asserted, "one continent becomes old, another rises into youth and perfection. But the perfected continent will in its turn correct the other." Monarchies became republics; republics in turn crumbled into monarchies. His response to Soulavie's queries were all painfully slow in coming but, thought his visitor, richly worth the wait. And so Soulavie ventured what he knew must sound like an irrelevant question: What did Franklin make of the prediction that France would one day suffer a revolution even greater than America's? Personally he had some forebodings. France was too strongly constituted to allow for either reform or revolution in their lifetimes, Franklin assured his guest. He made very clear his admiration for Louis XVI, pronouncing the French sovereign "the founder of the liberties of the United States."

The rainy evening of June 8 found Franklin in Paris, for a production of Gluck's *Orpheus*. Minutes after the final curtain a fire broke out in the Opéra; the building was instantly ablaze. As Franklin and Temple had seats in the balcony they were among the last to escape the theater, a cloud of dense, black smoke billowing on their heels. Before they were installed in their carriage the flames shot into the sky, rising to columns of three hundred feet, tossing sparks and burning embers all over the Montmartre neighborhood. "Had it happened 15 minutes earlier," Franklin allowed, "the pandemonium would likely have prevented the safe exit of a large number of spectators, and we would have been grilled." Typically he turned the close call to his own ends. Later in the year David Hartley, the old friend with a peace proposal in every pocket, submitted a plan for fireproofing theaters. Franklin considered his suggestions, but put their

---

*On at least one occasion Mrs. Wright was the victim of her own genius. Having carried the likeness to Passy to compare it with the original—"twin brothers" was the verdict—she returned alone, on foot, to Paris, her sculpture neatly wrapped in a napkin. At the barrier that evening she was stopped by the customs agents. She resisted all efforts to examine her bundle. Her objections only excited curiosity, which led to the obvious conclusion: Mrs. Wright "was an escaped maniac, who had committed murder, and was about concealing the head of her victim." All was explained in due course, but only after Mrs. Wright had enjoyed a police escort to her hotel.

work in perspective. He had very nearly lost his life in one such conflagration, and that under circumstances that would have particularly gratified his enemies, who imagined him nightly at the Opéra. "But what are the lives of a few idle haunters of play-houses," asked the man who had founded a fire company a half century earlier, "compared with the many thousands of worthy men and honest industrious families butchered and destroyed by this devilish war!" That was the blaze he would like to extinguish. He was as single-minded with his report on the evening at another address. Madame Brillon was in the south of France but knew that her dear friend was to have attended the theater on June 8. She was worried sick. Franklin set her mind at ease, at least in part. He was entirely well. All the same he had to admit that he had attended the Opéra only as he had been deprived of his private one, at her home. Had he perished she would have had some accounting to do. Her absence had nearly killed him.

He dined more frequently with Madame Helvétius than with anyone else but thought a great deal, and more tenderly then ever, of the radiant Madame Brillon, the relationship in no way impaired by the failed matchmaking. For much of the year she was away from Paris, but Franklin discovered that—contrary to his inclination—his feelings remained undiminished. "There is an absence in my life which my other friends cannot fill. I love you too much," he wrote on July 15. He was impatient for her return; it was time again to remind his friend that he had been afflicted with his love of her for four years. (He did not acknowledge her affliction, the nervous breakdown that had set her traveling.) During that period he had been sustained by little more than jibes about his constancy. He was dying of malnutrition. He was only too happy to offer up a little parable to illustrate her lack of charity. He was a beggar; she a rich and miserly bishop. And Madame Brillon was only too happy to point up the flaws in his logic, to which she was immune. She had by no means been uncharitable. She had simply refused to comply with all his demands. "You will not suffer by my refusals," she chided her American friend. He was the kind of beggar who—on being given one coin— grumbles that he has not been given two.

With Madame Brillon alone Franklin lamented the state of his French, with which he was deeply dissatisfied. His jokes, he feared, came out as stupidities, and he could not correct them. He could express only half of what he had to say. He found himself beyond the age when he could make any progress. If anything, he seemed to be regressing. It is unclear if he regretted the poverty of his French with Madame Brillon because he could be most candid with her or because he felt more stymied with her. "It is always very good French to say, '*Je vous aime*,'" she had counseled early on; by 1781 Franklin groused that he could not be bothered with those three words, so inadequate to his sentiments. At times he sounds to be searching for a vocabulary he did not command in the first place. He sent her all the "tender *amitiés* that I cannot express in your language, and only with difficulty in my own." On the other hand, despite his protests, he sounded very much like a man who had mastered the local idiom. She had been out in a sailboat; he encouraged her to conquer her seasickness, so that he might spirit her off to America. He devoutly hoped she might return a little more libertine from her travels. Many mutual friends entrusted him to send on their love to her, commissions he would happily perform, with interest. At her instruction he gave his Wednesdays to Madame Le Veillard and his Saturdays to Madame Helvétius, but all would change on her return. He had been loyal in the extreme, without having procured the favors to which his constancy should entitle him. The attachment was as warm as ever.

Franklin's family had heard he was to return to America, but from his end the postresignation correspondence is notably devoid of any imagined or anticipated reunions, as of the brand of homesickness that had plagued him in England. He applied only for grafts of Newton Pippins, to which no French apple could compare. (It was an easier commission than that submitted by his successor. Determined to combat all the New World misconceptions past which Franklin amiably glided, Thomas Jefferson would send for a seven-foot New Hampshire stuffed moose. The carcass stood guard over the entry hall of his Paris home, shedding miserably.) Indeed between the day Franklin set his resignation to paper and the day six months later that he had his answer, there were no explosions about other people's vagaries or the perils of stumbling in the dark, but neither was there more than a scant syllable of longing for America. He was "among a people that love me, and whom I love."

~⁂~

Early in August Franklin learned from Vergennes that Congress had refused his resignation. There was no more talk of repose, no more grousing of responsibilities too heavy for elderly shoulders. To his mind the message was clear, and comforting. He had stepped aside so that Congress might find a fitter man. They had declined the offer. Ergo, there was no fitter man. He congratulated himself on having made his point, as on something else as well. "I fancy it may have been a double mortification to those enemies you have mentioned to me, that I should ask as a favor what they hoped to vex me by taking from me; and that I should nevertheless be continued," he exulted to Carmichael, of all people. With his next line he cut short his celebration—"But these sort of considerations should never influence our conduct"—before throwing down the gauntlet. The appointment struck him as a greater honor than his first, as all his enemies together had been insufficient to prevent it. In fact it included as well a new responsibility. Simultaneously he was joined to the peace commission, of which appointment he notified Adams. Where did matters stand on that front?

Many in Congress read Franklin's resignation in the spirit it was intended: as a canny riposte to the recall discussion. The desire to remain abroad was much remarked upon; it reinforced the impression that poker-faced Franklin, Franklin the silent and subtle, was bluffing. Joining the Temple request to the resignation convinced those inclined to believe as much that he was not only bluffing but scheming as well. That school included whole families. In mid-June Arthur Lee's older sister wrote a Massachusetts friend: "This is probably no more than a state trick to fix him more firm in the saddle. He says perhaps he is too old, but he does not perceive anything like it himself; and then gives a strong proof of it by recommending his grandson as the person who will, in a year or two, be most fit for our plenipotentiary. From this recommendation one or the other of these two things is clear: Either Mr. Franklin's faculties are impaired, or he thinks ours are." By error the letter was delivered to Abigail Adams, who, as it happened, simultaneously received word of Franklin's year-old report on her husband's collision with Vergennes. It was her opinion that Franklin should have forwarded Vergennes's reprimand without comment. Why had he felt it necessary to blacken Adams's reputation in Congress? What had her husband ever done to Franklin? Had he monopolized his women? Outwitted him in court intrigue? Was he too honest, too dedicated, too little inclined to dissipation? "I can only say that those who have no private interest to serve, no friends to advance, no grandson to plenipotentiarise, no views incompatible with the welfare of their country, will judge I hope more favorably of a gentleman whose heart and mind are truly republican," she raged. She was equally astonished that Franklin had enlisted Luzerne to his cause. No honest man was safe with the unprincipled Franklin, his "sly secret malice" more dangerous than the open attacks of the English. She ranked him alongside Benedict Arnold.

It was not Franklin who had enlisted Luzerne, but rather that envoy who enlisted Franklin. If Mrs. Adams was in the market for "sly secret malice" she would have been better advised to look to the French foreign ministry and its Philadelphia representative. For months the prudent and amiable Luzerne labored to impress upon Congress the French distaste for its appointed peace commissioner. Unfit for any sane negotiation, Adams might well cost the colonies a reasonable peace. Those discussions were well under way before the arrival of Franklin's resignation; the two questions came before Congress at the same time. Valiantly Luzerne lobbied for a check on Adams, suggesting alternatives to the abrasive New Englander. Faced with the recall of a representative, Congress reverted to its usual practice; it opted to send additional personnel instead. John Jay was appointed unanimously, but the efforts of New Hampshire's General John Sullivan to make Franklin a third met with difficulties. Jefferson and Henry Laurens were proposed, despite the rather inconvenient fact that Laurens was at the time a prisoner in the Tower of London. A deadlock ensued, at which point Sullivan forcefully renewed his case. Congress should remember Franklin's reputation, as well as the insult of the Laurens appointment. The arguments for continuity and sympathy went only so far; in the end Sullivan was reduced to manipulating the voting slates to ease Franklin past his enemies.* Sullivan had plenty of incentive to do so, as he was bribed by Luzerne.

And Luzerne milked Adams's intractability for all it was worth. Although Adams was joined to three presumably reasonable men, Luzerne managed to have the peace commissioners—in the end they would be Adams, Franklin, Laurens, and Jay—placed squarely under Vergennes's thumb. The Americans were instructed to negotiate only in conjunction with the French minister, to whose wisdoms they were to submit. Even

---

*Only four states voted for Franklin's inclusion.

after he had learned of the double shackles Vergennes continued to rail against that bull in the china shop of European diplomacy. "I am as sure as one can humanly be," he maintained, after Franklin had been settled firmly back in place, and Adams contained, "of the integrity and the wisdom of M. Franklin, and it is highly desirable that this minister should have a dominant influence over his colleagues." It was a mantra Vergennes could not repeat often enough. It seemed to calm his nerves. The alternative was in any case a nightmare. The particular concerns of any overly ambitious American could scuttle a peace and involve France in an endless war. Vergennes was not mistaken in his assessment. In an elegant bow to news of the enlarged commission, which was equally his demotion, Adams acknowledged that Congress may have been wise. "My talent, if I have one, lies in making war," he sighed, taking to his bed for six weeks, with what he described as a nervous ailment. He was silent until early October.

To merit the new confidence with which Congress honored him, Franklin vowed to redouble his efforts on America's behalf. He began by spreading a little goodwill, reminding Congress both of Louis XVI's generosity and of Vergennes's integrity. The latter was the most upright of men, "who never promised me anything which he did not punctually perform." He had no idea of the extent of his debt but some idea of the burden of the new commission. He had never known a peace, even the most advantageous, which was not deemed inadequate, its authors defamed as injudicious and corrupt.

Franklin was all the more eager to comply with his new assignment as he felt restored, both in body and spirit. The diversions of summer had worked wonders. Buckling back to work agreed less well with Temple, who succumbed to a persistent bout of jaundice. He found his secretarial duties a hindrance to his recovery, which no purgative seemed to facilitate; on October 14 his grandfather shipped him off to Chaumont's Loire estate, for a recuperative hunting trip. That departure left the Valentinois short-staffed, and Franklin to trudge through the aftermath of the Gillon mess on his own. Having spent weeks coaxing Vergennes to replace the supplies that had been lost with the captured *Lafayette*, Franklin now broke the devastating news that Gillon had not only abandoned the matériel he was meant to convey to America but scrapped his plan to sail west in favor of a little privateering. He was presently refitting in north-western Spain. Could France possibly lend a hand?

He applied for relief as well to Adams, who was after all based in Holland, along with the two vessels of misbegotten goods. It was a subtle attempt at buck-passing, as Adams noticed, lobbing the matter back to Passy. He was the first to agree that Gillon's was "a most ruinous and affecting affair." On the other hand, he had had no part in the transaction, over which Franklin and Laurens had alone presided. Franklin retreated nimbly, with a solicitousness that suggests he had a clear sense of where his intermittent colleague now stood. He by no means intended to trouble his co-commissioner, had referred the matter to Adams "really because I thought you understood such business better than myself, were on the spot, and equally concerned for the advantage of our constituents." He had been reluctant to do business with Gillon but allowed Laurens to convince him otherwise. "I find myself confoundedly pinched, but I deserve it in some degree for my facility and credulity," he asserted, rushing to assume responsibility.

Yet again he was without funds that might have alleviated the problem; he had only, as Adams suggested, to purchase the ships that should have sailed with Gillon, and then resell them in America. Franklin prayed that a Dutch loan would come through to relieve his multitude of embarrassments. Until then, he conceded, "I must scuffle and shift as I can." (The loan came through in 1782.) Franklin begged Robert Morris to take some measures toward self-sufficiency; he could not forever be on Vergennes's doorstep. Surely the Americans could exercise a little economy? Realistic as ever, he then caught himself: "But that is wishing mankind more sense than God has been pleased to give them and more than they desire, for they have not enough to know they want it; and one may as well wish them more money." (It was additionally unrealistic as the American economy was on the verge of collapse.) The Enlightenment embodied, he had no inordinate faith in human reason. Matters were complicated by the fact that Morris could not decipher some of the terms of the Franco-American loans, on which Franklin could shed only the dimmest of light: "For when we first arrived and did not well understand one another's language, it was easy to misapprehend, and suppose things said that were not, and indeed after such a length of time to forget some that were." It was probably no coincidence that Franklin that fall advised his Philadelphia grandson to master French and accounting. He asked Benny as well to assure him that he was learning arithmetic. It was a subject with which Franklin always felt uneasy.

☙

On October 22, 1781, after eleven years of marriage and just over an hour of labor, Marie Antoinette gave birth to a son. The rejoicing was such that perfect strangers stopped each other to exchange good wishes on the street; the delirium was universal. Every ambassador and public official journeyed to Versailles the following morning to congratulate the king and gaze upon the dauphin. Cheerfully Franklin assumed his place in the infant's adoration: "Before he was yet a day old, I was there, not in the capacity of an Eastern King, but rather the contrary, and from the West," he reported to Madame Brillon. It was a thrilling event for France, and for the queen, and thus by extension for him, "who loves them both, and who is always joyous when he sees his friends happy."

In equally high spirits he wrote Temple from his Versailles hotel room that late October afternoon. While playing magus, Franklin had received word of auspicious events closer to home. De Grasse had defeated the British in the Battle of the Chesapeake on September 5, a victory that opened the way for the French to continue on toward Cornwallis, in Virginia. Through other channels Franklin learned that Rochambeau and his troops were close to joining forces with Lafayette, in Williamsburg. Unless Cornwallis fled to the Carolinas, his army was in some danger of being trapped. Franklin was cautiously optimistic, not a poor mood in which to observe the masses and feasts and concerts given throughout Paris to celebrate the birth of the dauphin. By the king's command the entire city was brilliantly illuminated for the next weeks, which would have facilitated Temple's return from his hunting holiday. Paris was visible for miles around.*

---

*Generally returns tended to defy Temple, and this one was no exception; the trip from the Loire met with every manner of delay. Unable to book a seat to Paris on any regular conveyance, Temple arranged finally to lease a local postmaster's cabriolet, an expensive alternative, for which he overpaid dearly. He kept the carriage for three weeks, lost the harness, and left the Chaumonts to settle his bill for him, a year later. The talent for misplacing things extended even to his recently acquired Newfoundland puppy, which turned up at the home of friends in a neighboring village.

The household was complete again save one. Early in October, Silas Deane decamped for the Netherlands. It is unclear if Franklin requested that he do so but plain he should have. While Vergennes labored to rein in Adams, Deane lodged ten miles from the French court, rehashing old grudges and manufacturing new ones, a pen permanently affixed to his hand. Having run out of people to blame for his miseries, he turned to France. Had no one else noticed that America was more servile in 1781 to Louis XVI than she had ever been to George III? His countrymen were fooling themselves if they believed they had any chance at the negotiating table. Congress itself was in the pay of France, as was the American army, as were—it was the closest Deane came to maligning his host— America's European ministers. Were America not to make peace with England immediately, she would feel the full weight of French despotism, far heavier than its English cousin. His countrymen were but the tools of France and cheap ones too, the cheapest ones available, cried Deane, forgetting in his misery that France was also a rich savior, the richest one available, which was why he had landed on her shores in 1776. There was every reason to abandon the alliance and rejoin the British Empire, he argued, as loudly as he could, which was too loudly. When some of his intercepted letters turned up on George III's desk, the British monarch deemed them useless for propaganda purposes. They overshot the mark.

Luzerne speculated that Congress would order Franklin to have Deane arrested, which it did not, even after Deane's intercepted letters began to appear in America. Those missives delighted no one more than Franklin's enemies, who blamed him for having entrusted their affairs to a traitor. Even Bancroft began to distance himself from his childhood tutor and the colleague with whom he had done so much business, both officially and unofficially. Franklin continued to defend Deane—from Madrid Jay did the same—but could not have been anything other than relieved when Deane removed himself to Ghent.* Friendless, twice exiled, impoverished, he continued on in his campaign, "deadly hostile to his native land," as Franklin heard, on numerous occasions. He could not bring

---

*Deane's best defender may have been Beaumarchais, who granted him a share of any monies he might manage to extract from the Americans. What was it about that "miserable new republican country" that drove those who tried to help her to desperation?

himself to believe as much, even while Deane was eviscerated by his enemies. They made mincemeat of him, delighting in reports that he lived in abject poverty, with a prostitute and among thieves, who stole his papers.

It was with news of Deane's descent into misanthropy that a young merchant arrived at the Valentinois on the afternoon of November 19. The New York–born, Nantes-based Elkanah Watson alighted in Passy that Monday to find Franklin in what was clearly a favorite posture. He looked just as he did in a well-known 1766 engraving: Framed by a doorway, his left arm on the table, chin supported by his right thumb, the fleshy American ambassador sat intent on the book open before him. Instantly he set his visitor at ease. Just as quickly he cut short the report on his recent houseguest, whom Watson had found raving like a traitor in Ghent. Franklin had the perfect means with which to divert a conversation: Did Watson know he was a musician? He led the handsome twenty-three-year-old across the room to his glass armonica, an invention of which he was particularly proud and which Watson encouraged him to play. Without ceremony Franklin seated himself before the five-foot-long instrument, where he moistened the tips of his fingers on a piece of sponge. He then began to play, his right foot "bearing upon a treadle fixed in the manner of a spinning wheel, which turned a set of musical glasses, presenting their edges in perpendicular positions, in the shape of saucers graduated of different sizes, so as to produce all the requisite tones." From the colored glasses swelled a delicate rendition of a Scottish pastorale. To Watson it made for a thrilling spectacle. To Franklin's ears the sweet, muted tones were far preferable to tales of Deane's apostasy.

The conversation that afternoon turned quickly to Franco-American efforts to rout Cornwallis. Various reports had confirmed that de Grasse and his fleet of twenty-eight ships of the line were in the Chesapeake, Washington's and Rochambeau's armies marching together toward Virginia, and a French squadron under the comte de Barras sailing from Rhode Island to join de Grasse. Their maps spread before them, Watson, Bancroft, and Franklin spent hours working up every scenario. An avid Franklin weighed two radically different conclusions, sinking at times into utter gloom, to blossom minutes later into a state of exhilaration. "His whole machinery," remarked Watson, "appeared in a state of elasticity, and in active play." That the future of America depended to a great extent on the outcome of the impending engagement was clear to all; Watson understood how fierce were each of his host's competing emotions, "as Franklin's great influence at the court of France was the primary cause of producing this bold enterprise." The celebrated equanimity was nowhere in sight. In the end the same dismal conclusion repeatedly presented itself, however. All signs pointed to the British intercepting Barras, overwhelming de Grasse, and subduing Washington and Rochambeau, at which point the American cause was as good as lost. On that cheerless note Watson took his leave. He looked at his watch. It was eleven in the evening.

In Paris Watson went to bed "sighing over the distresses of my bleeding country." It is unlikely that Franklin got that far. Just before midnight a courier knocked at his door, with a note from Vergennes. It contained glorious news. After a three-week siege, the combined armies of France and America, 16,000 men in all, had forced Cornwallis to surrender at Yorktown, where on October 19 cries of *"Vive le Roi!"* had alternated with those of "God and liberty!" Immediately Franklin set to disseminating the word. Cornwallis's defeat arrived four years to the day after Burgoyne's, and technology had come a long way; the American minister put Watt's copying machine to good work. Watson was among those woken by a furious rapping at his door and the fruit of those late-night labors; he rode immediately out to Passy. Already Franklin was surrounded by well-wishers and "in an ecstasy of joy." Repeatedly he exulted in two observations. "There is no parallel in history of two entire armies being captured from the same enemy in any one war," he cried, always quick to summon the historical context. As he more than anyone knew, the triumph was remarkable as well on a practical plane. Yorktown represented a miracle of execution, in which three armies and two navies had, in a complex maneuver, converged over 1,600 miles, to unite two generals who could communicate only with the help of a translator. (Lafayette was at the ready.) That battle represented the flawless coordination that had for so long eluded the alliance; the delirium was all the greater for the joint triumph of planning and execution.* Also for the first time the Americans

---

*Not only was the maneuver perfectly executed, noted Franklin, but Cornwallis's army had been obliging enough "to quit a situation from whence it might have escaped, and place itself in another from whence an escape was impossible."

looked impressive, in their French-made brown and blue uniforms. The members of one regiment had carefully powdered their hair.

As if in acknowledgment the two celebrations blurred into one. Paris was illuminated by three nights of fireworks; various maps of North America went on sale, on which to locate the British embarrassment. Rochambeau's blockade was laid out in sugar by a master confectioner, a new bonbon offered up in Washington's honor. When Watson returned to Nantes he found every city along his route ablaze in light. Franklin would have had the sense that all of France was celebrating with him. He could not sufficiently express his delight. Louis XVI was surely, he assured Vergennes, in French-speckled English, "*le plus grand faiseur d'heureux* that this world affords." It was unlike him to conflate the two languages, but altogether appropriate to the occasion.

To Madame Brillon he wrote not at all, which prompted a scolding. He captured whole armies in America, and she was left to read of his stunning success in the papers? On the balmiest of Christmas Days—Franklin dined that afternoon with friends, the doors and windows flung open as if in summer—he attempted to redeem himself. He was by no means unaware of the magnitude of the victory. But his friend should recall his approach to the chessboard. He never renounced a match until it was over. Nor did he celebrate until success was certain. And while Yorktown was clearly a momentous victory it was not yet, in the final days of 1781, a decisive one. Franklin begged his compatriots not to relax their efforts for a spring campaign. He set a persevering example. In the only letter he wrote that Christmas, Franklin conceded that he no longer coveted the Brillon house as once he had. His feelings for his neighbor's wife remained constant, however. If in her travels she was to meet the Holy Father, he hoped she might petition him for a repeal of the Ten Commandments. They were miserably inconvenient.

X

Those Who in Quarrels Interpose May Get Bloody Nose

1782

Resentment is a passion, implanted by nature for the preservation of the individual. Injury is the object which excites it. Injustice, wrong, injury excites the feeling of resentment, as naturally and necessarily as frost and ice excite the feeling of cold, as fire excites heat, and as both excite pain. A man may have the faculty of concealing his resentment, or suppressing it, but he must and ought to feel it. Nay he ought to indulge it, to cultivate it. It is a duty.
—John Adams

Franklin allowed himself a rare moment of self-indulgence in the first days of the New Year. Something possessed America's eldest peace commissioner—the man who claimed it more beneficial to kiss and make up than to prolong a quarrel; who believed polemic a waste of time; who prided himself on his dispassionate nature—to draw up a list of a dozen names. The first were those who had lied to him in borrowing money. To them Franklin joined George Lupton, who had spied on him at his own dinner table; Digges, who had absconded with funds; Gillon, who had absconded without supplies; Captain Hynson, whose treachery was nearly unequaled. Among Franklin's swindlers and scoundrels and saboteurs figure neither America's greatest enemies nor his acknowledged ones; the roundup is significantly shorter than it could have been. He had been imposed upon by a multitude of people, the majority of them American. He may have compiled the inventory in self-rebuke; certainly it stands as a testimony to his credulousness. He had come a long way since his conviction, as a twenty-year-old, that honesty could not be counterfeited. In any event having assembled his rogues' gallery Franklin—in a gesture either of excorcism or of embarrassment—crossed out the names, with a single vertical line.

Amid a season of celebrations, at a time when American affairs looked bright, he remained very much on guard. He did not think it possible to overestimate the animus of the British monarch. "For depend upon it," he assured Robert Morris, "the King hates us cordially, and will be content with nothing short of our extirpation." He was not surprised that the first peace offers that came his way after Yorktown attempted to separate America from France, a strategy at which he squawked in disgust. He felt (or so he supposed) as would an honest woman whom an expert seducer entertained with arguments "in which infidelity to her husband would be justifiable." Several such overtures were made to him; he remained deaf to them all. And he went the extra mile, reminding David Hartley that negotiations could be undermined by overly severe terms. He took as a case in point the onerous terms the British had imposed on the French in 1763. "I do think a faithful ally, especially when under obligations for such a great and generous assistance as we have received, should fight as long as he is able to prevent (as far as his continuing to fight may prevent) his friends being compelled again to suffer such an insult," he contended. He was the lone envoy who implied—and who even believed—that America was fighting for France as much as France was fighting for America.

At the same time he reprised a familiar role. While he made clear that America would not be swayed by tawdry proposals, he assured Hartley that he was open to honest ones. Those should come from England, the older and wiser party. America was but the novice in these matters as Lord Stormont—Franklin forgot little, an insult least of all—had been so good as to remind him. Were the British to propose reasonable and equitable terms, they would be greeted reasonably and equably. With Congress he assumed another persona, one that revealed a different motive for the reluctance to finger any olive branches. England appeared humbled now, but with a little success would be as insolent as ever. "I remember that when I was a boxing boy, it was allowed after an adversary said he had enough, to give him a rising blow. Let ours be a douser," entreated the self-proclaimed pacifist.

Franklin was clear about how he felt that final blow should be administered. It was time for America to fend for herself. He had spent five years begging; neither a momentous victory, nor a superintendent of finance, nor even a peace negotiation seemed to raise him from his knees. France had granted America massive funds, a fleet, and an army, "and yet," he reminded Morris, "I am obliged to worry with my solicitations for more, which makes us appear insatiable." He enclosed with his letter the coldest document he was ever to receive from Vergennes, who wrangled with his disappointment. Lafayette made a triumphant return to France on January 21, in time for the celebrations, and for a promotion. Vergennes was frank with the youngest French marshal: "I am not marvelously pleased with the country that you have just left. I find it barely active and very demanding," he scolded. Days after his return Lafayette called on Franklin, who begged his assistance in soliciting funds. Both men knew that Lafayette could carry America's case to deeper recesses at court; in any event Franklin was too mortified to put in an appearance. And he was in a bind. His own funds would carry him only through the end of February. (It was a test of his loyalty that he refrained from comment on the dauphin's layette, all 1.5 million livres of which made its way to Versailles in a procession of superb carriages. For the same sum Franklin could have had nearly one hundred tons of saltpeter.)

In mid-January Franklin explained to John Jay that he had delayed writing him for an unconscionable two months because he was too pained by what he had to report. Jay was wholly sympathetic: "Our credit in Holland leans upon you on one hand and, in Spain, on the other—thus you continue like the key stone of an arch, pressed by both sides and yet sustaining each." He was all the more compassionate in that he knew what it was like to bleed a stone. For his twenty-nine months in Spain Jay had not a penny in assistance to show; Franklin advised him to apply for a recall. The begging was no easier on Adams, who compared his Amsterdam existence to "that of a man in the midst of an ocean negotiating for his life among a school of sharks." If only Spain and Holland would admit that they did not intend to support America, he and Jay could go home and stop diverting from Franklin funds that would better serve the American army.

The begging Franklin had found unseemly in 1776 was moreover painful by 1782; there were fewer excuses for the disorder, the miscalculations, the vagueness on the new republic's side. He was made wretched by a reluctance that Luzerne best articulated from Philadelphia: "The Americans suffer the torching of their farms, the loss of their ships, and endure all the trials of war with courage, of which they haven't enough to levy taxes, which would prevent the greater part of their calamities." By contrast they seemed to think France infinitely rich. Franklin was mortified to learn that in the congressional opinion the American war was but a negligible line item in the French budget. In truth it was every bit as expensive to that power as had been the Seven Years' War. And Franklin was not the only one to practice hit-or-miss bookkeeping. Massive obscurity reigned in Congress as to how much aid France had extended America, and on what terms. Alarmed, Luzerne begged for a full accounting; the numbers grew vaguer every day. Vergennes promptly complied: As of March 1782, the king of France had advanced or gifted America a total of 28 million livres. And still, as Franklin explained to the newly arrived and highly competent American consul, Thomas Barclay, the demands of their countrymen were unceasing. A million livres of crucial, Laurens-acquired stores might well be sitting abandoned in Amsterdam. But delaying the departure of those goods remained, to Franklin's mind, a preferable alternative to declaring bankruptcy.

It was Lafayette who saved the financial day, convincing Vergennes to extend Franklin another 6 million livres loan on March 1. Almost simultaneously Franklin received word that the House of Commons had voted against pursuing the war. Vergennes may have heard sooner; in any event it was not confidence in France's ally so much as a lack thereof that elicited the new funds. Vergennes extended the loan to strengthen American resolve, of which success appeared to have sapped the nascent republic. To his mind it would likely fall to pieces when relieved of the British menace. Crediting Lafayette for the coup, Franklin took pains to remind Morris that the monies constituted half of what had been requested. Morris should take appropriate precautions at his end. To the happy news he attached a little psychological primer, to be applied to international relations. In his book nations had feelings too. They should be respected. There was nothing to be gained by making a man feel unkind for having to refuse a favor, or weak in revealing his inability to do so.

He proceeded to offer up an analysis of France that was as unerring as his approach to the Brillons had been misguided. "This is really a generous nation, fond of glory and particularly that of protecting the oppressed," Franklin asserted, pointing up a crucial distinction between the two lands: "Trade is not the admiration of their noblesse who always govern here." To assure France that it was in her interest to assist her ally for profit's sake was to insult her. He derived infinite pleasure from the new-found harmony between French and American troops; the officers who returned in 1782 had nothing in common with the disgruntled crew whom Deane had dispatched in 1776. They were starry-eyed and admiring, the envy of their countrymen. Indeed both nations had evolved to some extent. The French officers had grasped that the supreme compliment in America was to tell a man he was "sensible." They understood it was incumbent upon them to admire the excellent sidewalks of Philadelphia. There was a glimmer of enlightenment on the American side too. Their saviors were as robust as they, and knew a thing or two about military discipline.

On that new rapport Franklin was forthright: "It should be carefully cultivated. I hope nothing will happen to disturb it." Aware of how closely Vergennes parsed Luzerne's words, Franklin reminded all concerned that it behooved them to maintain warm relations with the emissary in their midst. Deference, if not honest gratitude, was surely due to a party who had now advanced 34 million livres. "I find by experience that great affairs and great men are sometimes influenced by small matters, and that it is not good to differ with or disoblige them or even their secretaries," he prodded Morris on March 9. Two weeks later he had some proof of that theorem. Madame Brillon had written him of a fine young Englishman with whom she had been much taken in Nice. A British army colonel, Lord Cholmondeley shared her admiration for Franklin, whom he would love nothing more than to meet. The two men had another friend in common, Cholmondeley explained; he was an intimate of the Earl of Shelburne, at whose country estate Franklin had first made the acquaintance of the abbé Morellet. Might Madame Brillon arrange for young Cholmondeley to call at Passy? On March 22 Franklin welcomed his admirer to the Valentinois for tea. Before leaving that morning, Cholmondeley asked if his host might care to send a word with him to Shelburne. Franklin penned a brief note, expressing his wish that the world might be set aright. He pledged to do all in his power. As quickly he forgot about the communication, saddled as he was with a new assignment. Cholmondeley had only just left when Franklin received a petition from Madame Brillon. Did he really need to be reminded of his promise to suspend his courtship of beautiful women for fifteen minutes every other week in order to write her? She claimed damages, issuing an ultimatum for one long letter before twenty-four hours were out, or six shorter letters, on the subject of his choice.

Before Franklin had complied he learned that the British government had fallen, in a scene of high drama. The old friend whom he had earnestly if offhandedly addressed on March 22 had been named—several hours before Cholmondeley lifted his teacup in Passy—home and colonial secretary. Shelburne received Franklin's incidental note on April 5 and had an emissary at the Valentinois in just over a week. "Great affairs sometimes take their rise from small circumstances," Franklin concluded, granting Madame Brillon pride of place in his journal of the peace negotiations. Inadvertently, she had set the ball in motion.

～～

Early April found Franklin much pleased that every British peace probe met with the same considered response. Adams held the same line in Amsterdam as did Franklin in Passy and Vergennes at Versailles. France and America had no interest in a separate peace. In the flurry of overtures Franklin correctly read British desperation; in the stonewalling of the allies he read a favorable negotiating position. Without saying as much he sensed that he had the upper hand. He whispered that he might even obtain more at the negotiating table than his country expected. The paper flowed from his desk in record quantity and yet he found a few moments to attempt a primitive sketch of the Valentinois garden; he profited from the half-peace to contact long-lost friends in Britain. He renewed two propositions to which he was much attached. If England truly meant to reconcile, he suggested to David Hartley, a voluntary gesture of goodwill would make for a promising start. What about the release of those long-suffering prisoners? To Polly Hewson went a familiar request. Spring was coming. Was it not time for a visit?

Only on April 14 did he have reason to be reminded of the note he had dashed off to Shelburne. That Sunday Franklin was surprised by a visit from Caleb Whitefoord, his old London friend and next-door neighbor. Whitefoord had been dispatched to Paris to introduce Shelburne's peace emissary, Richard Oswald. Both were inspired choices. Whitefoord was a wit and a Franklin intimate, Oswald a seventy-six-year-old Scottish merchant, a modest man of calm bearing and liberal opinions who had lived for a time in America. Neither titled nor a diplomat, he was credited with being "versed in the world; and yet devoid of the pride of aristocracy, without being suspected of democracy," a description that for many years would have fit Franklin as well. Would Franklin agree to meet Oswald the following morning? asked Whitefoord. Franklin performed his little dance about the multitude of peace feelers and the mangled reports that followed upon their visits, but agreed all the same to see the Scot. He came at eleven, bearing not only Shelburne's testimony to his integrity but that of a designated American peace commissioner as well. Henry Laurens had been Oswald's American agent in the slave trade; the two were life-long friends. It was Oswald who had stood bail for Laurens, released on the last day of December 1781, after fifteen months in the Tower of London. (He emerged in shattered health and in no mood to submit to the wranglings in Paris, all the more so as he doubted that Adams and Franklin would be able to come to terms with each other.*) He was happy to vouch for Oswald, however, as to sing his compatriot's praises. Franklin had a fair reputation in England for malice and cunning. Laurens assured Oswald there was no cause for alarm. "Doctor Franklin knows very well how to manage a cunning man, but when the doctor converses or treats with a man of candor there's no man more candid than himself," he promised.

Laurens predicted that the two would like each other and was right. Franklin took immediately to the widely read, practical-minded Oswald, another man of few words. Affably, respectfully, they traded silences. Franklin was hungry to know what Shelburne had in mind, which Oswald was too cautious to reveal; Oswald was desperate to assess the American commitment to France, which Franklin was too cautious to reveal. The awkward dance repeated itself at Versailles that Wednesday, when Franklin escorted Oswald to Vergennes's office. In English Oswald

---

*In a matter of months he would be crushed as well by the loss of his favorite son. John Laurens was to die in a minor skirmish in August 1782, a loss that aged his father dramatically. Devastated, Laurens could say little more than "Thank God I had a son who dared to die in defense of his country," a line that must have felt like a lashing to Franklin. They had both lost sons in the war, very differently.

begged for proposals he might carry back to London; in French Vergennes reminded him that it was up to England to make those overtures. England was now engaged against four nations, not so much America's allies as her cobelligerents, whose conflicting demands would need to be reconciled. (Holland too had entered the war, and, like Spain, had her own agenda.) As England was acting alone, it made more sense for her to initiate the process. It would be weeks before anyone said as much, but Oswald's real question was whether France meant to continue her war against Britain. Vergennes made clear that his nation had no intention of humiliating her rival but rather—the distinction was interesting—expected to undo the damage of 1763. On that note the French minister was happy to leave the matter.

Franklin was not. He paid Oswald a call the following morning, ostensibly to deliver a letter for Shelburne. His real motive was to broach a topic Oswald had studiously and expertly avoided: Canada, that Franklinian hobbyhorse. He arrived in Saint-Germain well prepared, his mini-discourse written out in advance. In it he drew a distinction he considered vital. Peace was one thing, reconciliation another. The latter was the far sweeter entity. And what better way for Britain to reconcile with her colonies than by offering up voluntary reparations for the atrocities she had committed? The British could not compensate for the villages and towns they had wantonly destroyed, but they did have Canada. Oswald had himself noted that the landmass had played a crucial role from the start; France's concession of it to England had advanced the cause of the American Revolution. (Had it remained French, he might just as well have argued, Versailles would not have ridden to the American rescue.) That was true, acknowledged Franklin, tenacious as ever; and the longer Britain held on to Canada, the stronger would be American ties with France. Did it not make more sense to cede that territory to the colonies now, as a mark of goodwill and in lieu of pecuniary compensation for the Loyalists, which a strapped Great Britain was in no position to offer?

It was an audacious opening, the more so for what came next. Oswald asked if he might carry Franklin's notes back to Shelburne. Gratified, Franklin parted with his scrap of paper. It was, he realized immediately, a colossal mistake, one that went unmentioned in the progress report he submitted the next morning to Adams. Franklin had had no authority from Congress to discuss reparations for the Loyalists, for whom there was little sympathy in America. Nor had he conferred with Vergennes, despite his congressional instructions. Were Shelburne to share his propositions he would incur the wrath of France; anyone at Versailles would have choked on the cession of Canada alone. He was furious with himself for having overreached, ashamed to have been so imprudent as to have allowed the paper out of his hands. Oswald was to return within two weeks to continue discussions, but Franklin was miserable in the interval.

He atoned for his sins constructively. Oswald had not yet crossed the English Channel when Franklin began circulating a *Boston Independent Chronicle* excerpt, authentic-seeming down to the marginal advertisements. It catalogued British-encouraged Indian atrocities in lurid detail. The careful reader might have recognized the Parisian typeface, as some in London twigged immediately to the first-rate prose. Franklin mailed out copies left and right; he was a little sheepish, but reasoned that it was the British who ought to be ashamed of themselves. There was after all a great deal of truth in his little fiction. At the same time and possibly also on account of his lapse, he begged Jay to join him in Paris. Laurens had made his distaste for the commission clear. Adams was in the midst of loan negotiations. Franklin had no interest in standing alone. "Spain has taken four years to consider whether she should treat with us or not. Give her forty. And let us in the meantime mind our own business," he urged Jay. To his appeal he added Vergennes's endorsement. And he made a point of advertising his Spanish sentiments, sending Jay's envelope through channels he knew could be relied upon for their indiscretion.

Six years as a supplicant left Franklin no more comfortable on his knees than he had ever been. He made no note of what Adams described as the typical reception at Versailles, "those lowering countenances, solemn looks, distant bows, and other peculiarities, which have been sometimes diverting and sometimes provoking for so many years." As he could be brutally reminded, he wore still the scarlet A among the diplomatic corps, however. He caused a minor scandal when the grand duke of Russia, later to become Czar Paul I, made a state visit to Paris that spring. The grand duke's calling card was delivered to all the representatives of nations with whom the court of Saint Petersburg had relations, in which rounds the Valentinois was included. Upon receipt of his card, Franklin rode to the Russian ambassador's home, to have his name inscribed in the guestbook, as protocol required. Several days later a frantic servant arrived at the Valentinois. He had made a dreadful mistake, for which he would surely be fired. As the court of Saint Petersburg had not yet acknowledged America's existence, Franklin's name could not soil the porter's book. Franklin calmed him; the servant had only to erase his name. For his part he would burn the grand duke's card. Franklin had little patience for the customs of the Old World, although he was finally able to parse them. It was not lost on him that—as of 1782—the Spanish ambassador had begun to hold the door for him.*

Nor was American dignity, or fear of his own inadequacy, the only reason Franklin begged for his colleagues to join him. Peacemaking was a thankless profession. He expected to be pilloried no matter how he fared. He pleaded with Laurens to make the Paris trip; Laurens's reputation for integrity would help to defend him against his enemies. He was correct at least about the tirelessness of his detractors: In America Arthur Lee continued on the warpath against "that old, corrupt serpent." Why had Congress entrusted Franklin with the negotiation on which the nation's existence depended when "they had the fullest evidence and conviction that Dr. Franklin was both a dishonest and incapable man?" He could be counted upon to exercise his malignant magic, to toady to the French, to attend to his own accounts. In the course of the next months Lee would attempt another recall effort.

Meanwhile Franklin discovered that the dearth of American colleagues was nothing compared to the proliferation of British emissaries. Oswald returned as promised on May 4, Franklin's scrap of paper in hand. Happily, Shelburne alone had read it. Exceeding his own instructions, Oswald gave Franklin to believe that the Canada proposal had been well received (which was highly improbable), suggesting that its discussion await the end of the negotiation. Oswald brought with him as well the news that Shelburne's rival, the new foreign secretary, Charles James Fox, was sending his own man to Paris. Franklin was to expect

---

*The Russian ambassador was all grateful apologies after the incident. He made a point to include Franklin in an entertainment held in the grand duke's honor, for which the ambassador's carved and gilded home was gorgeously illuminated, the guests superbly attired, the ladies dripping in diamonds, a scene which was, Franklin noted, acknowledging what he had been missing, "altogether the most splendid spectacle my eyes ever beheld."

Dr. FRANKLIN, prefents his Compliments to
and defires the honour
of   Company at Dinner, on Monday the 5th
of *July*; in order to celebrate the ANNIVERSARY of the
DECLARATION of AMERICAN INDEPENDENCE.

Paffy,   1779.

An Anfwer if you pleafe.

Franklin's invitation to his lavish 1779 Independence Day dinner (duck, chicken, quail, turkey, and pigeon, veal and lamb), and the first known imprint of the press he quietly set up at the Valentinois.

The portrait of General Washington with which Lafayette returned to France in 1779, and that presided over Franklin's Independence Day celebration. Underfoot Washington tramples Britain's conciliatory bills; he holds aloft the Declaration of Independence and the Franco-American treaties.

Madame Brillon's house and terrace, in a gouache most likely of her own composition. At the top of her 150 steps Franklin installed himself on summer evenings, to revel in the view, the gardens, and his neighbor's sparkling conversation.

A nineteenth-century engraving of Franklin at the French court, a tableau accurate only in spirit. Louis XVI appears seated, with Marie Antoinette at his side; the comte de Maurepas can be glimpsed in profile, just above his sovereign. Vergennes stands to the right of the woman crowning Franklin with laurels.

John Adams, Franklin's erratic and irascible colleague. In 1776 Adams extolled Franklin's talents; the Philadelphian was the ideal American representative. By 1782 Adams was less admiring. "As far as cruel fate shall compel me to act with him in public affairs," he wrote of Franklin, "I shall treat him with decency and perfect impartiality. Further than that I can feel for him no other sentiments than contempt and abhorrence."

The marquis de Lafayette, the younger face of Franco-American amity. The twenty-year-old major general helped to shoulder many of Franklin's burdens even while he succinctly grasped the difficulties inherent in the alliance. "I cannot deny that the Americans are somewhat difficult to handle," warned Lafayette, "especially for a Frenchman."

Monsieur Franklin's French calling card.

Antoine Borel's allegorical print of 1778, for which Franklin posed but which he begged not be dedicated to him. Instead Borel dedicated the piece to Congress while granting Franklin mythic status. In Roman garb he prevails over the "triumph of reason and humanity." His right hand rests on America's shoulder; with his left he directs Mars, who fells Britain and Neptune. Minerva assists from on high.

Franklin again in his allegorical glory, in an etching based on Fragonard's early 1778 design. From his throne Franklin heads off tyranny and avarice; a poised and decidedly docile America views her liberation from a perch at his knee. As with the medal Franklin himself designed later, America's dirty work falls to the nonnationals.

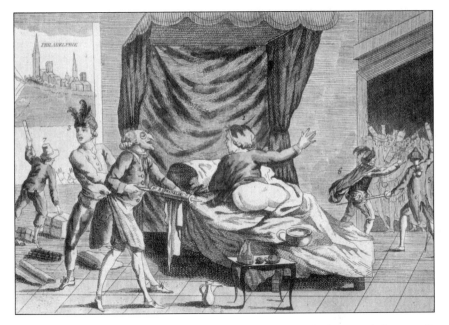

The less vulgar version of a 1778 political cartoon. Sick in bed, an Englishman calls for a remedy to his ills. Obligingly the apothecary steps in—with a syringe labeled "Dr. Franklin"—to be forcibly restrained by an American. An army of doctors arrives to save the day but is held off by a Spaniard and a Frenchman, épée in hand. Meanwhile a Dutchman profits from the chaos.

The eighteenth century wrote its history in its hairstyles. Left, the *coiffure à l'indépendence américaine* and, right, an aerostatic lady of 1783, sporting a hot-air-balloon hat, tethered to her belt with silk sashes.

Benjamin West's unfinished portrait of the peace commissioners who assembled in Paris on November 30, 1782. Left to right, Jay, Adams, Franklin, Henry Laurens, and William Temple Franklin.

Thomas Jefferson, America's second minister plenipotentiary to the court of France and the only colleague other than Deane with whom Franklin enjoyed warm relations. To the question, "Is it you, Sir, who replaces Dr. Franklin?" Jefferson took to answering: "No one can *replace* him, Sir; I am only his successor."

Franklin was among those assembled on the morning of November 21, 1783, when Pilâtre de Rozier and the marquis d'Arlandes's seventy-foot balloon rose from the garden of La Muette, bottom left. Right, the balloon as seen from Franklin's terrace, the steeples of Notre Dame and Saint-Sulpice in the distance.

"Magnetism Unveiled," a 1784 engraving in which Franklin plays the central role, brandishing the Mesmer report. In its harsh light both the deluded and the forces of evil flee. The task was in truth less neat; deceptions were more tenacious—and more lucrative—than even a born hoaxer had imagined.

Louis XVI, twenty-three years old at the time he entered into the American alliance, as depicted in the portrait he sent Franklin in 1785, a parting gift. Originally the portrait was surrounded by 408 diamonds; Franklin left the miniature to his daughter, with the proviso that she not use the gems for ornamentation, "and thereby introduce or countenance the expensive, vain, and useless fashion of wearing jewels in this country." Sally sold them instead, evidently to finance a trip to France.

Three renditions of the fur-hatted Franklin. France came to know the American primarily through the Nini medallion, above. As Franklin's family noted, the artists seemed more interested in his headgear than in any accurate depiction of their celebrated relative's physiognomy. In the end the lack of resemblance mattered little. The subject's sister observed that the face appeared in a thousand variations, "however if it is called Dr. Franklin, it will be revered."

A drawing of one of Houdon's 1778 Franklin busts, which all of Paris raced to examine, and which were said to bear a striking resemblance to its subject, at once frank and dispassionate, earthy and wise.

Thomas Grenville immediately. That envoy happened to be the son of Franklin's nemesis, George Grenville, author of the Stamp Act. Franklin stumbled not at all over the young man's pedigree, declaring Grenville intelligent and judicious. He appeared to carry no more specific proposals than did Oswald, however. Franklin hoped he might be more forthcoming with Vergennes, to whom he introduced Grenville on May 9. Two hours passed in which the new envoy revealed no terms, arguing only that as England was prepared to grant America her independence, France should ready herself to return the British island she had conquered and call it quits. With a smile Vergennes noted that granting American independence hardly qualified as a concession on Britain's part. It was already won. "There is Mr. Franklin, he will answer you as to that point," he asserted, passing the baton. Franklin relayed him expertly. "To be sure," he said, "we do not consider ourselves as under any necessity of bargaining for a thing that is our own, and which we have bought at the expense of so much blood and treasure, and which we are in full possession of."

Vergennes drew a parallel with the previous war. That conflict had erupted over some obscure tracts of land on the Ohio River and in Nova Scotia. Yet Britain had walked away from it (in a treaty Grenville knew well; it had been negotiated by his uncle) with miles and miles of new territory, including Canada, Louisiana, and Florida. She had checked and constrained France in every part of the globe. Surely Britain did not expect lands to be restored to her after she had waged a war that was both unsuccessful and unprovoked? At the second adjective Grenville jumped. But the French had been only too happy to incite the Americans to revolt! Vergennes tensed. France had done no such thing. He defied the world to prove otherwise. "There sits," he fumed, "Mr. Franklin, who knows the fact and will contradict me if I do not speak the truth." Franklin held serenely still in his chair. Endorsing hypocrisy did not figure in his instructions.

Grenville was sullen on the carriage ride back to Paris. Surely the Americans did not mean to reject attractive English offers only to gratify the ambitions of the Bourbon kings? France would presumably insist on concessions utterly foreign to the alliance, with which America was under no obligation to assist. He offered up that paternalistic advice with a smile, one that faded as Franklin startled the twenty-six-year-old with a discourse on obligation and gratitude. There were things in the world greater than money, he lectured, demonstrating that a debt could not always be discharged by repayment alone. Grenville protested that Franklin was carrying his benevolence rather too far in applying it to Franco-American relations, especially when Louis XVI acted purely from self-interest. Franklin would have none of it. And Grenville was no more pleased to learn, from the conde de Aranda, that Spanish claims were equally separate from American independence. Toward the ambitions of that ally Franklin was less deferential. He supposed that Spain would ask for Gibraltar, an idea that left Grenville aghast. Briskly Franklin added that it did not matter to him one way or another who wound up with that particular pile of stone.

Unable to flush out either Fox's or Shelburne's agenda, Franklin had reason all the same to believe that the end was in sight to a ruinous war. The goodwill was there even if the terms were missing; on May 9 he began a journal of the peace proceedings. He obliged the public's hopes, commenting after Grenville and his delegation were sighted at the Valentinois: "They came to take my temperature, which they certainly did not find feverish." Soon enough it became clear even to a temperate man, however, that while there was much talk, there was little progress. The British appeared to be stalling in the grant of the obvious. Grenville thought he heard in Franklin's conversations hints that America might be less likely to support the Bourbon claims were independence granted immediately, which he may indeed have heard; Shelburne remained opposed to that concession. Fox had long been more willing to accommodate on the American front and had further reason to as well. Once America was independent, her affairs would fall to him in his capacity as secretary of state. While all British emissaries warned Franklin against allowing his country to become a European football, America's independence was tossed back and forth between British ministries, in a Whitehall turf war. That only partly explained the fumbling over the wording of British instructions, which could not address the riddle of how to negotiate with a nation England refused to recognize as one. From the Hague Adams summed up Franklin's predicament clearly. He was appalled by all the dancing about. If Britain wanted a peace she had only to declare America independent. Otherwise all that will happen, carped Adams, is to "nibble and piddle and dribble and fribble."

That comment might just as well have been inspired by the weather, which was uncommonly cool and unremittingly sodden; the rains that began in mid-March continued without intermission through June. All was mud outdoors, dampness within. Throughout Paris the fires burned steadily. With the unseasonable chill came an influenza epidemic that incapacitated Europe; by summer 100,000 Parisians were laid low, police chief Lenoir among them. Accounts of the capture of Admiral de Grasse in the Antilles only dampened soggy spirits; the hero of Yorktown had been soundly defeated in April. On May 27 Franklin dined next door at d'Estaing's, amid a group of dejected French naval officers. He attempted to cheer the table with the tale of a sixteenth-century Turkish defeat at the hands of the Venetians—the Turks suffered massive losses, to reemerge with a larger fleet the following year—but soon enough began to suspect that Britain's late triumph had doused the peace initiative. He could see no other reason why she failed to authorize her emissaries to negotiate with an independent America. Grenville did his best to attribute the reluctance to transcription errors, assuring Franklin that he was wrong to question British sincerity. Their victory in the Antilles in no way dissuaded anyone from making peace. Nor could any envoy impress upon Franklin how highly he was esteemed by the British cabinet. It was unlikely, Oswald assured him, that any single man had ever had in his hands the opportunity to do as much good as did he at that moment. Those encomia sounded different to Franklin in 1782 than they might have decades earlier. He felt he had nothing to prove. He was beyond ambition, a useful place to be.

As talks remained agreeable, informal, and altogether unforthcoming, he prepared to break off negotiations. Clearly Britain was too exhausted to pursue the war but too proud to make peace. Late in May came the happy news that John Jay was en route from Madrid, as well as a *London Evening Post* report that Franklin had agreed to forsake the alliance. Assuming that untruth had come directly from Grenville, Franklin made a radical suggestion to Vergennes. It struck him as likely that after the peace Britain meant to attack one or the other country separately. Before any peace was signed, would it not make sense for the allies to agree that "we who are at war against England should enter into another treaty, engaging ourselves that in such case we should again make it a common cause, and renew the general war"? It was a proposal that would have made his compatriots shudder; Franklin was volunteering to wade into European politics for her allies' sake. The proposal doubtless made Vergennes shudder too; it revealed a thorough misunderstanding of the treaty of 1778. The Franco-American alliance was a perpetual one. On paper it did not end with American independence, although it clearly did in Franklin's mind. Misplaced though it was, Franklin's query was a fitting revenge on a peace commissioner who was at that moment avoiding him because his questions were too good. "I have already felt myself under some embarrassment respecting Mr. Franklin," admitted Grenville, who knew full well that he was selling a shoddy piece of goods, and to a master craftsman.

To his mounting political frustration Franklin joined a more personal one. The British emissaries brought with them an easy correspondence with a lost world, so close and yet just beyond his grasp. When Polly Hewson begged off from making the French trip, a disappointed Franklin could only admire her practical sense: "In this affair I now doubt my own head, and suspect it was rather a project of my heart. The truth is, I love you both very much, and wish to be with you anywhere." At his request the family of Jonathan Shipley, in whose home Franklin drafted the first pages of his *Autobiography* in 1771, sent on their silhouettes. Franklin propped them on the Valentinois mantel, "so that I have not only you always in my mind, but constantly before my eyes." (A framed print of Polly Hewson's late husband hung as well in his study.) To Shipley, the father of five sparkling and impeccably educated girls, Franklin lamented that he sorely missed his own daughter. He claimed he "would give the world for one," a sentiment he did not communicate to Philadelphia. The embrace of surrogate family was as much on display as ever. While he issued a brief to Polly Hewson on the importance of educating one's offspring, he sounded few concerned notes about Benny at that singular moment when Geneva qualified as a political hotspot. Franklin considered sending for the thirteen-year-old, but on that count his heart by no means got the better of his head.

Another frustration presented itself as well. Deciphering France's early overtures proved nearly as difficult as deciphering England's late ones. In

America Robert Morris continued to scratch his head over the Beaumarchais account, which he begged Franklin to resolve. At the end of June Franklin paid the playwright two million livres, but he could no sooner solve the larger financial mystery than he could deliver up a peace treaty. Convinced that sloppy bookkeeping was to blame at Beaumarchais's end— "He has often promised solemnly to render me an account in two or three days. Years have since elapsed and he has not yet done it"—he begged that someone else try his luck. He was caught up in his own tangle of accounts, the time having come to settle up with Chaumont, a process that generated a new season of ill will at the Valentinois. Petitions and counterpetitions flew back and forth down the hallway, the titles of which—"Response of Mr. Franklin to the reply of M. Chaumont regarding the memorandum of Mr. Franklin addressing the observations of M. Chaumont"—spoke for themselves. Franklin found the process infuriating, the more so as Chaumont's niggling brought out equally unattractive behavior in himself. And the closer the matter came to a settlement, the more frequently the entrepreneur changed his mind.* Only on a July morning did landlord and tenant, zealous supplier and uneasy procurement officer, sit down with their respective notaries to settle their differences. They agreed to submit to an arbitrator's decision; should either party fail to do so, he would be subject to a penalty of 10,000 livres. Forty-eight hours later Chaumont was again revising his figures. Franklin let the matter drop. The tug-of-war revealed him to be as reluctant to condemn as he had been with Silas Deane, who lived still—even after Franklin admitted that his ex-colleague sat "croaking at Ghent, chagrined, discontented, and dispirited"—on handouts from the Valentinois. As severe as he was with family, friends could rarely do wrong. Franklin continued to believe his landlord naturally honest, "driven into knavery by the effect of imprudent speculations."†

---

*"One is never sure of having finished any thing [with] M. C. He is forever renewing old demands or inventing new ones," Franklin complained to Jonathan Williams in mid-June, his patience exhausted, and about to be tried again. In reply to his granduncle's queries regarding the Chaumont account, Williams revealed that the America-bound cargoes had included goods smuggled aboard without his knowledge. Indeed it was difficult to construe 4,694 ostrich feathers, 32 silk umbrellas, 80 bundles of artificial flowers, or 2 leopard skins as military supplies.

†So far as Franklin's rent was concerned, America got a bargain. Chaumont billed Franklin 20,000 livres for five years. The least extravagant of the foreign diplomats paid several times as much. Franklin protested the bill, and in May 1784 finally paid 15,000 livres.

Fortunately Paris was alive with distractions that spring and summer. In March Franklin met several times with Alessandro Volta, who was to create the chemical battery. He followed the progress of a nearby inventor, perfecting his flying boat. In the first warm days of April, before any notaries were yet in sight, he ventured with Chaumont to his Passy limestone quarry. In the course of their tour Franklin learned that the workers had recently liberated several toads from solid rock. He lost no time in interrogating one of the men. Indeed four live toads had been unearthed from cavities fifteen feet below ground. Could there have been an opening in the rock, inquired Franklin, by which the animal had entered? None at all, the laborer assured him. Had he ever seen such a thing before, in any other quarry? He had not. Could Franklin examine the toads? The workman clambered up the stone, where he located two of the former captives, tossed, by the toes, down to the American. One was quite dead, the other plump and alive. Franklin was befuddled; it was understood that animals that did not perspire, such as turtles and snakes, could live for long intervals without food. If the creatures had remained in the rock since its formation, reasoned the seventy-six-year-old scientist, they must be nearly immortal. Having asked the workman to alert him if he met with any future specimens, Franklin headed off with his toads. The live one did not appear to survive the carriage ride home but revived briefly as wine was poured over him, flouncing about for a few minutes before expiring. Franklin was enchanted, preserving the specimens and writing up the incident for the Académie des Sciences. He was still talking years later about the discovery, for which he had all the curiosity that did not extend to naval affairs.

On a summer Friday he sat down to add a few last lines to a letter to Joseph Priestley, the theologian and respected British chemist. The cruelties of war and British dithering had taken a toll; no more disillusioned document would issue from Franklin's pen. He envied Priestley his engagement with the natural world, so superior to that of men. "The more I discovered of the former, the more I admired them; the more I know of the latter, the more I am disgusted with them. Men I find to be a sort of beings very badly constructed, as they are generally more easily provoked than reconciled, more disposed to do mischief to each other than to make reparation, much more easily deceived than undeceived, and having more pride and even pleasure in killing than in begetting one another, for without a blush they assemble in great armies at noon day to destroy, and when they have killed as many as they can, they exaggerate the number to augment the fancied glory; but they creep into corners, or cover themselves with the darkness of night when they mean to beget, as being ashamed of a virtuous action." He was not altogether convinced the species worth preserving. It was not impossible that Priestley would come to the same conclusion one day, and wish he had sacrificed boys and girls in his experiments instead of murdering "honest harmless mice."

At the end of May a peculiar caller materialized at the gates of the Valentinois. "A man very shabbily dressed—all his dress together was not worth five shillings—came and desired to see me," Franklin recalled. The unprepossessing visitor had walked from the south of France, bearing with him his forty-six-page plan for universal peace. Three years earlier he had sent Franklin a draft of that opus, at which time he had signed himself "Galley slave number 1336." So Pierre Gargaz had been for twenty years, condemned to a forced labor sentence for a murder he had not committed. On his release, having lost his wife and children, the fifty-two-year-old former schoolmaster hiked to Passy with his proposal for what was essentially a model United Nations. He envisioned an authority that would peaceably resolve all international differences; its presiding officer would be the representative of the oldest sovereign. Among other oddities the plan called for canals to be dug at Panama and Suez. (Only a united Europe might accomplish those projects, theorized Gargaz, who held they would stimulate economies, and satisfy monarchical egos, more effectively than war.) In June 1782 those pages intrigued Franklin more than did any documents that came his way from Britain. Eagerly he printed up Gargaz's idealistic proposal, the whole of which, like the story behind it, struck some as so unlikely that it was taken later as a Franklinian hoax.

So it might seem were there no material evidence of Gargaz's visit. In the course of it the former galley slave and the American peace commissioner lingered over another common obsession: a phonetic alphabet, a project with which Franklin had toyed for years. He jotted down French homonyms, which Gargaz reworked according to his system. Franklin made some attempts to adopt Gargaz's alphabet, by which, for example, *"ils mangeroient"* became *"iƺ manjeren."* The unlikely visitor met with his wholehearted approbation. Here was a man, mused Franklin, who "asks for nothing, expects nothing, and does not even desire to be known." By

1782 he had himself developed a quintessentially French taste. He pronounced himself in awe of the simple provincial emissary, "this *véritable philosophe.*"

~~*~~

Tall, wiry, sharp-featured, John Jay arrived in Paris on June 23. The thirty-seven-year-old New Yorker, resolute and dignified, a sober study in black and white, settled his wife and family in the hotel rooms Temple had located for them and hurried out to Passy to spend the afternoon with Franklin. Jay was displeased to find that British enthusiasm for a peace seemed to have evaporated since Franklin had so urgently summoned him, and that Fox and Shelburne were working at cross-purposes. With his partner in what he termed "the skirmishing business" he was, however, delighted. "He is in perfect good health, and his mind appears more vigorous than that of any man of his age I have known. He certainly is a valuable minister, and an agreeable companion," Jay assured America's first secretary of foreign affairs, Robert Livingston.

As his colleague settled in near the Louvre, Franklin absorbed the news that Congress expected him to obtain additional funds. He had been repeatedly warned at Versailles that he was on no condition to count on further assistance. "Under this declaration with what face could I ask for another six millions?" he moaned. Within days he also fixed on a means for doing so. Ostensibly to assure Vergennes that Congress would resist all British efforts to divide the two countries, he submitted his recent correspondence to the King's Council. He had only ulterior motives, "which was that they should see I have been ordered to demand further aids, and had foreborne to make the demand." It was a fine maneuver; he could win points simultaneously for frankness and reserve, while allowing France the gracious gesture of offering up aid unasked.

July deprived Franklin and Oswald each of a colleague. The influenza epidemic that made the tour of Europe disabled both John and the pregnant Sally Jay for three weeks. (Theirs was an early bow to fashion, quipped the effervescent Mrs. Jay.) In London the epidemic claimed the life of the prime minister, leaving Shelburne in the ascendant and ending Grenville's commission. The cleared field worked wonders for Franklin, who invited Oswald to the Valentinois on the morning of July 10, to offer up terms for a peace. Those he divided into necessary and advisable articles. The first conformed to Congress's directions—the nonnegotiable articles were complete independence; the evacuation of British troops from American soil; boundaries that took the country to the Great Lakes and the Mississippi, doubling its size; the right to fish off Newfoundland—while the second constituted a liberal set of Franklin-designed extras. That list included an apology. Simultaneously Franklin corrected two of his errata. Despite Oswald's entreaties, he kept his notes to himself. And he changed tack completely on the issue of Loyalist compensation, on which he never again wavered. He was cheerful and sanguine, confident that matters could be sorted out quickly, an analysis with which Oswald agreed. His instructions were to see to it that America in no way wind up as a satellite of France, an alternative less palatable even than independence. For his part, Franklin warned Oswald that America had no intention of winding up as an Ireland, Shelburne's preferred solution. To discourage that eventuality, Franklin burnished the French connection for the next emissary in town, who happened to be his great friend and publisher Benjamin Vaughan, a Shelburne protégé and a distant relative of Laurens's. In six years, marveled Franklin, Vergennes had never once let him down. The first French officers may have failed to endear themselves to America, but the second wave had enchanted her entirely. Not only was France unceasingly, uncommonly generous, she made it a habit—the shame and dread of his supplications were nowhere in sight—of "always throwing in a million or two when closing their accounts."

At the end of the month came Shelburne's approval to proceed on Franklin's terms. Also at the end of the month Jay returned to the negotiating table. It took him little time to establish his distrust for Shelburne, who continued to offer American independence as a treaty term rather than as a preexisting condition. Jay would proceed only on an equal footing. Franklin was more pliable; he saw no reason to continue a bloody war, which three million people were eager to end, on account of a technicality. The British were equally startled by Jay's lack of warmth toward the mother country. As even the amiable Oswald noted, the New Yorker was "as much alienated from any particular regard for England, as if he had never heard of it in his life." After one intemperate exchange, Franklin found himself assuring a stunned Oswald that his younger colleague was a perfectly reasonable individual. He might well sound severe, he was perhaps a bit of a stickler, but he was a lawyer after all, explained the man who rarely allowed a detail to get in his way, and who preferred to proceed affably and obliquely, forever reaching into his grab bag of allegories and anecdotes.

It took the eminently sensible Jay only slightly longer to develop a distrust of Vergennes, one that mutated quickly into contempt. He believed that the French minister was poised to sell out the Americans to Spanish interests. Vergennes indeed found himself between a rock and a hard place—commonly known as Gibraltar and the Appalachians, Spain's obsessions—but Franklin could not believe he would forsake his young ally. While he recognized France's self-interest he did not doubt her good faith. He saw no reason for the Americans to undermine themselves by separating from her ally, while Jay saw no reason they should embarrass themselves by submitting to her. He attempted to reason with his colleague about France: "If we lean on her love of liberty, her affection for America, or her disinterested magnanimity, we shall lean on a broken reed, that will sooner or later pierce our hands," Jay insisted, years of elegantly expressed pro-French sentiment dissolving on contact with French soil. By August he had come to rail equally against the Bourbon powers and his undignified instructions. Did he really prefer to break with those instructions? Franklin challenged. Indeed Jay did, refusing to continue until American independence was taken as a given and until he could negotiate without Vergennes. He would prefer to resign, he insisted, than to serve manacled to the French. Franklin had invoked the same language when it came to proceeding *without* the French.

It would be entirely thanks to Jay that Oswald was finally empowered to negotiate with the Americans as representatives of a sovereign nation rather than of British colonies. And it would be largely Jay who—trading marked-up maps with the conde de Aranda—firmly established that the western border of the new country would include all lands to the Mississippi, as well as the right to navigate that river. He took the lead in negotiations partly of necessity; Franklin fell ill at the end of the summer with kidney stones, a malady he feared would be his last. As he did so, Vergennes fell out of the equation. Early in September Jay discovered that Vergennes had secretly dispatched one of his trusted undersecretaries, forty-six-year-old Joseph-Mathias Gérard de Rayneval, the younger brother of the former Philadelphia envoy, to London. Rayneval could only have headed off, reasoned Jay, to undermine American objectives. (Rayneval was in truth charged with a parallel negotiation. As always with France, American interests were secondary.) Jay buttressed his case the following day when a French paper came to hand—supplied by the British, who had helpfully deciphered it as well—that argued against American claims to the Newfoundland fisheries. That document was a 1782 dispatch submitted to Vergennes by a subordinate, but Jay read it as a position paper.

Franklin wrote the document off as a hoax. Jay begged to differ, and behind his colleague's back dispatched Vaughan to London, to frustrate Rayneval's efforts. He knew well that Franklin would have blocked such a measure, which was daring; Jay had enlisted Shelburne's emissary to his own ends. With Congress he was forthright about his suspicious. He hastened to add that his venerable colleague saw things very differently, believing that France meant to confine herself to conduct that was impeccably "friendly, fair and honorable." One of them, Jay concluded, was wrong. Especially after Rayneval's secret mission, there was no question in his mind who that was. After two years of chasing the Spanish court from one of its five royal residences to another, never to be received, never to be granted a cent, and never to conquer his aversion to gazpacho, Jay had had enough of Bourbon princes; he may have been inclined to make France pay a little for his Spanish humiliation.* He began to wish for the sane and potent presence of John Adams, whom he summoned to Paris, as yet unaware of any bad blood between his colleagues.

By contrast Franklin—whose ductility so often made him appear suspect—remained steadfast in his commitment to France. Warmly he acknowledged the summer festivities held throughout America to celebrate the birth of the dauphin, celebrations set off by a parade of Washington's troops in West Point. Boston had come a long way since the ladles of fresh frog; the city awoke on June 12 to the boom of cannon and the peals of church bells, and crawled into bed that night fortified by ample toasts, after a dazzling display of fireworks. In Philadelphia Robert

---

*Known for his obstinacy, Jay had already performed one about-face on France's count. Descended from Huguenots, he had effectively tamped down a personal prejudice in 1778; at the time of the Deane–Lee imbroglio, Jay was elected to succeed Laurens as president of Congress because he was believed to be ardently pro-French. In 1780 he confessed to Franklin that he was attached to that kingdom to a degree he "could not have thought myself capable of ten years ago." He would love France as long as he lived; she was America's first, best, "and almost only friend." Yet again, Vergennes was to pay the price for Spanish recalcitrance.

Morris marveled over the incongruity of those events; to some it seemed as if human nature had been turned inside out. (To others it seemed as if the celebrations were staged purely for Britain's sake.) Franklin had little difficulty with the contortionism, against which he was warned in a private letter from Morris. Franklin's enemies industriously published that he was too grateful to be effective, too much in the thrall of the French to press forcefully for American aid. Increasingly, allowed Morris, by way of consolation, those who censured Franklin were those who censured France.*

Franklin had not hesitated to exceed, or ignore, his instructions in the past. He had acknowledged that America held a strong negotiating hand; Jay had made a convincing case for French duplicity. If America had no further reason to fear England she had no further reason either to cultivate France. Why then the stubborn loyalty? Gratitude played a large part. Franklin saw America's commitment to France not as an entangling alliance but as a godsend. She would be nowhere without her. He sincerely meant what he said about Vergennes. The French minister had never once let him down, and had always dealt fairly, a refrain Franklin's colleagues knew to be among his favorites. He did not need anyone to remind him of how America would appear were she to comport herself differently, but one scientific friend did. He had recently heard it asserted that America "has taken a French instead of an English husband, but that she did not like her spouse and was determined to cuckold him very soon, grow rid of him, and marry a good one. I told him that if his prediction should prove true, America could never place herself among the venerable matrons, the other republics, without blushing, as being an adulteress and vile prostitute." Franklin assured his correspondent that American independence would never be founded on flightiness or infidelity. In part too Franklin was spiteful, reluctant to give the British what they wanted. And by 1782 the British were more intent on breaking up a Franco-American alliance than they were on resisting American independence.

"Let us be honest and grateful to *France*, but let us think for *our-*

---

*That Franklin had stubborn enemies in Philadelphia was driven home vividly that spring, when lightning struck Luzerne's rented home at the corner of Chestnut and Seventh Streets, causing considerable damage. In loud advertisement of its owner's politics, the house did not sport a lightning rod. Appropriately enough, the result was a fried French artillery officer.

selves," went the upright Jay's argument. Franklin did not believe the two mutually exclusive. Like many of his countrymen, Jay was eager to secure his nation's independence and pack up and go home. Franklin had some inkling that America would never be able entirely to do so; he knew the ocean of fire that Jefferson wished might separate the two worlds would never materialize. While his colleagues had no taste for any kind of postwar European involvement, the end of the year found Franklin proposing a quadruple alliance among France, Spain, Holland, and the United States, in the event that England attempted to avenge herself on any single party. Nothing would so effectively guarantee world peace. From a purely practical standpoint, Franklin doubtless understood that forsaking France did nothing to strengthen America's bargaining position.

Was he mistaken? He was about the fisheries document, which was very real. France had long had an overriding interest in the Newfoundland coast and the Saint Lawrence, although there is no evidence that Vergennes meant to insist on any rights that would have interfered with America's in 1782. His plans for Canada were indeed diametrically opposed to Franklin's; from the start, Vergennes was committed to keeping that territory, including the Great Lakes, out of American hands, as he was to keeping his intentions an impenetrable secret. And if France's first priority was to humble England, her second was to guarantee that no new power rise in the west. To that Franklin appeared oblivious. He was equally so to Vergennes's desperation to make a prompt peace. The French treasury had been bled dry, and Vergennes was eager to direct his attention to the east, where Russia was reviving from a closely monitored slumber. Jay was equally ignorant of those considerations. Well into the fall he continued to believe that France had no inclination toward peace when the opposite was true. Neither envoy had any grasp of the fuller picture; Vergennes was perfectly within his rights noting that the Americans were not conspicuous for their understanding of the world political scene. It has been argued that—had Franklin and Jay better understood how eager Vergennes was to attend to eastern Europe, had they moved more quickly—southern Ontario would today be American.

Could Franklin have endangered his country's interests? It is uncertain if Vergennes could have manipulated him, if ever he meant to; all evidence points to the foreign minister's having been in a compromising rather than a conspiring mood. Franklin was no less passionate than his

colleagues, but he was more covert. Fundamentally, he was not an ideo-
logue. And in a way his attitude toward Vergennes was a nonissue. He
trusted Shelburne, with whom he felt confident negotiating. Shelburne
was an old friend, a kindred spirit, a free trader, and an admirer of many
things American. He was no favorite of George III's. Franklin believed
him sincerely bent on peace, as indeed Shelburne was; he had no interest
in pursuing any kind of revenge. Essentially Jay and Franklin would proceed from different angles: Franklin tilted always at Canada, intent on a
British concession, while Jay focused on the American West, more concerned with blunting Spanish ambitions. In the process Jay tripped as
much over his Spanish spite as his colleague did over his French loyalty.
So Jay submitted an extraordinary proposal. In October, he outright encouraged the English to direct their troops from Charleston and New
York south, to seize Florida from the Spanish, which was to say from the
clutches of America's ally. He preferred to share that tract of land with a
declared enemy than with a Bourbon king.

On October 14 Franklin alerted Congress that preliminary terms had
gone off to England. He had little hope they would be accepted, as they
were not. Shelburne either believed that Oswald had been dominated by
the Americans or felt less accommodating once he sensed Jay's distaste for
France; he was in less of a position to be generous than he had been earlier. The same day Vergennes assured Luzerne, in Philadelphia, that the
king had every intention of again subsidizing the Americans but no intention yet of letting them know as much, the better to manipulate them. He
conveyed to Congress his astonishment that an independence-obsessed
republic continued to draw for its defense on a foreign monarch rather
than taxing its citizens. Luzerne should see to it as well that Congress remind its commissioners of their obligations. The American told him nothing. "But you will take the greatest care," he specified, "not to present what
I tell you as a complaint, and you will pray Mr. Livingston not to make
any reproach to Messrs. Franklin and Jay, because that would give them
dissatisfaction, which must be avoided." (Livingston promised a discreet
and delicate slap on the wrist. The commissioners' instructions were crystal clear. They were to place "the most absolute confidence" in Vergennes.)

Vergennes did not know that Congress was squirming equally in its
ignorance of the envoys' discussions. As troubling from the American
side was that there were four men in Europe to negotiate a peace, of which

only two were in Paris. Why was Adams holding off? And why did Laurens refuse to serve? As the southern states were quick to note, discussions thereby remained entirely in the hands of northerners. There was additional cause for alarm as reports circulated that Franklin was in much-diminished health. Frail and lame, he was practically immobile. Some who saw him early in the fall suspected that he would not live to see a peace. Unable to sit comfortably at table, he had abandoned his practice of gathering the American community together on Sundays; very little made its way out of his wine cellar that fall, which customarily yielded a dozen bottles of beer, wine, and Madeira at week's end. Was it possible, Congress fretted, that its representatives were quarreling? That assembly had no inkling that Franklin's chant of "the British are trying to divide us" had yielded to Jay's "the French are trying to deceive us." Despite their uncongenial views the two remained on good terms, however. Firm but fair-minded, Jay kept his concerns about his colleague to himself. The two men differed in opinion but did not distrust each other. And then, through the mud which was western Europe, a morass that even six horses navigated with difficulty and that swallowed whole carriage wheels, transforming a three-day jaunt into a ten-day ordeal, rode John Adams.

He arrived in Paris on October 26. Three things had kept him in Amsterdam until Jay's summons. He had not judged a peace likely for most of the summer. His loan was in its final stages; early in October he signed a treaty of commerce with the Dutch. And he had developed a violent aversion to Franklin. He was livid that Franklin had conveyed Vergennes's complaints against him to Congress, equally furious that Franklin had for so long failed to mention doing so. Franklin had been under no obligation to share those libels; no government could require as much of a foreign ambassador. If Vergennes had a complaint, argued Adams, he should have filed it with his own envoy. (Vergennes had.) Adams braced himself for a role familiar to him from 1778: "Between two as subtle spirits as any in this world, the one malicious, the other I think honest, I shall have a delicate, a nice, a critical part to act. F[ranklin]'s cunning will be to divide us. To this end he will provoke, he will insinuate, he will intrigue, he will maneuver. My curiosity will at least be employed in observing his invention and his artifice."

With relief he discovered that Jay—a colleague he had previously dismissed as a lightweight and a latecomer, and who hailed from an opposing congressional faction—shared his suspicions about French designs. The two men fell into each other's arms. Three days after his arrival Adams had practically to be dragged from his place du Carrousel hotel to call on his elder colleague. Reminded by a well-meaning friend that the call was necessary, he rejoined that it had hardly been necessary to assassinate his character. But it was essential to present a united front to the world, he was upbraided, at which he relented a little: Franklin was welcome to come to him. But the immutable laws of Paris obliged the last comer to make the first visit, as he well knew. He might be the last to have arrived in Paris but he was the first commissioner to have been appointed, objected Adams. How was Franklin to call on him when he was not aware that Adams was in Paris? Adams bowed to logic as he had not to etiquette, although even after pulling on his coat he shrank again from his odious obligation. He had for Franklin "no other sentiments than contempt or abhorrence." He prided himself on having been forthright; he had complained of Franklin equally to American, French, and Spanish colleagues. Despite himself he was fitted back into his coat and trundled off for an evening at Passy, where he found Franklin looking decrepit, and in the course of which Adams made his opinions of the French court abundantly and no doubt unnecessarily clear. He intended to support Jay wholeheartedly. He was appalled by the concept of submitting to Vergennes. Franklin heard him out in silence.* At a later and equally critical date, Franklin was perfectly philosophical on the subject: "For when you assemble a number of men to have the advantage of their joint wisdom, you inevitably assemble with those men all their prejudices, their passions, their errors of opinion, their local interests, and their selfish views."

Formal negotiations resumed on October 30 and continued over the next week, at a vigorous pace and with barely a pause, from eleven in the morning until well into the evening. On alternate days meetings were held at Jay's or Oswald's Left Bank quarters, at Adams's rooms in central Paris, or at the Valentinois. Perceived to have been too lenient, Oswald was joined in Paris by Undersecretary Henry Strachey, thought to be

---

*He would have been within his rights reminding the new arrival that it had been Adams himself who—before any Declaration was signed in 1776—had waxed eloquent about America's "natural ally."

made of sterner stuff. (He was familiar to both Adams and Franklin from Staten Island, having served as Admiral Lord Howe's secretary in 1776.) The British caviled with each of the major issues from the preliminary terms; a good deal therefore went back on the negotiating table, where it was heatedly and loudly debated, as those in neighboring rooms testified. The schedule was exhausting, especially for Oswald and Jay, who regularly drafted through the night in preparation for the next day's discussions. Still weak, nearly paralyzed on his left side, suffering from various urological ills, Franklin put in only irregular appearances. Early on it became clear that the greatest bones of contention were the fishing rights off Newfoundland and the Loyalists; as Adams was to remember, the days passed in "a constant scuffle, morning noon and night about cod and haddock on the Grand Bank, deerskins on the Ohio, and pine trees at Penobscot, and what were worse than all the refugees." Within the first week other matters too became clear. The issues were at times esoteric and the Americans without any diplomatic training, but the new nation's interests hardly went neglected. "These Americans are the greatest quibblers I ever knew," sighed an exhausted Strachey, who would vow never again to involve himself in a peace negotiation. Two American lawyers did him in. He was heartened at least by the anti-French sentiment across the table. It was evident to him that Jay distrusted the French even more than the English.

Adams noted as much as well, remarking that Jay disliked the French every bit as much as had Izard and Lee. "Our allies don't play fair," Jay assured the Bostonian, who did not disagree, and who inveighed even more loudly than had the New Yorker against his orders to make no peace without Vergennes. (Somehow Adams never received his official copy of those instructions. He would deduce they had been purposely concealed from him.) Did Congress really mean to make them look like idiots in the eyes of Europe? Why not simply appoint Vergennes to negotiate for them? If the French told them to cede the Mississippi to Spain, were they to do so? If so he preferred to resign, he yelped, knowing full well that a resignation submitted early in November 1782 would be read in America over the first days of the New Year, at the earliest. Nor was it sufficient for Adams to share his indignation with his American colleagues. On November 6 he called on Oswald to let the Scot know that neither he nor Jay had any attachment to the French court. Vergennes meant only to clip America's wings.

Adams was clear that his distress with France equaled, and in some way fell out from, his disregard for Franklin. Indeed it was difficult to see where one ended and the other began. Only so as to dupe America did the French see to it that "one man, who is submission itself, is puffed up to the top of Jacob's ladder in the clouds, and every other man depressed to the bottom of it in the dust." And there was no question that Adams felt himself in the dust. He could not differentiate between America serving as a football among European powers and his own vanity being trampled in the process; from his correspondence it nearly seems as if he and Jay squared off in the peace negotiation against Vergennes and Franklin. Adams took it as a point of honor that he collided regularly and violently with two men whom he was enjoined to approach with "passive obedience." Any honest man, he swore, would have the same trouble.

The aversion was to Franklin the idol more than Franklin the man, as was obvious in November, when Vergennes shrewdly neutralized the great Adams ego. With Vergennes too the Bostonian spurned protocol, pointedly omitting a courtesy call at Versailles. The foreign minister waited some time before making known his displeasure, which was great; he deplored the manners of a man who called himself a diplomat and yet spent weeks in Paris "without fancying that he owed me a mark of attention." As did Lafayette, Franklin nudged his colleague, reminding him finally on November 9 that Vergennes should not be left to hear of Adams's activities from the Paris police. The following morning Adams rode nervously out to Versailles, expecting a scolding. Instead—Vergennes was nothing if not a master diplomat—Adams met with an effusive welcome. Never had the comte been so attentive. He invited Adams to stay to Sunday dinner, briefing him on each course as it was served, offering up cakes and claret and Madeira. Even the comtesse doted upon Adams. He was infinitely pleased with the reception, on which he reported widely. No one was as ingenious at compliments as the French, Adams marveled, enchanted by every one that came his way. To his zero-sum mind they had a very viable use. "A few of these compliments would kill Franklin if they should come to his ears," he calculated, sounding as if he might like that very much indeed.*

Even as Adams raged against his instructions, even as he warned that

---

*The account did not kill Franklin but did come to haunt Adams, who accidentally submitted his puffed-up diary entry to Congress. It was read aloud there in 1783, to guffaws.

England and France could be relied upon to involve America in their future wars, he had to concede that Franklin was full of surprises. By November he had quickly and entirely come around regarding Vergennes. Outvoted, Franklin had of course little choice but to submit to his colleagues' wishes. He had been overruled before; the French mission itself had been something he opposed. He continued to feel as awkward about forsaking the French as Adams and Jay did about consulting with them. But for weeks he kept his distance from Vergennes, and—like his colleagues—separated himself even from Lafayette, whom Jay suspected of leaking information to Versailles. Lafayette had delayed his return to the Continental army, believing himself more useful to his adopted country in his native one. To Adams and Jay he appeared overly inquisitive and endlessly interfering, suspect on account of the same court connections that made him invaluable on the financial front; the man who had seen to it that young Georges de Lafayette's first word was "Washington" was to Adams a dubious "mongrel character." All three found themselves exasperated with the war hero after he implied that he remained in Europe at their request, when the opposite was true. (Fortunately none of the commissioners knew that Lafayette had lobbied hard in America to be named to their ranks.) Lafayette elicited a display of vanity even on the part of Franklin, who felt muscled aside on the loan-procuring front. Here finally was an issue on which the three men could agree.

Once the decision to circumvent Vergennes was made, all proceeded with unanimity; throughout November Franklin astonished his colleagues with his cogent arguments and his staunch positions. Adams rated his performance as nothing short of noble. On no point was that sturdy resolve more pronounced than on the issue of Loyalist compensation, about which Franklin was particularly severe. Were the British to insist on reparations, would they, challenged Franklin, care to discuss American towns burned, plantations devastated? He had a small document in his pocket, on which he had set out some of those damages. The man who insisted he made it a practice never to confuse personal and public resentments included in that inventory even the plundering of his own Philadelphia library. Franklin's contention was all the more remarkable as he was the only American commissioner with a Loyalist son. In itself William Franklin's bold stance may have accounted for his father's intransigence; word of the self-appointed Loyalist leader's activities made the Paris papers throughout the fall. In any event Franklin atoned for his indiscretion of June many times over.

At Versailles Vergennes fretted over the leisurely pace with which the Americans appeared to pursue their negotiation. He wished he could press them—he was only too aware who would foot the bill if the new republic continued in her struggle—but confined himself to recommending the virtues "of moderation and justice," the same banner, as it happened, under which he had waged a war. He kept his distance; to do otherwise would be to risk the commissioners' mistrust. He was flabbergasted then when a note arrived from the Valentinois on November 29, following a month of silence. Franklin was delighted to report that the Americans had agreed to preliminary peace terms. Before the shock had worn off at Versailles, Adams, Franklin, and Jay made their separate ways through a wet snow to Oswald's hotel, on what is today the rue Bonaparte, where they were joined by the newly arrived Henry Laurens.* There on November 30, under sullen skies and without ceremony, first by Oswald and then in alphabetical order by the Americans, a preliminary document was signed. It granted the United States all the terms Franklin had set out in his necessary articles of June. Afterward the commissioners rode out for a celebratory meal at the Valentinois, much pleased, as they should have been, with their achievement and with each other. Jay pronounced himself gratified by the perfect harmony with which they had proceeded, citing in particular Adams's help with the fisheries and Franklin's "firmness and exertions on the subject of the Tories." (Jay was himself stunning on the border dispute.) He marveled afresh at Franklin's acuity and spirit. There was ample reason for Jay's generosity. In their perfect unanimity the commissioners had defied not only Congress but the treaty Franklin had come to negotiate exactly six years earlier. Surely it was better to hang together.

The trip to Versailles fell to Franklin. If the terms of the peace rank as America's greatest diplomatic triumph—and they were nothing less in the eyes of Europe—Franklin's management of Vergennes may rank as his. In December 1776 he had journeyed to Versailles to grovel on behalf of a country that could promise only her everlasting friendship and grati-

---

*The last-minute arrival may have been a blessing. Laurens was a brawler.

tude. Now he paid a call to explain away her infidelity. Vergennes had every reason to deplore American selfishness; he felt utterly betrayed. He made Franklin understand that the commissioners' behavior "had not been very obliging of the King." Lightly, amiably, Franklin offered the best excuses he could for the commissioners. He was unfailingly polite. Vergennes contented himself finally with dissuading Franklin from submitting the preliminary terms until France and England had concluded their negotiations; the former were after all contingent on the latter, and he was intent on all parties finishing together. Franklin left him with his assurances.

Vergennes was at once delighted and appalled by the American terms, which exceeded all he thought possible. He sniffed that the British were purchasing rather than negotiating a peace; his very astonishment gave the envoys additional cause for celebration. He wanted Congress apprised immediately of the irregular conduct of those emissaries, however. To Luzerne went his indictment of the three men, with a request that they be censured by Congress. Vergennes was unable to contain either his surprise or horror when next he heard from Franklin, ten days later. Crisply Franklin advised him that the treaty was to sail immediately for America. To his announcement he added a most presumptuous request: Would it be possible to send funds over in the same vessel? Congress would be reduced to despair were no monies to be forthcoming. "I am rather at a loss, Sir, to explain your conduct and that of your colleagues on our account," Vergennes rebuked the man who had begun his year with his inventory of those who had traduced and abused him. "You are wise and discreet, Sir; you understand the proprieties; you have fulfilled your duties all your life. Do you think you are satisfying those that connect you to the King?"

Franklin could have expected nothing less. Nor could he have addressed Vergennes's perfectly valid points with more canniness or grace. His fragility, the lameness was much remarked upon, and yet in his awkward shuffling he was more than ever nimble in his reasoning. On December 17 he convened his colleagues at noon, in Laurens's rooms, to vet the paragraphs he had drafted to atone for their collective sins. His lines were unanimously approved, and dispatched to Versailles. After the sermon he had delivered, Vergennes expected the Americans to ask after the status of French negotiations, a negotiation that might have been concluded long before had the king been as inconsiderate as his allies. He was shocked by a very different communication. Nothing in the preliminaries, Franklin asserted, undermined the interests of France, nor was any peace to be concluded before that of France. And surely Vergennes would agree that it was incumbent on the commissioners to keep Congress expeditiously informed of their progress. "Your observation is however apparently just," Franklin conceded. In not consulting with him the Americans had indeed acted improperly, an award-winning euphemism for what was an outright betrayal. But as they had not done so for the wrong reasons—they meant no disrespect to the king, whom they universally loved and honored—was it too much to hope that they might be forgiven? To that wish Franklin joined a tour de force of casuistry. It would be a terrible shame if the king's glorious project—Franklin made it sound as if American independence had been the private brainchild of Louis XVI—was to "be ruined by a single indiscretion of ours." To which he added not only his most effusive praise for the French sovereign but—in another logistical backflip—what could be read as an implicit threat: "The English, I just now learn, flatter themselves they have already divided us. I hope this little misunderstanding will therefore be kept a perfect secret; and that they will find themselves totally mistaken."

Two days later Franklin and Vergennes met privately for dinner. Vergennes was utterly distraught and thoroughly embarrassed; the strain showed in his face. He assumed the American had come to grovel, "perceiving the irregularity of the conduct for which I had reproached him." Instead Franklin was all sweetness and light, assuring the French statesman that—desperate though they were for peace—nothing came before any of the commissioners' fidelity to France. To a man, they would rather renounce their engagements than in any way offend Louis XVI. They would be "inconsolable if their conduct should have displeased the King, and cooled his affection for the United States." The implication was that they may well have acted foolishly but—what could you expect?—they were babes in the woods. Vergennes agreed to countermand his prior letter to Luzerne; a censure would be unnecessary. It was of course easier to be sweetness and light as Franklin had the foreign minister over a barrel. As much as he might argue that American haste impeded his own negotiation—and it indeed strengthened Shelburne's hand—Vergennes was desperate for peace. For a multitude of reasons that stretched from the French West Indies to eastern Europe, he anticipated only English victories in the year to come. The American navy might well be reduced to one ship, but the French navy was exhausted as well. Affairs in eastern Europe demanded his attention. And he had plenty of his own enemies at court, including the colleague who advised Louis XVI to suspend Vergennes's talks, as France seemed to lose a colony with each session. While it pained him to do so, he agreed to the dispatch of the preliminaries before a general peace was resolved. To do otherwise was to risk the impression that the king of France stood where the king of England once had: between America and her future happiness. Franklin rode out to Passy after a perfectly amiable dinner to assure his colleagues that he had not only calmed the waters, but arranged for the first installment of a new loan to sail across them. "All is fair weather," rejoiced Adams.

Over the next days Franklin alone disserted on the importance of the French connection. He had reason to; he was the one who had claimed that "an honest American would cut off his right hand" rather than sign an agreement with England contrary to the alliance, then proceeded to do so. America was well on her way to a good peace, one for which he took no individual credit; neither in the groveling to Vergennes nor in his triumphant report to America did he distinguish himself from his colleagues. He gloried instead in his country's fortune. "Our independence is acknowledged, our boundaries as good and extensive as we demanded; and our fishery more so than the Congress expected," he wrote Samuel Cooper in Boston. He was generous in his inclusion of his colleagues, including even Laurens, who had been in Paris for one day. Franklin would have found it an impossible strain to continue discussions on his own.* He made a case as well for another kind of generosity: "It is our firm connection with France that gives us weight with England, and respect throughout Europe. If we were to break our faith with this nation *on whatever pretence*, England would again trample on us, and every other nation despise us." Private resentments must be barred from public counsels. Whatever was said to the contrary, the king of France was America's

---

*It took Adams only another few weeks to carp that discussions would still be ambling on had Franklin been left to handle them alone. In an unsent letter, he would also contend that Franklin had told Vergennes everything in advance.

friend. Vergennes took a more realistic view of the double-dealing. The preliminaries had only just headed out to sea when he prophesied: "If we judge the future from what is now passing before our eyes, we shall be poorly repaid for what we have done for the United States of America and for securing them their existence."

XI

The Absent Are Never Without Fault

1783

There is no excess in the world so commendable as excessive gratitude.
—*La Bruyère*

Seventeen eighty-three was the year of miracles. It began with feverish whispers of a peace; by December all attention had turned to aerial navigation. ("Anyone who wants to talk of anything other than balloons," noted one paper, "doesn't interest us.") If three million people on the far reaches of the globe had played the greatest powers of Europe against each other to achieve what seemed a dream, was anything impossible? The "miracle in human affairs" that Franklin had advertised in 1777 had come to pass; American independence was hailed as an event without parallel in the history of the world. It was as if a new planet had joined the solar system. No political power had emerged, matured, and burst onto the world stage in so short a time. Republics as history knew them were a rare phenomenon, fragile and short-lived, preludes to dictatorships. The birth of the United States did nothing less than invalidate that hoary wisdom: There *was* something new under the sun. Or so it seemed in January.

Late on Saturday evening, January 18, Franklin received an urgent summons from Vergennes. He hoped to see whatever commissioners were in town first thing on Monday, along with Temple, who would be needed to translate. Vergennes said no more, allowing only that the matter was of great import to the United States. Laurens and Jay were away; Franklin arranged for Adams to join him at the Valentinois before dawn that Monday, so that the two might be on the road to Versailles by eight. From the British Franklin learned why he should make every effort to be punctual. Vergennes had tied up his own negotiation; Franklin would likely that morning have the good fortune of concluding the peace. Indeed he and Adams were joined in Vergennes's office by Aranda and the British representative. There the preliminaries were signed, without ceremony, and in Adams's opinion, "in as short a time as a marriage settlement," although they more accurately constituted the opposite. Louis XVI announced the news that evening at table with the royal family; Franklin celebrated with Vergennes. Definitive terms would not be agreed upon until the fall, but peace was at hand. Lenoir saw to it that word went out to the cafés and theaters of Paris, where it was met with jubilation. Adroitly the news was slipped into that evening's performance of *King Lear*.

Franklin comported himself modestly but was radiant with delight. Embraced by the ever-charming duc de la Rochefoucauld, he sighed, "Could I have hoped, at my age, to enjoy such a happiness?" On hearing the news the duc de Cröy galloped out to Passy, where the two men embraced repeatedly, Franklin marveling that all had finished so well and so rapidly. Everything he had hoped for had been achieved. The success was all the richer for the desperate straits in which America had begun the war. Cröy could only remark breathlessly, "It's a country which has appeared as a dream!" That Friday, Franklin and the abbé Morellet meandered into a discussion of how much food a man needed to survive. Morellet was less startled by his friend's answer—as a journeyman, Franklin had subsisted for three weeks on a modest quantity of bread and water—than by the circumstances under which it was related.* The minister plenipotentiary of the newly recognized United States had not for a minute lost sight of

---

*According to Franklin, friends had asked his mother what could have overtaken her son. "He's read some crazy philosopher, someone named Plutarch. But I'm leaving him alone, he'll get tired of it soon enough." In the *Autobiography* the experiment is one Franklin gleaned from Thomas Tryon.

the fact that he had once been a printer's apprentice, of itself a revolutionary idea for Europe, where the two never met.

Franklin had an astounding diplomatic victory to celebrate and a multitude of callers. (He had as well a new and clearly quite necessary maître d'hôtel. When Bancroft stopped in at the Valentinois to extend his New Year's greetings, he found Franklin out, and not a soul at hand who might take a message.) The congratulations poured in from all over, as did praise for Franklin's triumph, praise he redirected. It was, he assured one well-wisher, purely the work of God and the king of France. The analysis was not the product of modesty alone. Vergennes was correct in sniffing that the British had bought a peace; as much as Adams prided himself on American astuteness—"we were better tacticians than was imagined," he crowed—Shelburne played as large a role in the negotiation as did American ingenuity. (For those efforts Shelburne would be out of office in a matter of months.) The credit for the victory lay as much with British strategy as with the abilities of three amateur statesmen who had been lucky and tenacious enough to manage an end run past their allies, gliding on Shelburne's handsome assist. And the credit for the peace was as well a different entity from its rewards. Once again, Vergennes was left to appease Spain, squawking that she had been left out in the cold. In Madrid's view the French ministry had been too hasty in beginning the war and too hasty in ending it.* Vergennes bribed that power toward a settlement by relinquishing French conquests; the war had not been one of expansion for France, and the peace would not be either. Vergennes got solely and purely what he wanted from the seven-year conflict. He redressed a wrong.† Paradoxically, in his crusade to restore Versailles to its rightful position at the center of the universe, he put America on the map.

---

*Franklin had his own strong opinions about Madrid's preferred tempo. In a rare display of bad manners, he dismissed a Spaniard's congratulations on the happy events. "So at last you're independent," commented the well-wisher, at Versailles. "We have been for some time now," snapped Franklin, turning his back.

†In addition to revenge, France got the island of Tobago, several African trading posts, and the right again to fortify Dunkirk, the single greatest sore of 1763 and the reward for which Vergennes admitted he had aimed from the start. Also from the start he had insisted that France could not lose. Even if the war ended badly, Vergennes had argued, an independent America was reward enough. Elsewhere in Paris many felt France had proved the purity of her intentions. The peace was not advantageous. But France had claimed herself to be disinterested, and so she had emerged.

Franklin was as clear-eyed about what he wanted from the peace as he had been about what he had wanted from the war. Even before the preliminaries were signed he begged to come home. Failing that, he was eager to leave Paris. Naturally enough he thought first of London and of old friends, applying in the first days of January to Polly Hewson, the daughter of his London landlady, for advice. Would it be prudent for him to make an appearance in England? Were he to do so, might he stay with her family? Polly's mother had been dead a week when Franklin invited himself to rejoin the household; bowing either to that loss or to a delicacy of feeling, he opted to postpone a British excursion, "so as not to insult anyone."* He contemplated a trip to Italy, assured by both the Tuscan and Venetian envoys, with whom he enjoyed warm personal relations, that the welcome there would be royal.

Franklin held that Mrs. Stevenson constituted his primary reason for visiting England, a claim that pointed up one of two obvious omissions from his itineraries. He made no acknowledgment of the fact that he had a son in London, one reported to be unwell. In Geneva Benny Bache knew what he wanted from the peace: the visit his grandfather had promised for four years, and of which Benny waited to hear with every post. Forlorn and forgotten, he could not interest Franklin even in sending him a book he much desired, which a teacher bought for him instead. No one wrote him. (It was a common complaint—Franklin's sister would go nearly three years without word from him—but Benny was thirteen years old. And there was no Atlantic Ocean between Paris and Geneva.) His existence was moderately happier after the arrival of another American student, in 1781. But the desire for a family reunion was acute, as was one other. From a world horological capital Benny pleaded, at the end of January, for a good gold watch, one of which he vowed, in stilted English, to take special care. The desire was strong. He waited a month before begging, pathetically, if his grandfather might permit him as well to accompany him to London. He had every reason to believe Franklin headed in

---

*From the British vantage point there was more to be dreaded in his return to his homeland. As a British negotiator put it: "Dr. Franklin seems anxious to return to America, which I am sorry for, being persuaded that he will do his utmost, when there, to prevent a revival of goodwill and cordiality with the mother country, his rancor and inveteracy against which are as violent as ever."

that direction. All the papers of Europe reported as much; many went so far as to supply his street address. Benny waited another month before emitting a muffled cry. Was anyone out there?

It was May 2 before Franklin finally replied, gently to one question, brutally to the other. He was not headed to England but would certainly take Benny with him when he was. As for the watch, it was Sally and the feathers all over again. He could not afford to give gold watches to children: "When you are more of a man, perhaps, if you have behaved well, I may give you one or something that is better. You should remember that I am at a great expense for your education, to pay for your board and clothing and instruction in learning that may be useful to you when you are grown up, and you should not tease me for expensive things that can be of little or no service to you." A bit of the steeliness that would distinguish the adult Benny glinted in his reply. All his friends had watches. So did the younger boys. That said, he bowed to the wisdom of his grandfather, who he hoped would forgive the brevity of his letter. He had had a fever, and was unwell. It was that illness that would release Benny finally from his exile; in June Franklin was alarmed to hear from a well-intentioned Englishman who had hosted Benny on several occasions. Benny's health was fragile, no surprise given "his unhealthy dwelling, improper diet, and ignorance on the part of his tutors." Under the circumstances it was a miracle he had not succumbed to plague. It seemed that his grandson was farther from the reaches of opulent Paris than Franklin had intended. His room, on a dark alley, resembled nothing so much as a prison cell.

Not everyone got such immediate gratification, and no one was as vocal about his displeasure as John Adams. He too clamored to return home. That came as no surprise to Congress, newly in receipt of his prodigious correspondence of September and as yet ignorant of the happy outcome of the negotiations that had followed. James Madison marveled over Adams's torrent of words, "not remarkable for anything unless it be a display of his vanity, his prejudice against the French court, and his venom against Dr. Franklin." The peace commissioner who had sat out his commission scratched his head over how Adams would proceed in Paris. "He hates Franklin, he hates John Jay, he hates the French, he hates the English," acknowledged Jefferson. With whom would he side? None of them could have guessed that peace would prove as taxing to Adams's nerves as a revolution had been. The negotiation behind him, the ingredients Madison so aptly isolated began to combine in the New Englander's mind, explosively and thunderously.

"I shall forever be a dull man in Europe," Adams lamented a week after affixing his signature to the preliminaries. He always choked on the distinction of others; he held a parallel grudge against Washington. It irked him even that the English congratulated themselves for having separated the Americans from the French, comments Franklin let pass. (They were correct, after all.) Lafayette's sin was to have "gained more applause than human nature at twenty-five can bear." But nothing so fed Adams's insecurity, so unsettled his discerning mind, as the celebrity of his eminent colleague. Generally Adams was a man to whom virtue and unpopularity were synonymous. At the same time, he felt every laurel bestowed on Franklin as a personal affront. That was an unfortunate state of affairs when his colleague was hailed throughout Europe as the "founder of the American Republic." There was no escaping the florid reports of a prestigious Masonic society's March meeting, a brilliant tribute to American independence. Four hundred of Paris's most eminent diplomats and intellectuals were in attendance, along with the most beautiful women in the city, for an evening of literature and music. After the orchestra and before the late-evening meal, all glasses rose to Franklin's glory. Amid plaudits and to a musical accompaniment, a palm branch was placed in his hand and a crown of laurels on his head. Franklin gratified his delirious admirers with a few words, restating his wish for an everlasting union between the two countries.

The next day found Adams at his desk, offering up a rethinking of American foreign policy since 1776. He was sorry to note that it had been shamefully conducted. He would have done it all very differently. He could certainly have seen to it that the war had ended far sooner. (He was inconsistent in his views of a French alliance, having initially proposed only recognition and aid, an idea to which now, in peacetime, he returned.) He was very clear in identifying a culprit: "I must and do most solemnly deliver it as my opinion that French policy has obstructed the progress of our cause in Europe, more than British." It was high time America acknowledged as much. In the weeks that followed the blasts would multiply, as Adams worked his way down two paths that met at the Valentinois door. Vergennes's reputation sat as badly with him as any other outsized one. If he had made a peace when he did it was only for the sake of keeping his job, and so as to obtain "the miserable gloriole of being the pacificateur of Europe." Gleefully (and erroneously) Adams predicted that Vergennes would be removed from office before the fall. His goal had been to secure for France America's fisheries and western territories. Adams's attachment to those entities had alone cost him the minister's good graces in 1780. "The pretense that I had given offense," Adams charged, despite a lengthy paper trail, "was a mere fiction."* He had never offended anyone! He was simply known as a man who could not be "deceived, wheedled, flattered, or intimidated," the implication being that someone else all too easily could be.†

Franklin had a fair idea of his colleague's sentiments, as well as a job to do. And the two were very much at odds. If the war was to be continued, it would be so at the expense of France. Were peace achieved, only France could enable Congress to discharge the army. Franklin was back at Versailles in January, having squeezed six million livres out of Vergennes. He was astonished by his success and too a little on the defensive. France could not meet its own expenses, he reminded Morris, "yet it has advanced six millions to save the credit of ours." He allowed himself a few words on "the ravings of a certain mischievous madman here against France and its ministers, which I hear of every day." He hoped they would be given little weight in America. He made no reference to Adams's personal attacks, which he acknowledged only privately, to Laurens: "I hear frequently of his ravings against M. de Vergennes and me whom he suspects of plots against him which have no existence but in his own troubled imagination. I take no notice, and we are civil when we meet."

---

*Adams had a way with words. Decades later—while still holding that he had not offended—he would assert that on receipt of his advice in 1780, "the count fell into a passion, and wrote me a passionate and ungentlemanly reply." To which Adams, piqued, offered up "a gently tingling rejoinder."

†Vergennes entertained a different view of that history. He assumed that it was precisely his earlier reprimand of Adams that set him on the warpath now. And the American could not forgive him for having saddled him with colleagues in his peace commission. Adams was bent on vengeance, and would do all in his power to make France appear odious and untrustworthy. Impatiently Vergennes awaited the day the New Englander might sail homeward. In his offices it was generally understood that Franklin drove Adams to distraction as much on account of his *belle réputation* as because he stood as a monument to Franco-American amity.

At the end of March Franklin applied to Vergennes for permission to publish a complete translation of the United States constitutions in French, the only language in which they could be widely read. He was eager to correct Europe's misapprehensions about the new nation; he knew as well that he was offering up an advertisement for American trade and immigration. It was a project of which Vergennes disapproved, but Franklin persisted. After a sustained arm-wrestle he got his way, again to his surprise. (Even the king's printer sympathized, reminding Franklin that Paris by no means resembled Philadelphia. Clearly a second Franklin was necessary to relieve France of its shackles, a rather impertinent suggestion from the royal printer.) Copies went out over the summer to the entire diplomatic corps and, in extravagantly bound editions, to Louis XVI and Marie Antoinette. The most influential of Franklin's European publications, the constitutions were universally well received. Their editor was gratified to discover that they were an astonishment to many, "who had conceived mean ideas of the state of civilization in America, and could not have expected so much political knowledge and sagacity had existed in our wilderness."

In April he negotiated and signed a treaty of amity and commerce with Sweden, America's first with a foreign power; he looked forward to negotiating trade agreements with Denmark and Portugal.* Together Adams and Franklin discussed the future of Anglo-American commercial relations, an issue left outstanding in the fall and never to be settled. Franklin held off the multitudes who hoped to settle in America or to serve as her consul in one European port or another, along with the usual swarms of applicants. For every Frenchman who hoped to open a sugar refinery in Philadelphia or a glass manufactory in Virginia there was another who was running away from his multiple wives and who hoped to plant vines in the New World, or who inquired if it were true that America were distributing vast tracts of land for nothing. They were followed by the industrious souls who had devised the means to blow up Gibraltar, a

---

*Adams drilled him like a schoolmaster on the latter. Had he discussed Brazil and the Portuguese islands? Unsatisfied by his answers, Adams implored Congress to read the treaty closely before signing it. He dearly wished that the Portuguese had sent an envoy directly to Philadelphia, so that America's advantages were not lost "by this method of preparing treaties here, by ministers who have made no particular study of the objects of them."

method to transform ordinary table salt into saltpeter, liquids that could fireproof wood. Most of Europe looked upon Passy as a kind of political Lourdes; as usual, every hard-luck story in Europe came Franklin's way, along with volumes of unsolicited advice.* "Let there be no lawyers or professors of law in the country under pain of death," warned one impassioned expert on nation building, preaching to the converted.

～ンベ～

Over the same weeks, by his own admission "weary, disgusted, affronted and disappointed," Adams kept up a regular correspondence with William Lee, in Brussels. Lee was happy to resurrect all his earlier griefs. And although never at a loss for words, Adams was happy to avail himself of the disgruntled ex-commissioner's vocabulary. On March 27, Lee— who shared Adams's view that the United States owed France nothing— insisted that Franklin was "a scourge to America." Two weeks later Adams had improved on that formula. Franklin was "the demon of discord among our ministers, and the curse and scourge of our foreign affairs." He would remain so as long as he lived. By April Adams made the leap from illiberal to unbalanced. Vergennes was deceitful and despotic, Franklin no less so. "I never know when he speaks the truth, and when not," huffed Adams. Assuming Lee's grudge, he asserted that Franklin's laziness and inactivity led him to consider every American envoy who set foot in Europe as his enemy. (There was a certain contradiction between the charges of laziness and monopolizing, but then there was a certain discrepancy between Franklin's languor and his enormous aptitude for work.) The love child of Machiavelli and the Jesuits, Franklin was the greatest imposter on earth since Mahomet. He was an insidious man, and impossible to remove. For both reasons Adams could only wish with all his heart that Franklin was already out of office, repenting for his sins, and preparing for the next world.

Franklin began a French translation of the Book of Job in 1782, but it

---

*Franklin had a light touch with the hard-luck stories. He provided one needy soul with a modest sum, on the condition that the young man repeat the gesture when he could afford to do so. "This is a trick of mine for doing a deal of good with a little money. I am not rich enough to afford *much* in good works and so am obliged to be cunning and make the most of a *little*," Franklin explained.

was his colleague who, adrift and on edge, catalogued his trials. They amounted to nothing less than the martyrdom of John Adams. While he had suffered before in public life, no ordeal bore comparison with what he had endured in Europe, "the greatest and worst part of which has been caused by the ill dispositions of the C[ount] de Vergennes, aided by the jealousy, envy, and selfish servility of Dr. Franklin." Time and again he had been sacrificed at the altar of Franklin's vanity. That commissioner's subtle corruption—and Congress's humiliating instructions—had undermined his health. They had nearly poisoned him. Given the "malice of enemies, the finesse of allies, and the treachery of a colleague," it should not be imagined that he slept on a bed of roses. Rather he was stretched on the rack of Franklin's popularity, broken on the wheel of his taciturnity. He had been pierced by arrows aimed his way in the darkness. For some time he had been haunted by the image of running a race, breathless and barefoot, over burning ground, jealousy, avarice, treachery, tyranny, insolence, lashing him all the way. The electrical conjurings at Passy—in Adams's mouth that leafy suburb sounded like the seat of a foreign power—were perilous. He determined to remain beyond striking distance. Franklin had fed him to "a furnace of affliction," an image that recurred with Adams. He would prefer to be a doorkeeper in Congress than continue as he was in Paris.

By his own admission Adams was in a grim mood that spring, one that darkened as Congress remained unforthcoming regarding its plans for him, as with its gratitude. (Had he only been willing to sell out his country, he would be praised to the skies, feted by the great, immortalized on snuffboxes, applauded at the opera.) Outside his place du Carrousel window the carriages thundered incessantly; he felt the infernal roar of the Parisian street would do him in. It was like Niagara Falls, and quiet for only three hours in the middle of the night. Sleep was impossible. Paris traffic was one ill for which he did not blame Franklin, but Franklin suffered for it all the same. William Lee was happy to further poison Adams's addled mind, dilating on charges as wide-ranging as they were vague. Lee insisted on financial impropriety, an accusation for which there was no basis but which Adams was only too willing to echo. Had there been some mismanagement, Jay would presumably have reported it as well; he registered no complaints. He also moved his family into the Valentinois early in the summer, which he presumably would not have done had he believed Franklin was embezzling American funds. (Jay was eager to escape the confines of filthy Paris, and his wife was expecting her baby in August.)

At the same time, Franklin was guilty on the usual charges. He was secretive, he was peremptory, he was maddeningly vague. He focused more on pleasing Versailles than his colleagues, or even his countrymen; innumerable Americans in Paris voiced their displeasure with their minister, who was so seldom willing to gratify their wish for a court presentation and so evasive about his reluctance. In Europe that privilege would have fallen to those of noble birth; when pressed, Franklin argued that as class distinctions did not exist in America, only those in public service should be presented. Presumably he meant only to spare himself the unnecessary ceremony, but he was typically slow to explain his hesitation. He continued to wash his hands of shipping and maritime details, almost a relief to the consul, Thomas Barclay, whose job it was to clarify them. And Franklin took no pains to pacify Adams. He may even have incited his colleague. At one juncture he informed Adams that America ought to commit to joining France in two future wars against Britain, "the first to pay the debt we owe her for making war for us and the second to show ourselves as generous as she had been," an assertion that—for all its prescience—was so out of keeping with everything Franklin believed in or discussed with others that it may have constituted an attempt at Adams-baiting.

Franklin had the confident man's ease about affecting subservience; he made it his business publicly to acknowledge the gratitude he genuinely felt. As Adams steeped and stewed, Franklin—judging that Europe would respond to a durable monument to the alliance—distributed commemorative coins throughout Paris. On hearing of Cornwallis's surrender the first image that had leapt to his mind was a classical one; in 1782 he envisioned a coin "representing the United States by the figure of an infant Hercules in his cradle, strangling the two serpents, and France by that of Minerva, sitting by as his nurse, with her spear and helmet, and her robe specked with a few *fleurs-de-lis*." Over the months that followed he vetted a variety of sketches, appending to his favorite a line from Horace. He intended his commemorative piece to serve "as a monumental acknowledgement which may go down to future ages, of the obligations we are under to this nation." Designed before the peace, the medal was meant both to celebrate the birth of America and to cement Franco-American relations; struck after the peace, it assumed a different purpose. As he did the state constitutions, Franklin used the medal to grease the wheels of foreign relations. America was a country that did not forget its benefactors. She took her friendships seriously.

By the time the medals were struck—in gold for Louis XVI and Marie Antoinette; in silver for the French ministers and the president of Congress; and in copper (Franklin's favorite) for the members of that assembly and the ambassadors of Europe—the imagery had also undergone a metamorphosis. Ultimately Hercules was dwarfed, with what appear to be two toy snakes. The battle belongs to Minerva, who valiantly fends off the enemy, over the infant America's head. The composition represented a twist on Franklin's original proposal, but the elegant keepsake could have met with no more effusive reception; its imagery was so popular that it was incorporated into toile de Jouy fabrics. The Homeric borrowing in particular met with raves, so dulcet was it to European ears. That line too—"Not without divine help is the infant courageous"—significantly altered the narrative, just as it significantly assisted the diplomatic agenda. Only one element was missing from the tribute. Franklin made no official mention of Congress, which did not sanction the piece. Even after it was cast he hoped he might hear otherwise; he could easily revise the die. Foreign affairs secretary Livingston sent only regrets. It was one thing to conceal treaty terms from America's ally, quite another to grant her the dominant role in the narrative. What in the world was Minerva doing at center stage?*

Adams left no opinion of the medal, but as the weeks passed intensified his assaults on Franklin. His humor had no bearing on the two men's public demeanor. They continued to socialize and collaborate. Together they appeared at court, and together they braved the sweltering heat to make their official calls on the other European powers. They were still to stumble upon the servant who could not decide if His Excellency was or was not in for the Americans, the ambassador who preferred to send up his card rather than return a state visit in person, but by August most of the uneasi-

---

*The design, caviled Livingston, though never to Franklin, "keeps out of sight what we should most pride ourselves upon: that the first serpent was strangled before France had armed in our defense and when our infant Hercules received nothing more from her than now and then a spoonful of pap."

ness had evaporated, a point of etiquette—and American statehood—settled conclusively at last. Jointly Adams and Franklin celebrated July 4 in the company of a number of French officers who had served in America and with the assistance of Madame Brillon's piano, sent over for the occasion. The abbé Morellet proposed a little music before they dined that joyous afternoon; with much tenderness, Franklin offered up a toast, in verse, to the French officers. Afterward Adams went home to continue with his torrent of anti-French vitriol. Franklin submitted a new request for funds to Versailles, one he knew Vergennes would find as painful as did he.

Ultimately a season of Adams's maledictions took its toll. At the end of July Franklin warned Livingston of his colleague's shrill and very public pronouncements, his conviction that "gratitude to France is the greatest of follies," his delusions that Franklin and Vergennes were plotting against him, his conviction that he was being crucified in the press. (Adams was always highly attuned to the press, which Franklin cited only for its ineptitude. He heartily enjoyed each of the various and detailed accounts he had read of his own funeral.) Were he not so well aware that the French treasury was empty, he might suspect that those detonations accounted for Vergennes's sudden bout of frugality. It took a great deal to move Franklin to ad hominem attack, the more so as he judged Adams a redoubtable foe. But late in July he finally offered up the analysis of his colleague on which no one has improved. Adams meant well for his country, "is always an honest man, often a wise one, but sometimes and in some things, absolutely out of his senses."* His language was temperate in comparison with Adams's appraisal of him: "If I was in Congress, and this gentleman and the marble Mercury in the garden of Versailles were in nomination for an embassy, I would not hesitate to give my vote for the statue, upon the principle that it would do no harm."

~ぷ~

Mid-April brought word to the American people that a preliminary peace had been signed in Paris and that all hostilities were to cease. Precisely

---

*After seven months in Paris Jefferson would offer an analysis of Adams that reversed Franklin's terms but was not dissimilar: "He is vain, irritable, and a bad calculator of the force and probable effects of the motives which govern men. This is all the ill which can possibly be said of him."

eight years had elapsed since Lexington and Concord; the news was met with rapture. Congress alone found itself torn between back-slapping and hand-wringing. No one could complain of the results, but a fair number of delegates were pained by the methodology. The envoys were not to have proceeded without France. Inexplicably they had done so, proceeding in a manner "inconsistent with the spirit of the alliance, and a dishonorable departure from the candor, rectitude and plain dealing professed by Congress." A vigorous debate followed as to whether a censure was in order. Congress could neither disavow its representatives nor account for their rogue behavior; they had hardly comported themselves like virtuous Rousseau-inspired rustics, realizing their "natural right" to freedom.* Some insisted that the four men be reprimanded. Others felt they should be notified of their country's disappointment "and left to get over their embarrassment as best they could." Early in the debate one member of Congress asked outright if the court of France intended to file an official complaint against the commissioners. From Luzerne's aide came the answer that "great powers never *complained* but that they *felt and remembered*," a distinction that would point up the immaturity of the more amnesia-prone America in 1783. Jay came in for a particular drubbing, widely understood to have initiated the defection, in which Adams had happily followed, dragging Franklin along. Even those who disapproved of the envoys' instructions railed against their violation. The question remained: Had duplicity really been necessary? What had the commissioners been thinking?

Together the Parisian envoys addressed that question. Standing in a different light, they naturally saw things differently; they were quick to assure Livingston that he would understand if he knew the circumstances. "Since we have assumed a place in the political system of the world let us move like a primary and not like a secondary planet," they petitioned, a line that was almost certainly Jay's. They continued to believe honesty the

---

*Arthur Lee contended that it was improper to censure men who had haggled well. Moreover, Vergennes was himself too expert a negotiator not to admire the Americans' coup. To Lee's mind it was France who had first acted dishonorably. She was an ally, not a patron; the relationship by no means called for obsequiousness. Alexander Hamilton too argued against a censure, on the grounds that the commissioners would, in their disgust, return to foment parties in America. He had his eye less on Adams than on Jay.

best policy, but insisted that the maxim did not apply in this case; the inhabitants of the new star in the solar system had taken quickly to diplomacy. Separately Jay justified his behavior with a logic worthy of a future chief justice of the Supreme Court. The commissioners were under instructions to consult with France, as doing so would be to their advantage. All signs pointed to France's undermining American claims. Therefore, the instructions no longer applied. Moreover, as the French minister did not confer with the Americans about his articles, "our giving him as little trouble about ours did not violate any principle of reciprocity." They had conformed to the spirit, if not the letter, of their instructions. Adams backed up his colleague: "We might have more confidence in them, if they had any in us." It had been commendable to break with their infamous orders. Adams had the studious man's partiality to sports metaphors; French strategy had gone awry, he gloated, "and no wrestler was ever so completely thrown upon his back as the c[omte] de Vergennes."

Franklin alone addressed the contretemps as if it had occurred between friends rather than belligerent parties. He took full responsibility for a faux pas not his own: "We did what appeared to all of us best at the time, and if we have done wrong, the Congress will do right, after hearing us, to censure us." For the record, he permitted himself to add that he at no time shared his colleagues' suspicions of the French. He also counseled Jay not to make too much of their behavior. Congress had not officially blamed them, and he had placated Vergennes. Why cast aspersions on France, or muddy the waters? He felt at ease with the matter, especially as Versailles had filed no complaint. Congress was still debating a censure when news of the signing of the preliminaries arrived, at which juncture Luzerne borrowed Franklin's argument of December. England would be only too happy to see the allies at each other's throat. The question was best swept under the carpet.

By the time he proffered his explanation Franklin had begun to understand that his fondest hope was unlikely to be realized in 1783. An audible groan went up from the Valentinois, shrouded like all of France that summer in an eerie, persistent fog. He was as impatient for his resignation to be accepted as for the final treaties to be signed. He was sorely tempted when a New England captain offered to convey him to America but in no position to accept, as he could not leave Europe without Congress's permission. He was very clear about his desire. "The French are an amiable people to live with: They love me, and I love them," he conceded. He was much cosseted, "yet I do not feel myself at home." He was by no means a dull man in Europe—he knew that he would be a less exalted figure in Philadelphia—but he was a deracinated one, the more so as he had now a country from which to be expatriated. Reluctantly he planned to settle in for an eighth winter of exile. His disappointment was of a piece with Temple's. "As to my grandfather and myself," the twenty-three-year-old moaned, "I hardly know what will become of us." Temple banked ardently on a London trip. Even a week would do. As soon as it might decently be arranged, he looked forward to a visit with his father. He had made no effort to contact him, which restraint he hoped his father would approve.

Both Franklins' spirits were lifted that summer by a different reunion. On July 19 Benny rolled into the Valentinois courtyard, a taller, French-speaking version of the awkward, light-haired child packed off four and a half years earlier. His delicate health was restored, as Franklin suggested it might be, by the ten-day carriage ride across hazy Europe. On the whole Benny was an advertisement for the salutary effects of travel: The cold, self-contained Genevan was in Passy sweet-tempered and obliging. He was weeks away from his fourteenth birthday but seemed far younger, evidently a family trait. Within days of his arrival Benny noted that his grandfather was not like other old people. "For they were fretting and complaining, and dissatisfied," he explained, "and my grandpapa is laughing, and cheerful, like a young person." Benny was without many near-contemporaries but amused himself launching kites over, fishing in, and swimming across the Seine, on one occasion with his clothes on his head. He doted on the four canaries he kept in his room, experimented in the Valentinois garden with bows and arrows, and succumbed entirely to the thrall of his cousin, who had adopted their grandfather's passions along with his mannerisms. For Benny's amusement, Temple made a great show of knocking out a mouse with helium, then reviving the animal, only to finish him off with an electrical spark. "I am sure my cousin would pass for a conjurer in America," Benny assured his parents. His shyness alone followed him to Paris. He remained intimidated by titles, alarmed by royalty. When the brother of the king of Prussia came to call, Benny refused to put in an appearance. He cowered instead at the far end of the house, chagrined when the affable prince sought him out.

Initially Franklin thought of the Passy stay as an interlude in Benny's Swiss education. By the time he had realized that the young American could nimbly translate Latin into French but was at a perfect loss in English, he considered entrusting him instead to Polly Hewson. By summer's end Benny had so thoroughly charmed his cousin and grandfather that they were no more willing to part with him than he was again to be exiled. Benny settled down to a standard-issue French education, adding dancing, fencing, and drawing to his Swiss curriculum. At no juncture was he allowed to forget he was an American, however. From Philadelphia his father sternly reminded him that if he did not recover his English, neither parent would be able to converse with him on his return, "and should this be the case, we shall all of us be in a very awkward situation." In the future he was to write home in his native language, and often.

In a move that confounded his French friends, Franklin arranged for a printing apprenticeship for Benny, at the press he had established at the Valentinois. Benny took to the work quickly and with a diligence he had not applied to his studies; in 1784 he would be entrusted to the best printer in Paris, to return to Passy only on Saturdays. With that arrangement Franklin paid tribute to the craft by which he had risen in the world and for which his passion continued. He acknowledged another concern as well. He had sacrificed Temple's career to America's business; in having failed to provide him a secretary, Congress had left him little choice but to recruit his grandson. In that role Temple was impeccable: diligent, knowledgeable, genteel, affable, ingratiating. Contrary to myth, he was very capable, with penmanship for which history will always be grateful. And too a funny thing had happened in the course of his service. So many years had been lost to Temple's opportunity to study the law, and "his habits of life become so different," as Franklin put it, that a diplomatic career seemed more in order. Days after Benny's Geneva return Franklin ventured a bald request of Livingston. Could something be done for his elder grandson? Both the Swedes and the Danes had made clear that they would be honored to receive him as America's ambassador. (Indeed the Danes were counting already on his dispatch to Copenhagen.) Clearly Franklin felt indebted to Temple, who was unceasing in his attentions, and who had served both his grandfather and his country faithfully and uncomplainingly, at a nominal salary, while every American envoy to Paris—for what Franklin legitimately pointed out was a fraction of the work—paid his secretary 24,000 livres a year.* He did not feel he was overstepping his bounds by requesting a prompt reply. He was not soliciting anything, just attempting to firm up plans. He had long promised Temple an Italian tour. If Congress did not intend to put him to work, Franklin hoped to be able to make good on his word, while he still had the strength.

The founding of America was very much a family affair. Jay's private secretary in Spain was his (intractable) brother-in-law; Jefferson invited a distant relative as his clerk when he sailed to Paris in 1784. To Benny's delight, seventeen-year-old John Quincy Adams returned to Paris in August, having served as private secretary on a futile American mission to Russia. But Temple posed a special case for several reasons. He had spent only eighteen months of his life in America; the habits to which Franklin so charmingly alluded were European habits. Temple knew the difference between a fashionable and an unfashionable collar. He was a connoisseur of shoe buckles. Doubtless he would have been one of his tailor's favorites, had he only paid his bill. Even his closest Parisian friends thought he stood to benefit from the occasional sermon on responsibility. He had been brought up in opulence; he had known only good fortune. He lived entirely in the present. A man should not be judged by his shopping list, but Temple was never shy about specifying that he should like his "razors to be bought at the most renowned cutler's, and the bridle and spurs to be of the *dernier goût*." He sounded nothing like his grandfather, on that or on a second count. Everyone was impressed by Temple's fine command of French, the one essential for a diplomatic career. He was the likely candidate for the gay-hearted Sally Jay to recruit when organizing a celebratory ball; Jefferson deferred to him on all the points of etiquette. Inadvertently, Franklin had raised a French aristocrat.

Paris was as charmed by Temple as the Americans in Europe were put off. Everyone was struck by the young man's resemblance to his grandfa-

---

*Initially Temple worked gratis. When he turned twenty, Franklin took the liberty of compensating him, modestly. For that year Temple earned 3,400 livres, a salary that rose, by 1780, to 6,000 livres. In 1781 he settled on 7,200 livres, as that was what Congress paid William Lee's secretary, "who couldn't have had a quarter as much to do." By Franklin's September 1776 instructions, the mission secretary was to be allowed a salary of 1,000 pounds sterling, or 24,000 livres. Congress provided the salary but not the secretary.

ther, but not everyone was charmed by his habit of recycling Franklin's witticisms. He had more polish and less philosophy than his model. He made of his proximity to a great man more than seemed appropriate; he was quick to point up the pretensions of the American ladies abroad, who piled on the rouge and the jewelry.* He far preferred the graces of French-women, or seemed anyway to enjoy telling the Americans in town as much. He could be less than discreet, overly eager to assert his authority over public arrangements. Franklin would have been livid had he known that Temple had pulled aside a British peace commissioner in 1782, to ask privately if something might be done for his father. William Franklin had been the only British governor to persuade his state assembly to obey the Stamp Act, to offer the unvarnished truth on prewar colonial affairs. Might not something be found for him—the intergenerational irony was poignant—in the diplomatic corps? The appeal spoke loudly to the burden under which Temple labored in Passy, unable so much as to mention at the dinner table the father he yearned to see. It made him fair game to an extremist like Arthur Lee, always happy to probe the perfidious side of the Franklin dynasty. "Thus while Governor Franklin is planning our destruction in London," Lee sputtered, "his father and son are entrusted with all our secrets in Paris." Franklin might well justify that confidence but Temple (who, Lee raged, "has no character at all,") did not.

The truth was that Temple bore two characters, a substantially more awkward legacy. Over the summer of 1783 he fell—for his own reasons and not his grandfather's, progress of a kind—head over heels for the Brillons' younger daughter, Aldegonde. The passion was as serious as the affection for Aldegonde's sister had been practical, but the romance was discouraged on the same grounds. Temple was not enough a Frenchman to hope to marry into that family, friends reminded him. They acknowledged that he was in a blind fit of passion, also that—aside from the impossibility of his establishing a proper career in France—the matter of religion loomed large. Passions were short-lived, their consequences longer. Temple risked poisoning the rest of his days. He was too much the foreigner to qualify as a Brillon son-in-law, too much the Frenchman to pass for an American.

---

*He was not alone in remarking on that ostentation. As the Adamses sighed separately, it only made the American ministers look shabbier.

Of course Temple suffered from an additional stigma. He was not only, as Arthur Lee had it, "a[s] young insignificant boy as any in existence," but, as William Lee helpfully added, a bastard, twice over. His illegitimacy had always sat poorly with Adams; it was of a piece with Franklin's casual approach to his desk, his corpulence, his lack of discipline. At the end of 1782 Franklin had engaged in a little strong-arming. With the consent of Jay but without asking or notifying Adams, he had taken it upon himself to appoint Temple as secretary of the peace commission. In Adams's view that was a lucrative and coveted appointment, one that he, as the first peace commissioner to have been appointed, was entitled to fill. (He had his own candidate in mind, a cousin of his wife's.) He resented Franklin's unilateral decision but vowed to make no trouble and—having expressed his disapproval—never to mention the matter again.*

By the time Temple landed on his doorstep in January 1783, to request that Adams sign off retroactively on his commission, Adams was hysterical. Temple took every pain to be deferential—he had come to discuss a subject on which he did not speak easily or often—but managed only further to affront Adams, who let him know as much. He had been attacked by Vergennes, disgraced by Congress, treated shabbily by his colleagues. He could bear it no longer. He would, he explained to the well-meaning Franklin look-alike before him, "wear no livery with a spot upon it." Temple attempted to defuse the situation by allowing that his grandfather was weary and had asked to be relieved of his post. Not to be outdone, Adams replied that he, too, was weary. He had submitted the same request. Nor was he impressed with the document Temple delivered to him, in which Franklin testified to his grandson's "sagacity beyond his years, diligence, activity, fidelity, genteel address, facility in speaking French." Adams came away from the encounter convinced rather that Franklin's resignation was a sham, that—the idea originated with William Lee—Franklin was plotting to have Temple named in his stead at Versailles so

---

*That was in November 1782. Adams never tired of reminding the world that "the Dr., who knows better than I do how to provide for himself and his connections, got his son [*sic*] appointed," a subject on which he was still dilating in 1811. By which time he implied as well that Franklin appointed Temple to spy on him, a familiar theme. After the fact, Adams asserted that Franklin had hired Gellée, the young clerk, to the same end.

that he might accede to the same position in London. On that count he was mistaken. London was not a posting Franklin wanted (although it was one Adams coveted). What was true was that Adams had good reason to feel manipulated. Obviously Franklin had some inkling of how his colleague would take to having Temple forced upon him; Temple was asked to keep his new appointment secret for some time. (He failed to do so.) And Franklin, his memory about such matters rarely clouded, would misremember this one. Later he would recall of Temple that "three of my colleagues, without the smallest solicitation from me, chose him secretary of the negotiation for treaties." There was no question that his grandson was uniquely qualified for the post, also no question that in appointing him in the fashion he did Franklin had blundered.

It was a small step from Adams's legitimate sense that he was being manipulated to his 1783 have-you-no-decency cry. Franklin's whole life had been "one continued insult to good manners and to decency," he roared, putting Boston on the map. Borrowing again from Lee's vocabulary, Adams denounced his colleague's "effrontery" in forcing his illegitimate offspring on the world. Here at hand was one incontrovertible sign of Franklin's depravity, which set Adams to ranting about "outrages to morality and decorum, which would never have been forgiven in any other American." As a congressional ally put it, inflamed by Adams's blasts and by Franklin's campaign for Temple: "It is said he has served an apprenticeship; but with such a master, and such examples, he must be tenfold the worse for it."

Temple was fortunate in one respect. So fixated were his grandfather's enemies on his peccadillos that they had little time for Temple's own. He came of age in a city that could try any young man's morals, and he did it justice. His friends wished that he could join them in their travels, where they met women even looser than those in Paris, "which was saying a good deal." The same companions quibbled with Temple's choice of lovers. Did he not understand that easy conquests were drab conquests? These matters required contradiction, to give them piquancy. As for his violent attachment to Mademoiselle Brillon, already it had caused him to miss out on two very interesting adventures, which he could easily have concealed from an inexperienced fifteen-year-old. When it came to sentimental matters, Temple had none of the diffidence on doorsteps that he had displayed on Adams's. August 1783 found him utterly infatuated with

Aldegonde Brillon, and also tangling with a cuckolded husband. Early in August Sir James Nicolson, a wealthy Scot, called on Franklin to register a complaint about Temple's attentions to Lady Nicolson. It was arranged between the two older men that Temple would in future refrain from calling on her ladyship, an edict that was insufficiently impressed upon Temple. He not only returned immediately to her side (to be received by her) but secured as well a miniature of his paramour. (She had one already of him.) Nicolson insisted that Franklin arrange for the portrait's return, along with his wife's letters, which Temple refused to surrender. Conceding that his wife had been imprudent, Nicolson sent his servant to the Valentinois with an ultimatum. He appealed to Temple as a man of honor. Surely he grasped the proprieties of the situation. "Return what does not belong to you," implored Nicolson, to whom the incident was most disagreeable, the more so as it had some precedent. Lady Nicolson had also melted into the arms of John Paul Jones.

Nicolson was startled by the response of his wife's admirer, who waged his own assault on good manners and decency, at least as they applied to eighteenth-century adultery. It did not strike Temple as remotely correct that he return her ladyship's portrait. "A more proper and delicate method for all parties, according to my ideas of propriety (and the only one I shall ever comply with), would be for her to send me back *my* portrait first: this would convince me she did not wish me to retain hers," insisted Temple, suddenly an authority on decorum. His impudence was presumably not sanctioned by Franklin, who knew better than to send angry letters, and would never have signed off on one washing his hands of a "puerile affair, which has already taken up too much of my time" when that affair concerned another man's wife. Temple was not put off by Nicolson, although his attention was soon enough diverted by the wife of a famed actor who lived nearby. In 1784 Temple had a torrid affair with Blanchette Caillot, one that would preserve a family tradition. In February 1785 Madame Caillot bore Franklin's illegitimate son's illegitimate son an illegitimate son, of whose existence the child's great-grandfather seems to have been unaware.*

---

*By contrast Temple was well aware of the tradition he was upholding. On the day his son was born he made a curious notation in his datebook: "B a B of a B . . . ," a line that begs to be read "born a bastard of a bastard." While Franklin may not have known of the new addition to the family, the Americans' banker was. Temple was discreet about conveying funds to Blanchette.

Franklin made no secret of the fact that his grandson's presence consoled him for the loss of his son, or that he inclined toward leniency. He left the sermons entirely to Temple's cohorts. Franklin knew a thing or two about wild oats; he was an admirer of high spirits. When it came to neighbors' wives, his own divertissements were of the more subtle kind. That fall he flirted on every possible occasion with the blond, angelic-looking Sally Jay, whom he forbade to mention as much to her husband, then in Great Britain. The effusive, attractive, Shakespeare-reading daughter of an intellectual, Mrs. Jay was of a breed to which Franklin was partial. In company one November afternoon he held up two magnets, each of which he claimed represented a Jay. Placed nearby, they were immediately drawn to each other. Separating them, he produced a third magnet, which he dubbed "an English lady." The wandering magnet flew to it instantly. Thrilled by his demonstration, Franklin's company urged Sally Jay to avenge herself. Instead she wrote of it to her husband, as of the fact that Dr. Franklin was on his way over for tea, despite a torrential storm. Franklin failed to make of Mrs. Jay a European, but regularly succeeded in manifesting the insidious charm over which Adams so wrung his hands. He was always a flirt. It took John Adams to turn him into a womanizer.

※

In writing to women Franklin had long held that he wished himself twenty years younger. Everything about the fall of 1783 made him feel he had been born too soon, a different regret. The summer's baffling haze left the country in an unsettled mood; for weeks on end the sun emitted only a feeble glow, one that yielded no clue as to what time of day it was. Well into July Franklin was still lighting fires. Perplexed, he attempted to quantify the murk; he found that the sun's rays were "so faint in passing through it that when collected in the focus of a burning glass they would scarce kindle brown paper." Violent thunderstorms followed, as did an earthquake in eastern France, and a volcanic eruption. While the commissioners waited impatiently for an American response to their negotiations, a feeling of apocalypse hung heavy in the air. Under the circumstances there was every reason why the villagers outside Lyons, glimpsing what appeared to be a giant house sailing through the sky, should conclude that the moon had detached itself from the firmament and that the last judgment was upon them. Soon enough that ominous vision acquired a name. The Rhône villagers had been among the first to glimpse the aerostatic machine of the Montgolfier brothers. Local paper manufacturers, Joseph-Michel and Jacques-Etienne Montgolfier had wondered what might happen if they inflated a piece of ordinary silk with forty cubic feet of heated air. So as to avert further instances of mass terror, the government issued a statement: "Far from being a terrifying phenomenon, this is nothing but a machine made of light cloth and taffeta, covered in paper, which can cause no harm, and which presumably some day will serve a useful purpose for society."

Within a matter of weeks France found itself in the grip of balloon fever, of which Paris was, as ever, the epicenter. There was nowhere else on earth a man of science would have wished to be. So massive was the curiosity about the phenomenon that crowds nearly broke through the barricades surrounding the balloon of the chemist Jacques-Alexandre Charles, moved under cover of darkness to the Champ de Mars on August 25. Two days later a multitude crammed the field under a teeming rain, feathers wilting, lorgnettes dripping, for the balloon's ascension. Franklin enjoyed an unobstructed view from his terrace, as just after five that Saturday afternoon the gleaming silk orb, twelve feet in diameter, rose majestically skyward. Days later he was able to report on the fate of the hydrogen-filled marvel. At an altitude of three thousand feet the balloon had traveled for twelve miles, where it fell to earth in a village northeast of Paris. Its girth loomed larger than royal reassurances. The cart drivers who witnessed its descent were petrified, the more so as the colossus lumbered directly toward them, surging in several directions at once and nimbly averting their first blows. They went at the giant with rock and knives, until it emitted "a death rattle."

A joint attack of gout and kidney stones kept Franklin at home that day, where he welcomed two young Englishmen. John Baynes and Samuel Romilly called at the Valentinois early that afternoon; dressed in a nightshirt, Franklin received them in his bedroom, his inflamed feet wrapped in flannel and propped on a pillow. In their late twenties, Baynes and Romilly were scholars of the first rank. Baynes had just been called to the bar and would go on to become an eminent jurist; classicists both, the two read Tacitus together in the evenings. They were to discover that a few hours' conversation with Franklin was a pleasure unlike any other. As the crowds assembled on the Champ de Mars, Baynes and Romilly were treated to a marvel of a different kind: a wide-ranging discourse on parliamentary reform (of which Franklin thought Britain incapable), a discussion of the odious American slave trade. On exhibit was the glinting wit and the cantering intelligence. With those callers Franklin would argue that the laws of primogeniture were a hindrance to any nation's well-being, and would hold forth on the superiority of European printing and engraving. To prove his point he pulled out his newly acquired five-volume set of *Don Quixote*, a marvel of typography. He read aloud passages of the United States constitutions. Prescribing a difficult course, Franklin vowed that his countrymen should "keep themselves out of European politics as much as possible, and that they should make a point of adhering to their treaties." Britain aside, he was optimistic about the future. He felt wars would become less frequent, a conviction that recalled to mind Pierre Gargaz, moralist and galley slave. That tale he related in full, extracting Gargaz's pamphlet from the closet. In high spirits, he made no mention of several subjects that preoccupied him, foremost among which was the lack of conciliatory spirit among his countrymen and their concurrent refusal to support themselves. It seemed America had sunk into the ocean. Where, finally, were those treaties?

Three days later he had his answer. The British were at last ready to sign a definitive peace, although for reasons of their own they insisted on doing so in Paris. Would September 3 be agreeable, at the hotel of Franklin's old friend Hartley, who had replaced Oswald? Temple promised that his grandfather, although frail, would make every effort to attend, as indeed he did. On Wednesday morning, September 3, Franklin, Adams, and Jay converged on the rue Jacob to affix their signatures to what was to be known as the Treaty of Paris, identical to the preliminaries negotiated a year earlier, and America's effective declaration of independence. Later that afternoon, in Vergennes's offices, France and Britain signed the document to which their parallel negotiation had led, to be known as the Treaty of Versailles. All parties swore that such a global cataclysm as they had just survived would not repeat itself. Well into the celebratory evening, the duc de Cröy congratulated Vergennes on his good work: "I cannot say how this peace will reflect on you today, but in a hundred years it will be to your honor." With a moment's hesitation Vergennes replied, "I count on it reflecting well upon me at least then!"* In his ecstasy Franklin would propose to Hartley a three-way family compact, joining England, France, and America. What better way to preclude the folly of war? He was sincere about an Anglo-French entente, doubtless also aware that one would have very much pleased Vergennes.

He was not wholly conciliatory. Amid the mutual congratulation of early September he sent on a message to Charles James Fox, restored to his post as foreign secretary. Fox should not underestimate the Americans. "We are more thoroughly an enlightened people, with respect to our political interests, than perhaps any other under heaven. Every man among us reads, and is so easy in his circumstances as to have leisure for conversations of improvement, and for acquiring information. Our domestic misunderstandings, when we have them, are of small extent, though monstrously magnified by your microscopic newspapers. He who judges from them that we are on the point of falling into anarchy, or returning to the obedience of Britain, is like one who being shown some spots on the sun, should fancy that the whole disk would soon be overspread by them, and that there would be an end of daylight." All of which to say that it was high time the British evacuated New York, as they had promised to do nine months earlier.† And no sooner was the peace signed than Franklin turned to another piece of unfinished business. He had known for weeks of allegations registered against him regarding the negotiation. It had not been difficult to guess at their source, "but conscious of my innocence, and unwilling to disturb public operations by private resentments or contentions, I passed them over in silence." On September 10 he allowed himself a step "towards my vindication."‡

Adams had accused him of having obstructed America's claims to the fisheries and the western territories, asserting that Franklin either favored

---

*In the immediate and despite Adams's predictions, he got something more tangible: Maurepas's old title, which made him de facto prime minister.

†The last of the British troops left New York only on November 25, 1783.

‡As the French saw it, "Dr. Franklin had at last roused himself from the apathy with which, until now, he seems to have regarded the attacks of his colleague." Perhaps the least flattering take on his imperturbability was preserved by a Loyalist, citing a female friend in Paris. Franklin's insouciance was such that "the universe could collapse around him without his being disturbed in the least, provided there remained on earth a few people with whom he might play chess."

or did not oppose French claims, and "that it was entirely owing to the firmness, sagacity and disinterestedness of M. Adams, with whom Mr. Jay united, that we have obtained those important advantages." The accusation was tantamount to treason, and Franklin addressed it as such. "As to the two charges of age and weakness, I must confess the first; but I am not quite so clear in the latter; and perhaps my adversaries may find that they presumed a little too much upon it when they ventured to attack me," wrote the man who, under fire, was suddenly more vital than the one who had resigned months earlier, on account of his infirmity. To each of his co-commissioners went identical notes. Franklin had no interest in debating the question of who should receive what share of credit for the treaty they had mutually negotiated. But after fifty years in public office nor had he any intention of going to his grave under a cloud of suspicion. From each colleague he requested an affidavit, one sufficiently forceful to "entirely destroy the effect of that accusation."

Jay had an unequivocal statement to that effect on Franklin's desk the next day. Laurens—as eager to remain above the fray as he had been to remain far from the welter of negotiation—advised Franklin to ignore the calumnies. His conduct spoke for itself. Adams was less eager to gratify, as might be expected from the man who—on the day Franklin was firing off that challenge—was again deploring his "low cunning, and mean craft," insisting that Franklin was "secretly contriving" to negotiate all American trade agreements on his own. "I could have formed no idea that jealousy, envy, and vanity could have gone to such lengths," muttered Adams, sounding ill inclined toward apology. He was sorry to say he could do no better for his colleague than to quote his diary entry of November 30, 1782, in which he had announced to Franklin that he intended to follow Jay in all matters. "The Dr. heard me patiently but said nothing," Adams had noted. He was always ready to hold Franklin's taciturnity against him. It unnerved him every bit as much as did the excruciating crash of traffic at his hotel.

It was as unlike Franklin to dip a toe into the polemical surf as it was unlike Adams to retreat; Franklin would have been better served by submitting to Laurens's advice. Adams was too communicative, and too quotable. Soon enough he would reduce Franklin to a man "enfeebled with age, the stone, and the gout, and eaten with all the passions which may prey upon old age unprincipled, until it is no longer under the restraint even of hypocrisy." To those familiar with Adams, Franklin's humiliating appeal was unnecessary. Fourteen years later Jefferson was to note of the newly elected president of the United States: "Mr. Adams is vain, irritable, stubborn, endowed with excessive self-love, and still suffering pique at the preference accorded Franklin over him in Paris." All the same there was no question that—either in forcing the matter out in the open or in eliciting the reassurances he had—Franklin felt better. He sensed he had isolated, or at least better revealed, his colleague. When next he felt it incumbent on him to mention his fears for the Franco-American alliance, he permitted himself a more dismissive tone. Adams continued to engage in "extravagant and violent language" in public. "Luckily here, and I hope there, it is imputed to the true cause; a disorder in the brain; which though not constant has its fits too frequent."

With his young British admirers he identified a related pathology. Baynes declared that he always assumed a man to act from pure motives unless presented with reason to believe otherwise. "Yes," concurred Franklin, "so would every honest man." Lord North had operated from the opposite conviction, added Romilly; the former British prime minister had believed that all men were corrupt. And understandably so, opined Franklin, the natural man who had never read Rousseau. North's administration extrapolated from what it knew. "A man," he added, "who has seen nothing but hospitals, must naturally have a poor opinion of the health of mankind." There was every reason why Baynes would hope to continue his acquaintance with such an incisive sage, and he returned to the Valentinois on September 15. The Swiss Guard who greeted him at the door sent him upstairs, where a servant would direct him to Dr. Franklin. Upstairs all was silent and deserted, as Baynes reported to the Swiss. He was led back to the living quarters, and pointed toward a door. Behind it he would find Dr. Franklin. As the approach was rather unorthodox, Baynes asked to be announced. "Oh! *Monsieur*, that's not necessary, just go in, go in," insisted Franklin's doorman, leaving Baynes to barge in on an old man fast asleep on his couch. Franklin was all grace and apologies, explaining that he had risen early that morning and succumbed to the stifling heat. Within minutes his caller was swept into a discussion of the Quakers, of Franklin's firm conviction that government office should be unsalaried. He was happy to discourse on Irish politics, on America's lack of need for a standing army, on property rights in China, on English poetry, on debtor's prison, which he thought an abomination. Little escaped his attention. Hours after Baynes took his leave, Franklin was toying in his bedroom with a small balloon, which Temple had inflated with hydrogen. It rose happily to the ceiling, where it bounced about for some time.

⁓ꞋꞋꞋꞋ⁓

Paris was jubilant in the weeks following the peace, all spirits buoyed by the wonders in the air. Those were not exclusively of the political, or even of the aerostatic, variety. Earlier in the year Franklin had made the acquaintance of Wolfgang von Kempelen, the Hungarian inventor who conquered Paris with his chess-playing automaton. Franklin was duly impressed by the turbaned, pipe-smoking master, his body evidently composed of a system of wheels, springs, and levers, which whirred formidably every time he took a turn. (And among which, unknown to Franklin or to anyone else for half a century, was concealed a prodigy of a chess-playing child.) Of the pageant of talking automatons, the masterwork was the double-headed contraption Franklin examined in midsummer. Both its message and its ingenuity met with his approval. A perfectly comprehensible dialogue ensued when one head announced, "The king has brought peace to Europe," to which its mechanical interlocuter replied, with equal distinction, "The peace crowns the king with glory." Next in line was the enterprising Lyons water-walker, who proposed to demonstrate his elastic clogs under the Pont-Neuf. From his balcony Franklin followed a clumsy boat propelled by a set of windmill vanes as it made a speedy crossing of the Seine, a trip he clocked at three minutes. (The sight must have been particularly gripping to the seventy-eight-year-old who, in his youth, had swum from one side of a Boston pond to the other with a kite in his hand.) For the most part, however, all eyes turned skyward, for a display that seemed, most dramatically, to announce a new age. "We think of nothing here at present but of flying," Franklin reported to Laurens, unapologetically.

From across the Channel came word that an Englishman had walked on the ocean floor, news that elicited the inevitable gibe: The English were profound, the French entirely weightless. A peace may have been signed, but the rivalry lived on. With it an enduring anxiety raised its head. What if England was to be the first to perfect France's fabulous discovery, and usurp the air as she had for too long ruled the seas? Surely the peace commissioners should have given that a little thought, as opposed to some of the less essential matters that had so preoccupied them. It would not be Franco-British rivalry but a healthy competition between two Frenchmen that drove the flying frenzy forward, pitting the Montgolfiers and their heated air against the hydrogen balloons of Jacques-Alexandre Charles and Noel Robert. Franklin may have felt more intimate with Charles—the former financier claimed to have embraced science out of admiration for the American—but was as ever diplomatic. It was entirely natural, he quipped, that the new arrival should have two parents.

He had great expectations for manned flight and fortunately no great distance to travel; the next turn fell to Pilâtre de Rozier and the marquis d'Arlandes, on the great lawn at La Muette, two hundred paces from Franklin's back door. Minutes after their ascension on November 21 a gust of wind swept the machine into the upper reaches of the manicured chestnut trees, tipping the basket sideways and ripping the balloon. Franklin was in great distress for the men, assuming they would be burned to a crisp. Instead the balloon was swiftly repaired, setting off a second time without incident. It passed directly over Franklin's head, affording him a fine view of the fire that kept the machine afloat, which was considerable. (Equally great was the aeronauts' consideration for the anguished silence below. To reassure the crowd, d'Arlandes waved his arms about, until reprimanded by his partner. "You're doing nothing, and we're not rising!" shouted Pilâtre.) Continuing on its way, the blue sphere soared past the dome of the Invalides and across Paris, for an eventless seventeen-minute flight.

Hours later Franklin was honored by a visit from the marquis d'Arlandes, who assured him that the men had made a gentle landing. Their brilliantly decorated balloon had suffered little from the initial collision. Franklin had seen many things in his day but had never before entertained a man who had drunk champagne in a wicker basket and bickered with a colleague while flying three thousand feet above the earth. It was abundantly clear to him that a new age had dawned. All that remained to be seen was how far progress might go. "A few months since the idea of witches riding through the air upon a broomstick, and that of philosophers upon a bag of smoke, would have appeared equally impossible and ridiculous," he reminded his friend Joseph Banks, president of the Royal Society, in London.* Evidently it was well before the La Muette ascension that Franklin uttered the bon mot that would attach him eternally to the balloons of 1783, a scientific experiment to which he came not in his American role, as scientist, but in his European role, as propagandist. "What good were these experiments?" went the skeptic's question. To which Franklin replied, "What good is a new-born babe?" In some versions he continued: "He may be an imbecile, or a man of great intelligence. Let us wait for him to complete his studies before judging him."

Already he had himself proved a truth posited by Descartes: Disinterested research could be counted upon to yield practical results. The unknown should not be scorned, argued the man whose mind was so open it seemed to some devoid of principles. By the time d'Arlandes and Pilâtre had sailed over his head at La Muette he was a convert. "This experience is by no means a trifling one. It may be attended with important consequences that no one can foresee," Franklin assured London friends, a little elbow to the ribs. In the same spirit he followed the early aeronauts closely, if not exactly with the fervor of the Parisians. Around him balloons sprouted where once his face had appeared, on fans, clocks, birdcages. Plays and poems were offered up to the aeronauts; piles of love letters landed on Charles's doorstep. A new liqueur (*crème aérostatique*) was baptized, along with new ballads and a new hat.†

From the beginning Franklin reported half seriously on some of the applications suggested by the ballooning craze. Was this not a promising breakthrough for asthmatics, a treatment for those who suffered from ennui at lower altitudes? One chemist experimented in his laboratory with hail and snow, proposing to control the weather from a balloon. Henceforth royalty would travel in airborne carriages, drawn by eagles; owls would convey philosophers and doctors. Balloons anchored in the air could preserve food and ices until needed. To a degree Franklin joined in

---

*In February 1780 Franklin had speculated that man might one day "learn to deprive large masses of their gravity and give them absolute levity, for the sake of easy transport." He gave the human race a thousand years to work that magic.

†As one newspaper had it, "The Montgolfiers' invention has so addled the French mind that it has bestowed vigor on the aged, wit on pedants, and constancy on our women."

the light-headedness. Here finally was a productive application of hot air, a quality with which Paris was so generously endowed. During the fall he composed a satire that made its way into the *Journal de Paris*, a pitch-perfect proposal of a "lady correspondent" who understood that the search was under way for better sources of inflammable air. She had a worthy suggestion: "If you want to fill your balloons with an element ten times lighter than inflammable air, you can find a great quantity of it, and ready made, in the promises of lovers and of courtiers and in the sighs of our widowers; in the good resolutions made during a storm at sea, or on land, during an illness; and especially in the praise to be found in letters of recommendation."

With the first frosts Franklin's health took a turn for the worse, but even his disability could not keep him from the long-promised ascent of Charles and Robert. For the first display of a manned hydrogen balloon, he headed to the Tuileries on the raw morning of December 1. Given the cold he opted to remain in his carriage, which he stationed at an optimum vantage point, near the statue of Louis XV. His frailty saved him from the crush of 200,000 spectators, a throng that overspilled the gardens and seemed to Franklin infinite, as well it might have; it was five times the population of Philadelphia. (And was said to include even the most delicate of Parisian ladies, those who normally could not find it within their power to rouse themselves before noon, but who were that morning suddenly impervious to cold, wet, or fog.) Franklin looked around to see that all of Paris was out, if not in the Tuileries then on the quais and bridges, in the streets and at windows or hanging from the tops of houses. "Never before," he delighted, "was a philosophical experiment so magnificently attended." His uncomfortable wait bore a splendid reward. At noon the fog cleared; an hour later the yellow and red balloon rose, calmly and majestically, into a brilliantly clear sky, a display hailed as the most astonishing science had yet delivered the world. On the ground the audience alternately waved in admiration and fell to their knees with emotion. At two hundred feet the aeronauts displayed a white flag, to which the crowd responded with thunderclaps of applause. The Tuileries guards waved their sabers frantically in the air. Transfixed, Franklin followed the balloon's horizontal progress with his folding telescope, for an hour, until the globe disappeared from view.

It did not escape his notice that the machine in which Charles and

Robert made their historic flight failed to correspond perfectly to the one pictured on his admission ticket, which he corrected. Nor did it escape his notice that the two had covered a distance greater than that between Calais and Dover, or that the aeronauts could have traveled farther still. The implications for his own situation were obvious. Already Jonathan Williams had proposed a carriage for his granduncle based on a design Williams had seen, in which a bed was suspended on springs. Franklin's discomfort had become chronic; he was much at the mercy of the stone in his bladder, which by December must have been the size of a small egg. The wait at the Tuileries had been an uneasy one; the motion of a carriage on pavement was excruciating; he was no longer at ease confined to a room. That week he excused himself from putting in a personal appearance at Versailles, explaining—with eighteenth-century unsqueamishness—that on account of the stone and bloody urine, he was sending Temple in his stead.

As always however it was to the greater good that Franklin looked as men began to sail through the sky. He wondered if balloons might one day carry an engineer over an enemy's lines, or convey intelligence from a town under siege. If nothing else they should impress upon kings the folly of war. What ruler could defend himself against ten thousand men descending from the clouds? He had always distinguished himself for his unbridled faith in progress and did so now; he did not sound like a man who begrudged science for having nearly occluded the official celebrations for the peace. Several times delayed, they took place finally on December 15. From the aeronautics epidemic Franklin instead extracted a few cardinal rules; he was neither blown off course nor carried away by ideological ferment. He swatted at British temerity. A little daring was a good thing. At the same time it was essential not to disappoint one's public. After a failed ascension in the Luxembourg Gardens, spectators had rioted, overturning chairs and shredding a balloon. They would have done the same with the aeronauts had the guards not stepped in. (Even on December 1 there had been whispers of "If they don't go up, we'll have to hang them.") As always Franklin cited pride as an impediment to progress. And as ever he was a genius of perspective: "Beings of a rank and nature far superior to ours have not disdained to amuse themselves with making and launching balloons, otherwise we should never have enjoyed the light of those glorious objects that rule our day and night, nor have had the pleasure of riding round the sun ourselves upon the balloon we now inhabit."

He might well have added a reminder that men were fickle. It was imperative to enjoy their good grace while it lasted. Soon enough balloons would waft over Paris without turning a single head below. Already it was clear that that other great experiment of 1783—the work of a daring set of pioneers in a different realm, whose hot air had so improbably lifted the roof off an empire and provided Europe with a glimpse of another empyrean—was less miraculous than it had seemed. After 1783 the fervent Americanism of the revolutionary years was never to return. With some asperity the Paris commissioners warned Congress that "the situation of the army, the reluctance of the people to pay taxes, and the circumstances under which Congress removed from Philadelphia" were all public relations disasters. In foreign relations as in science, Franklin could not argue forcefully enough for humility. Britain was not yet reconciled to the loss of her colonies, he was again appealing to Vergennes for funds, and yet General Washington failed to acknowledge French aid in disbanding the army.* Evidently it was indeed great powers alone that felt and remembered. In the first three months of their existence, noted one paper, the Americans had yielded already to the depravities of age. They were lax, they were unconciliatory, they neglected their duties, they revolted against authority, they were bankrupts. It came as an equally wondrous revelation of 1783 that the New World rather resembled the Old.

---

*By December 1783 a Massachusetts delegate to Congress could already be heard denouncing the snare France had set for America. The colonies' position had been deplorable and their spirits low; the French had awaited only the "fatal moment" to intervene, manipulating Congress to their own ends. As John Adams would howl in 1784, the peace was far more advantageous to their ally than his compatriots realized. France "has raised herself by it from the deepest prostratation in the dust, to the highest elevation she ever obtained."

XII

Creditors Have Better Memories Than Debtors
1784–1785

When men of sober age travel, they gather knowledge which they may apply usefully for their country; but they are subject ever after to recollections mixed with regret; their affections are weakened by being extended over more objects; and they learn new habits which cannot be gratified when they return home.
—Thomas Jefferson

During the 1783 Christmas season John Jay heard in England that Franklin was seriously unwell. With some alarm he inquired after his colleague. He also satisfied Franklin's curiosity on an outstanding question: In what esteem was he held in Britain? "There are many in this country who speak of you with great respect," Jay allowed, and "there are others who like you as little as the eagle did the cat, and probably for the same reasons." Franklin was all good cheer in his reply. While his stone was a hindrance—it made carriage rides and sudden movements an agony—he was by no means ready to consider treatment. "You may judge that my disease is not very grievous," he mused, "since I am more afraid of the medicines than of the malady." He was equally unafflicted by Jay's report: "I have, as you observe, some enemies in England, but they are my enemies as *an American*; I have also two or three in America, who are my enemies as *a minister*: but I thank God there are not in the whole world any who are my enemies as a *man*." He continued to believe himself beyond reproach, a secret of a kind to happiness, and one appropriate to the season. It was Poor Richard who had noted that "a good conscience is a continual Christmas." Franklin welcomed John Paul Jones and others to the Valentinois that afternoon, for a holiday dinner of delicacies, pheasant and partridge, thrush and duck.

For the rest of his time in France he was not to venture far beyond the neighborhood. When he did he got no farther than the Adams or Helvétius households, a mile away in Auteuil; Paris had always been willing to come to him, and henceforth would be obliged to. (The corollary was that Franklin was at the mercy of every manner of caller. "Celebrity may for a while flatter one's vanity, but its effects are troublesome," he lamented.) Temple filled in for him at Versailles, a particular relief; Vergennes was eager to discuss America's repayment of her debt, a conversation Franklin was equally eager to avoid. While he never complained of the senselessness of court ritual, he found it debilitating. His fellow ambassadors breezed through the palace at an impressive clip. He lagged well behind them all, struggling especially on the stairs.

"All the desire in the world can't get me to Paris just now," Franklin explained early in February 1784, to his friend Antoine-Alexis-François Cadet de Vaux, the *Journal de Paris* founder and editor. An accomplished chemist and pharmacologist, Cadet de Vaux was as well a professor of baking. In collaboration with police chief Lenoir, he had long hoped to reproduce Franklin's smokeless, carbon-burning stove. There was additional reason for Cadet de Vaux's curiosity in the New Year. Christmas 1783 ushered in the most brutal winter in living memory. For ten weeks the temperature remained well below freezing. The storms were constant, the winds fierce, and—with firewood scarce—the misery rampant. An epidemic of broken limbs further incapacitated Paris. (Never a man to let a phenomenon traipse by without attaching a theory to it, Franklin speculated that the summer fogs were responsible for the arctic conditions.) Stiff with cold, he wondered if Cadet de Vaux might impose on Lenoir for a little coal. He would be greatly obliged. The streets impassable, Franklin was much on his own; even the stalwarts stayed away. And with business at a standstill, he fixed his attention not on Paris but on another unreachable city. On the back of a letter from Grand he calculated the date of his Philadelphia arrival six decades earlier. By his reckoning, Franklin had walked the streets of that city for the first time on October 6, 1723. To the dismay of friends he was intent on doing so again. No reasoning in the world would convince the man who could not make it to Paris that Philadelphia was beyond his reach.

As the snow fell and fell again, as a March thaw flooded the streets, isolating Passy entirely, the deferential request for a recall turned into a melancholy plea. Franklin did not mean to importune Congress. Nor did he care to be forgotten. The calendar loomed large; in order to sail over the summer he would need Congress's word by spring. Yet he heard nothing. He emerged from the winter disgruntled and diminished, hobbled again by gout, begging for a private hint of what he might expect, plainly envious of Jay and Laurens, soon to be America-bound. He asked both men to look into his situation and that of Temple, whose qualifications he again enumerated. (He also picked up on Laurens's offer to defend him, should ever there be need. Indeed he would be grateful if Laurens could neutralize any damage Adams might have done.) Soon enough he began to sound the scold. America needed to pay her debts, honor her treaties, insist on her gratitude, and resist all false sense of security. As for him, another winter like the one he had just endured and he could relinquish all hope of seeing his country again. By summer he was well beyond anthems to Temple. He hit a new note concerning the American government: "They should methinks reflect that if they continue me here, the faults I may henceforth commit through the infirmities of age will be rather theirs than mine."

Though flanked by his grandsons, he was less at home at the Valentinois than he had ever been. He had made a number of repairs to the property but it remained in need of work, to which Chaumont attended slowly. The paint was peeling; the floorboards in Temple's rooms crumbled underfoot. As any number of callers observed, Franklin had never mastered French household management, which to a lesser degree would defy both Jefferson and the invincible Abigail Adams as well. Over the course of 1783 Franklin eased more responsibility (and a grossly inflated salary) into the hands of Jacques Finck, the new maître d'hôtel; their agreement left Franklin to provide only for his liquor, wood, candles, and heating oil. At the same time Franklin discovered why the mistress of every French household wore the keys to her pantry around her wrist. Finck was a credit to his profession as defined by Mrs. Adams: The job of maître d'hôtel was to see to it that nobody in the household cheated more than himself. While he boasted daily of his honesty, Finck's demands were unceasing; Franklin discovered him to be as irritable when they were met as when they were not. (Only later did he discover that Finck had gambling and drinking habits.) Valets came and went, abusing their privileges and leaving bills in their wake. The gardener whom Benny sent to Paris for fishhooks one morning at ten o'clock returned at eleven in the evening, blind drunk, and having accomplished only half his mission. Franklin's coachman and kitchen boy worked out a long-standing grudge by attacking each other in the Valentinois kitchen, a scuffle from which the coachman emerged with serious head injuries.

In December the Valentinois was in an uproar when Chaumont's former errand boy was arrested. He had twice been caught carting leeks and turnips out of the garden. On the first occasion Chaumont delivered a thrashing; on the second he called the police. The entire household was deposed, as was the sixteen-year-old offender, who had a history of petty theft. The pathos of the situation would not have been lost on Franklin— Jean Grépillon had been born on the property and served Chaumont since the age of twelve; his crime was to have been homeless and hungry—but it is uncertain if he involved himself in the domestic drama. There was plainly no shortage of it at the Valentinois. (Benny was delighted at one point to retrieve a dueling sword from the bushes, the blade still streaked with blood.) What was clear by early 1784 was Franklin's determination to move, whether he was to remain in France or not. Madame Brillon offered up her home, while other friends pursued leads in Versailles. Always there was a discrepancy between what they thought fitting for America's minister plenipotentiary and what America's minister plenipotentiary thought fitting. One after another he rejected the options as too magnificent for his republican taste.*

Since Silas Deane's cry that he would prefer an American farm to a French dukedom, no American envoy had been comfortable in Paris. Even in the darkest hours Franklin refrained from the blanket condemna-

---

*While chained in place Franklin evidently had one foot out the Valentinois door. He was without any particular confidence in his poetic gift, but in April penned a piece of doggerel that stands as one of the more original lease-ending notices on record: "If life is compared to a feast, / Near fourscore years I've been a guest, / I've been regaled with the best, / And feel quite satisfied. / 'Tis time that I retire to rest; / Landlord, I thank ye! Friends, good night."

tions by his colleagues but in 1784, imperceptibly at first, he began to detach himself from France. He ventured only a rare comment on the poverty of the people, on the profusion of luxuries. He was gentle in dismissing precious French manners. At no time did he relinquish his sense that Louis XVI was a better friend to America than George III. How much he invested still in the rivalry between those two monarchs, and how much he had come to favor the former, can be read in the ballooning dispatches to London. After seven decades as a British subject Franklin affected a little nationalistic cross-dressing: "Your philosophy," he nudged Joseph Banks, "seems to be too bashful. In this country we are not so much afraid of being laughed at. If we do a foolish thing, we are the first to laugh at it ourselves, and are almost as much pleased with a *bon mot* or a good *chanson* that ridicules well the disappointment of a project, as we might have been with its success." He spared Banks a regret he voiced elsewhere. It was a shame that England had not taken to ballooning. Franklin had more faith in her mechanical genius than in that of France.

In March he unveiled for friends a piece he composed in self-defense. He was "pestered continually" by people from all over Europe who wished to settle in America, the silk makers, olive experts, laundresses, proofreaders, and obstetricians who had only the most outlandish ideas of what might await them there. Intended to set the record straight about the New World, the essay proved unexpectedly revealing of what Franklin thought of the Old. He reiterated familiar themes: It was a rule in much of America that no political office "should be so profitable as to make it desirable." Sobriety, frugality, and industry inevitably bore rewards; labor served to guard "the morals and virtue of a nation." America was fertile and edenic, rich, wide, and open. She offered cheap land and abundant employment, unprecedented religious, social, and commercial liberties. She made multitudes of poor immigrants wealthy. Contrary to myth, however, she was not the land of plenty imagined by the French, "where the streets are said to be paved with half-peck loaves, the houses tiled with pancakes, and where the fowls fly about ready roasted, crying, *come eat me!*" His nation stood as a corrective to what Franklin described (to a Spaniard) as the two most detrimental of European prejudices: the convictions that useful labor was disgraceful and that estates perpetuated families.

"Information to Those Who Would Remove to America" offers what may stand as the best one-line definition of the land of opportunity. In

Europe pedigree might be all, "but it is a commodity that cannot be carried to a worse market than to that of America, where people do not enquire concerning a stranger, *what is he?* but *what can he do?*" A useful man was always welcome in the New World, where no stigma attached to manual labor. A man who was interested only in rank, wrote Franklin, "will be despised and disregarded." It was not the place to come in search of a lucrative civil service position. (The majority of his French friends would have been without resources there.) He had hit some of the same notes in 1777 when comparing British and American credit, but generally these were not ideas Franklin publicized while abroad. The essay may have facilitated his job, but it risked clouding his reputation in Europe. Published anonymously in Paris, the piece could not pass the German censors. Franklin regretted that it appeared under his name in England.

His ode to the middle class was distributed widely, but he was advised to be more circumspect with a second composition of the winter. Just before Christmas, the Russian ambassador inquired if General Washington was really planning to decorate the French officers who had served in America with a hereditary honor. Tartly Franklin replied that he knew of no such thing. Soon enough he was working out the math, which he incorporated into his fiery blast against the Society of the Cincinnati, over which Washington had indeed agreed to preside. In his condemnation Franklin diverged even from Vergennes, who viewed the Cincinnati favorably; any institution that bound together Lafayette and Washington could only further Franco-American relations. Franklin was aghast that his countrymen had been seduced by "the ribbands and crosses they have seen among them, hanging to the button-holes of foreign officers." How could they have fallen for such frippery? He was of the firm conviction that distinctions were nontransferable. Settling honors on heirs was crippling to a people, "apt to make them proud, disdaining to be employed in useful arts, and thence falling into poverty, and all the meanness, servility and wretchedness attending it; which is the present case with much of what is called the *noblesse* in Europe." He had come a long way from the nation that had only one fault: that of pushing its compliments to the limit. Still, it took what he perceived to be his own country's missteps to move him to a blistering attack on his adopted one.

He returned to the Chinese example, with which he was so much taken. As such he proposed that if the Cincinnati founders were to persist in their plan, badges go to the parents of those who had served. While he was at it he blasted the laws of primogeniture, "another pest to industry and improvement of the country." He offered up mathematical evidence of the dilution of blood over nine generations, by which time one could too easily imagine what "number of rogues, and fools, and royalists and scoundrels and prostitutes" are mixed up with one's progeny, a list of which, at least on one count, he had some direct experience.* Franklin had come very far in the world but remained always a youngest son, born to a youngest son. He found moreover the manner in which America attempted to assume European airs an embarrassment. The Cincinnati's Latin inscription was inelegant and incorrect. His countrymen would have been better to content themselves with English. And the American eagle proposed for the enameled decoration more closely resembled a turkey. (He was right.) On his main point he was unwavering, and acerbic: Inherited honor was a bane to posterity. It led inevitably to "the odious mixture of pride and beggary and idleness," which he wanted kept from America.† Here was where he drew the line between the two worlds. Franklin was interested in thanking France, not in emulating her. He had as much difficulty with Washington's medal as Congress did with his numismatic labor.

At his request, the abbé Morellet dutifully translated the eleven-page document, which went back and forth between the two men throughout March. Morellet took pains to preserve Franklin's logic and what he read

---

*Again he was harping on ideas he had espoused decades earlier. Franklin first attacked the concept of hereditary nobility in Boston in 1723. In 1751 he had similarly offered up mathematical proof "that the pretension of such purity of blood in ancient families is a mere joke." He had additional reason for his blast in 1784; his anger with William would only have intensified his assault. Paradoxically, in a hereditary system a father has less control, too. He cannot so easily disavow a son.

†Not only did he oppose favoring firstborn children, but he recognized in that practice a geographical divide. "Since my being last in France," Franklin wrote a friend in July 1785, "I have seen several of our eldest sons spending idly their fortunes by residing in Europe, and neglecting their own country. These are from the southern States. The northern young men stay at home and are industrious and useful citizens, the more equal division of their father's fortune not enabling them to ramble and spend their shares abroad, which is so much the better for their country." The weight that Franklin's place in his own family bore on the argument is clear. For a 1783 visitor he recalled a discussion in the Massachusetts Assembly of the fair division of estates, a debate Franklin followed as a young clerk: "Some were for having the eldest son to have the extraordinary share; others were for giving it to the youngest son, which seemed indeed the most reasonable, as he was the most likely to want his education, which the others might probably have already had from their father."

as his sly humor, cutting the most explosive lines. Franklin's tongue was nowhere near his cheek, but he bowed to Morellet's judgment, which he trusted implicitly. At best, argued Morellet, a man generally not overeager to please, the document was disrespectful of the officers who had served in America. At worse it was subversive. The essay was likely to irritate many "you do not want to antagonize"; the European system was unlikely to appear so absurd to others as it did to him. Franklin took his point: "Your sentiments and mine, my dear friend, are exactly the same, respecting the imprudence of showing that paper; it has therefore, though written some months past, never been communicated to anyone but yourself, and will probably not appear till after my decease, if it does then."

So Franklin assured Morellet in March, flattering his friend that the translation read better than the original. All the same he was not as guarded with the essay as he professed to be. At some point over the next weeks he shared it with at least one great American admirer, Gabriel-Honoré Riquetti, comte de Mirabeau. The thirty-five-year-old former cavalry officer was the perfect candidate; at the request of his father, Mirabeau had spent most of Franklin's time in France in prison. He was also a conspicuous recruit; he was a cousin of Lafayette.* From Franklin's eleven pages emerged the comte's *Considerations on the Order of Cincinnatus*, a work for which the young aristocrat could not find a publisher, no surprise given that in elaborating on Franklin's arguments he drafted lines like: "Hence issued that swarm of counts, dukes, and marquises, which over-ran and desolated Europe." He added as well his own dose of strychnine. "A medal suspended by a ribband! Such then is the venerable monument of the greatest of revolution!" went Mirabeau's version, with which Franklin was much pleased. Repeatedly he recommended to London friends both the comte and his essay, which could not be published in France. Subject aside, Franklin's immodesty gave him away: "I find that some of the best judges think it extremely well written, with great clearness, force, and elegance." He was as audacious in his assault as he was

---

*In the preface to the text, Mirabeau boldly announced that for the first time in his literary life he was forgoing a pseudonym. Previously he had wanted neither to honor his father by lending their name to his literary pursuits nor even to be known as the marquis de Mirabeau's son. He too had reason to wish family names—like honors—incommunicable.

subtle in his methods. Reworked by Mirabeau but wholly recognizable, the essay caused a scandal on publication in Britain the following year.*

In February Cadet de Vaux demonstrated for Franklin the new oil lamps of Quinquet and Lange, which owed their revolutionary, smoke-free technology to Lavoisier. Having himself experimented with a similar contraption, Franklin responded not with a better lamp but with a modest proposal. Composed in mid-March, it was published anonymously in the April 26 *Journal de Paris*. Quinquet's lamp was all well and good, but why were the wise people of Paris relying so heavily on fuliginous, expensive light? The very morning after the Quinquet demonstration he had been startled awake at six to make a most astonishing discovery: The sun was already high in the sky at that hour. Doubtless his readers would find this as revelatory as did his friends, who had never in their lives seen a glimmer of light before noon. Franklin understood that he was up against tradition but appealed to that most reasonable of human sentiments: thrift. The man who rose with the sun could save six hours of candlelight. By Franklin's calculation, that added up to 96 million livres of tallow in six months alone. As much as anything he lunged at ostentatious consumption; his was a proposition that would have put the leisure class out of business. (To say nothing of the assault it represented on the previous generation, to which no honors ascended in this case: Franklin was a candlemaker's son.) Like so many things concerning Franklin, "An Economical Project" was different things in different countries. A satire in France, the piece earned its reform-obsessed author credit for inventing daylight saving time, one thing he did not do.†

~☙~

While John Adams had spent the better part of a year sputtering about a venal American conjurer with an approximate grasp of French, the rest of

---

*Samuel Romilly, Franklin's promising 1783 visitor, wound up as Mirabeau's translator. He found the essay's (presumed) author impossible to satisfy, no small wonder since the perfect pitch Mirabeau expected Romilly to re-create was—unknown to the translator—the English of Dr. Franklin.

†The piece was dusted off and republished in 1916 when—under wartime constraints—Franklin's wisdom seemed more apt than ever, and when daylight saving time was established in France.

Paris was transfixed by another. Unlike Franklin, this one came to Paris with sterling academic credentials. Franklin probably met Franz Anton Mesmer for the first time late in 1779, when he and Madame Brillon had called on the Viennese physician for what they assumed would be a discussion of glass armonicas. Mesmer was an accomplished musician; he promised he had amazing things to share with Franklin. The commanding young doctor with the prominent forehead and piercing eyes did not care to discuss armonicas, however. Rather he lectured his visitors on his sensational new discovery, a phenomenon he termed animal magnetism.

If Franklin performed his wizardry with newfangled Enlightenment ideals, Mesmer electrified the old-fashioned way. Having ascertained that a magnetic fluid coursed through nature, he concluded that all illness resulted either from its imbalance or from its faulty distribution. By manipulating a patient's fluids with his hands or with a special iron wand, he could restore that equilibrium, thereby alleviating any complaint, from rheumatism, gout, or asthma to blindness, epilepsy, or paralysis. (He drew the line at venereal disease.) Those miracles he accomplished in either individual or communal sessions in his apartment near Les Halles. Conveniently, the strength of Mesmer's ministrations increased when he treated a group of patients simultaneously; he arranged them cross-legged around one of the ten-foot wooden tubs, knees touching, hands linked, looped together by ropes, so as to form a sort of human electrical current. Various iron rods connected the invalids to magnetized water in the tubs. To musical accompaniment, in subdued light, and under controlled atmospheric conditions (as a rule, Mesmer never magnetized during storms), the miracle worker circulated in lilac silk gown, prodding his patients expertly with his gold wand. Soon enough the air filled with sighs, ecstatic shrieks, and hysterical laughter. Patients fell into trances, or succumbed to violent convulsions, at which point they were removed to silk-padded rooms.

Mesmer enjoyed exponentially more success with the Parisian public than with the scientific establishment, to whom Franklin's chess-playing neighbor, Le Roy, attempted to introduce him, with humiliating results. Even the acquisition of a French disciple, a handsome court physician named Charles Deslon, failed to bring Mesmer the legitimacy he craved. When he threatened to set up shop where his genius was better appreciated, the Vienna-born Marie Antoinette intervened for her countryman.

Mesmer wound up with something more valuable than the Academy's blessing: a handsome government pension. And while Franklin may have preferred his malady to the medicine, most Parisians evidently felt differently. In record number they flocked to Mesmer's door. He might just as well have discovered the fountain of youth. (To withstand the dawn-to-dusk magnetizing Mesmer took to subsisting on a potent brew of coffee, sugar, and egg yolk, of which he consumed several pots a day.) Of an evening one could meet any number of people who had been miraculously cured by magnetism. When one did not there was ample reason. Challenged to account for an unfortunate case, Deslon replied with effortless panache. The patient had indeed died, but he had died cured.

In order to address that brand of logic—and to put an end to the tales that inevitably attached themselves to practices involving communal tubs and mattress-lined rooms, presided over by foreigners—Louis XVI appointed two commissions to investigate mesmerism. The French sovereign was not eager for there to be too many new things under the sun; already the frenzy was excessive. Franklin's scientific career had played a vast role in his diplomatic one and now the equation reversed itself; in a signal honor, he was appointed in March to the royal commission. Among others that panel included Le Roy, Lavoisier, the astronomer Jean-Sylvain Bailly, and Joseph-Ignace Guillotin, the idealistic, literature-loving doctor who championed the device to which he lent his name, but Franklin's opinion carried the weight of his eight colleagues combined. No scientific commission would be complete without him. He made no secret of the fact that he doubted the existence of magnetic fluid, conceding only that mesmerism might be less dangerous than some of the quackery at loose in the world. He was equally unsurprised by its popularity. Mankind much enjoyed deceiving itself. That said, any delusion might well be useful while it lasted.

If Franklin tread softly it was in part because he understood the tenacity of superstition. Even as the appointment of the Mesmer commission made headlines, a well-informed Frenchman could be heard denouncing the lightning rod, more likely a hoax perpetuated by ironworkers than a beacon of the Enlightenment. If the conductors truly worked, should they not also be attached to carriages and hats? And if man could tame lightning, surely it stood to reason that he could also cure cancer—the kind of illogic that, in different hands, accounted for the stampede at

Mesmer's door. From northern France came the news of the celebrated case that had been winding its way through the courts since the summer of 1780, when a local inventor had erected a lightning rod on his house. His neighbors had petitioned him to dismantle the apparatus. It was certain to burn down the neighborhood; it was additionally known to cause miscarriages. The inventor refused. His lawyer argued the case of science brilliantly, sending his speeches on to Franklin. That lawyer's name was Maximilien de Robespierre. He would launch his career defending one of Franklin's principles, to make his reputation, under a slightly different name, mangling another.

Even while he marveled at the human capacity for deception, Franklin continued to bank personally on the virtues of transparency, accountability, and healthy disbelief. He was of the same school as the irreverent Morellet, who believed that all knowledge began with skepticism. (Morellet drew the line all the same at mesmerism. So great was the hysteria that he felt more comfortable keeping his doubts to himself.) That was not an analysis with which Franklin would have disagreed, as he made clear when a second commission began to coalesce that spring. In April the British indicated a new willingness to proceed with an American treaty of commerce, left unresolved at the peace. Franklin begged Henry Laurens to join him in Paris posthaste. "For Mr. Jay will probably be gone," he explained, "and I shall be left alone, or with Mr. A[dams], and I can have no favorable opinion of what may be the offspring of a coalition between my ignorance and his positiveness." Between those ills Franklin had a marked preference. He was of the school that doubted the existence of a stupid question. It was the too-ready answer that alarmed him. In that respect as well he caviled with France. Faced with a question he could not answer, an Englishman, observed Franklin, would readily admit to ignorance. "A Frenchman," he continued, "always replies as though he knows very well what you ask; but when pinned down to details and circumstances, he is frequently forced to admit that he is ignorant of the most important ones, even those which are indispensable to the giving of any kind of an answer."

Lavoisier assumed the direction of the Mesmer commission, studying the literature and devising a plan of inquiry. The distinguished chemist proposed not to focus on the alleged cures but on the existence of magnetic fluid itself, launching an inquest into the human imagination. Was it possible to pretend to magnetize someone? Could a subject be magnetized without his knowledge? (The language was not yet in place, but what Lavoisier introduced to the study of magnetism was a placebo control and a blind test.) In deference to Franklin, the commission divided its meetings between Paris and Passy; Franklin followed the sessions he could not attend in the investigators' record books. Consequently Mesmer's charismatic, blond-haired disciple headed to the Valentinois on April 15. With Deslon went seven invalids, magnetized in turn. None made a miraculous recovery, but three strongly sensed the effects of the treatment. On a subsequent visit Deslon magnetized Franklin, Madame Brillon, Temple, Benny, and an American officer (probably John Paul Jones), all of whom proved more resistant to his attentions. It remained possible that none of them was sufficiently sensitive or sick; it was equally possible that public treatments tended to exacerbate the effects of magnetism. On a brilliant May Saturday Deslon rode out to Passy to prove how powerful mesmerism could be on a suitable subject. With him went a twelve-year-old boy, said to have been partially paralyzed before submitting to magnetism.

As Mesmer had asserted that trees could be as effective as communal tubs, the commissioners escorted Deslon to Franklin's garden, to survey the options. The patient remained under observation indoors. Deslon settled on an isolated apricot, over which he passed his wand several times. The blindfolded boy was afterward led to various trees in the Valentinois orchard, each of which he embraced for several minutes. Deslon remained at a distance, from which he continued to focus his attention on and wave his wand at the magnetized apricot. At the first tree the young man began to sweat profusely, cough, and foam at the mouth. At the second he complained of dizziness. By the third he announced he was nearing the affected tree, as his symptoms increased dramatically. At the fourth he fainted dead away. He was laid out gently on the lawn, where he suffered a dramatic series of limb-stiffening spasms. Unfortunately he did so before the wrong tree—and twenty-four feet from the apricot. Deslon wrote the results down to natural magnetism, inherent in all nature, and a force that surged in his presence; the commissioners pointed out that that phenomenon should render it impossible for any sensitive soul ever to walk in a garden without experiencing violent convulsions.

Several weeks later the astronomer Bailly headed out to Passy to help

Franklin prepare for another round of examinations. At noon the remaining six commissioners reassembled with Deslon, who arrived with a group of poor patients; it had been noted that the less educated the subject, the more susceptible to magnetism. While Deslon attempted to magnetize Franklin, a woman was taken aside, blindfolded, and treated by a commissioner, impersonating Deslon. He managed to reduce her to a violent crisis in three minutes. In an adjoining room, two of his colleagues worked the same effect on a patient who believed that Deslon was magnetizing through the wall. So great were her convulsions that she left teeth marks on her hand. In another demonstration, a blindfolded laundress who had previously succumbed instantly to Deslon's ministrations proved impervious to his powers when treated, for thirty minutes, without her knowledge. Without yielding in his claims, Deslon largely admitted that imagination played a great role in the wonders of magnetism. The new agent might well exist only in the human mind, but its power was obviously greater than had ever been known. And if the imagination was the best therapy, argued Deslon that June afternoon, why not practice imaginary medicine?*

The failure of the demonstrations brought Lafayette to the door. His thirst for novelty appeared to know no bounds; from the start the suspiciously hale war hero was a Mesmer convert. Surely Franklin should observe Mesmer, the true master, and not the disciple? Mesmer had not been so much a fool as to impart all his secrets to his student, warned Lafayette, who had himself but dimly understood the American cause when first he fell under its spell. It behooved the commissioners to apply directly to Mesmer. (Their orders were to examine Deslon.) Lafayette made little headway and was unable to intercede further on science's behalf, as he sailed that summer for America. He did so with Mesmer's special cure for seasickness (embrace the mast), and burning to introduce his "grand philosophical discovery" to the New World. He vowed to proselytize for the master, an effort Jefferson blocked.

At the end of the summer a report circulated in a locked box among

---

*Franklin himself had toyed years earlier with electrotherapy, to conclude that (with one remarkable exception) the minimal results were psychosomatic. The effective component of his treatments had been the exercise his patients got in their daily trips to his house, and their hopes of success.

the commissioners, for their signatures. Although Franklin's name appeared first, the text was most likely Lavoisier's. The panel could find no truth in Mesmer's science, unanimously dismissed as quackery. As to whether the discipline was useful, it surely had something to contribute to the study of the human imagination. Hope was a powerful remedy. At the same time the practice's dangers appeared to outweigh its occasional benefits. Separately and for the sake of public decency, the commissioners drafted a secret article, intended for the king's eyes only. Already the panel had observed that women were more receptive to magnetism than men; female nerves and imaginations being what they were, the placement of a vulnerable patient in intimate contact with a man charged, behind closed doors, with inflaming her senses, who palpated her legs and her thighs, while staring into her eyes, his breath intermingling with hers, was a source of some concern. The commissioners' gentle implication was that what passed in Mesmer's rooms for convulsion—lowered eyelids, a complete disordering of the senses, heavy breathing, tensed limbs, violent tremors followed by lassitude—was orgasm. The possibility for abuse was great. That article went unpublished for fifteen years.*

The official report was much praised for its impartial, moderate tone; the talk of Paris, it sold in record numbers, and in pirated editions. Delighted, Franklin forwarded a copy to the Royal Society in London. He brushed off any concerns the inquiry might raise for religion. It was unlikely to undermine the Bible or weaken human faith in miracles. "Some think it will put an end to mesmerism. But there is a wonderful deal of credulity in the world, and deceptions as absurd have supported themselves for ages," he added, well aware that skepticism was a harder sell than the supernatural. While all of Paris applauded the report, the unflappable Mesmer conceived a series of experiments on horses, to prove that the force of the human imagination had no bearing on his practice. His popularity continued unabated. The exercise of reason—and well-planned inquiry—could not eradicate superstition. That spring sensible and influential men took Franklin to task for having signed the ill-advised Mesmer report. It was a shame that in pronouncing on the Austrian wizard the American one had sided with the Establishment.

---

*Some would draw a straight line from the attachment the commissioners identified in their secret article to what a later Viennese physician was to term transference.

Even Franklin would be surprised at the persistence of delusion, a more lucrative business than he had imagined. And he failed as well to grasp that a certain floodgate had opened. He made no note of a sensational play being performed in the heart of Paris, in which another assault was made on hereditary privilege, one as fierce as his Cincinnati piece. The theatrical sensation of 1784 was Beaumarchais's *The Marriage of Figaro*; Franklin owned a copy of the play but was among the few in the capital not to have seen it performed.* In his rousing last-act monologue, Figaro daily brought down the house when he reminded his employer that the count had done nothing to merit his advantages in life aside from having taken the trouble to be born. Beaumarchais's was a triumph of insolence rather than ignorance over the established order; he had found it more difficult to have the play staged than to coax millions of livres of munitions covertly across the Atlantic Ocean. A campaign of several years preceded the play's April debut. Earlier Louis XVI had fumed that the Bastille would have to be pulled down before *Figaro* was performed in public. He was mistaken only in his chronology.

And Franklin—who understood so well the power of charisma—had to look no further than his own household for evidence of Mesmer's. The enterprising physician formed a secret society along Masonic lines, with a limited membership, a prohibitive initiation fee, and branches all over France. It may have been a greater stroke of genius even than his brilliantly staged treatments, essentially a forerunner of hypnotism. The society's membership list was studded with familiar, America-loving names. Cabanis was 9th on the list, Lafayette 91st. The 103rd subscriber was Temple Franklin. To his grandfather Temple implied that he joined more out of fashion than out of conviction, or at least did after the royal commission weighed in.

❧

Midsummer found both Franklin and Adams of the mind that Congress had succumbed to a mesmerist trance of its own. The commissioners— one in Paris, the other in The Hague, each tending to convalescing Ameri-

---

*The Adamses (as well as their servants) attended. "It is from beginning to end a piece of studied deception and intrigue," concluded nineteen-year-old Nabby Adams, less than admiringly, but quite accurately.

can credit—had heard nothing since the peace. The Danish and Portuguese ambassadors had been waiting patiently for word on commercial treaties; Franklin was mortified to have no answers for them. Adams could not remember when he had last had a letter from Congress. He suggested that they renounce politics altogether and devote themselves to something more fashionable, perhaps "a course of experiments in physics and mechanics, of telescopical or microscopical observations."* Franklin's impatience divided between that with the English, who seemed so ambivalent about a commercial treaty, and that with Congress, who seemed generally so negligent. He had calculated that it would take him a year to organize America's diplomatic position in the world; the year had now passed, fruitlessly. There was every reason why he should resolve at the end of July that individuals managed their affairs more intelligently than did assemblies of men. Judging by the edicts passed to regulate commerce alone, Franklin stood ready to conclude that "an assembly of wise men is the greatest fool upon earth."

Late in June he again picked up the private journal he kept sporadically; at some point in the year he added a short section to what was to become his *Autobiography*, drafting the pages on the founding of the Philadelphia library and the section on moral perfection, which he considered the kernel of the book. Daily he fielded visits from the representatives of every nation on earth. "It is amazing," Franklin noted, having seen one visitor off on a summer Sunday, "the number of legislators that kindly bring me new plans for governing the United States." He attempted to alleviate the misery of two young Americans who aspired to become Episcopalian ministers. Already they had waited a year for a decision from London, where it was established that they could not be ordained as they refused to pledge their allegiance to the crown. The man who had in 1773 revised the Book of Common Prayer was not so easily daunted by orthodoxy; impishly Franklin inquired if the pope might lend a hand. Surely he knew full well

---

*That was no great stretch for Franklin, out of bed at the crack of dawn on July 12 so as to accompany his grandsons the few miles west to Saint-Cloud. There the duc de Chartres, the king's cousin and an eminent Mason, readied a cylindrical airship, complete with oars and a rudder, to be lifted by two enormous hydrogen-filled globes. The Franklins arrived to discover that the ascension would be postponed for several days; they returned to the Valentinois for breakfast, after which they launched a miniature hydrogen balloon of their own, which traveled over the house.

that the answer would be that "the thing is impossible, unless the gentlemen become Catholics," as indeed it was. Ultimately he suggested what had already become clear to some: Why the Church of England? Surely in a century's time, "when people are more enlightened, it will be wondered at that men in America, qualified by their learning and piety to pray for and instruct their neighbors, should not be permitted to do it till they had made a voyage of 6000 miles going out and home, to ask leave of a cross old gentleman at Canterbury." Under the circumstances it was also easy to see why the papal nuncio looked forward to the day when America's representative in France might be a Catholic. Their present representative was at best a heretic, at worst a Presbyterian.*

Late in July Franklin learned that Thomas Jefferson was en route to Paris but remained in suspense as to what that arrival meant for him. His hopes for a recall were dashed days before his new colleague materialized, when Congress delivered a bruising one-two punch. "You will see," Franklin warned Adams, with whom he shared their new instructions, "that a good deal of business is cut out for us, treaties to be made with I think 20 powers, in two years, so that we are not likely to eat the bread of idleness; and that we may not surfeit by eating too much, our masters have diminished our allowance." Personally he had no problem with a curtailed budget, which tallied with his conviction that, in public office, the less the salary the greater the honor.† He left it to his colleagues to rule on Congress's financial acumen, which they did with gusto. He suffered from a different malaise, the symptoms of which he described on August 6: "The readers of Connecticut newspapers ought not to be troubled with any more accounts of our extravagance. For my own part, if I could sit down to dinner on a piece of their excellent salt pork and pump-

---

*Generally, Franklin's allergy was to dogma rather than to sect. On occasion however he revealed a glimmer of a bias, at least when it came to proselytizing: "Our ancestors from Catholics became first Church-of-England-men, and then refined into Presbyterians. To change now from Presbyterianism to Popery seems to me refining backwards, from white sugar to brown."

†So he explained repeatedly to visitors, adding, "Persons will play at chess, by the hour, without being paid for it; this you may see in every coffee-house in Paris. Deciding causes is in fact only a matter of amusement to sensible men." He changed his tune a year later. Could it really be possible, he inquired of Barclay, the consul, that the congressional cutback applied to him? It was impracticable to cut his expenses by a fifth.

kin, I would not give a farthing for all the luxuries of Paris." It was obvious by that Friday that he was also past the point of a 1784 return.

That afternoon Jefferson rode into Paris, in an American-made phaeton. The red hair had faded to a coppery gray, but the forty-one-year-old remained a red-cheeked, long-legged study in taut lines and chiseled features. The French were as quick to respond to Jefferson's physical presence as was he to the beauty of Paris, a mutual attraction that went a great way toward obliterating a language barrier.* For guidance Jefferson relied from his first hours on Temple, to whom he deferred on all details. The Franklins hung no less on what Jefferson had to say. He was appointed minister plenipotentiary to negotiate the clutch of trade agreements, which was to say that he was in Paris to join, not replace, Franklin. He had word regarding Temple, too. Congress had appointed David Humphreys, a thirty-two-year-old Connecticut native and former member of Washington's staff, as secretary of the new commission. (A tortured explanation from Washington would follow.) Jefferson confessed himself surprised by the decision; Temple was disappointed. Franklin was livid. He had asked precisely one favor, to which Congress had not deigned to reply, save, finally, to circumvent his request. Humphreys had fine military credentials but—as Franklin pointed out much later, the wound still raw—"certainly had none in the diplomatic line, and had neither the French language, nor the experience, nor the address proper to qualify him for such an employment."

Temple came away from the announcement with the sense that a visit to America "to make myself a little known there" might be well advised, an idea that would seem to indicate that Jefferson had been sparing with his explanations. The animus against Temple had nothing to do with the twenty-four-year-old himself. Nor was it bound up either with his father's dishonor or his grandfather's honor. As one of Adams's fire-breathing friends explained, the fear was that Temple would undermine John Adams, where another man would not. That colleague—it was Massachusetts's Elbridge Gerry, who continued in the divisive vein worthy

---

*Even after five years abroad Jefferson was never certain he understood what was said to him in French, or that a Frenchman found his replies intelligible. He doubted that his written French conveyed his original meaning, or any meaning at all.

of a man whose gift to posterity would be the word *gerrymandering*—snorted that Dr. Franklin was unlikely this time to mistake Congress's message. He was not in that assembly's good graces. "Indeed," continued Gerry, "we have not been reserved in Congress with respect to the Doctor, having declared, in so many words, that so far advanced in years and so tractable is he, as that it has become a matter of indifference to us whether we employ him or the c[oun]t de V[ergenne]s to negotiate our concerns at the c[our]t of V[ersaille]s."

Gerry neglected to cite an odd 1784 law of congressional physics. The Lees were reluctant to allow Adams's release for fear of leaving Franklin unsupervised. Franklin's supporters refused to permit Franklin to be recalled unless Adams was as well. The two were held hostage to their own differences, a perfectly appropriate punishment, but one that was to survive the most virulent days of the relationship. Even before Jefferson's appearance the two were on comfortable terms and best behavior, a little too much so. Noting that Franklin had been "lately more than commonly smooth and gracious," Adams was on guard. What was he up to? Confronted by the same phenomenon Franklin entertained the opposite possibility: Perhaps Adams liked him just a little? Adams might still emit the occasional shriek—his colleague had "done mischief enough"; he was insolent, and it was time he went home—but generally those cries were followed by a muffled whimper, then silence. It was something of a measure of Franklin's infirmity that by midyear Adams had entirely mellowed on his account. There were to be no more diatribes.

He was tamer still for the August arrival of Abigail Adams and their children. A happier man, Adams was a more agreeable colleague. Setting up house with his family put a number of issues in perspective as well. On August 17 the family moved into a handsome white stone mansion with a magnificent, five-acre garden, an estate that Adams judged "adequate to his station." (It was also a home so large that after three weeks Mrs. Adams had yet to set foot in every room. There were fifty.) From that Auteuil address it was more difficult to condemn the extravagance of Franklin's shabbier quarters a mile up the hill.* And Mrs. Adams impressed on her husband the extraordinary expense of life abroad, beyond

---

*Adams took the opposite tack. Always competitive, he found the three-story Auteuil house more luxurious than Franklin's lodgings. He boasted that the rent was lower too, which was untrue.

the wildest imaginings of a woman who had until that time barely ventured beyond Braintree, Massachusetts. It was her understanding that Jay had gone home because he could not support his family on his salary— and she was now to make do on less. With Yankee ingenuity she managed to bribe her maître d'hôtel to serve also as footman, but even with eight in staff it was difficult to get by. "With less we should be hooted at as ridiculous, and could not entertain any company," she sighed. Already their paltry salaries made them appear poorer than common merchants or housekeepers, lower even than "the genteel girls of the town," groused Adams. The discomfort weighed more heavily in Auteuil than it did in Passy, where personal prestige compensated for the absence of liveried ranks. Abigail Adams and Franklin saw eye to eye on a related issue, however. Given the fact that the cook refused to scrub a dish, or the charwoman to make a bed, Mrs. Adams estimated that her staff was idle two-thirds of the time. When precisely the French worked remained a mystery to her.

The Paris appointment of Franklin, Jefferson, and Adams—a reunion of three of the patriots who had drawn up the Declaration of Independence, eight years after the fact—has been hailed as the most brilliant collection of intellectual power in the history of American diplomacy. Certainly Congress congratulated itself on its wisdom. "At length our foreign affairs are put upon as excellent an establishment as we could desire," Virginia's James Monroe rejoiced, noting that, in addition to their combined intellectual weight and moral eminence, the public servants in Paris perfectly represented the three different regions of the country. It was indeed an extraordinary array of talent, but an underutilized one as well. On August 30 the envoys assembled in Passy to review their instructions, line by line. They determined to meet daily thereafter, until discussions were on a firm footing; the following morning they resolved to notify Vergennes of their objectives and to nudge the British. So they did, but treaties of commerce were to prove another chimera of 1784. The Americans were up against entrenched habits on the one side, massive ignorance on their own. Congress was sanguine about the possibilities of negotiating with some two dozen nations, few of whom were disposed to negotiate with it. Essentially what the envoys had to offer was a continuation of the Revolution in the commercial realm; they proposed to drive a stake in the heart of the old imperial system of exclusive trade privileges.

It came as a shock to that assembly that no one—at least no one with colonies of her own—was interested. The bulk of the American overtures went nowhere. The Venetian ambassador transmitted a draft treaty to the doge early in January; a year passed before anyone so much as acknowledged it, after which it was never mentioned again. Only after all three envoys had left Paris would a treaty be completed with England. America and Spain signed their agreement in 1795.

It was not so easy to build the world anew; America might well be independent, but she commanded little respect. Her own financial mismanagement was in part to blame, as Franklin never tired of pointing out on one side of the ocean, Alexander Hamilton on the other. Partly Europe could not take seriously a government that combined thirteen far-flung states that demonstrated little taste for central authority and less desire to act collectively. From the New World came frequent hints of disarray and dissolution; even the diligent Bancroft, who crossed the ocean in 1783, reported back on the republic's pains. And partly the new nation was the victim of a very excitable, very effective British press, which fattened itself on tales of American anarchy. That hatred continued to pollute the Continent. Nearly a year into his stay Jefferson had to concede that he had not "been able to discover the smallest token of respect towards the United States in any part of Europe." There was but one exception to the rule. Jefferson exulted that there was "more respect and veneration attached to the character of Dr. Franklin in France than to that of any other person in the same country, foreign or native."

The commissioners met Europe's disregard with odes to self-reliance. Jefferson concluded that sagging credit abroad would curb America's "disposition to luxury" and encourage his countrymen to look to Congress for leadership. For all his own very legitimate dissatisfaction with Congress, Franklin was delighted as well. He had hoped from the start to compromise neither American industry nor ingenuity; he had long placed a federal authority above those of individual states. It was an unpopular stand, to which were due many of the accusations of scheming and monopolizing. Just as he had failed to endear himself with the state representatives who had come to France to solicit wartime aid, he chased off a new breed of beggars. In turn Dartmouth, Dickinson, Princeton, Columbia came calling for European funds. Franklin shuddered at their appeals. Massively in debt as she was to Europe, America should think only of bolstering her credit. She could provide for herself; it was imperative she let Europe know as much. As for Congress, Franklin was a fount of loyalty. When a British friend cracked a joke about that assembly's wanderings—in the previous three years it had had four addresses—Franklin conceded he had a point. But it should be remembered that that body could not be dissolved by the whim of a minister. Nor should it be forgotten that a Virginia planter who had never set eyes on Europe had chased away five of the best generals Britain had to offer.

What Jefferson had to report was disheartening, but his presence was a tonic, and a well-timed one. In September Franklin had made the mistake of believing he was well enough for a carriage ride to Auteuil, only to reconsider hours afterward. He had better luck a few days later, when he and Benny walked that mile to join the newly installed Adamses, with whom, Franklin was quick to note, he got on swimmingly. "I wish this calm may continue and believe it will," Adams too remarked, in a letter that—the two men had different ideas of détente—included a swipe at Franklin. With Jefferson there was no such ambivalence. For the first time Franklin had a colleague who respected him completely, who shared his intellectual preoccupations, and who—despite a greater age and socio-economic gap than the one that divided Adams and Franklin—saw foreign affairs similarly. As were most men, Jefferson was more judgmental than Franklin, but he confined his displeasure to the French weather (insufferable), the French government (abominable), French morals (pestilent), and French poverty (unspeakable), before falling, as soon as the sun came out, head over heels in love with Paris.

It fell to Jefferson to illuminate Franklin on the two matters closest to his heart. His recall was nowhere on the table. Franklin began to despair he would ever obtain one. The requests for a discharge only brought new commissions, which he met with none of the puffed-out satisfaction of 1779. He let it be known that he had served his purpose in France. Any number of men could replace him. And surely two representatives were as good as three, the more so given the state of their affairs. The new ones made little progress, and the old ones "seem now to be rather going backward." That he himself could not budge from Paris was dismal enough; at some point early in the fall he shared his disappointment over Temple's fate with Jefferson, who urged him not to mention the matter again to Congress. That discussion presumably followed an August report from the assembly's secretary, Charles Thomson. Thomson had no doubt that Temple was a most admirable young man. That said, it would be wise for his grandfather to make other plans for him, plans that did not involve Congress.

The blow was fierce enough to provoke another unsent letter, the humblest Franklin ever wrote. Nowhere did he sound so contrite. With recourse to two most un-Franklinian words he chastised himself for having appealed to Congress on a personal matter: "I am sorry and ashamed that I asked any favor of C[ongress] for him." He had been too long abroad; he had yielded to the mores of France, where the patronage system ruled. (He deplored that system. Nothing could be done in France without resort to it, cried Franklin, who had worked its every angle to America's advantage for seven years.) "It was the first time I ever asked promotion for myself or any of my family," he swore, mangling the truth, and adding, inaccurately, that it would be the last. For a man who had so passionately denounced hereditary privilege his was doubtless an uncomfortable confession. The regret colored Benny's future: "I had thoughts of bringing him up under his cousin, and fitting him for public business," Franklin explained to the fourteen-year-old's parents, "thinking he might be of service hereafter to his country. But being now convinced that 'Service is no inheritance,' as the proverb says, I have determined to give him a trade that he may have something to depend on, and not be obliged to ask favors or offices of anybody." He could not however have been unaware of the plea Jefferson composed the same day. "Can nothing be done for young Franklin?" Jefferson implored Monroe. Not only was Temple "sensible, discreet, polite, and good-humored," he was as qualified as anyone could be. His grandfather had no official secretary. Lest there be any mistake, Jefferson added of his colleague: "He is most sensibly wounded at his grandson's being superseded."

That was nowhere so clear as in Franklin's unsent letter, in which figured his single most pained protest against ingratitude. "I flattered myself vainly that the Congress would be pleased with the opportunity I gave them of showing that mark of their approbation of my services. But I suppose the present members hardly know me or that I have performed any," he lamented. He could do the math; he had been away from America for most of those colleagues' lifetimes. In the fall he referred to himself for the first time as being "an exile."

That with Congress was not to be Franklin's most bruising brush with ingratitude. Late in the summer he received a letter from London that could not have been entirely unexpected. Its tone may have been. With peace at hand, fifty-four-year-old William Franklin hoped that his father might care "to revive that affectionate intercourse" that William valued above all else. Franklin's former best friend, his aide in matters military, mercantile, and Masonic, William was conciliatory but unrepentant. The words "sorry" and "ashamed" were nowhere in sight. The former royal governor went further still. Mistaken though his conduct may have been, he pronounced himself happy to have "uniformly acted from a strong sense of what I conceived my duty to my king," a line that would have obliterated any goodwill that preceded it. Were it all to happen again tomorrow he would act no differently. He flattered himself that his father might like to reconcile, as he had evidently done with others. Would he approve of William making the trip to Paris? There was much to discuss.

Already Franklin seemed to have resigned himself to the fact that parenting was an inexact science.* He had made clear that he had come to replace William with Temple, to whom he reflexively referred, much of Paris following him, as his son. The exchange made the congressional rebuff all the more painful. In large part William had been thrown the New Jersey governorship in the hopes that it might quiet his rebellious father. Franklin was unable to obtain from a republican government the kind of favor for his grandson that he had managed to obtain from a monarchy for his son. There was all the more reason that he should abhor the patronage system he now decried. It had cost him a child.

His was hardly the only family torn apart by the war—of the five American peace commissioners, all but Adams had Loyalist relatives— but his situation was beset by its own cluster of ironies. William Franklin was a moderate man, sympathetic to early colonial grievances. He was

---

*As he put it later: "When we launch our little fleet of barks into the ocean, bound to different ports, we hope for each a prosperous voyage; but contrary winds, hidden shoals, storms, and enemies come in for a share in the disposition of events; and though these occasion a mixture of disappointment, yet, considering the risk where we can make no insurance, we should think ourselves happy if some return with success."

also a forgiving man, one who expressed no anger at his father for having stolen off with his child. In the contest between loyalty to his father and loyalty to the crown, his own interests lay more closely with the former. No favorite among the royal governors, William was one of the worst paid; in New Jersey he had dipped deeply into his own (which was to say his father's) funds. He was also understandably eager to be judged on his own merits, which could never have been easy. He was forever stepping into posts that his father had recently vacated. And he did not take well to being forced into a corner, less so by a man who considered himself the soul of affability. It was his father who, after the Boston Tea Party, lobbed at William an insult that William found excruciating: "But you who are a thorough courtier, see every thing with government eyes." It was his father who took him to task for his aristocratic pretensions. Faced with a heart-wrenching decision, William came down finally on the side of what he believed was the legitimate government. Having already paid for one of his father's missteps he was doubtless reluctant to be complicit in another. He appears to have acted from personal rather than political reasons. He wanted to forge his own way in the world, a phenomenon not unknown in the Franklin family. William's vote for independence simply took him in a different direction. His rebellion against authority made of him a Loyalist.

Franklin waited a week before replying, and did so in as unsatisfying a manner as his son had addressed him. He too would delight in a restored relationship, especially as William's apostasy had caused him infinite pain. It caused him something else as well: "Indeed nothing has ever hurt me so much and affected me with such keen sensations, as to find myself deserted in my old age by my only son; and not only deserted, but to find him taking up arms against me, in a cause wherein my good name, fortune and life were all at stake." He could not begrudge William his political convictions. Those were his prerogative. Franklin was not the first father to sire a child of a violently different political stripe. Nor did he intend to be the first to let his son walk off easily without feeling the full weight of his wrath. Having introduced guilt and shame into the picture, Franklin added disgrace. Underscoring his words, he reminded William that "*there are natural duties which precede political ones, and cannot be extinguished by them.*" (It was a rich statement for a man who had put his service to his country before his wife's illness, death, or funeral—which he had left William to manage—and before both of his children's weddings.) Sounding like nothing so much as the France that had reminded her delinquent ally that great powers never complained but felt and remembered, he proposed to drop the matter. It made for a painful subject.*

He also rebuffed William's suggestion of a visit. Franklin may have been unwilling to engage with his own anger; he may have feared indulging his detractors with a reunion. (There were still those who accused father and son of having taken opposite sides on purpose.) His own fury on the subject burned brightly still. He believed as staunchly as ever that America owed the Loyalists nothing. So far as he was concerned, they were misnamed, better termed Royalists. "The true *loyalists* were the people of America against whom they acted," he huffed. He had one concession to offer, however. He was sending Temple to England. (Although he did so at Temple's insistence, he announced that he was sending William's son over "to pay his duty.") Of course William would see to it that the young man not consort with any improper company. And Franklin having determined that Temple was to study law, William was to provide his son with the texts Franklin indicated. As if to drive home his point, Franklin added that he was in France "among a people who love and respect me." He could get from that nation what his own son alone in the world begrudged him.

Temple was packed and ready to leave for London before his grandfather was prepared to let him go. Resorting to a trick he knew from his early years, Franklin delayed the departure by insisting Temple wait for his letters. With that bundle of correspondence and a commission for new ice skates for Benny, Temple rode off on August 23. He did so supplied with addresses of the best hatters and boot makers and taverns in London, as with other essentials as well: "And when lewd," one friend counseled, "go to the two following safe girls who I think are very handsome." Those visits, if ever they were made, had to wait; Temple spent his first London week sick in bed, tenderly nursed by his father and his father's

---

*Intentionally or not, his words were an echo of his son's. Franklin's actual 1784 line was, "This is a disagreeable subject. I drop it." A wounded William had replied to his father's barb about his being a "courtier" on Christmas Eve 1774. Writing of the politics that were about to divide them he concluded: "However it [is] a disagreeable subject, and I'll drop it." It was not unlike Franklin to recall as much, especially under the circumstances.

landlady. Which led him to pose the inevitable question, seven days into his visit: Might he extend his stay? Permission was granted on the condition that Temple write religiously. He was unable to do so, given a most exacting social schedule; it seemed that all of his grandfather's friends wanted him for their own. In Passy Franklin awaited each mail with impatience, to be regularly disappointed. He was humiliated to have nothing to tell Temple's legion of well-wishers, or so he claimed; he may have heard the silence as something more ominous. He was distinctly on edge. After three weeks that he counted as a month he played the guilt card. "Judge what I must feel, what they must think, and tell me what I am to think of such neglect," he chastised. By the time he did so Temple had already apologized for his silence—and begun angling to stay in London until mid-November. Again Franklin agreed, but only until mid-October, and again attaching a condition to his consent. Temple was to make the trip to Hampshire, to see the Shipleys, early advocates of American independence. It had been at their country home that Franklin began his *Autobiography* in 1771; it was the learned Jonathan Shipley's letters that Franklin read and reread, when loneliness struck in Passy.

Temple agreed to the assignment but persisted in a little tug-of-war. As the Shipley visit would require extra time, he would plan to return to Paris early in November, a date that was soon to slip again. How could his grandfather begrudge his accompanying the beloved Shipley to court, where a family case was to be heard on November 8? He was aware of having tried his grandfather's patience but able to report too that his dilatoriness had borne unexpected benefits. Franklin had had reasons of his own to send Temple to London: His proxy was to judge what kind of reception Franklin himself might meet there. On his behalf Temple was dispatched on every kind of errand, from the printers whose font casting his grandfather hoped to introduce in France to the manufacturers of the roof tiles he hoped to introduce in America. If possible Temple was also to escort the Hewsons back to Paris. Polly began at once to prepare for the trip but then lost her nerve, of which cowardice she made light. "To have such a young man ready to run off with one, and yet to stay behind, argues great virtue or great stupidity," she laughed. At forty-five she felt prudence became her, however. Temple's extended stay allowed her a second chance to change her mind; the party assembled in Dover at the end of November, to arrive in Passy on December 2. Franklin's delight in receiving Polly—jovial, well read, unaffected, and at ease before a chessboard—was not immediately matched by Benny, who noted coolly that his cousin had returned "with a lady and three children, who have come to spend the winter with my grandfather." (It may not have helped that Polly's eldest son was Franklin's godson, his younger brother a frighteningly precocious eleven-year-old, and their sister Benny's childhood fiancée.) Benny was less accustomed to makeshift family than was his grandfather. Franklin found the winter of 1784 the shortest he had ever known.

It was a very practical salvage operation; Franklin had lost one child but gained another. The substitution was more appropriate than probably even he acknowledged. Decades earlier he had encouraged William to marry the nimble-minded if awkward-looking Polly. On that front too William had defied him. Disappointed, Franklin made no effort to attend William's wedding to the wife he chose for himself, the wealthy daughter of a Barbados planter. (By contrast Franklin was on hand to walk Polly down the aisle at hers.) In early 1785 Franklin's intransigence would deprive him of another honor. Ballooning had finally made its way to England, where William's friend Dr. John Jeffries proposed to cross the Channel. "I dare say," wrote William to his Passy-based son excitedly, after midnight on December 16, "you will like to be one of the first who gets a letter across the British Channel by this means of aerial conveyance." He appears to have thought better of writing his father. The distinction of having received history's first airmail letter therefore fell not to America's first postmaster general but to Temple. Franklin would remember differently.

༺ ༻

With a French associate, Jeffries crossed the Channel in under three hours on January 7, a feat he recounted in detail a week later at Franklin's table, the new toast of the town cordially received by its most celebrated man of science. (The embrace crossed political lines as well. The unprepossessing Jeffries was a Boston-born Loyalist.) Franklin's guests were spellbound before the aeronaut's account of the near-catastrophic flight. With Calais in sight, the balloon had plunged four thousand feet in a matter of minutes. The fliers scurried to jettison all they could; the airship's damask curtains and garlands went first, followed by the provisions and brandy, the books, and most of the men's clothing. At one point a mere sixty feet separated them from the water. By the time they came safely to rest in the Calais tree from which they were carried a half hour later in triumph, the fliers were in their shirtsleeves.

For the next weeks Jeffries made his way about Paris on the arm of Temple, who took a helpful interest in his practical affairs. Franklin focused instead on Jeffries's feat. The relative ease with which the Massachusetts native had wafted across the English Channel must have been almost painful to listen to; equally so would have been Pilâtre's proposal for a Calais-to-Boston flight, a crossing the former chemistry professor boasted he could make in forty-eight hours. Franklin heard of those projects at a time when he strained piteously against his moorings. Nor was he envisioning a mere jaunt to Paris. The Adamses were all of them astounded that a man in his condition could remain so determined to return to America. He could neither walk nor ride in a carriage, and yet he continued to insist that the motion of a boat would not be painful to him. Many had trouble believing he could travel as far as London.

His health had unquestionably disintegrated, and with it his effectiveness. Increasingly he was prone to painful and urgent voiding of the bladder; he could feel the weight of the stone as he turned in bed; he was listless. He was truly comfortable only when prone, and even then found that the pain interfered with his train of thought. It was at times intolerable. He began to experiment with remedies, and was soon to apply to the experts for relief. Did any chemical exist that might dissolve the deposit? How could he minimize his discomfort? (Five of the most eminent medical minds in Great Britain could do no more for the patient than he had already done for himself.) He had of course a second set of chains still to slip. Adams visited with his broken-down colleague on January 30, when Franklin was suffering from a violent stomach virus. His colleague came away that afternoon convinced that "Dr. F[ranklin] is at present too much an object of compassion to be one of resentment." He might this time even be sincere in his request to resign, "for a voyage seems to be the only chance he has for his life. He can now neither walk nor ride, unless in a litter, but he is strong and eats freely, so that he will soon have other complaints besides the stone if he continues to live as entirely without exercise as he does at present." Adams was pleased to find his colleague humbled, and consequently on best behavior.

Privately Franklin complained that his age was showing. His originality had always been less impressive than his memory, which he felt began to fail him, one observation no one else shared. He was as charming and curious as ever, if more easily exhausted by the ceaseless visits. No matter who the caller, he remained eager, in his heteroclite French, to steer the conversation to America. He entertained regularly, hosting large dinners at which the Adamses, the Lafayettes, and John Paul Jones were the mainstays. On the page he remained lucid and logical, if not infallible; he theorized that Frenchwomen were flat chested because they did not breast-feed their children. He undertook a study of the penal code; he expounded—to Cadet de Vaux, who would publish the piece— on the uses of corn. (Those he had ample reason to advertise; America was well equipped to export that grain to France.) He discoursed with color on the force and the fecundity of the new nation, especially when it came to the navigation of the Mississippi, a right the Spaniards resisted. Franklin warned that the robust American economy could not be contained: "If you put up dams, it will break through them; it will come crashing through sooner or later with a thunderous noise." He remained faithful to his first principles. The residents of a new town in eastern Massachusetts had named itself after him. They proposed to build a steeple on their meetinghouse if he would donate a bell. Eight years in France had left few marks; Franklin advised that they spare themselves the expense and accept "books instead of a bell, sense being preferable to sound."

At the end of April 1785 the Hewsons reluctantly took their leave, a tearful parting that Franklin trusted was provisional. He leaned on Polly to rejoin him in America. In her family's absence the household felt quiet, more so than he could bear. He missed the "cheerful prattle" and—Temple sick, Benny lodging in Paris with Le Roy, so as to be near the printshop on the rue Jacob—felt lonelier than ever. "I have found it very *triste* breakfasting alone, and sitting alone, and without any tea in the evening," he admitted, although by the time he did so he also knew that relief was in sight. On April 26 Adams learned that he was appointed to represent

America at the court of Saint James's.* With that news came unofficial word that Franklin's recall was to be accepted. He dropped a first hint that he might be headed somewhere into a letter to Cadet de Vaux, who had delivered his newest corn confection. Much impressed, Franklin promised to take a quantity of the biscuits to sea. The happy news sent him back to his desk, where over the course of the next days he composed and illustrated a colossal letter to the Dutch scientist and physician Jan Ingenhousz, the kind of missive that could have issued only from Franklin's pen. A manic tying-up of loose ends, the letter veered from (inadvertently administered) electric shocks to uncollected debts to three-wheeled clocks to the effect of the equinox on gravity to infectious disease to America's embrace of free trade to mesmerism. He was still adding to it on Monday, May 2, when he received the authorization to return to America as soon as was convenient. The pen practically skips across the page: "Rejoice with me, my dear friend, that I am once more a free man; after fifty years in public affairs."†

He lost no time in setting the wheels in motion for a June departure. Immediately he tried outfitting a carriage with a mattress, only to find the jolting unbearable. Once again his grandnephew was enlisted to find a vessel, although there was this time none of the faux diffidence with which Franklin had left America in 1776: "I shall need the most comfortable accommodation the ship can afford, being so old and infirm, and I expect to pay accordingly." He did not believe he could survive a trip like the one that had delivered him to France. He was indifferent as to whether he sailed to Boston or Philadelphia, although Temple was not.‡ Within a matter of days Benny had disassembled and crated a printing press;

---

*His reputation preceded him. On being presented for the first time to George III, Adams was taken aback when His Majesty remarked, familiarly, almost laughingly, on the new ambassador's distaste for France. Adams was superb: "I must avow to your Majesty," he replied, "I have no attachment but to my own country." To which George III rejoined, "quick as lightning, 'An honest man will never have any other.'"

†The request had been referred to a committee on December 1, 1784, but not brought up for discussion until January, when it was held hostage to debates over how to fill the European diplomatic posts. Franklin's resignation was accepted finally in March 1785, over the objections of Massachusetts and Rhode Island, which firmly opposed his bid to return. Some confusion followed as to whether anyone had remembered to tell Franklin of the decision.

‡Separately Temple instructed Williams to hold out for Boston. If his grandfather landed in Philadelphia, "you may rely on it, he will not budge."

Franklin was in a flurry of packing when, in mid-May, he bid goodbye to the London-bound Adamses, and, separately, to John Quincy, who was to enter Harvard in the fall. Franklin was intent on his cases, determined to get to the coast as quickly as possible, to wait for the first available ship, when on May 17 Jefferson was received at Versailles as the new American minister plenipotentiary. Wisely the Virginian began that tenure with a bon mot. To the often-asked question "Is it you, Sir, who replaces Dr. Franklin?" Jefferson took to answering: "No one can *replace* him, Sir; I am only his successor."

❧

There was no final embrace of Vergennes, with whom Franklin exchanged only warm letters. Invited to dine with Franklin on June 9, the king's chief of protocol delivered the parting gift for which Vergennes had arranged, a portrait of Louis XVI encircled by diamonds, a case said to be worth 24,000 livres. In any event Franklin was overwhelmed by the practical obligations of closing up a household. He knew well the chaos of departures, the quicksand of unfinished business; his counsel for an extended voyage was to keep that trip secret as long as possible. In a perfect world the traveler would be left to make his preparations without interruption, and to bid his goodbyes only when ready. In his own case the departure was accompanied by a storm of farewell letters as fierce as had been the welcoming verse.

The packing was complete by June 8, but there remained still the matter of conveyance to the coast. The spring of 1785 brought with it a devastating drought; the country was reduced to a heap of ashes. All navigation via the Seine was impossible in so parched a season. A ship was scheduled to leave for America from Lorient at the end of the month, but Franklin knew he could not tolerate the trip overland to that western port. Under the circumstances he began to contemplate a 1786 departure, an idea he shared with the sprightly Madame Chaumont, who was lobbying to join him in his travels. Were he to delay, would she be willing to put up with him in the country for a few weeks? He knew that from the Chaumonts' Loire estate he could make the trip to Nantes entirely on water. He was helped out of his quandary by the king's equerry, who late in June offered a mule-drawn, curtained coach from the time of Louis XIV. In that litter a passenger could sit or recline, on a mound of pillows.

Benny woke at four o'clock on June 29 to greet the horse-drawn barge that was to transport the luggage to the coast but no vessel showed; it had run aground on a sandbar. The captain sent word that Benny should have the crates hauled to the water to await his arrival. Franklin's two tons of baggage—including twenty-three cases of books, four of scientific instruments, saddles and harnesses, a dismantled printing press, Temple's cabriolet, a selection of printer's type, and supplies of Passy water, each case numbered and emblazoned with a bold "BF"—spent that Wednesday night at river's edge, under guard, to be loaded under Benny's supervision the next day. It was perfectly appropriate that the fifteen-year-old should have been pressed into service; he had every reason to expedite the return. He had been away from his parents—and the four siblings he had never met—for more than half his lifetime. That Temple should have spent the last Passy weeks in bed, under care of a hired nurse, was no less apt. If he had reason to leave France he had none to do so for America. It was not his native country; both his family and his childhood memories were elsewhere. He had no great expectations for that wilderness. And his future was as unsettled as ever. Friends expected him to return to France as an ambassador; certainly that was how the system worked in Europe. "Mr. Franklin has been so long in France that he is more a Frenchman than an American," observed John Quincy Adams, who predicted, "I doubt whether he will enjoy himself perfectly if he returns to America."*

As determined as was Franklin to set eyes upon the nation he had known only as a British colony, he was uneasy about the return. Already it was an established truth that no one left Paris without a pang of sorrow; Franklin had enjoyed in France a respect and adulation that he could not

---

*Temple's example helped seventeen-year-old John Quincy to decide to return to America, separately from his family, to continue his studies. As difficult as he suspected it would be to submit to "the dry and tedious study of the law" after freely roaming about Europe for three years, he did not care to depend on anyone else for an honorable living, to loiter away his precious time abroad and head home only when forced. That alternative was sobering: "I have before me a striking example of the distressing and humiliating situation a person is reduced to by adopting a different line of conduct and I am determined not to fall into the same error." He does not appear to have noticed Benny, who was at the time working from dawn until seven in the evening in the printshop, while John Quincy Adams was devoting himself to Latin translation, charging through Molière and Racine, and serving as an amateur theater critic.

expect again to taste in his lifetime. He had known demotions before. He had also known regret. Waiting in England for a wind to waft him to America in 1762, he had confessed to mixed emotions; reason was on one side of the water, inclination on the other. There was little hesitation, but plenty of uncertainty. "I promise myself, or rather flatter myself, that I shall be happy when at home," he told friends, sounding like a man who had done his moral algebra but wished for a different result. He hoped he was doing the right thing. He was aware that he might well feel a stranger at home; he knew nothing of what to expect even of his own house, which the British had occupied and partly plundered. He had outlived the great majority of his friends. He was heading off not for a reunion with the past but for a glimpse of the future.

Those around him fixed on another concern. The duchesse d'Enville let slip a remark about prophets without honor; Morellet fretted openly about American ingratitude. Jefferson felt it necessary to remind his countrymen that the eyes of all Europe would be upon them. Friends presented eloquent cases for his remaining in France, adding that he was likely to meet with envy, and enmity, in America. Franklin acknowledged their point. He also promised that no amount of bitterness could undermine his joy. To the satisfaction of seeing the nation he had done so much to create, to the reunion with his family, he joined something else, something he could not explain. It was universal to think one's own home best, he mused, citing the example of the Greenlanders, who lived on sheer rock, which they preferred to all of Europe. He might be unsure of the reception but the curiosity was overpowering. To those who tried to hold him back he explained, tears in his eyes: "My task is not finished. The little which remains of my life I owe to those who have entrusted me with their own." His last official act was the signing of a treaty of amity and commerce with Prussia on July 9. He set July 12 for the departure.

The goodbyes were wrenching. Madame Brillon preferred not to attempt one in person. Already she was inconsolable; that scene would only be an agony to them both. At Madame Helvétius's as elsewhere there were floods of tears. To the last there were accounts to be settled and cheeks to be kissed and, on Franklin's part, praise for the king, whose wisdom he defended on the eve of his departure: "Perhaps no sovereign born to reign ever felt so much for other men or had more of the milk of human nature than Louis XVI." The litter arrived for him at four in the morning on the twelfth, but business kept Franklin from settling into it until well after five that evening. After a last dinner together he and Chaumont were still discussing broken windowpanes and costs of lightning rods. Finally Franklin climbed into the outmoded conveyance, surrounded by an enormous crowd in the Valentinois courtyard. Le Veillard, Benny, Temple, and a servant boarded a carriage behind him. Into a wagon went all the personal effects, among them an additional twenty-seven pieces of luggage, two of Temple's angora cats, and a crate of his fruit trees, which traveled less well than did the angoras. A solemn silence reigned, interrupted only by sobs. Pulled by two large mules and led by a muleteer on a third animal, the coach set out, followed by a vast procession, through the Bois de Boulogne and to the Porte Maillot, where Franklin said another set of goodbyes before heading north, on the Saint-Germain road. At a decidedly unambitious pace he jogged his way toward Le Havre, surprisingly comfortable, accompanied on various legs of the journey by friends, admirers, and local dignitaries. The valedictions followed all the way to the coast.

Not so much by invitation as by decree, he spent the night of July 14 at the exquisitely appointed château of the cardinal de la Rochefoucauld, archbishop of Rouen and the grandson of the duchesse d'Enville. La Rochefoucauld's was a superb, beautifully preserved fifteenth-century structure with exquisite views of the rich countryside; it was a dynasty, and a magnificence, Franklin was never to see again. From the road he continued in the relic-distributing he had begun in Passy; already his tea table had gone to Madame Le Veillard, his cane to Cabanis, Temple's English-born bulldog to Madame Helvétius, where the animal wasted no time in attacking the gentle abbé de la Roche.* Although he could very well have walked to Le Havre more quickly than he rode in the antiquated litter—these were the same 120 miles across which Beaumarchais had in 1776 hurdled in forty crucial hours, but then Beaumarchais moved always to a different tempo—nothing could dampen Franklin's spirits. In Le Havre he was joined by Houdon, set to sail as well to America, where the

---

*Temple's chamois went to the king's menagerie, in the hope that they would one day be transported to America, an opportunity that never arose. Temple carried his animal loving to genteel extremes; in May he had also commissioned a portrait of his horse.

artist was to sculpt a bust of Washington. Before stepping off the continent for the last time Franklin penned a mischievous letter to Madame Le Veillard. Her husband was meant to have turned back already but was continuing on with him across the Channel. Should he keep going, Franklin counseled Madame Le Veillard to find a discreet lover. He could think of no one better qualified than the neighborhood priest.

By the time the jewel-like splendor of the Isle of Wight, all velvety hills and emerald fields, sparkled before him, Franklin was in exquisite spirits. He felt better than he had in years. From Southampton's Star Inn he wrote to Madame Helvétius, as he had done from Le Havre. He was fighting still the tug of Passy. He was clear about his regret, poised as he was to leave her, and "the country that *I love most* in the world." He bid an emotional farewell to "my very, very, very dear friend." She was to instruct the abbés to pray for him. That was, after all, their métier. "I shall always love you," added Franklin, about to embark. Having postponed the goodbye as long as he could, Le Veillard carried that letter back to Passy, which he found disconsolate, a village, as Jefferson put it, that had lost its patriarch.*

≈

In well-tended Southampton there was another goodbye to be said. On the evening of July 24 Temple ran into his father on the street; William Franklin was poised to sail for the Isle of Wight, where he had heard he might find his father. The reunion was a chilly one, in the course of which Franklin and his son disentangled their financial affairs and sidestepped emotional ones. For a pitiful sum, Franklin arranged for William's vast New Jersey properties to be sold to Temple, to whom Franklin advanced the necessary funds. By the time Captain Thomas Truxton arrived, in the newly built London *Packet*, a ship generously provisioned with herds of sheep and pigs and fowl—there would be no need to resort to salt beef on this crossing—Franklin was surrounded by old friends. From Hampshire came Jonathan Shipley, his wife, and daughter, bearing a copy of Paley's

---

*And one in which there was some scuffling over relics. The blame would be assigned soon enough. Madame Helvétius could not hear Franklin's name without crying, "Oh that great man, that poor dear man, we will never see him again!" She would be silenced by Brillon. "That is entirely your fault, Madame," he quipped.

Moral Philosophy and a ginger cake. With his publisher, Benjamin Vaughan, Franklin discussed lead poisoning, promising an essay on the subject. That affectionate company and several others boarded the *Packet* on July 27. They stayed for supper and much later; Franklin left them to Captain Truxton when he retired for the evening. His guests crept off at four, to avoid an impossible goodbye. Shortly thereafter Truxton raised the anchor. Franklin woke to find himself alone and at sea.

~※~

Six weeks later a light morning breeze lifted the *Packet* above Virginia's Gloucester Point and into the Chesapeake, affording Franklin a full view of Philadelphia. Word of his arrival had preceded him; in the harbor he was greeted by salutes of every nation. Even the four British ships in Philadelphia displayed their colors. The bells pealed their welcome and the cannon boomed; the entire city seemed to materialize at the wharf. Temple could not see through his tears, nor Benny express his joy. Franklin burst with pleasure, even as his self-possession dissolved under the assault of acclaim and affection. His face was bathed in tears as the cheering crowd carried him to his Market Street courtyard, where Sally, paralyzed by emotion, awaited him. In those first days Franklin resembled no one more than Rip Van Winkle, who had also missed the American Revolution, though to different effect.

The disorientation was profound. The faces were nearly all new, the voices alone familiar. Even the language had evolved over what was nearly a nine-year absence. The acclamations and congratulations were familiar enough, however; in the days that followed, delegations of every kind flocked to Franklin's door, eager to expound on the "steady and painful services" he had rendered his country. (Richard Henry Lee, then president of Congress, found himself in Philadelphia that week. So it was that in his official capacity Lee was among the first to welcome back a man he would have preferred never to see again.) To each delegation Franklin replied with dignity and gratitude. He was delighted to have served his country in so remarkable a contest. A self-professed committee man to the end, he added a dollop of modesty. "My principal merit," Franklin assured one delegation, "if I may claim any, in public affairs, is that of having been always ready and willing to receive and follow good advice." He was overwhelmed by the reception, which exceeded his wildest expectations. Evidently there *was* such a thing on earth as gratitude. And while reports of American prosperity had reached Paris, nothing had prepared him for what Philadelphia had become in his absence, a flourishing city with thousands of new homes, an orderly market, and a cluster of public buildings, amid which poverty had no place and tolerance reigned, another bold guess amply realized, in every respect the promised land.

Epilogue

Histories of lives are seldom entertaining, unless they contain something either admirable or exemplary.
—*Benjamin Franklin, April 16, 1722*

For the last five years of his life Franklin made himself at home in the comfortable Market Street house he had built two decades earlier but barely occupied. And having vowed to retire, he was within a month of his arrival back in political office, elected president of the Executive Council of Pennsylvania, essentially governor of the state. It was the kind of affirmation he was unable to resist. He was proud to be unanimously reelected a year later, the more so as he knew public opinion to be fickle. He congratulated himself on having made the right decision to return.

He confessed to the occasional pang of regret, most sharply on Wednesdays, at ten in the morning, when he thought reflexively of his other, charmed life, at Madame Helvétius's exuberant table. That world was present to him at all times. The first report on the election to his new office went to Auteuil; over the Market Street mantel were aligned wax and plaster busts of his European idols. While he was pleased again to be of use to his country, he could not help but wish at times that he had accepted Madame Helvétius's invitation to remain in France. The longing was a general one, which he shared with Madame Brillon as well. He reveled in the presence of Sally and his grandchildren, "but as for every-thing else," he admitted in October 1785, "I was happier in France." Temple suspected that his grandfather missed his friends; he was notably less buoyant than he had been in Passy. Franklin sparkled as ever on the page but never dazzled as he had in France; there were to be no Philadelphia bagatelles. He was every bit the old conjurer who had broken his staff and thrown his book of charms to the sea, to rejoin the world of men. He served three terms as president of the Executive Council of Pennsylvania, after which he sat for four months in the Constitutional Convention.

He was shocked to discover that, as he put it, "I seem to have intruded myself into the company of posterity." Statistically speaking, he should have been long gone, as were most of his friends. Had he died before sailing to France, he reminded himself, he would however have been deprived of the most active years of his life. That was one way of seeing things. To his colleagues he was simply ancient. Hailed in Europe as the founder of a new order, an unlikely emissary of the avant-garde, he was in America an antique. There was nothing to compare with the sight of Franklin being transported through the newly planted yard of the Philadelphia State House to the Constitutional Convention in a Paris-built sedan chair, held aloft by four hulking prisoners from the Walnut Street jail. While it was true that he occupied an apse comparable only to Washington's, Franklin was less a father than a grandfather to his country. He was forty years older than most of the delegates at that 1787 assembly. Never a natural parliamentarian, he contributed little to the convention, which he blessed primarily with his presence, and his sane paeans to compromise.

Louis Otto, the new French envoy to Philadelphia, predicted that Franklin's enemies would pounce as soon as the first blush of delirium wore off. Indeed as the supplies of Passy mineral water began to run low on Market Street, Franklin discovered that he had spoken too soon in defense of gratitude. Once the applause of 1785 quieted, there was a resounding silence on the subject of his French odyssey. His accounts had been approved before he left France; America owed him a substantial sum. Franklin dispatched Temple promptly to New York, to submit his ledgers to Congress. No reimbursement materialized. Instead reports circulated that the former French minister was in debt to America, a debt he refused to settle.

By the end of 1788 he was reduced to petitioning his government for some recognition of his services, an indignity no other Founding Father would suffer. With reason Franklin considered the French posting the most taxing assignment of his life; he was forthright in his expectations. "I must own, I did hope that as it is customary in Europe to make some liberal provision for ministers when they return home from foreign service, during which their absence is necessarily injurious to their private affairs, the Congress would at least have been kind enough to have shown their approbation of my conduct by a grant of a small tract of land in their western country, which might have been of use and some honor to my posterity," he allowed. That was not exclusively a European custom; he knew well that both Arthur Lee and John Jay had been handsomely remunerated for their tours of duty.* On his return from England in 1762 Franklin had been accorded the title of postmaster general, which he had left to his son-in-law. Unable to recall Franklin in 1782, his enemies had retaliated by unseating Richard Bache. Franklin wondered if Bache might now be restored to his position, a request George Washington pointedly ignored.

There would be no reward, no settling of accounts, nor—most stunning—a syllable of gratitude for the French mission. As always the chief concern remained for Temple; Franklin could not understand why his grandson made little impression on Congress in the fall of 1785. He lobbied for him again in December, to no avail. Congress's neglect was most unkind, Franklin grumbled, although he had to admit that had he known of it beforehand he would hardly have served his country any less zealously. On his grandson's account Franklin was undermined even by his friends; evidently Temple did not improve on closer observation. He returned to America in 1785 with two letters from Jefferson to James Monroe. The first was a warm letter of introduction. The second was a coded document, on the same subject. "I have never been with him enough to unravel his character with certainty," cautioned Jefferson. It seemed essentially good, although like his grandfather, Temple was difficult to pen-

---

*He also noted that their compensations were but trifles compared with what Louis XVI had offered Gérard on his return, from a posting that more closely resembled Franklin's.

etrate. More to the point: "His understanding is good enough for common uses but not great enough for uncommon ones."*

"Having served a long and busy apprenticeship in it," Temple himself remained intent on a diplomatic career. At the same time he preferred not to be humiliated by an outright refusal. (The slights were generally more subtle. The Pennsylvania delegation nominated him as secretary to the Constitutional Convention; Washington's man—the energetic Amsterdam shopper William Jackson—prevailed in his stead.) As Congress continued unforthcoming, Franklin counseled his grandson to establish himself on his six hundred New Jersey acres, an honest, independent gentleman who had no need to ask favors of anyone. He did so, restlessly. Franklin could not seem to wean him of his taste for Europe. And Temple would prove Jefferson's concerns well founded. While Franklin labored to assure even the closest of French friends that all was well in America, the country satisfied with her revolution and little afflicted by partisan politics, Temple whispered that affairs at home were not on quite so solid a footing as his grandfather asserted. The new republic was thoroughly riven by factions. Were some foreign power to attempt to conquer America she would doubtless succeed. He was all the more sour for his personal predicament; Congress was in such an unruly state that he hesitated even to press his case. His grandfather's friends could only join him in deploring private influence in that body. Jefferson was blatantly two-faced on the subject. Having expressed his ambivalence to Monroe he could not enough impress his regret on Temple. He wished with all his heart that Temple might be called into the diplomatic line. It was disgraceful that nothing had worked out. What about Portugal? In October 1790 Temple was still confiding in Jefferson. His highest ambition, the one on which he had set his sights from the start, was "to be appointed to the court of France." Holland was his second choice. He hoped Jefferson would not mind his broad hints.

Unsettled though it was, the American government appeared solid in

---

*No one was truly willing to go out on a limb for Temple. As early as 1781 Jay happily conceded that Franklin's grandson was a fine writer, toward whom he was well inclined. He also stopped markedly short of singing Temple's praises, engaging in some elaborate contortions on the page to excuse the young man's fondness for "dress and diversions."

comparison to the French monarchy. To the extent of that unrest Franklin was oblivious; the man who had tamed the lightning proved deaf to the rolling of thunder in the distance. In July 1788 the duc de la Rochefoucauld provided him with the fullest account he yet had of affairs in Paris. Franklin thanked him; he hoped all would turn out well for a nation he held so dear and thought of so tenderly; he continued to extol Louis XVI as the father of America. "Now, even in my sleep, I find that the scenes of all my pleasant dreams are laid in that city, or in its neighborhood," he assured Madame Helvétius. In his daydreams he traveled to her dinner table, her sitting room, her garden. He could not envision that robust nation crumbling under the will of her people. (In that he was not alone. On July 14, 1789, the Bastille fell. In Paris two weeks later Jefferson so persisted in his faith in human reason that he swore "to be stoned as a false prophet if all does not end well in this country.") Already Franklin had taken to teasing his French friends. Why had Le Roy fallen silent? Was his head, joked Franklin, being paraded about on a stick by a mob? Had Le Veillard been arrested? Was he languishing in the Bastille?

Jefferson had inherited Franklin's eminent circle as well as the claims of Beaumarchais, the perpetual fallout from Landais, the messy matter of the American debt, and the unsettled claims of every Passy merchant with whom Franklin had had an account, each of whom Finck, the maître d'hôtel, had bilked.* By the time he returned to America to report on those sagas, and with the news that France was irretrievably changed, his predecessor was confined to his bed. In Philadelphia at the end of March 1790, Jefferson found Franklin frail and emaciated—by his own description he was a bag of bones, subsisting on opium—and as hypermnesic as ever. At his bedside Jefferson sketched a Paris in which all frivolities had yielded to politics. Franklin took a lively interest in the account, his face flushing often he plied his successor with questions. He was most anxious about the fate of friends. "He went over all in succession with a rapidity and animation," Jefferson observed, "almost too much for his strength." Still the two were of the same mind; it was necessary to upset a few apple

---

*The fruit seller, baker, wood merchant, and butcher had all tried to see Franklin on the eve of his departure, to be headed off by Finck. He subsequently fled, and proceeded to bury his former employer in abuse. Even his maître d'hôtel would attempt to blacken Franklin's reputation in the eyes of Congress.

carts in the name of progress. That week Jefferson reminded Lafayette that one did not travel "from despotism to liberty in a feather-bed." Fifteen days later Franklin died in his own, late on the evening of April 17, surrounded by friends and family, age eighty-four, lucid to the end.*

He was laid to rest in Christ Church burial ground; twenty thousand people turned out for the Philadelphia funeral, the largest public gathering America had yet seen. Within a matter of days it became clear that the popular hero was not a darling of the government, however. The eulogies fell to Franklin's enemies. Only in France would he be remembered as he had hoped to be, without his errata. In the course of the next two centuries he would have plenty of detractors, on plenty of counts. They had plenty of weighty names—Keats, Melville, Emerson, Poe, D. H. Lawrence among them—but all had Anglo-Saxon names. Even the unlikeliest of Frenchmen and Frenchwomen sanctified Franklin. George Sand and Laclos applauded him. Stendhal ranked him among history's greats.

From Franklin's adopted country came tales of the most effusive of eulogies. The National Assembly publicly mourned a commoner; Mirabeau's splendid oration to "the genius who liberated America and poured upon Europe torrents of light" became an anthem of the French Revolution. When that oration crossed the ocean it initiated a game of hot potato. Washington declined to open the evelope, directing it instead to the Senate, which sent it back to him. Washington returned the packet unopened. When finally the tribute was read in Congress it was delivered, with chilling apathy, by John Adams. One Pennsylvania delegate wondered what the French would say when they discovered that Americans were cold at heart and cared "not a fig about them, Franklin, or freedom." The House of Representatives voted to wear mourning for a month. In the Senate the motion to do so was withdrawn before Lee, Izard, or Adams had yet to open his mouth. In France the apotheoses continued for months.

It is unlikely that Franklin received the 1790 letters from friends who

---

*He was as well unforgiving to the end. In his will he disinherited the son he had already once disinherited, adding that he felt obliged to leave William "no more of an estate he endeavored to deprive me of." He also canceled William's debt to him, one which—it would be a relief to think sloppy bookkeeping was to blame—William had already repaid. The bulk of the estate went to Sally and her family, a nice twist on the laws of primogeniture.

wished he were still on hand, who warned that France was at a critical stage and in need of his guidance. His image towered over that contest; Franklin statuettes went on sale, carved of "authentic" stones of the Bastille. A prophet of a revolt he had not foreseen, he joined Rousseau and Voltaire in the holy trinity of the French Revolution. It was a legacy he had never meant to impart; from under the marten fur cap escaped those rasping furies, liberty, equality, fraternity. Having sailed east as a British traitor Franklin returned home as a French saint. In a life of protean transformations, it was perhaps his greatest conjuring act.

~ ~ ~

He would be some time in shaking off charges of heresy in America. The French years provided his detractors precisely what they needed: proof that the ur-American was un-American. Franklin was the Founding Father who had come the furthest, which makes him today the most compelling; he was also the Founding Father who traveled the farthest, which in his own century made him the most suspect. Few other homes in Philadelphia sported both Réaumur and Fahrenheit thermometers. The story goes that when Franklin proposed that Congress open its meetings with a prayer, Alexander Hamilton quipped that that body had no need of "foreign aid." The story may be apocryphal but the sentiment was real. The expatriate patriot, Franklin was associated in many minds with the dependent chapter of American independence, one better expunged from the record. It was certainly a chapter that Washington had no particular interest in promoting. America did not care to be the courageous child, aided by the powerful gods. She preferred a different myth, one of self-realization and self-actualization, of having sprung fully formed from her own high-blown ideals. Doubtless something else was at work too. Among marquises and counts and dukes Franklin was a gem. Among the American gentry he distinguished himself as a lowborn upstart.

Having made an astonishing and unorthodox dash through the ranks, he left his grandsons to scramble for their bearings. Temple and Benny returned to America with French as their common language. To his family Benny billed himself as an "Anglo-Frenchman."* Submitting to his

---

*Benny himself had trouble with his identity, or at least the nomenclature. Above "Anglo-Frenchman" he wrote "Franco-American." He let both terms stand.

grandfather's wishes, Temple did his best to establish a European-style hunting lodge on his newly acquired lands. It proved no easier to transplant a Franklin than a French roebuck to southern New Jersey; the aspiring diplomat hankered increasingly for Paris, to which he returned in 1796, although Blanchette Caillot and his son did not await him. Their child had died, for which Temple could not forgive Blanchette. Franklin's prophecy for Temple—that he would grow up to become a distinguished gentleman—proved wide of the mark. Having inherited his grandfather's invaluable papers Temple made no timely efforts to publish them (Jefferson believed he was bribed to suppress them); he dabbled in French real estate; he sired a second illegitimate child, whom he entrusted, in family fashion, to his father, in London.* In his will Franklin had attempted to nudge Temple toward a more settled future; William did the same, urging him toward marriage. Temple demurred until such time as he found an heiress. The two men fell out and went without speaking for fourteen years. Again in family fashion, William wrote Temple out of his will.

Father and son never reconciled. William died in obscurity in London in 1813, Temple in Paris in 1823, where he is buried beside the woman he had married several days earlier. A kind friend covered the burial costs. Everything about the life was an insult to the teachings of Poor Richard, although it is unclear if Franklin might have noticed. In the 1760s he had complained of his own double identity—in England he was suspect for being too much an American, in America of being too much an Englishman—and he bequeathed a similar burden to his progeny. For his service abroad he wound up with a British son and a French grandson. In Temple's case geography was not solely to blame. In 1776 Franklin had pried Temple away from his father (and ostensibly back to school) with a few sage words of advice: "This is the time of life in which you are to lay the foundations of your future improvement, and of your importance among men. If this season is neglected, it will be like cutting off the spring from the year." He had then swept the sixteen-year-old off to Paris, for his own reasons, and to the same end.

Benny too defied predictions. Along with his apathy he shed his youthful timidity; the sluggish Swiss student became a Philadelphia firebrand.

---

*Ellen Franklin was born in 1798. Her mother was the sister of William Franklin's second wife, which made William Franklin both her uncle and her grandfather.

And to the regret of John Adams, he very much recovered his English. After Franklin's death Benny established the Philadelphia *General Advertiser*, later the *Aurora*, a paper that had no rival in its savage attacks on Washington and Adams. Dubbing the latter "the Duke of Braintree," Benny upheld a different family tradition: that of making himself obnoxious to the authorities. His efforts earned him the name "Lightning Rod, Jr." With him the Adams–Franklin enmity continued. To Adams's mind Benny Bache was a malicious libeler, settled into his career by "his grandfather, from whom he inherited a dirty, envious, jealous and revengeful spite against me for no other cause under heaven than because I was too honest a man to favor or connive at his selfish schemes of ambition and avarice." Benny was arrested and jailed, under the Alien and Sedition Acts, for libeling Adams.* He died soon after of yellow fever, at thirty.

Of Franklin's French family only Jonathan Williams landed on his feet. He felt a perfect stranger on his 1785 arrival in America but soon recovered. The makeshift commercial agent wound up as the first superintendent of West Point, under Jefferson, as consistently devoted to Franklin's grandnephew as he was wary of Franklin's grandson. Williams went on to organize the defenses of New York and Philadelphia for the War of 1812. He was for many years ranking engineer of the army, providing the brand of expertise for which Franklin had been dispatched to France in 1776.

Generally those who invested most in the American contest emerged with the least. Having sacrificed the better part of his fortune to America, Chaumont sent his twenty-five-year-old son to Congress to press his claim. Jacques Le Ray de Chaumont arrived in 1785. Four frustrating years later Franklin attempted to intervene on his behalf, reminding George Washington that his former landlord "was the first in France who gave us credit, and before the court showed us any countenance trusted us with 2000 barrels of gunpowder, and from time to time afterwards exerted himself to furnish the Congress with supplies of various kinds, which, for want of due returns, they being of great amount, has finally

---

*Adams's final take on Franklin was clear. Vain, ambitious, and scheming, Franklin had "entered into partnership with the count de Vergennes, the most powerful minister of state in Europe, to destroy the character and power of a poor man almost without a name, unknown in the European world, born and educated in the American wilderness, out of which he had never set his foot till 1778."

much distressed him in circumstances." Was it possible to settle the matter? Yet again he wrote in vain. Chaumont's claims wound their way through committee after committee. In August 1790, the United States Treasury accorded him a nominal sum. The Valentinois was seized by his creditors; Chaumont removed to his Loire estate where he died, nearly penniless, in 1803.

Silas Deane died of unknown causes in 1789, addled and derelict, having boarded the ship on which he hoped finally to return to North America. Even in his lifetime no irregularities were found in his accounts, which were no better or worse than anyone else's. Some thought him a martyr to the cause, others a traitor. His heirs pursued his claims for payment of 3.3 million livres. In 1842 Congress issued an apology, and just under half that sum. Beaumarchais met with as little satisfaction. He had first approached Deane on July 14, 1776—an oddly mongrel date—to pledge his assistance to the Americans in their "sublime project." Fifty years later his role was still under discussion. His was a debt on which it was difficult to make good as it had officially never been incurred. From the start the visionary playwright had adopted the language of the munificent fairy, which was how Congress treated him. They could be excused for assuming Beaumarchais to be a fiction; there was no other way to account for him. He continued in his pathetic, irate, and explosive appeals to Congress, where in 1787 his file was passed on to Arthur Lee. Lee was quick to determine that his sworn enemy owed America money rather than the other way around. Five years later Hamilton proved a more able accountant, determining that America owed Beaumarchais more than 2.2 million livres. Discussed nineteen times between 1806 and 1831, the claim was finally settled in 1835, with a quarter of that sum. America was equally laggard with her debt payments to France, although she could be said to have redeemed herself belatedly, under Woodrow Wilson.

Having arguably contributed more to American independence than anyone besides George Washington or George III, Vergennes went forgotten, unsung, and unheralded, save by Louis XVI, so stricken by the loss of his trusted minister that he did not hunt on the day of his death. Rarely has the law of unintended consequences worked to such striking effect as it did in the case of the powerful French foreign minister. The most conservative of men, and the most frugal—Vergennes was famed for not throwing away a taper until he had used it several times—he took a rash step to maintain a balance of power that he was inadvertently to destroy, by bankrupting his nation. He had been of the conviction that even if the war ended badly France would have a great deal to gain from an independent America; he turned out to be the pragmatist who cleared the way for the ideologues. Along with Franklin he would discover that diplomats make dull heroes. Vergennes is paraded out when the occasion requires, as it did in 1917. He tends to be exhumed in anniversary years.

The only one of the Passy intimates to fare well was Edward Bancroft, the diligent secretary with the disarming smile. As Franklin might have demonstrated with his Euclidean logic, Bancroft turned out to be twice as loyal as anyone, as he was so to both sides. It was he who had made the Tuesday evening jaunts to the Tuileries, to slip rolls of correspondence into bottles and to lower those bottles into the ground. As Edward Bancroft he transcribed Franklin's papers and shared in his secrets; as "Edward Edwards" he conveyed every detail of the mission—there are no better accounts of the negotiations with Versailles and Madrid, the shipping details, the intramural squabbling—to London. There was good reason why Bancroft should regularly have complained that his hand was falling off. As late as 1783 he was contributing pro-British pieces to American newspapers. His accomplishment was not lost on him; his confession survives in his request for a continuation of his generous British pension, despite the fact that he spent the war on both nations' payrolls. (And despite the fact that he managed to put his own stock speculations before his duties to either set of employers. The British Secret Service read his personal correspondence as eagerly as his official one.) With his combined salaries Bancroft outearned even Paul Wentworth, the master spy who had recruited him in 1776. From the start Wentworth had been intent on a seat in Commons or a title. He got the former, although never the chance to occupy it. He went on to become a trustee of Dartmouth College and—after another bout of French intrigue, which left him persona non grata in England—to finish his long life on his plantation in Surinam, where he had met Bancroft in the first place.

As for the heartfelt wishes that Louis XVI and Franklin exchanged on March 20, 1778—that their pact would be for the good of both countries, and that America would be meticulous in honoring her engagement—one man failed to deliver on his promise. Despite the hundreds of pages consecrated to it at Versailles, the trade of America was a dowry that never materialized; American commerce with Britain returned to prewar levels within years of the peace. For her American alliance France got only an empty treasury, Franklin's greatest tangible contribution to the French Revolution. By 1787 Versailles could not meet the interest payments on her debts from the American contest, which claimed half of her annual budget. To address that crisis Louis XVI had no choice but to call the Assembly of Notables, then to convoke the Estates-General. In 1789 the French monarch conceded that he never thought about the American contest without regret. He had little chance to reproach himself. Almost exactly ten years after the peace was signed he mounted the guillotine, from what was then the place Louis XV, would soon be the place de la Révolution, and is today the place de la Concorde—there where Franklin had followed Charles and Robert's balloon as it melted into the sky.

Fortunately for him, Franklin was never to know the fates of his French friends. Other than Lee's restless and colorful cohort, the duck-beheading comte de Lauraguais, few went peacefully to their graves. (Lauraguais lived to a ripe old age in a garret, a tribute to the life-enhancing powers of eccentricity. The chevalière d'Eon too died an impoverished little old lady, in London—at which point he turned out to be a little old man, to the astonishment of the widow with whom he had long shared a room.) For the rest penury would have been a happy fate. The chemist Lavoisier was guillotined, as were his Mesmer co-commissioners, the astronomer Bailly, and Dr. Guillotin himself. The mathematician Condorcet died in jail; Luzerne, the envoy to America, had already died but did so again. He was dug up, his remains thrown in the Seine. Le Veillard mounted the scaffold. The enlightened la Rochefoucauld, translator of the American constitutions, was stoned to death and disemboweled, before his family, of whom Franklin was so fond. The mother and sister of Madame de Lafayette were put to death. American heroes were not exempt: D'Estaing was executed, Rochambeau imprisoned. Charged with treason, Lafayette spent five years in an Austrian dungeon, his fortune confiscated. His reputation did not survive in France, although it did in America, to which he made a triumphant return in 1824.

✦

Hours after John Adams heard the news of Franklin's death, he was again wheezing that his former colleague's career was that of neither an honest man nor a sensible one. As ever he was the more vocal of the two states-men. The charges of libertinism and depravity were ones Franklin never entirely shook.* In Adams's estimation it was as if America had sent Fal-staff (and Prince Hal) to represent her abroad. Benny was said to be "the son of one of Dr. Franklin's bastards," Franklin "his crafty and lecherous old hypocrite of a grandfather, whose very statue seems to gloat on the wenches as they walk the State House yard." History belongs to the elo-quent, all the more to the prolifically so. To a large extent Adams's Franklin has been the one to survive. His was a cruder, more satisfying version of a nuanced story. No one was at hand to absorb Jefferson's qui-eter assertion that Franklin was the sole exception to the rule that seven years abroad spoiled an American.

In part Franklin had himself to blame; he had as much difficulty finish-ing what he had written as Adams did in separating pen from page. French friends had entreated Franklin to devote the trip home to his *Auto-biography*; it was essential that he offer his version of the life. Instead he turned out a series of treatises on ship design and stoves and chimneys, in the greatest burst of scientific writing of his career; the outer world was always more appealing to him than the inner one. He was charming in his own defense. It was true that he had not set his most important acts to pa-per, but he had done something better. The years that raised him from ob-scurity were those he considered most vital. They were by far the most useful, he argued, stressing as they did the "the effects of prudent and im-prudent conduct in the commencement of a life of business." He did not foresee that those same pages might earn him a reputation for prose-over-poetry pragmatism. In the Anglo-Saxon world he would be kidnapped by his own creation, charged with philistinism. (The accusation was curi-ously at odds with those leveled by Adams.) Franklin had won Europe to America's side; he had brought respect and affection to the table. Para-doxically it was only at home that he came to stand for a creature the Con-

---

*And, as ever, taciturnity grated on Adams's nerves. What had become of the good old days of oratory? he sputtered. "Secrecy! Cunning! Silence! *Voilà les grands* [sic] *sciences des temps mod-erns*. Washington! Franklin! Jefferson! Eternal silence! Impenetrable secrecy! Deep cunning!" he exploded in 1806. "These are the talents and virtues which are triumphant in these days." After the negotiations of 1778, Gérard paid tribute to Franklin as a marvelous actor, "whose silence and reserve were among his greatest assets."

tinent knew well. One thing Franklin did not invent was the ugly American, that uncouth, incurious, chest-jabbing chauvinist, spiritually bankrupt and materially insatiable, given to baseball hats, sports metaphors, and sanctimoniousness.

From the start the Franco-American alliance played itself out with all the grace of a three-legged race; without Franklin's participation it stumbled soon enough. France and Britain were again at war in 1793. That April a French envoy disembarked in Philadelphia on an oddly familiar mission. "Genêt came to this country with the affectation of not desiring to embark us in the war," noted Hamilton, "and yet he did all in his power by indirect means to drag us into it." Indeed Genêt hoped to drum up support for a revolution, and to encourage America to harass British shipping. The treaty of 1778 notwithstanding, America opted for neutrality. Under Adams's presidency the former allies came as close as they ever would to an open conflict, one that the American leader skillfully averted. As ever, Gallic misdemeanors served as a divisive issue in America and as a boon to Adams; his popularity soared on the same anti-French sentiment that transformed Franklin into the bête noire of the Federalist Party.

After 1945 it was America's turn to hold France in contempt as a military ally, France's to prove that ingratitude is a universal. The May 8, 1945, Paris headlines hailed the German defeat rather than the Allied victory, a perfectly legitimate riposte to Washington's discharge of his troops in 1783 without a nod to France.* It would be only another few years before the former insurgents attempted their clandestine "Coca-Colonization" of France. Vergennes had had his revenge, but saddled France with American hegemony in place of British rivalry. And America had learned little along the way. In 1952 France was "morally debilitated and half agnostic or atheistic" even in the estimation of the campaigning Dwight Eisenhower.

While they created an independent nation, Franklin's French years established a second entity as well. Lord Stormont had good reason to

---

*Vergennes seemed to live on in the pages of *Paris-Match*, which in 1952 ably summed up the resentments of the postwar scene: "No country was worse prepared than America for the worldwide role that she brusquely had to play, and on so immense a scale. The Americans are leaders through the force of events, but without having the desirable first-rate qualities like sure judgment and a cool head." Those were precisely the qualities the French foreign minister had praised in Franklin in 1776.

wring his hands over the American's insidious ability to assume any shape. As a journalist noted of Franklin in 1926, "If by chance he had been sent to China, he would almost certainly have left there ranking higher in Chineseness than Confucius." He was indeed a man of frightening versatility, more difficult to embrace for his very breadth. He was a natural American in only one respect: He proved that there is no such thing. He was willing at all times to put practice before theory, especially in France, when his country's fate hung in the balance. To the end he favored modest experience over grandiose hypotheses. The latter were all too pleasing "till some experiment comes and unluckily destroys them," he observed, proof that he was not a Frenchman after all. He was no less the revolutionary for being a congenial and cool-headed late bloomer. He never allowed himself to be constrained by accepted practice or prevailing ethos; he was always prepared to throw piety out the window. He preferred dialogue to dogma. To that extent the charges of heresy were in order. The supreme gift was his very flexibility. He was the opportunistic envoy from the land of opportunity, that pluralistic singularity that is the United States. His was an initial display of America's scrappy, improvisatory genius; it is the gift Falstaff gives Hal. Exercising to the last his right to alter and abolish, Franklin's final speech was an attack on slavery, a resounding vote for free and independent men, and in 1790 another dissident act. "In this world," he reminded a French friend, "it is not faith that saves us, but defiance."

Chronology

1706 Franklin born January 17, in Boston. Tenth and youngest son of a candle- and tallow-maker.

1716 Serves as his father's assistant; dislikes the business.

1718 Apprenticed to his older brother's press.

1722 Silence Dogood makes regular appearances in the *New England Courant*.

1723 Franklin briefly assumes management of the *New England Courant*. Flees to Philadelphia after a quarrel with his brother.

1724–26 First trip to London.

1728 Opens print shop in Philadelphia.

1729 Becomes publisher of the *Pennsylvania Gazette*. First experiments with color and heat.

1730 Son William born; Franklin marries Deborah Read, his former fiancée.

1731 Founds America's first circulating library.

1732 *Poor Richard's Almanack* appears. Frances Franklin and George Washington born.

1735 John Adams born.

1736 Franklin founds fire company. Frances Franklin dies of smallpox.

1737 Appointed Philadelphia's postmaster.

1739 Design of the Franklin stove.

1743 Sarah Franklin, Thomas Jefferson born. Franklin examines astronomical and meteorological phenomena; founds American Philosophical Society.

1745 First electrical experiments. John Jay born.

1747 Franklin organizes first Pennsylvania militia.

1748 Retires from business.

1749 Proposes an academy, to become the University of Pennsylvania.

1751 Elected to Pennsylvania Assembly. *Experiments and Observations on Electricity* published in London.

1752 Follows electrical research with kite experiment; adds lightning rod to his home; founds first fire insurance company.

1753 Appointed deputy postmaster general of the colonies; receives honorary degrees from Harvard and Yale.

1754 French and Indian War; Franklin unsuccessfully proposes Albany Plan of Union for protection of colonies. Birth of Louis XVI.

1755 Franklin aids colonies in defending against French and Indian attacks; writes on population. John Adams graduates Harvard.

1757 William in tow, Franklin departs for London, as agent for Pennsylvania Assembly. Writes *The Way to Wealth*. Lodges with Mrs. Stevenson, on Craven Street.

1760 Temple Franklin born in London, to an unknown mother.

1761 Franklin visits Holland and Belgium.

1762 William Franklin appointed royal governor of New Jersey. Marries following his father's departure for America. Franklin designs glass armonica, his favorite invention.

1763 French and Indian War ends. Franklin returns to Philadelphia, tours northern colonies.

1764 Defeated in Pennsylvania elections. Returns to London, ultimately as agent for Massachusetts, New Jersey, Pennsylvania, and Georgia. John Jay graduates college.

1765 Stamp Act passed; Franklin fights for its repeal.

1767 First trip to France, August 28 to October 8; presented to Louis XV at court. Sally Franklin marries, in her father's absence. Stamp Act repealed; Townshend Revenue Act passed.

1769 Second trip to France, July 14 to August 23. Benny Franklin Bache born.

1770 Boston Massacre. Franklin campaigns against Townshend duties, repealed in April.

1771 Composes first pages of the *Autobiography*.

1773 Dubourg publishes *Oeuvres de M. Franklin* in Paris. Tea Act passed; Boston Tea Party.

1774 Franklin savagely denounced in Privy Council by British solicitor general; loses post office position. Coercive Acts passed. Widowed on December 19, having not seen Deborah in a decade. First meeting of Continental Congress. Louis XVI ascends to throne of France.

1775 Franklin returns to America with Temple; learns of battles of Lexington and Concord on arrival. Elected to Second Continental Congress, serves on multiple subcommittees, including that for production of saltpeter in colonies. First meets John Adams. Submits Articles of Confederation. Breaks with William Franklin. Howe, Clinton, and Burgoyone arrive in Boston; George Washington named commander in chief of army. Battle of Bunker Hill.

1776 Beaumarchais passes on first funds from French government. Franklin makes punishing, futile Canada trip; meets with Vergennes's secret representative. Presides at Pennsylvania Constitutional Convention; signs Declaration of Independence. William Franklin arrested. Deane arrives Paris, to meet with Vergennes on July 11. Battle of Long Island. Franklin appointed to negotiate a French treaty, along with Deane and Arthur Lee; departs October 26. Two days later, Americans defeated at White Plains. Two months later, Washington crosses the Delaware. Franklin to Versailles for clandestine meeting, December 28.

1777 France grants additional secret aid in January. Franklin moves to Passy; hears happy news of Trenton and Princeton in March. Lafayette sails for America. Congress establishes Committee for Foreign Affairs. Burgoyne captures Ticonderoga; Howe occupies Philadelphia. On October 17 Burgoyne surrenders at Saratoga; news reaches Paris on December 6. Washington spends winter at Valley Forge.

1778 British peace commission dispatched under Lord Carlisle. Treaties of amity and commerce signed in February, ratified by Congress in May. Voltaire returns to Paris. American independence recognized at Versailles, March 20. Adams replaces Deane. Outbreak of Franco-British hostilities, June 17; d'Estaing arrives in America with Gérard two weeks later. French fleet dispersed off Rhode Island in August. Deane publishes his address to the American people.

1779 Franklin officially learns he has been appointed sole minister plenipotentiary; presents credentials in March. Simultaneously

Congress debates his recall. Elected grand master of his Masonic lodge. Spain declares war on England on June 21. Temple prepares to serve with Lafayette; invasion of England scuttled. Jones defeats British at Flamborough Head. Franco-American forces fail in assault on Savannah, October 9.

1780 Jay arrives in Spain; Adams returns to Paris. British take Charleston, May 12; Franklin hears news in July. Rochambeau's forces land in Rhode Island. Franklin struggles with Landais; Lee departs; Deane returns to Paris. Congress depreciates currency forty to one. Defection of Benedict Arnold. Jay named minister to Spain. Franklin's recall again discussed; John Laurens elected special envoy to France.

1781 Pennsylvania and New Jersey troops mutiny. Articles of Confederation, drafted in 1776, ratified in March. Franklin resigns as minister plenipotentiary; John Laurens arrives. Congress appoints Jay, Henry Laurens, Adams, Jefferson, and Franklin to negotiate a peace. De Grasse sails for America. Dauphin born. After three-week siege, Cornwallis surrenders at Yorktown, October 19.

1782 Shelburne becomes prime minister on July 11 and peace discussions open. Franklin falls ill; Jay negotiates. Adams arrives Paris, October 26. American commissioners sign peace preliminary articles without consulting Versailles, November 30.

1783 Benny returns to Paris after four-year absence. Definitive peace signed, September 3. Washington disbands army, returns to Mount Vernon.

1784 Franklin begs to retire, adds to *Autobiography*. Mesmer commission named. Peace ratified in May. Mrs. Adams meets Madame Helvétius. Jefferson arrives. Polly Hewson and family spend winter in Passy.

1785 Jefferson named minister plenipotentiary to France; Franklin leaves Passy in July. After a brief, cold encounter with William, arrives Philadelphia, September 14, to deafening ovations. Elected president of Executive Council of Pennsylvania, October 11.

1786 Builds an addition to his home, with an ample library.

1787 Oldest delegate to Constitutional Convention. Vergennes dies, February 12.

1788 First five states ratify the Constitution, in effect as of June 21. Franklin serves his last weeks in Executive Council of Pennsylvania in October.

1789 Bastille falls on July 14. Franklin submits first three parts of *Autobiography* to French friends. Subsists on diet of laudanum.

1790 Dies of pleurisy, April 7, in Philadelphia.

Notes

Except where indicated, all Franklin citations may be found, in manuscript or in copies, in the editorial offices of the Papers of Benjamin Franklin, Yale University Library. Correspondence through August 15, 1782, has been published in thirty-seven magnificently annotated volumes, as *The Papers of Benjamin Franklin* (New Haven: Yale University Press, 1959–2003), a project originally under the direction of Leonard W. Labaree, today under that of Ellen R. Cohn. The collection in its entirety is now searchable on CD-ROM. Additional original and family materials make their home at the American Philosophical Society, in Philadelphia. For the most part I have otherwise reconstructed Franklin's French stay from documents in the following archives:

AAE	Archives des Affaires Etrangères, Quai d'Orsay, Paris
AN	Archives Nationales, Paris
APS	American Philosophical Society, Philadelphia
BL	British Library, London
BN	Bibliothèque Nationale, salle des manuscrits, Paris
DR	Sächsisches Hauptstaatsarchiv, Dresden
InF	Institut de France, Paris
NYPL	New York Public Library
PRO	Public Record Office, Kew, England
WLF	Niedersächsisches Staatsarchiv, Wolfenbüttel

Substantial portions of the French and British materials have been published in two collections: Mary A. Guinta et. al., eds., *The Emerging Nation: A Documentary History of the Foreign Relations of the United States Under the Articles of the Confederation, 1780–89* (Washington: National Historical Publications and Records Commission, 1996), 3 vols. (hereafter "Guinta"); and Benjamin F. Stevens, ed., *Facsimiles of Manuscripts in European Archives Relating to America, 1773–1783* (London, 1889–98), 25 vols. (The most comprehensive source of published materials in the AAE, BL, and PRO; hereafter "Stevens.") American materials have been drawn largely from Francis Wharton, ed., *The Revolutionary Diplomatic Correspondence of the United States* (Washington: Government Printing Office, 1889), 6 vols. ("Wharton"); and from Edmund C. Burnett, ed., *Letters of Members of the Continental Congress* (Washington: Carnegie Institute, 1921–36), 8 vols. ("Burnett").

Also among key texts—as much for colorful as for accurate reporting—are the following periodicals and gossip sheets, abbreviated where indicated: Louis-Petit de Bachaumont, *Mémoires secrets pour servir à l'histoire de la république des lettres* (London, 1781–89), 36 vols. ("Bachaumont"); Lescure, *Correspondance secrète inédite sur Louis XVI, Marie Antoinette, la cour et la ville* (Paris: Plon, 1866), 2 vols. ("Lescure"); Linguet, *Annales politiques, civiles et littéraires du 18ème siècle,* 14 vols. ("Linguet"); François Métra, *Correspondance secrète, politique et littéraire* (Geneva: Slatkine Reprints, 1967), 3 vols. ("Métra"); Pidanzat de Mairobert, *L'Espion Anglais, ou Correspondance secrète entre Milord All'Eye et Milord All'Ear* (London: John Adamson, 1777–85), 10 vols. (*"Espion Anglais"*); *Le Courrier d'Avignon; Le Courrier de l'Europe; La Gazette de France; Le Journal de Bruxelles; Le Journal de Genève; Le Journal de Paris; Le Mercure de France;* and *Nouvelles Extraordinaires de Divers Endroits.*

Two hundred and thirty years of documentation can add up to as many pages of source notes. Where much material has been compressed into little, chapter headnotes indicate central texts; volumes that have shaped the text as a whole or that have been consulted regularly appear in the selected bibliography that follows. Those titles appear in the notes in abbreviated form. For a complete bibliography, see Melvin H. Buxbaum, *Benjamin Franklin: A Reference Guide* (Boston: G. K. Hall, 1983–88), 2 vols. In addition to diplomatic dispatches, intelligence reports, and correspondences, I have relied heavily on four modern mainstays. The work of Gilbert Chinard and A. O. Aldridge has been essential; that of Jonathan Dull and Claude Lopez informs every one of these pages.

Spellings have been Americanized and on occasion modernized. If Franklin wrote "oeconomy" the word appears as "economy"; Lafayette's "schokingly nack'd" is here "shockingly naked." For the sake of clarity I have on occasion lightly tampered as well with punctuation. Translations from the French are my own and may vary from published texts. For translations from other languages I am indebted to Zulema Seligsohn (Spanish), John Ottosson (Swedish), Ana Morais (Portuguese), Jennifer Hohensteiner and Liselotte Davis (German), Karina Attar (Italian), Tom Buk-Swienty (Danish), May Bletz (Dutch), and Stanley Rosenberg (Greek).

Names of principal correspondents are rendered as follows:

JA	John Adams
BB	Benjamin Bache
BEAU	Pierre-Augustin Caron de Beaumarchais
SD	Silas Deane
BF	Benjamin Franklin
WTF	William Temple Franklin
RI	Ralph Izard
JJ	John Jay
TJ	Thomas Jefferson
LF	Marquis de Lafayette
HL	Henry Laurens
AL	Arthur Lee
RL	Richard Henry Lee
WL	William Lee
RM	Robert Morris
ST	Lord Stormont
VRG	Comte de Vergennes

GW   George Washington
PW   Paul Wentworth

INTRODUCTION

2 best orator in Congress: Richard Henry Lee to Landon Carter, June 2, 1776, Burnett, I, 469. Edward Rutledge to JJ, June 8, 1776, Burnett, I, 476.

3 "I could as easily": BF to Jane Mecom, December 24, 1767.

   "politically he was an American": Ormond Seavey, cited in Edmund S. Morgan, *The Genuine Article* (New York: Norton, 2004), 173.

   "The greatest revolution": Richard Henry Lee, *The Life of Arthur Lee* (Boston: Wells & Lilly, 1829), I, 345.

4 "The essence of the whole": JA to Benjamin Rush, April 4, 1790, in L. H. Butterfield, ed., *Letters of Benjamin Rush* (Princeton: Princeton University Press, 1951), I, 1207.

   "the first to lay": Cited in Nian-Sheng Huang, *Benjamin Franklin in American Thought and Culture, 1790–1990* (Philadelphia: American Philosophical Society, 1994), 33.

5 cost of the Revolution: The total cost of the American Revolution to France has been estimated at between 1 and 1.3 billion livres, exclusive of debt interest. Overall gifts totaled 47.5 million livres; Schaeper, *France and America in the Revolutionary Era: The Life of Jacques-Donatien Leray de Chaumont* (Providence: Berghahn Books, 1995), has calculated that 38 million livres passed through the hands of Ferdinand Grand.

I: THE FIRST MISTAKE IN PUBLIC BUSINESS IS THE GOING INTO IT

For SD's trials and BEAU's operations, I have drawn largely on the New-York Historical Society's five volumes of the *Deane Papers* (New York: Collections of the New-York Historical Society for the years 1886–90); on Beaumarchais's published and unpublished correspondences, in Brian N. Morton, ed., *Beaumarchais Correspondence*, 4 vols., the last in collaboration with Donald C. Spinelli (Paris: Nizet, 1969–78); vol. 5 in its unpublished form, courtesy of Spinelli; Morton and Spinelli's masterful *Beaumarchais and the American Revolution* (Lanham, Md.: Lexington Books, 2002); on Jacques Léon Donvez's unpublished doctoral dissertation, Université de Paris III, "La Politique de Beaumarchais" (1978); on Stormont's reports and on those of Whitehall's informers (BL and PRO, especially Stormont to Weymouth, SP 78/300 and SP 78/301); on French police reports (Contrôle des étrangers, AAE); and on the dispatches of various foreign ambassadors to Versailles, chief among them the dispatches of Mercy d'Argenteau, Oesterreichisches Staatsarchiv, Vienna. Aranda's dispatches have been published in Juan F. Yela Utrilla, *España ante la independencia de los Estados Unidos* (Lérida: Mariana, 1925), 2 vols.

    For the Auray arrival, I am indebted to William Bell Clark's very good *Lambert Wickes: Sea Raider and Diplomat* (New Haven: Yale University Press, 1932), as well as to Theodore Sizer, ed., *Autobiography of Colonel John Trumbull* (New Haven: Yale University Press, 1953). Among guides to Franklin's daily and commercial life there is no better source than Thomas J. Schaeper, *France and America in the Revolutionary Era: The Life of Jacques Donatien Leray de Chaumont* (Providence: Berghahn Books, 1995). For Dubourg, see Alfred Owen Aldridge's excellent "Jacques Barbeu-Dubourg: A French Disciple of Benjamin Franklin," *Proceedings of the American Philosophical Society*, Aug. 1951, 331–92; and J. C. Lettsom, "Memoirs of Jacques Barbeu Dubourg," *Memoirs of the Medical Society of London*, I, Feb. 25, 1787, 476–91. There is a fine, unpublished L'Air de Lamotte sketch of Dubourg, written after December 13, 1779, in the Yale Franklin papers.

7 "If something foreign": Paget Toynbee, ed., *Letters of Horace Walpole* (Oxford: Clarendon Press, 1905), V, 205.

invisible ink: SD's ink was provided by JJ's (Loyalist) brother, Sir James Jay. For more on SD's technique, L. Bendikson, "The Restoration of Obliterated Passages and of Secret Writing in Diplomatic Missives," *The Franco-American Review*, I, 1937, 240–56, and Victor Hugo Paltsits, "The Use of Invisible Ink for Secret Writing During the American Revolution," *Bulletin of the New York Public Library*, May 1935, 361–64.

"We look only": Benjamin Rush to Dubourg, September 16, 1776, in *Letters of Benjamin Rush*, I, 110.

8 "so incapable of acting": SD to Simeon Deane, May 16, 1781, *Deane Papers*, IV, 337.

"See for yourself": Louis-Sébastien Mercier, *Tableau de Paris* (Geneva: Slatkine Reprints, 1979), I–II.

"but you know, Americans": SD to Messrs. Delap, July 30, 1776, *Deane Papers*, I, 169.

"For heaven's sake": SD to Committee of Secret Correspondence (hereafter CSC), Oct. 1, 1776, *ibid.*, 288.

9 "here where everything": SD to JJ, Dec. 3, 1776, *ibid.*

"Is not this a pretty": JA to Abigail Adams, May 10, 1777, Burnett, I, 359.

"the most silent": BEAU to VRG, Aug. 13, 1776, in Morton, II.

10 "moneyless, without credit": SD's narrative to Congress, in Edward D. Ingraham, ed., *Papers in Relation to the Case of Silas Deane* (Philadelphia: Collins, 1855), 21.

"one can connive": VRG to Dubourg, June 1776, cited in Albert Henry Smyth, *The Writings of Benjamin Franklin* (New York: Macmillan, 1907), X, 313.

Beaumarchais's math: BEAU to VRG, May 2, 1776, Morton, II, 198. Also BEAU to Louis XVI and Maurepas, early Sept. 1776, Donvez, 341–42.

"one of the most zealous": BEAU to CSC, Aug. 18, 1776, Morton, II, 244.

"My Lord, I have never": BEAU to VRG, May 3, 1776, Morton and Spinelli, II, 204.

11 "For the enemies": BEAU to CSC, Sept. 5, 1776, Wharton, II, 146.

"remove...all obstacles": BEAU to CSC, Aug. 18, 1776, Wharton, II, 129.

"better able than you": BEAU to CSC, Sept. 16, 1776, Wharton, II, 146.

Have you realized: BEAU to CSC, Aug. 18, 1776, Wharton II, 131.

12 "There is as much intrigue": JJ to GW, Apr. 26, 1779, Wharton, II.

13 "paroxysms of intemperance": SD to RM, Oct. 5, 1777, in Ingraham, 122.

"He is drunk": William McCreery to JA, Sept. 29, 1777; cited in JA, *Diary*, II, 368.

"without intelligence": SD to JJ, Dec. 3, 1776, *Deane Papers*, I, 395.

14 "You will be surprised": BF to Dubourg, Dec. 4, 1776.

16 "Let Old England": Cited in Clark, *Lambert Wickes*, 92.

17 a wrong he has been said: Richard Brookhiser, *Founding Father: Rediscovering George Washington* (New York: Free Press, 1997), 138.

18 "conceit, wrong-headedness": The charge was Lord Hillsborough's, according to Franklin. Cited in James Parton, *Life and Times of Benjamin Franklin* (New York: Mason Brothers, 1865), I, 505. The 1919 of its day, 1763 found another neat parallel in 1871, when the stain on French honor was Sedan. Gambetta's advice—"Never mention it, think of it always"—was a reprise of Vergennes's theme song.

"was too much for the nerves": Cited in George L. Clark, *Silas Deane: A Connecticut Leader in the American Revolution* (New York: Putnam's, 1913), 40. In Europe the Declaration of Independence was seen as a patent plea for aid. See Salken dispatch (Saxony), Jan. 7, 1777, DR.

19 their very nakedness: Cited in David Hackett Fischer, *Washington's Crossing* (New York: Oxford University Press, 2004), 155.

"This was kept secret": BF to Priestley, Jan. 27, 1777. On the nonsupply of gunpowder in the colonies, Orlando W. Stephenson, "The Supply of Gunpowder in 1776," *American Historical Review*, Jan. 1925, 271–81.

"with an easy air": JA, Sep. 17, 1776, *Autobiography*, III, 422.

20 "masterly acquaintance": JA to Warren, Feb. 18, 1776, Burnett, I.

"I am old and good": Benjamin Rush to Thomas Morris, Oct. 22, 1776, intercepted letter in CP Etats-Unis, I, f77, AAE. Stormont's information was so good that he was able to report, in his dispatch of Jan. 1, 1777, that BF had "told the Congress that all he could do was to go to France, and die there in their service, that the *fluff* was almost worn out, but that the last *thread* of it was at their disposal."

21 "Persuasion and goodness": Oct. 9, 1777, entry in "Georg Forster's Tagebucher," from Paul Zincke and Albert Leitzmann, eds., *Deutsche Literaturdenkmale* (Berlin: B. Berh, 1914).

"You know that Dr. Franklin's": Voltaire to Jean le Rond d'Alembert, Oct. 22, 1776, in Theodore Besterman, ed., *Voltaire correspondance* (Paris: Gallimard, 1964), vol. 95, 130–31.

22 "Dr. Franklin's landing": Lenoir to Vergennes, Dec. 14, 1776, AAE.

"an old man": *Nouvelles Extraordinaires*, Dec. 20, 1776, Dec. 24, 1776.

23 It was equally asserted: Zeno (Venice) dispatch of Dec. 30, 1776, Fond Italien 1982, filza 257, BN. To sue for peace: *Courrier d'Avignon*, Dec. 20, 1776; to ensure that future generations: *Espion Anglais*, V, 3. Saxon ambassador: Salken dispatch, Dec. 13, 1776, DR. Sardinian envoy: comte de Viry dispatch of Jan. 10, 1777, Archivio di Stato di Torino. Finish his days: Métra, Dec. 24, 1776. With a mission, or to settle in France: *Gazette d'Amsterdam*, Dec. 20, 1776; *Journal de Genève*, Dec. 17, 1776. Dispute with Congress: *Town and Country Magazine*, Jan., 1777. See also Journal of S-P Hardy, "Mes loisirs," Mss. Fr. 5582, BN; Stormont to Weymouth, Dec. 11, 1776, SP 78/300–382, PR.

no strategic advantage: Thulemeier (Prussia) to Frederick II, Jan. 3, 1777; Rep. 96, 41D, vol. XVI, fol. 2v, Geheimes Staatsarchiv, Berlin. Short of that: Braunschweig–Lueneburg dispatch, Dec. 15, 1776, WLF. Salken dispatch (Saxony), Jan. 12, 1777, DR.

24 expertly trained men: Creutz (Sweden) dispatch of Dec. 15, 1776, Riksarkivet. More resistance: Mercy d'Argenteau (Austria) dispatch, Jan. 17, 1777, Nouv. Acq., 6957, BN.

"I have helped": BF to John Hancock, Dec. 8, 1776.

"As he is a subtle": Stormont to Weymouth, Dec. 11, 1776, SP 78/300, PRO.

25 "wild, roving disposition": Stormont to Weymouth, Dec. 18, 1776, Wharton, XIV. On Stormont, see E. Maxtone Graham, *The Beautiful Mrs. Graham and the Cathcart Circle* (Boston: Houghton Mifflin, 1928). For his being shaken, Blome (Denmark) dispatch of Dec. 19, 1776, 631, Rigsarkivet, Copenhagen.

26 "I am about to begin": BEAU to SD, Dec. 17, 1776, *Deane Papers*, I, 423.

"God is a Bourbon": BEAU to VRG, Nov. 12, 1776, Wharton, IX.

27 "to go and meet": BEAU to VRG, Dec. 16, 1776, CP Angleterre, vol. 519, f343, AAE.

"No one knows": BEAU to SD, Dec. 17, 1776, *Deane Papers*, I, 424.

29 "to the end of": Cited in Elizabeth S. Kite, "French 'Secret Aid' Precursor to the French American Alliance 1776–1777," *French American Review*, Apr. 1948, 151.

a young rake: Dec. 27, 1776, Métra.

31 "He avoids direct falsehood": Stormont to Weymouth, Oct. 8, 1776, cited in *British Diplomatic Instructions, 1689–1789*, VII, France, part IV, 1745–89, Camden Third Series, London, 1934.

Vergennes opened the Saturday meeting: Vergennes to Ossun, Jan. 4, 1777, CP Espagne, vol. 583, f14, AAE. PW to Earl of Suffolk, Jan. 25, 1777, Auckland Mss. 34413, f161, BL. For Franklin's account, American Commissioners to CSC, Mar. 12–Apr. 9, 1777.

32 Cool-headed man: Mercy d'Argenteau dispatch, Jan. 17, 1777, Nouv. Acq. 6957, BN.

"In any event": VRG to Noailles, Jan. 10, 1777, CP Angleterre, vol. 521, AAE.

clucked about Beaumarchais: Mercy d'Argenteau dispatch, Jan. 17, 1777. Aranda (Spain) dispatch of Jan. 13, 1777, in Yela Utrilla. Most of the rest of Europe disapproved of French complicity; see for example Viry (Sardinia) dispatch, Feb. 21, 1777, Archivio di Stato di Torino.

"Wait now": Stormont to Weymouth, Jan. 22, 1777, SP 78/301, PRO.

33 "Franklin speaks" and "Either because": Aranda to Grimaldi, dispatches 938 and 939 of Jan. 13, 1777, in Yela Utrilla, II.

"much more specific": VRG to Ossun, Jan. 12, 1777, CP Espagne, vol. 583, f40, AAE.

34 "originally well-imagined": William Carmichael to Dumas, Jan. 21, 1777, *Deane Papers*, I, 465.

"God preserve us": Nicholas Rogers to SD, Jan. 9, 1777, *Deane Papers*, I, 454.

35 "My dear Sir": BEAU to SD, Jan. 5, 1777, Donvez, 403.

II : HALF THE TRUTH IS OFTEN A GREAT LIE

On Paris, Louis-Sebastien Mercier's supreme *Tableau de Paris* (Geneva: Slatkine Reprints, 1979), 12 vols. All of BF's letters combined do not pack the descriptive punch of a single Abigail Adams missive; I have plundered mercilessly from her pages, as from those of Gouverneur Morris, *Diary and Letters of Gouverneur Morris*, ed. Anne Cary Morris (New York: Scribner's, 1888), 2 vols. Otherwise I have deferred to a number of eighteenth-century travelers, among them Arthur Young, *Travels in France During the Years 1787, 1788, and 1789* (Garden City: Doubleday, 1969); John Moore, *A View of Society and Manners in France, Switzerland and Germany* (London: Cadill, 1786); William Greene, "Journal of a Visit to Paris," *Massachusetts Historical Society*, Oct. 1920, 84–138; William Cole, *A Journal of My Journey to Paris in the Year 1765* (New York: Richard R. Smith, 1931); Tobias Smollett, *Travels Through France and Italy*, ed. Frank Felsenstein (New York: Oxford University Press, 1979); *The French Journals of Mrs. Thrale and Dr. Johnson* (Manchester: Manchester University Press, 1932); Charles Kunstler, *La vie quotidienne sous Louis XVI* (Paris: Hachette, 1950); Winslow C. Watson, ed., *Men and Times of the Revolution, or Memoirs of Elkanah Watson* (New York: Dana, 1856); Benjamin Rush's unpublished account of his Paris journey, in the Morgan Library. Among modern sources: David Garrioch, *The Making of Revolutionary Paris* (Berkeley: University of California Press, 2002); Evelyn Farr, *Before the Deluge* (London: Peter Owen, 1994); Daniel Roche, *The People of Paris: An Essay in Popular Culture in the Eighteenth Century* (Berkeley: University of California Press, 1987); Olivier Bernier, *Pleasure and Privilege* (New York: Doubleday, 1981); and Pierre Gaxotte, *Paris au XVIIIème siècle* (Paris: Arthaud, 1968).

On Chaumont and the Valentinois: Again I am much indebted to the research of Thomas J. Schaeper. There is no better topography to BF's French life than Meredith (Martindale) Frapier; see Meredith Martindale, "Benjamin Franklin's Residence in France," *Antiques*, Aug. 1977, 262–73, and Meredith Martindale, "L'Hôtel de Valentinois et ses environs au temps de Benjamin Franklin," *Bulletin de la Société Historique d'Auteuil et de Passy*, XV, no. 2, 1978, 7–12. Equally essential is Howard C. Rice Jr., *Thomas Jefferson's Paris* (Princeton: Princeton University Press, 1976).

36 "set down in the tourbillion": BF to Le Veillard, Sept. 5, 1789, Morgan Library.
38 "against the hollow puffery": Anonymous to BF, Dec., 1776.
   "The first thing": JA, Oct. 26, 1782, *Diary*, III, 37.
   "dull razors": BF to Lord Kames, Feb. 28, 1768. Similarly, BF, *Autobiography* (New York: Modern Library, 2001), 140.
39 "Canada fur-cap": *Morning Post* (London), Jan. 12, 1779.
   Madame du Deffand encounter: Stormont to Weymouth, Jan. 1, 1777, Stevens XIV, 1408; Bancroft to SD, Feb. 28, 1777, in *Deane Papers*, II, 5; Madame du Deffand to Walpole, Dec. 31, 1776, and Jan. 26, 1777, in M. de Lescure, ed., *Correspondance complète de la marquise du Deffand* (Paris: Plon, 1865), II.
41 tackle asparagus: *Souvenirs de la marquise de Créquy* (Paris: Delloye, 1840), V, 178.
   "bizarre and dishonest" BEAU to Théveneau de Francy, Jan. 22, 1777, Donvez, 407.
   Franklin and Aranda: Aranda to Grimaldi, dispatch of Jan. 13, 1777, in Yela Utrilla, II.
42 "Our Delaware River": Vicomte de Grouchy and Paul Cottin, eds., *Journal inédit du duc de Cröy* (Paris: Flammarion, 1906), III, 300. Also Cröy, Ms. 1671, InF.
   He listened: See, among other examples, *Mémoires de Brissot sur ses contemporains et la révolution française* (Paris: Ladvocat, 1830), I, 231.
   Hence his theory: Creutz dispatches (Sweden), Dec. 22, 1776, and Jan. 7, 1778, Riksarkivet.
43 That week the papers: Bachaumont, Jan. 17, 1777, *Espion Anglais*, V, 5.
   "and who did not": JA, *Boston Patriot*, May 15, 1811. "When they spoke of him," continued JA, "they seemed to think he was to restore the golden age."
   "Congress did not want": Aranda to Grimaldi, Jan. 13, 1777, in Yela Utrilla, II.
44 "If you ever expect": Carmichael to SD, Jan. 19, 1777, *Deane Papers*, I, 463.
   "It is simply this": BF to Juliana Ritchie, Jan. 19, 1777.
45 "an appalling luxury": Voltaire to Philippe-Antoine de Claris, Mar. 15, 1778, in Theodore Besterman, ed., *Voltaire correspondance* (Paris: Gallimard, 1964), vol. 98, 141.
46 "All the splendors": Nicolai Karamzine, *Lettres d'un voyageur russe* (Paris: Quai Voltaire, 1991), 130.
   "vaulting across a river": Louis-Sebastien Mercier, *Tableau de Paris* (Geneva: Slatkine Reprints, 1979), I–II, 120.
47 "generally speaks at great length": Mercier, VII, 281. "to talk much": Oct. 16, 1777, *Life of Arthur Lee*, I, 339. Karamzine, 127.
   "is the very dirtiest": Abigail Adams to Lucy Cranch, Sep. 5, 1784, in Charles F. Adams, ed., *Letters of Mrs. Adams* (Boston: Little, Brown, 1840), 251.
   "I find the general fate": TJ to Charles Bellini, Sep. 30, 1785, in Adrienne Koch and William Peden, eds., *The Life and Selected Writings of Thomas Jefferson* (New York: Random House, 1944), 382.
48 "the most magically magical": BF to Peter Collinson, c. 1752.
49 "amuse those that make": BF to Juliana Ritchie, Jan. 19, 1777.
52 "While learning the language": TJ to Dugald Stewart, in *The Papers of Thomas Jefferson*, XV, 204.
53 "If you stand well": The translator was JA.
   "there to find": BF to Dumas, Jan. 28, 1777.

54 "refused so many people": Rulhière to VRG, Mar. 4, 1777, CP Etats-Unis, II, 130.

"Frequently if a man": BF to Dubourg, after Oct. 2, 1777.

"Sir, if you in America": Cited in Gilbert Chinard, "Abbé Lefebvre de la Roche's Recollections of Benjamin Franklin," *Proceedings of the American Philosophical Society*, June 1950, 221.

55 "The noise of every": BF to Dubourg, c. Oct. 2, 1777.

"Whoever writes": BF to unnamed correspondent, Apr. 6, 1777.

56 Just because Congress: James Lovell to BF, July 4, 1777.

"a delicate and perplexing": GW to BF, Aug. 17, 1777.

"The number of wild schemes": BF's journal, Dec. 13, 1777.

"I don't know what is is": Deborah Franklin cited in Morellet, Add. Mss. 6134, 100, BL. For a sympathetic appraisal of Deborah Franklin, see Jennifer Reed Fry, " 'Extraordinary Freedom and Great Humility': A Reinterpretation of Deborah Franklin," *The Pennsylvania Magazine of History and Biography*, Apr. 2003, 167–96.

58 "No one but me": BEAU to SD, Feb. 19, 1777, *Deane Papers*, I, 491.

Passy sanctuary: Stormont to Weymouth, Apr. 2, 1777. Creutz (Sweden) dispatch of Jan. 18, 1777, Riksarkivet. Count d'Haslang (Bavaria) dispatches of Jan. 25, 1777, Feb. 9, 1777, Bayerisches Haupstaatsarchiv. Salken dispatch, Jan. 26, 1777, DR. Deutsches Museum account cited in Roland Krebs, ed., *La Révolution américaine vue par les périodiques de langue allemande, 1773–1783* (Metz: Université de Metz, 1992), 4.

"I still don't know": VRG to Noailles, Feb. 22, 1779, CP Angleterre, vol. 520 supp., f339, AAE. Noailles was entirely correct. See Peter Orlando Hutchinson, ed., *The Diary of Thomas Hutchinson* (London: Sampson, Low, 1886), 237.

59 "You English consider us": Purported letter from Paris to a gentleman in London, printed in the *Public Advertiser*, Jan. 17, 1769.

"Franklin's customary strategy": Noailles to VRG, Feb. 28, 1777, CP Angleterre, Vol. 521, f366, AAE.

60 "I will deal confidentially": Stormont to Weymouth, Feb. 26, 1777, Stevens, XIV.

"A minister's residence": Stormont to Weymouth, Dec. 18, 1776, Stevens, XIV.

"some trouble and uneasiness": Commissioners to the CSC, March 12–April 9, 1777. On Vergennes's divertissement, VRG to Noailles, Mar. 22, 1777, Stevens, XV.

61 the Maurepas visit: Stormont to Weymouth, May 22, 1777, Stevens, XV.

"a clear head": JA, *Autobiography*, IV, 73.

62 "This is what is happening": Stormont to Weymouth, Apr. 9, 1777, SP 78/302, PRO.

63 "for we know that separated": Sir Philip Gibbes, minutes of a conversation with BF, on or before Feb. 5, 1777. Similarly, BF to Hartley, Mar. 21, 1779.

"Dr. Franklin had invented": Walpole to William Mason, Feb. 27, 1777, Paget Toynbee, *Letters of Horace Walpole*, X, 22. Also *New Jersey Gazette*, Dec. 31, 1777.

"All the better": Lescure, I, Feb. 6, 1777.

64 "All Europe is for us": BF and SD to the CSC, Mar. 12, 1777, Auckland Mss., 34413, f311, BL. Similarly, BF to Cooper, May 1, 1777. Before sailing for France BF had proposed a seal for the new republic in which Moses commands the seas to part, and overwhelm the pharoah.

Notes

III: THREE CAN KEEP A SECRET, IF TWO OF THEM ARE DEAD

On the press, the seminal work of Robert Darnton, in particular *The Business of Enlightenment* (Cambridge: Harvard University Press, 1979), *The Literary Underground of the Old Regime* (Cambridge: Harvard University Press, 1982), and Darnton and Daniel Roche, eds., *Revolution in Print: The Press in France, 1775–1800* (Berkeley: University of California Press, 1989). On the same front, David T. Pottinger, *The French Book Trade in the Ancien Régime, 1500–1791* (Cambridge: Harvard University Press, 1958). For the long arm of the Paris police, Alan Williams, *The Police of Paris, 1718–89* (Baton Rouge: Louisiana State University Press, 1979); Darnton, "The Memoirs of Lenoir, Lieutenant de Police de Paris," *English Historical Review*, July 1970, vol. 85, 532–59; Maxime de Sars, *Le Noir, lieutenant de police, 1732–1807* (Paris: Hachette, 1948); J. Peuchet, *Archives de la police de Paris* (Paris: Levfavasseur, 1838), II–III; Pierre Manuel, *La police de Paris dévoilée* (Paris: Garnery, 1791), 2 vols. Nearly everyone's movements around Paris can be read in the police reports, Contrôle des étrangers, AAE. On Le Veillard: Leroux-Cesbron, "Un ami de Franklin: Le Veillard," *Bulletin de la Société Historique d'Auteuil et de Passy*, X, no. 2, 1921.

65 full catalogue: See VRG to Ossun, Apr. 12, 1777, CP Espagne, vol. 584, f65, AAE.
67 "We were poorly armed" to "to make the effort": Cröy, *Journal*, III, 302–03.
    "the division of the young": William S. Stryker, cited in David Hackett Fischer, *Washington's Crossing* (New York: Oxford University Press, 2004), 439.
    British atrocities: Abbé Niccoli, in Antonio Pace, *Benjamin Franklin and Italy* (Philadelphia: American Philosophical Society, 1958), 99.
68 "the old veteran": *Morning Post* (London), Jan. 12, 1779.
    "You being at so great": RM to the American commissioners, Mar. 28, 1777.
69 Was it not time: BEAU to VRG, Apr. 15, 1777, Morton, III, 93.
    "whose heart is formed" to "France and America": BEAU to Maurepas, Mar. 30, 1777, Stevens, XV.
70 "in a state of some perplexity": VRG to Ossun, Apr. 12, 1777, CP Espagne, vol. 583, f65, AAE.
    "Only small minds": Cited in Gilbert Chinard, "Adventures in a Library," *The Newberry Library Bulletin*, Mar. 1952, 233.
    "which sets him chatting": Cited in Lewis Einstein, *Divided Loyalties* (New York: Russell and Russell, 1970), 423.
71 "He thinks we shall derive": Carmichael to "Jean Tourville," Nov. 1, 1777, Auckland Mss. 34414, f298, BL.
    "I had rather be sent": Carmichael to Dumas, May 9, 1777, Wharton, II.
    "When you hear not": Committee for Foreign Affairs to the commissioners, May 30, 1777.
72 the packet boat: See Ellen R. Cohn, "Benjamin Franklin, Georges-Louis Le Rouge and the Franklin/Folger Chart of the Gulf Stream," *Imago Mundi*, no. 52, 2000, 124–42.
73 For the Berlin heist: BL, Auckland Mss., SF 1451–1481, BL.
    "We have no time": Cited in Burton J. Hendrick, *The Lees of Virginia* (New York: Halcyon House, 1935), 284.
    "He was an honest rascal": Earl of Suffolk to Eden, Oct. 23, 1777, Stevens, III.
74 odd, repulsive-looking caller: *Courrier de l'Europe*, July 18, 1777; PW to Suffolk, July 17, 1777, Stevens II, 182. Contrôle des étrangers, July 25, 1777, vol. 16, and Aug. 1, 1777, vol. 17, AAE. Evidently there is a report in the *Nouvelles Extraordinaires*, Aug.

20, 1777, on sinister characters lurking at Passy and on the stepped-up security there, but I have never found it.

75 "every transaction": Reproduced in S. F. Bemis, "British Secret Service and the French-American Alliance," *American Historical Review*, XXIX, 1924, 494. The instructions for transmitting reports are in the Auckland Mss. 34413, f104ff, BL.

a branch of British intelligence: Dull, "Franklin the Diplomat: The French Mission" (Philadelphia: Transactions of the American Philosophical Society, 1982), 33.

76 "There is one Hynson here": PW to the Earl of Suffolk, Apr. 14, 1777, Stevens, III, 250.

"He speaks French": BEAU to VRG, Dec. 17, 1777, Morton, III, 230.

77 "of the first birth": Col. Smith (?) to Eden, Mar. 28, 1777, Auckland Mss. 34413, f341, BL.

On Lafayette: Louis Gottschalk, *Lafayette Comes to America* (Chicago: University of Chicago Press, 1935), and *Lafayette Joins the American Army* (Chicago: University of Chicago Press, 1937); Stanley J. Idzerda, ed., *Lafayette in the Age of the American Revolution* (Ithaca: Cornell University Press, 1977), 5 vols.

78 "Lord Stormont appears": Vergennes to Noailles, May 2, 1777, CP Angleterre, vol. 523, AAE.

79 "Luckily his age": Noailles to Maurepas, Apr. 8, 1777, Stevens, XV, 1509.

"Of course it's madness": Madame du Deffand to Walpole, M. de Lescure, ed., *Correspondance complète de la marquise du Deffand* (Paris: Plon, 1865), Mar. 31, 1777, 598.

80 "There is more support": Abbé Morellet to Shelburne, May 4, 1777, in Dorothy Medlin et al., *Lettres d'André Morellet* (Oxford: Voltaire Foundation, 1991), I. The observation was not lost on Britain, *Courrier de l'Europe*, May 9, 1780.

"that there is an unaccountable": Stormont to Weymouth, May 14, 1777, Stevens, XV, 1531.

"industriously propagated": Stormont to Weymouth, Mar. 21, 1777, Grantham Papers, 24163, f68, BL.

81 The number of printers: For the most vivid depiction of the publishing scene, Darnton, *The Literary Underground of the Old Regime*. Before the censors: Bureau de la librairie, notes et avis des censeurs, Mss. Fr. 22015, BN.

"Except at mealtimes": Morellet, *Mémoires inédites* (Paris: Badouin, 1823), I, 97; the translation is Francis Steegmuller's, from *A Woman, a Man, and Two Kingdoms: The Story of Madame d'Epinay and the Abbé Galiani* (New York: Knopf, 1991).

82 In the official press: *Courrier de l'Europe*, Apr. 11, 1777.

83 "Deane is managing": *Espion Anglais*, V, 13.

Tory press: Soon enough the British press would assert (Jan. 12, 1779) that BF and Maurepas had hatched the plan for the American Revolution during the course of BF's London posting. It was praise of a kind that the *Morning Post* classed BF together with the sublimely manipulative French minister: "There is not, perhaps, two geniuses existing so similar in vindictive subtlety, watchfulness, and political trick."

On *Les Affaires de l'Angleterre et de l'Amérique*: Chinard, "Adventures in a Library," 223–38. Also Chinard in *American Philosophical Society Year Book*, 1943, 84–106.

84 Polly Baker: For a delicious account of Polly Baker and Beaumarchais, see Agnes G. Raymond, "Figaro, fils naturel de Polly Baker?" *Comparative Literature Studies*, Mar. 1975, 33–43. Morellet, Add. Mss. 6134, 576, BL. On the Raynal conversation, Koch and Peden, 169.

85 "This short volume": Bureau de la librairie, notes et avis des censeurs, Apr. 24, 1777, Mss. Fr. 22015, f 257, BN.

86 "Dr. Franklin is a man": *Town and Country Magazine*, Sept. 1777, 453.

86 prisoner exchange: On the ill-fated American prisoners, Catherine M. Prelinger, "Benjamin Franklin and the American Prisoners of War in England During the American Revolution," *William and Mary Quarterly*, Apr. 1975, 261–94, and Sheldon S. Cohen, "William Hodgson: An English Merchant and Unsung Friend to American Revolutionary Captives," *Pennsylvania Magazine of History and Biography*, Jan.–Apr. 1999, 57–85. "The King's Ambassador": Cited in Prelinger, 263.

88 "At whatever moment": Cabanis, *Oeuvres Posthumes* (Paris: Didot, 1825), 269.
"We do not take kings": *The Life and Selected Writings of Thomas Jefferson*, 167.
"of the largest sizes": Hortalez invoice of May 18, 1778, CP Etats-Unis, IV, f266, AAE.

89 "It would appear": Cited in Louis Guimbaud, "Benjamin Franklin et les artistes," *Art et Curiosité*, July 1925, 3.
"This popularity": BF to Sally Bache, June 2, 1779. Similarly BF to Jane Mecom, Oct. 25, 1779.
As one diplomat noted: Zeno (Venice) dispatch of Dec. 30, 1776, Fond Italien 1982, filza 257, BN.
"The curiosity of the people": *New Jersey Gazette*, Dec. 31, 1777.

90 "The air of Passy": WTF to Jonathan Williams Sr., May 27, 1777.

91 "I still imagine" to "making them interminable": Cited in Chinard, "Abbé Lefebvre de la Roche," 221.

IV: THE CAT IN GLOVES CATCHES NO MICE

On the privateering maelstrom, correspondence in the AAE; Stormont dispatches, BL. A great deal of the story can be read in William Bell Clark, *Ben Franklin's Privateers* (Baton Rouge: Louisiana State University Press, 1956), and in Ruth Y. Johnston's "American Privateers in French Ports," *The Pennsylvania Magazine of History and Biography*, vol. 53, no. 4, 352–74. On the alliance in general: The incisive work of Jonathan R. Dull; William C. Stinchcombe's *The American Revolution and the French Alliance* (Syracuse: Syracuse University Press, 1969); Ronald Hoffman and Peter J. Albert, eds., *Diplomacy and Revolution: The Franco-American Alliance of 1778* (Charlottesville: University Press of Virginia, 1981). Arthur Lee's running commentary is invaluable, *Life of Arthur Lee*.

94 "I've always found": BEAU to VRG, July 14, 1775, in Morton, *Beaumarchais Correspondence* (Paris: Nizet, 1969–78), II, 129.
"pretend to hold": SD to RM, Aug. 23, 1777, *Deane Papers*, II, 106.

95 "Scarcely more could": July 4, 1777, in *British Diplomatic Instructions, 1689–1789*, VII, France, part IV, 1745–89, Camden Third Series, London, 1934.
"You are too well-informed": VRG to BF and SD, July 16, 1777, CP Angleterre vol. 524, AAE. The censure was sent as well to Noailles in London, and no doubt intended largely for use at that address.

96 "I think our sentiments": VRG to Grand, Aug. 21, 1777, Wharton, II.

97 craven tribute: Bachaumont, XI, 45.
briefed Louis XVI: Memo of July 23, 1777, CP Espagne, vol. 585, f95, AAE.
Vergennes in his element to "that licentious spirit": Stormont to Weymouth, Aug. 20, 1777, Stevens, XVIII.

98 It was Forth: See Marion Ward's terrific *Forth* (London: Phillimore, 1982); also Aug. 1777, France, Mémoires et Documents, vol. 531, AAE; Aranda to Grimaldi, vol. 72, August 26, 1777, in Yela Utrilla, II.

98 "Instill in the American": VRG to Ossun, Aug. 26, 1777, CP Espagne, vol. 585, f329, AAE. Similarly VRG to Ossun, Sept. 19, 1777, CP Espagne, vol. 586, f120, AAE.

    to Vergennes's mind: VRG to Ossun, Sept. 26, 1777, CP Espagne, vol. 586, f147, AAE.

99 "Everyone does what he has": VRG to Ossun, Aug. 22, 1777, CP Espagne, vol. 585, f290, AAE.

    Reports had it: Grand to VRG, Sept. 24, 1777, CP Angleterre, vol. 524, f542, AAE.

100 "It is vexing": BF and SD to Jonathan Williams, Aug. 7, 1777.

    "Mr. Franklin seems to have lost": Sept. 26, 1777, Contrôle des étrangers, vol. 18, AAE. On Lauraguais: *Chronique Scandaleuse*, I, 1785, 125; Paul Robiquet, *Théveneau de Morande* (Paris: Quantin, 1882). The best description may be that of the comte de Ségur, *Mémoires, ou Souvenirs et anecdotes* (Paris: Henri Colburn, 1825), 132.

101 "There is nothing better": Cited in Lauraguais to Vergennes, Sept. 20, 1777, CP Angleterre, vol. 524, f534, AAE.

    could afford to alienate: VRG to Ossun, Sept. 26, 1777, CP Espagne, vol. 586, f147, AAE.

102 "indifferent to the" and the Morris encounter: SD to RM, Oct. 1, 1777, *Deane Papers*, II, 155. Lupton to Eden, Sept. 23, 1777, Auckland Mss. 34414, f176, BL.

103 refused to say more: RI to BF, June 18, 1778, and Lupton to Eden, Oct. 15, 1777, Auckland Mss. 34414, f234, BL. RM would apologize, profusely, *Deane Papers*, II, 254.

104 Bancroft's complaint: Bancroft to the commissioners, Oct. 3, 1777, Historical Society of Pennsylvania.

    "I must look on myself": Stephen Sayre to BF, Jan. 13, 1779, Wharton, I, 615.

    "well-nigh discouraged": SD, Narrative read before Congress, *Deane Papers*, III, 178.

105 all a sort of confidence game: BEAU to VRG, Oct. 1, 1777, Morton, III, 203.

    He was colorful: *Espion Anglais*, vol. XI, 59. Zeno (Venice) dispatch of Dec. 8, 1777, Fond Italien 1982, filza 257, BN.

    "civil wars": PW to Eden, Oct. 20, 1777, Auckland Mss. 34414, f342, BL.

106 "such a miracle": *Life of Arthur Lee*, I, 345.

107 "Oh that! My dear": Cited in Vincent Le Ray de Chaumont, *La semaine des familles*, I (1859), 385–87. See also Lopez, *Mon Cher Papa: Franklin and the Ladies of Paris* (New Haven: Yale University Press, 1966), 214, and Franklin, "The Morals of Chess."

    "Never again": BF to Madame Brillon, Nov. 29, 1777.

    "must end in total confusion": AL to Samuel Adams, Nov. 29, 1777, Samuel Adams Papers, NYPL.

108 "The Americans are doomed": Nov. 3, 1777, Lescure, I.

    "drank and smoked": Cited in C. H. Van Tyne, "French Aid Before the Alliance of 1778," *American Historical Review*, XXXI, 1925, 38.

109 "I'm doing my best": Cited in Michel de Decker, *Madame le chevalier d'Eon* (Paris: Perrin, 1987), 210. On d'Eon and Vergennes, Blome (Denmark) dispatch of Dec. 4, 1777, Rigsarkivet.

    Jonathan Loring Austin and "Sir, *is* Philadelphia taken": See WTF, *Memoirs*, II, 56; *Deane Papers*, II 269; Austin journal, reprinted in *Boston Monthly Magazine*, July 1826, 57–66.

110 "to cheer up General Burgoyne": Madame Brillon to BF, Dec. 4, 1777.

110 "Oh! Mr. Austin": Austin journal, *Boston Monthly*, 59.

Paris's daily paper: *Journal de Paris*, Dec. 9, 1777. Bachaumont, Dec. 8, 1777; *Nouvelles Extraordinaires*, Dec. 12, 1777; Lescure, Dec. 4, 1777. Blome (Denmark) dispatch of Dec. 7, 1777, Rigsarkivet.

111 "with a friend who could be": VRG to Montmorin, Dec. 5, 1777, CP Espagne, vol. 587, f140, AAE.

"was received in France": WTF, *Memoirs*, II, 59.

112 "But we must not": VRG to Noailles, Dec. 20, 1777, CP Angleterre, vol. 526, AAE.

"the French officers had fled": Linguet, II, 127.

referred to the Americans: *Life of Arthur Lee*, I, 358.

fussed over afterward: *Courrier de l'Europe*, Dec. 23, 1777.

113 Vergennes read through: VRG to Montmorin, Dec. 13, 1777, CP Espagne, vol. 587, f188, AAE. Also *Life of Arthur Lee*, I, 362.

114 a German paper: *Deutsches Museum*, Dec. 12, 1777, cited in Roland Krebs, *La Révolution américaine vue par les périodiques de langue allemande, 1773–1787* (Metz: Université de Metz, 1992). On the yearning for peace, see also Horace Walpole to the countess of Upper Ossory, Dec. 11, 1777, in Paget Toynbee, ed., *Letters of Horace Walpole* (Oxford: Clarendon Press, 1905), X, 166.

the taciturn Dr. Franklin: BEAU to VRG, Dec. 7, 1777, CP Angleterre, Vol. 526, AAE.

115 an unusual ally: VRG to Montmorin, Dec. 13, 1777, and Dec. 27 1777, CP Espagne, vol. 587, f188 and f307, AAE.

volunteers began lining up: For Pulteney's trip, Frederick B. Tolles, "Franklin and the Pulteney Mission: An Episode in the Secret History of the American Revolution," *Huntington Library Quarterly*, 1953, 37–59. The correspondence is in the Huntington Library.

"one of the cleverest": BEAU to VRG, Dec. 17, 1777, Morton, III, 230.

"We have often been asked": Eden to PW, Dec. 5, 1777, Auckland Mss., SF 483, BL.

116 "and frequently tread" to "always quoting": PW to Eden, Dec. 17, 1777, Auckland Mss., 34414, f433, BL.

117 Favier emerged: Favier to VRG, Jan. 11 and Jan. 15, 1778, France, Mémoires et Documents, vol. 410, f149ff, AAE.

"his dinner was": Favier to VRG, Jan. 10, 1778, Stevens, XXI.

"unfaithful in friendship": PW to Eden, Dec. 22, 1777, Auckland Mss., 34414, f448, BL.

118 the *Amphitrite* stores: BF to RM, Aug. 12, 1782; BEAU to Francy, Dec. 20, 1777, Donvez, 510; *Life of Arthur Lee*, I, Dec. 24, 1777, 368.

"Would you believe, Gentlemen": BEAU to the Committee for Foreign Affairs, Dec. 1777, Donvez, 522.

"all life": Lupton to Eden, Dec. 31, 1777, Auckland Mss., 34414, BL.

"parading and gasconading": PW to Eden, Jan. 7, 1778, Auckland Mss., 34415, BL.

"We have severed one" to "except your life": Braunschweig envoy, dispatches of Feb. 19, 1778, and Feb. 26, 1778, WLF.

119 "And if you please": George Lupton to Eden, Dec. 31, 1777, Auckland Mss., 34414, BL.

"his urbanity and the sweetness": Sousa Coutinho (Portugal) dispatch of Dec. 30, 1777, Instituto dos Arquivos Nacionais, Torre do Tombo, Lisbon.

120 "the Court neither loved": *Espion Anglais*, IX, 18. Bachaumont, XI, Jan. 10, 1778.

120 "There were 13 carriages": Kendall to George Frend, Jan. 7, 1778, in Frederic R. Kirkland, ed., *Letters on the American Revolution in the Library at Karolfred* (Philadelphia, 1941), II, 44.

"I know the door": Samuel Petrie, Jan. 4, 1778, cited in Dixon Wecter, "Burke, Franklin, and Samuel Petrie, *Huntington Library Quarterly*, Apr. 1940, 328.

"Mr. Franklin plays": Blome (Denmark) dispatch of Jan. 1, 1778, Rigsarkivet. Similarly, Creutz (Sweden) dispatch of Jan. 7, 1778, Riksarkivet.

"You have only left us": Chaumont to VRG, Jan. 5, 1778, Stevens IV, 771.

121 dissolved in tears: Braunschweig dispatch, Feb. 19, 1779, WLF; Hutton to BF, Jan. 24, 1783. For a thumbnail account of the visit: John Jordan, "James Hutton's Visit to Franklin, in France, in December of 1777," *The Pennsylvania Magazine of History and Biography*, vol. 32, no. 2, 223–32.

"I observe much eagerness": Chaumont to VRG, Jan. 5, 1778, CP Etats-Unis, III, AAE.

"a man of genius": VRG to Montmorin, Jan. 2, 1778, CP Espagne, vol. 588, AAE.

"72 [Franklin] is taciturn": PW to Eden, Jan. 4, 1778, BL.

122 "I never knew him": PW to Eden, Jan. 7, 1778, Auckland Mss., SF 489, BL.

"We are new at treaty": Sir Philip Gibbes, minutes of a conversation with BF, Jan. 5, 1778.

123 "I don't know that I" to "fears the most": Vergennes to Montmorin, Jan. 8, 1778; CP Espagne, vol. 588, ff17–19, AAE.

124 Vergennes respectfully reminded: France, Mémoirs et Documents, vol. 446, f351, AAE. Similarly, VRG to Montmorin, Apr. 3, 1778, CP Espagne, vol. 589, f11, AAE. taken advantage of his youth: John Hardman and Munro Price, eds., *Louis XVI and the Comte de Vergennes: Correspondance, 1774–1787* (Oxford: Voltaire Foundation, 1998), 43. Regarding a similar opportunity in India, Louis XVI demurred: "Ceci ressemblerait trop à l'affaire de l'Amérique, à laquelle je ne pense jamais sans regret. On a un peu abusé de ma jeunesse dans ce temps-la; nous en portons la peine aujourd'hui. La leçon est trop forte pour l'oublier."

"to restore the honor": Louis XVI to Charles II, Apr. 25, 1780, CP Espagne, vol. 598, AAE.

"And what will you give us": Forth's diary, in Ward, *Forth*, 52–53. See also Aranda to Floridablanca, Mar. 7, 1778, in Yela Utrilla, II.

"but had the indiscretion": Vergennes to Montmorin, Jan. 16, 1778, CP Espagne, vol. 588, AAE.

125 "that the dependency": Franklin to Gibbes, Jan. 6, 1778, cited in *Life of Arthur Lee*, I, 374.

V: THERE IS NO SUCH THING AS A LITTLE ENEMY

In addition to BL reports, AAE files, and AL's diary, the *Letters of William Lee*. Generally I relied a great deal on JA's *Diary* but steered clear of the *Autobiography*, written later. For details on Gérard, Albert Krebs, "Un Alsacien trop oublié: Conrad-Alexandre Gérard, Artisan de l'indépendance des Etats-Unis," *Revue d'Alsace*, 95, 1956, 1–15.

126 "the bait of a false peace" to "as much as possible": Meeting reconstructed from Gérard account of interview, Jan. 9, 1778, Stevens, XXI, and from the commissioners' responses, *Papers of BF*, vol. XXV, 441. Also *Life of Arthur Lee*, I, 374ff; VRG's

correspondence with Montmorin, in CP Espagne, vols. 587 and 588; CP Etats-Unis, III, AAE.

128 "These people show themselves": Vergennes to Montmorin, Jan. 16, 1778, CP Espagne, vol. 588, AAE.

Vergennes claimed utter: Unsigned 1778 memoir, CP Angleterre, supp. vol. 14, f34, AAE.

129 " 'You' " explained Vergennes": Stormont to Weymouth, Dec. 24, 1777, Stevens, XX.

"But do you know": Bachaumont, XI, Feb. 1, 1778.

130 eye always on the Russians: Jonathan Dull has made a solid and ambitiously researched case for VRG's eastern Europe obsession. In *Louis XVI and the Comte de Vergennes: Correspondance, 1774–1787* (Oxford: Voltaire Foundation, 1998), John Hardman and Munro Price (eds.) argue that the king precipitated war when he did in order to avoid involving himself in supporting Austria.

the ambassadorial corps: Blome (Denmark) dispatches of Jan. 11 and Jan. 15, 1778, Rigsarkivet.

131 "Dr. F[ranklin] then, in a certain": *Life of Arthur Lee*, I, 384.

"the treaty upon" to "of their grandfathers": *Life of Arthur Lee*, I, 382–83.

132 "They play us off": Stormont to Eden, Jan. 23, 1778, Auckland Mss., 29475 add., BL.

"Are we to be beholden": JA to James Warren, May 3, 1777, *Papers of John Adams*, V, 174.

Could it be morally: RM to JJ, Sept. 23, 1776, in *Correspondence and Public Papers of John Jay*, I, 85.

133 He much relished: Vergennes to Montmorin, Jan. 30, 1778, CP Espagne, vol. 588, f207, AAE.

by rational men: See, for example, Mercy d'Argenteau (Vienna) dispatch, Nov. 19, 1777, Oesterreichisches Staatsarchiv; Cröy, entry of Mar. 13, 1778, *Journal*, IV, 73; Zeno (Venice) dispatch of Feb. 17, 1778, Fond Italien 1982, filza 257, BN; Blome, Dec. 25, 1777, Rigsarkivet.

"nothing ever persuade": David Hartley to BF, Feb. 3, 1778.

"America has been *forced*": BF to Hartley, Feb. 12, 1778.

134 acting like Don Quixote: Floridablanca, cited in Montmorin to Vergennes, Apr. 10, 1778, CP Espagne, vol. 589, f43, AAE. Floridablanca had made a similar accusation earlier, Montmorin to Vergennes, Dec. 23, 1777, CP Espagne, vol. 587, f262, AAE.

ancient, modern, or fairy: Walpole to the Reverend William Mason, in Paget Toynbee, *Letters of Horace Walpole*, Feb. 18, 1778.

135 "We most often understand": Vergennes to Montmorin, Mar. 6, 1778, CP Espagne, vol. 588, f338, AAE.

"We think Mr. Deane": BF and SD to AL, Feb. 26, 1778.

136 "and seeing no one": Lauraguais to Maurepas, Mar. 5, 1778, Stevens, VIII, 799.

137 "the worthiest man in America": Voltaire to Louis-Laurent Gaultier, Feb. 20, 1778, in Besterman, vol. 98, 110. On the encounter, Voltaire to Theodore Tronchin, Feb. 17, 1778, in Besterman, vol. 98, 91; Nicolas Louis François de Neufchâteau to *Journal de Paris*, in Besterman, vol. 98, 103; Voltaire to Philippe-Antoine de Claris, Mar. 15, 1778, in Besterman, vol. 98, 141. Every paper in Europe: Among them *Das Felleisen*, Mar. 10, 1778; *Espion Anglais*, VII, 297.

in a room together: Académie des Sciences, *pochette* for Apr. 29, 1778, including Etienne Baillat account, Apr. 28, 1778, InF. *Journal de Bruxelles*, May 15, 1778; *Journal de*

Genève, May 10, 1778; *Courrier de l'Europe*, May 15, 1778; *Espion Anglais*, IX, 183: JA *Autobiography*, IV, 81. See also Ernest Choullier, *Voltaire et Franklin à l'Académie des Sciences* (Troyes: Paul Nouel, 1898). The half cats appear in the *Journal de Genève*, May 10, 1778.

138 "The moment they appear": Madame d'Epinay to the abbé Galiani, May 3, 1778, in Francis Steegmuller, *A Woman, a Man, and Two Kingdoms: The Story of Madame d'Epinay and the Abbé Galiani* (New York: Knopf, 1991). The translation is Steegmuller's.

reception was the same: *Courrier d'Avignon*, Mar. 24, 1778; *Nouvelles Extraordinaires*, Mar. 20, 1778; SD to Congress, Dec. 21, 1778, *Deane Papers*, III; Bachaumont, XI, Feb. 25 and Mar. 20, 1778.

"There were many": Feb. 25, 1778, Bachaumont, XI.

Europe would not fail: Feb. 28, 1778, Linguet.

Much of the Continent: Braunschweig dispatch, Feb. 26, 1778, WLF.

139 "I live here": BF to Catharine Greene, Feb. 28, 1778.

"would subject France": Mar. 5, 1778, *Life of Arthur Lee*, I, 401.

buckling under: VRG to Montmorin, personal letter of Mar. 10, 1778, CP Espagne, vol. 588, AAE.

Tears of anger: Creutz (Sweden) dispatch of Mar. 26, 1778, Riksarkivet. For the declaration itself, and the "constant and sincere commitment," May, 1780, Linguet, VIII, 403ff. See also *Mémoires du duc de Lauzun, 1747–1783* (Paris: Poulet-Malassis et de Broise, 1858).

140 His departure was delayed: Braunschweig dispatch, Mar. 22, 1778, WLF; Ward, *Forth*, 73. Stormont's mood: Madame du Deffand to Walpole, Mar. 22, 1778, in M. de Lescure, ed., *Correspondance complète de la marquise du Deffand* (Paris: Plon, 1865), 648.

"Is it possible" to "any eventuality": Mar. 27, 1778, Métra.

"by signing" to "are arrested": Forth diary entry, Mar. 18, 1778, cited in Ward, *Forth*, 74–75. With thanks to Marion Ward for her generous assistance.

141 diplomatic norms: Creutz (Sweden) dispatches of Mar. 19 and Mar. 22, 1778, Riksarkivet; Zeno (Venice) dispatches of Mar. 23, 1778 and Apr. 6, 1778, Fond Italien 1982, filza 257, BN; Blome (Denmark) dispatch of Mar. 22, 1778, Rigsarkivet Braunschweig dispatch of Mar. 22, 1778, WLF. Amy A. Bernardy, "La Missione di Beniamo Franklin a Parigi," *Archivio storico italiano*, 77, 1920, 237–62. On the cut-rate ceremony: Aranda to Floridablanca, Mar. 23, 1778, document no. 1258, Archivo de Simancas, Valladolid. See also Jonathan Loring Austin's memoir, reprinted in *Boston Monthly Magazine*, July 1826. Madame du Deffand, Mar. 22, 1778 to Horace Walpole, in *Correspondance complète*, II, 648–49.

The Versailles appearance: See especially the duc de Castries, *La France et l'indépendence américaine* (Paris: Perrin, 1975), 186–90.

142 "Only the man": Cröy, Ms. 1673, InF.

At noon: *Journal de Genève*, Apr. 20, 1778; AL, entry of Mar. 20, 1778 (an account in which BF does not appear); *Life of Arthur Lee*, I, 403. On Louis XVI, Thomas Blaikie, *Diary of a Scotch Gardener at the French Court at the End of the 18th Century* (New York: Dutton, 1932), 133. Berkenroode (Holland) dispatch of Mar. 22, 1778, Nationaal Archief, the Hague; Austin journal; Cröy, Ms. 1673, InF.

"Please assure Congress": Cröy, "Mémoirs du duc de Cröy," Mar. 27, 1778, *La Nouvelle Revue Retrospective*, 1897; Braunschweig dispatch, Mar. 22, 1778, WLF.

"If all monarchies": Schönfeld (Saxon) dispatch, Mar. 27, 1778, DR.

Notes

143 Lady Stormont: Contrôle des étrangers, Mar. 27, 1778, vol. 21, AAE; Blome (Denmark) dispatch of Mar. 22, 1778, Rigsarkivet.
"But Franklin having skillfully": Cröy, Ms. 1673, InF. See also Anonymous, *Portrait du comte de Vergennes*, 1788 (BN catalogue no. 8-LN27-31339), 63; Abbé Georgel, *Mémoirs pour servir à l'histoire des événements de la fin du 18ème siècle* (Paris: Alexis Eymery, 1820), I, 430.

144 "united all parties": Edwards/PW to Eden, Mar. 26, 1778; Auckland Mss. 34415, f292, BL.
"Never have I seen": Le Roy, cited in Gilbert Chinard, "The Apotheosis of Benjamin Franklin: Paris, 1790–1791," *Proceedings of the American Philosophical Society*, Dec. 1955, 469.
"Never has England": Creutz (Sweden), Mar. 19, 1778, Riksarkivet.
"Many of the streets": Shaw, "Remembrance of Things Past," in Adam Gopnik, ed., *Americans in Paris: A Literary Anthology* (New York: Library of America, 2004), 487.
From the other side: BEAU to VRG, Mar. 13, 1778, in *Deane Papers*, II, 399ff.

145 would throw up his hands: RHL to JA, May 13, 1778, in James Curtis Ballagh, ed., *The Letters of Richard Henry Lee* (New York: Macmillan, 1911), I.

146 "but our tempers" to "we were separated": BF to RM, Dec. 21, 1777.
"rude and disgusting": SD's narrative for Congress, Dec. 20, 1776, *Deane Papers*, III, 189.
"no troops": SD to Congress, Dec. 21, 1778, cited in *Yale Library Gazette*, Apr. 1928, 61.

147 "guided by principles": RI to HL, June 28, 1778, in David Chesnutt and C. James Taylor, eds., *The Papers of Henry Laurens* (Columbia: University of South Carolina Press, 1992), vol. 13, 524.
"How does it happen": BEAU to VRG, Mar. 13, 1778, *Deane Papers*, II, 401.
"plenteously and without account": WL to RHL, Jan. 24, 1778, *Letters of William Lee*, I, 350.

148 "have put near a million": WL to BF, Mar. 11, 1778, *Letters of William Lee*, II, 398.
"might otherwise combine": AL to Samuel Adams, Feb. 28, 1778, NYPL.

149 "The sending persons": AL to comte de Sarsfield, 1777, in Burton J. Hendrick, *The Lees of Virginia* (New York: Halcyon House, 1935), 266.
"from being a clerk": WL to RHL, Oct. 15, 1778, *Letters of William Lee*, II. AL to Bland, Dec. 13, 1778, *ibid.*, 494.
"great wheel": AL to Samuel Adams, Oct. 4, 1777, *Life of Arthur Lee*, II, 113. Similarly, WL to RHL, Jan. 9, 1778, in *Letters of William Lee*, I. If the Feb. 1778 document not in his hand can be believed, RI requested outright that BF be removed and that room be made for RI at Versailles, RI to HL, *Deane Papers*, III, 206.
"to be done with this": Aranda to VRG, Dec. 11, 1777, CP Espagne 587, AAE.

150 "They will soon": PW to Eden, Sep. 24, 1777, Auckland Mss., 34414, f186, BL.
to be replaced by: Stormont to Weymouth, Mar. 11, 1778, Stevens, XXII.

151 "labored indefatigably": Bancroft to Samuel Adams, c. Mar. 1778, Adams Papers, NYPL.
Pulteney was in Paris: See Frederick B. Tolles, "Franklin and the Pulteney Mission: An Episode in the Secret History of the American Revolution," *Huntington Library Quarterly*, XVII, 1953, 37–59.

152 "probably have been accepted": BF to VRG, Apr. 1, 1778.
"Is this the example": AL to BF, Apr. 2, 1778.
"I do not like": BF to AL, Apr. 3, 1778.

152 "for this my terrible": BF to AL, Apr. 4, 1778.
"His disorder seems": BF to SD, Apr. 7, 1778.

153 Franklin barely glanced: For a different version of events, see TJ to Madison, Jan. 31, 1778, in *Papers of Thomas Jefferson*, VI, 226.
"always to *suppose*": BF to RI, Jan. 29, 1778.
"His tricks": RI to HL, June 28, 1778, South Carolina Historical Society.
"the most corrupt": AL to Samuel Adams, May 22, 1779, NYPL.

154 With Europe's attention: Feb. 15 and Mar. 30, 1778, Linguet, III.
"The Boston manner": BF to John Lathrop, May 31, 1788.

155 "that Dr. Franklin was one": JA, May 2, 1778, *Autobiography*, IV, 87.
"I wished to be": RI to HL, n.d., in *Deane Papers*, III, 206. The original appears to be in the hand of John Laurens but is an accurate echo of every letter of RI's.
"has too high": WL to AL, Apr. 23, 1778, *Letters of William Lee*, II, 420.
"nest of wretches": WL to RHL, May 30, 1778, *ibid.*, 443.
"rather more of animosity": JA to RHL, Aug. 5, 1778, Wharton, II.
"Children," Franklin held: Charles Pougens, *Lettres philosophiques à Madame X* (Paris: François Louis, 1826), 133.

156 "America had not": BF to la Rochefoucauld, Apr. 16, 1778, Mantes-la-Jolie.
"We've kept": Braunschweig dispatch, Apr. 12, 1778, WLF.
"A little, and if": JA, Apr. 13, 1778, *Diary*, II, 300, in French in the original. "Not a word," is from JA, May 8, 1778, *Autobiography*, IV, 92.

157 "But I did not": JA, Apr. 10, 1778, *Autobiography*, IV, 47.
"but he was active": JA, Apr. 21, 1778, *Diary*, II, 305.

158 "And that if she": BF to VRG, Apr. 24, 1778.
"more nobility, more candor": VRG to BF, Apr. 25, 1778, CP Etats-Unis, III, f230, AAE.
"a sort of tar-and-feather": BF to Charles de Weissenstein, July 1, 1778. Contrôle des étrangers, vol. 27, f42, AAE.

159 "the campaign of destiny": June 3, 1779, Métra.
"in my own country": BF to Antoine Borel, June 24, 1778. On Madame Bertin's playlet: Another American in the audience later claimed that JA had been so wounded by the piece that he feigned sickness and left the room. That reporter was Dr. James Smith, seated next to Adams at the time, also at the time a bane of BF's existence.
"I have long been": BF to Jane Mecom, Nov. 26, 1788.

160 "My venerable colleague": JA to Abigail Adams, Apr. 25, 1778, *Adams Family Correspondence*, ed. L. H. Butterfield (Cambridge: Harvard University Press, 1963), II. JA originally wrote that the ladies allowed BF "to buss them" as often as he pleased, then corrected himself.
"That is a great general" to "of Great Britain": JA, *Autobiography*, Apr. 29, 1778, IV, 80. VRG's line in French in the original. See also JA in *Boston Patriot*, May 15, 1811.

161 "Our affairs in this kingdom": JA to SA, May 21, 1778, Wharton, II.

162 "I was perfectly happy": D'Eon to Maurepas, cited in Gilles Perrault, *La revanche Américaine* (Paris: Fayard, 1996), 572.

163 "France by her open candor": RHL and James Lovell to the American commissioners, May 14, 1778, CP Espagne, vol. 590, AAE.
"To lay duties" to "my country": BF to James Lovell, July 22, 1778.

164 "I know all the gentlemen": HL to GW, June 8, 1778, Burnett, III.
"The longer I live": JA to James Warren, Aug. 4, 1778, *Warren-Adams Letters*, II, 40.

VI: ADMIRATION IS THE DAUGHTER OF IGNORANCE

For JA and much more, David McCullough's *John Adams* (New York: Simon & Schuster, 2001). On the evolution of JA's feelings toward BF, John Ferling's "John Adams, Diplomat," *The William and Mary Quarterly*, Apr. 1994, 227–52. All accounts of Mme. Brillon and BF begin and end as ever with the work of Claude Lopez. On the French language, Paul M. Spurlin, "The Founding Fathers' Knowledge of French," *French Review*, Dec. 1946, 120–28, and Spurlin, "The Founding Fathers and the French Language, *The Modern Language Journal*, Mar. 1976, 85–96; Morris Bishop, "Franklin in France," *Daedalus*, May 1957, 214–30; Dorothy Medlin, "Benjamin Franklin and the French Language," *French-American Review*, Fall 1977, 232–37. On the embrace of France and America: Durand Echeverria's still shining *Mirage in the West: A History of the French Image of American Society to 1815* (New York: Octagon Books, 1966); the chevalier de Pontgibaud, *A French Volunteer of the War of Independence* (New York, Bouton, 1897); the marquis de Chastellux, *Travels in North America*, ed. Howard C. Rice Jr. (Chapel Hill: University of North Carolina Press, 1963); Crèvecoeur, *Letters from an American Farmer*, ed. Susan Manning (Oxford: Oxford University Press, 1997); Eugene Parker Chase, ed., *Our Revolutionary Forefathers: The Letters of François, marquis de Barbé-Marbois, 1779–1785* (New York: Duffield, 1929); Echeverria, ed., "The American Character: A Frenchman Views the New Republic," *The William and Mary Quarterly*, July 1959, 376–413; Catherine Radziwell, *They Knew the Washingtons: Letters from a French soldier with Lafayette and from his family in Virginia* (Indianapolis: Bobbs-Merrill, 1926); Philippe Roger, *L'Ennemi américain* (Paris: Seuil, 2002).

165 "a good prognostic": John Carroll to BF, Jan. 18, 1778.
"You have come": Synopsis of Gérard dispatches, CP Angleterre, supp., vol. 14, f328, AAE.

166 "The favorable issue": GW to RHL, May 25, 1778, in John Fitzpatrick, ed., *Writings of George Washington* (Washington: Government Printing Office, 1937), vol. XI, 450. Harvard taught French: The research is not mine but Spurlin's, *French Review*, 120–21.

167 "farce of union": La Chardonier, Apr. 26, 1778, *Report on the Manuscripts of Mrs. Stopford-Sackville* (London: Mackie, 1910), II, 109.

168 "the French did the fighting": Cited in Orville T. Murphy, "The French Professional Soldier's Opinion of the American Militia in the War of the Revolution," *Military Affairs*, Feb. 1969, 195.
"honeymoon": SA to James Warren, Oct. 11, 1778, NYPL.
"have personally been put": LF to Alexander Hamilton, Aug. 26, 1778, cited in William C. Stinchcombe, *The American Revolution and the French Alliance* (Syracuse: Syracuse University Press, 1969), 52.
On the Lafayette challenge: Linguet, IV, 376ff.
"English as regards": De Fleury memoir, Nov. 16, 1779, cited in Stinchcombe, 60.
"Their character being": Crèvecoeur, cited in Ronald Hoffman and Peter J. Albert, eds., *Diplomacy and Revolution: The Franco-American Alliance of 1778* (Charlottesville: University Press of Virginia, 1981), 49.

169 "assemble only when the danger": Fersen letter of Jan. 9, 1781, in F. U. Wrangel, ed., *Lettres d'Axel Fersen à son père pendant la guerre d'indépendance d'Amérique* (Paris: Fimin Didot, 1929).

170 *"Mon Dieu! Une grenouille!"*: H. E. Scudder, ed., *Recollections of Samuel Breck* (London: Sampson, Low, Marston, Searle, 1877), 24.

171 "They contain particular": BF to Genet, Dec. 1, 1778.

exhaustive dispatches: See John J. Meng, ed., *Despatches and Instructions of Conrad Alexandre Gérard* (Baltimore, 1939).

172 "In fact," elaborated: Carmichael to TJ, Oct. 15, 1787, in *The Papers of Thomas Jefferson*, XII, 241. For TJ's account, *The Life and Selected Writings of Thomas Jefferson*, 169.

173 While posted to Constantinople: Henri Doniol, *Le comte de Vergennes et P. M. Hennin* (Paris: Colin, 1898); J. F. Labourdette, *Vergennes: Ministre principal de Louis XVI* (Paris: Editions Desjonquères, 1990); Orville T. Murphy, *Charles Gravier: Comte de Vergennes* (Albany: State University of New York Press, 1982); Pierre-Michel Hennin, "Eloge de Vergennes," Apr. 1787, Ms. 1223, f26 InF.

"I vow to you": VRG to Montmorin, Nov. 27, 1778, CP Espagne, vol. 591, AAE.

"our vices will have": Memo for Louis XVI, July 23, 1777, CP Espagne, vol. 585, f60, AAE.

174 "It pains me to have": Gérard to VRG, Aug. 12, 1778, CP Etats-Unis, IV, AAE.

175 "There is certainly scarce": BF as Silence Dogood, *New England Courant*, Apr. 9, 1722.

"by his debauchery": Mme. Brillon to BF, c. June 4, 1779. On her talent, Bruce Gustafson, "The Music of Madame Brillon," *Notes: The Quarterly Journal of the Music Library Association*, Mar. 1987, 522–43.

176 "I mean the one": BF to Mme. Brillon, Mar. 10, 1778.

"You renounce and" to "equal tenderness": BF to Mme. Brillon, July 27, 1778.

177 "I love you furiously," Mme. Brillon to BF, c. July 27, 1778.

"Half an hour": BF to Mme. Brillon, c. July, 1778.

178 "electrified the weather": Turgot to d'Enville, Aug. 26, 1778, in *Lettres de Turgot à la duchesse d'Enville* (Louvain: Université Catholique de Louvain, 1976).

"To me, after all": "The Ephemera," Sept. 20, 1778.

179 "Do you know": Mme. Brillon to BF, c. Dec. 20, 1778.

"As one day" to "this desire": BF to Mme. Brillon, Oct. 10, 1778.

180 "I think that a young": BF to Charles Dumas, Sept. 22, 1778.

"If you would be": BF to Vergennes, Oct. 20, 1778.

181 "had things been": RI to HL, Sept. 12, 1778, National Archives.

"Doing an injury": BF to Mme. Brillon, May 10, 1779.

182 "an affluent pillar": July 31, 1778, Contrôle des étrangers, vol. 23, AAE.

"as much vigor": BF's journal of his health, Oct. 4, 1778–Jan. 16, 1780.

"The one may be too": JA to Samuel Adams, Aug. 7, *Papers of John Adams*, VI, 354. See also JA in the *Boston Patriot*, May 15, 1811.

183 "It can not be expected" to "cultivate a harmony": JA to AL, Oct. 10, 1778, *Life of Arthur Lee*, II, 260.

184 "I find 11": AL to JA, Oct. 12, 1778, Wharton, II.

"I should be happy": BF to Mary Stevenson Hewson, Nov. 27, 1778.

185 "the copper pot lined": BF to Margaret Stevenson, Jan. 25, 1779.

"The tongues": Mme. Brillon to BF, c. Dec. 20, 1778.

"I want a faithful": Mme. Brillon to BF, c. Dec. 15, 1778.

186 "as a *matter of*" to "effectual assistance": Dec. 4, 1778, *Life of Arthur Lee*, I, 404.

"an excellent chance": Gerard W. Gawalt, ed., *John Paul Jones's Memoir of the American*

Revolution, Presented to King Louis XVI of France (Washington: Library of Congress, 1979), 14.

187 "If it should occasion": BF to Joseph Priestley, Feb. 8, 1780.
"If your French": Mme. Brillon to BF, c. Dec. 15, 1778.
"I always wish": JA, May 20, 1778, *Diary*, II.
"There was too much": JA, Apr. 19, 1778, *Autobiography*, IV, 66.

188 "It's too orderly": Janet Flanner, *Paris Was Yesterday* (New York: Harcourt Brace Jovanovich, 1972), 174.
"oppressive to industry": Cited in Beatrix Cary Davenport, ed., *A Diary of the French Revolution* (Westport, Conn.: Greenwood Press, 1972), 38.

189 "If only you Frenchmen": Le Roy, cited in Chinard, "Abbé Lefebvre de la Roche's Recollections of Benjamin Franklin," *Proceedings of the American Philosophical Society*, June 1950, 219.
retrospective report card: The eloquent grader was Morris Bishop, in his *Daedalus* piece, 221. On BF's French, see also *Espion Anglais*, XI, 1777, 61.
"For 60 years": BF to Mme. Brillon, Jan. 6, 1782.

190 "They talk very loud": JA, Aug. 23, 1774, *Diary*, II, 109.
"I find I can neither": JA, Dec. 8, 1760, *Diary*, I.

191 "His pronunciation too": JA, Apr. 16, 1778, *Diary*, II, 302.
"You speak slowly": JA, June 22, 1779, *Diary*, II, 389. In French in the original.
"Women, especially": La Roche papers, Ms. 2222, f74, InF.

192 "They make fine work": JA to Abigail Adams, Feb. 13, 1779, *Adams Family Correspondence*, III, 170. Similarly, Feb. 11, 1779, *Diary*, II, 352. JA was paraphrasing the *Morning Post* (London), Jan. 12, 1779.
a tirade: JA to Warren, Dec. 2, 1778.

193 "he cannot easily" to "present footing: JA to Samuel Adams, Dec. 7, 1778, NYPL.

194 "I fete everyone": Chaumont to VRG, Nov. 1778, CP Etats-Unis, V, f215, AAE.
"La Fête Bostonienne": Lenoir to Vergennes, Dec. 14, 1778; VRG to Lenoir, Dec. 18, 1778, in Wharton, XXIII.

195 "Our affairs are in": GW to Ben Harrison, Dec. 18, 1778, *Writings of George Washington*, vol. 13, 466.

VII: SUCCESS HAS RUINED MANY A MAN

The Letters of Richard Henry Lee (ed. Ballagh) and *Letters of William Lee* (ed. Ford) make for spellbinding reading; the diary of AL less so. The *Deane Papers* charts a life swerving garrulously out of control. On the Deane-Lee imbroglio, H. James Henderson, "Congressional Factionalism and the Attempt to Recall Benjamin Franklin," *The William and Mary Quarterly*, Apr. 1970, 246–67. See also Kalman Goldstein's perceptive "Silas Deane: Preparation for Rascality," *The Historian*, Nov. 1980, 75–97, and Edmund S. Morgan, "The Puritan Ethic and the American Revolution," *The William and Mary Quarterly*, Jan. 1967, 3–43. On the Fragonard allegory, Mary D. Sheriff, " 'Au Génie de Franklin': An Allegory by J-H Fragonard," *Proceedings of the American Philosophical Society*, 1983, 180–93.

197 "You are a gentleman": BF to RI, Jan. 4, 1779. For RI's side, see the collected Izard–Laurens correspondence, *The South Carolina Historical and Genealogical Magazine*, July 1921, 73–87.

198 "calmly suffer their authority". RI to HL, Jan. 16, 1779, South Carolina Historical Society.

199 "We are commanded": BF to Alexander Small, Nov. 5, 1789.

200 "gave universal disgust": *Pennsylvania Gazette*, Dec. 5, 1778.

201 thrilled to the sight: *London Packet*, Jan. 27, 1779; *London Chronicle*, Apr. 17 and Apr. 27, 1779.
"What egregious fools": Thomas Digges to BF, Jan. 31, 1779.

202 "I confess it" to "benefit of mankind": JA, Feb. 12, 1779, *Diary*, II, 353. Similarly, RI to HL, Feb. 18, 1779, South Carolina Historical Society. "ought to be hunted": JA, Feb. 8, 1779, *Diary*, II, 345.
"All the Parisian evils": JA to Abigail Adams, Feb. 9, 1779, in L. H. Butterfield, Marc Friedlaender, and Mary-Jo Kline, eds., *The Book of Abigail and John: Selected Letters of the Adams Family, 1762–84* (Cambridge: Harvard University Press, 1975), 235.

203 "a monopoly of reputation": JA to James Lovell, Feb. 20, 1778, in *Deane Papers*, III, 376.
the visit with Marat: François Sage, "Souvenirs d'un témoin oculaire," in *Analyse chimique et concordance des trois règnes* (Paris: Panckoucke, 1786), 118; *Nouvelles Extraordinaires*, Aug. 6, 1779.

204 "little, hissing, crooked": "The Petition of the Letter Z," after Feb. 12, 1779.
"The Americans are": Turgot to Du Pont, Feb. 23, 1779, in Gustave Schelle, ed., *Oeuvres de Turgot* (Paris: Felix Alcan, 1923), V.
"magnifying my own service": BF to Jonathan Williams, Feb. 13, 1778.

205 "I will try to see": Cröy, in Grouchy and Cottin, eds., *Journal inédit du duc de Cröy* (Paris: Flammarion, 1906), IV, 169.
"Petty disputes": BF to Stephen Sayre, March 31, 1779.
rumor attributed: Mar. 19, 1779, Contrôle des étrangers, vol. 28, AAE; *Courrier d'Avignon*, Apr. 2, 1779; Niccoli (Tuscany) dispatch of Mar. 22, 1779, cited in Pace; Zeno (Venice) dispatches of Mar. 8 and Mar. 29, 1778, Fond Italien 1983, filza 258, BN.
"rude or singular": BF's Journal of Peace Negotiations, May, 1782.

206 "Congress should set": WL to RHL, Mar. 25, 1779, *Letters of William Lee*, II, 597.
Separately Arthur Lee dilated: AL to Samuel Adams, May 22, 1779, Samuel Adams Papers, NYPL.

207 "should stand in need": RI to HL, June 3, 1779, Emmet Collection, NYPL.
"They quarrel *at*": BF to Carmichael, June 2, 1779.
"but my too great": BF to Richard Bache, June 2, 1779.
"a constant rule": BF to James Lovell, June 2, 1779.

208 "rescued a valuable": BF to Richard Bache, June 2, 1779.
"deprive an old man": BF to Sarah Bache, June 3, 1779.
"It is enough": BF to Richard Bache, June 2, 1779.

209 "Frenchmen and Americans": Pierre Landais to BF, Feb. 26, 1779.
"nobody expects them": BF to LF, Mar. 22, 1779.
"For there is not only" to "both of you": BF to John Paul Jones, Apr. 27, 1779. The best source on the *Bonhomme Richard* is Jean Boudriot, *John Paul Jones and the Bonhomme Richard* (Annapolis: Naval Institute Press, 1987). See also Gerald W. Gawalt, ed., *John Paul Jones's Memoir of the American Revolution, Presented to King Louis XVI of France* (Washington: Library of Congress, 1979).

210 "Does the old conjurer": JA, May 12, 1779, *Diary*, II, 369.

211 "And in truth": Chaumont to BF, May 14, 1779. In French in the original.

211 "For God's sake": LF to GW, June 12, 1779, in Stanley J. Idzerda, ed., *Lafayette in the Age of the American Revolution* (Ithaca: Cornell University Press, 1977), II, 277.

212 "He has the most": JA, May 10, 1779, *Diary*, II, 367.

213 "a most amiable": BF to John Quincy Sr., Apr. 22, 1779.
"As he is destined": BF to John Quincy Adams, Apr. 21, 1779. On the Passy pension, George Izard memoir, South Carolina Historical Society; Charles B. Cochran to Mary Cochran, Dec. 24, 1778, South Carolina Historical Society.

214 cooked up by: See LF to BF, Aug. 29, 1779, CP Etats-Unis, IX, AAE.
"I flattered myself": BF to LF, Oct. 1, 1779.

215 "disgusted me as much" to "modes and luxuries": BF to Sally Bache, June 3, 1779.
"What do you want": BF to Georgiana Shipley, Feb. 3, 1781.
day of fasting: HL notes of July 2, 1779, Burnett, IV, 294.

216 "It only proves": Sept. 26, 1779, Métra. John Paul Jones was probably not wrong when he later boasted that the beautifully finished blade with which Louis XVI honored him was "much more elegant than that presented to the marquis de Lafayette."
"A benevolent man": *Autobiography* (Modern Library, 2001), 98.
On Gellée: See Abigail Adams to Mercy Warren, Feb. 28, 1780, *Adams Family Correspondence*, III, 288.
"You have found out": BF to LF, Aug. 17, 1779.
"spirit of assassinating": James Lovell to BF, Apr. 29, 1779.
"I fear that the ease": Gérard to VRG, Mar. 4, 1779, CP Etats-Unis, VIII, f78, AAE.

217 "that Mr. Franklin": *Journals of the Continental Congress*, Mar. 24, 1779, XIII, 367.
"I must warn you": Gérard to VRG, July 18, 1779, CP Etats-Unis, IX, f106, AAE. See also Gérard to Vergennes, July 27, 1779, *ibid.*
"neither one nor the other": Gérard to VRG, Sept. 26, 1779, CP Etats-Unis, X, f127, AAE.

218 "I cannot deny": LF to VRG, July 18, 1779, Stevens, XVII.
"If Mr. Franklin": LF to VRG, Aug. 16, 1779, in Idzerda, *Lafayette in the Age of the American Revolution*, II, 301.

219 "the Congress has used": Bishop of Derry to Lord George Germain, Aug. 4, 1779, in *Report on the Manuscripts of Mrs. Stopford-Sackville*, II.
"But one is not to expect": BF to Jane Mecom, Oct. 25, 1779.
"Monsieur Franklin": July 2, 1779, Bachaumont, XX.

220 On Franklin and the Masons: *Espion Anglais*, X, 1784, 84–91; H. T. C. de Lafontaine's slightly off-center but well-researched "Benjamin Franklin," Ars Quatuor Coronatorum, XLI, 1929, 3–40; and Louis Amiable, *Une loge maçonnique d'avant 1789* (Paris: Felix Alcan, 1897).
"In short, Sir": [Richard Tickell], *La Cassette verte de M. Sartine* (London: Whiskerfeld, 1779), 7.

221 The story of a French louse: [Delauney], *History of a French Louse, or The Spy of a New Species, in France and England* (T. Becket: London, 1779).
"Since Dr. Franklin has ceded": Kenneth Scott, ed., *Rivington's New York Newspaper, New-York Historical Society* (New York: New-York Historical Society, 1973), 22.

222 "Dr. Franklin's knowledge": Burnett, IV, 412n.
"He is," allowed Adams: JA, June 23, 1779, *Diary*, II, 391.
"The history of our revolution": JA to Benjamin Rush, Apr. 4, 1790, in *Letters of Benjamin Rush*, II, 1207.
"were always attended": JA, June 23, 1779, *Diary*, II, 392.

223 "endeavor to give". BF to JJ, Oct. 4–28, 1779.
   assertions of futility: See Métra, Dec. 11, 1779; Bachaumont, Nov. 17, 1779.
   a little less ubiquitous: *La Chronique scandaleuse*, I, 1785, 256; Linguet, 1779, VII, 145.
225 "cool conduct": BF to Jones, Oct. 15, 1779.
   "Either Captain Landais": Jones to BF, Oct. 3, 1779. On the Jones–Landais fiasco,
   Richard B. Morris, "The Revolution's Caine Mutiny," *American Heritage*, Apr. 1960,
   10–13, 88–91.
226 "so many inconveniences": BF to Lovell, Oct. 17, 1779.
   "that there were": BF to Sartine, Nov. 28, 1779.
   "The way to insure": James Lovell to JA, Nov. 1, Paul H. Smith et al., eds., *Letters of
   Delegates to Congress* (Washington: Library of Congress, 1976), XIV, 139.
227 Dubourg died: See J. C. Lettsom, "Memoirs of Jacques Barbeau Dubourg," *Memoirs
   of the Medical Society of London*, I, Feb. 25, 1787, 476–91.
228 twelve colonies to go: The quip made the papers, Bachaumont, XXI, 152–53.
   "You began the war": BF to William Strachan, Jan. 24, 1780.
   At the same time: BF to David Hartley, Feb. 2, 1780.

VIII: EVERYONE HAS WISDOM ENOUGH TO MANAGE
THE AFFAIRS OF HIS NEIGHBORS

For the best account of BF's shipping travails, Claude-Anne Lopez, "Benjamin Franklin,
Lafayette, and the *Lafayette*," *Proceedings of the American Philosophical Society*, June 1964,
181–223.

229 James Baldwin, cited in Gopnik, ed., *Americans in Paris: A Literary Anthology*, 471.
   "Being arrived at 70": BF to Thomas Bond, Mar. 16, 1780.
   "Of course you know": Geneviève Le Veillard to BF, Nov. 18, 1779.
230 "Oh, to be 70": Lopez, *Mon Cher Papa*, 246. On the Helvétius household: Antoine
   Guillois, *Le Salon de Madame Helvétius* (Paris: Calmann Levy, 1894); Suzanne
   Burkard, ed., *Mémoires de la Baronne d'Oberkirch* (Paris: Mercure de France, 1970),
   415ff; Jules Bertaut, *Egeries du XVIIIème siècle* (Paris: Plon, 1928).
232 "If this lady": BF to Cabanis, Sept. 19, 1779, in French in the original.
   "It is worth": Cited in D. W. Smith et al., "La correspondance d'Helvétius," *Dix-
   Huitième Siècle*, no. 5, 1973, 342.
   "The Elysian Fields": See Dorothy Medlin, "Benjamin Franklin's Bagatelles for
   Madame Helvétius: Some Biographical and Stylistic Considerations," *Early American Literature*, Spring 1980, 42–58, and Gilbert Chinard, "Random Notes on Two
   'Bagatelles,'" *Proceedings of the American Philosophical Society*, Dec. 1959,
   727–60.
234 "bad habit I have long": BF to Bethia Alexander, June 24, 1782.
   Euclidian proof: BF to Mme. Brillon, Feb. 16, 1781.
235 "semi-serious declarations": Chinard, "Random Notes," 740.
   "he came home at all": JA, May 27, 1778, *Autobiography*, IV, 119.
   "'Ah! Mon Dieu!'" to "her favorite": Abigail Adams to Lucy Cranch, Sep. 5, 1784,
   V, 436. Similarly, Nabby Adams to Lucy Cranch, Sep. 4, 1784, *Adams Family Correspondence*, V, 430.
236 "The manners of women": JA, June 2, 1778, *Autobiography*, IV, 123.

236 "How would he": C. A. Helvétius, *De l'Esprit, or Essays on the Mind* (London: Richardson, 1809), 168.

"The purest": Cited in William Seward, *Anecdotes of Distinguished Persons, Chiefly of the Present and Two Preceding Centuries* (London: Cadell and Davies, 1796), III, 345.

Peter Allaire: See Lopez, *My Life with Benjamin Franklin* (New Haven: Yale University Press, 1966), 61–72. Allaire's extraordinary narrative, written in the Bastille, appeared in *Now and Then*, Apr., 1948, 296–303. BEAU to VRG, Feb. 4, 1780, CP Angleterre, vol. 533, f35, AAE.

239 "the dawdling manner": Mercy d'Argenteau dispatch of Mar. 18, 1780, Oesterreichisches Staatsarchiv, Vienna.

He devoutly hoped: Vergennes to Montmorin, Jan. 29, 1780, CP Espagne, vol. 597, f222, AAE.

"busy oneself furnishing": Cited in Edward S. Corwin, *French Policy and the American Alliance of 1778* (Gloucester, Mass.: Peter Smith, 1969), 274.

"I never heard": JA to Samuel Huntington, Feb. 15, 1780, *Autobiography*, IV, 241.

240 "But let me repeat": BF to Jones, Feb. 19, 1780.

"But the number": BF to Samuel Huntington, May 31, 1780.

"We live upon good": BF to Carmichael, Mar. 31 to Apr. 7, 1780.

241 "You would on this side": BF to GW, Mar. 5, 1780. Franklin went on to wax rhapsodic about America's future, a scene that he did not believe he would witness, but that GW would.

"Not being liked here": BF to Samuel Cooper, Mar. 16, 1780.

"And if the people remain": Jones to BF, Apr. 4, 1780.

242 "and yet everybody": BF to Williams, May 10, 1780.

"I find him so exceedingly": BF to Jones, Mar. 1, 1780.

243 his personal opinion: BF to Landais, Mar. 12, 1780.

"Take in good part": BF to the officers of the *Alliance*, June 7, 1780.

"Shut the door": Chevalier de Pontgibaud; *A French Volunteer of the War of Independence* (New York: Bouton, 1897), 83.

244 "You have shown": BF to Jones, June 12, 1780.

"Mr. Lee is at the bottom": Samuel Wharton to BF, June 14, 1780. Similarly, Jones to BF, Aug. 7, 1780.

The two men faced off: Chaumont to Rayneval, June 24, 1780, CP Etats-Unis, XII, f384, AAE. Also E. Brush and Joseph Brown Jr., testimony regarding duel by his seconds, June 20, 1780, Yale.

"if some of the many": BF to Samuel Wharton, June 17, 1780.

245 "And as a friend": Jones to BF, Aug. 7, 1780.

"If you come within": Cited in Richard Morris, "Revolution's Caine Mutiny," 13.

"my humanity would not suffer": Jones to RM, June 27, 1780, in Stan V. Henkels, *Confidential Correspondence of Robert Morris*, Auction Commission, Philadelphia, 1917.

"Thus does this fool": Williams to BF, June 23, 1780.

246 held his head high: Zeno (Venice) dispatch of May 8, 1780, Fond Italien 1983, filza 258, BN. Also Métra, Apr. 25, 1780.

an entire dinner: Turgot to Du Pont, June 28, 1780, in Gustave Schelle, *Oeuvres de Turgot* (Paris: Felix Alcan, 1923), V.

"I have been too long": BF to Williams, June 27, 1780.

247 "rather like women": Jones to Bancroft, June 27, 1780, cited in *The Papers of Benjamin Franklin*, vol. 33, 28n.

"Hereafter, if you": BF to Jones, July 5, 1780.

"to keep his hand": JA to Robert Livingston, Nov. 8, 1782, in Charles Francis Adams, ed., *The Works of John Adams* (Boston: Little, Brown, 1853), VIII.

"It is hard": BF to Samuel Wharton, June 17, 1780.

248 "give my poor opinion": JA to Vergennes, July 27, 1780, CP Etats-Unis, XIII, AAE.

said to be in the king's: Kaganeck to Baron Alstromer, in *Lettres de M. de Kaganeck au baron Alstromer* (Paris: Charpentier, 1884), July 17, 1780.

"The King has not": VRG to JA, July 29, 1780, *Papers of John Adams*, X, 57.

249 "As for myself": VRG to Luzerne, Aug. 7, 1780, Guinta, I, 3.

"a resolution that I believe": BF to VRG, Aug. 3, 1780.

"whether something might not be" to "please this Court": BF to Huntington, Aug. 9, 1780. The line got a rise out of JA's friends in Congress and, much later, out of JA himself. Evidently on receipt of BF's explanation, James Lovell could remark only that its author was "an old rascal." See T. Pickering to R. King, Nov. 19, 1808, in Charles King, ed., *Life and Correspondence of Rufus King* (New York: Putnam's, 1898), V, 108.

250 "He says the ideas": BF to Huntington, Aug. 9, 1780.

prize portion of the turkey: Pontgibaud, 83.

251 "Try if you can": BF to Williams, June 17, 1780.

"for sometimes people": BF to Williams, Nov. 1, 1780.

"never to go out": BF to Williams, Dec. 27, 1780.

252 "I, in all these mercantile": BF to Williams, Jan. 15, 1781.

a horse thief: JA, May 20, 1778, 314, *Diary*, II; JA, May 20, 1778, *Autobiography*, IV, 105; Pougens, *Lettres philosophiques*, 136.

"It is almost as great" to "soothe and conciliate": SD to JJ, Sept. 18, 1780, *Deane Papers*, IV, 228–29.

253 "actually mad, and more so": SD to JJ, Nov. 1780, *Deane Papers*, IV, 262.

some predicted: See, for example, Jehan de Witte, *Journal de l'abbé de Veri* (Paris: Editions Jules Tallandier, 1928), II, 319ff.

Congress pointed fingers: Marbois to VRG, Sept. 9, 1780, CP Etats-Unis XIII, AAE.

254 Lavoisier also happened: See Denis I. Duveen and Herbert S. Klickstein, "Benjamin Franklin (1706–1790) and Antoine-Laurent Lavoisier (1743–1794)," *Annals of Science*, June 1955, 103–28, and Dec. 1955, 271–308; also Jean-Pierre Poirier's fine *Lavoisier: Chemist, Biologist, Economist* (Philadelphia: University of Pennsylvania Press, 1996). Also, Lopez, "Saltpeter, Tin and Gunpowder: Addenda to the Correspondence of Lavoisier and Franklin," *Annals of Science*, June 1960, 83–94.

"and so much indisposed" to "all America": BF to JJ, Oct. 2, 1780.

255 "If they were the effects": BF to JA, Oct. 8, 1780.

"We are naked": LF to BF, Oct. 9, 1780.

256 "particularly when one finds": "The Deformed and Handsome Leg," before Nov. 23, 1780, Yale.

257 "When I was a young": BF to Mme. Brillon, c. Nov. 17, 1780.

258 "For God's sake": BF to Williams, Nov. 29, 1780.

"You know that I have": BF to Chaumont, Dec. 18, 1780.

"Affairs among friends": BF diary entry, Dec. 19, 1780.

"a number of unforeseen": BF to LF, Dec. 9, 1780.

IX: THE STING OF A REPROACH IS THE TRUTH OF IT

Claude Lopez is most eloquent on BF's end-of-year misery, "One Christmas Season in the Life of Benjamin Franklin," *Proceedings of the American Philosophical Society*, Oct. 1977, 373–76. On John Laurens, see Gregory D. Massey, *John Laurens and the American Revolution* (Columbia: University of South Carolina Press, 2000). On BB, Lopez, "A Story of Grandfathers, Fathers, and Sons," *The Yale University Library Gazette*, Apr. 1979, 177–95.

260 dragged himself: Franklin's journal, Dec. 18, 1780, to Jan. 29, 1781. So compromised was BF's health that among the diplomatic corps he was thought to have suffered a stroke.

"If my enemies": BF to Carmichael, Jan. 27, 1781.

261 "How long, my dear friend": RHL to Samuel Adams, Sept. 10, 1780, in Ballagh, II, 202.

"The truth is that": AL to Congress, Dec. 7, 1780, Wharton, IV.

(unfounded) attempts: RHL to AL, Aug. 31 1780, in *Letters of Richard Henry Lee*, II, 198. Also Lovell to Gerry, July 24, 1780, in Smith, *Letters of Delegates of Congress*, XV, 499.

262 With what sounds like: BF to Carmichael, Jan. 23, 1782.

"by his nonchalance": Luzerne to VRG, Dec. 15, 1780, Guinta, I.

proposed to pass Temple off: William Franklin to BF, c. Jan. 2, 1769.

263 "a want of confidence": McKean to JA, mid-Dec. 1780, Burnett, IV.

"In a word": Gouverneur Morris to Robert Livingston, Feb. 21, 1781, Box VI, Livingston Papers, New-York Historical Society.

make-nice letter: GW to BF, Jan. 15, 1781.

Wistfully, Franklin replied: BF to LF, Mar. 14, 1781.

264 the Virginia representative: See Philip Mazzei, *My Life and Wanderings* (Morristown, N.J.: American Institute of Italian Studies, 1980), and Howard R. Marraro, ed., *Philip Mazzei: Virginia's Agent in Europe* (New York: New York Public Library, 1935).

"Alas, sir, there are": James Searle to Joseph Reed, Feb. 14, 1781, from William B. Reed, ed., *Life and Correspondence of Joseph Reed* (Philadelphia: Lindsay and Blakiston, 1847), II, 455–57.

265 "I am grown old": BF to VRG, Feb. 13, 1781.

"Let them judge" to "opinions to Congress": VRG to Luzerne, Feb. 19, 1781, CP Etats-Unis, XV, AAE.

"If Dr. Franklin": *Pennsylvania Gazette*, Mar. 28, 1781.

266 "You should therefore": BF to Williams, Mar. 8, 1781.

no more American adventures: VRG to Montmorin, Apr. 12, 1781, CP Espagne, vol. 603, f47, AAE.

"deficient in that Christian": BF to Jane Mecom, Dec. 30, 1770.

267 "a signal" to "last to discover that": BF to Samuel Huntington, Mar. 12, 1781. It is difficult to believe BF did not have at hand JA's letter to McKean of Sep. 20, 1779, in which JA described his colleague's predicament: "He is too old, too infirm, too indolent and dissipated, to be sufficient for the discharge of all the important duties of ambassador, board of war, board of treasury, commissary of prisoners, etc. as he is at present in that department, besides an immense correspondence and acquaintance, each of which would be enough for the whole time of the most active man in the vigor of youth." As Luzerne noted, Franklin's resignation artfully focused his enemies on themselves.

268 Jay also shivered. JJ to Huntington, Apr. 21, 1781, in Henry Johnston, ed., *Correspondence and Public Papers of John Jay* (New York: Putnam, 1891), II, 17.

"like a common prostitute": SD to Jesse Root, May 20, 1781, *Deane Papers*, IV, 370. SD was quoting an assertion made six months earlier, in Congress.

269 "If such a fellow": BF to William Hodgson, Apr. 1, 1781.

depositions were taken: Chambre de la prevoté, document Y 18705B, Apr. 28, 1781, AN.

"In certain matters": SD to JJ, July 2, 1781, *Deane Papers*, IV, 445.

270 Comparing sect and ritual: BF to Mme. Brillon, before Apr. 20, 1781.

271 let Franklin down gingerly: Mme. Brillon to BF, Apr. 20, 1781.

"a mere white curd": Abigail Adams to James Lovell, June 30, 1781, *Adams Family Correspondence*, IV, 165.

"wicked unprincipled": Abigail Adams to JA, Oct. 21, 1781, in *Adams Family Correspondence*, IV, 230.

272 long hoped to make: WTF to Carmichael, Aug. 15, 1784.

"attend more nearly": BF to Sarah and Richard Bache, May 14, 1781.

"poor, and dirty": BF to BB, Sept. 25, 1780.

273 firing squad: BB diary, Oct. 9, 1782, APS.

"It may be declared": GW to John Laurens, Apr. 9, 1781, *Writings of George Washington*, vol. 21, 439.

On John Laurens at Versailles: VRG memoir of April 18, 1781, CP Etats-Unis, XVI, AAE.

275 "done more for the United States": Cited in BF to Jackson, July 6, 1781.

276 "to judge better" to "superior airs": BF to Jackson, July 10, 1781. For more on the episode, James A. Lewis, *Neptune's Militia* (Kent, Ohio: Kent State University Press, 1999).

277 "The public": BF to RM, July 26, 1781.

"cannot bear that": BF to Jan Ingenhousz, Oct. 2, 1781.

278 A visiting American: The episode is from Elkanah Watson, in Winslow C. Watson, ed., *Men and Times of the Revolution, or Memoirs of Elkanah Watson* (New York: Dana, 1856), 117–22. For more on Mrs. Wright, Charles Coleman Sellers, *Patience Wright: American Artist and Spy in George III's London* (Middletown, Conn.: Wesleyan University Press, 1976).

279 "one continent becomes old": Soulavie, *Memoirs of the Reign of Lewis XVI* (London: G. and J. Robinson, 1802), V, 162. "the founder of the liberties," *ibid.*, 179.

"Had it happened": BF to Mme. Brillon, June 7, 1781. On the fire, *Journal de Genève*, June 12, 1781.

280 "But what are the lives": BF to David Hartley, Dec. 15, 1781.

"There is an absence": BF to Mme. Brillon, July 15, 1781.

"You will not suffer": Mme. Brillon to BF, July 1, 1781.

281 "tender *amitiés* that I cannot": BF to M. and Mme. Brillon, Oct. 30, 1781. Similarly, BF to Mme. Brillon, Oct. 1, 1781.

"among a people": BF to Sarah and Richard Bache, May 14, 1781.

282 "I fancy it may": BF to Carmichael, Aug. 24, 1781.

"This is probably": Alice Lee Shippen to Elizabeth W. Adams, June 17, 1781, *Adams Family Correspondence*, IV, 154.

"I can only say" to "sly secret malice": Abigail Adams to Alice Lee Shippen, June 30, 1781, *Adams Family Correspondence*, IV, 167. See also Abigail Adams to James Lovell, June 30, 1781, ibid., 165.

283 On the peace commission: Luzerne to VRG, June 14, 1781, in Guinta, I, 191.

284 "I am as sure": VRG to Luzerne, Sept. 7, 1781, CP Etats-Unis, XVIII, f21, AAE.
"My talent, if I have one": JA to BF, Aug. 24, 1781. For a sensitive handling of the illness, see Ferling, "John Adams, Diplomat," 246.
"who never promised me": BF to Samuel Huntington, Sept. 13, 1781.

285 "a most ruinous": JA to BF, Oct. 25, 1781.
"really because I thought" to "shift as I can": BF to JA, Nov. 7, 1781.
"But that is wishing" to "some that were": BF to RM, Nov. 5, 1781.

286 "Before he was yet" to "his friends happy": BF to M. and Mme. Brillon, Oct. 30, 1781.

287 "miserable new republican": BEAU to VRG, Dec. 2, 1780, Donvez, 811.

288 "bearing upon a treadle" to "in any one war": Elkanah Watson, diary entry of Nov. 19, 1781, in *Papers of BF*, vol. 36, 73–75.

289 "to quit a situation": BF to JA, Nov. 26, 1781. Similarly Blome dispatch of November 23, 1781, Rigsarkivet. On the powdered hair, Christopher Hibbert, *Redcoats and Rebels* (New York: Norton, 1990), 327.

290 *"le plus grand faiseur"*: BF to VRG, Nov. 20, 1781.

X: THOSE WHO IN QUARRELS INTERPOSE MAY GET BLOODY NOSE

Discussions of the peace are reconstructed from and illuminated by BF's journal of the peace negotiations, vol. 37, 291ff; Guinta, vols. I and II; Richard B. Morris, ed., *John Jay: The Winning of the Peace, Unpublished Papers, 1780–1784* (New York: Harper & Row, 1980); Morris, *The Peacemakers: The Great Powers and American Independence* (New York: Harper & Row, 1965); Ronald Hoffman and Peter J. Albert, eds., *Peace and the Peacemakers: The Treaty of 1783* (Charlottesville: University Press of Virginia, 1986); Jonathan R. Dull, *The French Navy and American Independence,* especially 324–35; Herbert E. Klingelhofer, "Matthew Ridley's Diary During the Peace Negotiations of 1782," *William and Mary Quarterly,* Jan. 1963, 95–133; W. A. S. Hewins, ed., *The Whitefoord Papers* (Oxford: Clarendon Press, 1898); and Frank Monaghan, *The Diary of John Jay During the Peace Negotiations of 1782* (New Haven: Bibliographical Press, 1934). Andrew Stockley's *Britain and France at the Birth of America* (Exeter: University of Exeter Press, 2001) makes for a useful corrective to years of lopsided French and American accounts.

291 "Resentment is a passion": JA, Mar. 4, 1776, *Diary*, II, 236.
list of a dozen names: "List of Scoundrels," c. Jan. 4, 1782, *Papers of BF*, vol. 36, 375.

292 "For depend upon it": BF to RM, Mar. 4, 1782.
"in which infidelity" to "such an insult": BF to David Hartley, Feb. 16, 1782.
"I remember that": BF to RM, Mar. 9, 1782.

293 "and yet I am": BF to JJ, Jan. 19, 1782.
"I am not marvelously": VRG to LF, Jan. 23, 1782, in Louis Gottschalk, *Lafayette and the Close of the American Revolution* (Chicago: University of Chicago Press, 1942), 353.
"Our credit in Holland": JJ to BF, Jan. 30, 1782.
"that of a man": JA to BF, May 16, 1782.
"The Americans suffer": Luzerne to VRG, May 22, 1782, CP Etats-Unis, XXI, f227, AAE.

294 To his mind it would: VRG to Montmorin, Mar. 14, 1782, CP Espagne, vol. 606, AAE.

294 "This is really". BF to Robert Livingston, Mar. 4, 1782.

295 The French officers: Narrative of the Prince de Broglie, 1782, *Magazine of American History*, I, 1877, 231.
"It should be carefully": BF to Livingston, Mar. 4, 1782.
"I find by experience": BF to RM, Mar. 9, 1782.
on Cholmondeley: Mme. Brillon to BF, Feb. 1, 1782.

296 "Great affairs": BF's journal of the peace negotiations, 1782.

297 "versed in the world": Cited in Morris, *John Jay: The Winning of the Peace*, 345.
"Doctor Franklin knows": HL to BF, Apr. 7, 1782.
"Thank God": *The Papers of Henry Laurens*, vol. 16, xvi.

299 The careful reader: Horace Walpole to the countess of Upper Ossory, Oct. 1, 1782, *Letters of Horace Walpole*, vol. 12.
"Spain has taken four": BF to JJ, Apr. 22, 1782.
"those lowering": JA to Livingston, July 9, 1783, Wharton, VI, 531.

300 Laurens's reputation: BF to Laurens, May 25, 1782.
"that old, corrupt": AL to James Warren, June 15, 1781, *Warren-Adams Letters*, II, 167.
"they had the fullest": AL to Warren, July 1782, *Warren-Adams Letters*, II, 173.

301 "There is Mr. Franklin" to "speak the truth": From BF's journal of the peace negotiations, May 9, 1782.

302 "They came to take": *Courrier d'Avignon*, May 16, 1782.
"nibble and piddle": JA to Francis Dana, May 13, 1782, in Charles Francis Adams, ed., *The Works of John Adams*, VII, 584.

304 "we who are at war": BF's journal of the peace negotiations, June 11, 1782. On the varying perspectives on foreign affairs, Max Savelle, "The Appearance of an American Attitude Toward External Affairs," *The American Historical Review*, July 1947, 655–66.
Misplaced though it was: Jonathan Dull gets all credit for pointing out to me BF's lapse.
"I have already": Grenville to Fox, June 21, 1782, cited in Yale, vol. 37, 339.
"In this affair": BF to Mary Hewson, May 13, 1782.

305 "He has often promised": BF to RM, Aug. 12, 1782.
They agreed to submit: Agreement of July 7, 1782, M.C. XIII, 420, no. 16, AN.
"croaking at Ghent": BF to RM, Mar. 30, 1782.
"driven into knavery" to "new ones": BF to Jonathan Williams, June 13, 1782.
got a bargain: The Swedish ambassador paid 9,000 livres a year for an unfurnished house; Holland's ambassador paid 18,000 for a furnished one. At his most affordable address, TJ's annual rent was 7,400 livres.

306 "The more I discovered": BF to Priestley, June 7, 1782.

307 "A man very shabbily": John Baynes journal, in *The Life of Sir Samuel Romilly* (London: John Murray, 1842), 453.
"asks for nothing" to "*véritable philosophe*": BF to David Hartley, July 10, 1782.

308 "He is in perfect": JJ to Livingston, June 25, 1782, National Archives, Washington.
"Under this declaration": BF to Livingston, June 25, 1782.
"which was that": BF's journal of the peace negotiations, June 28, 1782.

309 "always throwing in": Cited in Vaughan to Lord Shelburne, July 31, 1782, Guinta, I, 485.

310 "If we lean on": JJ to Livingston, Nov. 17, 1782, Wharton, VI, 49. On the meeting with VRG, see JJ to Livingston, Nov. 8, 1782, in Henry Johnston, ed., *Correspondence and Public Papers of John Jay* (New York: Putnam, 1891), 371–73. As JA saw it in

1811, "upon this point, the whole negotiation was suspended and stood still, till my arrival from Holland."

311 "could not have thought": JJ to BF, Apr. 27, 1780.

ladles of fresh frog: See, for example, Fitz-Henry Smith Jr., "The French at Boston During the Revolution," *Bostonian Society Publications*, 1913, vol. 10, 9–75.

312 private letter from Morris: RM to BF, Sept. 28, 1782.

lightning struck: Howard C. Rice, ed., *Travels in North America*, by the Marquis de Chastellux (Chapel Hill: University of North Carolina Press, 1963), I, 293.

"has taken a French": Jan Ingenhousz to BF, Nov. 29, 1782, APS.

"Let us be honest": JJ to Livingston, Sept. 18, 1782, Guinta, I, 582.

313 It has been argued: See especially Dull, *French Navy and American Independence*, and Dull, "France and the American Revolution Seen as Tragedy," in Hoffman and Albert, eds., *Diplomacy and Revolution*, 73–106.

314 "But you will take": VRG to Luzerne, Oct. 14, 1782, CP Etats-Unis, XXII, AAE.

"the most absolute": Luzerne to VRG, Dec. 30, 1782, CP Etats-Unis, XXII, f605, AAE.

315 reports circulated: Luzerne to VRG, Sep. 22, 1782, CP Etats-Unis, XXII, f253, AAE.

He was livid: See especially Adams's later account, *Boston Patriot*, May 15, 1811.

"Between two as subtle": JA, Oct. 27, 1782, *Diary*, III, 38.

316 a well-meaning friend: The account is from Klingelhofer, "Matthew Ridley's Diary," 123.

"no other sentiments": JA to Edmund Jenings, July 20, 1782, Massachusetts Historical Society.

"For when you assemble": BF's speech in the Convention on the Constitution, Sept. 17, 1787.

317 "a constant scuffle": JA to Abigail Adams, *The Book of Abigail and John*, 327.

"Our allies": JA, Nov. 5, 1782, *Diary*, III, 47.

318 "one man, who is submission": JA to Livingston, Nov. 8, 1782, Wharton, V.

"without fancying": VRG to Luzerne, Dec. 19, 1782, CP Etats-Unis, XXII, f185, AAE.

No one was as ingenious: JA, Nov. 10, 1782, *Diary*, III, 50. Also Klingelhofer, "Matthew Ridley's Diary," 416–17.

"A few of these compliments": JA, Nov. 12, 1782, *Diary*, III, 53.

320 "firmness and exertions": JJ to Livingston, Dec. 12, 1782, Wharton, VI.

321 "had not been very obliging": VRG to Luzerne, Dec. 19, 1782, CP Etats-Unis, XXII, f185, AAE.

"I am rather at a loss" to "you to the King?": VRG to BF, Dec. 15, 1782, CP Etats-Unis, XXII, f180, AAE.

322 "Your observation" to "totally mistaken": BF to VRG, Dec. 17, 1782.

strain showed in his face: Ivan Bariatinskii dispatch, December 12, 1782, in Nina Bashkina et al., eds., *The United States and Russia: The Beginning of Relations, 1765–1815* (Washington: Department of State, 1980), 169.

"perceiving the irregularity" to "for the United States": VRG to Luzerne, Dec. 21, 1782, CP Etats-Unis, XXII, f189, AAE.

323 "All is fair": JA, Dec. 21, 1782, *Diary*, III, 98.

"an honest American": BF note [to Hartley] of May 4, 1779, CP Etats-Unis, XXII, f636, AAE. Privately he had also told JJ he did not disagree about the instructions, which he himself had ignored early on with Oswald.

"Our independence" to "despise us": BF to Samuel Cooper, Dec. 26, 1782.

324 "If we judge": VRG to Luzerne, Dec. 19, 1782, CP Etats-Unis, XXII, f185, AAE.

XI: THE ABSENT ARE NEVER WITHOUT FAULT

325 "Anyone who wants": *Courrier d'Avignon*, Dec. 26, 1783. On the American miracle, see, for example, Linguet, IX, 1783, 473; Linguet, X, 1783, 342.

326 "Could I have hoped": Cited in Gilbert Chinard, *L'apothéose de Benjamin Franklin* (Paris: Librairie orientale et américaine, 1955), 97.

"It's a country": Cröy, "Mémoirs du duc de Cröy," Mar. 1, 1779, *La Nouvelle Revue Retrospective*, 1897, 386; Vicomte de Grouchy and Paul Cottin, eds., Cröy, *Journal inédit du duc de Cröy* (Paris: Flammarion, 1906), IV.

meandered into a discussion: Morellet, Add. Mss. 6134–1635, BL.

327 "we were better tacticians": JA to Gerry, December 14, 1782, Massachusetts Historical Society.

"So at last": Apr. 28, 1783, Métra.

Also from the start: VRG to Montmorin, Dec. 27, 1777, vol. 587, f307, AAE.

328 "Dr. Franklin seems anxious": Alleyne Fitzherbert to Lord Grantham, Feb. 9, 1783, Guinta I, 766.

329 "When you are more": BF to BB, May 2, 1783.

"his unhealthy dwelling": Robert Pigott to BF, June 27, 1783, APS.

"not remarkable for anything": James Madison to TJ, Feb. 11, 1783, *Papers of Thomas Jefferson*, VI.

"He hates Franklin": TJ to JM, Feb. 14, 1783, *ibid.*

330 "I shall forever": JA to Abigail Adams, Jan. 29, 1783.

"gained more applause": JA to Warren, Apr. 16, 1783, *Warren-Adams Letters*, II, 213.

March meeting: Mar. 19, 1783, Métra.

"I must and do": JA to James Warren, Mar. 209, 1783, *Warren-Adams Letters*, II, 193.

331 "the miserable gloriole" to "or intimidated": JA to Warren, Mar. 21, 1783, *Warren-Adams Letters*, II, 195–97.

"the count fell": JA in *Boston Patriot*, May 15, 1811.

Impatiently Vergennes awaited: VRG to Luzerne, Sept. 7, 1783, CP Etats-Unis, XXV, f261, AAE. VRG was even less fond of JJ.

"yet it has advanced" to "hear of every day": BF to RM, Mar. 7, 1783, New Hampshire Historical Society.

"I hear frequently": BF to HL, Mar. 20, 1783, Princeton University Library.

332 "who had conceived": BF to Thomas Mifflin, Dec. 25, 1783, National Archives.

"by this method": JA to Livingston, July 12, 1783, Guinta, II, 185. For more on JA's complaints regarding BF and the treaties, Luzerne to VRG, Dec. 1, 1783, CP Etats-Unis, XXVI, f151, AAE, a passage that terminates: "Nous sommes ici comme autant de satellites tournant autour de la planète du vieux Docteur, et nous ne servons qu'à relever son éclat."

333 "This is a trick": BF to Benjamin Webb, Apr. 22, 1784, Library of Congress.

"Let there be": John Bourne to BF, Mar. 9, 1783, University of Pennsylvania Library. For its amusement Franklin periodically sent the most outlandish of these petitions to Congress, so that his colleagues might see "how people make shoes for feet they have never measured."

"weary, disgusted": JA, Feb. 18, 1783, *Diary*, III, 108.

"the demon of discord" to "and when not": JA to Warren, Apr. 13, 1783, *Warren-Adams Letters*, II, 209–211.

334 "the greatest and worst part": JA to Livingston, May 25, 1783, Massachusetts Historical Society.

"malice of enemies": JA to Warren, Apr. 9, 1783, *Warren-Adams Letters*, II, 206.

running a race: JA to Abigail Adams, Apr. 16, 1783, *Adams Family Correspondence*, V, 126–27.

335 "the first to pay": JA to AL/Osgood, Apr. 9, 1784, Massachusetts Historical Society.

"representing the United States": BF to Livingston, Mar. 4, 1782. Lester C. Olson is most eloquent on the medal, "Benjamin Franklin's Commemorative Medal *Libertas Americana*: A Study in Rhetorical Iconology," *Quarterly Journal of Speech*, Feb. 1990, 23–45. With thanks to the University of Delaware Library's Gregg A. Silvis, who supplied the text.

"as a monumental acknowledgement": BF to Livingston, Apr. 15, 1783.

336 "keeps out of sight": Livingston to Elias Boudinot, Sept. 29, 1783, Livingston Papers, New-York Historical Society.

337 "is always an honest man": BF to Livingston, July 22, 1783.

"If I was in Congress": JA to Livingston, May 25, 1783, Massachusetts Historical Society.

338 back-slapping and hand-wringing: See Samuel Osgood to JA, Dec. 7, 1783, Burnett, VII, 383–84.

"inconsistent with the spirit": See James Madison's Notes of Debates, Mar. 19, 1783, in Guinta I, 793. Also Osgood to JA, Dec. 7, 1783, Burnett, VII; VRG to Luzerne, Mar. 22, 1783, CP Etats-Unis, XXIII, f355, AAE.

"great powers never": James Madison's Notes of Debates, Mar. 12–15, 1783, Guinta I, 781.

"Since we have assumed": American commissioners to Livingston, July 18, 1873, in Morris, *John Jay: The Winning of the Peace*, 554.

339 "our giving him": JJ to Livingston, July 19, 1783; ibid., 561.

"and no wrestler": JA, Jan. 12, 1783, *Diary*, III, 105.

"We did what appeared": BF to Livingston, July 22, 1783.

Luzerne borrowed: Luzerne to VRG, Mar. 22 and Mar. 26, 1783, CP Etats-Unis, XXIII, f355 and f376, AAE.

"The French are": BF to Nathaniel Falconer, July 28, 1783, APS.

340 "As to my grandfather": WTF to Caleb Whitefoord, Aug. 7, 1783, Whitefoord Correspondence, 36593, BL.

"For they were": Cited in Dorcas Montgomery to Sarah Bache, July 26, 1783, APS.

"I am sure my cousin": BB to Richard and Sarah Bache, Oct. 30, 1783, APS.

341 "and should this": Richard Bache to BB, Nov. 5, 1783, APS.

In a move that confounded: See M. Flourens, *Eloge historique de Benjamin Delessert* (Paris: Didot Frères, 1850), 6. On the Passy press, William E. Lingelbach, "B. Franklin, Printer—New Source Materials," *Proceedings of the American Philosophical Society*, vol. 92, no. 2, May 1948, 79–100.

Contrary to myth: Both JA and TJ testified to his capabilities, TJ to Monroe, Nov. 11, 1784.

Indeed the Danes: Blome had told the Saxe ambassador as much, Apr. 18, 1783, DR; BF to Baron de Stael, June 16, 1783.

342 Even his closest Parisian friends: Le Veillard fils to WTF, Dec. 17, 1782, APS.

"razors to be bought": WTF to Whitefoord, July 12, 1782, Whitefoord Correspondence, 36593, BL.

343 more polish: Mary Hewson to BF, Oct. 25, 1784; Mary Hewson to Barbara Hewson, Jan. 25, 1785, APS; Ridley to RM, Feb. 16, 1782, *Papers of Robert Morris*, IV, 244; and Abigail Adams Smith, Mar. 17, 1785, *Journal and Correspondence of Miss Adams* (New York: Wiley, 1841), I, 61–64.

"Thus while Governor" to "any in existence": AL to Warren, Dec. 12, 1782, *Warren-Adams Letters*, II, 186.

344 "the Dr., who knows better": JA to RM, Sept. 14, 1783, *Papers of Robert Morris*, VIII, 516.

"wear no livery" to "in speaking French": JA, Jan. 11, 1783, *Diary*, III, 102.

345 "three of my colleagues": WTF, *Memoirs*, V, 212. JJ clearly regretted that he had so readily agreed to WTF's appointment, less because of doubts about his abilities than because of JJ's desire to act independently of BF.

"one continued insult": JA to Warren, Apr. 13, 1783, *Warren-Adams Letters*, II, 209.

"Effrontery" is from WL to JA, Mar. 27, 1783, *William Lee Letters*, III, 937.

"outrages to morality": JA to Warren, Apr. 13, 1783, in *Warren-Adams Letters*, II, 209.

"It is said": Sam Osgood to JA, Dec. 7, 1783, Burnett, VII, 388.

"which was saying": Le Veillard fils to WTF, Sept. 14, 1782.

346 "Return what does not": Sir James Nicolson to WTF, Aug. 13, 1783, APS.

"A more proper and delicate": WTF to Nicolson, Aug. 14, 1783, APS.

"B a B of a B": WTF's datebook, Feb. 22, 1785, APS.

347 "an English lady": Sally Jay to JJ, Nov. 18, 1783, Papers of John Jay, Columbia University.

"so faint in passing": BF, Meteorological Reflections, May 1784.

feeling of apocalypse: *Courrier d'Avignon*, July 17, 1784; *Journal de Genève*, July 22, 1784.

348 "Far from being": *Journal de Genève*, Sept. 2, 1784.

349 "keep themselves out": John Baynes, Sept. 23 entry, in Romilly, II, 452.

"I cannot say": Cröy, Ms. 1653, InF.

350 "We are more thoroughly": BF to David Hartley, Sept. 6, 1783.

"but conscious of my" to "my vindication": BF to Josiah Quincy Sr., Sept. 11, 1783, APS.

"Dr. Franklin had at last": Luzerne to VRG, Dec. 1, 1783, CP Etats-Unis, XXVI, f151, AAE.

"the universe could": Sept. 15, 1784, entry, in L. F. S. Upton, ed., *The Diary and Selected Papers of Chief Justice William Smith* (Toronto: Champlain Society, 1963), I, 137.

351 "that it was entirely": Samuel Cooper to BF, May 5, 1782.

"As to the two charges": BF to Quincy, Sept. 11, 1783, APS.

"low cunning": JA to Gerry, Sept. 10, 1783, Massachusetts Historical Society.

"secretly contriving" to "such lengths": JA to Warren, Sept. 10, 1783, *Warren-Adams Letters*, II, 222.

"enfeebled with age": JA to AL/Osgood, Apr. 9, 1784, Massachusetts Historical Society.

352 "Mr. Adams is vain": Cited in McCullough, *John Adams*, 489.

"Luckily here, and I hope": BF to RM, Dec. 25, 1783.

" 'Yes,' concurred Franklin" to "health of mankind": Baynes in Romilly, 448. "Oh, Monsieur," entry, Sept. 15, 1784, 449.

353 chess-playing automaton: *Journal de Genève*, May 3, 1783.

"The king has brought": *Journal de Genève*, July 15, 1783.

"We think of nothing": BF to HL, Dec. 6, 1783, South Carolina Historical Society.

353 inevitable gibe: *Journal de Genève*, Dec. 23, 1783.

354 should have two parents: Dec. 5, 1783, Bachaumont.

"You're doing nothing": *Courrier de l'Europe*, Nov. 29, 1783.

"A few months since": BF to Sir Joseph Banks, Nov. 21, 1783.

355 "learn to deprive": BF to Joseph Priestley, Feb. 8, 1780.

"What good is": Aug. 1783, cited in Maurice Tourneux, ed., *Correspondance littéraire, philosophique et critique par Grimm, Diderot, Raynal, etc.* (Paris: 1877–82), Vol XIII, 349. See also *Journal de Genève*, Sept. 23, 1783; *Nouvelles Extraordinaires*, Oct. 22, 1784; Bachaumont, XXIII, Sept. 24, 1783. For the last word on Franklin's utterance, Seymour L. Chapin, "A Legendary Bon Mot: Franklin's 'What Is the Good of a Newborn Baby?'" *Proceedings of the American Philosophical Society*, vol. 129, no. 3, 1985.

"This experience is": BF to Banks, Nov. 21, 1783.

"The Montgolfiers' invention": Feb. 18, 1784, Métra.

356 "If you want to fill": The discovery is that of the eagle-eyed Claude Lopez, Yale document 15943.

"Never before": BF to Banks, Dec. 1, 1783.

357 "Beings of a rank": BF to Banks, Nov. 21, 1783.

358 "the situation of the army": Commissioners to Boudinot, Sept. 10, 1783.

Washington failed: Luzerne to Vergennes, Nov. 11, 1783, CP Etats-Unis, XXVI, f112, AAE.

"fatal moment": Osgood to JA, Dec. 7, 1783, Burnett, VII, 379.

"has raised herself": JA to AL/Osgood, Apr. 9, 1784, Massachusetts Historical Society.

XII: CREDITORS HAVE BETTER MEMORIES THAN DEBTORS

On Mesmer: Robert Darnton, *Mesmerism and the End of the Enlightenment in France* (Cambridge: Harvard University Press, 1968); Jean Thuillier, *Franz Anton Mesmer, ou L'exstase magnétique* (Paris: Laffont, 1988); Louis Figuier, *Histoire des merveilleux* (Paris: Hachette, 1860); Jean-Nicolas Dufort de Cheverny, *Mémoires* (Paris: Les amis de l'histoire, 1970), 2 vols.; Charles Coulston Gillispie, *Science and Polity in France at the End of the Old Regime* (Princeton: Princeton University Press, 1980). For the best account of the voyage home, Charles Jenkins's impeccable "Franklin Returns from France, 1785," *American Philosophical Society Proceedings*, Dec. 1948, 417–32. Also BF's Private Journal, in WTF's *Memoirs*; BB's diary, APS; WTF's appointment book for 1785, APS; and JW's journal of a voyage, JW mss., Lilly Library, Indiana University. For TJ: *The Papers of Thomas Jefferson*; Howard C. Rice Jr., *Thomas Jefferson's Paris*; and William Howard Adams, *The Paris Years of Thomas Jefferson* (New Haven: Yale University Press, 1997). For more on the Adams family, Abigail Adams Smith, *Journal and Correspondence of Miss Adams: Daughter of John Adams* (New York: Wiley, 1841).

359 "When men of sober age": TJ to Peter Carr, Aug. 10, 1787, *Papers of Thomas Jefferson*, XII, 17.

"There are many": JJ to BF, Dec. 26, 1783, APS. In his diary JA had reverted to the same metaphor to describe the Anglo-American relationship.

"You may judge" to "as a *man*": BF to JJ, Jan. 6, 1784.

360 "Celebrity may for a while": BF to Jan Ingehousz, Apr. 29, 1785. On BF's immobility, JA to Elbridge Gerry, Nov. 4, 1784.

360 found it debilitating: BF to VRG, May 15, 1783.

"All the desire": BF to Antoine-Alexis-François Cadet de Vaux, February 5, 1784, Bibliothèque Municipale, Nantes.

On the back of a letter: The discovery is Claude Lopez's.

361 "They should methinks": BF to Livingston, July 22, 1783, cited in Continental Congress resolution on BF's retirement, Mar. 29, 1784.

the new maître d'hôtel: See agreement with Finck, Jan. 1784, Yale. On Finck's misbehavior, BF to Chaumont, Oct. 20, 1785. Also Bénard to BF, Mar. 31, 1781.

362 The gardener: BB diary, Sept. 9, 1784, APS. Franklin's coachman: Z-2-3880/A, AN. On Jean Grépillon: Y 18722C, AN.

"If life is compared": BF poem of Apr. 22, 1784, Berg Collection, NYPL.

363 "Your philosophy": BF to Banks, Nov. 21, 1783.

"where the streets": "Information to Those Who Would Remove to America," published anonymously in *Courrier d'Avignon*, May 4, 1784.

to a Spaniard: BF to Pedro Rodriguez, conde de Campomanes, June 5, 1784.

364 Franklin regretted that: BF to Vaughan, July 26, 1784.

"the ribbands" to "improvement of the country": BF to Sally Bache, Jan. 26, 1784. The irony of his deploring the laws of primogeniture to his daughter was lost on BF.

365 "that the pretension": *New England Courant*, Feb. 11, 1723.

"the odious mixture": BF to Sally Bache, Jan. 26, 1784.

"Since my being last": BF to Grenville Sharp, July 5, 1785.

"Some were for": Cited by Baynes, Romilly, II, 455.

366 "you do not want": Morellet to BF, Mar. 16, 1784, APS.

"Your sentiments and mine": BF to Morellet, Mar. 16, 1784, APS.

"Hence issued": See Mirabeau, *Considérations sur l'ordre de Cincinnatus* (London, 1784). Mirabeau called on BF on July 13, 1784; he appears to have worked not only from BF's text but from BF's letter to Sally Bache. BF had earlier critiqued the laws of primogeniture with Baynes, see Romilly, 455–56.

"I find that some": BF to Vaughan, Sept. 7, 1785.

367 "An Economical Project": Published under the rubric "Economie," *Journal de Paris*, Apr. 26, 1784. See A. O. Aldridge, "Franklin's Essay on Daylight Savings," *American Literature*, Mar. 1956, 23–29. On the dusting off, C. Couderc, "Economies proposées par Benjamin Franklin et Mercier de Saint-Léger pour l'éclairage et le chauffage, à Paris 1784," *Bulletin de la Société de l'Histoire de Paris*, 1916, 93–101.

368 Mesmer: See *Benjamin Franklin: Inquiry into Mesmerism, Seven Separate Original Pamphlets* (Paris, 1784).

369 No scientific commission: Even the Establishment-friendly Lavoisier had earlier appealed to BF for his imprimateur. "I could regard this revolution as much advanced or even entirely completed," he wrote BF in Feb. 1780, "if you take our side."

He was equally: BF to La Condamine, Mar. 19, 1784.

a well-informed Frenchman: Louis-Sebastien Mercier, *Tableau de Paris*, XII, 144.

370 From northern France: For a fine account of the St.-Omer case, see Charles Vellay, "Benjamin Franklin et le procès du paratonnere de St.-Omer, *Revue Historique de la Révolution Française*, Jan. 1914, 135–38.

"For Mr. Jay": BF to HL, Apr. 29, 1784.

"A Frenchman": BF to Morellet, cited in A. O. Aldridge, *Franklin and His French Contemporaries* (New York: New York University Press, 1957), 189.

371 The language: See Stuart Green, "The Origins of Modern Clinical Research," *Clinical Orthopaedics and Related Research*, no. 404, 2002.
Deslon settled on: BB diary, May 22, 1784, APS.

372 It behooved the: LF to BF, June 12, 1784.
"grand philosophical discovery": LF to GW, May 14, 1784, in W. W. Abbot, ed., *The Papers of George Washington* (Charlottesville: University Press of Virginia, 1992), 380.

373 "Some think it will": BF to WTF, Aug. 25, 1784.
took Franklin to task: Mar. 26, 1785, entry, *Diary of John Quincy Adams*, ed. Robert J. Taylor (Cambridge: Harvard University Press, 1981), II.

374 "It is from beginning": Abigail Adams Smith, entry of December 2, 1784, *Journal and Correspondence*, I, 36. On *Figaro*, Jean-François de La Harpe, *Correspondance littéraire* (Geneva: Slatkine, 1968), III, 210.

375 "a course of experiments": JA to BF, July 19, 1784.
"an assembly of wise": BF to Benjamin Vaughan, July 26, 1784.
"It is amazing": BF private journal, July 18, 1784.

376 "the thing is impossible" to "at Canterbury": BF to Mason Weems and Edward Gant, July 18, 1784.
at worst a Presbyterian: Pace, 112.
"Our ancestors": BF to Jonathan Williams Sr., Apr. 13, 1785.
"You will see": BF to JA, Aug. 6, 1784, Massachusetts Historical Society.
"Persons will play": Baynes in Romilly, Sept. 15, 1784, visit, 450. Similarly, BF to Strahan, Aug. 19, 1784.
"The readers of Connecticut": BF to JA, Aug. 6, 1784. The salary was cut from $11,000 to $9,000, on the motion of Elbridge Gerry, Massachusetts Historical Society.

377 A tortured explanation: GW to BF, June 2, 1784.
"certainly had none": BF to Charles Thomson, Dec. 29, 1788.
"to make myself": WTF to Carmichael, Aug. 15, 1784, APS.

378 "Indeed," continued Gerry: Elbridge Gerry to JA, June 16, 1784, Burnett, VII, 554.
The two were held: Luzerne to VRG, May 17, 1784, Guinta, II.
"lately more than": JA to Abigail Adams, July 9, 1783, *Adams Family Correspondence*, V, 198.
"done mischief": JA to AL/Osgood, Apr. 9, 1784, Massachusetts Historical Society.

379 "With less we should": Abigail Adams to Mary Cranch, Sept. 5, 1784, AFC, V, 439.
"the genteel girls": JA to Gerry, Dec. 12, 1783, cited in James T. Austin, *The Life of Elbridge Gerry* (Boston: Wells & Lilly, 1828), II, 401.
has been hailed: Joseph Ellis, *American Sphinx* (New York: Knopf, 1996), 78.
"At length our foreign": James Monroe, cited in Marie Kimball, *Jefferson: The Scene of Europe* (New York: Coward-McCann, 1950), 17.

380 "been able to discover" to "foreign or native": TJ to Dr. William Smith, n.d., WTF, *Memoirs*, II, 258–59.
new breed of beggars: See, for example, BF to the Regents of the University of the State of New York, Aug. 9, 1784.

381 "I wish this calm": JA to Gerry, Dec. 12, 1784, Massachusetts Historical Society.
"seem now to be": BF to JJ, Feb. 8, 1785.

382 "I am sorry" to "any of my family": Draft of BF to Charles Thomson, Oct.–Nov. 1784, APS.
"I had thoughts" to "offices of anybody": BF to Richard Bache, Nov. 11, 1784, BL.

382 "Can nothing be done" to "being superceded": TJ to Monroe, Nov. 11, 1784.
"I flattered myself" to "performed any": BF to Thomson, Oct.–Nov. 1784, APS.
"an exile": BF to Richard Bache, Nov. 11, 1784.

383 "to revive" to "duty to my king": William Franklin to BF, July 22, 1784.
"When we launch": BF to Jonathan Shipley, Feb. 24, 1786.

384 "But you who are": BF to William Franklin, Sept. 7, 1774. For more on William, see Claude-Anne Lopez and Eugenia W. Herbert, *The Private Franklin* (New York: Norton, 1975), and Sheila L. Skemp, *William Franklin: Son of a Patriot, Servant of a King* (New York: Oxford University Press, 1990). Especially good is Catherine Fennelly, "William Franklin of New Jersey," *The William and Mary Quarterly*, July 1949, 361–83.
"Indeed nothing has ever" to "*extinguished by them*": BF to William Franklin, Aug. 16, 1784, BL.

385 "This is a disagreeable": BF to William Franklin, Aug. 16, 1784, BL. "However it [is]": William to BF, Dec. 24, 1774. BF kept particularly close track of WTF's expenses in Paris, which bill he intended for William. A Loyalist offspring, no matter how great his service to a republic, was not to be supported by revolutionary coffers.
"The true *loyalists*": BF to Baron Francis Maseres, June 26, 1785.
"And when lewd": Henry Grand to WTF, Aug. 19, 1784, APS.

386 "Judge what I must": BF to WTF, Oct. 2, 1784, APS.
"To have such a young": Mary Hewson to BF, Oct. 25, 1784, APS.

387 "with a lady": BB diary, Dec. 2, 1784, APS.
found the winter: BF to Mary Hewson, May 5, 1785.
"I dare say". William Franklin to WTF, Dec. 16, 1784, APS. See also Doctor Jeffries, *A Narrative of the Two Aerial Voyages of Doctor Jeffries with Mons. Blanchard* (Robson: London, 1786), 75–82.

388 he was listless: Smith diary, Feb. 9, 1784, in L. F. S. Upton, ed., *The Diary and Selected Papers of Chief Justice William Smith* (Toronto: Champlain Society, 1963), I, 10. On Franklin's health, George W. Corner and Willard E. Goodwin, "Benjamin Franklin's Bladder Stone," *Journal of the History of Medicine and Allied Sciences*, Oct. 1953, 359–77.
"Dr. F[ranklin] is": JA to AL, Jan. 31, 1785, Massachusetts Historical Society.
"for a voyage": JA to Elbridge Gerry, Jan. 31, 1785, Massachusetts Historical Society.

389 No matter who the visitor: See Robert Kahn, "F. Grimm, and J. H. Landolt," *Proceedings of the American Philosophical Society*, Dec. 1955, 401–04. A British informer had noted the same years earlier: "I know not how it is, we always run into politics, though we set out with philosophy" (William Pulteney, May 26, 1778, Huntington Library).
"If you put up dams": *Nouvelles Extraordinaires*, Mar. 11, 1785; *Courrier d'Avignon*, Mar. 25, 1785.
"books instead": BF to Richard Price, Mar. 18, 1785, APS.
"I have found it": BF to Mary Hewson, May 5, 1785.

390 "I must avow" to "any other": JA to JJ, June 2, 1785, cited in *The Works of John Adams*, VIII, 258.
"Rejoice with me": BF to Jan Ingenhousz, Apr. 29, 1785.
"I shall need": BF to Jonathan Williams, May 5, 1785.
"you may rely on it": WTF to Jonathan Williams, May 6, 1785.

391 "Is it you, Sir": TJ to Dr. William Smith, WTF, *Memoirs*, II, 259.
his counsel for: BF to Le Roy, Feb. 1784. In WTF, *Memoirs*, VI, 470–71.

392 "Mr. Franklin has been": *Diary of John Quincy Adams*, I, Feb. 26, 1785.
"I have before me": *Diary of John Quincy Adams*, I, Apr. 26, 1785.

393 "I promise myself": BF to Mary Hewson, May 5, 1785. Similarly to Mme. Helvétius, July 19, 1785.

He also promised: See M. Flourens, *Eloge historique de Benjamin Delessert* (Paris: Didot Frères, 1850), 6.

Greenlanders: BF to George Whatley, May 23, 1785.

"My task is not": In Gilbert Chinard, "Abbé Lefebvre de la Roche's Recollections of Benjamin Franklin," *Proceedings of the American Philosophical Society*, June 1950, 221. Part of the remark found its way into the *Courrier de l'Europe*, May 30, 1785.

tears in his eyes: On the departure, René Desgenettes, *Souvenirs de la fin du XVII-Ième siècle* (Paris: Didot, 1836), I, 197; Cabanis, *Oeuvres Posthumes*, V; BB diary, July 12, 1785, APS.

"Perhaps no sovereign": R. W. Darwin, Nov. 1, 1803, in *Proceedings of the Massachusetts Historical Society*, XIX, 311.

394 solemn silence: BB diary, July 12, 1785, APS.

395 discreet lover: BF to Madame Le Veillard, July 22, 1785.

"the country that *I love*": BF to Mme. Helvétius, July 19, 1785.

"I shall always": BF to Mme. Helvétius, July 27, 1785.

"Oh that great man" to "your fault": Brillon to BF, December 30, 1785, APS.

396 The bells pealed: WTF to Le Veillard, Sept. 16, 1785, Morgan Library; WTF to Blanchette Caillot, Sept. 15, 1785; BB diary, Sept. 13, 1785; BF diary; JW to Mariamne Alexander Williams, Sept. 15, 1785, Lilly Library, Indiana University; BB to Robert Alexander, Oct. 30, 1785, APS; *Courrier d'Avignon*, Nov. 1, 1785; *Journal de Paris*, Oct. 21, 1785, and Oct. 22, 1785; *Nouvelles Extraordinaires*, Nov. 1, 1785; *The Freeman's Journal*, Sept. 21, 1785; *The Independent Chronicle and Universal Advertiser*, Sept. 29, 1785; *Maryland Gazette*, Sept. 17, 1785; *Pennsylvania Packet*, Sept. 15–23, 1785; J. Bennett Nolan, "Doctor Franklin Arrives from France," *The Historical Review of Berks County*, Jan.–Mar. 1951, 51.

"My principal merit": *Pennsylvania Gazette*, Sept. 21, 1785.

overwhelmed by the reception: BF to JJ, Sept. 21, 1785. BF to Edward Newenham, Oct. 3, 1785.

EPILOGUE

For the French reaction to BF's death, Gilbert Chinard, "The Apotheosis of Benjamin Franklin: Paris 1790–1791," *Proceedings of the American Philosophical Society*, Dec. 1955, 440–73. On the lack of apotheosis in America, Julian Boyd's masterful "Death of Franklin: The Politics of Mourning in France and the United States," in *Papers of Thomas Jefferson*, vol. 19, 78–106. For the last days of SD, Julian P. Boyd's three-part series, "Silas Deane: Death by a Kindly Teacher of Treason?" *The William and Mary Quarterly*, Apr., July, Oct., 1959. For fine analyses of BF's enduring influence and image: A. Aulard, "La Révolution américaine et la révolution française: Franklin," *La Révolution Française*, Sept.–Oct. 1918, 385–416; James A. Leith, "Le culte de Franklin en France avant et pendant la révolution française," *Annales Historiques de la Révolution Française*, July–Sept. 1976, 543–71; Philip Mark Katz, *The Image of Benjamin Franklin in the Politics of the French Revolution, 1776–1794* (Harvard University, BA essay, 1987).

399 "but as for": BF to Mme. Brillon, Oct. 20, 1785.

Temple suspected: WTF to Le Veillard, Jan. 18, 1786, Morgan Library.

399 "I seem to have intruded myself": BF to George Whatley, May 18, 1787.

enemies would pounce: Louis Otto to VRG, Sept. 17, 1785, CP Etats-Unis, vol. 30, AAE.

400 "I must own": BF to Charles Thomson, Dec. 29, 1788. GW's very specific oversight has been pointed out by Claude Lopez.

"I have never": TJ to James Monroe, July 5, 1785, *Papers of Thomas Jefferson*, vol. VIII, 261–62.

401 "dress and diversions": JJ to Samuel Huntington, Apr. 21, 1781, Morris, *John Jay: The Winning of the Peace*, 66.

"Having served": WTF to TJ, Jan. 18, 1786, *Papers of Thomas Jefferson*, vol. IX, 179. Temple whispered: WTF to Le Veillard, June 6, 1786, Morgan Library.

"to be appointed": Temple to TJ, Oct. 13, 1790, *Papers of Thomas Jefferson*, XVII, 591.

402 "Now, even in my sleep": BF to Mme. Helvétius, Oct. 25, 1788.

On Finck: Lamotte to WTF, Sept. 27, 1785.

"He went over all": TJ, *Autobiography*, in *The Life and Selected Writings of Thomas Jefferson*, 102.

403 "from despotism": TJ to LF, Apr. 2, 1790, *Papers of Thomas Jefferson*, XVI, 293.

"not a fig": William Maclay, Jan. 26, 1791, in Kenneth R. Bowling and Helen E. Veit, eds., *The Diary of William Maclay and Other Notes on Senate Debates* (Baltimore: Johns Hopkins University Press, 1988), IX, 369.

404 A prophet: For an account of BF's popularity during the Reign of Terror and the Revolution, see Kenneth N. McKee, "The Popularity of the 'American' on the French Stage During the Revolution," *Proceedings of the American Philosophical Society*, Sept. 1940, 479–91.

405 "This is the time": BF to WTF, Sept. 19, 1776.

406 "his grandfather": In Richard N. Rosenfeld, *American Aurora*, 235.

"entered into partnership": JA, *Boston Patriot*, May 15, 1811.

"was the first in France": BF to GW, June 3, 1789.

409 Hours after John Adams: JA to John Trumball, Apr. 25, 1790, in Ferling, 247.

410 "Secrecy! Cunning!": JA to Benjamin Rush, July 23, 1806, in John Schutz and Douglass Adair, *The Spur of Fame* (San Marion, Calif.: Huntington Library, 1966), 59.

"the son of" to "State House yard": *Porcupine's Gazette*, cited in Robert C. Alberts, *The Golden Voyage: The Life and Times of William Bingham* (Boston: Houghton Mifflin, 1969), 325.

"the effects of prudent": BF to la Rochefoucauld, Oct. 24, 1788, Bibliothèque de Mantes, Mantes-la-Jolie.

411 "Genêt came to": Cited in Ron Chernow, *Alexander Hamilton* (New York: Penguin, 2003), 438.

"morally debilitated": Janet Flanner, *Paris Journal, 1944–1955* (New York: Harvest, 1998), 179. "No country was worse": *Ibid.*, 184.

412 "If by chance": Phillips Russell, "Franklin in Paris," *McNaught's Monthly*, Sept. 1926, 76.

"till some experiment comes": BF to Parraud, June 14, 1783.

"In this world": Dubourg, *Calendrier de philosophie; ou le moraliste américain pour tous les jours de l'année* (Paris, 1785), 106. Similarly but not exactly, Cabanis cites Franklin, in *Oeuvres posthumes*, V, 266: "Si la foi sauve dans l'autre monde, elle perd dans celui-ci."

Selected Bibliography

Adams, John. *Diary and Autobiography.* Ed. L. H. Butterfield et al. Cambridge: Harvard University Press, 1961. 4 vols.

Adams, John Quincy. *Diary of John Quincy Adams.* Ed. Robert J. Taylor. Cambridge: Harvard University Press, 1981. 2 vols.

Adams Family Correspondence. Ed. L. H. Butterfield, Cambridge: Harvard University Press, 1963. 4 vols.

Aldridge, Alfred Owen. *Franklin and His French Contemporaries.* New York: New York University Press, 1957.

Bailyn, Bernard. *To Begin the World Anew.* New York: Knopf, 2003.

Ballagh, James Curtis, ed. *The Letters of Richard Henry Lee.* New York: Macmillan, 1911. 2 vols.

Bemis, Samuel Flagg. *The Diplomacy of the American Revolution.* New York: Appleton-Century, 1935.

Benjamin Franklin et la France: Exposition organisée pour le 250ème anniversaire de sa naissance. Paris: Les Presses Artistiques, 1956.

Bizardel, Yvon. *Les Américains à Paris sous Louis XVI et pendant la révolution.* Self-published, 1978.

Boyd, Julian P. "Silas Deane: Death by a Kindly Teacher of Treason?" *The William and Mary Quarterly*, series 3, XVI, Apr., July, Oct. 1959.

Cabanis, Pierre-Jean-Georges. *Oeuvres complètes.* Paris: Bossange Frères, 1825. V.

Chase, Eugene Parker, ed. *Our Revolutionary Forefathers: Letters of François, Marquis de Barbé-Marbois, 1779–1785.* New York: Duffield, 1929.

Chastellux, marquis de. *Travels in North America in the Years 1780, 1781, and 1782.* Ed. Howard C. Rice Jr. Chapel Hill: University of North Carolina Press, 1963. 2 vols.

Cogan, Charles. *French Negotiating Behavior.* Washington: U.S. Institute of Peace Press, 2003.

Conner, Paul W. *Poor Richard's Politicks: Benjamin Franklin and His New American Order.* New York: Oxford University Press, 1965.

Corwin, Edward S. *French Policy and the American Alliance of 1778.* Gloucester, Mass.: Peter Smith, 1969.

Deane, Silas. *Collections of the New-York Historical Society.* New York: 1886–90. 5 vols.

Dull, Jonathan R. *A Diplomatic History of the American Revolution.* New Haven: Yale University Press, 1985.

————. "Franklin in France: A Reappraisal." *Proceedings of the Annual Meeting of the Western Society for French History*, 1976. No. 4, 256–62.

————. *Franklin the Diplomat: The French Mission*. Philadelphia: Transactions of the American Philosophical Society, 1982. 1–76.

————. *The French Navy and American Independence: A Study of Arms and Diplomacy, 1774–1787*. Princeton: Princeton University Press, 1975.

Echeverria, Durand. *Mirage in the West: A History of the French Image of American Society to 1815*. New York: Octagon Books, 1966.

Elias, Robert H. and Eugene D. Finch, eds. *Letters of Thomas Attwood Digges*. Columbia: University of South Carolina Press, 1982.

Ford, Worthington Chauncey et al., eds. *Journals of the Continental Congress, 1744–1789*. Washington: Government Printing Office, 1904–37. 34 vols.

Fortescue, John William, ed. *The Correspondence of King George the Third from 1760 to 1783*. London: Macmillan, 1927–28. 6 vols.

Franklin, Benjamin. *The Autobiography of Benjamin Franklin*. New York: Modern Library, 2001.

————. *The Papers of Benjamin Franklin*. Ed. Ellen R. Cohn et al. New Haven: Yale University Press, 1959–present. 37 vols. to date.

Franklin, William Temple, ed. *Memoirs of the Life and Writings of Benjamin Franklin*. London: Henry Colburn, 1818. 6 vols.

Huang, Nian-Sheng. *Benjamin Franklin in American Thought and Culture, 1790–1990*. Philadelphia: American Philosophical Society, 1994.

Hudson, Ruth Strong. *The Minister from France: Conrad Alexander Gérard*. Euclid, Ohio: Lutz, 1994.

Jefferson, Thomas. *The Papers of Thomas Jefferson*. Ed. Julian P. Boyd et al. Princeton: Princeton University Press, 1950–present. 30 vols. to date.

Labourdette, Jean-François. *Vergennes: Ministre principal de Louis XVI*. Paris: Editions Desjonquères, 1990.

Laurens, Henry. *The Papers of Henry Laurens*. Ed. Philip M. Hamer et al. Columbia: University of South Carolina Press, 1968–present. 16 vols. to date.

Lee, Richard Henry. *The Life of Arthur Lee*. Boston: Wells & Lilly, 1829. 2 vols.

Lee, William. *Letters of William Lee*. Ed. Worthington Chauncey Ford. Brooklyn, N.Y.: Historical Printing Club, 1891. 3 vols.

Lopez, Claude-Anne. *My Life with Benjamin Franklin*. New Haven: Yale University Press, 2000.

————. *Mon Cher Papa: Franklin and the Ladies of Paris*. New Haven: Yale University Press, 1966. Published in expanded form as *Le sceptre et la foudre*. Paris: Mercure de France, 1990.

Lopez, Claude-Anne, and Eugenia W. Herbert. *The Private Franklin*. New York: Norton, 1975.

McCullough, David. *John Adams*. New York: Simon & Schuster, 2001.

Medlin, Dorothy, Jean-Claude David, and Paul LeClerc, eds. *Lettres d'André Morellet*. Oxford: Voltaire Foundation, 1991–96. I.

Meng, John J., ed. *Despatches and Instructions of Conrad-Alexandre Gérard*. Baltimore: Johns Hopkins University Press, 1939.

Mercier, Louis-Sebastien. *Tableau de Paris*. Geneva: Slatkine Reprints, 1979. 12 vols.

Morellet, André. *Mémoires inédits de l'abbé Morellet*. Paris: Badouin, 1823. 2 vols.

Morris, Robert. *The Papers of Robert Morris.* Ed. E. James Ferguson et al. Pittsburgh: University of Pittsburgh Press, 1973–present. 9 vols. to date.

Perkins, James Breck. *France in the American Revolution.* Boston: Houghton Mifflin, 1911.

Perrault, Gilles. *La Revanche américaine: Le Secret du Roi.* Paris: Fayard, 1996.

Plumb, J. H. "The French Connection." *American Heritage,* Dec. 1974. 27–87.

Price, Munro, and John Hardman, eds. *Louis XVI and the comte de Vergennes: Correspondance, 1774–1787.* Oxford: Voltaire Foundation, 1998.

Rice, Howard C., Jr. *Thomas Jefferson's Paris.* Princeton: Princeton University Press, 1976.

Roger, Philippe. *L'Ennemi américain: Généalogie de l'antiaméricanisme français.* Paris: Seuil, 2002.

Rosenfeld, Richard N. *American Aurora: A Democratic-Republican Returns.* New York: St. Martin's, 1997.

Schaeper, Thomas J. *France and America in the Revolutionary Era: The Life of Jacques-Donatien Leray de Chaumont.* Providence: Berghahn Books, 1995.

Schama, Simon. *Citizens: A Chronicle of the French Revolution.* New York: Knopf, 1989.

Schelle, Gustave. *Oeuvres de Turgot.* Paris: Felix Alcan, 1923. 5 vols.

Sellers, Charles Coleman. *Benjamin Franklin in Portraiture.* New Haven: Yale University Press, 1962.

Smith, Paul H. et al., eds. *Letters of Delegates to Congress.* Washington: Library of Congress, 1976. 26 vols.

Stinchcombe, William C. *The American Revolution and the French Alliance.* Syracuse: Syracuse University Press, 1969.

Stourzh, Gerald. *Benjamin Franklin and American Foreign Policy.* Chicago: University of Chicago Press, 1969.

Watson, Winslow C., ed. *Men and Times of the Revolution, or Memoirs of Elkanah Watson.* New York: Dana, 1856.

Yela Utrilla, Juan F. *España ante la independencia de los Estados Unidos.* Mariana: Lérida, 1925. 2 vols.

Van Alstyne, Richard W. "Great Britain, the War for Independence, and the 'Gathering Storm' in Europe, 1775–1778." *The Huntington Library Quarterly,* Aug. 1964, 311–46.

Van Tyne, C. H. "French Aid Before the Alliance of 1778." *American Historical Review* XXXI, 1925. 20–40.

Warren-Adams Letters, being Chiefly a correspondence among John Adams, Samuel Adams, and James Warren. Boston: Massachusetts Historical Society, 1925. 2 vols.

Acknowledgments

There are not many people you can call before nine in the morning to ask what kind of dog, precisely, perched on Madame Helvétius's lap (and performed so obligingly for Abigail Adams), but Claude Lopez ranks first among them. This book owes everything to her decades of astute scholarship, her round-the-clock advice, and her close reading. I am indebted as well to Jonathan Dull for his patience with my elementary questions, his equally patient reading, and his splendid research. On every conceivable count I am grateful to the rest of the team at the Papers of Benjamin Franklin, who set the gold standard for scholarly works. Editor in chief Ellen Cohn is a marvel, as are Karen Duval, Jennifer Macellaro, Kate Ohno, and Michael Sletcher.

For documents and in many cases for permission to quote from them, I would like to thank the following institutions: the American Philosophical Society and in particular Roy Goodman, Valerie-Anne Lutz, and Joseph-James Ahern; the Service des Archives, Ministère des Affaires Etrangères, Paris; Geneviève Hamon, at the Archives Municipales, Auray; the Archives Nationales, Paris; the Archivio di Stato, Florence; the Archivio di Stato, Venice; the Archivio di Stato di Torino; the Archivo de Simancas, Valladolid, Spain; the Bayerisches Hauptstaatsarchiv, Munich; the Bibliothèque de l'Académie Nationale de Médicine; the Bibliothèque de l'Arsenal, especially Danielle Muzerelle; the Bibliothèque du Grand Orient; the Bibliothèque Historique de la Ville de Paris; the Bibliothèque de l'Institut de France; the Bibliothèque Municipale de Lyon; the Bibliothèques Municipales d'Orléans; Marie-Françoise Rose at the Bibliothèque Municipale de Versailles; the staff of the salle des manuscripts at the Bibliothèque

Nationale, the Musée National de la Coopération Franco-Américaine, Château de Blérancourt; the British Library; Butler Library, Columbia University; Geheimes Staatsarchiv, Berlin; Jill Davis Adams at the Connecticut Historical Society; Lee Arnold, director of the Historical Society of Pennsylvania; the Huntington Library; the Instituto dos Arquivos Nacionais, Lisbon; the Library of Congress, manuscripts division; Becky Cape, and the Lilly Library, Indiana University; the Mairie de Mantes-la-Jolie; Paul Tsimahides and the Massachusetts Historical Society; the Morgan Library; Victor van den Bergh at the Nationaal Archief, The Hague; the Niedersächsisches Staatsarchiv, Wolfenbüttel; the manuscripts department of the New-York Historical Society; the New York Public Library, and the Berg Collection's Stephen Crook; the Oesterreichisches Stätsarchiv, Vienna; the Public Record Office, London; the Rigsarkivet, Copenhagen; the Riksarkivet, Stockholm; the Sächsisches Hauptstaatsarchiv, Dresden; Claude Lanzenberg, at the Société Historique d'Auteuil et de Passy; the South Carolina Historical Society and Carey Lucas Nikonchuk; Tim Murray at the University of Delaware, Special Collections.

It is a pleasure finally to acknowledge my debt to the Dorothy and Lewis B. Cullman Center for Scholars and Writers at the New York Public Library, which provided an idyllic writing year, and perhaps more access to materials than is healthy. Peter Gay and the center's staff have my enduring thanks, as does the library staff. Many individuals have contributed materials to this book, Susan Mary Alsop, Ron Blumer, Emmanuel and Marie Breguet, François Cornu, Mary Deschamps, H. George Fletcher, Claude Fohlen, Patti Foster, Meredith Frapier, Stuart Karu, Mary Jane Kinney, Dorothy Medlin, Muffie Meyer, Tom Puchniak, Thomas J. Schaeper, Marion Ward, Barbara Wheaton, and Chuck Yanikowski among them. I would still be wandering around the Archives Nationales in Paris were it not for the incomparable Gilles Dussert, whom I know only through Donald Spinelli, to whose Beaumarchais scholarship I am indebted. Mackenzie Pitcairn, Elizabeth Seay, and Mary Phillips-Sandy all tracked down American-side documents and battled microfilm machines; Monsieur and Madame Pierre Tugny opened the Vergennes family papers to me in France. Professor Steven Smith at Yale's Branford College provided housing. Much of the rest of the time I benefited from the collections of the New York Society Library and the University of Alberta Library. Lena Auerbach, Cecile Pozzo di Borgo, Jean-Paul

Cluzel, Raymonde l'Italien, Ambassador Olivier de La Baume, and the Honorable A. Anne McLellan intervened to make available copies of original documents at the Quai d'Orsay, a collection presided over by Monique Constant, who resisted all entreaties.

At Holt Jennifer Barth worked wonders with a pencil and anticipated every one of her author's anxieties. It has been a privilege to work with her and her colleagues, especially John Sterling, Maggie Richards, Richard Rhorer, Elizabeth Shreve, Christine Ball, Fritz Metsch, Eva Diaz, Tom Nau, Lucille Rettino, Denise Cronin, Janice O'Quinn, Kenn Russell, Chris O'Connell, and Sam Douglas. Lois Wallace remains the most attentive, and the most amusing, of agents. For indulgence, advice, close readings, and caffeine, I am indebted to Donald Antrim, Wendy Belzberg, Emily Braun, Tom Buk-Swienty, David Colbert, Benita Eisler, Harry Frankfurt, Susan Hertog, Mitch Katz, Franziska Kirchner, Elinor Lipman, Thomas Schaeper, and Strauss Zelnick. Emily de La Bruyère helped to check all Franklin citations, and, with her brother Max, graciously allowed the eighteenth century to take priority over hockey practice. It never will again. I thank their sister Jo for having had the wisdom to thrive on neglect. My debt to Marc de La Bruyère is equal only to my admiration for him.

Index

on parenting, 383n

Paris and, in early months, 36, 47–48

Passy withdrawal of, encouraged by
Vergennes, 57–60, 63–64

Paul, grand duke of Russia and,
299–300

peace celebrations and, 357–58

peace negotiations and, xiv, 282–84,
299–304, 308–27

personality of, 2–3, 5, 49–50, 67–69,
85–86, 131, 198, 269

phonetic alphabet and, 307

Polly Hewson visits, 386–87, 389

Poor Richard's wisdoms published in
France and, 85

popularity of, in France, 89–90, 159–60,
165, 192–93, 196, 199, 219

portraits of, 51, 88–89, 97, 159, 196,
234–35, 278–79

pragmatism of, 18, 21, 412

presented in court, after treaty
announcement, 141–44

presented in court, as sole
plenipotentiary, 206

press and propaganda and, 80–84

on primogeniture, 365, 403n

printing press of, at Passy, 278

prisoner exchange and, 86–87

privateers and, 16, 22, 94–97, 99–100,
107–8, 119, 182

psoriasis and, 90, 182, 199

on psychology in international
relations, 294–96

on public service, 277

quadruple alliance proposed by, 313

religion and, 49, 270–71, 375–76

reputation of, after death, 403–4, 412

Robert Morris and, 277

Sally Jay and, 347

Saratoga and, 109–13, 119–20

satirical pamphlets on, 220–21

scientific interests of, 48, 186–87, 278,
279, 306, 353, 360, 390

Searle and, 268

secretary needed by, 227, 263, 265

self-reliance and, 106

social life of, in France, 39–44, 91, 138,
140, 162–63, 277–79, 336–37

son William and, xiii, 74, 91–92, 297n,
383–85, 395–96

Spain and, 173, 174, 300

spies and, xiii, 44–45, 76

Stormont and, 42–43, 61, 62

supplies for America and, 223–24, 240,
251–59, 275–76, 284–86

taciturnity of, 412n

Thomas Morris affair and, 102–3

Treaty of Paris signing and, 349–50

vengefulness of, 198–99

Vergennes and, 18, 100–101, 111–14,
125, 320–24, 332

Voltaire and, 136–38, 159

war successes of 1777 and, 71–72

will of, 403n

workday of, in Passy, 86

writes "An Economic Project" on
lamps and daylight saving time
credit, 367

writes bagatelle on mayflies, 178–79

writes balloon satire, 356

writes "Bilked for Breakfast," 231

writes essay on corn, 389

writes essay on Society of the
Cincinnati, 364–67

writes "Information to Those Who
Would Remove to America," 363–64

writes on founding of Philadelphia
library and moral perfection, 375

writes satire of Izard, 204

writes "Sundry Moral and
Philosophical Christian Reflections,"
232

writes "The Deformed and Handsome
Leg," 256

writes "The Dialogue Between the
Gout and Mr. Franklin," 256–57

writes "The Elysian Fields," 232–33

writes "The Whistle" for Mme. Brillon,
230

writing of, after return home focuses on
science not life, 412

Yorktown victory news reaches, 288–91

Franklin, Deborah Read "Debbie" (wife),
xiii, 52, 56n, 176, 179n, 233

Franklin, Ellen (great-granddaughter),
405n

About the Author

STACY SCHIFF is the author of *Véra (Mrs. Vladimir Nabokov)*, which won the 2000 Pulitzer Prize in biography, and *Saint-Exupéry*, which was a finalist for the 1995 Pulitzer Prize. She has received fellowships from the Guggenheim Foundation and the National Endowment for the Humanities, and was a Director's Fellow at the Center for Scholars and Writers at the New York Public Library. Schiff lives in New York City.

Illustration Credits

M. and Mme. Brillon: Private collection

Mme. Helvétius: Centre des monuments nationaux, Paris

Arthur Lee: The Historical Society of Pennsylvania Collection, Atwater Kent Museum of Philadelphia

William Lee: Stratford Hall Plantation

Ralph Izard: Photograph © 2004 Museum of Fine Arts, Boston

Benny Bache: The American Philosophical Society

William Temple Franklin: Yale University Art Gallery, Trumbull Collection

William Franklin: Private collection

Gérard: Independence National Historical Park

Sculpture: Courtesy, Winterthur Museum

Place Louis XV: The Louvre, Paris

Invitation: American Philosophical Society

George Washington: Château de Blois

Mme. Brillon's house: Franklin Collection, Yale University Library

Franklin crowned: Franklin Collection, Yale University Library

Adams: Boston Athanaeum

Lafayette: Franklin Collection, Yale University Library

Calling card: American Philosophical Society

Borel and Fragonard: Franklin Collection, Yale University Library

Cartoon: Bibliothèque Nationale

Coiffure à l'indépendence américaine: Réunion des Musées Nationaux/Art Resource, New York

Balloon lady: U.S. Air Force Academy Library, Gimbel Collection

Group portrait: Courtesy, Winterthur Museum

Jefferson: National Portrait Gallery, Smithsonian Institution/Art Resource, New York

Balloon over garden: Bibliothèque Nationale

Balloon above the city: Franklin Collection, Yale University Library

"Magnetism Unveiled": Franklin Collection, Yale University Library

Illustration Credits

Louis XVI: American Philosophical Society

Fur-hatted Franklins, Nini medallion, and Houdon drawing: Franklin Collection, Yale University Library

A Note on the Type

A Great Improvisation was set in Fournier. Trained as an artist and engraver, Pierre Simon Fournier opened his own foundry in 1742, having developed a pioneering system of typographical measures, still in use today. In total he cut nearly 150 alphabets before patenting an original system of musical notation and before publishing his masterwork, *Manuel Typographique*. He died in 1768.

In 1777 Franklin obtained type for his Passy press from Fournier's son, who—with his mother—continued the family business. In 1780 the younger Fournier designed an ornate, script alphabet specifically for the American envoy, type the Frenchman christened "le Franklin."

Dr: Passy, Jan. 1. 1779

day	Money paid &c.	L.	S.	D.	day	Money received &c.	L.
C	Etrennes aux Bonshommes }	6				In hand	494 6
C	Petis poste & pour Alm. de Poche }	12				Rec'd of Mr Grand more	2400
X	Boyes 6 each —	12					
C	Bath —	3	12				
	Flower Woman —		12				
C	Other Etrennes —	323	4				
8	Coachman of Ctte Maille bois —	6					
	Advanc'd to Billy to buy things for me }	240					2900
		603	8	0	6	Jan. in hand — 22	96
C 7	Box for the Poor —	6	0	0			6 78
10	Error in reckoning what I had in hand }	72			10	In hand — 22	18
		681	8	0	14	Rec'd of Waites Money he had borrow'd of me 32 Louis —	768
16	Supply'd Mr Belton a poor ingenious American with 4 Louis }	96			C	And 5 Louis that he had taken of our Agent at Calais for which I am Dr to Congress }	120
17	Etrennes to the Servants of the Ministers at Versailles 8 Guineas }	192					
C 20	to Pierre Sajo, a Capt of Vessel who had been Prisoner	48					
		1017	8	0			31